Vauxhall Astra
Service and Repair Manual

Steve Rendle and Finn Deacon

(1832-336-4Y2)

Models covered

Vauxhall Astra models with petrol engines, including special/limited editions
Saloon, Hatchback, Estate and Van
1389 cc, 1598 cc & 1998 cc (SOHC and DOHC)

Does not Diesel engines or air conditioning
For information on 1992 Convertible and Astramax Van models, see OWM 1136

ABCDE
FGHIJ
K

© Haynes Publishing 1996

A book in the **Haynes Service and Repair Manual Series**

ISBN 1 85960 250 9

British Library Cataloguing in Publication Data
A catalogue record for this book is available from the British Library.

Printed by **J H Haynes & Co. Ltd, Sparkford, Nr Yeovil, Somerset BA22 7JJ**

Haynes Publishing
Sparkford, Nr Yeovil, Somerset BA22 7JJ, England

Haynes North America, Inc
861 Lawrence Drive, Newbury Park, California 91320, USA

Editions Haynes S.A.
147/149, rue Saint Honoré, 75001 PARIS, France

Contents

Contents

Introduction to the Vauxhall Astra

The Astra covered by this manual was first introduced to the European market in Autumn 1991. Although mechanically there is a fundamental similarity to the previous Astra/Belmont/Kadett models, the later version is much improved and refined in all respects. This manual covers models fitted with petrol engines, but other models in the range are available with diesel engines.

Five petrol engines are available in the Astra range, although not all of the engines are available in all markets. The engines available are 1.4, 1.6, 1.8 and 2.0 litre single overhead camshaft (SOHC) versions, and 1.6, 1.8 and 2.0 litre double overhead camshaft (DOHC) versions. All of the engines use fuel injection, and are fitted with a range of emission control systems, with the exception of a 1.4 litre carburettor engine available in certain markets. All the engines are of a well-proven design and, provided regular maintenance is carried out, are unlikely to give trouble.

The Astra is available in 4-door Saloon, 3- and 5-door Hatchback, Estate and Van bodystyles (although the GSi model is only available in Hatchback form), with a wide range of fittings and interior trim depending on the model specification.

Fully-independent front suspension is fitted, with the components attached to a subframe assembly; the rear suspension is semi-independent, with a torsion beam and trailing arms.

A five-speed manual gearbox is fitted as standard to all models, and four-speed electronically-controlled automatic transmission is available as an option on certain models.

A wide range of standard and optional equipment is available within the Astra range to suit most tastes, including an anti-lock braking system.

For the home mechanic, the Astra is a straightforward vehicle to maintain, and most of the items requiring frequent attention are easily accessible.

Your Vauxhall Astra Manual

The aim of this manual is to help you get the best value from your vehicle. It can do so in several ways. It can help you decide what work must be done (even should you choose to get it done by a garage). It will also provide information on routine maintenance and servicing, and give a logical course of action and diagnosis when random faults occur. However, it is hoped that you will use the manual by tackling the work yourself. On simpler jobs it may even be quicker than booking the car into a garage and going there twice, to leave and collect it. Perhaps most important, a lot of money can be saved by avoiding the costs a garage must charge to cover its labour and overheads.

New Astra GSi 16V

Astra LS estate

The manual has drawings and descriptions to show the function of the various components so that their layout can be understood. Tasks are described and photographed in a clear step-by-step sequence.

Acknowledgements

Thanks are due to Champion Spark Plug who supplied the illustrations showing spark plug conditions. Certain illustrations are the copyright of Vauxhall Motors Ltd, and are used with their permission. Thanks are also due to Sykes-Pickavant Limited, who provided some of the workshop tools, and to all those people at Sparkford who helped in the production of this manual.

We take great pride in the accuracy of information given in this manual, but vehicle manufacturers make alterations and design changes during the production run of a particular vehicle of which they do not inform us. No liability can be accepted by the authors or publishers for loss, damage or injury caused by any errors in, or omissions from, the information given.

Working on your car can be dangerous. This page shows just some of the potential risks and hazards, with the aim of creating a safety-conscious attitude.

General hazards

Scalding

• Don't remove the radiator or expansion tank cap while the engine is hot.
• Engine oil, automatic transmission fluid or power steering fluid may also be dangerously hot if the engine has recently been running.

Burning

• Beware of burns from the exhaust system and from any part of the engine. Brake discs and drums can also be extremely hot immediately after use.

Crushing

• When working under or near a raised vehicle, always supplement the jack with axle stands, or use drive-on ramps. *Never venture under a car which is only supported by a jack.*
• Take care if loosening or tightening high-torque nuts when the vehicle is on stands. Initial loosening and final tightening should be done with the wheels on the ground.

Fire

• Fuel is highly flammable; fuel vapour is explosive.
• Don't let fuel spill onto a hot engine.
• Do not smoke or allow naked lights (including pilot lights) anywhere near a vehicle being worked on. Also beware of creating sparks (electrically or by use of tools).
• Fuel vapour is heavier than air, so don't work on the fuel system with the vehicle over an inspection pit.
• Another cause of fire is an electrical overload or short-circuit. Take care when repairing or modifying the vehicle wiring.
• Keep a fire extinguisher handy, of a type suitable for use on fuel and electrical fires.

Electric shock

• Ignition HT voltage can be dangerous, especially to people with heart problems or a pacemaker. Don't work on or near the ignition system with the engine running or the ignition switched on.

• Mains voltage is also dangerous. Make sure that any mains-operated equipment is correctly earthed. Mains power points should be protected by a residual current device (RCD) circuit breaker.

Fume or gas intoxication

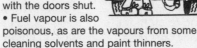

• Exhaust fumes are poisonous; they often contain carbon monoxide, which is rapidly fatal if inhaled. Never run the engine in a confined space such as a garage with the doors shut.
• Fuel vapour is also poisonous, as are the vapours from some cleaning solvents and paint thinners.

Poisonous or irritant substances

• Avoid skin contact with battery acid and with any fuel, fluid or lubricant, especially antifreeze, brake hydraulic fluid and Diesel fuel. Don't syphon them by mouth. If such a substance is swallowed or gets into the eyes, seek medical advice.
• Prolonged contact with used engine oil can cause skin cancer. Wear gloves or use a barrier cream if necessary. Change out of oil-soaked clothes and do not keep oily rags in your pocket.
• Air conditioning refrigerant forms a poisonous gas if exposed to a naked flame (including a cigarette). It can also cause skin burns on contact.

Asbestos

• Asbestos dust can cause cancer if inhaled or swallowed. Asbestos may be found in gaskets and in brake and clutch linings. When dealing with such components it is safest to assume that they contain asbestos.

Special hazards

Hydrofluoric acid

• This extremely corrosive acid is formed when certain types of synthetic rubber, found in some O-rings, oil seals, fuel hoses etc, are exposed to temperatures above 400°C. The rubber changes into a charred or sticky substance containing the acid. *Once formed, the acid remains dangerous for years. If it gets onto the skin, it may be necessary to amputate the limb concerned.*
• When dealing with a vehicle which has suffered a fire, or with components salvaged from such a vehicle, wear protective gloves and discard them after use.

The battery

• Batteries contain sulphuric acid, which attacks clothing, eyes and skin. Take care when topping-up or carrying the battery.
• The hydrogen gas given off by the battery is highly explosive. Never cause a spark or allow a naked light nearby. Be careful when connecting and disconnecting battery chargers or jump leads.

Air bags

• Air bags can cause injury if they go off accidentally. Take care when removing the steering wheel and/or facia. Special storage instructions may apply.

⚠️ *Warning: Never expose the hands, face or any other part of the body to injector spray; the fuel can penetrate the skin with potentially fatal results.*

Remember...

DO

• Do use eye protection when using power tools, and when working under the vehicle.

• Do wear gloves or use barrier cream to protect your hands when necessary.

• Do get someone to check periodically that all is well when working alone on the vehicle.

• Do keep loose clothing and long hair well out of the way of moving mechanical parts.

• Do remove rings, wristwatch etc, before working on the vehicle – especially the electrical system.

• Do ensure that any lifting or jacking equipment has a safe working load rating adequate for the job.

DON'T

• Don't attempt to lift a heavy component which may be beyond your capability – get assistance.

• Don't rush to finish a job, or take unverified short cuts.

• Don't use ill-fitting tools which may slip and cause injury.

• Don't leave tools or parts lying around where someone can trip over them. Mop up oil and fuel spills at once.

• Don't allow children or pets to play in or near a vehicle being worked on.

The following pages are intended to help in dealing with common roadside emergencies and breakdowns. You will find more detailed fault finding information at the back of the manual, and repair information in the main Chapters.

If your car won't start and the starter motor doesn't turn

☐ If it is a model with automatic transmission, make sure the selector is in the 'P' or 'N' position on the selector.
☐ Open the bonnet and make sure that the battery terminals are clean and tight.
☐ Switch on the headlights and try to start the engine. If the headlights go very dim when you are trying to start, the battery is probably flat. Try 'jump starting' (see next page), using another car.

If your car won't start even though the starter motor turns as normal

☐ Is there fuel in the tank, or is your fuel gauge faulty?
☐ Is there moisture on electrical components under the bonnet? Switch off the ignition, then wipe off any obvious dampness with a dry cloth. Spray a water repellent aerosol product (WD-40 or equivalent) on ignition and fuel system electrical connectors like those shown in the photos. Pay special attention to the ignition coil, DIS coil wiring connector and HT leads.

A Check that the spark plug HT leads are connected firmly.

B The fuel injection system wiring plug may cause problems if not connected securely.

C Check the ECU multi-plug for security (where fitted), with the ignition switched off.

Check that electrical connections are secure (with the ignition switched off) and spray with water dispersant if you suspect a problem due to damp.

D Check the security and condition of the battery connections.

E Check that the coils wiring plug is secure and spray with water-dispersant if necessary.

Jump starting

Jump starting will get you out of trouble, but you must correct whatever made the battery go flat in the first place. There are three possibilities:

1 *The battery has been drained by repeated attempts to start, or by leaving the lights on.*

2 *The charging system is not working properly (alternator drivebelt slack or broken, alternator wiring fault or alternator itself faulty).*

3 *The battery itself is at fault (electrolyte low, or battery worn out).*

When jump-starting a car using a booster battery, observe the following precautions:

✔ Before connecting the booster battery, make sure that the ignition is switched off.

✔ Ensure that all electrical equipment (lights, heater, wipers, etc) is switched off.

✔ Ensure that the battery may be jumped (see Chapter 5, Section 6)

✔ Make sure that the booster battery is the same voltage as the discharged one in the vehicle.

✔ If the battery is being jump-started from the battery in another vehicle, the two vehicles MUST NOT TOUCH each other.

✔ Make sure that the transmission is in neutral (or PARK, in the case of automatic transmission).

1 Connect one end of the red jump lead to the positive (+) terminal of the flat battery

2 Connect the other end of the red lead to the positive (+) terminal of the booster battery.

3 Connect one end of the black jump lead to the negative (-) terminal of the booster battery

4 Connect the other end of the black jump lead to a bolt or bracket on the engine block, well away from the battery, on the vehicle to be started.

5 Make sure that the jump leads will not come into contact with the fan, drive-belts or other moving parts of the engine.

6 Start the engine using the booster battery, then with the engine running at idle speed, disconnect the jump leads in the reverse order of connection.

Wheel changing

Some of the details shown here will vary according to model.

⚠️ *Warning: Do not change a wheel in a situation where you risk being injured by other traffic. On busy roads, try to stop in a lay-by or gateway. Be wary of passing traffic while changing the wheel. It is easy to become distracted by the job in hand.*

Preparation

☐ When a puncture occurs, stop when it is safe to do so.
☐ Park on firm level ground, if possible, and well out of the way of other traffic.

☐ Use hazard warning lights, if necessary.
☐ If you have one, use a warning triangle to alert other drivers of your presence.
☐ Apply the handbrake and engage first or reverse gear.

☐ Chock the wheel diagonally opposite the one being removed. A couple of large stones will do for this.
☐ If the ground is soft, use a flat piece of wood or paving to spread the load under the foot of the jack.

Changing the wheel

1 Clear the boot area, and remove the carpet and spare wheel cover.

2 Remove the tool holder and unscrew the spare wheel clamp

3 For safety, place the spare wheel under the car near the jacking point.

4 Remove the wheel trim (where fitted) and slacken each wheel bolt by half a turn.

5 Raise the jack whilst locating below the jacking point (ensure that the jack is on firm ground and located on the car correctly)

6 Turn the handle clockwise until the wheel is raised clear of the ground. Remove the bolts and lift the wheel clear.

7 Position the spare wheel and fit the bolts. Hand tighten with the wheel brace and lower the car to the ground. Tighten the wheel bolts in the sequence shown, fit the wheel trim and secure the punctured wheel in the boot.

Finally...

☐ Remove the wheel chocks. Stow the jack and tools in the appropriate locations in the car.
☐ Check the tyre pressure on the wheel just fitted. If it low, or if you don't have a pressure gauge with you, drive slowly to the nearest garage and inflate the tyre to the correct pressure. Have the damaged tyre or wheel repaired or replaced, as soon as possible.

Identifying leaks

Puddles on the garage floor or drive, or obvious wetness under the bonnet or underneath the car, suggest a leak that needs investigating. It can sometimes be difficult to decide where the leak is coming from, especially if the engine bay is very dirty already. Leaking oil or fluid can also be blown rearwards by the passage of air under the car, giving a false impression of where the problem lies.

 Warning: Most automotive oils and fluids are poisonous. Wash them off skin, and change out of contaminated clothing, without delay.

 HAYNES HiNT *The smell of a fluid leaking from the car may provide a clue to what's leaking. Some fluids are distinctively coloured. It may help to clean the car and to park it over some clean paper as an aid to locating the source of the leak. Remember that some leaks may only occur while the engine is running.*

Sump oil

Engine oil may leak from the drain plug...

Oil from filter

...or from the base of the oil filter.

Gearbox oil

Gearbox oil can leak from the seals at the inboard ends of the driveshafts.

Antifreeze

Leaking antifreeze often leaves a crystalline deposit like this.

Brake fluid

A leak occurring at a wheel is almost certainly brake fluid.

Power steering fluid

Power steering fluid may leak from the pipe connectors on the steering rack.

Towing

When all else fails, you may find yourself having to get a tow home – or of course you may be helping somebody else. Long-distance recovery should only be done by a garage or breakdown service. For shorter distances, DIY towing using another car is easy enough, but observe the following points:

☐ Use a proper tow-rope – they are not expensive. The vehicle being towed must display an 'ON TOW' sign in its rear window.
☐ Always turn the ignition key to the 'on' position when the vehicle is being towed, so that the steering lock is released, and

that the direction indicator and brake lights work.
☐ Only attach the tow-rope to the towing eyes provided.
☐ Before being towed, release the handbrake and select neutral on the transmission.
☐ Note that greater-than-usual pedal pressure will be required to operate the brakes, since the vacuum servo unit is only operational with the engine running.
☐ On models with power steering, greater-than-usual steering effort will also be required.
☐ Make sure that both drivers know the route before setting off.

☐ The driver of the car being towed must keep the tow-rope taut at all times to avoid snatching.
☐ Only drive at moderate speeds and keep the distance towed to a mimimum. Drive smoothly and allow plenty of time for slowing down at junctions.
☐ Never tow an automatic model backwards. If the transmission appears to be in working order, the vehicle can be towed for a maximum distance of 62 miles (100 km), at no more than 50 mph (80 km/h). The vehicle can be towed greater distances with the front wheels raised.

Introduction

There are some very simple checks that need only take a few minutes to carry out, but that could save you much inconvenience and expense.

These 'Weekly checks' require no great skill or special tools and the small amount of time they take to perform could prove to be very well spent, for example.

Keeping an eye on tyre condition and pressures, will not only help to stop them wearing out prematurely but could also save your life.

Many breakdowns are caused by electrical problems. Battery related faults are particularly common and a quick check on a regular basis will often prevent the majority of these.

If your car develops a brake fluid leak, the first time you might know about it is when your brakes do not work properly. Checking the level regularly will give warning of this kind of problem.

If the oil or coolant levels run low, the cost of repairing any engine damage will be far greater than fixing the leak, for example.

Underbonnet check points

C 14 NZ model

A Engine oil level dipstick

B Engine oil filler cap

C Coolant expansion cap

D Brake fluid reservoir

E Screen washer fluid reservoir

F Battery

C 16 SE model

A Engine oil level dipstick

B Engine oil filler cap

C Coolant expansion cap

D Brake fluid reservoir

E Screen washer fluid reservoir

F Battery

X 16 XEL model

A *Engine oil level dipstick*
B *Engine oil filler cap*

C *Coolant expansion cap*
D *Brake fluid reservoir*

E *Screen washer fluid reservoir*
F *Battery*

C 20 XE model

A Engine oil level dipstick

B Engine oil filler cap

C Coolant expansion cap

D Brake fluid reservoir

E Screen washer fluid reservoir

F Battery

Engine oil level

Before you start

✔ Make sure that your car is level ground.
✔ Check the oil level before the car is driven or at least 5 minutes after the engine has been switched off.

If the oil is checked immediately after driving the vehicle, some of the oil will remain in the upper engine components, resulting in an inaccurate reading in the dipstick!

The correct oil

Modern engines place great demands on their oil. It is very important that the correct oil for your car is used (See "Lubricants and Fluids").

Car Care

● If you have to add oil frequently, you should check whether you have any leaks. Note any stains already on the surface where you normally park and check for new stains in the morning. If there are no leaks, the engine may be burning oil (see "Fault Finding")
● Always maintain the level between the upper and lower dipstick marks (see photo 3). If the level is too low severe damage may occur. Oil seal failure may result if the engine is overfilled by adding too much oil.

1 The dipstick is often brightly coloured for easy identification (see "Underbonnet check points" on page 0.10 for exact location). Withdraw the dipstick.

2 Using a clean rag or paper towel remove all oil from the dipstick. Insert the clean dipstick into the tube as far as it will go, then withdraw it again.

3 Note the level on the end of the dipstick, which should be between the upper ("MAX") mark and lower ("MIN") mark.

4 Oil is added through the filler cap. Unscrew the cap and top-up the level. A funnel may help to reduce spillage. Add the oil slowly, checking the level on the dipstick frequently. Avoid overfilling (see "Car Care")

Coolant level

Warning: DO NOT attempt to remove the expansion tank pressure cap when the engine is hot, as there is a very great risk of scalding. Do not leave open containers of coolant about, as it is poisonous.

Car Care

● With a sealed type cooling system, adding coolant should not be necessary on a regular basis. If frequent topping-up is required, it is likely there is a leak. Check the radiator, all hoses and joint faces for signs of staining or wetness and rectify as necessary.

● It is important that antifreeze is used in the cooling system all year round, not just during the winter months. This is due to it's cooling and anti-corrosion properties. Do not top-up with water alone, as the antifreeze will become too diluted.

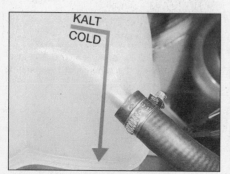

1 The coolant level varies with the temperature of the engine. When the engine is cold, the coolant level should be near the "COLD" (or "KALT") mark.

2 If topping-up is necessary, wait until the engine is cold. Slowly unscrew the cap to release any pressure present in the cooling system and remove it.

3 Add a mixture of water and antifreeze to the expansion tank until the coolant level is halfway between the level marks.

Brake fluid level

⚠️ *Warning: Brake hydraulic fluid can harm your eyes and damage painted surfaces, so use extreme caution when handling and pouring it. Do not use fluid that has been standing open for some time, as it absorbs moisture from the air that can cause a dangerous loss of braking effectiveness.*

HAYNES HiNT *Make sure that your car is on level ground. The fluid level in the master cylinder will drop slightly as the brake linings wear down, but the fluid level must never be allowed to drop below the "MIN" mark.*

Safety first

● If the reservoir requires repeated topping-up this indicates a fluid leak somewhere in the system, that should be investigated immediately.
● If a leak is suspected, the car should not be driven until the braking system has been checked. Never take any risks where brakes are concerned.

1 The "MIN" and "MAX" marks are indicated on the reservoir. The fluid level must be kept between the marks at all times.

2 If topping-up is necessary, first wipe clean the area around the filler cap to prevent dirt entering the hydraulic system. Unscrew the reservoir cap.

3 Carefully add fluid, taking care not to spill it onto the surrounding components. Use only the specified fluid; mixing different types can cause damage to the system. Then securely refit the cap and wipe off any spilt fluid.

Power steering fluid level

Before your start:
✔ Park the vehicle on level ground.
✔ Set the steering wheel straight ahead.
✔ The engine should be turned off.

Safety First!
● The need for frequent topping up indicates a leak, which should be investigated immediately.

1 The reservoir is located at the front left-hand side of the engine compartment, next to the battery. The power steering fluid level is checked with a dipstick attached to the reservoir filler cap. Unscrew the filler cap from the top of the reservoir, and wipe all the fluid from the end with a clean rag or paper towel. Refit the reservoir filler cap, then remove it once more. Note the fluid level on the dipstick. When the engine is cold, the fluid level should be up to the lower mark on the dipstick. When the engine is at normal operating temperature, the fluid level should be up to the upper mark on the dipstick.

2 Top-up with the specified type of fluid if necessary and securely refit the reservoir filler cap on completion.

Tyre condition and pressure

It is very important that tyres are in good condition, and at the correct pressure - having a tyre failure at any speed is highly dangerous. Tyre wear is influenced by driving style - harsh braking and acceleration, or fast cornering, will all produce more rapid tyre wear. As a general rule, the front tyres wear out faster than the rears. Interchanging the tyres from front to rear ("rotating" the tyres) may result in more even wear. However, if this is completely effective, you may have the expense of replacing all four tyres at once! Remove any nails or stones embedded in the tread before they penetrate the tyre to cause deflation. If removal of a nail does reveal that the tyre has been punctured, refit the nail so that its point of penetration is marked. Then immediately change the wheel, and have the tyre repaired by a tyre dealer.

Regularly check the tyres for damage in the form of cuts or bulges, especially in the sidewalls. Periodically remove the wheels, and clean any dirt or mud from the inside and outside surfaces. Examine the wheel rims for signs of rusting, corrosion or other damage. Light alloy wheels are easily damaged by "kerbing" whilst parking; steel wheels may also become dented or buckled. A new wheel is very often the only way to overcome severe damage.

New tyres should be balanced when they are fitted, but it may become necessary to re-balance them as they wear, or if the balance weights fitted to the wheel rim should fall off. Unbalanced tyres will wear more quickly, as will the steering and suspension components. Wheel imbalance is normally signified by vibration, particularly at a certain speed (typically around 50 mph). If this vibration is felt only through the steering, then it is likely that just the front wheels need balancing. If, however, the vibration is felt through the whole car, the rear wheels could be out of balance. Wheel balancing should be carried out by a tyre dealer or garage.

1 Tread Depth - visual check
The original tyres have tread wear safety bands (B), which will appear when the tread depth reaches approximately 1.6 mm. The band positions are indicated by a triangular mark on the tyre sidewall (A).

2 Tread Depth - manual check
Alternatively, tread wear can be monitored with a simple, inexpensive device known as a tread depth indicator gauge.

3 Tyre Pressure Check
Check the tyre pressures regularly with the tyres cold. Do not adjust the tyre pressures immediately after the vehicle has been used, or an inaccurate setting will result.

Tyre tread wear patterns

Shoulder Wear

Underinflation (wear on both sides)
Under-inflation will cause overheating of the tyre, because the tyre will flex too much, and the tread will not sit correctly on the road surface. This will cause a loss of grip and excessive wear, not to mention the danger of sudden tyre failure due to heat build-up.
Check and adjust pressures
Incorrect wheel camber (wear on one side)
Repair or renew suspension parts
Hard cornering
Reduce speed!

Centre Wear

Overinflation
Over-inflation will cause rapid wear of the centre part of the tyre tread, coupled with reduced grip, harsher ride, and the danger of shock damage occurring in the tyre casing.
Check and adjust pressures

If you sometimes have to inflate your car's tyres to the higher pressures specified for maximum load or sustained high speed, don't forget to reduce the pressures to normal afterwards.

Uneven Wear

Front tyres may wear unevenly as a result of wheel misalignment. Most tyre dealers and garages can check and adjust the wheel alignment (or "tracking") for a modest charge.
Incorrect camber or castor
Repair or renew suspension parts
Malfunctioning suspension
Repair or renew suspension parts
Unbalanced wheel
Balance tyres
Incorrect toe setting
Adjust front wheel alignment
Note: *The feathered edge of the tread which typifies toe wear is best checked by feel.*

Battery

Caution: Before carrying out any work on the vehicle battery, read the precautions given in the "Safety First" at the beginning of this manual.

✔ Make sure that the battery tray is in good condition and that the clamp and the battery itself can be removed with a solution of water and baking soda. Thoroughly rinse all cleaned areas with water. Any metal parts damaged by corrosion should be coated with a zinc based primer, then painted.

✔ Periodically (approximately every three months), check the charge condition of the battery, as described in Chapter 5.

✔ If the battery is flat and you need to "jump start" your vehicle, see "Roadside Repairs"

 HAYNES HiNT *Battery corrosion can be kept to a minimum by applying a layer of petroleum jelly to the clamps and terminals after they are reconnected.*

1 The battery is located at the front left-hand corner of the engine compartment.

2 Check that security and condition of the battery connections.

Electrical systems

✔ Check all external lights and the horn. Refer to the appropriate Sections of Chapter 12 for details of bulb and component replacement, if necessary.

✔ Visually check all accessible wiring connectors, harnesses and retaining clips for security and for signs of chafing or damage.

HAYNES HiNT *To check your rear lights unaided, back up to a wall and turn them on. The reflected light should show if they are working properly.*

1 Indicator lamp bulb replacement

2 The main fuses are located in the fusebox, at the lower driver's side: of the facia, under a removable cover.

3 Replacing a fuse

Screen washer fluid

Screenwash additives not only keep the windscreen clean during foul weather, they also prevent the washer system freezing in cold weather - which is when you are likely to need it most. Do not top-up using plain water as the screenwash will become too diluted and will freeze during cold weather. On no account use antifreeze in the washer system as this could discolour or damage the paintwork.

1 The screenwasher fluid reservoir is located at the rear right-hand corner of the engine compartment.

2 When topping-up the reservoir, a screenwash additive should be added in the quantities recommended on the bottle.

Wiper blades

1 Check the condition of the wiper blades; if they are cracked or show any signs of deterioration, or if the glass swept area is smeared, renew them. Wiper blades should be renewed annually.

2 To remove a windscreen wiper blade, pull the arm fully away from the screen until it locks. Swivel the blade through 90°, press the locking tab with your fingers and slide the blade out of the arm's hooked end.

3 Don't forget to check the tailgate wiper blade as well. To remove the blade, depress the retaining tab and slide the blade out of the hooked end of the arm.

Lubricants and fluids

Engine oil	Multigrade engine oil, viscosity SAE 10W/40 to 20W/50, to API SG/CD
Cooling system	Ethylene glycol based antifreeze
Manual Transmission Fluid	Gear oil, viscosity SAE 80 EP (i.e. Vauxhall P/N 90188629)
Automatic Transmission Fluid	Dexron II type ATF (i.e. P/N 90350342)
Braking system	Hydraulic fluid to SAE J1703F or DOT 4 (i.e. Vauxhall P/N 90007080)
Power Steering Fluid	Dexron II type ATF (i.e. Vauxhall P/N 90350342)
Adhesive Sealing Compound	Vauxhall P/N 90485251
Locking Compound	Vauxhall P/N 90167347
Longlife Grease	Molybdenum disulphide grease (MoS_2)
Sealing Compound	Vauxhall P/N 90094714 or 90350544
Silicone Grease	Vauxhall P/N 90167353
Special Grease	Vauxhall P/N 90094176

Tyre pressures

	Front	Rear
Saloon and Convertible:		
14 NV, C 14 NZ, 14 SE, C 14 SE, C 16 NZ and X 16 SZ	2.0 bars (29 psi)	1.7 bars (24 psi)
C 16 SE and C 18 NZ	2.2 bars (32 psi)	1.9 bars (27 psi)
C 18 XE, C 20 NE, C 20 XE and X 20 XEV	2.4 bars (35 psi)	2.1 bars (30 psi)
Estate and Van:		
14 NV, C 14 NZ, 14 SE, C 14 SE, C 16 NZ and X 16 SZ	2.0 bars (29 psi)	1.8 bars (26 psi)
C 16 SE and C 18 NZ	2.2 bars (32 psi)	2.0 bars (29 psi)
C 18 XE, C 20 NE, C 20 XE and X 20 XEV	2.2 bars (35 psi)	2.0 bars (29 psi)

Note: *The pressures quoted are for a normal load (up to 3 passengers). For full load pressures, consult your handbook or a Vauxhall dealer*

Chapter 1
Routine maintenance and servicing

Contents

Degrees of difficulty

Easy, suitable for novice with little experience	**Fairly easy,** suitable for beginner with some experience	**Fairly difficult,** suitable for competent DIY mechanic	**Difficult,** suitable for experienced DIY mechanic	**Very difficult,** suitable for expert DIY or professional

Servicing Specifications

Lubricants and fluids
Refer to "Weekly Checks"

Capacities

Engine oil

Capacity (including filter):

All 1.4 litre, C 16 NZ, C 16 SE and X 16 SZ models	3.5 litres
X 16 XEL models	3.25 litres
1.8 litre, C 20 NE, X 20 XEV and C 20 XE (without oil cooler) models	4.0 litres
C 20 XE (with oil cooler) models	4.5 litres

Difference between MAX and MIN dipstick marks:

All models	1.0 litre

Cooling system

	Manual transmission	Automatic transmission
All 1.4 litre models	5.8 litres	5.6 litres (C 14 SE only)
C 16 NZ, C 16 SE and X 16 SZ models	5.6 litres	6.3 litres (not C 16 NZ)
X 16 XEL models	6.0 litres	n/a
C 18 NZ models	7.0 litres	6.9 litres
C 20 NE models	6.5 litres	n/a
DOHC models (except X 16 XEL)	6.9 litres	6.9 litres

Fuel tank

Saloon and Hatchback models	52.0 litres
Estate and Van models	50.0 litres

Manual transmission

F10 and F13	1.6 litres
F15	1.8 litres
F16, F18, F18+ and F20	1.9 litres

Automatic transmission

AF13	5.0 litres (approx.)
AF20	7.0 litres (approx.)

Power steering fluid reservoir

All models	1.0 litre

Washer reservoirs

Windscreen and tailgate	2.3 litres
Headlamp (if fitted)	5.0 litres

Engine

Oil filter

14 NV, 14 SE, C 14 NZ, C 14 SE, C 16 NZ, C 16 SE and X 16 SZ	Vauxhall P/N 93156245
X 16 XEL	Vauxhall P/N 93156954
C 18 XE, C 18 XEL and C 20 NE	Vauxhall P/N 93156245
C 18 NZ and X 20 XEV	Vauxhall P/N 93156954
C 20 XE	Vauxhall P/N 93156245

Sump plug washer

All models	Vauxhall P/N 11023582

Cooling system

Antifreeze mixtures (antifreeze to Vauxhall specification GME L 6)	Antifreeze	Water
Protection to –10°C	20%	80%
Protection to –20°C	34%	66%
Protection to –30°C	44%	56%
Protection to –40°C	52%	48%

Note: *Refer to antifreeze manufacturer for latest recommendations.*

Fuel system

Idle speed

Note: *Ignition timing adjustment is not possible on models with fuel injection. Details shown for information only. For further details refer to Chapters 4A or 4B, as applicable.*

14 NV	900 to 950 rpm
14 SE	820 to 980 rpm
C 14 NZ	830 to 990 rpm
C 14 SE	820 to 980 rpm
C 16 NZ	830 to 990 rpm
C 16 SE	820 to 980 rpm
C 18 NZ:	
Manual transmission models	820 to 980 rpm
Automatic saloon models	750 to 910 rpm
Automatic estate models	650 to 810 rpm
C 18 XE and C 18 XEL	700 to 1000 rpm
C 20 NE	820 to 980 rpm
C 20 XE	860 to 1020 rpm
X 20 XEV	770 to 930 rpm

Idle mixture CO content

Carburettor models	max. 0.5%
Fuel injection engines (all models)	0.3% or less

Fuel octane requirement (refer to Chapter 4A for further details)

Carburettor engine	97 RON leaded (i.e. 4-star) or 95 RON unleaded (i.e. unleaded Premium)
Fuel injection engines (all models)	95 RON unleaded (i.e. unleaded Premium)

Ignition system

Firing order	1-3-4-2
Location of No 1 cylinder	Crankshaft pulley (timing belt) end
Direction of crankshaft rotation	Clockwise
Direction of distributor rotor arm rotation	Anti-clockwise
Ignition timing (stroboscopic, at idle speed, with vacuum hose disconnected):	
Carburettor engine	5° BTDC
Fuel-injection engines	Controlled by electronic control unit – no adjustment possible

Ignition system (continued)

Spark plugs

Type:

SOHC models (except C 18 NZ and C20NE)	Vauxhall P/N 91143775 (Champion WR7DC)
C 18 NZ and C 20 NE	Vauxhall P/N 90356323 (Champion WR8DC)
DOHC models	Vauxhall P/N 90444724 (Champion FR8LDC)
Electrode gap (all models)	0.8 mm

Clutch

Clutch pedal travel

Right-hand-drive models	134 to 141 mm
Left-hand -drive models	125 to 132 mm

Braking system

Minimum front brake pad lining thickness (including backing plate)

All models	7.0 mm

Minimum rear brake pad lining thickness (including backing plate)

All models	7.0 mm

Minimum rear brake shoe lining thickness

All models	0.5 mm above rivet heads

Suspension and steering

Power steering pump drivebelt deflection

All models	10.0 mm

Electrical system

Alternator drive belt deflection

All models	10.0 mm

Torque wrench settings	Nm	lbf ft
Alternator mounting nuts and bolts – SOHC models with V-belt:		
Alternator to bracket (M8)	30	22
Alternator to bracket (M10)	40	29
Engine oil drain plug	55	41
Power steering pump mounting bolts – 1.8 and 2.0 litre engine models:		
Bolts 'A' and 'C' (see illustration 18.5)	25	18
Bolts 'B' (see illustration 18.5)	40	30
Roadwheel bolts	110	81
Spark plugs	25	18

Maintenance schedule

The maintenance intervals in this manual are provided with the assumption that you, not the dealer, will be carrying out the work. These are the minimum maintenance intervals recommended by the manufacturer for vehicles driven daily. If you wish to keep your vehicle in peak condition at all times, you may wish to perform some of these procedures more often. We encourage frequent maintenance, because it enhances the efficiency, performance and resale value of your vehicle.

If the vehicle is driven in dusty areas, used to tow a trailer, or driven frequently at slow speeds (idling in traffic) or on short journeys, more frequent maintenance intervals are recommended. Vauxhall recommend that the service intervals are halved for vehicles that are used under these conditions.

When the vehicle is new, it should be serviced by a factory-authorised dealer service department, to preserve the factory warranty.

Maintenance is essential for ensuring safety and for getting the best in terms of performance and economy from your vehicle. Over the years, the need for periodic lubrication - oiling, greasing, and so on - has been drastically reduced, if not eliminated. This has unfortunately tended to lead some owners to think that because no action is required, components either no longer exist, or will last for ever. This is certainly not the case; it is essential to carry out regular visual examination comprehensively to spot any possible defects at an early stage before they develop into major expensive repairs.

The following service schedules are a list of the maintenance requirements, and the intervals at which they should be carried out, as recommended by the manufacturers. Where applicable, these procedures are covered in greater detail near the beginning of each relevant Chapter.

Every 250 miles (400 km) or weekly

- [ ] Refer to "Weekly checks"

Basic service, every 9000 miles (15 000 km) or 12 months - whichever comes sooner

- [ ] Renew the engine oil and oil filter (Section 3).
- [ ] Check all hoses and other components for fluid leaks (Section 4).
- [ ] Check the steering and suspension components (Section 5).
- [ ] Check the condition of the driveshaft rubber gaiters (Section 6).
- [ ] Check the automatic transmission fluid level (if applicable) (Section 7).
- [ ] Check the radiator for blockage (e.g. dead insects) and clean as necessary (Section 8).
- [ ] Check and adjust the idle speed and mixture (if applicable) (Section 9).
- [ ] Check the exhaust system for corrosion, leaks and security (Section 10).
- [ ] Check all wiring for condition and security (Section 11).
- [ ] Check and adjust the ignition timing (if applicable) (Section 12).
- [ ] Renew the brake fluid (Section 13).
- [ ] Check the brake pad friction material for wear (Section 14).
- [ ] Check the handbrake linkage (Section 15).
- [ ] Check the rear brake pressure-regulating valve adjustment (if applicable) (Section 16)
- [ ] Check the power steering fluid level (if applicable) (Section 17).
- [ ] Check the power steering pump drivebelt (if applicable), (Section 18).
- [ ] Check the rear suspension level control system height, if fitted (Section 19).
- [ ] Check the bodywork (Section 20).
- [ ] Lubricate all locks and hinges (Section 21).
- [ ] Check the alternator V-belt (Section 22).

- [ ] Check the headlamp alignment (Section 23).
- [ ] Renew the pollen filter (Section 24)
- [ ] Replace battery in the door-lock key (if applicable) (Section 25).
- [ ] Carry out a road test (Section 26).

Note: *Vauxhall specify that an Exhaust Emissions Test should be carried out at least annually. However, this requires special equipment, and is performed as part of the MOT test (refer to Chapter 4C and to the Reference Section).*

Full service, every 18 000 miles (30 000 km) or 24 months - whichever comes sooner

Along with the 'basic service', carry out the following:

- [ ] Renew the coolant (Section 27).
- [ ] Renew the air cleaner element (Section 28).
- [ ] Renew the fuel filter (Section 29).
- [ ] Renew the spark plugs (SOHC only) (Section 30).
- [ ] Distributor cap and HT lead check (Section 31).
- [ ] Check the clutch cable adjustment (Section 32).
- [ ] Check the manual transmission oil level (Section 33).
- [ ] Check the automatic transmission (Section 34).
- [ ] Check the brake drum shoe for wear (Section 35).
- [ ] Check the condition and operation of the seat belts (Section 36)

Major service, every 36 000 miles (60 000 km) or 48 months - whichever comes sooner

Along with the 'full service', carry out the following:

- [ ] Renew timing belt (Section 37).
- [ ] Renew the spark plugs (DOHC models only) (Section 38).
- [ ] Renew automatic transmission fluid*.

* Note: *If a vehicle is used for heavy-duty work (e.g. taxi work, caravan/trailer towing, mostly short-distance, stop-start city driving) the fluid must be changed every 36 months or 27 000 miles (45 000 km), whichever occurs first.*

1

Maintenance procedures

1 Introduction

1 This Chapter is designed to help the home mechanic maintain his/her vehicle for safety, economy, long life and peak performance.

2 The Chapter contains a master maintenance schedule, followed by Sections dealing specifically with each task in the schedule. Visual checks, adjustments, component renewal and other helpful items are included. Refer to the accompanying illustrations of the engine compartment and the underside of the vehicle for the locations of the various components.

3 Servicing your vehicle according to the mileage/time maintenance schedule and the following Sections will provide a planned maintenance programme, which should result in a long and reliable service life. This is a comprehensive plan, so maintaining some items but not others at the specified service intervals, will not produce the same results.

4 As you service your vehicle, you will discover that many of the procedures can - and should - be grouped together, because of the particular procedure being performed, or because of the proximity of two otherwise-unrelated components to one another. For example, if the vehicle is raised for any reason, the exhaust can be inspected at the same time as the suspension and steering components.

5 The first step in this maintenance programme is to prepare yourself before the actual work begins. Read through all the Sections relevant to the work to be carried out, then make a list and gather all the parts and tools required. If a problem is come across, seek advice from a parts specialist, or a dealers service department.

2 Maintenance

1 If, from the time the vehicle is new, routine maintenance schedule is followed closely, frequent checks made of fluid levels and high-wear items, as recommended, the engine will be kept in relatively good running condition. The need for additional work will be minimised.

2 It is possible that there will be times when the engine is running poorly due to the lack of regular maintenance. This is even more likely if a used vehicle, which has not received regular and frequent maintenance checks, is purchased. In such cases, additional work may need to be carried out, outside of the regular maintenance intervals.

3 If engine wear is suspected, a compression test (refer to Chapter 2A) will provide valuable information regarding the overall performance of the main internal components. Such a test can be used as a basis to decide on the extent of the work to be carried out. If, for example, a compression test indicates serious internal engine wear, conventional maintenance as described in this Chapter will not greatly improve the performance of the engine. It may also prove a waste of time and money, unless extensive overhaul work is carried out first.

4 The following series of operations are those most often required to improve the performance of a generally poor-running engine:

Primary operations

a) *Clean, inspect and test the battery (See "Weekly Checks")*

b) *Check all the engine related fluids (See "Weekly Checks")*

c) *Check the condition and tension of the auxiliary drivebelt (Sections 18 and 22, as appropriate).*

d) *Renew the spark plugs (Sections 30 and 38, as appropriate).*

e) *Inspect the distributor cap, rotor arm and HT leads, as applicable (Section 31).*

f) *Check the condition of the air filter, and renew if necessary (Section 28).*

g) *Check the fuel filter (Section 29).*

h) *Check the condition of all hoses, and check for fluid leaks (Section 4).*

i) *Check the idle speed and mixture settings, as applicable (Section 9).*

5 If the above operations do not prove fully effective, carry out the following secondary operations:

Secondary operations

All items listed under "Primary operations", plus the following:

a) *Check the charging system (Chapter 5).*

b) *Check the ignition system (Chapter 5).*

c) *Check the fuel system (Chapter 4).*

d) *Renew the distributor cap and rotor arm (Section 31).*

e) *Renew the ignition HT leads (Section 31).*

Engine compartment component locations (airbox removed) - C 14 NZ model

1 VIN plate
2 Air cleaner casing
3 Suspension strut top cover
4 Washer fluid reservoir
5 Brake fluid reservoir
6 Alternator
7 Throttle cable
8 Tie-rods

9 Fuel injection unit
10 Coolant expansion tank
11 Clutch cable
12 Ignition coil
13 Battery positive lead
14 Battery negative lead
15 Battery condition indicator

16 Distributor
17 Radiator
18 Cooling fan motor
19 Engine oil level dipstick
20 Engine oil filler cap
21 Oxygen sensor
22 Air cleaner hot air tube

1

Engine compartment component locations - C 16 SE model

1 VIN plate
2 Air cleaner casing
3 Suspension strut top cover
4 Washer fluid reservoir
5 Brake fluid reservoir
6 Throttle body
7 Inlet manifold
8 Tie-rods

9 Throttle cable
10 Coolant expansion tank
11 Clutch cable
12 Battery positive lead
13 Battery negative lead
14 Battery condition indicator
15 Power steering fluid reservoir

16 Ignition coil
17 Radiator
18 Cooling fan motor
19 Engine oil level dipstick
20 Engine oil filler cap
21 Fuel injectors
22 Fuel rail

Engine compartment component locations - C 20 XE model

1 VIN plate
2 Air cleaner casing
3 Suspension strut top cover
4 Windscreen/tailgate washer fluid reservoir
5 Brake fluid reservoir
6 Air mass meter
7 Airbox
8 Fuse/relay box

9 Coolant expansion tank
10 Headlight washer fluid reservoir
11 ABS hydraulic modulator
12 Ignition coil
13 Battery positive lead
14 Battery negative lead
15 Battery condition indicator

16 Power steering fluid reservoir
17 Distributor
18 Radiator
19 Engine oil level dipstick
20 Spark plug cover
21 Throttle cable
22 Engine oil filler cap

**Front underbody view -
C 16 SE model**

1 Brake caliper
2 Anti-roll bar securing nut
3 Suspensioh lower arm
4 Catalytic converter
5 Subframe
6 Power steering fluid cooler pipes
7 Oil filter
8 Clutch cover plate
9 Differential cover plate
10 Engine oil drain plug
11 Driveshaft
12 Rear engine/transmission mounting-to-
   subframe nuts
13 Exhaust sprung joint

1

Rear underbody view

1 Shock absorber
2 Exhaust expansion box
3 Fuel tank filler pipe
4 Torsion beam
5 Fuel filter
6 Fuel tank
7 Fuel tank securing straps
8 Handbrake cable
9 Coil spring
10 Trailing arm

3.4 Removing the engine undershield - DOHC models

3.7A Loosening the oil drain plug - SOHC models

3.7B Engine oil drain plug - DOHC models

Basic service, every 9000 miles (15 000 km) or 12 months

3 Engine oil and filter - renewal

Note: *Always buy a sump plug washer (and plug, if possible) when buying an oil filter.*

Removal

1 Ideally, the oil should be drained with the engine warm, just after the vehicle has been driven, as the oil will drain more easily, and most of any built-up sludge will be removed with it.

2 Make sure that you have plenty of clean rags and newspapers handy to mop up any spills.

3 Take care not to touch the exhaust or any other hot parts of the engine when working under the vehicle. To avoid any possibility of scalding, and to protect yourself from possible skin irritants and other harmful contaminants in used engine oils, it is advisable to wear gloves when carrying out this work. Access to the underside of the vehicle will be greatly improved if it can be raised on a lift, driven onto ramps, or jacked up and supported on axle stands. Whichever method is chosen, make sure that the vehicle remains level, or if it is at an angle, that the drain plug is at the lowest point. The drain plug is located in the rear face of the sump.

4 On DOHC engine models, release the securing clips, and remove the access hatch from the engine undershield for access to the oil drain plug **(see illustration)**.

5 Remove the oil filler cap from the camshaft cover (twist it through a quarter turn anti-clockwise and withdraw it).

6 Place a container beneath the oil drain plug at the rear of the sump.

7 Using a spanner, or preferably a socket and bar, slacken the drain plug about half a turn **(see illustrations)**. Remove the plug completely. If possible, try to keep the plug pressed into the sump while unscrewing it by hand the last couple of turns.

HAYNES HiNT

As the drain plug releases from the threads, move it away quickly so the stream of oil, running out of the sump, goes into the container not up your sleeve.

8 Allow ten to fifteen minutes for the oil to drain completely. It may be necessary to move the container as the oil flow slows to a trickle.

9 After all the oil has drained, wipe the drain plug and the sealing washer with a clean rag. Examine the condition of the sump plug and renew it if it shows signs of wear, especially rounding of the corners. Clean the area around the drain plug opening and refit the plug complete with the new washer. Tighten the plug securely, preferably to the specified torque using a torque wrench.

10 The oil filter is located at the front left-hand side of the engine on 1.4 and 1.6 litre engines, or on the right-hand side of the engine on 1.8 and 2.0 litre engines. On 1.8 and 2.0 litre models, improved access to the oil filter can be obtained by jacking up the front of the vehicle (if not already done) and removing the right-hand roadwheel.

11 On DOHC engine models, release the securing clips, and remove the access hatch to the right-hand side of the engine for access to the oil filter **(see illustration)**.

12 Move the container into position under the oil filter.

13 Use an oil filter removal tool to slacken the filter initially, then unscrew it by hand the rest of the way **(see illustrations)**. Empty the oil from the old filter into the container.

14 Use a clean rag to remove all oil, dirt and

3.11 Removing the access hatch for access to the oil filter - DOHC models

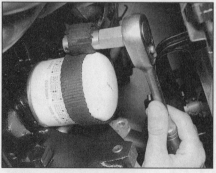

3.13A Using an oil filter removal tool to slacken the filter - SOHC models

3.13B Using an oil filter removal tool to slacken the filter - DOHC models

sludge from the filter sealing area on the engine. Check the old filter to make sure that the rubber sealing ring has not stuck to the engine. If it has, carefully remove it.

Renewal

15 Apply a light coating of clean engine oil to the sealing ring on the new filter, then screw the filter into position on the engine. Tighten the filter firmly by hand only – **do not** use any tools.

16 Remove the old oil and all tools from under the vehicle then, if applicable, lower the vehicle to the ground.

17 Fill the engine through the filler hole in the camshaft cover, using the correct grade and type of oil, as described in 'Weekly Checks'. Pour in half the specified quantity of oil first, then wait a few minutes for the oil to drain into the sump. Continue to add oil a small quantity at a time until the level is up to the lower mark on the dipstick. Adding a further 1.0 litre will bring the level up to the upper mark on the dipstick.

18 Start the engine and run it for a few minutes, while checking for leaks around the oil filter seal and the sump drain plug. Note that there may be a delay of a few seconds before the low oil pressure warning light goes out when the engine is first started. The oil circulates through the new oil filter and the engine oil galleries before the pressure builds up.

19 On DOHC engine models, refit the access hatches to the engine undershield after checking for oil leaks.

20 Stop the engine and wait a few minutes for the oil to settle in the sump again. With the new oil circulated and the filter now completely full, recheck the level on the dipstick and add more oil as necessary.

21 Dispose of the old engine oil safely; do not pour it down a drain.

Note: It is antisocial and illegal to dump oil down the drain. To find the location of your local oil recycling bank, call this number free.

4 Hose and fluid leak check

Engine

1 Visually inspect the engine joint faces, gaskets and seals for any signs of water or oil leaks. Pay particular attention to the areas around the camshaft cover, cylinder head, oil filter and sump joint faces. Remember that, over a period of time, some very slight seepage from these areas is to be expected –

what you are really looking for is any indication of a serious leak. Should a leak be found, renew the offending gasket or oil seal by referring to the appropriate Chapters in this manual.

2 Also check the security and condition of all the engine related pipes and hoses. Ensure that all cable ties or securing clips are in place, and in good condition. Clips that are broken or missing can lead to chafing of the hoses, pipes or wiring, which could cause more serious problems in the future.

Coolant

3 Carefully check the radiator hoses and heater hoses along their entire length. Renew any hose that is cracked, swollen or deteriorated. Cracks will show up better if the hose is squeezed. Pay close attention to the clips that secure the hoses to the cooling system components. Hose clips can pinch and puncture hoses, resulting in cooling system leaks. It is always beneficial to renew hose clips whenever possible.

4 Inspect all the cooling system components (hoses, joint faces, etc.) for leaks.

A leak in the cooling system will usually show up as white or rust coloured deposits on the area adjoining the leak .

5 Where any problems are found on system components, renew the component or gasket with reference to Chapter 3.

Automatic transmission

6 Where applicable, inspect the automatic transmission fluid cooler hoses for leaks or deterioration.

Fuel system

7 With the vehicle raised, inspect the petrol tank and filler neck for punctures, cracks and other damage. The connection between the filler neck and tank is especially critical. Sometimes a rubber filler neck or connecting hose will leak due to loose retaining clamps or deteriorated rubber.

8 Carefully check all rubber hoses and metal fuel lines leading away from the petrol tank. Check for loose connections, deteriorated hoses, crimped lines, and other damage. Pay particular attention to the vent pipes and hoses, which often loop up around the filler

neck and can become blocked or crimped. Follow the lines to the front of the vehicle, carefully inspecting them all the way. Renew damaged sections as necessary.

9 From within the engine compartment, check the security of all fuel hose attachments and pipe unions, and inspect the fuel hoses and vacuum hoses for kinks, chafing and deterioration.

Power steering

10 Where applicable, check the condition of the power steering fluid hoses and pipes.

5 Steering and suspension check

Front suspension and steering check

1 Raise the front of the vehicle, and securely support it on axle stands.

2 Visually inspect the balljoint dust covers and the steering rack-and-pinion gaiters for splits, chafing or deterioration. Any wear of these components will cause loss of lubricant, together with dirt and water entry, resulting in rapid deterioration of the balljoints or steering gear.

3 On vehicles with power steering, check the fluid hoses for chafing or deterioration, and the pipe and hose unions for fluid leaks. Also check for signs of fluid leakage under pressure from the steering gear rubber gaiters, which would indicate failed fluid seals within the steering gear.

4 Grasp the roadwheel at the 12 o'clock and 6 o'clock positions, and try to rock it **(see illustration)**. Very slight free play may be felt, but if the movement is appreciable, further investigation is necessary to determine the source. Continue rocking the wheel while an assistant depresses the footbrake. If the movement is now eliminated or significantly reduced, it is likely that the hub bearings are at fault. If the free play is still evident with the footbrake depressed, then there is wear in the suspension joints or mountings.

5.4 Checking the front wheel hub for wear

6.1 Check the condition of the driveshaft joint gaiters

A Gaiter   *B Retaining clips*

7.2 Withdrawing the automatic transmission fluid level dipstick

7.4 Automatic transmission fluid level dipstick markings

A Markings for fluid at operating temperature
B Markings for cold fluid

5 Now grasp the wheel at the 9 o'clock and 3 o'clock positions, and try to rock it as before. Any movement felt now may again be caused by wear in the hub bearings or the steering track-rod balljoints. If the inner or outer balljoint is worn, the visual movement will be obvious.

6 Using a large screwdriver or flat bar, check for wear in the suspension mounting bushes by levering between the relevant suspension component and its attachment point. Some movement is to be expected as the mountings are made of rubber, but excessive wear should be obvious. Also check the condition of any visible rubber bushes, looking for splits, cracks or contamination of the rubber.

7 With the car standing on its wheels, have an assistant turn the steering wheel back and forth about an eighth of a turn each way. There should be very little, if any, lost movement between the steering wheel and roadwheels. If this is not the case, closely observe the joints and mountings previously described, but in addition, check the steering column universal joints for wear, and the rack-and-pinion steering gear itself.

Suspension strut/shock absorber check

Note: *Suspension struts/shock absorbers should always be renewed in pairs on the same axle.*

8 Check for any signs of fluid leakage around the suspension strut/shock absorber body, or from the rubber gaiter around the piston rod. Should any fluid be noticed, the suspension strut/shock absorber is defective internally, and should be renewed.

9 The efficiency of the suspension strut/shock absorber may be checked by bouncing the vehicle at each corner. The body will return to its normal position and stop after being depressed. If it rises and returns on a rebound, the suspension strut/shock absorber is probably suspect. Examine also the suspension strut/shock absorber upper and lower mountings for any signs of wear.

6 Driveshaft gaiter check

1 With the vehicle raised and securely supported on stands, turn the steering onto full lock, then slowly rotate the roadwheel. Inspect the condition of the outer constant velocity (CV) joint rubber gaiters, squeezing the gaiters to open out the folds **(see illustration)**. Check for signs of cracking, splits or deterioration of the rubber, which may allow the grease to escape, and lead to water and grit entry into the joint. Also check the security and condition of the retaining clips. Repeat these checks on the inner CV joints. If any damage or deterioration is found, the gaiters should be renewed as described in Chapter 8.

2 At the same time, check the general condition of the CV joints themselves by first holding the driveshaft and attempting to rotate the wheel. Repeat this check by holding the inner joint and attempting to rotate the driveshaft. Any appreciable movement indicates wear in the joints, wear in the driveshaft splines, or a loose driveshaft retaining nut.

7 Automatic transmission fluid level check

Note: *The transmission fluid level can be checked either when it is cold (only below 35°C (100°F) outside temperature) or when it is fully warmed up to normal operating temperature (after driving for a distance of approximately 12 miles/20 km).*

 Be careful to keep loose clothing, long hair, etc., well clear of hot or moving components when working under the bonnet

Transmission cold

1 Park the vehicle on level ground and apply the handbrake firmly. With the engine running at no more than idle speed and your foot firmly on the brake pedal, move the selector lever through all positions, ending in position "P". Allow the engine to idle for one minute, then check the level within two minutes.

2 With the engine still idling and position "P" still selected, open the bonnet and withdraw the transmission dipstick from the filler tube located in the front of the transmission casing, at the left-hand end of the engine **(see illustration)**.

3 Note the fluid's condition (see below), then wipe clean the dipstick using a clean, non-fluffy rag, insert it fully back into the tube and withdraw it again.

4 The level should be up to the "MAX" mark on the "+20°C" side of the dipstick **(see illustration)**.

5 If topping-up is required, switch off the ignition and add only good quality fluid of the specified type through the filler tube. If significant amounts of fluid are being lost (carefully note the amounts being added, and how often), check the transmission for leaks and either repair the fault or take the vehicle to a Vauxhall dealer for attention.

6 When the level is correct, ensure that the dipstick is pressed firmly into the filler tube.

Transmission fully warmed up

7 Work exactly as described above, but take the level reading from the "+ 80°C" side of the dipstick. In this case, the level must be between the dipstick "MAX" and "MIN" marks.

Checking the fluid's condition

8 Whenever the fluid level is checked, examine the condition of the fluid and compare its colour, smell and texture with that of new fluid.

9 If the fluid is dark, almost black, and smells burnt, it is possible that the transmission friction material is worn or disintegrating. The

vehicle should be taken to a Vauxhall dealer or automatic transmission specialist for immediate attention.

10 If the fluid is milky, this is due to the presence of emulsified droplets of water. This may be caused either by condensation after a prolonged period of short journeys or by the entry of water through the dipstick/filler tube or breather. If the fluid does not revert to its normal appearance after a long journey it must be renewed or advice should be sought from a Vauxhall dealer or automatic transmission specialist.

11 If the fluid is varnish-like (i.e. light to dark brown and tacky) it has oxidised due to overheating or to over- or under-filling. If renewal of the fluid does not cure the problem, the vehicle should be taken to a Vauxhall dealer or automatic transmission specialist for immediate attention.

12 If at any time on checking the fluid level or on draining the fluid, particles of dirt, metal chips or other foreign matter are found in the fluid, the vehicle must be taken to a Vauxhall dealer or automatic transmission specialist for immediate attention. It may be necessary to strip, clean and reassemble at least the valve body, if not the complete transmission, to rectify any fault.

8 Radiator inspection and cleaning

1 Inspect radiator for leaks or corrosion, especially around the outlet or inlet connectors.

2 Clean the radiator with a soft brush or compressed air. Remove any debris, like dead insects or leaves.

3 If leaks are visible, replace radiator. Refer to Chapter 3, if necessary.

9 Idle speed and mixture - adjustment

> ⚠ *Warning: Certain procedures in this Section require the removal of fuel lines and connections, which may result in some fuel spillage. Before carrying out any operation on the fuel system, refer to the precautions given in 'Safety first!' at the beginning of this manual, and follow them implicitly. Petrol is a highly dangerous and volatile liquid, and the precautions necessary when handling it cannot be overstressed.*

Note: *Certain adjustment points in the fuel system are protected by tamperproof caps, plugs or seals. In some territories, it is an offence to drive a vehicle with broken or missing tamperproof seals. Before disturbing a tamperproof seal check that no local or national laws will be broken by doing so, and fit a new tamperproof seal after adjustment is complete, where required by law. Do not break tamperproof seals on an engine that is still under warranty. To carry out the adjustments, an accurate tachometer and an exhaust gas analyser (CO meter) will be required.*

Adjustment

Carburettor models

1 In order to check the idle speed and mixture adjustment, the following conditions must be met.

(a) *The engine must be at normal operating temperature.*

(b) *All electrical consumers (cooling fan, heater blower, headlights, etc.) must be switched off.*

(c) *The ignition timing and spark plug gaps must be correctly adjusted – see Sections 12 and 30 or 38.*

(d) *The throttle cable free play must be correctly adjusted – see Chapter 4A.*

(e) *The air intake components must be free from leaks, and the air cleaner filter element must be clean.*

(f) *The fast idle speed adjustment screw must not touch the fast idle cam during the procedure.*

2 Connect a tachometer and an exhaust gas analyser to the vehicle in accordance with the manufacturer's instructions.

3 Start the engine and run it an 2000 rpm for approximately 30 seconds, then allow it to idle. If the idle speed is outside the specified limits, adjust by means of the throttle stop screw **(see illustration)**.

4 When the idle speed is correct check the CO level in the exhaust gas. If it is outside the specified limits, adjust by means of the idle mixture adjustment screw **(see illustration)**. Turn the screw in very small increments until the CO level is correct.

5 With the idle mixture correct, readjust the idle speed if necessary.

6 If the cooling fan cuts in during the adjustment procedure, stop the adjustments and continue when the cooling fan stops.

7 When both idle speed and mixture are correctly set, stop the engine and disconnect the test equipment.

8 Fit new tamperproof seals to the adjustment screws, where this is required by law.

Fuel injection models

9 On all fuel injection engines, the idle speed and mixture are controlled by the electronic control unit (ECU), and no adjustment is possible. If any problems are suspected, the vehicle should be taken to a Vauxhall dealer who will have the necessary specialist test equipment to carry out system checks and fault diagnosis. Refer to Chapter 4B for further details of the fuel injection systems.

10 Exhaust system check

1 With the engine off, check the security of the exhaust system. Pay particular attention to the rubber mountings that suspend the exhaust.

2 Start the engine and check underneath for leaks, which can be heard. This job is made easier if you have access to a ramp.

3 Listen for exhaust leaks from around the front pipe to exhaust manifold joint.

4 For further information, refer to Chapter 4C

11 Wiring check

1 Check all wiring in both the engine compartment and under the car.

2 Ensure that all wiring clips or clamps are secure.

3 Pay particular attention to wiring near components that get hot, i.e. exhaust systems.

4 Make sure that electrical connections are secure and undamaged.

9.3 Carburettor idle speed adjustment (throttle stop) screw (arrowed)

9.4 Tamperproof plug (arrowed) covering carburettor idle mixture adjustment screw

1

12 Ignition timing

⚠️ **Warning: Voltages produced by an electronic ignition system are considerably higher than those produced by conventional ignition systems. Extreme care must be taken when working on the system with the ignition switched on. Persons with surgically implanted cardiac pacemaker devices should keep away from the ignition circuits, components and test equipment.**

Note: *A tachometer and a timing light will be required during this procedure.*

Carburettor engine

Check

1 Start the engine and run it until it reaches normal operating temperature, then switch off.
2 Disconnect the vacuum pipe from the distributor vacuum unit.
3 Connect a tachometer and a stroboscopic timing light to the engine, in accordance with the equipment manufacturer's instructions. Note that the timing light should be connected to No 1 cylinder HT circuit (No 1 cylinder is nearest the timing belt end of the engine).
4 Start the engine, and check that the idle speed is between 700 and 1000 rpm.
5 Point the timing light at the timing pointer on the rear timing belt cover, and check that the pointer is aligned with the upper notch in the crankshaft pulley, representing 5° BTDC. There are two notches on the pulley representing 5° and 10° BTDC, refer to Chapter 5, for further details.

Adjustment

6 If the notches and the pointer are not aligned as previously described, loosen the distributor clamp nut and turn the distributor body slightly in the required direction to align the notches and pointer.
7 Tighten the distributor clamp nut, and check that the notches and pointer are still aligned.
8 Stop the engine and disconnect the timing light and the tachometer, then reconnect the vacuum pipe to the distributor vacuum diaphragm unit.

Fuel injection engines

9 No adjustment of the ignition timing is possible on fuel injection engines, as the adjustment is carried out automatically by the electronic control unit.
10 If a fault is suspected, the ignition timing can be checked by a Vauxhall dealer, using dedicated test equipment.

13 Brake fluid renewal

⚠️ **Warning: Brake hydraulic fluid can harm your eyes and damage painted surfaces, so use extreme caution when handling and pouring it. Do not use fluid that has been standing open for some time, as it absorbs moisture from the air. Excess moisture can cause a dangerous loss of braking effectiveness.**

> **HAYNES HiNT** *Old hydraulic fluid is usually darker in colour than new fluid.*

1 Renew the brake and bleed the system. Refer to Chapter 9 for full details.

14 Brake pad check

> **HAYNES HiNT**
For a quick check, the thickness of the friction material on each brake pad can be measured through the aperture in the caliper

1 With the front or rear (as applicable) of the vehicle raised, remove the wheels and check brake pads for wear. Renew the pads if the lining is below that specified. See Chapter 9, for specifications and full details.

15 Handbrake linkage check

1 With the vehicle raised, check the operation of the handbrake and lubricate the linkages. Refer to Chapter 9, for further details.

16 Rear brake pressure-regulating valve check (Estate and Van models only)

Check

1 To check the adjustment of the valve, the vehicle must be unladen (i.e. there should be

16.4 Rear brake pressure-regulating valve components - Estate and Van models

1 Operating lever	3 Plastic bushes
2 Spring	4 Bracket

no luggage or passengers in the vehicle) and the fuel tank should be a maximum of half-full. On models fitted with manual rear suspension level control, check that the system is pressurised to a minimum of 0.8 bars (see Section 19).
2 The vehicle must be standing on its wheels.
3 To check the operation of the valve, fully depress the brake pedal, then quickly release it.
4 The valve operating lever **(see illustration)** should move. If the lever does not move, the valve is faulty, and should be renewed.

Adjust

5 To adjust the valve, ensure that the valve operating lever is resting against its stop - if necessary, press the operating lever up to its stop, towards the front of the vehicle. The ends of the spring should lie in the plastic bushes in the valve operating lever and the bracket on the rear suspension torsion beam, and the spring should be free of play, and free from tension.
6 If necessary, loosen the nut securing the spring bracket to the rear suspension torsion beam, and move the bracket backwards or forwards as necessary until the spring is free of play and free from tension. Tighten the bracket securing nut on completion of adjustment.

17 Power steering fluid check

1 The power steering fluid level is checked with a dipstick attached to the reservoir filler cap. The reservoir is located at the front left-hand side of the engine compartment, next to the battery.
2 The fluid level should be checked with the engine stopped.
3 Unscrew the filler cap from the top of the

17.3 Power steering fluid level dipstick markings

A   Level with engine cold
B   Level with engine at operating
temperature

reservoir, and wipe all the fluid from the end with a clean rag or paper towel. Refit the reservoir filler cap, then remove it once more. Note the fluid level on the dipstick. When the engine is cold, the fluid level should be up to the lower mark on the dipstick. When the engine is at normal operating temperature, the fluid level should be up to the upper mark on the dipstick **(see illustration)**.
4 Top-up with the specified type of fluid if necessary **(see illustration)**, and securely refit the reservoir filler cap on completion.
5 If frequent topping-up proves to be necessary, this indicates that there is a leak in the hydraulic system, which should be located and rectified without delay.

18 Power steering pump drivebelt check

Note: *On some models, the pump is driven by the same belt that drives the alternator. For further details on checking, refer to Section 22.*

18.5 Mounting and adjuster bolts (arrowed) must be loosened to adjust power steering pump drivebelt tension - 1.8 and 2.0 litre SOHC models

For A, B and C see 'Torque wrench settings'

17.4 Topping-up the power steering fluid level

Check

2 Correct tensioning of the drivebelt will ensure that it has a long life. Beware, however, of over-tightening, as this can cause excessive wear in the pump.
3 The belt should be inspected along its entire length regularly, and if it is found to be worn, frayed or cracked, it should be renewed as a precaution against breakage in service.
4 Although special tools are available for measuring the belt tension, a good approximation can be achieved if the belt is tensioned so that there is approximately 10.0 mm of free movement under firm thumb pressure at the mid-point of the belt run between pulleys. If in doubt, err on the slack side, as an excessively tight belt may cause damage to the pump.

Adjust

5 If adjustment is required, or if the belt is to be renewed, slacken the adjuster and mounting bolts shown in **(see illustration)**.
6 Slacken the adjuster nuts, and adjust the length of the threaded rod in order to tension or remove the belt, as necessary **(see illustration)**.
7 Where applicable, fit the new belt around the pulleys, then tension the belt as described previously. On DOHC models remove the air cleaner assembly.
8 Tighten the adjuster nuts, and tighten the adjuster and mounting bolts to the specified torque on completion.

18.6 Adjusting the length of the power steering pump threaded rod - 1.8 and 2.0 litre SOHC models

9 If a new drivebelt has been fitted, recheck the tension after a few hundred miles.

19 Rear suspension level control system check

1 The rear suspension level control system pressure is checked using a tyre pressure gauge on the inflation valve located in the rear right-hand side of the luggage compartment floor. The check should be carried out with the vehicle unladen.
2 Remove the cap from the valve, and check that the system pressure is 0.8 bars (11.6 Ibf/in^2). The pressure must never be allowed to drop below this value, even with the vehicle unladen. Adjust if necessary using a tyre pump.

20 Bodywork check

1 Clean the outside of the vehicle. If possible, clean underneath as well. If using a pressure cleaner take care not to damage any electrical components, especially in the engine compartment.
2 Check all around for signs of damage or corrosion and treat accordingly. Repair stone chips when you can to prevent rusting.
3 The wax-based underbody protective coating should be inspected annually, preferably just prior to Winter, when the underbody should be washed down as thoroughly as possible without disturbing the protective coating. Any damage to the coating should be repaired using a wax-based sealer. If any of the body panels are disturbed for repair or renewal, do not forget to replace the coating and to inject wax into door panels, sills and box sections, to maintain the level of protection provided by the vehicle manufacturer.
4 Refer to Chapter 11, for more details.

21 Lock and hinge check

1 Lubricate locks and hinges on all doors, tailgates (or boot lid) and bonnet.
2 Check for wear or damage and ensure correct operation of safety catches.
3 Check security of the bonnet stay and it's securing clip.
4 Read Chapter 11, for further details.

1

22.9 Sliding the drivebelt from the alternator pulley - C 16 SE model with power steering

24.2 Lifting the pollen filter from its housing

25.3 Replacing the battery in the door key
1 Battery (note, positive '+' side up)   2 Bulb

22 Alternator V-belt check

Note: *The new ribbed V-belt, fitted to later and DOHC models, is automatically adjusted by a tension roller.*

Check

1 Correct tensioning of the alternator drivebelt will ensure that it has a long life. Beware, however, of over-tightening, as this can cause excessive wear in the alternator.
2 On some models, the alternator drivebelt also drives the power steering pump.
3 Disconnect the air intake trunking from the air cleaner, and the airbox or the throttle body, as applicable, and remove it for improved access.
4 The belt should be inspected along its entire length regularly, and if it is found to be worn, frayed or cracked, it should be renewed as a precaution against breakage in service. It is advisable to carry a spare drivebelt of the correct type in the vehicle at all times.
5 Although special tools are available for measuring the belt tension, a good approximation can be achieved if the belt is tensioned so that there is approximately 13.0 mm of free movement under firm thumb pressure at the mid-point of the longest run between pulleys. If in doubt, err on the slack side, as an excessively tight belt may cause damage to the alternator.

Adjustment

6 If adjustment is required, loosen the alternator upper and lower mounting nuts and bolts, and with the mounting bolts just holding the unit firm, lever the alternator away from the engine using a wooden lever at the mounting bracket until the correct tension is achieved. Then tighten the mounting nuts and bolts. On no account lever at the free end of the alternator, as serious internal damage could be caused to the alternator.

Removal

7 If applicable, first remove the power steering pump drivebelt as described in Section 18.
8 Disconnect the air intake trunking from the air cleaner, and the airbox or the throttle body,

as applicable, and remove it for improved access. Loosen the alternator upper and lower mounting nuts and bolts sufficiently to allow the alternator to pivot towards the engine.
9 Slide the belt from the pulleys **(see illustration)**.

Refitting

10 Fit the new belt around the pulleys, and take up the slack in the belt by swinging the alternator away from the engine and lightly tightening the mounting nuts and bolts.
11 Tension the drivebelt as described previously in this sub-Section, and recheck the tension after a few hundred miles.
12 If applicable, refit the power steering drivebelt as described in Chapter 10.

23 Headlamp alignment

1 Refer to Chapter 12 for details.

24 Pollen filter renewal

Removal

1 Open the bonnet, and remove the scuttle water deflector panels, noting how they are located over the flanges on the scuttle.
2 Release the securing clips at the front of the now-exposed pollen filter, and carefully lift the filter from its housing **(see illustration)**.

Refitting

3 Fit the new filter using a reversal of the removal procedure, ensuring that the water deflector panels are correctly located on the scuttle.

25 Door lock key battery - renewal

1 Carefully prise open the outer cover from the key. Take care not to lose any of the internal components, as they are loose.
2 Remove the battery and discard it safely.
3 Place the new battery, "+" side up **(see**

illustration). Check the operation of the key. If the bulb does not light obtain a replacement.
4 Replace the outer cover.

26 Road test

Instruments and electrical equipment

1 Check the operation of all instruments and electrical equipment.
2 Make sure that all instruments read correctly, and switch on all electrical equipment in turn to check that it functions properly.

Steering and suspension

3 Check for any abnormalities in the steering, suspension, handling or road "feel".
4 Drive the vehicle, and check that there are no unusual vibrations or noises.
5 Check that the steering feels positive, with no excessive "sloppiness", or roughness, and check for any suspension noises when cornering, or when driving over bumps.

Drivetrain

6 Check the performance of the engine, clutch, transmission and driveshafts.
7 Turn the radio/cassette off and listen for any unusual noises from the engine, clutch and transmission.
8 Make sure that the engine runs smoothly when idling, and that there is no hesitation when accelerating.
9 Check that the clutch action is smooth and progressive, that the drive is taken up smoothly, and that the pedal travel is not excessive. Also listen for any noises when the clutch pedal is depressed.
10 Check that all gears can be engaged smoothly, without noise, and that the gear lever action is not abnormally vague or "notchy".
11 Listen for a metallic clicking sound from the front of the vehicle, as the vehicle is driven slowly in a circle with the steering on full lock. Carry out this check in both directions. If a clicking noise is heard, this indicates wear in a driveshaft joint, in which case, the complete driveshaft must be renewed (see Chapter 8).

Full service, every 18 000 miles (30 000 km) or 24 months

27 Coolant renewal

⚠ **Warning: Wait until the engine is cold before starting the procedure. Do not allow antifreeze to come in contact with your skin or with painted surfaces of the vehicle. Rinse off spills with plenty of water. Never leave antifreeze lying around in an open container. Always clean spilt fluids, as it can be harmful if swallowed.**

1 Refer to Chapter 3 for details.

28 Air cleaner element - renewal

1 The air cleaner assembly is located at the front right-hand side of the engine compartment.
2 Release the clips securing the cover to the air cleaner casing, then lift the cover sufficiently to remove the element **(see illustrations)**.
3 Wipe clean the inside surfaces of the cover and the main casing, and check that there is no foreign matter visible in the inlet duct.
4 Fit the new element, noting that the rubber locating flange should be uppermost, then refit the air cleaner cover and secure with the clips.

29 Fuel filter renewal

⚠ **Warning: Before carrying out the following operation, refer to the precautions given in "Safety first!" at the beginning of this manual, and follow them implicitly. Petrol is a highly dangerous and volatile liquid, and the precautions necessary when handling it cannot be overstressed.**

Carburettor models

Removal

1 The fuel filter is located in the carburettor fuel inlet pipe.
2 Disconnect the trunking from the air cleaner, then disconnect the vacuum pipe and breather hose from the airbox. Extract the three securing screws and lift off the airbox, complete with air trunking.
3 Place a wad of rag under the fuel inlet pipe at the carburettor to catch any fuel that may be spilled during the procedure.
4 Disconnect the fuel inlet hose from the carburettor. Be prepared for fuel spillage, and clamp or plug the end of the hose to reduce

unnecessary fuel loss. Take adequate fire precautions.
5 To remove the filter, carefully screw an M3 bolt approximately 5.0 mm into the end of the filter, and pull on the bolt to withdraw the filter from the end of the inlet pipe **(see illustration)**.

Refitting

6 Push the new filter into the inlet pipe, ensuring that it engages securely, then reconnect the fuel inlet hose, and refit the airbox.

Fuel injection models

Removal

7 The fuel filter is located on a bracket attached to the right-hand side of the fuel tank **(see illustration)**.
8 Clamp the fuel hoses at either end of the filter to minimise fuel loss when the hoses are disconnected, then place a container beneath the filter to catch the fuel that will be released.
9 Disconnect the fuel hoses from the filter. Be prepared for fuel spillage, and take adequate fire precautions.
10 Note the orientation of the filter (note the orientation of any flow direction markings that may appear on the filter body), then unscrew the clamp bolt, and withdraw the filter from its bracket. Note that the filter will still contain some petrol, which should be drained safely

into a container. Dispose of the old filter safely.

Refitting

11 Position the new filter in the retaining strap, ensuring that it is orientated correctly (make sure that the flow direction arrow(s) are correctly orientated, where applicable), then tighten the retaining strap screw to secure the filter.
12 Reconnect the hoses to the filter.
13 Run the engine and check for leaks on completion. If leakage is evident, stop the engine immediately, and rectify the problem without delay.

30 Spark plug renewal (SOHC)

Removal

1 The correct functioning of the spark plugs is vital for the correct running and efficiency of the engine. It is essential that the plugs fitted are appropriate for the engine. If the engine is in good condition, the spark plugs should not need attention between scheduled service intervals. Spark plug cleaning is rarely necessary and should not be attempted unless specialised equipment is available, as damage can easily be caused to the firing ends.

28.2A Release the clips securing the cover to the air cleaner casing . . .

28.2B . . . then lift the cover sufficiently to remove the element

29.5 Removing the fuel filter from the carburettor fuel inlet pipe

29.6 Fuel filter location

30.3 Removing a spark plug - SOHC models

30.9A Measuring a spark plug electrode gap using a feeler gauge

Refitting

11 Screw in the plugs by hand, then tighten them to the specified torque. Do not exceed the torque figure.

12 Push the HT leads firmly onto the spark plugs, ensuring that they are connected to their correct cylinders.

31 Distributor cap and HT lead check

HAYNES HiNT	*Number the HT leads before removal to ensure correct refitting.*

2 Identify each HT lead for position so that the leads can be refitted to their correct cylinders. Then disconnect the leads from the plugs by pulling on the connectors, not the leads.

3 Clean the area around each spark plug using a small paintbrush, then using a plug spanner (preferably with a rubber insert), unscrew and remove the plugs **(see illustration)**. Cover the spark plug holes with a clean rag to prevent the ingress of any foreign matter.

4 The condition of the spark plugs will tell much about the overall condition of the engine.

5 If the insulator nose of the spark plug is clean and white, with no deposits, this is a sign of a weak mixture, or too hot a plug. A hot plug transfers heat away from the electrode slowly and a cold plug transfers heat away quickly.

6 If the tip and insulator nose is covered with hard black-looking deposits, then this is indicative that the mixture is too rich. Should the plug be black and oily, then it is likely that the engine is fairly worn, as well as the mixture being too rich.

7 If the insulator nose is covered with light tan to greyish brown deposits, then the mixture is correct, and it is likely that the engine is in good condition.

8 The spark plug gap is of considerable importance, because if it is either too large or too small, the size of the spark and its efficiency will be seriously impaired. The spark plug gap should be set to the figure given in the Specifications.

9 To set it, measure the gap with a feeler gauge and then bend open, or close, the outer plug electrode until the correct gap is achieved. The centre electrode should never be bent, as this may crack the insulation and cause plug failure, if nothing worse **(see illustrations)**.

10 Before fitting new spark plugs check that their threaded connector sleeves are tight.

It is very often difficult to insert spark plugs into their holes without cross-threading them. To avoid this, fit a short length of 8 mm (internal diameter), rubber hose over the end of the spark plug. The flexible hose acts as a universal joint to help align the plug correctly. Should the plug begin to cross-thread, the hose will slip on the spark plug, preventing damage to the thread in the cylinder head.

1 Remove the distributor cap and HT leads, and wipe them clean. On DOHC models, unscrew the spark plug cover for access to the HT leads **(see illustration)**.

2 Check the HT leads one at a time. Remove the leads by gripping them on the spark plug connector and not the lead. This should prevent damage.

3 Wipe clean the coil connections. Remove the rotor arm, then visually check the distributor cap, rotor arm and HT leads for hairline cracks, signs of arcing and corrosion.

4 When refitting the distributor cap, check that the ends of the HT leads are fitted securely to the cap, plugs and coil. Also make sure that the spring-tensioned carbon brush in the centre of the distributor cap moves freely, and that the HT segments are not worn excessively.

5 Inspect the electrical and vacuum connections of the ignition/engine management systems, and make sure that they are clean and secure.

32 Clutch cable adjustment

1 Working inside the vehicle, ensure that the clutch pedal is in its normal rest position, then measure the distance from the centre of the

30.9B Measuring a spark plug electrode gap using a wire gauge

30.9C Adjusting a spark plug electrode gap using a special tool

31.1 Releasing a distributor cap securing clip

32.1A Measure the distance from the centre of the top edge of the pedal to the lowest point of the steering wheel . . .

32.1B . . . then fully depress the pedal and repeat the measurement

32.3 Removing the clip from the clutch cable threaded rod. Threaded rod adjuster flats arrowed

top edge of the pedal to the lowest point of the steering wheel. Fully depress the pedal, and repeat the measurement **(see illustrations)**. The measurements can be taken using a strip of wood or metal, as the important figure is the *difference* between the two measurements, i.e. the movement (stroke) of the pedal.

2 The difference between the two measurements must be as given in the Specifications. If not, adjust the clutch cable as follows to achieve the specified pedal movement.

3 Working in the engine compartment, remove the clip from the threaded rod at the clutch release arm on the transmission, then turn the threaded rod as required, using a spanner on the flats provided **(see illustration)**. Turn the rod clockwise to increase pedal movement, or anti-clockwise to decrease pedal movement. Recheck the pedal movement, and then refit the clip to the threaded rod on completion.

4 On a vehicle in which the clutch has covered a high mileage, it may no longer be possible to adjust the cable to achieve the specified pedal movement, and this indicates that the clutch friction disc requires renewal. *Note that when correctly adjusted, the clutch pedal will rest slightly higher than the brake pedal – it is incorrect for the two pedals to be in alignment. If the pedals are*

aligned, the cable requires adjustment. Note also that there should be no play in the clutch pedal.

5 Check also, the condition of the cable. Inspect the cable strands for fraying, and ensure that the cable is correctly routed, to avoid chafing against surrounding components. Renew the cable, as described in Chapter 6, if excessive wear or damage is evident.

33 Manual transmission fluid check

Note: *Models built after 1994 it is no longer necessary to check levels.*

1 Ensure that the vehicle is on level ground. On DOHC models remove the engine undershield as described in Chapter 11.

2 Unscrew the transmission oil level plug, which is located in the rear left of the differential housing on F10 and F13 transmissions, and in the rear right of the differential housing on F16 and F20 transmissions **(see illustrations)**. The oil level should be up to the bottom of the level plug orifice.

3 If necessary, top up the oil level through the breather/filler orifice in the gear selector cover. Unscrew the breather/filler plug, and top up with the specified grade of oil, until oil

just begins to run from the level plug orifice. Refit the level plug and the breather/filler plug on completion **(see illustrations)**.

4 Renewal of the transmission oil is not specified by the manufacturers, and no drain plug is provided. If necessary, renew the oil as a precaution. The oil may be drained by removing the differential cover plate. Use a new gasket when refitting the cover plate. Fill the transmission through the breather/filler orifice, as described previously in this Section.

5 Periodically inspect the transmission for oil leaks, and check the gear selector linkage components for wear and smooth operation.

6 On DOHC engine models, refit the engine undershield.

33.2A Removing the transmission oil level plug - F13 type transmission

33.2B Transmission oil level plug (arrowed) - F16 type transmission (viewed from below, with driveshaft removed)

33.3A Unscrew the breather/filler plug . . .

33.3B . . . and top-up with the specified grade of oil

35.2 Removing the sealing grommet from the inspection hole in the rear brake backplate

34 Automatic transmission check

1 Carry out a thorough road test, ensuring that all gearchanges occur smoothly, without snatching and with no increase in engine speed between changes.
2 Check the operation of the kickdown. Check that all gear positions can be engaged at the appropriate movement of the selector lever and with the vehicle at rest, check that the operation of the parking pawl in position "P" prevents it from being moved. Ensure that the starter motor will work only with the selector lever in positions "P" or "N", and that

the reversing lamps light only when position "R" is selected.
3 The manufacturer's schedule calls for a regular check of the electrical control system using the special Vauxhall test equipment; owners will have to have this check carried out by a Vauxhall dealer.
4 Periodically inspect the transmission casing, checking all joint surfaces and seals for signs of fluid leaks. If any are found, the fault must be rectified immediately.
5 Check also that the transmission breather hose (under the battery mounting bracket) is clear and not blocked, kinked or twisted.
6 To check the fluid level, the vehicle must be parked on level ground with the handbrake applied.

35 Brake shoe check

Note: *On models fitted with rear brake pads, the handbrake operates brake shoes that are located inside the rear brake discs.*
1 Jack up the rear of the vehicle and support it securely on axle stands.
2 For a quick check, the thickness of friction material remaining on one of the brake shoes can be observed through the hole in the brake backplate that is exposed by prising out the sealing grommet **(see illustration)**. If a rod of

the same diameter as the specified minimum friction material thickness is placed against the shoe friction material, the amount of wear can be assessed. A torch or inspection light will probably be required to help observation. If the friction material on any shoe is worn down to the specified minimum thickness or less, all four shoes must be renewed.
3 For a comprehensive check, the brake drum should be removed and cleaned. This will allow the wheel cylinders to be checked, and the condition of the brake drum itself to be fully examined (see Chapter 9).

36 Seat belt check

1 Carefully examine the seat belt webbing for cuts or any signs of serious fraying or deterioration. If the seat belt is of the retractable type, pull the belt all the way out, and examine the full extent of the webbing.
2 The seat belts are designed to lock up during a sudden stop or impact, yet allow free movement during normal driving. Fasten and unfasten the belt, ensuring that the locking mechanism holds securely and releases properly when intended. Check also that the retracting mechanism operates correctly when the belt is released.

Major service, every 36 000 miles (60 000 km) or 48 months

37 Timing belt renewal

1 To minimise risk of major damage to the engine, the timing belt (or cambelt, as it is sometimes called), needs replacing at least, on every major service.
2 It is good practise however, not only to renew the belt whenever major engine work is carried out, but also if you buy a used car with unclear service history.

On models without automatic tensioners, correct tensioning of the drivebelt will ensure prolonged life. A belt too slack will slip and squeal. Overtightening will cause excessive wear in the alternators bearings.

3 Some models are fitted with an inspection cover to view the condition of the belt. Whilst others involve a lot more work.
4 Full details on checking and replacement are shown in Chapters 2A or 2B, as appropriate.

38 Spark plug renewal (DOHC)

1 This procedure is basically the same shown in Section 30. However on these models, a spark plug cover needs to be removed from the camshaft cover before the plugs can be removed.

2 A special tool (No. KM-836) is available to safely and easily pull the HT leads from the plugs. If not available, do not overstrain the connector as internal damage to the lead may occur. Take great care when removing and refitting spark plugs on these engines. Hairline cracks in the ceramic of the plug can cause occasional or complete ignition failure. Damage to the catalytic converter may also occur.

3 Special tool (Vauxhall No. KM-194-B), with a 3 part conical sliding element have been made available, to reduce the risk of plug damage **(see illustration)**.

4 After refitting the spark plugs, remember to replace the plug cover.

38.3 Removing spark plugs using special adapter (DOHC models)

A Torque wrench
B Extension
C Joint
D Special adaptor (P/N KM-194-B)

Chapter 2 Part A
Engine - SOHC

Contents

Degrees of difficulty

Easy, suitable for novice with little experience	Fairly easy, suitable for beginner with some experience	Fairly difficult, suitable for competent DIY mechanic	Difficult, suitable for experienced DIY mechanic 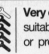	Very difficult, suitable for expert DIY or professional

Specifications

General

Type
All models . . . . Four-cylinder, in-line, water-cooled, transversely mounted at front of vehicle. Single belt-driven overhead camshaft, acting on hydraulic valve lifters.

Manufacturer's engine codes
Note: *The code can be found on the cylinder block, in front of the clutch housing.*

14 NV	1.4 litre (1389 cc) + carburettor
14 SE	1.4 litre (1389 cc) + Multi-point fuel injection (MPi)
C 14 NZ	1.4 litre (1389 cc) + catalytic converter + Central fuel injection (CFi)
C 14 SE	1.4 litre (1389 cc) + cat + MPi
C 16 NZ	1.6 litre (1598 cc) + cat + CFi
C 16 SE	1.6 litre (1598 cc) + cat + MPi
X 16 SZ	1.6 litre (1598 cc) + cat + CFi
C 18 NZ	1.8 litre (1796 cc) + cat + CFi
C 20 NE	2.0 litre (1998 cc) + cat + MPi

Pistons

	Bore (mm)	Stroke (mm)
14 NV, 14 SE, C 14 NZ and C 14 SE	77.6	73.4
C 16 NZ, C 16 SE and X 16 SZ	79.0	81.5
C 18 NZ	84.8	79.5
C 20 NE	86.0	86.0

Compression ratio

14 NV and C 14 NZ	9.4 : 1
14 SE	9.8 : 1
C 14 SE	10.0 : 1
C 16 NZ, C 18 NZ and C 20 NE	9.2 : 1
C 16 SE models	9.8 : 1

Maximum power

14 NV	55 kW at 5800 rpm
14 SE	60 kW at 5600 rpm
C 14 NZ	44 kW at 5200 rpm
C 14 SE	60 kW at 5800 rpm
C 16 NZ	55 kW at 5200 rpm
C 16 SE	74 kW at 5800 rpm
X 16 SZ	52 kW at 5000 rpm
C 18 NZ	66 kW at 5400 rpm
C 20 NE	85 kW at 5400 rpm

Maximum torque

14 NV	110 Nm at 3000 rpm
14 SE	115 Nm at 3400 rpm
C 14 NZ	103 Nm at 2800 rpm
C 14 SE	113 Nm at 3400 rpm
C 16 NZ	125 Nm at 2800 rpm
C 16 SE	135 Nm at 3400 rpm
X 16 SZ	128 Nm at 2800 rpm
C 18 NZ	145 Nm at 3000 rpm
C 20 NE	170 Nm at 2600 rpm

Firing order

All models	1 3-4-2 (No 1 cylinder at timing belt end)

Direction of crankshaft rotation

All models	Clockwise

Maximum compression pressure difference between cylinders

All models	1.0 bar

Camshaft

Camshaft bearing journal diameter (mm)

1.4 and 1.6 litre models:

No 1	39.435 to 39.455
No 2	39.685 to 39.705
No 3	39.935 to 39.955
No 4	40.185 to 40.205
No 5	40.435 to 40.455

C 18 NZ and C 20 NE models:	Standard	0.1 mm undersize
No 1	42.455 to 42.470	42.355 to 42.370
No 2	42.705 to 42.720	42.605 to 42.620
No 3	42.955 to 42.970	42.855 to 42.870
No 4	43.205 to 43.220	43.105 to 43.120
No 5	43.455 to 43.470	43.355 to 43.370

Camshaft bearing diameter in housing (mm)

1.4 and 1.6 litre models:

No 1	39.500 to 39.525
No 2	39.750 to 39.775
No 3	40.000 to 40.025
No 4	40.250 to 40.275
No 5	40.500 to 40.525

C 18 NZ and C 20 NE models:	Standard	0.1 mm undersize
No 1	42.500 to 42.525	42.400 to 42.425
No 2	42.750 to 42.775	42.650 to 42.675
No 3	43.000 to 43.025	42.900 to 42.925
No 4	43.250 to 43.275	43.150 to 43.175
No 5	43.500 to 43.525	43.400 to 43.425

Maximum permissible radial run-out (mm)

All models	0.03

Endfloat (mm)

All models	0.09 to 0.21

Cylinder block

Material	Cast iron
Maximum cylinder bore ovality	0.013 mm
Maximum cylinder bore taper	0.013 mm
Maximum permissible rebore oversize	0.5 mm

Cylinder head

Material	Light alloy
Maximum permissible distortion of sealing face	0.025 mm
Overall height of head	96.00 ± 0.1 mm

Timing belt

Tension using gauge KM-510-A (C 18 NZ and C 20 NE models, refer to text)

New belt, cold	4.5
New belt, warm	7.5
Used belt, cold	2.5
Used belt, warm	7.0

Flywheel

Maximum permissible lateral run-out of starter ring gear

All models	0.5 mm

Refinishing limit (maximum depth of material that may be removed from clutch friction surface)

All models	0.3 mm

Lubrication system

Minimum permissible oil pressure at idle speed, with engine at operating temperature (at least 80°C)

All models	1.5 bars

Oil pump type

All models	Gear type, driven from crankshaft

Oil pump clearances

Inner-to-outer gear teeth clearance (backlash)	0.10 to 0.20 mm
Gear-to-housing clearance (endfloat):	
1.4 and 1.6 litre models	0.08 to 0.15 mm
C 18 NZ and C 20 NE models	0.03 to 0.10 mm

Torque wrench settings

Note: *Use new bolts where marked with an asterisk (*).*
The torque settings stated are only applicable to latest specification cylinder head bolts, available from Vauxhall. Earlier type or alternative make, head bolts may require different torques. Consult your supplier.

	Nm	lbf ft
Air intake shroud to exhaust manifold	8	6
Adjuster bracket to alternator and inlet manifold:		
1.4 and 1.6 litre models	25	18
C 18 NZ and C 20 NE:		
Pre 1993 models	25	18
1993-on models	18	13
Adjuster bracket to alternator and intake pipe (1993-on models)	20	14
Alternator to bracket:		
M10 bolts	40	29
M8 bolts	30	22
Alternator and inlet manifold bracket (1993-on models):		
1.4 and 1.6 litre models	20	14
C 18 NZ and C 20 NE models	18	13
Alternator bracket to cylinder block:		
M8 (C 18 NZ and C 20 NE models)	25	18
M10 (1.4 and 1.6 litre models)	40	29
M12 (C 18 NZ and C 20 NE models)	40	29
Big-end bearing cap: *		
1.4 and 1.6 litre models:		
Stage 1	25	18
Stage 2	Angle tighten by a further 30°	
C 18 NZ and C 20 NE models:		
Stage 1	35	25
Stage 2	Angle tighten by a further 45°	
Stage 3	Angle tighten by a further 15°	

2A

Torque wrench settings (continued)

	Nm	lbf ft
Camshaft housing cover to housing	8	6
Camshaft pulley to camshaft	45	33
Camshaft thrust plate	8	6
Coolant outlet to thermostat housing:		
C 18 NZ and C 20 NE models	8	6
Coolant pump to block:		
M6 (1.4 and 1.6 litre models)	8	6
M8 (C 18 NZ and C 20 NE models)	25	18
Cylinder head to block: *		
1.4 and 1.6 litre models:		
Stage 1	25	18
Stage 2	Angle tighten by a further 60°	
Stage 3	Angle tighten by a further 60°	
Stage 4	Angle tighten by a further 60°	
C 18 NZ and C 20 NE models:		
Stage 1	25	18
Stage 2	Angle tighten by a further 90°	
Stage 3	Angle tighten by a further 90°	
Stage 4	Angle tighten by a further 90°	
Driveplate to crankshaft (refer to text)	60	43
Engine bracket (rear) to transmission (renew lockplates)	60	43
Engine bracket (right) to cylinder block	60	43
Engine mounting (left and right) to body (refer to text)	65	47
Engine mounting (left) to engine bracket	60	43
Engine mounting (rear) to engine bracket	45	33
Engine mounting (rear) to crossmember	40	29
Engine mounting (right) to engine bracket	35	25
Engine mounting to engine bracket:		
C 18 NZ and C 20 NE models	65	47
Engine mounting bracket to engine bracket:		
C 18 NZ and C 20 NE 1993-on models	60	43
Engine mounting bracket (left) to transmission	60	43
Engine mounting bracket to power steering pump support (1993-on models)	60	43
Engine support bracket to camshaft housing	15	11
Exhaust downpipe to manifold	25	18
Exhaust manifold to cylinder head *	22	16
Flywheel to crankshaft: *		
1.4 and 1.6 litre models:		
Stage 1	35	25
Stage 2	Angle tighten by a further 30°	
Stage 3	Angle tighten by a further 15°	
C 18 NZ and C 20 NE models:		
Stage 1	65	47
Stage 2	Angle tighten by a further 30°	
Stage 3	Angle tighten by a further 15°	
Fuel pump to camshaft housing	18	13
Inlet manifold to cylinder head	22	16
Knock sensor to cylinder block:		
X 16 SZ models	13	9
Main bearing cap to block: *		
Stage 1	50	36
Stage 2	Angle tighten by a further 45°	
Stage 3	Angle tighten by a further 15°	
Oil intake pipe to oil pump (refer to text)	8	6
Oil intake pipe to block	6	4
Oil pressure relief valve plug	30	22
Oil pressure switch to oil pump:		
1.4 and 1.6 litre models	30	22
C 18 NZ and C 20 NE models	40	29
Oil pump to block	6	4
Oxygen sensor to exhaust manifold (refer to text)	30	22
Power steering pump adjuster to support:		
C 18 NZ and C 20 NE models	18	13
Power steering pump bracket to block (1993-on models)	35	25

Torque wrench settings (continued)

	Nm	lbf ft
Power steering pump to bracket (1993-on models):		
1.4 and 1.6 litre models	20	14
C 18 NZ and C 20 NE models	25	18
Ribbed V-belt pulley to timing belt drive:		
C 18 NZ and C 20 NE models	20	15
Ribbed V-belt pulley with timing belt drive to crankshaft:		
C 16 NZ (with power steering, up to 1993): *		
Stage 1	55	40
Stage 2	Angle tighten by a further 45°	
Stage 3	Angle tighten by a further 15°	
1993-on models	55	40
Ribbed V-belt tension roller to power steering pump support		
1993-on models	18	13
Spark plugs	25	18
Starter bracket to block	25	18
Starter to block (engine side)	45	32
Starter to block (transmission side)	60	43
Sump drain plug	55	40
Sump to block:		
1.4 and 1.6 litre models	8	6
C 18 NZ and C 20 NE models (refer to text):		
Baffle plate with attached seal	5	4
Baffle plate with vulcanised seal	10	7
Temperature sender to inlet manifold	10	7
Thermostat housing to cylinder head:		
1.4 and 1.6 litre models	10	7
C 18 NZ and C 20 NE models	15	11
Timing belt cover (rear) to oil pump and camshaft housing	12	9
Timing belt drive to crankshaft:		
C 18 NZ and C 20 NE models: *		
Stage 1	130	94
Stage 2	Angle tighten by a further 40° to 50°	
Timing belt tension roller to oil pump	20	14
Transmission to block:		
M10	45	32
M12	60	43
V-belt pulley to timing belt drive:		
C 18 NZ and C 20 NE models	20	15
V-belt pulley with timing belt drive to crankshaft	55	40

2A

1 Description - general

1 The engine is of four-cylinder, in-line single or double overhead camshaft type (depending on model), mounted transversely at the front of the vehicle.

2 The crankshaft runs in five shell-type bearings and the centre bearing incorporates a thrust bearing shell to control crankshaft endfloat.

3 The connecting rods are attached to the crankshaft by horizontally split shell-type big-end bearings. On single overhead camshaft (SOHC) models, the pistons are attached to the connecting rods by gudgeon pins, which are an interference fit in the connecting rod small-end bore. The aluminium alloy pistons are fitted with three piston rings: two compression rings and an oil control ring.

4 The camshaft on SOHC models is driven from the crankshaft by a toothed composite rubber belt. Each cylinder has two valves (one inlet and one exhaust), operated through rocker arms that are supported at their pivot ends by hydraulic self-adjusting valve lifters (tappets), (see illustrations).

5 The inlet and exhaust valves are each closed by a single valve spring and operate in guides pressed into the cylinder head.

6 A gear-type oil pump is located in a housing attached to the front of the cylinder block and is driven directly from the crankshaft. A full-flow type oil filter is fitted.

7 The distributor is driven directly from the end of the camshaft. On carburettor models, the mechanical fuel pump is operated from the front end of the camshaft. The coolant pump is located at the front of the cylinder block and is driven by the timing belt.

8 Chapter 2A describes the SOHC model repair procedures. Many repairs and specifications to the DOHC engine are similar to the SOHC. However where they differ, details can be found in Chapter 2B.

Repair operations possible with the engine in the vehicle

The following operations can be carried out without having to remove the engine from the vehicle.

(a) Removal and refitting of the cylinder head.
(b) Removal and refitting of the timing belt and gears.
(c) Removal and refitting of the camshaft.
(d) Removal and refitting of the sump.
(e) Removal and refitting of the big-end bearings, connecting rods and pistons *.
(f) Removal and refitting of the oil pump.
(g) Renewal of the engine mountings.
(h) Removal and refitting of the flywheel/driveplate.

* Although the operation marked with an asterisk can be carried out with the engine in the vehicle (after removal of the sump), the procedure is easier if the engine is removed.

1.4A Side sectional view of a C 16 SE model

1.4B Front sectional view of a C 16 SE model

2 Compression test - description and interpretation

Description

1 When engine performance is down, or if it is misfiring, check the ignition or fuel systems. If no fault can be found, a compression test can provide diagnostic clues as to the engine's condition. If the test is performed regularly, it can give early warning of trouble before causing major damage to the engine.

2 The engine must be fully warmed-up to normal operating temperature, the battery must be fully charged and all the spark plugs must be removed (Chapter 1). Assistance will also be required.

3 Disable the ignition system by disconnecting the ignition HT coil lead from the distributor cap and earthing it on the cylinder block. Use a jumper lead or similar wire to make a good connection.

2.4 Compression tester fitted to No 1 spark plug hole

4 Fit a compression tester to the No 1 cylinder spark plug hole. The type of tester that screws into the plug thread will be easier to use **(see illustration)**.

5 Have the assistant hold the throttle wide open and crank the engine on the starter motor. After one or two revolutions, the compression pressure should build up to a maximum figure and then stabilise. Make a note of the highest reading.

6 Repeat the test on the remaining cylinders, recording the pressure on each.

Interpretation

7 All cylinders should produce very similar pressures; a difference of more than 2 bars between any two cylinders indicates a fault. The compression should build up quickly in a healthy engine. Low compression on the first stroke, followed by gradually increasing pressure on successive strokes, indicates worn piston rings. A low compression reading on the first stroke, which does not build up during successive strokes, indicates leaking valves or a blown head gasket (a cracked head could also be the cause). Deposits on the undersides of the valve heads can also cause low compression.

8 Although Vauxhall do not specify exact compression pressures, as a guide, any cylinder pressure of below 10 bars can be considered as less than healthy. Refer to a Vauxhall dealer or other specialist if in doubt whether a particular pressure reading is acceptable.

9 If the pressure in any cylinder is low, carry out the following test to isolate the cause. Introduce a teaspoonful of clean oil into that cylinder through its spark plug hole and repeat the test.

10 If the addition of oil temporarily improves the compression pressure, this indicates that bore or piston wear is responsible for the pressure loss. No improvement suggests that leaking or burnt valves, or a blown head gasket, may be to blame.

11 A low reading from two adjacent cylinders is almost certainly due to the head gasket having blown between them. The presence of coolant in the engine oil will confirm this.

12 If one cylinder is about 20 percent lower than the others and the engine has a slightly rough idle, a worn camshaft lobe could be the cause.

13 If the compression reading is unusually high, the combustion chambers are probably coated with carbon deposits. If this is the case, the cylinder head should be removed and decarbonised.

14 On completion of the test, refit the spark plugs and reconnect the ignition system.

3 Top dead centre (TDC) - general

1 Top dead centre (TDC) is the highest point in the cylinder that a piston reaches as the crankshaft turns. Each piston reaches TDC at the end of the compression stroke and again at the end of the exhaust stroke. However for the timing of the engine, TDC refers to the position of No 1 piston at the end of its compression stroke. On all models, No. 1 piston and cylinder are at the timing belt end of the engine.

2 All engine overhaul procedures use the

3.6 Crankshaft pulley 10° BTDC notch aligned with pointer on rear timing belt cover - 14NV model

3.7A TDC pointer on timing belt cover aligned with timing notch in TDC sensor wheel (arrowed) - C 16 SE model

3.7B TDC pointer on timing belt cover aligned with timing notch in crankshaft pulley (arrowed) - C 20 NE model

factory timing marks, which vary according to engine type.

3 Disconnect both battery leads.

4 Remove the outer timing belt cover (it is only necessary to remove the upper cover on SOHC models), as described in Section 7.

5 Using a spanner or socket on the crankshaft pulley or gear bolt, rotate the crankshaft to bring No. 1 piston to TDC as follows, according to engine type. On manual transmission models, the crankshaft can be turned by engaging top gear and pushing the vehicle backwards or forwards.

14 NV models

6 The pointer on the rear timing belt cover must be aligned with the 10° BTDC notch in the crankshaft pulley **(see illustration)** and the timing mark on the camshaft gear must be aligned with the notch in the timing belt rear cover. When the timing marks are aligned as described, although No 1 piston is positioned 10° BTDC, this is acceptable for all the tasks in this manual requiring No 1 piston to be positioned at TDC.

All models except 14 NV models

7 The pointer on the timing belt cover must be aligned with the notch in the crankshaft pulley, or the timing mark on the TDC sensor wheel, as applicable. The timing mark on the camshaft gear must be aligned with the notch in the timing belt rear cover **(see illustrations)**.

4 Camshaft cover - removal and refitting

Note: *A new gasket will almost certainly be required after removing the cover.*

Removal

1 Disconnect the breather hoses from the camshaft cover **(see illustrations)**.

2 Take note of the positions of all brackets and clips secured by the camshaft cover bolts, then unscrew and remove the bolts, along with all clips and brackets, as applicable **(see illustration)**.

3.7C Timing mark on camshaft gear aligned with notch in timing belt rear cover (arrowed) - C 16 SE model

3 Lift the camshaft cover from the cylinder head **(see illustration)**. If the cover is stuck, do not lever between the cover and camshaft housing mating surfaces. If necessary, gently tap the cover sideways to free it. Remove the old gasket/rubber seal.

Refitting

4 Before starting refitting, examine the inside of the cover for a build-up of oil sludge or any other contamination. Examine the condition of the crankcase ventilation filter inside the camshaft cover, if fitted. If the filter is too contaminated, renew it. Using paraffin or a water-soluble solvent, clean the cover (and filter) and dry the cover thoroughly before refitting.

4.1A Disconnect the breather hoses . . .

4.1B . . . from the camshaft cover - C 16 SE model

4.2 Note the positions of any brackets and clips (arrowed) secured by the camshaft cover bolts - C 16 SE model

4.3 Lifting the camshaft cover from the cylinder head

2A

4.5 Tag on seal (arrowed) engages with notch in camshaft cover - C 16 SE model

5.3 Withdrawing the underwing shield - C 16 SE model

5.8 Removing the crankshaft pulley bolt and washer - C 16 SE model

5 Examine the condition of the rubber seal and if necessary, renew it. On some models, the seal rests in a groove in the cover and a tag on the seal engages with the notch in the cover when the seal is correctly positioned **(see illustration)**. If a cork gasket was fitted, it should always be renewed on refitting.

6 Thoroughly clean the mating faces of the camshaft housing and the cover.

7 Position the cover on the camshaft housing, noting that the breather pipe stubs should be nearest the timing belt end of the engine.

8 Refit the securing bolts, ensuring that any clips and/or brackets are in place under their heads as noted before removal and tighten the bolts to the specified torque in a diagonal sequence.

9 Reconnect the breather hoses.

5 Crankshaft pulley - removal and refitting

Note: *On 1.4 and 1.6 litre models, a new securing bolt may be required when refitting the crankshaft pulley.*

Removal

1 Disconnect the battery negative lead.

2 For improved access, raise the front right-hand side of the vehicle and support securely on axle stands. Remove the roadwheel.

3 Unscrew the securing screws (or remove the plastic clips, as applicable) and withdraw the underwing shield **(see illustration)**.

4 If necessary, rotate the crankshaft (using a socket or spanner on the crankshaft pulley or gear bolt, as applicable) until the relevant timing marks align (see Section 3).

5 If fitted, remove the power steering pump drivebelt as described in Chapter 10.

6 Remove the alternator drivebelt as described in Chapter 1.

7 To prevent the crankshaft from turning as the pulley bolt is unscrewed, either select top gear and have an assistant apply the brakes hard (manual transmission models only), or remove the starter motor and lock the ring gear teeth using a large screwdriver.

8 On 1.4 and 1.6 litre models, unscrew the pulley bolt and remove the washer fitted behind it, then remove the pulley **(see illustration)**.

9 On 1.8 and 2.0 litre models, unscrew the four (or six) bolts securing the pulley to the crankshaft gear, using an Allen key or hexagon bit, then remove the pulley.

Refitting

11 On refitting, ensure that the notch in the pulley fits over the locating lug on the crankshaft gear.

12 On 1.4 and 1.6 litre models, it may be necessary to use a new bolt to secure the pulley, depending on the type of bolt originally fitted. Refer to 'Specifications'.

13 Prevent the crankshaft from turning as during removal, then fit the pulley securing bolt(s), ensuring that the washer is in place under the bolt head where applicable.

14 Tighten the bolt(s) to the specified torque, in stages where applicable. Refer to 'Specifications'.

15 Refit and tension the alternator drivebelt, as described in Chapter 1.

16 Where applicable, refit and tension the power steering pump drivebelt as described in Chapter 10.

17 Refit the underwing shield.

18 Refit the roadwheel and lower the vehicle to the ground.

19 Reconnect the battery negative lead.

6 Timing belt upper outer cover - removal and refitting

14 NV, C 14 NZ, C 16 NZ and X 16 SZ models

Removal

1 For improved access, remove the air cleaner assembly, as described in Chapter 4A or 4B.

2 If required, remove the alternator drivebelt as described in Chapter 1. On models with power steering, remove the power steering pump pulley and loosen the pump securing bolts. This will allow the pump to be moved

away from the timing belt cover. There is no need to disconnect the fluid pipes. If the timing belt is to be removed, the power steering pump must be removed completely.

3 Unscrew the securing bolt and unclip the upper timing belt cover from the rear cover and lower cover.

Refitting

4 Refitting is a reversal of removal, but where applicable, refit and tension the alternator and power steering pump drivebelt, as described in Chapters 5 and 10.

14 SE, C 14 SE and C 16 SE models

Removal

5 Disconnect the battery negative lead.

6 For improved access, remove the air cleaner assembly, as described in Chapter 4B.

7 Remove the alternator drivebelt, as described in Chapter 1.

8 On models with power steering, remove the power steering pump pulley and loosen the pump securing bolts to enable the pump to be moved away from the timing belt cover. There is no need to disconnect the fluid pipes.

9 Unscrew the three securing bolts and unclip the lower edge of the upper cover from the lower cover. Withdraw the upper cover **(see illustrations)**.

Refitting

10 Refitting is a reversal of removal, but refit and tension the alternator drivebelt as described in Chapter 1.

C 18 NZ and C 20 NE models

Removal

11 Disconnect the battery negative lead.

12 For improved access, remove the air cleaner assembly as described in Chapter 4B.

13 Remove the power steering pump drivebelt as described in Chapter 10.

14 Remove the alternator drivebelt, as described in Chapter 1.

15 Disconnect the wiring from the temperature gauge sender.

16 Release the securing clips and remove the upper timing belt cover.

6.9A Unscrew the three securing bolts (arrowed) . . .

Refitting

17 Refitting is a reversal of removal, but refit and tension the alternator drivebelt as described in Chapter 1.

7 Timing belt lower outer cover - removal and refitting

14 NV, C 14 NZ, C 16 NZ and X 16 SZ models

Removal

1 For improved access, raise the front right-hand side of the vehicle and support securely on axle stands. Remove the roadwheel.
2 Remove the underwing shield (see Chapter 11).
3 Remove the crankshaft pulley as described in Section 5.
4 Unscrew the two securing bolts and unclip the lower timing belt cover from the upper cover and rear cover.

Refitting

5 Refitting is a reversal of removal, but where applicable, refit the crankshaft pulley using a new securing bolt as described in Section 5.

14 SE, C 14 SE and C 16 SE models

Removal

6 Disconnect the battery negative lead.
7 For improved access, raise the front right-hand side of the vehicle and support securely on axle stands. Remove the roadwheel.
8 Remove the underwing shield (see Chapter 11).
9 Remove the crankshaft pulley as described in Section 5.
10 Where applicable, unclip the TDC sensor wiring from the lower timing belt cover.
12 Unscrew the four securing bolts and remove the lower timing belt cover.

Refitting

13 Refitting is a reversal of removal, but where applicable, refit the crankshaft pulley using a new securing bolt as described in Section 5.

6.9B . . . and withdraw the upper timing belt cover - C 16 SE model

C 18 NZ and C 20 NE models

Removal

14 Remove the upper timing belt cover as described previously in Section 6, then unclip the lower cover from the coolant pump.

Refitting

15 Refitting is a reversal of removal, but refit and tension the alternator drivebelt as described in Chapter 1.

8 Timing belt rear cover - removal and refitting

14 NV, C 14 NZ, C 16 NZ and X 16 SZ models

Removal

1 Remove the outer covers as described previously in Sections 6 and 7, but note that where applicable, the power steering pump must be removed completely, as described in Chapter 10.
2 Remove the timing belt as described in Section 9.
3 Remove the timing belt gears as described in Sections 12 and 13.
4 Unscrew the securing bolt and remove the timing belt tension indicator assembly from the cylinder block.
5 Unscrew and remove the screws securing the rear timing belt cover to the camshaft housing and cylinder block, then withdraw the cover.

8.8 Unscrewing a rear timing belt cover upper securing screw - C 16 SE model

Refitting

6 Refitting is a reversal of removal, remembering the following points.
(a) Refit and tension the timing belt as described in Section 9.
(b) Refit the outer timing belt covers as described previously.
(c) Where applicable, refit the power steering pump and bleed the fluid circuit as described in Chapter 10.

14 SE, C 14 SE and C 16 SE models

Removal

7 Proceed as described in paragraphs 1 to 4 inclusive.
8 Unscrew the two upper and two lower screws securing the rear timing belt cover **(see illustration)**.
9 Withdraw the rear cover and where applicable, unclip the TDC sensor wiring from the rear of the cover **(see illustration)**.

Refitting

10 Proceed as described in paragraph 6.

C 18 NZ and C 20 NE models

Removal

11 Remove the outer timing belt covers as described previously in Sections 6 and 7.
12 Remove the timing belt as described in Section 10 or 11.
13 Remove the timing belt gears as described in Sections 12 and 13.
14 Where applicable, disconnect the wiring plug from the TDC sensor and unclip the wiring from the rear belt cover.
15 Unscrew the two upper and two lower securing bolts and withdraw the cover, manipulating it from the smaller rear cover on the coolant pump.
16 The smaller rear belt cover can be removed from the coolant pump, after unscrewing the securing bolt, by rotating it to disengage it from the retaining flange on the pump.

Refitting

17 Refitting is a reversal of removal, but refit and tension the timing belt as described in Section 10 or 11.

8.9 TDC sensor wiring clipped to rear of rear timing belt cover - C 16 SE model

2A

9.6 Using a pin punch to lock the timing belt tensioner indicator arm in position - C 16 SE model

9.8 Sliding the timing belt from the camshaft gear - C 16 SE model

9.9 Arrow on crankshaft gear aligned with notch in rear timing belt cover (arrowed) with No 1 piston at TDC - C 16 SE model

9 Timing belt (1.4 and 1.6 litre models) - removal, refitting and adjustment

Removal

1 Disconnect the battery negative lead.
2 If fitted, remove air intake hose, shroud and air filter housing.
3 Remove the outer timing belt covers as described in Sections 6 and 7. On models fitted with power steering, note the running direction of the belt, before removal and then remove the pump. Refer to Chapter 10 for further details.
4 Remove the V-belt from the alternator.
5 Turn the crankshaft to bring No 1 piston to top dead centre, as described in Section 3. If necessary, temporarily refit the crankshaft pulley and its securing bolt to enable the timing mark to be viewed and the crankshaft to be turned.
6 Insert a tool (such as a pin punch) into the hole in the timing belt tension indicator arm, then lever the arm clockwise to its stop and lock in position by inserting the tool into the corresponding hole in the tension indicator backplate **(see illustration).** Leave the tool in position to lock the tension indicator until the belt is refitted.
7 Loosen the three coolant pump securing bolts, using an Allen key or hexagon bit, then

9.20 Using special tool KM-421-A to turn the coolant pump - C 16 SE model

turn the pump to relieve the tension in the timing belt.
8 Slide the timing belt from the gears and withdraw it from the engine **(see illustration).** Take note of any arrows marked on the belt to indicate the direction of rotation.

Refitting

9 Ensure that No 1 piston is still positioned at top dead centre, as described in Section 3. Note that the arrow cast into the front face of the crankshaft gear must be aligned with the corresponding notch in the bottom of the rear timing belt cover **(see illustration).**
10 Refit the timing belt around the gears, starting at the crankshaft gear.
11 Adjust the timing belt tension, as described in paragraphs 16 to 25 inclusive.
12 Refit the outer timing belt covers, as described in Sections 6 and 7.
13 Where applicable, refit the power steering pump and belt, as described in Chapter 10.
14 If applicable, refit the air filter housing, shroud and intake pipe.
15 Reconnect the battery negative lead and where applicable, bleed the power steering fluid circuit, as described in Chapter 10.

Adjustment

Note: *The engine must be cold when carrying out checking and adjustment of the timing belt tension.*

9.23 Turn the coolant pump (special tool shown) anti-clockwise until the tension indicator pointer (1) is positioned in the centre of the 'V' (2) - 1.4 and 1.6 litre models

16 With the outer timing belt covers removed as described in Sections 6 and 7, continue as follows.
17 Turn the crankshaft to bring No 1 piston to top dead centre, as described in Section 3. If necessary, temporarily refit the crankshaft pulley and its bolt to enable the timing mark to be viewed and the crankshaft to be turned.
18 To make the crankshaft easier to turn during the following procedure, remove the spark plugs as described in Chapter 1.
19 Loosen the three coolant pump securing bolts, using an Allen key or hexagon bit, but do not remove them.
20 Turn the coolant pump clockwise to increase the belt tension until the tensioner indicator arm moves fully clockwise to its stop (i.e. the holes in the indicator arm and the tensioner backplate are aligned). Note that a special tool is available to turn the coolant pump (Vauxhall tool KM-421-A or equivalent), **(see illustration).**
21 Tighten the coolant pump securing bolts sufficiently to prevent the pump from moving during the following operation.
22 Using a socket or spanner on the crankshaft pulley bolt, turn the crankshaft clockwise through two complete revolutions, until No 1 piston is again positioned at top dead centre. Turn the crankshaft smoothly without jerking, to avoid the belt jumping on the pulleys.
23 Carefully turn the coolant pump anti-clockwise to slacken the belt, until the tension indicator pointer is positioned in the centre of the 'V' on the tensioner backplate **(see illustration),** then tighten the coolant pump securing bolts to the specified torque.
24 Turn the crankshaft clockwise through two complete revolutions, as described previously and check that the tension indicator pointer is still positioned as described in paragraph 23. If not, the procedure described in paragraphs 19 to 23 inclusive must be repeated until the pointer aligns correctly.
25 On completion, refit the spark plugs (where applicable) and refit the outer timing belt covers as described in Sections 6 and 7.

10.5 Loosening a coolant pump securing bolt - C 20 NE model

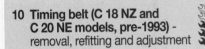

10 Timing belt (C 18 NZ and C 20 NE models, pre-1993) - removal, refitting and adjustment

Note: A puller may be required to remove the crankshaft gear.

Removal

1 Disconnect the battery negative lead. Disconnect wiring from the air flow meter and air temperature sensor, if fitted.
2 Remove the air intake hose and air filter housing. Remove the outer timing belt covers, as described in Sections 6 and 7.
3 Turn the crankshaft to bring No 1 cylinder to top dead centre, using a socket or spanner on the crankshaft gear bolt, as described in Section 3.
4 Remove the crankshaft pulley, as described in Section 5.
5 Loosen the three coolant pump securing bolts, using an Allen key or hexagon bit **(see illustration)**, then turn the pump to relieve the tension in the timing belt.
6 Slide the timing belt from the gears and withdraw it from the engine. Take note of any arrows marked on the belt to indicate the direction of rotation.

Refitting

7 Ensure that No 1 cylinder is still positioned at top dead centre, as described in Section 3.
8 Refit the timing belt around the gears, starting at the crankshaft gear.
9 Adjust the timing belt tension, as described in paragraphs 13 to 25, or 26 to 30, as applicable.
10 Refit the crankshaft pulley, as described in Section 5.
11 Refit the outer timing belt covers, as described in Sections 6 and 7.
12 On completion, reconnect the battery negative lead.

Adjustment

Adjustment using Vauxhall tool KM-510-A

Note: The tension of a new belt must be adjusted with the engine cold. The tension of

10.17 Tension gauge KM-510-A correctly positioned on timing belt. Belt must pass through points A, B and C - C 20 NE model

a used belt must be checked with the engine at normal operating temperature. The manufacturers specify the use of a special gauge, Vauxhall tool KM-510-A, for checking the timing belt tension. If access to a gauge cannot be obtained. it is strongly recommended that the vehicle is taken to a Vauxhall dealer to have the belt tension checked at the earliest opportunity.

13 With the outer timing belt covers removed as described in Sections 6 and 7, continue as follows.
14 To make the crankshaft easier to turn during the following procedure, remove the spark plugs as described in Chapter 1.
15 Read the instructions supplied with the gauge before proceeding.
16 Turn the crankshaft through at least quarter of a turn clockwise, using a socket or spanner on the crankshaft gear bolt.
17 Place the locked gauge at the centre of the belt run between the coolant pump and the camshaft gear. The gauge should locate on the timing belt as shown **(see illustration)**.
18 Slowly release the operating lever on the gauge, then lightly tap the gauge two or three times and note the reading on the scale **(see illustration)**.
19 If the reading is not as specified, loosen the three coolant pump securing bolts, using an Allen key or hexagon bit (if not already done) and rotate the coolant pump in the

10.18 Note the reading on the scale of the tension gauge - C 20 NE model

required direction to achieve the necessary reading on the gauge. Rotate the pump clockwise to increase the belt tension, or anti-clockwise to decrease the tension. A special tool is available to turn the coolant pump (Vauxhall tool KM-421-A or equivalent).
20 Lightly tighten the coolant pump securing bolts sufficiently to prevent the pump from moving.
21 Remove the tensioning gauge and turn the crankshaft through on complete revolution clockwise.
22 Re-check the belt tension as described in paragraphs 17 and 18.
23 If the tension is not as specified, repeat paragraphs 19 to 22 inclusive until the required reading is obtained.
24 On completion of adjustment, remove the checking gauge and tighten the coolant pump bolts to the specified torque.
25 Refit the spark plugs and refit the outer timing belt covers as described in Sections 6 and 7.

Temporary adjustment

26 With the outer timing belt covers removed as described in Sections 6 and 7, continue as follows.
27 If the special gauge is not available, the timing belt tension can be checked approximately by twisting the belt between the thumb and forefinger, at the centre of the run between the coolant pump and the camshaft gear. It ought to be just possible to twist the belt through 90° using moderate pressure **(see illustration)**.
28 If adjustment is necessary, continue as described previously for adjustment using the special gauge (i.e., adjust the tension by moving the coolant pump), but have the belt tension checked by a Vauxhall dealer at the earliest opportunity.
29 If in doubt, err on the tight side when adjusting the tension as if the belt is too slack, it may jump on the gears, which could result in serious engine damage.
30 Ensure that the coolant pump bolts are tightened to the specified torque before refitting the outer timing belt covers as described in Sections 6 and 7.

10.27 Checking the timing belt tension by twisting the belt through 90° between thumb and forefinger - C 20 NE model

2A

11.8A Timing belt automatic tensioner details (alternative type)

A Alignment lugs on coolant pump and cylinder block
B Tensioner pointer aligned with notch in tensioner bracket
1 Move the tensioner arm anti-clockwise to release the belt tension
2 Move the tensioner arm clockwise to tension the belt

11.8B Timing belt adjustment

1 Alignment for new belts
2 Alignment for 'run-in' belts (gap is approximately 4 mm to the left of centre)

---

11 Timing belt (C 18 NZ and C 20 NE models, 1993-on) - removal, refitting and adjustment

Removal

1 An alternative type of spring loaded automatic timing belt tensioner is fitted to these engines, from 1993 onward. The tensioner assembly is similar to other automatic tensioners, but the removal and refitting procedures vary as follows.

2 The timing belt main outer cover may be secured either by clips or by hexagon-headed screws to the rear cover; in some cases, a combination of clips and screws may be used.

3 To release the belt tension before removal, unscrew the timing belt tensioner securing bolt slightly then, with a tool inserted in the slot on the tensioner arm, turn the tensioner arm until the timing belt is slack. If necessary, remove completely and examine the tensioner for wear.

Refitting

4 Refit the tensioner into position and tighten the securing bolt slightly.

5 Ensure that the coolant pump is correctly positioned by checking that the lug on the coolant pump flange is aligned with the corresponding lug on the cylinder block. If this is not the case, slacken the coolant pump mounting bolts slightly and move the pump accordingly (see Chapter 3). Tighten the bolts to the specified torque on completion.

6 Refit the timing belt then tension it as follows.

Adjustment

7 Slacken the automatic tensioner securing bolt and move the tensioner arm anti-clockwise, until the tensioner pointer lies at its stop. Tighten the tensioner securing bolt to hold the tensioner in this position.

8 Turn the crankshaft through two complete revolutions in the normal direction of rotation, and check that with the crankshaft pulley TDC mark aligned with the pointer on the rear timing belt cover. The TDC mark on the camshaft gear is still aligned with the notch in the timing belt rear cover.. Slacken the automatic tensioner securing bolt again and move the tensioner arm clockwise, until the tensioner pointer is aligned with the notch in the tensioner bracket. In the first few hours of operation a new belt will be subjected to 'settling-in', (known as the running-in procedure). If you are refitting a used belt (one that has been 'run-in'), align the pointer to approximately 4 mm to the left of the notch **(see illustrations)**

9 Tighten the tensioner securing bolt securely. Turn the crankshaft through one complete revolution, in the normal direction of rotation, and check that the crankshaft and camshaft timing marks still align. Then refit the remainder of the components.

10 With the timing belt adjustment set in this way, correct tension will always be maintained by the automatic tensioner and no further checking or adjustment will be necessary.

---

12 Camshaft gear - removal and refitting

Removal

1 With the outer timing belt covers removed as described in Sections 6 and 7, continue as follows.

2 Turn the crankshaft to bring No 1 piston to top dead centre, as described in Section 3.

3 On 1.4 and 1.6 litre models, insert a tool (such as a pin punch) into the hole in the timing belt tension indicator arm, then lever the arm clockwise to its stop and lock in position by inserting the tool into the corresponding hole in the tension indicator

backplate. Leave the tool in position to lock the tension indicator until the camshaft gear is refitted.

4 Loosen the three coolant pump securing bolts, using an Allen key or hexagon bit, then turn the pump to relieve the tension in the timing belt.

5 The camshaft must be locked into position, as the gear bolt is unscrewed and this can be achieved in one of two ways as follows.

(a) Make up a tool similar to that shown and use it to hold the gear stationary by means of the holes in the gear face **(see illustration)**.

(b) Remove the camshaft cover as described in Section 4 and prevent the camshaft from turning by holding it with a spanner on the flats provided between Nos 3 and 4 camshaft lobes.

12.5 Improvised tool being used to hold the camshaft gear stationary

12.8 Lug (1) on camshaft engages with hole (2) in gear

12.9 Tightening the camshaft gear securing bolt while holding the camshaft using a spanner on the camshaft flats

13.6A Remove the crankshaft gear . . .

2A

6 Unscrew the camshaft gear bolt and withdraw it, noting the washer under the bolt head.

7 Withdraw the gear from the end of the camshaft, manipulating the timing belt from the gear as it is withdrawn.

Refitting

8 Begin refitting by offering the camshaft gear to the camshaft, making sure that the lug on the end of the camshaft engages with the corresponding hole in the camshaft gear **(see illustration)**.

9 Refit the gear securing bolt, ensuring that the washer is in place and tighten the bolt to the specified torque, preventing the camshaft from turning as during removal **(see illustration)**.

10 Where applicable, refit the camshaft cover as described in Section 4.

11 Ensure that the TDC marks on the camshaft gear and crankshaft gear are still aligned (No 1 piston at TDC) as described in Section 3, then slip the timing belt over the camshaft gear.

12 Adjust the timing belt tension as described in Section 9, 10 or 11.

13 Refit the outer timing belt covers as described in Sections 6 and 7.

13 Crankshaft gear - removal and refitting

Note: *A puller may be required to remove the gear on C 18 NZ and C 20 NE models. New securing bolts may be required when refitting the crankshaft pulley or gears - refer to Sections 5 and 13.*

Removal

1 With the outer timing belt covers removed as described in Sections 6 and 7, continue as follows.

2 Turn the crankshaft to bring No 1 piston to top dead centre, as described in Section 3.

3 Remove the crankshaft pulley, as described in Section 5.

4 On C 18 NZ and C 20 NE models, the crankshaft gear bolt must now be unscrewed. To prevent the crankshaft from turning as the gear bolt is unscrewed, either select top gear and have an assistant apply the brakes hard (manual transmission models only), or remove the starter motor and jam the ring gear teeth using a tool, like a large screwdriver. Unscrew the gear bolt (taking care as it is very tight) and remove the washer from under the bolt head.

5 Loosen the belt as described in para-

graphs 3 and 4, of Section 9, then slip the timing belt from the gear.

6 Remove the gear from the end of the crankshaft, using a puller if necessary. Where applicable, remove the Woodruff key and the thrust-washer from the end of the crankshaft **(see illustrations)**.

Refitting

7 On 1.4 and 1.6 litre models, where applicable refit the Woodruff key to the end of the crankshaft, then refit the crankshaft gear with the locating flange and locating lug for the crankshaft pulley outermost **(see illustration)**.

8 On C 18 NZ and C 20 NE models, refit the thrustwasher and the Woodruff key to the end of the crankshaft, then refit the crankshaft gear and tighten a new securing bolt to the specified torque in the two stages given in the Specifications. Ensure that the washer is in place under the bolt head and prevent the engine from turning as during removal.

9 Ensure that the TDC marks on the camshaft gear and crankshaft gear are still aligned (No 1 piston at TDC) as described in Section 3 (temporarily refit the crankshaft pulley if necessary), then slip the timing belt over the crankshaft gear.

10 Refit the crankshaft pulley as described in Section 5.

13.6B . . . Woodruff key . . .

13.6C . . . and thrustwasher from the end of the crankshaft - C 20 NE model

13.7 Refitting the crankshaft pulley with locating flange and locating lug for pulley (arrowed) outermost

14.2 Withdrawing the timing belt tension indicator - C 16 SE model

14.3 Lug (1) on tension indicator backplate must engage with hole (2) in oil pump - C 16 SE model (shown with engine removed from vehicle)

15.3 Extracting the camshaft front oil seal using a self-tapping screw - C 16 SE model

11 Adjust the timing belt tension as described in Section 9, 10 or 11.
12 Refit the outer timing belt covers as described in Sections 6 and 7.

14 Timing belt tension roller (1.4 and 1.6 litre models) - removal and refitting

Removal

1 Remove the timing belt as described in Section 9.
2 Unscrew the central securing bolt and withdraw the tension roller (see illustration).

Refitting

3 Refit the tension roller, ensuring that the lug on the roller backplate engages with the corresponding hole in the oil pump (see illustration).
4 Refit the tension roller securing bolt and tighten it to the specified torque.
5 Refit and tension the timing belt and adjust the tension as described in Section 9.

15 Camshaft oil seals - renewal

Front oil seal

Removal

1 Remove the camshaft gear as described in Section 12.
2 Punch or drill a small hole in the centre of the now-exposed oil seal.
3 Screw in a self-tapping screw and pull on the screw with pliers to extract the seal (see illustration).
4 Clean the oil seal seat with a wooden or plastic scraper.

Refitting

5 Wind a thin band of tape around the end of the camshaft, to protect the lips of the new oil seal as it is fitted.
6 Grease the lips of the new seal and drive it into position until it is flush with the housing, using a socket or tube (see illustration). Take care not to damage the seal lips during fitting.
7 Carefully remove the tape from the end of the camshaft.
8 Refit the camshaft gear as described in Section 12.

Rear oil seal - 1.4 and 1.6 litre models

Removal

9 Remove the distributor, or coil, as applicable, from the end of the camshaft housing, as described in Chapter 5.

Refitting

10 On 1.4 litre, C 16 NZ and X 16 SZ models, the camshaft rear oil seal takes the form of an O-ring on the rear of the distributor body. Prise off the old O-ring using a screwdriver (see illustration), then fit the new O-ring and refit the distributor as described in Chapter 5.
11 On C 16 SE models, the camshaft rear oil seal takes the form of an O-ring on the rear of the coil mounting plate. Unscrew the three coil mounting plate securing bolts and withdraw the plate from the end of the camshaft housing (see illustration). Prise off the old O-ring using a screwdriver, then fit the new O-ring and refit the coil mounting plate. Refit the coil to the mounting plate, referring to Chapter 5 if necessary.

Rear oil seal - C 18 NZ and C 20 NE models

Removal

12 Remove the distributor components, as described in Chapter 5.

15.6 Fitting a new camshaft front oil seal using a large socket - C 16 SE model

15.10 Removing the O-ring/camshaft rear oil seal from the rear of the distributor - 14 NV model

15.11 Coil mounting plate removed for access to O-ring/camshaft rear oil seal (arrowed) - C 16 SE model (shown with camshaft housing removed from engine)

15.13 Removing the camshaft rear oil seal - C 20 NE model (shown with camshaft housing removed from engine)

16.9 Camshaft thrustplate and securing bolts - C 16 SE model

16.10 Removing the camshaft thrustplate - C 20 NE model

13 Prise the seal from the camshaft housing **(see illustration)**.

14 Clean the oil seal seat with a wooden or plastic scraper.

Refitting

15 Grease the lips of the new seal and drive it into position until it is flush with the end of the camshaft housing, using a socket or tube. Take care not to damage the seal lips during fitting.

16 Refit the distributor components as described in Chapter 5.

16 Camshaft - removal, inspection and refitting

Note: The front (and rear, where applicable) camshaft oil seal(s) should be renewed on refitting.

Removal

1 The camshaft can only be removed without disturbing the housing if a special tool (Vauxhall P/N 603 850, or equivalent) is available to depress the cam followers whilst the camshaft is withdrawn.

2 If such a tool is not available, the camshaft housing must be removed. Since the cylinder head bolts must be removed, it is strongly recommended that a new cylinder head gasket is fitted. If the gasket is not renewed

and it 'blows' on reassembly, the cylinder head will have to be removed to renew the gasket and another new set of bolts will have to be obtained for refitting. *You have been warned!*

3 Removal and refitting of the camshaft housing is described in Section 17, along with cylinder head removal and refitting. If it is decided not to disturb the cylinder head, the relevant paragraphs referring specifically to cylinder head removal and refitting can be ignored. It is strongly recommended that the cylinder head is clamped to the cylinder block using four head bolts and some spacers to reduce the possibility of the seal between the head and the block being broken.

4 With the camshaft housing removed, continue as follows.

5 On 14 NV models, remove the fuel pump as described in Chapter 4A.

6 Remove the distributor, distributor components, or coil (as applicable) from the end of the housing.

7 On C 16 SE models, unscrew the three securing bolts and remove the coil mounting plate from the end of the camshaft housing.

8 On C 18 NZ and C 20 NE models, prise out the camshaft rear oil seal.

9 Working at the distributor/coil end of the camshaft, unscrew the two camshaft thrustplate securing bolts, using an Allen key or hexagon bit **(see illustration)**.

10 Withdraw the thrustplate, noting which way round it is fitted **(see illustration)**.

11 Carefully withdraw the camshaft from the distributor/coil end of the housing, taking care not to damage the bearing journals **(see illustration)**.

Inspection

12 With the camshaft removed, examine the bearings in the camshaft housing for signs of obvious wear or pitting. If evident, a new camshaft housing will probably be required. Also check that the oil supply holes in the camshaft housing are free from obstructions **(see illustration)**.

13 The camshaft itself should show no marks or scoring on the journal or cam lobe surfaces. If evident, renew the camshaft. Note that if the camshaft is renewed, all the rocker arms should also be renewed.

14 Check the camshaft thrustplate for signs of wear or grooves and renew if evident.

Refitting

15 It is advisable to renew the camshaft front oil seal as a matter of course if the camshaft has been removed. Prise out the old seal using a screwdriver and tap in the new seal until it is flush with the housing, using a socket or tube.

16 Begin refitting by liberally oiling the bearings in the housing and the oil seal lip.

17 Carefully insert the camshaft into the housing from the distributor/coil end, taking care to avoid damage to the bearings.

18 Refit the thrustplate and tighten the

2A

16.11 Withdrawing the camshaft from the housing - C 20 NE model

16.12 Oil supply hole (arrowed) in camshaft housing

16.18A Tightening a camshaft thrustplate securing bolt - C 16 SE model

16.18B Checking the camshaft endfloat using a feeler gauge - C 16 SE model

17.8 Loosening a camshaft cover breather hose clamp - C 20 NE model

17.9 Unbolting a wiring harness earth lead from the camshaft housing - C 16 SE model

securing bolts. Check the camshaft endfloat by inserting a feeler gauge between the thrustplate and the camshaft end flange. If the endfloat exceeds that specified, renew the thrustplate **(see illustrations)**.

19 On C 18 NZ and C 20 NE models, fit a new camshaft rear oil seal to the housing, using a socket or tube. The oil seal should be flush with the end of the camshaft housing.

20 On C 16 SE models, examine the condition of the O-ring on the rear of the coil mounting plate and renew it if necessary, then refit the coil mounting plate.

21 Refit the distributor, distributor components or coil, as applicable, as described in Chapter 5.

22 On 14 NV models, refit the fuel pump as described in Chapter 4.

23 Where applicable, remove the bolts and spacers clamping the cylinder head to the block.

24 Refit the camshaft housing, as described in Section 17.

25 If a new camshaft has been fitted, it is important to observe the following running-in schedule (unless otherwise specified by the manufacturer) immediately after initially starting the engine:

(a) One minute at 2000 rpm.
(b) One minute at 1500 rpm.
(c) One minute at 3000 rpm.
(d) One minute at 2000 rpm.

26 Change the engine oil (but not the filter,

unless due in any case) approximately 600 miles (1000 km) after fitting a new camshaft.

17 Cylinder head - removal and refitting

Note: *Do not remove the cylinder head from a hot engine. New cylinder head bolts and a new cylinder head gasket must be used on refitting and sealer (Vauxhall P/N 90094714, or equivalent), will be required when refitting the camshaft housing.*

Note: *The torque settings stated are only applicable to latest specification head bolts, available from Vauxhall. Earlier type or alternative make head bolts may require different torques. Consult your supplier.*

Removal

1 Disconnect the battery negative lead.

2 Drain the cooling system as described in Chapter 3.

3 Disconnect the exhaust downpipe from the manifold, referring to Chapter 4C.

4 The cylinder head can be removed complete with the manifolds, or the manifolds can be detached from the cylinder head before removal, with reference to Chapter 4C. If no work is to be carried out on the inlet manifold, it can be unbolted from the cylinder

head and supported to one side out of the way. This will avoid the need to disconnect the relevant hoses, pipes and wiring.

5 If the cylinder head is to be removed complete with the manifolds, disconnect all relevant hoses, pipes and wiring from the inlet manifold and associated components. On carburettor models, disconnect the hot air hose from the shroud on the exhaust manifold.

6 If the inlet manifold is to be left in the engine compartment, continue as follows otherwise, continue to paragraph 15.

7 Disconnect the air cleaner trunking from the airbox on the carburettor or fuel injection unit, or directly from the throttle body (as applicable).

8 Disconnect the camshaft cover breather hose(s) from the camshaft cover **(see illustration)**.

9 Where applicable, on fuel injection models, unbolt the wiring harness earth lead(s) from the camshaft housing **(see illustration)**.

10 On 1.4 and 1.6 litre models, disconnect the crankcase breather hose from the stub at the rear of the camshaft housing **(see illustration)**.

11 Loosen the alternator mountings, then unbolt the upper alternator mounting bracket from the inlet manifold **(see illustration)**.

12 Where applicable, unclip the fuel injector wiring harness from the brackets on the camshaft cover, then separate the two halves of the harness connector and release the

17.10 Loosening the crankcase breather hose clamp from the camshaft housing stub - C 16 SE model

17.11 Unbolt the upper alternator mounting bracket (bolt arrowed) from the inlet manifold

17.12A Unclip the fuel injector wiring harness from the brackets on the camshaft cover . . .

17.12B ... then separate the two halves of the wiring connector - C 16 SE model

17.13 Inlet manifold moved to one side to enable removal of the cylinder head - C 16 SE model

17.19A Disconnecting the crankcase breather hose from the camshaft housing - C 20 NE model

connector from the clip on the camshaft cover **(see illustrations)**.

13 Make a final check to ensure that all necessary hoses, pipes and wires have been disconnected. Then unscrew the securing nuts, noting the location of any brackets (e.g., engine lifting bracket) attached to the studs in the cylinder head and lift the inlet manifold from the cylinder head. Ensure that the manifold is properly supported, taking care not to strain any of the hoses, pipes and wires, etc., which are still connected **(see illustration)**.

14 Remove the manifold gasket from the cylinder head.

15 If necessary, remove the exhaust manifold with reference to Chapter 4C.

16 Remove the camshaft gear as described in Section 12.

17 Unscrew the two upper rear timing belt cover securing bolts from the camshaft housing.

18 Disconnect the HT leads from the spark plugs and the coil, labelling them if necessary to aid refitting and where applicable remove the distributor cap with reference to Chapter 1. Where applicable, disconnect the distributor or coil (C 16 SE models) wiring plug.

19 If not already done, disconnect the crankcase breather hose from the camshaft housing and on C 18 NZ and C 20 NE models.

Unscrew the bolt securing the crankcase breather tube bracket to the end of the cylinder head **(see illustrations)**.

20 Disconnect the coolant hose(s) from the thermostat housing **(see illustration)**.

21 On 14 NV models, disconnect the fuel hoses from the fuel pump. Be prepared for fuel spillage and plug or clamp the open ends of the hoses to prevent further fuel loss and dirt ingress.

22 Where applicable, disconnect the wiring plug from the coolant temperature sensor lin the end of the cylinder head **(see illustration)**.

23 Make a final check to ensure that all

17.19B Unbolting the crankcase breather tube bracket from the cylinder head - C 20 NE model

relevant hoses, pipes and wires, etc., have been disconnected.

24 Working from the outside inwards in a spiral pattern as shown **(see illustration)**, loosen all the cylinder head bolts by a quarter of a turn, then loosen all the bolts by half a turn and finally loosen and remove the bolts. Remove the washers.

25 Lift the camshaft housing from the cylinder head **(see illustration)**. If necessary, tap the housing gently with a soft-faced mallet to free it from the cylinder head, but **do not** lever at the mating faces. Note that the camshaft housing is located on dowels.

26 Lift the cylinder head from the cylinder

17.20 Disconnecting the coolant hose from the thermostat housing - C 16 SE model

17.22 Disconnecting the wiring plug from the coolant temperature sensor - C 16 SE model

17.24 Cylinder head bolt loosening sequence

17.25 Lifting the camshaft housing from the cylinder head - C 16 SE model

2A

17.26 Lifting the cylinder head from the cylinder block - C 16 SE model

17.27A Lift the rocker arms . . .

17.27B . . . and their thrust pads from the cylinder head - C 16 SE model

block **(see illustration)**. If necessary, tap the cylinder head gently with a soft-faced mallet to free it from the block, but **do not** lever at the mating faces. Note that the cylinder head is located on dowels.

27 Lift the rocker arms and their thrust pads from the cylinder head, keeping them in order so that they can be refitted in their original positions **(see illustrations)**.

28 Lift the hydraulic valve lifters from the cylinder head and keep the lifters in order, so that they can be refitted in their original positions **(see illustration)**.

29 Remove the cylinder head gasket and discard it.

Refitting

30 Clean the cylinder head and block mating faces and the camshaft housing and cylinder head mating faces, by careful scraping. Take care not to damage the cylinder head and camshaft housing, which are made of light alloy and are easily scored. Cover the coolant passages and other openings with masking tape or rag to prevent dirt and carbon falling in. Mop out all the oil from the bolt holes; if oil is left in the holes, hydraulic pressure could crack the block when the bolts are refitted.

31 Begin refitting by locating a new cylinder head gasket on the block so that the word

'OBEN' or 'TOP' can be read from above **(see illustrations)**.

32 With the mating faces scrupulously clean, locate the cylinder head on the block so that the positioning dowels engage in their holes.

33 Before refitting the hydraulic valve lifters, it is advisable to dismantle and clean them as described in Section 31.

34 Refit the hydraulic valve lifters, thrust pads and rocker arms to the cylinder head in their original positions. Liberally oil the valve lifter bores. Lubricate the contact faces of the valve lifters, thrust pads and rocker arms with a little long life paste (MoS_2), **(see illustration)**.

35 Temporarily refit the crankshaft gear and ensure that the timing marks are still positioned with No 1 piston at top dead centre (see Section 3).

36 Apply sealing compound (Vauxhall P/N 90094714, or equivalent) to the cylinder head top mating face **(see illustration)**, then refit the camshaft housing to the cylinder head.

37 Fit the **new** cylinder head bolts, ensuring that the washers are in place under their heads and screw the bolts in *by hand* as far as possible **(see illustration)**.

38 Tighten the bolts as shown **(see illustration)**. Tighten the bolts in the four stages given in the Specifications - i.e.

17.28 Lift the hydraulic valve lifters from the cylinder head - C 16 SE model

17.31A Cylinder head gasket 'OBEN/ TOP' markings

17.31B Cylinder head gasket correctly located over dowels (arrowed) in cylinder block - C 16 SE model (shown with engine removed from vehicle)

17.34 Lubricate the valve lifter contact faces with molybdenum disulphide grease - C 16 SE model

17.36 Apply sealing compound to the cylinder head top mating face - C 16 SE model

17.37 Fit new cylinder head bolts, ensuring that the washers are in place - C 20 NE model

17.38A Tighten the cylinder head bolts to the specified torque . . .

17.38B . . . then through the specified angle - C 20 NE model

2A

tighten all bolts to the Stage 1 torque, then tighten all bolts to Stage 2 and so on **(see illustrations)**. Additional tightening is not required.

39 Further refitting is a reversal of the removal procedure, remembering the following points.

40 Ensure that the ignition HT leads are reconnected to their correct cylinders.

41 Refit the camshaft gear as described in Section 12.

42 Where applicable, refit the manifolds to the cylinder head with reference to Chapter 4C, using new gaskets.

43 Reconnect the exhaust downpipe to the manifold, using a new gasket, with reference to Chapter 4C.

44 Refit the upper alternator mounting bracket to the inlet manifold and then adjust the alternator drivebelt tension as described in Chapter 1.

45 Refill the cooling system as described in Chapter 3.

46 On completion, check that all relevant hoses, pipes and wires, etc., have been reconnected.

47 When the engine is started, check for signs of leaks.

48 Once the engine has reached normal operating temperature, check and if necessary adjust the idle speed and mixture (where possible), as described in Chapter 4A.

---

18 Sump and oil pick-up pipe - removal and refitting

Note: *A new sump gasket and sump baffle gasket (C 18 NZ and C 20 NE models) must be used on refitting. Sealant (Vauxhall P/N 90485251, or equivalent) will be required to coat the cylinder block face (see text) and thread-locking compound (P/N 90167347) will be required to coat the sump securing bolt threads.*

Removal

1 Disconnect the battery negative lead.

2 Drain the engine oil, with reference to Chapter 1 if necessary, then refit and tighten the drain plug.

3 Apply the handbrake, then jack up the front of the vehicle and support securely on axle stands.

4 Remove the front section of the exhaust system as described in Chapter 4C.

5 Where applicable, disconnect the wiring from the oil level sensor mounted in the sump.

6 Unscrew the securing bolts and remove the engine-to-transmission blanking plate from the bellhousing **(see illustration)**.

7 Unscrew the securing bolts and withdraw the sump **(see illustration)**. If necessary, tap the sump with a soft-faced mallet to free it from the cylinder block. *Do not* lever between

17.38C Cylinder head bolt tightening sequence

the sump and cylinder block mating faces. On C 18 NZ and C 20 NE models, the sump baffle will probably be pulled away from the cylinder block with the sump, but cannot be removed until the bracket securing the oil pick-up pipe has been removed.

8 Remove the gasket.

9 On C 18 NZ and C 20 NE models, to remove the sump baffle, unbolt the bracket securing the oil pick-up pipe to the cylinder block **(see illustration)**. The baffle can then be manipulated over the oil pick-up pipe. Remove the sump baffle gasket.

10 The oil pick-up pipe can be removed by unscrewing the single bolt securing the support bracket to the cylinder block (if not already done) and the two bolts securing the

18.6 Removing the engine-to-gearbox/transmission blanking plate from the bellhousing - C 20 NE model

18.7 Withdrawing the sump - C 16 SE model

18.9 Removing the bracket securing the oil pick-up pipe to the cylinder block - C 20 NE model

18.12A Applying sealing compound to the joint between the oil pump and cylinder block - C 20 NE model

18.12B Apply sealing compound to oil pump and rear main bearing cap joints before refitting sump

18.14A Fit a new O-ring to the oil pick-up pipe . . .

end of the pipe to the oil pump. Remove the O-ring.

Refitting

11 Clean all traces of old gasket from the mating faces of the cylinder block, sump baffle (where applicable) and sump.

12 Begin refitting by applying sealing compound (Vauxhall P/N 90485251, or equivalent) to the joints between the oil pump and cylinder block and the rear main bearing cap and cylinder block **(see illustrations)**.

13 On C 18 NZ and C 20 NE models, fit a new sump baffle gasket, if necessary applying a little sealing compound to hold it in place. Then offer the sump baffle up to the cylinder block, manipulating it over the oil pick-up pipe where applicable. Locate the remaining gasket on the sump baffle, but do not use sealing compound.

14 If the oil pick-up pipe has been removed, refit it to the oil pump using a new O-ring **(see illustrations)**.

15 Where applicable, refit the bracket securing the oil pick-up pipe to the cylinder block, ensuring that it passes through the relevant hole in the sump baffle on C 18 NZ and C 20 NE models.

16 Coat the sump securing bolts with thread-locking compound, then refit the sump and tighten the securing bolts to the specified torque.

17 Further refitting is a reversal of removal, but refit the front section of the exhaust

system with reference to Chapter 4C and on completion, refill the engine with oil as described in Chapter 1.

19 Oil pump - removal and refitting

Note: *A new oil pump gasket, a new front crankshaft oil seal and on C 18 NZ and C 20 NE models, a new oil filter must be used on refitting.*

Removal

1 Remove the rear timing belt cover as described in Section 8.

2 Remove the sump, oil pick-up pipe and sump baffle (where applicable) as described in Section 18.

3 On C 18 NZ and C 20 NE models, unscrew the oil filter from its mounting on the oil pump, with reference to Chapter 1 if necessary.

4 Disconnect the wiring from the oil pressure switch mounted in the oil pump.

5 Remove the securing bolts and withdraw the oil pump from the cylinder block. Remove the gasket.

Refitting

6 Thoroughly clean the mating faces of the oil pump and cylinder block, then locate a new gasket on the block **(see illustration)**.

7 Wind a thin layer of tape around the front

edge of the crankshaft, to prevent damage to the oil seal lips as the pump is refitted.

8 With a new oil seal fitted to the pump, as described in Section 20, grease the oil seal lips, then refit the pump, ensuring that the inner gear engages with the flats on the crankshaft **(see illustration)**.

9 Tighten the securing bolts to the specified torque, then carefully remove the tape from the front of the crankshaft.

10 Reconnect the wiring to the oil pressure switch.

11 On C 18 NZ and C 20 NE models, fit a new oil filter, with reference to Chapter 1.

12 Refit the sump baffle (where fitted), oil pick-up pipe and sump, as described in Section 18.

13 Refit the rear timing belt cover as described in Section 8.

20 Oil pump - dismantling, inspection and reassembly

Note: *A new pressure relief valve sealing ring should be used on reassembly and sealing compound (Vauxhall P/N 90094714, or equivalent) will be required to coat the pump housing mating face.*

19.8 Refitting the oil pump - 1.6 litre model (shown with engine removed from vehicle)

1 Tape wound around crankshaft
2 Flats on crankshaft engage with inner oil pump gear

18.14B . . . and refit the pick-up pipe to the oil pump - C 16 SE model

19.6 Locate a new oil pump gasket on the cylinder block - C 20 NE model

20.2 Removing an oil pump rear cover securing screw

20.3 Oil pressure relief valve components

1 Plunger	*3 Sealing ring*
2 Spring	*4 Plug*

20.5 Check the clearance between the inner and outer gear teeth . . .

Dismantling

1 With the oil pump removed as described in Section 19, continue as follows.

2 Remove the securing screws **(see illustration)** and withdraw the rear cover. The screws may be very tight, in which case it may be necessary to use an impact driver to remove them.

3 The oil pressure relief valve components can be removed from the pump by unscrewing the cap. Withdraw the cap, sealing ring, spring and plunger **(see illustration)**.

4 Prise the crankshaft front oil seal from the pump using a screwdriver.

Inspection

5 Check the clearance between the inner and outer gear teeth (backlash) using a feeler gauge **(see illustration)**.

6 Check the clearance between the edges of the gears and the housing (endfloat) using a straight edge and a feeler gauge **(see illustration)**.

7 If any of the clearances are outside the specified limits, renew the components as necessary.

8 Examine the pressure relief valve spring and plunger and renew if any sign of damage or wear is evident.

Reassembly

9 Ensure that the interior of the pump body is scrupulously clean before beginning reassembly.

10 Discard the old pressure relief valve sealing ring, then thoroughly clean the pressure relief valve components and lubricate them with clean engine oil before refitting. Use a new sealing ring.

11 Ensure that the gears are clean. Then lubricate them with clean engine oil and refit them to the pump body, noting that the outer gear is marked with a punch dot to indicate its outer face (i.e., the face nearest the pump cover), **(see illustration)**.

12 Ensure that the mating faces of the rear cover and the pump housing are clean, then coat the pump housing mating face with sealing compound (Vauxhall P/N 90094714, or equivalent) and refit the rear cover. Refit and tighten the securing screws.

13 Fit a new crankshaft front oil seal to the recess in the pump body, using a socket or tube, so that the seal is flush with the outer face of the housing **(see illustration)**.

20.6 . . . and between the edges of the gears and the housing

---

21 Crankshaft oil seals - renewal

Front oil seal

Removal

1 Remove the crankshaft gear as described in Section 13. Ensure that, where applicable, the Woodruff key is removed from the end of the crankshaft.

2 On C 18 NZ and C 20 NE SOHC models, remove the rear timing belt cover with reference to Section 8.

3 Punch or drill a small hole in the centre of the now-exposed oil seal.

4 Screw in a self-tapping screw and pull on the screw with pliers to extract the seal **(see illustration)**. Several attempts may be necessary. Be careful not to damage the sealing face of the crankshaft.

Refitting

5 Clean the oil seal seat with a wooden or plastic scraper.

6 Wind a thin band of tape around the end of the crankshaft to protect the lips of the new oil seal as it is fitted.

20.11 Gear outer face identification mark (arrowed)

20.13 Fitting a new crankshaft front oil seal to the oil pump

21.4 Using a self-tapping screw and a pair of pliers to extract the crankshaft front oil seal - C 16 SE model

2A

21.7 Tapping a new crankshaft front oil seal into position - C 16 SE model

7 Grease the lips of the new seal and tap it into position until it is flush with the outer face of the oil pump body, using a socket or tube **(see illustration)**. Take care not to damage the seal lips during fitting.

8 Carefully remove the tape from the end of the crankshaft.

9 On C 18 NZ and C 20 NE models, refit the rear timing belt cover, with reference to Section 8.

10 Where applicable, refit the Woodruff key and refit the crankshaft pulley, as described in Section 13.

Rear oil seal
Removal

13 Remove the flywheel/driveplate as described in Section 22.

22.13A Tool for preventing flywheel from turning, using engine-to-gearbox bolt - C 16 SE model

22.13B Tighten the flywheel securing bolts to the specified torque . . .

21.15 Fitting a new crankshaft rear oil seal (viewed with engine removed from vehicle and sump removed). Note tape on end of crankshaft

14 Proceed as described in paragraphs 3 to 5 inclusive of this Section.

Refitting

15 Grease the lips of the new seal, then tap the seal into position using a tube, until flush with the outer faces of the cylinder block and rear main bearing cap **(see illustration)**.

16 Refit the flywheel/driveplate as described in Section 22.

22 Flywheel/driveplate - removal, inspection and refitting

Note: *New flywheel securing bolts must be used on refitting.*

 Warning: Take care when removing the flywheel, as it is very heavy.

Removal

1 Remove the starter motor as described in Chapter 5.

2 Remove the clutch as described in Chapter 6, or the automatic transmission as described in Chapter 7B, as applicable.

3 If the transmission is still attached to the engine, remove the clutch release bearing and its guide sleeve, as described in Chapter 6.

4 Although the flywheel bolt holes are offset so that the flywheel can only be fitted in one position, it will make refitting easier if alignment marks are made between the flywheel and the end of the crankshaft.

22.13C . . . and then through the specified angle - C 16 SE model

22.6 Removing the flywheel - C 16 SE model

5 Prevent the flywheel from turning by jamming the ring gear teeth using a large screwdriver or similar tool. Access is most easily obtained through the starter motor aperture.

6 Unscrew the securing bolts and remove the flywheel **(see illustration)**.

Inspection

7 If the teeth on the flywheel starter ring are badly worn, or if some are missing, then it will be necessary to remove the ring and fit a new one.

8 The old ring can be split with a cold chisel, after making a cut with a hacksaw blade between two gear teeth. Take great care not to damage the flywheel during this operation and use eye protection at all times. Once the ring has been split, it will spread apart and can be lifted from the flywheel.

9 The new ring gear must be heated to between 180° to 230°C and unless facilities for heating by oven or flame are available, leave the fitting to a Vauxhall dealer or engineering works. The new ring gear must not be overheated during this work, or the strength of the metal will be affected.

10 The ring should be tapped gently down onto its register and left to cool naturally. The contraction of the metal on cooling will ensure that it is a secure and permanent fit.

11 If the clutch friction disc contact surface of the flywheel is scored, or on close inspection, shows signs of small hair cracks (caused by overheating), it may be possible to have the flywheel surface-ground, provided the overall thickness of the flywheel is not reduced too much. Consult a Vauxhall dealer or a specialist engine repairer and if grinding is not possible, renew the flywheel complete.

Refitting

12 Offer the flywheel to the end of the crankshaft and align the previously made marks on the flywheel and crankshaft.

13 Fit new flywheel securing bolts and tighten them to the two stages given in the Specifications, whilst preventing the flywheel from turning as during removal **(see illustrations)**.

14 Where applicable, refit the clutch release

23.7 Right-hand engine mounting bracket (1) and mounting block (2) - C 16 SE model (viewed from underneath)

23.15 Left-hand engine/transmission mounting bracket (1) and mounting block (2) - 1.6 litre model (viewed from underneath)

bearing and its guide sleeve, as described in Chapter 6.

15 Refit the clutch as described in Chapter 6 or the automatic transmission as described in Chapter 7B, as applicable.

16 Refit the starter motor (Chapter 5).

23 Engine/transmission mountings - inspection and renewal

Note: *Thread-locking compound will be required to coat the threads of the mounting to body bolts on refitting. New mounting to body bolts must be used on refitting.*

Inspection

1 To improve access, raise the front of the vehicle and support it securely on axle stands.

2 Check the mounting rubbers to see if they are cracked, hardened or separated from the metal at any point. Renew the mounting if any such damage or deterioration is evident.

3 Check that all the mounting securing nuts and bolts are securely tightened, using a torque wrench to check if possible.

4 Using a large screwdriver, or a similar tool, check for wear in the mountings by carefully levering against them to check for free play. Where this is not possible, request assistance to move the engine/transmission assembly back and forth and from side to side, while you observe the mountings. While some free play is to be expected, even from new components, excessive wear should be obvious. If excessive free play is found, check first to see that the securing nuts and bolts are correctly tightened, then renew any worn components as described below.

Renewal

Right-hand mounting

5 If not already done, apply the handbrake, then raise the front of the vehicle and support securely on axle stands.

6 Attach lifting tackle to the engine lifting brackets on the cylinder head and support the weight of the engine.

7 Working under the vehicle, unbolt the engine mounting bracket from the cylinder block and unbolt the mounting from the body, then withdraw the bracket/mounting assembly **(see illustration)**.

8 Unbolt the mounting from the bracket.

9 Fit the new mounting to the bracket and tighten the securing bolts to the specified torque.

10 Refit the mounting bracket to the cylinder block and tighten the securing bolts to the specified torque.

11 Coat the threads of the mounting to body bolts with Locking Compound, then refit them and tighten to the specified torque.

12 Disconnect the lifting tackle and hoist from the engine.

13 Lower the vehicle to the ground.

Left-hand mounting

14 Proceed as described in paragraphs 5 and 6.

15 Working under the vehicle, unbolt the engine/transmission mounting bracket from the transmission and unbolt the mounting from the body, then withdraw the bracket/mounting assembly **(see illustration)**.

16 Unbolt the mounting from the bracket.

17 Fit the new mounting to the bracket and tighten the securing bolts to the specified torque.

18 Before refitting the bracket/mounting assembly, check that the original bolts that

secured the mounting to the body rotate freely in their threaded bores in the body. If necessary, recut the threaded bores using an M10 x 1.25 mm tap.

19 Refit the mounting bracket to the transmission and tighten the securing bolts to the specified torque.

20 Fit *new* mounting to body bolts and tighten them to the specified torque.

21 Disconnect the lifting tackle and hoist from the engine. Lower the vehicle to the ground.

Rear mounting

22 Proceed as described in paragraphs 5 and 6.

23 Working under the vehicle, unbolt the mounting from the front subframe and the mounting bracket and withdraw the mounting **(see illustrations)**.

24 Fit the new mounting to the subframe and mounting bracket and tighten the securing bolts to the specified torque.

25 Disconnect the lifting tackle and hoist from the engine. Lower the vehicle to the ground.

24 Engine overhaul - general

1 The following sections include details of engine removal and refitting and general overhaul procedures for the cylinder head, cylinder block/crankcase and internal engine components.

2 The information ranges from advice concerning preparation for an overhaul and the purchase of replacement parts, to detailed step-by-step procedures covering removal, inspection, renovation and refitting of internal engine components.

3 The Sections are based on the assumption that the engine has been removed from the vehicle.

4 It is not always easy to determine when, or if, an engine should be completely overhauled, as a number of factors must be

23.23A Rear engine mounting block-to-front subframe nuts (arrowed) - viewed from underneath

23.23B Rear engine mounting bracket (arrowed) - C 16 SE model (viewed from underneath)

2A

considered. Also remember that it may prove more economical to buy a reconditioned engine than to carry out a full overhaul. This cannot be accurately determined until the engine has been fully dismantled.

5 High mileage is not necessarily an indication that an engine overhaul is required, while low mileage does not preclude the need for an overhaul. Frequency of servicing is the most important consideration. An engine that has had regular and frequent oil and filter changes, besides the other specified maintenance (see Chapter 1), is likely to give many thousands of miles of reliable service. Conversely, a neglected engine may require an overhaul very early in its life.

6 Excessive oil consumption is an indication that piston rings, valve seals and/or valve guides are in need of attention. Make sure that oil leaks are not responsible before deciding that the piston rings and/or valve guides are worn. Perform a cylinder compression check to determine the extent of the work required (refer to Section 2).

7 Check the oil pressure using a gauge fitted in place of the engine oil pressure switch (follow the equipment manufacturer's instructions) and compare it with the figure given in the Specifications. If the oil pressure is extremely low, the main and big-end bearings and/or the oil pump are probably worn.

8 Loss of power, rough running, knocking or metallic engine noises, excessive valve gear noise, or high fuel consumption may also point to the need for an overhaul, especially if all the conditions are present at the same time. If a complete service does not remedy the situation, overhaul is the only course of action available.

9 A full engine overhaul involves restoring the specifications (clearances, endfloats, etc.) of the internal components to the standards used in a new engine. During a complete overhaul, the pistons and piston rings are renewed and the cylinder bores are reconditioned. New main bearings and big-end bearings are generally fitted and if necessary, the crankshaft may be reground to compensate for wear in the bearing journals. The valves should also be inspected and serviced as well, since they are usually in less-than-perfect condition if the engine has reached the stage where overhaul is required. Always pay careful attention to the condition of the oil pump when overhauling the engine and renew it if in any doubt as to its service-ability. If a complete overhaul is carried out, the result should be to the standard of a new engine and should provide many trouble-free miles of service.

10 Before beginning engine overhaul, carefully read through all the procedures involved to familiarize yourself with the scope and requirements of the job. Overhauling an engine is not difficult if you follow all the instructions carefully, have the necessary tools and equipment ready to hand and pay

close attention to all the recommended specifications. Engine overhaul can be time-consuming. Plan on the vehicle being off the road for a minimum of two weeks, especially if parts must be taken to an engineering works for repair or reconditioning. Check on the availability of new parts and make sure that any necessary special tools and equipment are obtained in advance. Most work can be done with typical hand tools, although a number of precision measuring instruments will be required to inspect parts to determine whether renewal is required. Often, an engineering works will handle the inspection of parts and offer advice concerning reconditioning and renewal.

11 Always wait until the engine has been completely dismantled and all components, especially the cylinder block, have been inspected before deciding which service and repair operations must be entrusted to an engineering works. Since the condition of the cylinder block will be the major factor to consider when determining whether to overhaul the original engine or buy a reconditioned unit, do not buy parts or have overhaul work done on other components until the block has been thoroughly inspected. As a rule, time is the primary cost of an overhaul, so it does not pay to fit worn or sub-standard parts.

12 Critical cooling system components such as the hoses, thermostat and water pump should be carefully inspected and if necessary renewed when an engine is overhauled. The radiator should be checked carefully to ensure that it is not clogged or leaking.

13 As a final note, to ensure maximum life and minimum trouble from an overhauled engine, everything must be assembled with care in a spotlessly clean environment.

25 Engine removal, methods and precautions - general

1 If you have decided to remove an engine for overhaul or major repair work, several preliminary steps should be taken.

2 Finding a place to work is extremely important. Adequate working space, along with storage space for the vehicle, will be required. If a garage is not available, at the very least a flat, level, clean work surface is required.

3 Cleaning the engine compartment and engine before beginning the removal procedure will help to keep tools clean and organised.

4 An engine hoist or an A-frame will also be required. Make sure that the equipment is rated more than the combined weight of the engine and transmission. Safety is of primary importance, considering the potential hazards involved in lifting the engine out of the vehicle.

If the engine is being removed by a novice, an assistant should be available.

5 Advice and assistance from someone more experienced would also be helpful. There are many instances when one person cannot simultaneously perform all the operations required when lifting the engine out of the vehicle. Plan the operation carefully before beginning.

6 Obtain all the tools and equipment required before beginning the job. Equipment necessary to perform engine removal and installation safely and with relative ease includes (in addition to an engine hoist) a heavy-duty trolley jack, complete sets of spanners and sockets as described in the Reference section of this manual, wooden blocks and plenty of rags and cleaning solvent to cope with spilled oil, coolant and fuel. If the hoist is to be hired, make sure that you arrange for it in advance and perform all the operations possible without it beforehand. This will save you money and time.

7 Plan for the vehicle to be out of use for some time. An engineering works may be required to perform some of the work that the DIY enthusiast cannot accomplish without special equipment. These establishments often have a busy schedule, so it would be a good idea to consult them before removing the engine, to gain a rough estimate of the amount of time required to overhaul or repair components that may require attention.

8 Always be extremely careful when removing and refitting the engine. Serious injury can result from careless actions. By planning ahead and taking plenty of time, the job (although major) can be accomplished successfully.

26 Engine - removal and refitting (leaving manual transmission in vehicle)

Removal

1 Disconnect both battery leads.

2 Drain the cooling system and remove the radiator as described in Chapter 3.

3 Drain the engine oil as described in Chapter 1 and, on C 18 NZ and C 20 NE models, remove the oil filter.

4 Remove the air cleaner assembly from the body panel and remove the air inlet trunking and the airbox from the carburettor or throttle body, referring to Chapter 4A or 4B, as applicable.

5 On carburettor and single-point fuel injection models, disconnect the hot air hose from the exhaust manifold hot air shroud and the air cleaner and remove the hose.

6 Remove the alternator as described in Chapter 5.

7 Remove the power steering pump, if fitted, as described in Chapter 10.

26.8 Disconnecting the brake servo vacuum hose from the inlet manifold - C 16 SE model

26.10 Disconnecting the MAP sensor vacuum hose from the throttle body - C 16 SE model

26.11 Disconnecting a coolant hose from the throttle body - C 16 SE model

8 Disconnect the brake servo vacuum hose from the inlet manifold **(see illustration)**.

9 Disconnect the throttle cable from the throttle lever and the bracket on the carburettor or inlet manifold, as applicable.

10 Disconnect the vacuum pipe(s) from the carburettor or throttle body (as applicable), noting their locations **(see illustration)**.

11 Disconnect the coolant hose(s) from the inlet manifold and/or throttle body, as applicable **(see illustration)**.

12 On 14 NV models, disconnect the coolant hoses from the automatic choke housing and disconnect the wiring from the automatic choke heater and the choke pull-down solenoid. Disconnect the airbox vacuum pipe from the carburettor.

13 Depressurise the fuel system as described in Chapter 4B. Then disconnect the fuel hoses from the fuel pump and vapour separator on carburettor models, or from the fuel injection unit or the pipes on the inlet manifold on fuel injection models. Be prepared for fuel spillage and take adequate fire precautions. Plug or clamp the open ends of the pipes and hoses to prevent dirt ingress and further fuel leakage.

14 On fuel injection models, disconnect all relevant wiring connections and plugs, noting their locations and move the fuel injection wiring harness to one side.

15 Release the securing clips and withdraw the wiring harness from the brackets on the camshaft cover, if applicable.

16 Disconnect the heater coolant hoses from the coolant gallery at the rear of the cylinder block and from the cylinder head or inlet manifold, as applicable **(see illustration)**.

17 Disconnect the wiring from the following components (if not already done). Note that on certain models, a large single plug can be disconnected to separate the engine wiring loom from the main wiring harness (the connector can usually be found clipped to a bracket on the battery tray). This will leave the wiring loom attached to the engine, avoiding the need to remove the plugs and connections from individual components.

(a) *Starter motor.*
(b) *Distributor/coil (as applicable, note HT lead positions).*
(c) *Oil pressure switch.*
(d) *TDC sensor (if fitted).*
(e) *Oil level sensor (if fitted).*
(f) *Coolant temperature sensor (if fitted).*
(g) *Temperature gauge sender.*
(h) *Knock sensor (if fitted)*

18 Make a final check to ensure that all relevant hoses, pipes and wires have been disconnected and that they are positioned clear of the engine.

19 Unscrew and remove the three upper engine-to-transmission bolts accessible from the engine compartment, noting the locations of any brackets that may be secured by the bolts **(see illustration)**.

20 If not already done, apply the handbrake,

then jack up the front of the vehicle and support securely on axle stands.

21 Remove the crankshaft pulley, with reference to Section 5.

22 Remove the front section of the exhaust system, as described in Chapter 4C.

23 On models where it is possible to remove the clutch with the engine and transmission in the vehicle, remove the clutch as described in Chapter 6.

24 On models where it is not possible to remove the clutch with the engine and transmission in the vehicle, pull the transmission input shaft from engagement with the splined hub of the clutch friction disc. This procedure is described in Chapter 6, as part of the clutch removal procedure for models where it is possible to remove the clutch with the engine and transmission in the vehicle.

25 Unbolt and remove the transmission bellhousing cover plate.

26 Attach a hoist and lifting tackle to the engine lifting brackets on the cylinder head and support the weight of the engine.

27 Support the transmission using a trolley jack with a block of wood to spread the load.

28 Unbolt the right-hand engine mounting from the cylinder block and the body and withdraw the mounting bracket **(see illustration)**.

29 Unscrew and remove the four lower engine-to-transmission bolts (again noting the location of any brackets that may be secured

26.16 Disconnecting the coolant hose (arrowed) from the inlet manifold - C 16 SE model

26.19 Three upper engine-to-gearbox bolts (arrowed)

26.28 Right-hand engine mounting bracket (arrowed) - SOHC model

2A

26.30 Lifting the engine from the vehicle – 1.6 litre multi-point fuel injection engine

by the bolts), then manipulate the engine as necessary to separate it from the transmission. The transmission locates on dowels in the cylinder block.

30 Carefully raise the hoist and lift the engine from the vehicle, taking care not to damage any of the surrounding components in the engine compartment **(see illustration)**.

31 With the engine removed, the transmission can be supported by placing a length of wood between the bellhousing and the front suspension subframe. Once the wooden support is in place, remove the trolley jack from under the transmission.

Refitting

Note: *Thread-locking compound will be required to coat the threads of the right-hand engine mounting-to-body bolts.*

32 With the front of the vehicle raised and supported on axle stands, support the transmission with a trolley jack and block of wood and remove the previously positioned support from between the transmission bellhousing and the subframe.

33 Support the engine with the hoist and lifting tackle and gently lower the engine into position in the engine compartment.

34 Mate the engine and the transmission together, ensuring that the transmission locates on the dowels in the cylinder block. Then refit the three upper engine-to-transmission bolts (ensuring that any brackets noted during removal are in place) do not fully tighten the bolts at this stage.

35 Refit the four lower engine-to-transmission bolts (again ensuring that any brackets noted during removal are in place), but again do not fully tighten them at this stage.

36 Fit the right-hand engine mounting bracket to the cylinder block and tighten its securing bolts to the specified torque.

37 Coat the engine mounting-to-body bolts with thread-locking compound, then manipulate the engine and transmission as necessary to enable the bolts to be fitted. Fit the bolts and tighten them to the specified torque.

38 Tighten all the engine-to-transmission bolts to the specified torque, then disconnect the lifting tackle and hoist from the engine and

remove the trolley jack from beneath the transmission.

39 Refit the transmission bellhousing cover plate.

40 Refit the clutch, if applicable and engage the transmission input shaft with the splined hub of the clutch friction disc (as described in Chapter 6).

41 Refit the front section of the exhaust system, as described in Chapter 4C.

42 Refit the crankshaft pulley, with reference to Section 5.

43 Lower the vehicle to the ground.

44 Refit and reconnect all relevant pipes, wires and hoses, etc., using a reversal of the removal procedure described in paragraphs 8 to 17 inclusive.

45 Where applicable, refit the power steering pump and on C 18 NZ and C 20 NE models, tension the pump drivebelt, as described in Chapter 10.

46 Refit the alternator and tension the drivebelt, as described in Chapter 1.

47 Refit the air cleaner components, referring to Chapter 4A or 4B, if necessary and on carburettor models, reconnect the hot air hose to the exhaust manifold hot air shroud.

48 Fill the engine with oil and where applicable fit a new oil filter, as described in Chapter 1.

49 Refit the radiator and refill the cooling system as described in Chapter 3.

50 Refit the bonnet as described in Chapter 11.

51 Reconnect the battery leads.

52 On completion, if applicable, bleed the power steering fluid circuit as described in Chapter 10.

27 Engine/manual transmission assembly - removal and refitting

Note: *New bolts must be used to secure the left-hand engine/transmission mounting to the body on refitting and new locking plates must be used on the bolts securing the rear engine/transmission mounting to the transmission. Thread-locking compound will be required to coat the threads of the right-hand engine mounting-to-body bolts. An M10 x 1.25 mm tap may be required during this procedure - refer to the text.*

Removal

1 Proceed as described in Section 26, paragraphs 1 to 17 inclusive.

2 Working in the engine compartment, make alignment marks between the gear selector rod and the clamp sleeve, then loosen the clamp bolt and disconnect the gear selector rod from the clamp sleeve **(see illustration)**.

3 Remove the retaining clip, then slide the clutch cable from the release lever, pushing the release lever back towards the bulkhead if necessary to allow the cable to be disconnected. Pull the cable support from the bracket on the transmission casing, then

move the cable to one side out of the way, taking note of its routing.

4 Disconnect the wiring from the reversing light switch, which is located at the front of the transmission casing.

5 Unscrew the securing sleeve and disconnect the speedometer cable from the transmission.

6 Unscrew the retaining nut and disconnect the earth strap from the transmission endplate.

7 Make a final check to ensure that all relevant pipes, hoses, wires, etc., have been disconnected and that they are positioned clear of the engine and transmission.

8 Proceed as described in Section 26, paragraphs 20 to 22 inclusive.

9 Disconnect the inboard ends of the driveshafts from the differential, referring to the relevant paragraphs of Chapter 8. Be prepared for oil spillage as the driveshafts are withdrawn and plug the apertures in the differential, to prevent further loss of oil and dirt ingress. Support the driveshafts by suspending them with wire or string. *Do not* allow them to hand down under their own weight.

10 Attach a hoist and lifting tackle to the engine lifting brackets on the cylinder head and support the weight of the engine.

11 Remove the left-hand engine/transmission mounting completely by unscrewing the two bolts securing the rubber mounting to the vehicle body and the three bolts securing the mounting bracket to the transmission.

12 Unbolt the right-hand engine mounting from the body and from the cylinder block and withdraw the mounting bracket.

13 Working under the vehicle, unscrew and remove the two nuts securing the engine/transmission rear mounting to the front subframe and the three bolts securing the mounting bracket to the transmission, then withdraw the mounting bracket.

14 Carefully swing the engine/transmission assembly across the engine compartment as necessary, to allow the assembly to be lifted vertically from the vehicle by raising the hoist. Take care not to damage any of the surrounding components in the engine compartment.

27.2 Gear selector rod clamp sleeve (arrowed)

15 With the engine/transmission assembly removed, support the assembly on blocks of wood positioned on a workbench, or failing that, on a clean area of the workshop floor.

16 Clean away any external dirt using paraffin or a water-soluble solvent and a stiff brush.

17 Unbolt and remove the transmission bellhousing cover plate.

18 Ensure that both engine and transmission are adequately supported, then unscrew and remove the engine-to-transmission bolts, noting the locations of any brackets that may be secured by the bolts.

19 Carefully withdraw the transmission from the engine, ensuring that the weight of the transmission is not allowed to hang on the input shaft while it is engaged with the clutch friction disc. Note that the transmission locates on dowels positioned in the cylinder block.

Refitting

20 Before starting the refitting operations, check that the two original bolts that secure the left-hand engine/transmission rubber mounting to the vehicle body rotate freely in their threaded bores in the body. If necessary, re-cut the threaded bores using an M10 x 1.25 mm tap.

21 On models where the clutch can be removed and refitted with the engine and transmission in the vehicle, if the clutch has been removed, it will prove easier to refit after the engine/transmission assembly has been refitted to the vehicle.

22 Carefully offer the transmission to the engine until the bellhousing is located on the dowels in the cylinder block, then refit the engine-to-transmission bolts and tighten them to the specified torque. Make sure that any brackets secured by the bolts are correctly positioned as noted before removal. If the clutch is still bolted to the flywheel, ensure that the weight of the transmission is not allowed to hang on the input shaft as it is engaged with the clutch friction disc.

23 If the clutch is in place, refit the transmission bellhousing cover plate.

24 With the front of the vehicle raised and supported on axle stands, support the engine/transmission assembly with the hoist and lifting tackle, then gently lower it into position in the engine compartment.

25 Working under the vehicle, refit the rear engine/transmission mounting to the transmission, using new locking plates under the bolt heads and tighten the bolts to the specified torque.

26 Fit the two bolts securing the engine/transmission rear mounting to the front subframe, but do not fully tighten them at this stage.

27 Fit the right-hand engine mounting bracket to the cylinder block and tighten the securing bolts to the specified torque.

28 Coat the right-hand engine mounting-to-body bolts with thread-locking compound,

then fit the bolts, but do not fully tighten them at this stage.

29 Fit the left-hand transmission mounting bracket to the transmission and tighten the securing bolts to the specified torque.

30 Fit new left-hand transmission mounting-to-body bolts and tighten them to the specified torque.

31 Tighten the right-hand engine mounting and the rear engine/transmission mounting-to-front subframe bolts to their specified torques, then remove the lifting tackle and the hoist from the engine.

32 Where applicable, the clutch can now be fitted and/or the transmission input shaft can be pressed into engagement with the splined hub of the clutch friction disc, as described in Chapter 6. Refit the transmission bellhousing cover plate, where applicable.

33 Reconnect the inboard ends of the driveshafts to the differential, with reference to the relevant paragraphs in Chapter 8, using new snap-rings.

34 Refit the front section of the exhaust system, as described in Chapter 4C.

35 Refit the crankshaft pulley, with reference to Section 5.

36 Reconnect the transmission earth strap and tighten the securing nut.

37 Lower the vehicle to the ground.

38 Reconnect the speedometer cable to the transmission and tighten the securing sleeve.

39 Reconnect the reversing light switch wiring.

40 Refit the clutch cable to the bracket on the transmission casing, then reconnect the cable to the release lever and adjust the cable as described in Chapter 6. Ensure that the cable is routed as noted during removal.

41 Reconnect the gear selector rod to the clamp sleeve, ensuring that the marks made before disconnection are aligned and tighten the clamp bolt.

42 Proceed as described in Section 26, paragraphs 44 to 49 inclusive.

43 Top-up the transmission oil level, as described in Chapter 1.

44 Refit the bonnet as described in Chapter 11.

45 Reconnect the battery leads.

---

28 Engine - removal and refitting (leaving automatic transmission in vehicle)

Note: *New torque converter-to-driveplate bolts must be used on refitting and if the original torque converter is being used, an M10 x 1.25 mm tap will be required. Thread-locking compound will be required to coat the threads of the right-hand engine mounting-to-body bolts.*

Removal

1 Proceed as described in Section 26, paragraphs 1 to 17 inclusive.

2 Make a final check to ensure that all

relevant hoses, pipes and wires have been disconnected and that they are positioned clear of the engine.

3 Unscrew and remove the three upper engine-to-transmission bolts, accessible from the engine compartment, noting the location of any brackets that may be secured by the bolts.

4 Proceed as described in Section 26, paragraphs 20 to 22 inclusive.

5 Unbolt and remove the transmission bellhousing cover plate.

6 If the original torque converter and driveplate are to be refitted, make alignment marks between the torque converter and the driveplate, to ensure that the components are reassembled in their original positions.

7 Working through the bottom of the bellhousing, unscrew the three torque converter-to-driveplate bolts. It will be necessary to turn the crankshaft using a spanner or socket on the crankshaft pulley or gear bolt (as applicable), to gain access to each bolt in turn through the aperture. Use a screwdriver or a similar tool to jam the driveplate ring gear, preventing the driveplate from rotating as the bolts are loosened. Discard the bolts.

8 Attach a hoist and lifting tackle to the engine lifting brackets on the cylinder head and support the weight of the engine.

9 Support the transmission using a trolley jack with a block of wood to spread the load.

10 Unbolt the right-hand engine mounting from the cylinder block and the body and withdraw the mounting bracket.

11 Unscrew and remove the lower engine-to-transmission bolts, then manipulate the engine as necessary to separate it from the transmission, noting that the transmission locates on dowels in the cylinder block. Ensure that the torque converter is held firmly in place in the transmission casing as the engine and transmission are separated, otherwise it could fall out, resulting in fluid spillage and possible damage. Retain the torque converter while the engine is removed by bolting a strip of metal across the transmission bellhousing end face.

12 Carefully raise the hoist and lift the engine from the vehicle, taking care not to damage any of the surrounding components in the engine compartment.

13 With the engine removed, the transmission can be supported by placing a length of wood between the bellhousing and the front suspension subframe. Once the wooden support is in place, remove the trolley jack from under the transmission.

Refitting

14 With the front of the vehicle raised and supported on axle stands, support the transmission with a trolley jack and a block of wood. Remove the axle stands from beneath the transmission bellhousing and the subframe.

15 If the original torque converter is still in place, begin refitting by recutting the torque converter-to-driveplate bolt threads in the torque converter using an M10 x 1.25 mm tap.

16 Support the engine with the hoist and lifting tackle and gently lower the engine into position in the engine compartment.

17 Where applicable, remove the strip of metal retaining the torque converter in the transmission casing and hold the torque converter in position as the engine is mated to the transmission.

18 Ensure that the transmission locates on the dowels in the cylinder block, then refit the three upper engine-to-transmission bolts (ensuring that any brackets are in place as noted before removal) - do not fully tighten the bolts at this stage.

19 Refit the lower engine-to-transmission bolts (again ensuring that any brackets are in place), but again do not fully tighten them at this stage.

20 Fit the right-hand engine mounting bracket to the cylinder block and tighten its securing bolts to the specified torque.

21 Coat the engine mounting-to-body bolts with thread-locking compound, then manipulate the engine and transmission as necessary to enable the bolts to be fitted. Fit the bolts and tighten them to the specified torque.

22 Tighten all the engine-to-transmission bolts to the specified torque, then disconnect the lifting tackle and hoist from the engine and remove the trolley jack from beneath the transmission.

23 If the original torque converter and driveplate have been refitted, carefully turn the crankshaft to align the marks made before removal before fitting the torque converter-to-driveplate bolts.

24 Fit **new** torque converter-to-driveplate bolts and tighten them to the specified torque. Turn the crankshaft for access to each bolt in turn and prevent the driveplate from turning as during removal.

25 Refit the transmission bellhousing cover plate.

26 Proceed as described in Section 26, paragraphs 41 to 52 inclusive.

27 Check the transmission fluid level and top-up if necessary, as described in Chapter 1.

29 Engine/automatic transmission assembly - removal and refitting

Note: *New torque converter-to-driveplate bolts must be used on refitting. New bolts must be used to secure the left-hand engine/transmission mounting to the body on refitting and new locking plates must be used on the bolts securing the rear engine/transmission mounting to the transmission. Thread-locking compound will be required to coat the threads of the right-hand engine mounting-to-body bolts. An M10 x 1.25 mm tap may be required during this procedure. Refer to the text.*

Removal

1 Proceed as described in Section 26, paragraphs 1 to 17 inclusive.

2 To reduce fluid spillage as the driveshafts are withdrawn from the transmission, drain the transmission fluid as described in Chapter 7B.

3 Unscrew the securing sleeve and disconnect the speedometer cable from the transmission.

4 If not already done, apply the handbrake, then jack up the front of the vehicle and support securely on axle stands.

5 Remove the crankshaft pulley, with reference to Section 5.

6 Remove the front section of the exhaust system, as described in Chapter 4C.

7 Disconnect the transmission fluid cooler hoses either at the transmission or at the radiator, noting their routing. Clamp or plug the hoses to minimise fluid loss and dirt ingress.

8 Disconnect the transmission wiring harness connector and unbolt the two wiring harness brackets from the transmission casing.

9 Disconnect the vent hose from the transmission (the vent hose is located below the battery tray), noting its routing.

10 Remove the retaining clamp and the washer and disconnect the selector cable from the actuating lever on the transmission. Move the cable to one side away from the transmission.

11 Make a final check to ensure that all relevant pipes, hoses, wires, etc., have been disconnected and that they are positioned clear of the engine and transmission.

12 Proceed as described in Section 26, paragraphs 9 to 14 inclusive.

13 With the engine/transmission assembly removed, support the assembly on blocks of wood positioned on a workbench, or failing that, on a clean area of the workshop floor.

14 Clean away any external dirt using paraffin or a water-soluble solvent and a stiff brush.

15 Unbolt and remove the transmission bellhousing cover plate.

16 If the original torque converter and driveplate are to be refitted, make alignment marks between the torque converter and the driveplate, to ensure that the components are reassembled in their original positions.

17 Ensure that both the engine and transmission are adequately supported, then working through the bottom of the bellhousing, unscrew the three torque converter-to-driveplate bolts. It will be necessary to turn the crankshaft using a spanner or socket on the crankshaft pulley or gear bolt (as applicable), to gain access to each bolt in turn through the aperture. Use a screwdriver or a similar tool to jam the driveplate ring gear, preventing the driveplate from rotating as the bolts are loosened. Discard the bolts.

18 Unscrew and remove the engine-to-transmission bolts, noting the locations of any brackets that may be secured by the bolts.

19 Carefully pull the engine and transmission apart, ensuring that the torque converter is held firmly in place in the transmission casing, otherwise it could fall out, resulting in fluid spillage and possible damage. It may be necessary to rock the units slightly to separate them. If the transmission is to be left removed for some time, retain the torque converter by bolting a strip of metal across the bellhousing end face.

Refitting

20 If the original torque converter is being refitted, begin refitting by recutting the torque converter-to-driveplate bolt threads in the torque converter using an M10 x 1.25 mm tap.

21 If a new transmission is being fitted, the manufacturers recommend that the radiator fluid cooler passages are flushed clean before the new transmission is installed. Ideally, compressed air should be used (in which case, ensure that adequate safety precautions are taken). Alternatively, the cooler can be flushed with clean automatic transmission fluid until all the old fluid has been expelled and fresh fluid runs clear from the cooler outlet.

22 Check that the two original bolts that secure the left-hand engine/transmission rubber mounting to the vehicle body rotate freely in their threaded bores in the body. If necessary, re-cut the threaded bores using an M10 x 1.25 mm tap.

23 Carefully offer the transmission to the engine until the bellhousing is located on the dowels in the cylinder block (ensure that the torque converter is held firmly in place in the transmission casing as the engine and transmission are connected). Then refit the engine-to-transmission bolts and tighten them to the specified torque. Make sure that any brackets secured by the bolts are correctly positioned as noted before removal.

24 If the original torque converter and driveplate are being refitted, carefully turn the crankshaft to align the marks made before removal, before fitting the torque converter-to-driveplate bolts.

25 Fit **new** torque converter-to-driveplate bolts and tighten them to the specified torque. Turn the crankshaft for access to each bolt in turn and prevent the driveplate from turning as during removal.

26 Refit the transmission bellhousing cover plate.

27 Attach the lifting tackle to the engine/transmission assembly, then lower the assembly into the engine compartment and reconnect the mountings as described in Section 26, paragraphs 24 to 31 inclusive.

28 Reconnect the inboard ends of the driveshafts to the differential, with reference Chapter 8, using new snap-rings.

29 Reconnect the transmission vent hose, ensuring that it is routed as noted before removal.

30 Reconnect the selector cable to the

actuating lever on the transmission and adjust the cable as described in Chapter 7B.

31 Refit the transmission wiring harness brackets and reconnect the transmission wiring harness connector.

32 Reconnect the transmission fluid cooler hoses, using new sealing washers where applicable and making sure that they are correctly routed.

33 Refit the front section of the exhaust system, as described in Chapter 4C.

34 Refit the crankshaft pulley, with reference to Section 5.

35 Lower the vehicle to the ground.

36 Reconnect the speedometer cable and tighten the securing sleeve.

37 Proceed as described in Section 26, paragraphs 44 to 49 inclusive.

38 Refill the transmission with the correct quantity and type of fluid, through the dipstick tube.

39 Refit the bonnet as described in Chapter 11.

40 Make a final check to ensure that all hoses, pipes and wires have been correctly reconnected.

41 Reconnect the battery leads.

42 On completion, where applicable bleed the power steering fluid circuit as described in Chapter 10 and top-up the automatic transmission fluid level as described in Chapter 1.

---

30 Engine overhaul - dismantling

Note: *When removing the ancillary components from the engine, pay close attention to details that may be helpful or important during refitting. Note the fitted position of gaskets, seals, spacers, washers, bolts and other small items.*

Dismantling

1 It is far easier to dismantle and work on the engine if it is mounted on a portable engine stand. These stands can often be hired from a tool hire shop. Depending on the type of stand used, the flywheel/driveplate may have to be removed from the engine to allow the engine stand bolts to be tightened into the end of the cylinder block.

2 If a stand is not available, it is possible to dismantle the engine while supported on blocks on a sturdy workbench or on the floor. Be extra careful not to tip or drop the engine when working without a stand.

3 Before starting the overhaul procedure, the external engine ancillary components must be removed. This is the case even if a reconditioned engine is to be fitted, in which case, the components from the old engine must be transferred to the reconditioned unit. These components include the following.

(a) *Alternator and mounting bracket (see Chapter 5).*

(b) *Starter motor (see Chapter 5).*

(c) *Rear coolant gallery and hoses.*

(d) *Inlet and exhaust manifolds (see Chapter 4C).*

(e) *Oil filter (see Chapter 1).*

(f) *Distributor/coil components (as applicable), HT leads and spark plugs (see Chapter 1 or 5).*

(g) *Engine mounting (see Section 23).*

(h) *Oil pressure switch (see Chapter 5).*

(l) *Crankcase breather tube.*

(j) *Engine lifting brackets.*

(k) *TDC sensor and bracket (where fitted) (see Chapter 5).*

(l) *Coolant temperature sensor (where fitted) (see Chapter 5).*

(m) *Knock sensor (where fitted) (see Chapter 5).*

(n) *Thermostat and cover (C 18 NZ and C 20 NE models), (see Chapter 3).*

(o) *Fuel pump (14 NV models) (see Chapter 4A).*

(p) *Power steering pump mounting bracket (C 18 NZ and C 20 NE models) (see Chapter 10).*

(q) *Power steering pump (where fitted) (see Chapter 10).*

(r) *Wiring harnesses.*

(s) *Dipstick.*

4 If a 'short' engine is being obtained (which consists of the cylinder block, crankshaft, pistons and connecting rods all assembled as a unit), then the cylinder head, sump, timing belt and possibly other components (such as the oil pump) will have to be removed from the old unit and fitted to the new unit.

5 Before beginning the dismantling and overhaul procedures, make sure that all the correct tools have been obtained. Refer to the Reference Chapter of this manual for further information.

6 If a complete overhaul is being planned, the engine can be dismantled using the following sequence.

(a) *Inlet and exhaust manifolds (see Chapter 4C).*

(b) *Timing belt and gears (see Sections 12 and 13).*

(c) *Cylinder head (see Section 17).*

(d) *Flywheel/driveplate (see Section 22).*

(e) *Sump (see Section 18).*

(f) *Oil pump (see Section 19).*

(g) *Piston/connecting rod assemblies (see Section 32).*

(h) *Crankshaft (see Section 34).*

---

31 Cylinder head - dismantling, inspection and reassembly

Note: *New and reconditioned cylinder heads are available from the manufacturers and from engine overhaul specialists. Some specialist tools are required for the dismantling and inspection procedures and new components may not be readily available. It may be more practical and economical for the home mechanic to buy a reconditioned head rather than to dismantle, inspect and recondition the original head. A valve spring compressor tool will be required for this operation.*

Be sure to perform all the inspection procedures before deciding that the services of a specialist are required. Make a list of all items that require attention.

New valve stem oil seals should be used on reassembly.

Dismantling

1 With the cylinder head removed as described in Section 17, clean away all external dirt and remove the following components, if not already done.

(a) *Remove the manifolds (see Chapter 4C).*

(b) *Remove the spark plugs (see Chapter 1).*

(c) *Remove the thermostat housing **(see illustration)** and on 1.4 and 1.6 litre models, the thermostat (see Chapter 3).*

2 To remove a valve, fit a valve spring compressor tool. Ensure that the arms of the compressor tool are securely positioned on the head of the valve and the spring cap **(see illustration)**.

3 Compress the valve spring to relieve the pressure of the spring cap acting on the collets. If the spring cap sticks to the valve stem, support the compressor tool and give the end a light tap with a soft-faced mallet to help free the spring cap.

31.1 Removing the thermostat housing from the cylinder head - C 20 NE model

31.2 Valve spring compressor tool fitted to No 1 exhaust valve - C 20 NE model

31.4 Extracting a split collet - SOHC model

31.5A Remove the spring cap . . .

31.5B . . . spring . . .

4 Extract the two split collets, then slowly release the compressor tool **(see illustration)**.
5 Remove the spring cap, spring, valve stem oil seal and the spring seat, then withdraw the valve through the combustion chamber **(see illustrations)**.
6 Repeat the procedure for the remaining valves, keeping all components in strict order so that they can be refitted in their original positions, unless all the components are to be renewed.

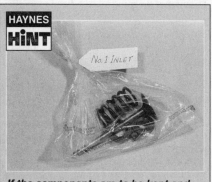

If the components are to be kept and used again, place each valve assembly in a labelled polythene bag or a similar small container. Note that as with cylinder numbering, the valves are normally numbered from the timing belt end of the engine.

Inspection

7 Thorough cleaning of the cylinder head and valve components, followed by a detailed inspection, will enable a decision to be made on whether further work is necessary before reassembling the components.
8 Scrape away all traces of old gasket material and sealing compound from the cylinder head surfaces. Take care not to damage the cylinder head surfaces, as the head is made of light alloy.
9 Scrape away the carbon from the combustion chambers and ports, then wash the cylinder head thoroughly with paraffin or a solvent.
10 Scrape off any heavy carbon deposits that may have formed on the valves, then use a power-operated wire brush to remove deposits from the valve heads and stems.
11 Inspect the head very carefully for cracks, evidence of coolant leakage and other damage. If cracks are found, a new cylinder head should be obtained.
12 Use a straight-edge and feeler blade to check that the cylinder head surface is not distorted **(see illustration)**. If the specified distortion limit is exceeded, it may be possible to have the cylinder head resurfaced, provided that the overall height of the head is not reduced to less than the specified minimum.
13 Examine the valve seats in each of the combustion chambers. If the seats are severely

pitted, cracked or burned, then they will need to be recut by an engine overhaul specialist. If only slight pitting is evident, this can be removed by grinding the valve heads and seats together with coarse then fine grinding paste, as described later in this Section.
14 If the valve guides are worn, indicated by a side-to-side motion of the valve, the guides can be reamed and valves with oversize stems can be fitted. This work is best carried out by an engine overhaul specialist. A dial gauge may be used to determine whether the amount of side play of a valve exceeds the specified maximum.
15 Check the valve lifter bores in the cylinder head for wear. If excessive wear is evident, the cylinder head must be renewed. Also check the valve lifter oil holes in the cylinder head for obstructions.
16 On C 18 NZ and C 20 NE models, an oil pressure regulating valve is fitted to the oil gallery in the cylinder head **(see illustration)**. This valve can be renewed if it appears to be damaged, or if its operation is suspect and access is gained via the circular plug covering the end of the valve. The old valve must be crushed, then its remains extracted and a thread (M10) cut in the valve seat to allow removal using a bolt. A new valve and plug can then be driven into position. In view of the intricacies of this operation, it is probably best to have the valve renewed by a Vauxhall dealer if necessary.

31.5C . . . valve stem oil seal (arrowed) . . .

31.5D . . . and spring seat

31.12 Checking the cylinder head surface for distortion

31.16 Cylinder head oil pressure regulating valve (1) and plug (2) - C 20 NE model

31.17 Renewing the thermostat housing sealing ring - C 20 NE model

31.18 Measuring a valve stem diameter

2A

17 On C 18 NZ and C 20 NE models, always renew the sealing ring between the cylinder head and the thermostat housing when the head is removed for overhaul **(see illustration)**.

18 Examine the head of each valve for pitting, burning, cracks and general wear and check the valve stem for scoring and wear ridges. Rotate the valve and check for any obvious indication that it is bent. Look for pitting and excessive wear on the end of each valve stem. If the valve appears satisfactory at this stage, measure the valve stem diameter at several points using a micrometer **(see illustration)**. Any significant difference in the readings obtained indicates wear of the valve stem. Should any of these conditions be apparent, the valve(s) must be renewed. If the valves are in good condition, they should be ground onto their respective seats to ensure a smooth gas-tight seal.

19 Valve grinding is carried out as follows. Place the cylinder head upside-down on a bench, with a block of wood at each end to give clearance for the valve stems.

20 Smear a trace of coarse grinding paste on the seat face in the cylinder head and press a suction grinding tool onto the relevant valve head. With a semi-rotary action, grind the valve head to its seat, lifting the valve occasionally to spread the grinding paste **(see illustration)**. When a dull, matt, even surface is produced on the faces of both the valve seat and the valve, wipe off the paste and repeat the process with fine grinding paste. A

light spring placed under the valve head will greatly ease this operation. When a smooth unbroken ring of light grey matt finish is produced on both the valve and seat faces, the grinding operation is complete. Carefully clean away every trace of grinding paste, taking great care to leave none in the ports or in the valve guides. Clean the valves and valve seats with a paraffin-soaked rag, then with a clean rag and finally, if an air line is available, blow the valves, valve guides and cylinder head ports clean.

21 Check that all the valve springs are intact. If any one is broken, all should be renewed.

22 If possible, check the free height of the springs against new ones, then stand each spring on a flat surface and check it for squareness. If a spring is found to be too short, or damaged in any way, renew all the springs as a set. Springs suffer from fatigue and it is a good idea to renew them even if they look serviceable.

23 Check the rocker arm and thrust pad faces (the areas that contact the valve lifters and valve stems) for pits, wear, score-marks or any indication that the surface-hardening has worn through. Check the rocker arm camshaft contact faces in the same manner. Clean the oil hole in the top of each rocker arm using a length of wire. Renew any rocker arms or thrust pads which appear suspect.

24 Proceed as described in paragraph 15.

25 On models that have covered a high mileage, or for which the service history

(particularly oil changes) is suspect, it is possible for the valve lifters to suffer internal contamination, which in extreme cases may result in increased engine top-end noise and wear. To minimise the possibility of problems occurring later in the life of the engine, it is advisable to dismantle and clean the hydraulic valve lifters as follows whenever the cylinder head is overhauled. No spare parts are available for the valve lifters and if any of the components are unserviceable, the complete assembly must be renewed **(see illustration)**.

26 Carefully pull the collar from the top of the valve lifter cylinder. It should be possible to remove the collar by hand if a tool is used, take care not to distort the collar.

27 Withdraw the plunger from the cylinder and remove the spring.

28 Using a small screwdriver, carefully prise the cap from the base of the plunger. Remove the spring and ball from under the cap, taking care not to lose them as the cap is removed.

29 Carefully clean all the components using paraffin or a solvent, paying particular attention to the machined surfaces of the cylinder (internal surfaces) and piston (external surfaces). Thoroughly dry all the components using a lint-free cloth. Carefully examine the springs for damage or distortion - the complete valve lifter must be renewed if the springs are not in perfect condition.

30 Lubricate the components sparingly with clean engine oil of the correct grade, then reassemble as follows.

31 Invert the plunger and locate the ball on its seat in the base of the plunger **(see illustration)**.

31.20 Grinding-in a valve seat

31.25 Hydraulic valve lifter components - SOHC model

1 Collar
2 Plunger
3 Ball
4 Small spring
5 Plunger cap
6 Large spring
7 Cylinder

31.31 Locate the ball (1) on its seat (2) in the base of the plunger

31.32A Locate the cap flange in the plunger groove

31.32B Spring (1) located in plunger cap, and ball (2) located on seat in plunger

31.33A Locate the spring over the plunger cap . . .

32 Locate the smaller spring on its seat in the plunger cap, then carefully refit the cap and spring, ensuring that the spring locates on the ball. Carefully press around the flange of the cap, using a small screwdriver if necessary, until the flange is securely located in the groove in the base of the plunger (see illustrations).

33 Locate the larger spring over the plunger cap, ensuring that the spring is correctly seated and slide the plunger and spring assembly into the cylinder (see illustrations).

34 Slide the collar over the top of the plunger and carefully compress the plunger by hand, until the collar can be pushed down to engage securely with the groove in the cylinder (see illustration).

Reassembly

35 With all the components cleaned, starting at one end of the cylinder head, fit the valve components as follows (see illustration).

36 Insert the appropriate valve into its guide (if new valves are being fitted, insert each valve into the location to which it has been ground), ensuring that the valve stem is well lubricated with clean engine oil (see illustration). If the original components are being refitted, all components must be refitted in their original positions.

37 Fit the spring seat (see illustration).

38 New valve stem oil seals should be supplied with a fitting sleeve, which fits over the collet groove in the valve stem, to prevent

damage to the oil seal as it is slid down the valve stem (see illustration). If no sleeve is supplied, wind a short length of tape round the top of the valve stem to cover the collet groove.

39 Lubricate the valve stem oil seal with clean engine oil, then push the oil seal down the valve stem using a tube or socket until the seal is fully engaged with the spring seat (see illustrations). Remove the fitting sleeve or the tape, as applicable, from the valve stem.

40 Fit the valve spring and the spring cap (see illustrations).

41 Fit the spring compressor tool and compress the valve spring until the spring cap passes beyond the collet groove in the valve stem.

31.33B . . . then slide the plunger and spring assembly into the cylinder

31.34 Slide the collar (1) over the top of the plunger and engage with the groove (2) in the cylinder

31.35 Inlet (1) and exhaust (2) valve components - SOHC model

31.36 Inserting an exhaust valve into its guide - SOHC model

31.37 Fitting a valve seat (exhaust valve shown) - SOHC model

31.38 Slide the oil seal fitting sleeve down the valve stem . . .

31.39A Fit the valve stem oil seal . . .

31.39B . . . and push onto the spring seat using a socket - SOHC model

31.40A Fit the valve spring . . .

42 Apply a little grease to the collet groove, then fit the split collets into the groove, with the narrow ends nearest the spring. The grease should hold them in the groove **(see illustration)**.

43 Slowly release the compressor tool, ensuring that the collets are not dislodged from the groove. When the compressor is fully released, give the top of the valve assembly a tap with a soft-faced mallet to settle the components.

44 Repeat the procedure for the remaining valves, ensuring that if the original components are being used, they are all refitted in their original positions.

45 Refit the following components as applicable (these components can be refitted after refitting the cylinder head).

(a) *Refit the thermostat housing, (see Chapter 3).*

(b) *Refit the spark plugs (see Chapter 1).*

(c) *Refit the manifolds (see Chapter 4C).*

32 Pistons and connecting rods - removal and refitting

Note: *New big-end cap bolts must be used on refitting*

Removal

1 Remove the cylinder head, as described previously in this Section 17.

2 Remove the sump, oil pick-up pipe and sump baffle (where applicable), as described in Section 18.

3 If the connecting rods and big-end caps are not marked to indicate their positions in the cylinder block (i.e. cylinder numbers), centre-punch them at adjacent points either side of the cap/rod joint. Note to which side of the engine the marks face **(see illustration)**.

4 Unscrew the big-end cap bolts from the first connecting rod, and remove the cap. If the bearing shells are to be re-used, tape the cap and shell together.

5 Check the top of the piston bore for a wear ridge. If evident, carefully scrape it away with a ridge reaming tool, otherwise as the piston is pushed out of the block, the piston rings may jam against the ridge.

6 Place the wooden handle of a hammer against the bottom of the connecting rod, and push the piston/rod assembly up and out of the cylinder bore. Recover the bearing shell, and tape it to the connecting rod if it is to be re-used.

7 Remove the remaining three assemblies in a similar way. Rotate the crankshaft as necessary to bring the big-end bolts to the most accessible position.

8 The piston can be separated from the connecting rod by removing the circlips that secure the fully floating gudgeon pin. Note the orientation of the piston and connecting rod before separation, and if necessary, make alignment marks. Reassembly is a reversal of

dismantling ensuring that the piston and connecting rod are correctly orientated.

9 The pistons and connecting rods can be examined for wear and damage, as described in Section 33, and the bearings can be examined as described in Section 35.

Refitting

10 Begin reassembly by laying the piston/connecting rod assemblies out in their correct order, complete with bearing shells, ready for refitting into their respective bores in the cylinder block.

11 Ensure that the seats for the bearing shells are absolutely clean, and then fit the shells into the seats.

12 Wipe out the cylinder bores and oil them. Oil the piston rings liberally, and ensure that the ring gaps are positioned as described in Section 33.

13 Fit a piston ring compressor tool to the first assembly to be installed.

14 Insert the rod and piston into the top of the cylinder bore, so that the base of the compressor stands on the block. Check that the connecting rod markings are towards the side of the engine noted during removal. Note that the arrow or notch, as applicable, on the piston crown should point towards the timing belt end of the engine, and the lugs on the connecting rods should point towards

31.40B . . . and spring cap

31.42 Use a little grease to hold the split collets in place

32.3 Big-end cap centre punch identification marks (circled) - C 20 NE model
Note that lug on bearing cap faces flywheel end of model

2A

32.14A Piston crown arrow must point towards timing belt end of model - C 16 SE model

32.14B Lugs (arrowed) on connecting rod and big-end cap must point towards flywheel end of model - C 16 SE model

32.15 Tapping a piston into its bore - C 16 SE model

the flywheel end of the engine **(see illustrations)**.

15 Apply the wooden handle of a hammer to the piston crown and tap the assembly into the bore, at the same time releasing the compressor **(see illustration)**.

16 Oil the relevant crankpin, then guide the big-end of the connecting rod near to the crankpin, and pull it firmly onto the crankpin. Ensure that the bearing shell remains in position in the connecting rod.

17 Fit the big-end cap, with the markings towards the side of the engine noted during removal. Note that the lug should point towards the flywheel end of the engine.

18 Fit new big-end cap bolts, and tighten them to the specified torque in the two stages given in the Specifications **(see illustrations)**.

19 Repeat the procedure on the remaining three assemblies.

20 Refit the sump baffle (where applicable), oil pick-up pipe and sump, as described in Section 18.

21 Refit the cylinder head, as described previously in this Section 17.

33 Pistons and connecting rods - examination and renovation

Examination

1 Examine the mating faces of the big-end caps to see if they have ever been filed, in a mistaken attempt to take up bearing wear. This is extremely unlikely, but if evident, the

offending connecting rods and caps must be renewed.

2 Check the alignment of the rods visually, and if all is not well, take the rods to a Vauxhall dealer for a more detailed check.

3 The gudgeon pins are an interference (shrink) fit in the connecting rod small ends. Separation of the pistons and rods is a job for a dealer due to the special tools required, as is any remedial action required if the gudgeon pin is no longer an interference fit in the rod.

4 Examine the pistons for ovality, scoring and scratches.

5 If new rings are to be fitted to the existing pistons, expand the old rings over the tops of the pistons. The use of two or three old feeler gauges will be helpful in preventing the rings dropping into empty grooves. Note that the oil control ring is in three sections, and note which way up each ring is fitted, for use when refitting **(see illustrations)**.

Renovation

6 Before fitting the new rings to the pistons, insert them into their relevant cylinder bores, and check that the ring end gaps are within the specified limits using a feeler gauge **(see illustration)**. Check the ring gaps at the upper and lower limits of the piston travel in the bores.

7 If any of the ring end gaps exceed the specified tolerance, the relevant rings will have to be renewed, and if the ring grooves in the pistons are worn, new pistons may be required.

32.18A Tighten the big-end bearing cap bolts to the specified torque . . .

32.18B . . . then through the specified angle - C 16 SE model

33.5 Using a feeler gauge to aid removal of a piston ring

33.5 Sectional view showing correct orientation of piston rings - all models

33.6 Measuring a piston ring end gap using a feeler gauge

8 Clean out the piston ring grooves using a piece of old piston ring as a scraper. Take care not to scratch the surface of the pistons. Protect your fingers, piston ring edges are sharp. Also probe the groove oil return holes, to ensure that they are not blocked.

9 Check the cylinder bores for signs of wear ridges towards the top of the bores. If wear ridges are evident, and new piston rings are being fitted, the top ring must be stepped to clear the wear ridge, or the bore must be de-ridged using a scraper.

10 Fit the oil control ring sections with the lower steel ring gap offset 25 to 50 mm to the right of the spreader ring gap and the upper steel ring gap offset by the same distance to the left of the spreader ring gap.

11 Fit the lower compression ring, noting that the ring is tapered or stepped. The ring should be fitted with the word "TOP" uppermost.

12 Fit the upper compression ring, and offset the ring gap by 180° to the lower compression ring gap. If a stepped ring is being fitted, fit the ring with the smaller diameter of the step uppermost.

13 If new pistons are to be fitted, they must be selected from the grades available, after measuring the cylinder bores as described in Section 36.

14 Normally the appropriate oversize pistons are supplied by the dealer when the block is rebored.

15 Whenever new piston rings are being installed, the glaze on the original cylinder bores should be "broken", using either abrasive paper or a glaze-removing tool in an electric drill. If abrasive paper is used, use strokes at 60° to the bore centre line, to create a cross-hatching effect.

34 Crankshaft and bearings - removal and refitting

Note: *New main bearing cap bolts must be used on refitting*

Removal

1 With the engine removed from the vehicle, continue as follows.

2 Remove the cylinder head, as described previously in Section 17.

34.8 Main bearing cap identification marks (arrowed) - C 16 SE model

3 Remove the sump, oil pick-up pipe and sump baffle (where applicable), as described in Section 18.

4 Remove the oil pump, as described in Section 19.

5 Remove the flywheel or driveplate (if applicable), as described in Section 22.

6 Remove the pistons and connecting rods, as described in Section 32.

7 Invert the engine so that it is standing on the top face of the cylinder block.

8 The main bearing caps are numbered 1 to 4 from the timing belt end of the engine. The rear (flywheel end) cap is not marked. To ensure that the caps are refitted the correct way round, note that the numbers are read from the coolant pump side of the engine with the engine inverted **(see illustration)**.

9 Unscrew and remove the main bearing cap bolts, and tap off the bearing caps. If the bearing shells are to be re-used, tape them to their respective caps.

10 Note that the centre bearing shell incorporates thrust flanges to control crankshaft endfloat.

11 Lift the crankshaft (complete with timing sensor wheel, if fitted), from the crankcase **(see illustration)**.

12 Extract the upper bearing shells, and identify them for position if they are to be re-used.

13 The crankshaft and bearings can be examined for wear and damage, as described in Section 35, and the cylinder block and bores can be examined as described in Section 36.

34.11 Lifting the crankshaft from the crankcase

Refitting

14 Begin refitting by ensuring that the crankcase and crankshaft are thoroughly clean, and that all oilways are clear. If possible, blow through the oil drillings with compressed air, and inject clean engine oil into them.

> **HAYNES HINT** *A good alternative to compressed air is to use a water dispersing lubricant spray into each hole, using the spout provided.*

15 If the crankshaft is being replaced, where applicable, transfer the timing sensor wheel and tighten to correct torque.

16 Wipe clean the bearing shell seats in the crankcase and the bearing caps, then fit the upper bearing shells to their seats.

17 Note that there is a tag on the back of each bearing shell, which engages with a groove in the relevant seat in the crankcase or bearing cap **(see illustration)**.

18 If new bearing shells are being fitted, wipe away all traces of protective grease.

19 Note that the central bearing shells have thrust flanges which control crankshaft endfloat **(see illustration)**. Note also that the shells fitted to the crankcase all have oil duct holes, while only the centre main bearing cap shell has an oil duct hole.

20 When the shells are firmly located in the crankcase and the bearing caps, lubricate them with clean engine oil **(see illustration)**.

34.17 Fitting a main bearing shell to the cylinder block

34.19 Main bearing shell (A) and central main bearing shell (B) with thrust flange

34.20 Lubricate the main bearing shells before fitting the crankshaft

34.25A Fill the side grooves of the rear main bearing cap with RTV jointing compound . . .

34.25B . . . and the lower surfaces with sealing compound

34.25C Fitting the centre main bearing cap

21 Fill the lips of a new crankshaft rear oil seal with grease, and fit it to the end of the crankshaft.

22 Carefully lower the crankshaft into position in the crankcase.

23 If necessary, seat the crankshaft using light blows with a rubber hammer on the crankshaft balance webs.

24 Lubricate the main bearing journals and shells, and then fit numbers 2, 3 and 4 main bearing caps, and tighten the new bolts as far as possible by hand.

25 Fill the side grooves of the rear main bearing cap with jointing compound (Vauxhall P/N 90485251, or equivalent). Coat the lower surfaces of the bearing cap with sealing compound (Vauxhall P/N 90350544, or equivalent) (see illustrations). Fit the bearing cap, and tighten the new bolts as far as possible by hand.

26 Fit the front (No 1) main bearing cap, and tighten the new bolts as far as possible by hand, ensuring that the bearing cap is exactly flush with the end face of the cylinder block.

27 Working from the centre bearing cap outwards, tighten the bearing cap securing bolts to the specified torque in the two stages given in the Specifications; i.e. tighten all bolts to Stage 1, then tighten all bolts to Stage 2 and Stage 3 (see illustrations).

28 When all bolts have been fully tightened, inject further jointing compound into the side grooves of the rear main bearing cap, until it is certain that they are full.

29 Now rotate the crankshaft, and check that it turns freely, with no signs of binding or tight spots.

30 Check that the crankshaft endfloat is within the specified limits, using a dial gauge, or by inserting a feeler gauge between the thrust flange of the centre main bearing shell and the machined surface of the crankshaft (see illustrations). Before measuring, ensure that the crankshaft is fully forced towards one end of the crankcase, to give the widest possible gap at the measuring location. Incorrect endfloat will most likely be due to crankshaft wear or to incorrect regrinding, assuming that the correct bearing shells have been fitted.

31 Refit the previously removed components, referring to the relevant Sections of this Chapter.

35 Crankshaft and bearings - examination

1 Examine the crankpin and main journal surfaces for signs of scoring or scratches, and check the ovality and taper of the crankpins and main journals. If the bearing surface dimensions do not fall within the tolerance ranges given in the Specifications at the beginning of this Chapter, the crankpins and/or main journals will have to be reground.

2 Big-end and crankpin wear is accompanied by distinct metallic knocking, particularly noticeable when the engine is pulling from low revs, and some loss of oil pressure.

3 Main bearing and main journal wear is accompanied by severe engine vibration rumble - getting progressively worse as engine rev's increase - and again by loss of oil pressure.

4 If the crankshaft requires regrinding, take it to an engine reconditioning specialist, who will machine it for you and supply the correct undersize bearing shells.

5 Inspect the big-end and main bearing shells for signs of general wear, scoring, pitting and scratches. The bearings should be matt grey in colour. With lead-indium bearings, should a trace of copper colour be noticed, the bearings are badly worn, as the lead bearing material has worn away to expose the indium underlay. Renew the bearings if they are in this condition, or if there are any signs of scoring or pitting. *You are strongly advised to renew the bearings - regardless of their condition at time of major overhaul. Refitting used bearings is a false economy.*

6 The undersizes available are designed to correspond with crankshaft regrind sizes. The bearings are in fact, slightly more than the stated undersize, as running clearances have been allowed for during their manufacture.

7 Main and big-end bearing shells can be identified as to size by the marking on the back of the shell. Standard size shell bearings are marked STD or .00, undersize shells are marked with the undersize such as 0.020 u/s. This marking method applies only to replacement bearing shells, and not to those used during production (see illustrations).

8 An accurate method of determining bearing wear is by using a Plastigage. The crankshaft is located in the main bearings (and, if necessary, the big-end bearings), and the Plastigage filament is located across the journal. Vauxhall recommend that the crankshaft journal and bearing shells are lightly lubricated, to prevent the Plastigage from tearing as the bearing cap is removed. The bearing cap should be fitted, and the

34.27A Tighten the main bearing cap bolts to the specified torque . . .

34.27B . . . then through the specified angle - C 20 NE model

35.7A Typical main bearing shell . . .

35.7B . . . and main thrust bearing shell identification marks -
C 16 SE model

35.8 Using the scale on the envelope
provided to check (at its widest point) the
width of the crushed Plastigage and
measure the bearing running clearance

bolts tightened to the specified torque. The
cap is then removed, and the width of the
filament is checked against a scale that shows
the bearing running clearance. The clearance
should be compared with that given in the
Specifications.

9 Where applicable, check the teeth of the
crankshaft TDC sensor wheel for damage. If
evident, the crankshaft must be renewed.

10 Similarly, check the condition of the pins
in the front crankshaft balance weight,
which serve as detent points for the
plug-in diagnostic sensor used by Vauxhall
dealers.

36 Cylinder block and bores -
examination

1 Examine the cylinder bores for taper,
ovality, scoring and scratches. Start by
carefully examining the top of the cylinder
bores. If they are at all worn, a very slight

ridge will be found on the thrust side. This
marks the top of the piston ring travel. The
owner will have a good indication of the bore
wear before dismantling the engine, or
removing the cylinder head. Excessive oil
consumption, accompanied by blue smoke
from the exhaust, is a sure sign of worn
cylinder bores and piston rings.

2 Measure the bore diameter across the
block, and just below any ridge. This can be
done with an internal micrometer or a dial
gauge. Compare this with the diameter of the
bottom of the bore, which is not subject to
wear. If no measuring instruments are
available, use a piston from which the rings
have been removed, and measure the gap between it and the cylinder wall with a feeler
gauge. Refer to the Specifications. If the
cylinder wear exceeds the permitted
tolerances, then the cylinders will need
reboring, in which case note the following
points:

a) Piston and cylinder bores are closely
matched in production. The actual
diameter of the piston is indicated by
numbers on its crown; the same numbers
stamped on the crankcase indicate the
bore diameter

b) After reboring has taken place, the
cylinder bores should be measured
accurately and oversize pistons selected
from the grades available to give the
specified piston-to-bore clearance

c) For grading purposes, the piston diameter
is measured across the bottom of the skirt

3 If the wear is marginal and within the
tolerances given, new special piston rings can
be fitted to offset the wear.

4 Thoroughly examine the crankcase and
cylinder block for cracks and damage, and
use a piece of wire to probe all oilways and
waterways to ensure that they are
unobstructed.

5 On some models a rubber plug located next
to the bellhousing flange on the cylinder block
covers the aperture for the installation of a
diagnostic TDC sensor. The sensor, when
connected to a monitoring unit, indicates TDC
from the position of the pins set into the
crankshaft balance weight.

37 Examination and renovation
- general

1 With the engine completely stripped, clean
all components and examine them for wear.
Each component should be checked, and
where necessary renewed or renovated, as
described in the relevant Sections of this
Chapter.

2 Renew main and big-end bearing shells as
a matter of course, unless it is known that
they have had little wear, and are in perfect
condition.

3 If in doubt whether to renew a component
that is still just serviceable, consider the time
and effort that will be incurred should the
component fail at an early date after rebuild.
Obviously, the age and expected life of the
vehicle must influence the standards applied.

4 Gaskets, oil seals and O-rings must all be
renewed as a matter of routine. Flywheel,
cylinder head, and main and big-end bearing
cap bolts must be renewed, because of the
high stress to which they are subjected.

5 Renew the engine core plugs while they are
easily accessible, if they show signs of
leakage. Knock out the old plugs with a
hammer and chisel or punch. Clean the plug
seats, smear the new plugs with sealing compound, and tap them squarely into position.

38 Initial start-up after major overhaul or repair

1 Make a final check to ensure that everything has been reconnected to the engine, and that no rags or tools have been left in the engine compartment.

2 Check that oil and coolant levels are correct.

3 Start the engine. This may take a little longer than usual, as fuel is pumped to the engine.

4 Check that the oil pressure warning lamp goes out when the engine starts. This may take a few seconds as the new oil filter fills with oil.

5 Run the engine at a fast tickover, and check for leaks of oil, fuel and coolant. If a new camshaft has been fitted, pay careful attention to the running-in procedure given in Section 16, paragraphs 25 and 26. Where applicable, check the power steering and/or automatic transmission fluid cooler unions for leakage. Some smoke and odd smells may be experienced, as assembly lubricants and sealers burn off the various components.

6 Bring the engine to normal operating temperature. Check the ignition timing, idle speed and the mixture (where applicable), as described in Chapter 4A or 4B.

7 Allow the engine to cool, then recheck the oil and coolant levels. Top up if necessary

8 If new bearings, pistons, etc., have been fitted, the engine should be run-in at reduced speeds and loads for the first 500 miles (800 km) or so. It is beneficial to change the engine oil and filter after this mileage.

Chapter 2 Part B
Engine - DOHC

Contents

Degrees of difficulty

Easy, suitable for novice with little experience	**Fairly easy,** suitable for beginner with some experience	**Fairly difficult,** suitable for competent DIY mechanic	**Difficult,** suitable for experienced DIY mechanic	**Very difficult,** suitable for expert DIY or professional

Specifications

General
Note: *All specifications as for SOHC engines (refer to Chapter 2A), except where shown below.*

Type
All models . . . . Four-cylinder in-line, water-cooled. Double belt-driven overhead camshafts, acting on hydraulic valve lifters.

Manufacturer's engine code
Note: *The code can be found on the cylinder block, in front of the clutch housing.*
X 16 XEL ('Ecotec') . . . . 1.6 litre (1598cc) + catalytic converter + Multi-point fuel injection (MPi)
C 18 XE . . . . 1.8 litre (1796 cc) + cat + MPi
C 18 XEL ('Ecotec') . . . . 1.8 litre (1796 cc) + cat + MPi
C 20 XE . . . . 2.0 litre (1998 cc) + cat + MPi
X 20 XEV ('Ecotec') . . . . 2.0 litre (1998 cc) + cat + MPi

Pistons	Bore (mm)	Stroke (mm)
X 16 XEL	79.0	81.5
C 18 XE and C 18 XEL	81.6	86.0
C 20 XE and X 20 XEV	86.0	86.0

Compression	Ratio
X 16 XEL	10.5
C 18 XE and C 18 XEL	10.8
C 20 XE	10.5
X 20 XEV	10.8

Maximum power
X 16 XEL . . . . 74 kW at 6200 rpm
C 18 XE . . . . 92 kW at 5600 rpm
C 18 XEL . . . . 85 kW at 5400 rpm
C 20 XE . . . . 110 kW at 6000 rpm
X 20 XEV . . . . 100 kW at 5400 rpm

Maximum torque

X 16 XEL	148 Nm at 3500 rpm
C 18 XE	168 Nm at 4800 rpm
C 18 XEL	168 Nm at 4000 rpm
C 20 XE	196 Nm at 4600 rpm
X 20 XEV	185 Nm at 4000 rpm

Firing order

All models . . . . 1-3-4-2 (No 1 cylinder at timing belt end)

Direction of crankshaft rotation

All models . . . . Clockwise

Maximum compression pressure difference between cylinders

All models . . . . 1.0 bar

Crankshaft pulse pick-up gap

X 16 XEL . . . . 1.0 ± 0.7 mm

Camshafts

Note: *All specifications as for SOHC engines (refer to Chapter 2A), except where shown below.*

Camshaft bearing journal diameter (mm)

X 16 XEL and C 18 XEL	Not available (n/a)
C 18 XE, C 20 XE and X 20 XEV	27.939 to 27.960

Camshaft bearing diameter in housing (mm)

X 16 XEL and C 18 XEL	n/a
C 18 XE, C 20 XE and X 20 XEV	27.000 to 28.021

Maximum permissible radial run-out (mm)

X 16 XEL and C 18 XEL	n/a
C 18 XE and X 20 XEV	0.06
C 20 XE	0.04

Endfloat (mm)

X 16 XEL and C 18 XEL	n/a
C 18 XE, C 20 XE and X 20 XEV	0.040 to 0.144

Torque wrench settings

Note: *All specifications as for SOHC engines (refer to Chapter 2A), except where shown below.*
Use new bolts (or nuts, if applicable), where marked with an asterisk (*).
The torque settings stated are only applicable to latest specification cylinder head bolts, available from Vauxhall. Earlier type or alternative make, head bolts may require different torques. Consult your supplier.

	Nm	lbf ft
AIR metal pipe bracket to exhaust manifold:		
X 16 XEL (refer to text)	20	15
AIR valve support to exhaust manifold:		
X 16 XEL	8	6
Alternator adjuster arm:		
X 16 XEL	20	15
C 18 XE, C 18 XEL and C 20 XE	25	19
C 18 XE, C 18 XEL and C 20 XE (M10)	40	30
Alternator adjuster arm to alternator and inlet manifold:		
C 18 XE, C 18 XEL and C 20 XE	18	13
Alternator bracket to cylinder block:		
X 16 XEL	35	26
Alternator mounting (lower)	35	26
Big end bearing cap: *		
X 16 XEL:		
Stage 1	25	19
Stage 2	Angle tighten by a further 30°	
C 18 XE, C 18 XEL, C 20 XE and X 20 XEV:		
Stage 1	35	26
Stage 2	Angle tighten by a further 45°	
Stage 3	Angle tighten by a further 15°	
Brake servo line to inlet pipe:		
C 18 XE, C 18 XEL and C 20 XE	20	15
Camshaft gear to camshaft: *		
Stage 1	50	37
Stage 2	Angle tighten by a further 60°	
Stage 3	Angle tighten by a further 15°	

Torque wrench settings (continued)

	Nm	lbf ft
Camshaft sensor to cylinder head:		
C 18 XE, C 18 XEL and C 20 XE	15	11
Camshaft bearing cap:		
X 16 XEL, C 18 XE, C 18 XEL and X 20 XEV	8	6
C 20 XE (M8)	20	15
C 20 XE (M6)	10	7
Combination valve bracket to exhaust manifold:		
X 16 XEL (refer to text)*	8	6
Coolant flange to cylinder head:		
X 16 XEL	25	19
C 18 XE, C 18 XEL and C 20 XE:		
M8	20	15
M10	30	22
Coolant pipe to cylinder block:		
C 18 XE, C 18 XEL, C 20 XE and X 20 XEV	20	15
Coolant pump to cylinder block:		
X 16 XEL	8	6
C 18 XE, C 18 XEL, C 20 XE and X 20 XEV	25	19
Cover to cylinder head:		
M8 nuts	22	16
M6 bolts	9	7
Cover to exhaust manifold	8	6
Crankshaft gear with timing disc:		
X 16 XEL: *		
Stage 1	95	70
Stage 2	Angle tighten by a further 30°	
Stage 3	Angle tighten by a further 15°	
Crankshaft pulse pick-up bracket to oil pump		
X 16 XEL	6	4
Crankshaft pulse pick-up disc to crankshaft:		
C 18 XE, C 18 XEL, C 20 XE and X 20 XEV	13	10
Cylinder head bolts: *		
Stage 1	25	19
Stage 2	Angle tighten by a further 90°	
Stage 3	Angle tighten by a further 90°	
Stage 4	Angle tighten by a further 90°	
Cylinder head cover	8	6
DIS module to bracket to cylinder head	8	6
Engine cover to cylinder head cover:		
X 16 XEL	8	6
Engine mounting bracket to engine:		
X 16 XEL	60	44
Engine mounting to engine mounting bracket:		
X 16 XEL	35	26
C 18 XE, C 18 XEL and C 20 XE	65	48
Engine mounting to crossmember:		
X 16 XEL (refer to text)	65	48
Exhaust joint:		
C 20 XE	12	9
Exhaust manifold to cylinder head:		
X 16 XEL*	22	16
Flywheel to crankshaft: *		
X 16 XEL:		
Stage 1	35	26
Stage 2	Angle tighten by a further 30°	
Stage 3	Angle tighten by a further 15°	
C 18 XE, C 18 XEL, C 20 XE and X 20 XEV:		
Stage 1	65	48
Stage 2	Angle tighten by a further 30°	
Stage 3	Angle tighten by a further 15°	
Guide sleeve (thrust bearing to transmission housing)	22	16
Inductive pulse pick-up to cylinder block:		
C 18 XE, C 18 XEL and C 20 XE	8	6
Inlet manifold (lower) to cylinder head:		
X 16 XEL*	20	15

2B

Torque wrench settings (continued)

	Nm	lbf ft
Inlet manifold (upper) to cylinder head cover and to lower inlet manifold:		
X 16 XEL	8	6
Inlet manifold to cylinder head:		
C 20 XE*	22	16
Inlet manifold to bracket:		
C 20 XE	20	15
Inlet pipe to cylinder head:		
C 18 XE, C 18 XEL and C 20 XE	22	16
Intermediate shaft bracket to cylinder block:		
C 18 XE, C 18 XEL and C 20 XE	55	41
Knock sensor to cylinder block:		
X 16 XEL	13	10
C 18 XE, C 18 XEL and C 20 XE	25	19
Oil cooler pipes	30	22
Oil dipstick guide to cylinder block	25	19
Oil intake pipe bracket to cylinder block	6	4
Oil intake pipe to oil pump (refer to text)	8	6
Oil pressure switch to oil pump:		
C 18 XE, C 18 XEL and C 20 XE	40	30
Oil pump adaptor:		
C 18 XE, C 18 XEL and C 20 XE (refer to text)	23	17
Oil pump cover to pump	6	4
Oil temperature switch to cylinder block	30	22
Power steering pump to support:	25	19
Power steering pump adjuster to support:		
X 16 XEL	20	15
C 18 XE, C 18 XEL and C 20 XE	18	13
Road wheel	110	81
Ribbed V-belt pulley to timing gear drive:		
C 18 XE, C 18 XEL and C 20 XE	20	15
Ribbed V-belt roller support to cylinder block:		
C 18 XE, C 18 XEL and C 20 XE	25	19
Ribbed V-belt roller to support:		
X 16 XEL	20	12
C 18 XE, C 18 XEL and C 20 XE	18	13
Spark plug lead cover to cylinder head cover:		
C 18 XE and C 18 XEL	3	2
C 20 XE	8	6
X 20 XEV	6	4
Starter motor bracket to cylinder block:		
C 18 XE, C 18 XEL, C 20 XE and X 20 XEV	25	19
Starter motor to cylinder block:		
X 16 XEL	25	19
C 18 XE, C 18 XEL, C 20 XE and X 20 XEV	45	33
Sump to cylinder block:		
X 16 XEL	8	6
Sump to oil pump and cylinder block:		
C 18 XE, C 18 XEL, C 20 XE and X 20 XEV (refer to text)	15	11
Sump to transmission housing		
X 16 XEL	40	30
Sump drain plug	45	33
Support bracket to cylinder block	35	26
Temperature regulator plug (M20):		
C 18 XE, C 18 XEL, C 20 XE and X 20 XEV	30	22
Thermostat housing cover to housing:		
X 16 XEL	8	6
C 18 XE, C 18 XEL and C 20 XE	15	11
Thermostat housing to cylinder head:		
X 16 XEL	20	15
C 18 XE, C 18 XEL, C 20 XE and X 20 XEV	15	11
Throttle body to flange to inlet manifold:		
X 16 XEL	8	6
Timing belt cover - upper to lower to rear:		
X 16 XEL	4	3
Timing belt cover (rear) to cylinder head and oil pump:		
C 18 XE, C 18 XEL and C 20 XE	6	4

Torque wrench settings (continued)

	Nm	lbf ft
Timing belt cover to cylinder head and oil pump:		
X 16 XEL	6	4
C 18 XE, C 18 XEL, C 20 XE and X 20 XEV	8	6
Timing belt drive to crankshaft (refer to text): *		
Stage 1	250	185
Stage 2	Angle tighten by a further 40° to 50°	
Timing belt guide roller to cylinder block (pre-1993 models only): *		
Stage 1	25	19
Stage 2	Angle tighten by a further 45º	
Stage 3	Angle tighten by a further 15º	
Timing belt guide rollers to bracket to cylinder block:		
C 18 XE, C 18 XEL and C 20 XE	25	19
Timing belt guide rollers to cylinder head:		
X 16 XEL	25	19
Timing belt roller support to cylinder block:		
X 16 XEL	35	26
Timing belt tension roller to cylinder block (pre-1993 models only): *		
Stage 1	25	19
Stage 2	Angle tighten by a further 45º	
Stage 3	Angle tighten by a further 15º	
Timing belt tension roller to oil pump:		
X 16 XEL	20	15
Thermostat (with outlet) to housing:		
C 18 XE, C 18 XEL and C 20 XE	8	6
Transmission to cylinder block:		
C 18 XE, C 18 XEL, C 20 XE and X 20 XEV	60	44
V-belt pulley to timing belt drive	20	15

1.1 Front sectional view of C 20 XE model

1 Description - general

1 In 1993 the C 20 XE was introduced. Based on the C 20 NE engine, it shares many lower engine components. Later in this year, the C 18 XE engine was introduced. Like the C 20 XE, it uses the cylinder block from the SOHC, C 20 NE model **(see illustration)**.

2 During 1995, a new 1.6 litre DOHC engine (the X 16 XEL), was introduced to replace the C 16 SE model. This engine is part of the 'Ecotec' range, designed to meet tough new emission standards required from 1996. The range was supported during this year with the C 18 XEL and X 20 XEV. Both these models use a new engine management system, the Simtec 56.1, which offers improved fuel consumption.

3 Both camshafts on these engines are driven from the crankshaft by one toothed composite rubber belt. Each cylinder has four valves (two inlet and two exhaust), operated directly from the camshafts by hydraulic self-adjusting valve lifters. One camshaft operates the inlet valves, and the other operates the exhaust valves.

4 DOHC models are fitted with a remotely mounted oil cooler.

5 The distributor (if fitted), is driven directly from the exhaust camshaft.

6 This Chapter describes procedures that are specific to DOHC models. It should be read in conjunction with Chapter 2A. Many of the procedures require the engine undershield to be removed.

2B

7 Both the ribbed V-belt and the timing belt have automatic tensioners and once set, should not require further adjustments. However it is important that to avoid major damage to the engine, the timing belt should be replaced, at least at the stated service intervals. Refer to Chapter 1.

2 Timing belt covers (X 16 XEL) - removal and refitting

Upper outer cover

Removal

1 On X 16 XEL models the outer timing belt cover is split into two. The top part can be removed without having to remove to ribbed V-belt.
2 Remove the air cleaner and intake pipe, as described in Chapter 4B.
3 Undo the three retaining bolts from the cover.
4 Unclip the cover from the rear cover and remove.

Refitting

5 Refitting is a reversal of removal.

Lower outer cover

Removal

6 Remove the upper, outer cover as described above.
7 Remove the ribbed V-belt, as described in Chapter 5, remembering to mark the running direction of the belt.
8 Jack up the front of the vehicle and remove the right front wheel.
9 Unbolt and remove the engine access panel.
10 Remove the timing disc, from the crankshaft.
11 Select third gear to stop the engine from rotating.
12 The two bolts from the lower cover can now be removed.
13 Unclip the cover and remove.

Refitting

14 Refitting is a reversal of removal. However measure the gap of the crankshaft pulse pick-

3.4A Unscrewing an outer timing belt cover securing screw (C 20 XE models)

up, as described in Section 4, before replacing the engine access panel.

Rear cover

Removal

15 Remove both camshaft gears as described in Section 7.
16 Unbolt the guide roller from the inlet side of the cylinder head (see illustration).
17 Remove the timing belt tension roller from the oil pump and the timing belt drive gear from the crankshaft.
18 The two retaining bolts in the cylinder head and the two in the oil pump can now be removed.
19 The rear cover can now be lifted upwards.

Refitting

20 Refitting is a reversal of removal.

3 Timing belt covers (except X 16 XEL) - removal and refitting

Outer cover

Removal

1 Disconnect the battery negative lead.
2 For improved access to the timing belt cover bolts, remove the air cleaner assembly as described in Chapter 4B.
3 Remove the ribbed V-belt.

3.11A Timing belt cover fixings (C 20 XE models)

1　Cover screw upper stud
2　Rear belt cover upper securing bolts

3.4B Recover the rubber grommets if they are loose (C 20 XE models)

4 Remove the securing screws and withdraw the outer timing belt cover. Recover the rubber grommets if they are loose (see illustrations).

Refitting

5 Refitting is a reversal of removal, but examine the condition of the rubber seal on the cover and renew if necessary (see illustration). Ensure that the rubber grommets are in place in the cover securing screw holes and refit and tension the ribbed V-belt as described in Chapter 5.

Rear cover

Removal

6 Remove the outer timing belt cover as described previously in this section.
7 Remove the timing belt, as described in Section 5.
8 Remove the timing belt gears, as described in Sections 8 and 18.
9 Remove the timing belt tensioner and the idler gear, as described in Section 11.
10 Unscrew the upper and middle studs for the timing belt outer cover screws. Note that the upper stud simply unscrews from the cylinder head, but the middle stud is secured by a bolt.
11 Unscrew the two upper and single lower right-hand rear belt cover securing bolts (see illustrations) and withdraw the rear belt cover.

3.5 Removing the rubber seal from the outer timing belt cover (C 20 XE models)

3.11B Rear timing belt cover lower right-hand securing bolt (arrowed) (C 20 XE models)

Refitting

12 Refitting is a reversal of removal, remembering the following points.

(a) Refit the belt tensioner and the idler gear as described in Section 11.

(b) Refit the timing belt gears as described in Sections 8 and 18.

(c) Refit and tension the alternator drivebelt as described in Chapter 5.

4 Timing belt (X 16 XEL) - removal, refitting and adjustment

HAYNES HINT *Always replace the timing belt if you are unsure of it's history and condition.*

Removal

1 Remove negative battery lead

2 Remove air intake pipe and air cleaner assembly. Refer to Chapter 4B for details.

3 Remove the upper timing belt cover. Refer to Section 2 for details.

4 Remove the ribbed V-belt. Refer to Chapter 5 for details. Remembering to note running direction of the ribbed V-belt.

5 Apply the handbrake and jack up the front of the car.

6 Remove the right hand front wheel and unbolt engine access panel.

7 Unbolt the timing disc from the crankshaft

8 Select 3rd gear to stop the engine from turning.

9 Unbolt the lower timing belt cover.

10 Replace the timing disc's bolt into the timing belt drive and turn the crankshaft, in clockwise direction, to the 'TDC' mark **(see illustration)**.

11 The marks on the camshaft gears, must be opposite each other and align with the upper edge of the cylinder head. Turn crankshaft slowly and smoothly.

12 Take great care when turning the crankshaft or camshafts, as damage to pistons and valves may occur.

13 Loosen the tension roller and turn the tensioner arm clockwise until the pointer lies at the left stop.

14 Remove the timing belt and check for wear.

Refitting

15 Check the position of the coolant pump. The mark on the pump should align with the mark on the cylinder block **(see illustration)**.

16 Replace the timing belt, ensuring that the belt on the side opposite the coolant pump is taut. Always make sure that the gears are still in the correct position, by checking the timing marks.

17 Move the tensioner arm in an anti-clockwise direction, until pointer is at the right stop position.

4.10 Top dead centre (TDC) marks on X 16 XEL models

1 Marks on camshaft gears aligned with top face of cylinder head

2 Mark on crankshaft gear aligned with mark on cylinder block

18 Tighten securing bolt of the roller.

19 Turn the crankshaft slowly and smoothly two complete turns back to 'TDC' and check that the timing marks on all three gears line up, as before.

Adjustment

20 Loosen the rollers securing bolt again and turn its tensioner arm, clockwise. If a new timing belt has been fitted the pointer should

4.20 Timing belt tensioner marks (1993-on models)

I   Location for new belts

II Location for 'run-in' belts (gap = 4.0 mm to left of pointer)

4.15 Coolant pump location marks (X 16 XEL models)

1 Mark on cylinder block

2 Mark on coolant pump

be lined up with the notch. If replacing a 'run-in' belt (one that has been used for more than a few hours), move the pointer approximately 4 mm to the left of the notch **(see illustration)**.

21 Tighten the tension roller to the oil pump to the correct torque.

22 Turn the crankshaft two complete turns, in the engines normal direction of rotation (clockwise) and check the timing marks again.

23 Use a new bolt on the crankshaft gear.

24 Measure the crankshaft pulse pick-up gap using a feeler gauge. If it outside of it's nominal range (see Specifications), replace the pick-up's bracket.

25 Replace components in the reverse order to removal. Noting the running direction of the ribbed V-belt.

26 Tighten all fixings to their correct torque.

5 Timing belt (except X 16 XEL) - removal, refitting and adjustment

Note: *Always replace the timing belt if you are in any doubt about it's condition or history. A puller may be required to remove the crankshaft gear. The timing belt tension on all models built from 1993-on have automatic tension adjusters fitted. Therefore once fitted, should require no further maintenance.*

Pre-1993 models

Note: *Vauxhall specify the use of a special adjustment wrench (P/N KM-666), for adjusting the timing belt tension after fitting. If this tool is not available, have the belt replaced by a dealer. The following procedure describes belt replacement on the assumption that the tool is available. It details replacement of a new belt only. No specifications are available for replacement of part worn belts. Adjust the belt when the engine is cold.*

2B

5.6A Timing pointer on rear timing belt cover aligned with notch in crankshaft pulley (arrowed) (C 20 XE models)

5.6B Timing marks on the camshaft gears. Aligned with notches in the camshaft cover (arrowed) (C 20 XE models)

5.7 Crankshaft pulley and securing bolts (viewed through wheel arch with wheel removed) (C 20 XE models)

Removal

1 Disconnect the battery negative lead.
2 Remove the air intake hose and air cleaner assembly, as described in Chapter 4B.
3 Remove the V-belt from the alternator. Refer to Chapter 5 for details.
4 Remove the outer timing belt cover, as described in Section 3.
5 Remove the engine undershield, if fitted.
6 Turn the crankshaft to bring No 1 cylinder to top dead centre (TDC), using a socket or spanner on the crankshaft gear (or pulley) bolt. The mark on the crankshaft pulley should line up with the pointer on the rear timing belt cover. At the same time the notches on the camshaft gears should line up with the marks on the cylinder head cover **(see illustration)**. Turn the crankshaft slowly and evenly.
7 Remove the power steering belt. Before removing the V-belt pulley, note the position of the marks in relation to the marks on the camshaft gears **(see illustration)**.
8 Loosen the securing bolt **(see illustration)**, release the timing belt tensioner gear, then slide the belt from the camshaft and crankshaft gears.

Refitting

9 Fit the timing belt so that the side opposite the tensioner (i.e. the driving side) is taut.
10 Whilst fitting the belt, ensure that the timing marks stay in position.

11 Locate the special tool on the tension roller, as described in the tool manufacturers instructions.
12 Starting at the TDC mark on the exhaust camshaft gear, mark the 8 tooth anti-clockwise from the TDC mark.
13 Turn the crankshaft gear two complete turns clockwise. Turn slowly and evenly. Continue turning so that the reference mark made earlier, is flush with the notch on the cylinder head cover **(see illustration)**.
14 Remove the tool.
15 Turn the camshaft gears to TDC. Check that the mark on the crankshaft pulley is flush with the pointer.
16 Replace the V-belt pulley. Use open ended spanner to hold the crankshaft gear.
17 Tighten the timing belt tensioner in three stages, using a new bolt. Firstly tighten the bolt to the specified torque. Then angle tighten by the specified degrees.
18 Replace the remaining components in the reverse order to removal.

1993-on models

Removal

19 Disconnect the battery negative lead.
20 Disconnect the air temperature sensor and the hot film mass air flow meter wiring plugs (if fitted).
21 Remove the air intake hose and air cleaner assembly, as described in Chapter 4B.

22 Remove the engine undershield.
23 Mark the direction of rotation on the ribbed V-belt and remove it from the alternator pulley. Details in Chapter 5.
24 Remove the front timing belt cover.
25 Using the crankshaft gear bolt rotate the engine, slowly and evenly to TDC. Notches on camshaft gears and crankshaft pulley, should align with marks on cylinder head cover and rear timing belt cover, respectively.
26 Remove the crankshaft pulley. Use an open ended spanner to hold the pulley, whilst releasing the tension.
27 Remove the timing belt.

Refitting

28 Check the position of the coolant pump. The lug on the pump should be aligned with the lug on the cylinder block.
29 Fit the timing belt, keeping the side opposite the coolant pump, taut.
30 Ensure that the timing marks remain in position.
31 Slacken the tensioner roller and move the tensioner arm anti-clockwise, until the tensioner pointer lies at its right stop. Tighten the tensioner securing bolt to hold the tensioner in this position.
32 Turn the crankshaft through two complete revolutions in the normal direction of rotation, and check that the timing marks are still aligned. In the first few hours of operation a new belt will be subjected to 'settling-in', (known as the running-in procedure). If you are refitting a used belt (one that has been 'run-in'), align the pointer to approximately 4 mm to the left of the notch **(see illustration)**.
33 Tighten the tensioner roller securing bolt securely to the oil pump. Turn the crankshaft through one complete revolution, in the normal direction of rotation, and check that the crankshaft and camshaft timing marks still align. Then refit the remainder of the components, in the reverse order to which they were removed.
34 With the timing belt adjustment set in this way, correct tension will always be maintained by the automatic tensioner and no further checking or adjustment will be necessary.

5.8 Loosening the timing belt tensioner pulley securing bolt (C 20 XE models)

5.13 Working anti-clockwise from the TDC mark on the exhaust camshaft gear, mark the eighth tooth (pre-1993 models)

5.32 Timing belt tensioner marks (1993-on models)

I   Location for new belts
II Location for 'run-in' belts (gap = 4.0 mm to left of pointer)

6 Camshaft cover - removal and refitting

Removal

1 Remove the outer timing belt cover, as described in Section 2 or 3.

6.2A Disconnecting the larger breather hose from the rear of the camshaft cover (C 20 XE models)

6.2B Crankcase breather hoses (X 16 XEL models)

1   Ventilation tube clamp
2   Cylinder block ventilation hose

2 Disconnect the breather hoses from the camshaft cover (see illustrations).
3 Using an Allen key, or a hexagon bit, unscrew the two securing bolts and withdraw the spark plug cover (see illustrations). If necessary, mark the spark plug HT leads for position (to avoid confusion when refitting) then disconnect them from the plugs and unclip them from the end of the camshaft cover. Take care not to loose the two bushes on X 16 XEL models.
4 Using an Allen key or a hexagon bit, unscrew the securing bolts and withdraw the camshaft cover (see illustration).
5 Remove the one-piece (two on X 16 XEL models) rubber gasket (see illustration).

Refitting

6 Before starting refitting, examine the inside of the cover for a build-up of oil sludge or any other contamination and if necessary clean the cover with paraffin, or a water-soluble

6.3A Withdrawing the spark plug cover (C 20 XE models)

6.4 Unscrewing a camshaft cover securing bolt

1   Engine cover
2   Camshaft cover
3   Engine cover securing bolts
4   Engine cover bolt bushes
5   Camshaft cover bolts
6   Camshaft cover washers
7   Camshaft cover gaskets (2)

6.3B Engine and camshaft covers (X 16 XEL models)

6.5 Camshaft cover removed to show one-piece rubber gasket (C 20 XE models)

2B

7.10 Camshaft timing belt gears (X 16 XEL models)

1 Exhaust side gear
2 Inlet side gear
3 Extension piece for camshaft sensor

8.2 Spanner positioned to counterhold exhaust camshaft (C 20 XE model)

8.3 Withdrawing the camshaft gear bolt and washer . . .

solvent. Dry the cover thoroughly before refitting.

7 Thoroughly clean the mating faces of the camshaft cover and cylinder head.

8 Examine the condition of the camshaft cover rubber seal and if necessary renew it.

9 Refit the camshaft cover, then refit the securing bolts and tighten them to the specified torque.

10 Refit the HT leads to the spark plugs (ensuring that they are refitted to their correct cylinders), then clip the leads to the end of the camshaft cover, refit the camshaft cover and tighten the securing bolts.

11 Reconnect the breather hoses to the camshaft cover.

12 Refit the outer timing belt cover, as described in Section 2 or 3.

7 Camshaft gears (X 16 XEL) - removal and refitting

Removal

1 Disconnect the battery negative lead.

2 Turn crankshaft to sixty degrees before TDC.

3 Remove timing belt. Refer to Section 4, for details.

4 Remove top of inlet manifold. Refer to Chapter 4C.

5 Remove spark plug leads. As detailed in Chapter 1.

6 Disconnect the crankcase vent hose from the cylinder head cover. Then remove the cover.

7 Each gear can now be removed. Use an opened ended spanner behind the gear to counterhold the bolt whilst undoing the bolts.

Refitting

8 When refitting the gears, make sure that the timing marks face outwards.

9 Ensure that the hole in the gear fits over the camshafts guide pin.

10 The exhaust camshaft gear has an extension piece built on for the camshaft sensor (**see illustration**).

11 Replace the camshaft gear's with new bolts.

12 Fit a new gasket to the head cover.

13 Replacement of remaining components is a reversal of removal.

8 Camshaft gears (except X 16 XEL) - removal and refitting

Note: *A new camshaft gear securing bolt and a new timing belt must be used on refitting.*

Removal

1 Remove the timing belt as described in Section 5.

2 Prevent the camshaft from turning as the gear bolt is unscrewed, by holding the camshaft with an open ended spanner. Noting that the flats provided to hold the camshaft stationary are located in front of No 1 cam lobe (**see illustration**).

3 Unscrew the camshaft gear bolt and withdraw it, noting the washer under the bolt head (**see illustration**).

4 Withdraw the gear from the end of the camshaft (**see illustration**).

8.4 . . . and the camshaft gear

Refitting

5 Begin refitting by offering the camshaft gear to the camshaft, making sure that the lug on the end of the camshaft engages with the corresponding hole in the camshaft gear.

6 Fit a new gear securing bolt, ensuring that the washer is in place and tighten the bolt to the specified torque in the two stages given in the Specifications, preventing the camshaft from turning as during removal.

7 Fit a new timing belt and adjust the tension, as described in Section 5.

9 Camshaft front oil seals - renewal

Removal

1 Remove the relevant camshaft gear as described in Section 7 or 8.

2 Punch or drill a small hole in the centre of the now-exposed oil seal.

3 Screw in a self-tapping screw and pull on the screw with pliers to extract the seal (**see illustration**).

4 Clean the oil seal seat with a wooden or plastic scraper.

Refitting

5 Ensure that the locating peg for the gear in the end of the camshaft is uppermost.

6 Grease the lips of the new seal, then fit the

9.3 Removing a camshaft front oil seal

9.6 Using the camshaft gear bolt, washer, and a tube to fit a new camshaft front oil seal

11.2 Timing belt pulley components (pre-1993 models)

1 Tensioner pulley securing bolt
2 Tensioner pulley mounting plate
3 Idler pulley securing bolt

11.3 Belt tensioner pulley and spacer sleeve. Note that smaller diameter of spacer fits against pulley (pre-1993 models)

seal using a tube or socket of similar diameter with a washer and the camshaft gear bolt. Screw the camshaft gear bolt into the end of the camshaft to draw the oil seal into position on its shoulder **(see illustration)**.

7 Refit the camshaft gear as described in Section 7 or 8.

10 Camshaft rear oil seal - general

General

1 No rear camshaft oil seals are fitted to DOHC models, although an O-ring is fitted to the rear of the distributor body. The distributor is driven from the end of the exhaust camshaft.

2 To renew the O-ring, remove the distributor. Then prise off the old O-ring using a screwdriver. Fit the new O-ring and refit the distributor, as described in Chapter 5.

11 Timing belt tensioner and idler pulley - removal and refitting

Note: *The pulley securing bolt(s) and the timing belt must be renewed on refitting.*

Removal

1 Remove the timing belt as described in Section 4 or 5.

2 To remove the belt tensioner or the idler

pulley, simply unscrew the securing bolt from the centre of the pulley, then withdraw the tensioner assembly or pulley, as applicable **(see illustration)**. Recover the spacer sleeve from the bolt.

Refitting

3 Refit the belt tensioner or idler pulley, as applicable, using a new bolt, noting that the spacer sleeve should be fitted with the smaller diameter against the pulley **(see illustration)**.

4 Tighten the securing bolt to the specified torque in the two stages given in the Specifications, except when refitting the belt tensioner. In which case do not fully tighten the bolt until the timing belt has been fitted and tensioned.

5 Fit a new timing belt and adjust the tension as described in Section 4 or 5.

12 Camshafts - removal and refitting

Removal

1 Remove the camshaft housing cover. Refer to Section 6, for details.

2 Before removing timing set the crankshaft gear to sixty degrees before TDC **(see illustration)**.

3 Remove the timing belt as described in Section 4 or 5, remembering to mark the direction of rotation on the belt before removal.

4 Remove the camshaft gears as described in Section 7 or 8.

5 If the exhaust camshaft is to be removed, remove the distributor and camshaft sensor disc (if fitted), as described in Chapter 5.

6 Check the camshaft bearing caps for identification marks and if none are present, make corresponding marks on the bearing caps and the top surface of the cylinder head using a centre-punch. Note the orientation of the bearing caps before removal, as they must be refitted in exactly the same positions from which they are removed. The inlet camshaft caps are usually numbered 1 to 5 and the exhaust camshaft caps 6 to 11, with corresponding numbers cast into the cylinder head **(see illustration)**.

7 Before removing the camshaft, check the endfloat using a dial gauge or a feeler gauge. If the endfloat is outside the specified limits, the camshaft must be renewed.

8 Loosen the relevant camshaft bearing caps in half-turn stages. For example, loosen all the nuts by half a turn, then loosen all the nuts by a further half turn and so on (this is necessary to slowly relieve the tension in the valve springs). Note that the exhaust camshaft rear bearing cap, which also supports the distributor, is secured by four nuts **(see illustration)**.

2B

12.2 Crankshaft at sixty degrees before TDC

12.6 Corresponding identification marks (arrowed) on camshaft bearing cap and cylinder head

12.8 Exhaust camshaft rear bearing cap securing nuts (arrowed)

12.9 Removing a camshaft bearing cap

9 Remove the bearing cap nuts (noting the washers under them) and the bearing caps, then carefully lift the relevant camshaft evenly from the cylinder head, complete with the oil seal **(see illustration)**.

Inspection

10 With the camshaft removed, examine the bearing surfaces in the cylinder head for signs of obvious wear or pitting. If evident, the cylinder head and all the bearing caps must be renewed as a matched set, as it is not possible to renew the bearings individually.
11 The camshaft should show no marks or scoring on the journal or cam lobe surfaces. If evident, renew the camshaft.
12 It is advisable to renew the camshaft front oil seal as a matter of course. Prise the old seal from the front of the camshaft and discard it.

Refitting

13 Begin refitting by liberally coating the contact faces of the hydraulic valve lifters with Longlife Paste (MoS$_2$).
14 Coat the mating faces of the bearing cap which house the oil seal (No 1 or 6, depending on which camshaft has been removed) and in the case of the exhaust camshaft, the bearing cap which houses the distributor drive (No 11) with sealing compound (Vauxhall P/N 90350544, or equivalent).

12.15 Position camshaft gear locating pins towards the inlet and exhaust manifolds (C 18 XE, C 18 XEL and X 20 XEV models)

1 Camshaft gear locating pins

15 Oil the bearing surfaces and the lobes of the camshaft, then place the camshaft in position on the cylinder head. On C 20 XE models turn the camshafts so the gear locating pins are uppermost. On C 18 XE, C 18 XEL and X 20 XEV models the locating pins are pointing towards the manifolds **(see illustration)**.
16 Refit the bearing caps in their original positions as noted during removal.
17 Fit the bearing cap washers and nuts and tighten the nuts progressively to the specified torque in half-turn stages (as when loosening), **(see illustration)**. Note that when refitting the exhaust camshaft, the two smaller rear bearing cap securing nuts should be tightened after all the main camshaft bearing cap nuts have been tightened. Note also that the two smaller nuts should be tightened to a lower torque wrench setting than the main nuts. On X 16 XEL models, tighten the bearing caps in a spiral pattern, from the inside out **(see illustration)**.
18 Lubricate the lips of a new camshaft front oil seal with a little grease and fit the oil seal as described in Section 9.
19 Where applicable, refit the distributor as described in Chapter 5.
20 Refit the camshaft gear as described in Section 8.
21 Replacing remaining components in the reverse order to which they were removed.

13 Cylinder head (X 16 XEL) - removal and refitting

Note: *Do not remove the cylinder head from a hot engine. New cylinder head bolts and a new cylinder head gasket must be used on refitting and sealer (Vauxhall P/N 90094714, or equivalent), will be required when refitting the camshaft housing.*
Note: *The torque settings stated are only applicable to latest specification head bolts, available from Vauxhall. Earlier type or alternative make, head bolts may require different torques. Consult your supplier.*

12.17A Tightening a camshaft bearing cap securing nut (C 20 XE model)

Removal

1 Disconnect negative lead from battery.
2 Place a container beneath the lower radiator hose. Undo the hose clamp and release it from the radiator, allowing the coolant to drain into the container.
3 Remove the upper part of the inlet manifold. Refer to Chapter 4C, for details.
4 Disconnect the air intake pipe and air cleaner assembly. Refer to Chapter 4B for details.
5 Mark the running direction of the ribbed V-belt and remove it by moving the tension roller.
6 Disconnect the earth lead from the wiring harness bracket. Then remove the bracket from the inlet manifold.
7 Remove the alternator adjuster, unbolt the lower mounting bolt and place the alternator to one side. Secure with tape or string.
8 Disconnect the upper radiator hose from the coolant flange.
9 Remove the wiring trunking bracket complete with air intake pipe from the lower part of the inlet manifold.
10 Disconnect the pipe and remove the cable with bracket from the throttle body.
11 Remove the wiring trunking.
12 Unbolt the four bolts from the throttle body flange and place it with the air intake pipe securely to one side.
13 Clamp the fuel pipe and disconnect the lines from the distributor pipe and pressure regulator. Take great care not to allow fuel to spill, collect in a separate container.
14 Disconnect wiring plugs from both the potentiometer and idle stepper motor **(see illustration)**.
15 Remove the wiring harness plug from the crankshaft pulse pick-up bracket.
16 Disconnect spark plugs. Use a specially designed tool (i.e. KM-836), if available. If not, take care and do not overstretch the leads.
17 Remove DIS module from its bracket.
18 Undo the clamps and remove the crankcase vent hose from the cylinder head cover. Then remove the cover.
19 Remove the air duct and vacuum hose from the AIR combination valve.

12.17B Camshaft bearing cap tightening sequence (X 16 XEL model)

13.14 Wiring plugs

1 Stepper motor
2 Throttle valve potentiometer

13.22 Temperature sender and sensor wiring plugs

1 Temperature sender
2 Temperature sensor

13.23 Timing marks on crankshaft at sixty degrees before TDC (X 16 XEL model)

20 Disconnect the wiring plug for the oxygen sensor.

21 Remove completely the upper radiator hose.

22 Disconnect the wiring plugs from the coolant temperature sensor and sender (see illustration).

23 Before removing the timing belt, turn the crankshaft so that the timing mark is 60 degrees before the TDC mark (see illustration).

24 Remove the timing belt rear cover. Refer to Section 2, for details.

25 Disconnect the front pipe from the exhaust.

26 Place a container beneath the sump drain plug, release it and allow the engine oil to drain.

27 Loosen the cylinder head bolts, first by quarter of a turn then by half at a time, in the sequence shown (see illustration).

28 Carefully remove the cylinder head, taking care not to damage the machined face.

Refitting

29 Inspect the condition of the head, including all sealing surfaces, the bores and threads. Ensure that they are all clean and all old gasket has been removed. Refer to

Section 15 for details on how to dismantle the head.

30 Check the cylinder block for damage and wear. Again, refer to Chapter 2A for details.

31 Place the new cylinder head gasket, on the block with the 'TOP', (or 'OBEN') mark on top and at the timing belt end of the engine.

32 Carefully replace the cylinder head, taking care not to drop it too quickly or at an angle.

33 Always use new head bolts. Tighten them gradually, in the order shown (see illustration). The first stage of tightening is tighten each one to it's correct torque. Then using an angle gauge or home made equivalent, tighten further each bolt in turn, through ninety degrees, three times. Always tighten in the order shown. No further retightening is necessary.

34 Clean the area around the sump plug and refit the plug using a new washer. Tighten to the correct torque.

35 Reconnect the exhaust front pipe.

36 Replace the timing belt rear cover.

37 Before replacing the timing belt turn the crankshaft to the TDC mark. Ensure also that the camshaft gears are also in their correct position (see illustration).

38 Replace remaining components in the reverse order to which they were removed.

39 Tighten bolts (and nuts, if applicable) to their correct torques. See Specifications.

40 Renew gaskets, clamps and other fixings if they show any signs of damage or wear.

41 Check that all wiring connections are firm. If any appear to be dirty or damp, use a water dispersing cleaning spray to ensure good electrical contact can be made.

42 Renew the coolant if it appears to be contaminated or if it has passed it's working life (read manufacturers instructions). If in any doubt, replace it. Refer to Chapter 3, for further details.

43 Use only specified engine oil and top-up to the 'MAX' mark on the dipstick.

44 Finally check for engine oil, coolant and fuel leaks both before starting the engine and whilst it is running.

45 Dispose of the old engine oil correctly, do not pour it down the drain.

14 Cylinder head (except X 16 XE) - removal and refitting

Note: *Do not remove the cylinder head from a hot engine. New cylinder head bolts and a new cylinder head gasket must be used on refitting and sealer (Vauxhall P/N 90094714, or equivalent), will be required when refitting the camshaft housing.*

13.27 Loosening sequence for cylinder head bolts (X 16 XEL model)

13.33 Tightening sequence for cylinder head bolts (X 16 XEL model)

13.37 TDC timing marks (X 16 XEL model)

I Camshaft gears (arrows pointing to top face of cylinder head
II Crankshaft gear

2B

14.5 Unbolting the inlet manifold support bracket from the manifold (viewed from underneath)

14.17 Rotate engine to sixty degrees before TDC (C 20 XE model)

14.20 Removing the timing belt outer cover upper stud

Note: *The torque settings stated are only applicable to latest specification head bolts, available from Vauxhall. Earlier type or alternative make, head bolts may require different torques. Consult your supplier.*

1 Disconnect the battery negative lead.

2 Drain the cooling system as described in Chapter 3.

3 Remove the front section of the exhaust system as described in Chapter 4C.

4 The cylinder head can be removed complete with the inlet manifold, or the inlet manifold can be detached from the cylinder head before removal, referring to Chapter 4C. If no work is to be carried out on the inlet manifold, it can be unbolted from the cylinder head and supported to one side out of the way. This avoids the need to disconnect the relevant hoses, pipes and wiring.

5 If the cylinder head is to be removed complete with the inlet manifold, disconnect all relevant hoses, pipes and wiring from the inlet manifold and associated components, referring to Chapters 4B and 4C. Unbolt the manifold support bracket from the manifold **(see illustration)**. Loosen the alternator mountings, then unbolt the upper alternator mounting from the inlet manifold.

6 If the inlet manifold is to be left in the engine compartment, continue as follows - otherwise go on to paragraph 17.

7 Disconnect the wiring plug from the airflow meter and the breather hose from the airbox on the throttle body. Then disconnect the air cleaner trunking and remove the airflow

meter/airbox assembly, referring to Chapter 4B, if necessary.

8 Disconnect the end of the throttle cable from the throttle valve lever, then unbolt the throttle cable support bracket and remove it from the inlet manifold.

9 Unscrew the two earth lead securing nuts from the fuel rail (one at each end of the rail) and disconnect the three earth leads.

10 Disconnect the wiring plug from the throttle position switch.

11 Pull up on the wiring harness housing and disconnect the wiring plugs from the fuel injectors by compressing the retaining clips. Move the wiring harness to one side.

12 Disconnect the two breather hoses from the camshaft cover.

13 Loosen the alternator mountings, then unbolt the upper alternator mounting from the inlet manifold.

14 Unbolt the manifold support bracket from the manifold.

15 Make a final check to ensure that all necessary hoses, pipes and wires have been disconnected, then unscrew the securing nuts and lift the inlet manifold from the cylinder head. Ensure that the manifold is properly supported, taking care not to strain any of the hoses, pipes and wires, etc., which are still connected.

16 Remove the manifold gasket from the cylinder head.

17 Rotate the engine so that the timing mark on the crankshaft gear is at sixty degrees before TDC **(see illustration)**. Note the

running direction of the timing belt. Remove the timing belt and camshaft gears as described in Sections 5 and 8.

18 On C 18 XE, C 18 XEL and X 20 XEV models, remove the camshafts, as described in Section 12.

19 Remove the timing belt tensioner and the idler pulley, as described in Section 11.

20 Unscrew the upper and middle studs for the timing belt outer cover screws. Note that the upper stud simply unscrews from the cylinder head, but the middle stud is secured by a bolt **(see illustration)**.

21 Unscrew the two upper rear timing belt cover securing bolts from the cylinder head.

22 Remove the distributor cap, HT leads and disconnect the distributor wiring plug, as described in Chapter 5.

23 Disconnect the coolant hose from the cylinder head.

24 Unscrew the bolt securing the crankcase breather tube bracket to the end of the cylinder head.

25 Disconnect the radiator top hose from the thermostat housing. Disconnect the wiring plugs from the temperature gauge sender and the coolant temperature sensor (both located in the thermostat housing), **(see illustration)**.

26 Make a final check to ensure that all relevant hoses, pipes and wires have been disconnected.

27 Using a Torx socket and working in the order shown, loosen all the cylinder head bolts by a quarter of a turn, then loosen all the bolts by half a turn and finally loosen and

14.25 Disconnecting the radiator top hose from the thermostat housing

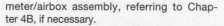

14.27A Loosening sequence for cylinder head bolts (C 20 XE models)

14.27B Loosening sequence for cylinder head bolts (C 18 XE, C 18 XEL and X 20 XEV models)

14.27C Removing a cylinder head bolt and washer

14.28 Lifting the cylinder head from the cylinder block (C 20 XE model)

14.31 New cylinder head gasket in position

remove the bolts. Remove the washers (see illustrations).

28 Lift the cylinder head from the cylinder block (see illustration). If necessary, tap the cylinder head gently with a soft-faced mallet to free it from the block, but do not lever at the mating faces. Note that the cylinder head is located on dowels.

29 Recover the cylinder head gasket and discard it.

Refitting

30 Clean the cylinder head and block mating faces by careful scraping. Take care not to damage the cylinder head, which is made of light alloy and is easily scored. Cover the coolant passages and other openings with

masking tape or rag, to prevent dirt and carbon falling in. Mop out all the oil from the bolt holes; if oil is left in the holes, hydraulic pressure could crack the block when the bolts are refitted.

31 Begin refitting by locating a new cylinder head gasket on the block so that the word 'OBEN' or 'TOP' is uppermost at the timing belt end of the engine (see illustration).

32 With the mating faces scrupulously clean, locate the cylinder head on the block so that the positioning dowels engage in their holes.

33 Temporarily refit the crankshaft gear and the camshaft gears and ensure that No 1 piston is still positioned at top dead centre (see Section 5).

34 Fit the new cylinder head bolts, ensuring that the washers are in place under their heads and screw the bolts in by hand as far as possible.

35 Tighten the bolts in the order shown. Tighten the bolts in the stages given in the Specifications - i.e., tighten all bolts to the Stage 1 torque, then tighten all bolts to Stage 2 and so on (see illustrations).

36 Further refitting is a reversal of removal, remembering the following points.

37 Refit the timing belt tensioner and idler gear as described in Section 11.

38 Refit the camshaft gears as described in Section 8.

39 Initial start-up after major overhaul or repair

40 Where applicable, refit the inlet manifold to the cylinder head, referring to

Chapter 4C, using a new gasket.

41 Refit the front section of the exhaust system as described in Chapter 4C, using a new gasket.

42 Refit the upper alternator mounting to the inlet manifold (where applicable), then adjust the alternator drivebelt tension as described in Chapter 5.

43 Refill the cooling system as described in Chapter 3.

44 On completion, check that all relevant hoses, pipes and wires, etc., have been reconnected.

45 When the engine is started, check for signs of leaks.

46 Using the latest specification head bolts, retightening is no longer necessary.

15 Cylinder head - dismantling and reassembly

Note: New and reconditioned cylinder heads are available from the manufacturers and from engine overhaul specialists. Some specialist tools are required for the dismantling and inspection procedures and new components may not be readily available. It may be more practical and economical for the home mechanic to buy a reconditioned head rather than to dismantle, inspect and recondition the original head. A valve spring compressor tool will be required for this operation.

14.35A Cylinder head bolt tightening sequence (C 20 XE models)

14.35B Cylinder head bolt tightening sequence (C 18 XE, C 18 XEL and X 20 XEV models)

14.35C Tighten the cylinder head bolts to the specified torque . . .

14.35D . . . and then through the specified angle

2B

15.2A Using a rubber suction plunger tool to remove a valve lifter

⚠️ *Warning: The exhaust valves fitted to DOHC models are filled with sodium to improve heat transfer. Sodium is a highly reactive metal, which will ignite or explode spontaneously on contact with water (including water vapour in the air). Valves containing sodium must NOT be disposed of with ordinary scrap seek advice from a Vauxhall dealer if the valves are to be disposed of.*

Dismantling

1 With the cylinder head removed as described in Section 13 or 14. Clean away all external dirt and remove the following components.
(a) Remove the manifolds (see Chapter 4C).
(b) Remove the engine cover or spark plug cover as applicable (see Section 6)
(c) Remove the AIR metal pipe and combination valve support (where applicable).
(d) Remove the spark plugs (see Chapter 1).
(e) Remove the thermostat housing and coolant flange, if fitted (see Chapter 3).
(f) Remove the camshafts (see Section 12).
(g) Remove the DIS bracket, if applicable (see Chapter 5).

2 Remove the hydraulic valve lifters from their bores using a rubber suction plunger tool **(see illustration)** do not invert the cylinder head to remove the valve lifters. Keep the valve lifters upright at all times **(see illustration)** and immerse them in order of removal in a

17.2 Sump to transmission fixings
1 Sump to transmission bolts

15.2B The valve lifters should be kept upright with the oil groove (arrowed) at the bottom

container of clean engine oil until they are to be refitted.
3 To remove a valve, fit a valve spring compressor tool. Ensure that the arms of the compressor tool are securely positioned on the head of the valve and the spring cap.
4 Compress the valve spring to relieve the pressure of the spring cap acting on the collets. If the spring cap sticks to the valve stem, support the compressor tool and give the end a light tap with a soft-faced mallet to help free the spring cap.
5 Extract the two split collets, then slowly release the compressor tool.

 HAYNES HiNT *Place each valve and valve component in a labelled polythene bag or a similar small container. The valves are normally numbered from the timing belt end of the engine. Make sure that the valve components are identified as inlet and exhaust, as well as numbered.*

6 Remove the spring cap, spring, valve stem oil seal and the spring seat, then withdraw the valve through the combustion chamber.
7 Repeat the procedure for the remaining valves, keeping all components in strict order so that they can be refitted in their original positions, unless all the components are to be renewed.

Reassembly

8 Inspect and recondition the head as described in Chapter 2A.
9 Before refitting the valves, coat each one in new engine oil.
10 Make sure that each valve and valve component is replaced in the same location from where it was removed.
11 Insert the valve seats.
12 Always renew the valve stem oil seals. If they were supplied with an assembly sleeve, place it on the valve and coat with new engine oil. Place the oil seal over the sleeve and push it down onto it's seat.
13 Replace the remaining valve components using the compressor.
14 Coat the surfaces of the hydraulic lifters and camshaft with Longlife Paste (MoS_2).
15 Insert the camshaft carefully in the head. Refer to Section 12.
16 Replace the camshaft bearing caps with

Sealing Compound (i.e. Vauxhall P/N 90350544) applied to the sealing surfaces of the guide bearing. When replacing the caps, ensure that the numbers on the caps match those on the head.
17 Tighten caps to their correct torque.
18 Coat the new camshaft oil seal lip with grease and insert using a large socket or similar tool.
19 Replace remaining components using new gaskets where applicable.

16 Hydraulic valve lifters - general

Note: *The valve lifters should always be stored upright in a container of clean engine oil while removed from the cylinder head.*
1 Inspect the valve lifters for obvious signs of wear on the contact faces and check the valve lifter oil holes for obstructions, particularly for oil sludge. If excessive wear is evident (this is unlikely), all the valve lifters must be renewed as a set.
2 Refit the hydraulic valve lifters to the cylinder head in their original positions. Liberally oil the valve lifter bores and if new valve lifters are being fitted, initially immerse each one in a container of clean engine oil and compress it (by hand) several times to charge it.

17 Sump (X 16 XEL) - general

1 The procedure is the same as for SOHC models (refer to Chapter 2A), except for the following.
2 The sump bolts directly onto the transmission **(see illustration)**. There is no blanking plate fitted.
3 As with SOHC models, remember to ensure that all old gasket remnants are removed and all sealing surfaces are clean. Use new gaskets.
4 To ensure that the sump fits correctly onto the transmission when refitting, first partially tighten all bolts. Then tighten the bolts to the transmission, then the bolts to the cylinder block, to their correct torques.

18 Crankshaft gear - removal and refitting

Note: *A new camshaft gear securing bolt and a new timing belt must be used on refitting.*

Removal

1 Remove the timing belt as described in Section 4 or 5.
2 The crankshaft gear bolt must now be unscrewed. To prevent the crankshaft from turning as the gear bolt is unscrewed, either

select top gear and have an assistant apply the brakes hard (manual transmission models only), or remove the starter motor and jam the ring gear teeth, using a large screwdriver.

3 Using a Torx socket, unscrew the gear bolt (taking care as it is very tight) and recover the washer from under the bolt head.

4 Withdraw the gear from the end of the crankshaft, using a puller if necessary.

Refitting

5 Refit the crankshaft gear to the end of the crankshaft.

6 Apply a little grease to the threads of a new gear securing bolt and tighten it to the specified torque in the two stages given in the Specifications. Ensure that the washer is in place under the bolt head and prevent the crankshaft from turning as during removal.

7 Fit a new timing belt and adjust the tension as described in Section 4 or 5.

19 Oil pump - removal and refitting

Note: *A new oil pump gasket, a new front crankshaft oil seal and on C 18 NZ and C 20 NE models, a new oil filter must be used on refitting. Sealing Compound (Vauxhall P/N 90350544, or equivalent) will be required to coat the face of the crankshaft spacer washer.*

Removal

1 Remove the rear timing belt cover as described in Section 2 or 3.

2 Remove the sump, oil pick-up pipe and sump baffle (where applicable) as described in Section 17.

3 On C 18 NZ and C 20 NE models, unscrew the oil filter from its mounting on the oil pump, referring to Chapter 1 if necessary.

4 Disconnect the oil cooler pipe unions from the oil pump and move the pipes to one side out of the way **(see illustration)**.

5 Disconnect the wiring from the oil pressure switch mounted in the oil pump.

6 Remove the spacer washer from the end of the crankshaft.

7 Remove the securing bolts and withdraw the oil pump from the cylinder block. Remove the gasket.

Refitting

8 Thoroughly clean the mating faces of the oil pump and cylinder block, then locate a new gasket on the block.

9 Wind a thin layer of tape around the front edge of the crankshaft, to prevent damage to the oil seal lips as the pump is refitted.

10 With a new oil seal fitted to the pump, as described in Chapter 2A, grease the oil seal lips, then refit the pump, ensuring that the inner gear engages with the flats on the crankshaft.

11 Tighten the securing bolts to the specified torque, then carefully remove the tape from the front of the crankshaft.

12 Coat the oil pump mating face of the spacer ring with sealing compound (Vauxhall P/N 90350544, or equivalent), then push the washer onto the end of the crankshaft until it is seated against the end of the oil pump **(see illustration)**.

13 Reconnect the wiring to the oil pressure switch.

14 Reconnect the oil cooler pipes to the oil pump and tighten the unions.

15 Fit a new oil filter, referring to Chapter 1.

16 Refit the sump baffle (where applicable), oil pick-up pipe and sump, as described in Section 17.

17 Refit the rear timing belt cover as described in Section 2 or 3.

20 Crankshaft oil seals - renewal

Note: *Sealing compound (Vauxhall P/N 90350544, or equivalent) will be required to coat the face of the crankshaft spacer washer.*

Front oil seal
Removal

1 Remove the crankshaft gear as described in Section 18.

2 Ensure that, where applicable, the Woodruff key is removed from the end of the crankshaft.

3 Remove the spacer washer from the end of the crankshaft.

4 Punch or drill a small hole in the centre of the now-exposed oil seal.

5 Screw in a self-tapping screw and pull on the screw with pliers to extract the seal. Several attempts may be necessary. Be careful not to damage the sealing face of the crankshaft.

Refitting

6 Clean the oil seal seat with a wooden or plastic scraper.

7 Wind a thin band of tape around the end of the crankshaft to protect the lips of the new oil seal as it is fitted.

19.4 Oil cooler pipe unions at oil pump

8 Grease the lips of the new seal and tap it into position until it is flush with the outer face of the oil pump body, using a socket or tube. Take care not to damage the seal lips during fitting.

9 Carefully remove the tape from the end of the crankshaft.

10 Coat the oil pump mating face of the spacer washer with sealing compound (Vauxhall P/N 90350544, or equivalent), then push the washer onto the end of the crankshaft until it is seated against the end of the oil pump.

11 Where applicable, refit the Woodruff key and refit the crankshaft gear, as described in Section 18.

Rear oil seal
Removal

12 Remove the flywheel/driveplate as described in Chapter 2A.

13 Proceed as described in paragraphs 4 to 6 inclusive of this Section.

Refitting

14 Grease the lips of the new seal, then tap the seal into position using a tube, until flush with the outer faces of the cylinder block and rear main bearing cap.

15 Refit the flywheel/driveplate as described in Chapter 2A.

21 Engine with transmission - removal and refitting

Note: *Due to the fitment of 'pot-type' flywheels, the engine and transmission must be removed as an assembly on later models (i.e. from 1993). For details on engine removal without transmission, for earlier models, refer to Chapter 2A.*

Removal

1 Disconnect the negative lead from the battery

2 Remove the air intake pipe and air cleaner assembly. Refer to Chapter 4B for details.

19.12 Oil pump securing bolts (arrowed)
A Crankshaft spacer ring

2B

21.4 Engine compartment wiring plugs - X 16 XEL models

1 Engine (2-pin)	5 Crankshaft pulse pick-up	8 Engine (3-pin)
2 Knock sensor	6 Earth cable	9 Oxygen sensor
3 Earth cable	7 Controlled canister purge	10 DIS ignition module
4 EGR Valve	valve	11 Camshaft sensor

3 Remove the engine cover from the cylinder head cover.

4 Carefully disconnect all the engine wiring plugs **(see illustration)**.

5 Unclip the wiring trough and lay to one side, if fitted.

6 Disconnect the vacuum hose from the AIR switchover and canister purge valve.

7 Disconnect the vacuum pipe and the pressure sensor vacuum hose from the inlet manifold.

8 Remove the accelerator cable and it's bracket.

9 Remove completely the positive cable from the battery.

10 Disconnect the engine multiplug.

11 Clamp the fuel pipes and disconnect them from the fuel pressure regulator. Take care to avoid spillage.

12 Disconnect the clutch and speedometer cables. Remove also, the transmission shift rod and guide. Refer to Chapter 7A or 7B, as applicable.

13 Place a container under the lower radiator hose. Loosen the clamp, carefully disconnect the hose and allow the coolant to drain into the container. Remove both radiator hoses completely.

14 If applicable, place a container underneath the oil cooler and disconnect the pipes from the adapters.

15 Remove the air duct and vacuum hose from the AIR combination valve.

16 Remove the engine cover plate.

17 Remove the ribbed V-belt. Refer to Chapter 5 for details, remembering to note the direction of rotation before removal.

18 Undo the power steering mounting bolts, remove and suspend it securely to one side.

19 Apply the handbrake and jack up the front of the vehicle.

20 Release the front exhaust pipe.

21 Suspend engine, using a hoist or engine holder.

22 Remove the front suspension cross-member. Refer to Chapter 10, for details.

23 Remove driveshafts. Refer to Chapter 8, for details.

24 Detach heater hoses from the heater radiator.

25 Place trolley jack underneath and slightly raise the engine and transmission assembly. Use a piece of wood between the jack and the engine for protection.

26 Remove the engine to crossmember mountings.

27 Disconnect the hoist or engine holder.

28 Lower the engine and transmission assembly carefully and remove the assembly from under the vehicle.

Refitting

29 Slide engine and transmission assembly from below up into the engine compartment.

30 Attach the hoist or engine holder.

31 Ensure that the threads for the engine mounting to crossmember are clean. Recut the threads if necessary. Refit the mounting,

replacing the bolts using Locking Compound (i.e. P/N 90167347).

32 Replace the heater hoses.

33 Refit the driveshafts. Refer to Chapter 8.

34 Replace the front suspension cross-member. Follow instructions in Chapter 10.

35 Refit the front exhaust pipe.

36 Remove the hoist or engine holder.

37 Replace the remaining components in the reverse order to which they were removed.

38 Check that when replacing components, they show no signs of damage or excessive wear. Renew where necessary.

39 Tighten all components to there correct torque. Refer to Specifications.

40 Check engine oil levels.

41 Top up cooling system. Refer to Chapter 3 for details.

42 Check for fuel, coolant and engine oil leaks, before and after engine has been started.

43 Refer to Chapter 2A, Section; 'Initial start-up after major overhaul or repair', for further information.

22 Oil cooler - removal and refitting

Removal

1 To gain sufficient access to enable the oil cooler to be removed, the radiator must be removed, as described in Chapter 3, or alternatively, the front bumper must be removed, as described in Chapter 11.

2 With the appropriate components removed for access, unscrew the oil cooler pipe unions from the oil cooler. Be prepared for oil spillage and plug the open ends of the pipes, to prevent further oil leakage and dirt ingress.

3 If necessary, unbolt the oil cooler pipes from their brackets, to allow sufficient space for the oil cooler to be removed **(see illustration)**.

4 Unscrew the two securing nuts and withdraw the oil cooler from its mounting brackets **(see illustration)**.

Refitting

5 Refitting is a reversal of removal, but on completion, check and if necessary top-up the engine oil level, as described in Chapter 1.

22.3 Oil cooler pipe bracket viewed through front bumper

22.4 Oil cooler fixings (viewed through front bumper)

1 Pipe union   2 Oil cooler securing nut

Chapter 3
Cooling, heating and ventilation systems

Contents

Degrees of difficulty

Easy, suitable for novice with little experience	**Fairly easy,** suitable for beginner with some experience	**Fairly difficult,** suitable for competent DIY mechanic	**Difficult,** suitable for experienced DIY mechanic	**Very difficult,** suitable for expert DIY or professional 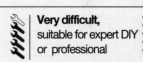

3

Specifications

System type . . . . Pressurised, with front-mounted radiator, remote expansion tank, and electric cooling fan. Coolant pump driven by timing belt

Thermostat
Type . . . . Wax
Start-to-open temperature (all models) . . . . 92°C
Fully-open temperature (all models) . . . . 107°C

Electric cooling fan
Switches on at (all models) . . . . 100°C
Switches off at . . . . 95°C

Torque wrench settings

	Nm	lbf ft
Coolant flange to cylinder head:		
X 16 XEL	25	18
C 18 XE, C 18 XEL and C 20 XE:		
M8 bolts	20	15
M10 bolts	30	22
Coolant outlet to thermostat housing	8	6
Coolant pump to cylinder block:		
1.4 and 1.6 litre (M6)	8	6
C 18 NZ, C 20 NE, C 18 XE, C 18 XEL, C 20 XE and X 20 XEV (M8) . .	25	18
Cover plate to cylinder head:		
C 18 XE, C 18 XEL, C 20 XE and X 20 XEV:		
M6 bolts	9	7
M8 nuts	22	16
Oil pipes to radiator (where applicable)	22	16
Thermostat housing to cylinder head		
1.4 and 1.6 litre SOHC models	10	7
X 16 XEL	20	15
C 18 NZ, C 20 NE, C 18 XE, C 18 XEL, C 20 XE and X 20 XEV	15	11
Thermostat housing cover (X 16 XEL)	8	6
Thermostat housing cover Allen key:		
X 16 XEL (refer to text), C 18 XE, C 18 XEL and C 20 XE	15	11

1 Cooling system - general

1 Engine cooling is achieved using a pump-assisted system, in which the coolant is pressurised. The system consists of a radiator, a coolant pump driven by the engine timing belt, an electric cooling fan, a thermostat, an expansion tank, and connecting hoses.

2 The system works in the following way. Cold coolant from one side of the radiator, which is mounted at the front of the engine compartment, passes to the coolant pump, which forces the coolant through the coolant passages in the cylinder block and cylinder head. The coolant absorbs heat from the engine, and then returns to the radiator via the heater system. As the coolant flows across the radiator, it is cooled, and the cycle is repeated.

3 Air flows through the radiator, to cool the radiator as a result of the vehicle's forward motion. However, if the coolant temperature exceeds a given figure, a temperature-sensitive switch in the radiator switches on the electric cooling fan, to increase the airflow through the radiator. The fan only operates when necessary, with a consequent reduction in noise and energy consumption.

4 To reduce the time taken for the engine to warm up when starting from cold, the thermostat, located in the cylinder head outlet, prevents coolant flowing to the radiator until the temperature has risen sufficiently. Instead, the outflow from the cylinder head bypasses the radiator and is redirected around the engine. When the temperature reaches a given figure, the thermostat opens, to allow coolant to flow to the radiator. The thermostat is operated by the expansion of a temperature-sensitive wax capsule.

5 An expansion tank is incorporated in the system, to allow for coolant expansion. The system is topped-up through a filler cap on the expansion tank.

6 On 1.8/2.0 litre SOHC and X 20 XEV models, the cooling system bleeds itself during engine 'warm-up'. The procedure for bleeding other systems are described in the refilling part of Section 3.

7 On models fitted with automatic transmission, the radiator incorporates a heat exchanger to cool the automatic transmission fluid.

8 Antifreeze must be used in the cooling system all year round. It not only prevents the system from freezing during cold weather, but also contains products to reduce overheating and protect against internal corrosion.

2 Precautions - warnings

1 *Do not attempt to remove the expansion tank filler cap or disturb any part of the cooling system while the engine is hot, as there is a high risk of scalding. If the expansion tank filler cap must be removed before the engine and radiator have fully cooled (even though this is NOT recommended) the pressure in the cooling system must first be relieved. Cover the cap with a thick layer of cloth, to avoid scalding, and slowly unscrew the filler cap until a hissing sound can be heard. When the hissing has stopped, indicating that the pressure has reduced, slowly unscrew the filler cap until it can be removed; if more hissing sounds are heard, wait until they have stopped before unscrewing the cap completely. At all times. keep well away from the filler cap opening.*
2 *Do not allow antifreeze to come into contact with skin or painted surfaces of the vehicle. Rinse off immediately with plenty of water. Never leave antifreeze lying around in an open container or in a puddle on the driveway or garage floor. Children and pets are attracted by its sweet smell, but antifreeze can be fatal if ingested.*
3 *If the engine is hot, the electric cooling fan may start rotating even if the engine is not running, so be careful to keep hands, hair and loose clothing well clear when working in the engine compartment.*

3 Cooling system - draining, flushing and refilling

![warning triangle] **Warning: Wait until the engine is cold before starting this procedure. Do not allow antifreeze to come in contact with your skin, or with the painted surfaces of the vehicle. Rinse off spills immediately with plenty of water. Never leave antifreeze lying around in an open container, or in a puddle in the driveway or garage floor. Children and pets are attracted by its sweet smell but antifreeze is fatal if ingested. Refer to Chapter 1, for capacity and mixture details.**

Draining

1 To drain the cooling system, carefully remove the expansion tank filler cap.
2 On DOHC models, remove the engine undershield. Refer to Chapter 11 for details.
3 Position a container beneath the radiator bottom hose connection. Then slacken the hose clip and ease the hose from the radiator stub. If the hose joint has not been disturbed for some time, it may be necessary to twist the hose to break the joint. Allow the coolant to drain into the container.

4 As no cylinder block drain plug is fitted, and the radiator bottom hose may be situated above the bottom of the radiator, the system cannot be drained completely. Care should therefore be taken when refilling the system to maintain antifreeze strength.
5 If the coolant has been drained for a reason other than renewal, then provided it is clean and less than two years old, it can be re-used. Vauxhall do not specify renewal intervals for the coolant installed in the system when the vehicle is new, so renewal is up to the discretion of the owner.

Flushing

6 If coolant renewal has been neglected, or if the antifreeze mixture has become diluted, then in time, the cooling system may gradually lose efficiency, as the coolant passages become restricted due to rust, scale deposits, and other sediment. The cooling system efficiency can be restored by flushing the system clean.
7 The radiator should be flushed independently of the engine, to avoid unnecessary contamination.
8 To flush the radiator, disconnect the top hose at the radiator. Disconnect the bottom hose. Then insert a garden hose into the radiator top inlet. Direct a flow of clean water through the radiator and continue flushing until clean water emerges from the radiator bottom outlet. If after a reasonable period, the water still does not run clear, the radiator can be flushed with a flushing solution. Available at all good motorist outlets. It is important that the cleaning agent manufacturer's instructions are followed carefully. If the contamination is particularly bad, insert the hose in the radiator bottom outlet, and flush the radiator in reverse ('reverse-flushing').
9 To flush the engine, proceed as follows, according to model.

1.4 and 1.6 litre models

10 Remove the thermostat as described in Section 7, then temporarily refit the thermostat cover.
11 With the radiator top and bottom hoses disconnected from the radiator, insert a hose into the radiator bottom hose. Direct a clean flow of water through the engine, and continue flushing until clean water emerges from the radiator top hose.
12 On completion of flushing, refit the thermostat, referring to Section 7 and reconnect the hoses.

1.8 and 2.0 litre models

13 Remove the thermostat and cover assembly, as described in Section 7.
14 With the radiator bottom hose disconnected from the radiator, insert a hose into the radiator bottom hose. Direct a flow of clean water through the engine and continue flushing until clean water emerges from the thermostat housing. It is advisable to place a sheet of plastic under the thermostat housing to deflect water away from the engine and

3.17A Bleeding the cooling system by removing the temperature sender unit - C 16 SE model

3.17B Location of the Allen key bolt for bleeding the cooling system - C 20 XE model

surrounding components during the flushing process.

15 On completion of flushing, refit the thermostat and cover assembly, reconnect the hoses and remove the plastic sheet.

Refilling

16 Before attempting to fill the cooling system, make sure that all hoses and clips are in good condition, and that the clips are tight. Antifreeze must be used all year round, to prevent corrosion of the alloy engine components.

17 On 1.4 and 1.6 litre models, disconnect the wire and unscrew the coolant temperature sender from the inlet manifold. On X 16 XEL, C 18 XE, C 18 XEL and C 20 XE models, remove the Allen bolt in the thermostat housing cover **(see illustrations)**.

18 Remove the expansion tank cap, and fill the system by slowly pouring the coolant into the expansion tank to prevent airlocks from forming.

19 If the coolant is being renewed, begin by pouring in a couple of litres of water, followed by the correct quantity of antifreeze, then top-up with more water.

20 Refit the coolant temperature sender when coolant free of air bubbles emerges from the bore of the manifold (or thermostat housing). Where applicable, replace the Allen bolt with Sealing Compound (i.e. Vauxhall P/N 90094714), when coolant flows free of bubbles.

21 Top-up the coolant level to the 'KALT' (or 'COLD') mark on the expansion tank, then refit the expansion tank cap.

22 Start the engine and run it until it reaches normal operating temperature, then stop the engine and allow it to cool.

23 Check for leaks, particularly around disturbed components. Check the coolant level in the expansion tank, and top-up if necessary. Note that the system must be cold before an accurate level is indicated in the expansion tank. if the expansion tank cap is removed while the engine is still warm, cover the cap with a thick cloth and unscrew the cap slowly to gradually relieve the system pressure (a hissing sound will normally be

heard). Wait until any pressure remaining in the system is released, then continue to turn the cap until it can be removed.

24 On DOHC models, refit the engine undershield on completion.

4 Cooling system hoses - general

Note: *Refer to the warnings given in Section 2 before proceeding.*

General

1 If the checks described in Chapter 1 reveal a faulty hose, it must be renewed as follows.

2 First drain the cooling system (see Section 3). If the coolant is not due for renewal, it may be re-used if it is collected in a clean container.

3 To disconnect a hose, use a screwdriver to slacken the clips, then move them along the hose, clear of the relevant inlet/outlet. Carefully work the hose free **(see illustration)**. While the hoses can be removed with relative ease when new, or when hot, **do not** attempt to disconnect any part of the system while it is still hot.

4 Note that the radiator inlet and outlet stubs are fragile; do not use excessive force when attempting to remove the hoses. If a hose proves to be difficult to remove, try to release it by rotating the ends on the relevant inlet/outlet before attempting to free it. If all else fails, cut the hose with a sharp knife, then slit it so that it can be peeled off in two pieces. Although this may prove expensive if the hose is otherwise undamaged, it is preferable to buying a new radiator.

5 When fitting a hose, first slide the clips onto the hose, then work the hose into position. If clamp type clips were originally fitted, it is a good idea to replace them with screw type clips when refitting the hose. If the hose is stiff, use a little soapy water as a lubricant, or soften the hose by soaking it in hot water.

6 Work the hose into position, checking that it is correctly routed, then slide each clip along the hose until it passes over the flared end of the relevant inlet/outlet, before tightening the clip securely.

7 Refill the cooling system with reference to Section 3.

8 Check thoroughly for leaks as soon as possible after disturbing any part of the cooling system.

5 Radiator - removal, inspection and refitting

Note: *Refer to the warnings given in Section 2 before proceeding. Minor leaks from the radiator can be cured without removing the radiator, using a liquid based sealant, available from all good motorist outlets. Where applicable, new sealing rings must be used when reconnecting the automatic trans-mission fluid cooler hoses.*

Removal

1 The radiator can be removed complete with the cooling fan and shroud if there is no need to disturb the fan. The fan and its shroud can be removed from the radiator with reference to Section 8.

2 Disconnect the battery negative lead.

3 Drain the cooling system as described in Section 3.

4 Where applicable, disconnect the wiring plugs from the cooling fan and the cooling fan switch mounted in the bottom right-hand side of the radiator. Remove also the air duct hose, AIR combination valve and AIR switchover valve bracket, if fitted.

5 Disconnect the top hose from the radiator.

6 On models with automatic transmission, clamp the transmission fluid cooler hoses. Then disconnect them from the cooler in the side of the radiator. Be prepared for fluid spillage, and plug the open ends of the cooler and hoses immediately, to minimise fluid loss and prevent dirt ingress.

7 Unscrew the two top radiator mounting bracket securing bolts, and lift the brackets

4.3 Disconnecting the radiator top hose

3

5.7 Removing a top radiator mounting bracket

5.8 Withdrawing the radiator

from the radiator rubber mountings **(see illustration)**.

8 Lift the radiator to disengage the lower securing lugs, and withdraw it from the vehicle **(see illustration)**.

Inspection

9 If the radiator has been removed due to suspected blockage, reverse flush it as described in Section 3. Clean dirt and debris from the radiator fins, using an air line (in which case, wear eye protection) or a soft brush. Be careful, as the fins are easily damaged, and are sharp.

10 If necessary, a radiator specialist can perform a 'flow test' on the radiator, to establish whether an internal blockage exists.

11 A leaking radiator must be referred to a specialist for permanent repair. Do not attempt to weld or solder a leaking radiator, as damage to the plastic components may result.

12 In an emergency, minor leaks from the radiator can be cured by using a radiator sealant in accordance with its manufacturer's instructions with the radiator *in situ*.

13 If the radiator is to be sent for repair or renewed, remove all hoses and the cooling fan switch.

14 Inspect the condition of the radiator mounting rubbers, and renew them if necessary **(see illustration)**.

Refitting

15 Refitting is a reversal of removal, bearing in mind the following points.

16 Ensure that the radiator rubber mountings are in good condition and renew if necessary, and ensure that the lower securing lugs engage correctly as the radiator is refitted.

17 Where applicable, use new sealing rings when reconnecting the automatic transmission fluid cooler hoses, and on completion check and if necessary top-up the fluid level as described in Section 3.

18 Refill the cooling system as described in Section 3.

---

6 Expansion tank - removal and refitting

Note: *Refer to the warnings given in Section 2 before proceeding.*

Removal

1 Where applicable, disconnect the battery negative lead, and disconnect the coolant level sensor wiring plug from the expansion tank filler cap.

2 Unscrew the two securing nuts, and lift the expansion tank clear of the body for access to the two coolant hose connections.

3 Where applicable, unclip the octane coding plug assembly from the side of the expansion tank.

4 Disconnect the hose from the side of the tank, then clamp or plug the hose, and suspend it as high as possible above the height of the engine to prevent coolant loss.

5 Position a container beneath the tank, then disconnect the bottom hose and allow the contents of the tank to drain into the container. Clamp or plug the bottom hose, then suspend the hose as high as possible above the engine to prevent coolant loss.

6 Withdraw the expansion tank from the engine compartment.

Refitting

7 Refitting is a reversal of removal, but on completion, check and if necessary top-up the coolant level, as described in Section 3. The coolant drained from the expansion tank during removal can be re-used, provided that it has not been contaminated.

---

7 Thermostat - removal, testing and refitting

Removal

1.4, 1.6 litre SOHC models

1 Partially drain the cooling system with reference to Section 3.

2 Remove the rear timing belt cover as described in Chapter 2A.

3 Unscrew and remove the two thermostat housing securing bolts, and lift off the thermostat housing **(see illustration)**.

4 Disconnect the coolant hose from the thermostat housing, and remove the housing.

5 Withdraw the thermostat from the cylinder head, noting that coolant may be released from the radiator bottom outlet as the thermostat is withdrawn, even though the cooling system has been partially drained.

6 Remove the sealing ring from the edge of the thermostat.

7 The thermostat can be tested, as described later in this Section.

1.8, 2.0 litre SOHC and all DOHC models

8 Partially drain the cooling system with reference to Section 3.

9 Disconnect the radiator top hose from the thermostat cover.

10 Unscrew and remove the three thermostat

5.14 Radiator mounting rubber (arrowed) in lower body panel

7.3 Lifting off the thermostat housing to expose the thermostat (arrowed) - C 16 NZ model

7.10A Withdraw the thermostat cover complete with the thermostat . . .

7.10B ... and recover the O-ring - C 20 NE model

7.14A Testing the thermostat opening temperature

7.14B View of thermostat showing opening temperature markings

cover securing bolts, and withdraw the cover complete with the thermostat. Recover the O-ring **(see illustrations)**.

11 The thermostat can be tested as described later in this Section.

12 If it is necessary to renew the thermostat, the complete cover and thermostat must be renewed as an assembly, as the two components are not available separately.

Testing

13 A rough test of the thermostat may be made by suspending it with a piece of string in a container full of water. Heat the water to bring it to the boil - the thermostat must open by the time the water boils. If not, renew it.

14 If a thermometer is available, the precise opening temperature of the thermostat may be determined, and compared with the figures given in the Specifications. The opening temperature is also marked on the thermostat **(see illustrations)**.

15 A thermostat which fails to close as the water cools must also be renewed.

Refitting

16 Refitting is a reversal of removal, but use a new sealing ring, and bearing in mind the following points.

17 Ensure that the lugs on the thermostat engage with the corresponding cut-outs in the cylinder head.

18 Where applicable, refit the rear timing belt cover as described in Chapter 2A.

19 Refill the cooling system with reference to Section 3.

---

8 Cooling fan - testing, removal and refitting

Testing

1 The cooling fan is supplied with current via the ignition switch and fuse 11 (which may be mounted in the fusebox, or under the fusebox, depending on model see Chapter 12). The circuit is completed by the cooling fan thermostatic switch, which is mounted in the lower right-hand side of the radiator **(see illustration)**.

2 If the fan does not appear to work, run the engine until normal operating temperature is reached, then allow it to idle. If the fan does not cut in within a few minutes, switch off the ignition and disconnect the wiring plug from the cooling fan switch. Bridge the two contacts in the wiring plug using a length of spare wire, and switch on the ignition. If the fan now operates, the switch is probably faulty and should be renewed.

3 If the fan still fails to operate, check that full battery voltage is available at the brown and white wire terminal of the switch; if not, then there is a fault in the feed wire to the switch (possibly due to a fault in the fan motor, or a blown fuse). If there is no problem with the feed, check that there is continuity between

the switch brown wire terminal and a good earth point on the body; if not, then the earth connection is faulty and must be re-made.

4 If the switch and the wiring are in good condition, the fault must lie in the motor itself. The motor can be checked by disconnecting it from the wiring loom, and connecting a 12-volt supply directly to it. If the motor is faulty, it must be renewed, as no spares are available.

Removal

5 Disconnect the battery negative lead.

6 Disconnect the wiring from the cooling fan **(see illustration)**.

7 Unscrew the two fan shroud securing bolts, then tilt the assembly back slightly towards the engine, and withdraw it upwards away from the radiator **(see illustrations)**.

8.1 Cooling fan thermostatic switch (arrowed)

8.6 Disconnecting the cooling fan wiring plug

8.7A Cooling fan shroud securing bolt (arrowed) - C 20 XE model

8.7B Withdrawing the cooling fan shroud assembly - C 16 NZ model

3

8.10 Ensure that the left-hand lower end of the fan shroud locates correctly in the clip on the radiator

8 To separate the fan motor from the shroud, unscrew the three securing nuts.
9 No spare parts are available for the motor, and if the unit is faulty, it must be renewed.

Refitting

10 Refitting is a reversal of removal, but ensure that the left-hand lower end of the fan shroud locates correctly in the clip on the radiator **(see illustration)**.
11 On completion, start the engine and run it until it reaches normal operating temperature, then continue to run the engine and check that the cooling fan cuts in and functions correctly.

9 Cooling fan thermostatic switch - testing, removal and refitting

Testing

1 Testing of the switch is described in Section 8, as part of the cooling fan test procedure.

Removal

2 The switch is located in the lower right-hand side of the radiator. The engine and radiator should be cold before removing the switch.
3 Either partially drain the cooling system (as described in Section 3) to just below the level of the switch, or have ready a plug which can be used to plug the switch aperture in the radiator while the switch is removed. If a plug is used, take great care not to damage the radiator, and do not use anything which will allow foreign matter to enter the radiator.
4 Disconnect the battery negative lead.
5 Disconnect the wiring plug from the switch.
6 Carefully unscrew the switch from the radiator, and recover the sealing ring.

Refitting

7 Refitting is a reversal of removal, but use a new sealing ring, and refill the cooling system as described in Section 3.
8 On completion, start the engine and run it until it reaches normal operating temperature, then continue to run the engine and check that the cooling fan cuts in and functions correctly.

10 Coolant temperature gauge sender - testing, removal and refitting

Note: *Sealant will be required to coat the sender threads when refitting. Some models are fitted with a separate temperature sensor, which sends readings direct to the ECU. Refer to Chapter 4B for further details.*

Testing

1 The coolant temperature gauge, mounted in the instrument panel, is fed with a stabilised voltage supply from the instrument panel feed (via the ignition switch and a fuse), and its earth is controlled by the sender.
2 The sender is screwed into either the inlet manifold, the thermostat housing or on the coolant flange, depending on model **(see illustrations)**. The sender contains a thermistor, which consists of an electronic component whose electrical resistance decreases at a predetermined rate as its temperature rises. When the coolant is cold, the sender resistance is high, current flow through the gauge is reduced, and the gauge needle points towards the blue (cold) end of the scale. If the sender is faulty, it must be renewed.
3 If the gauge develops a fault, first check the other instruments. If they do not work at all, check the instrument panel electrical feed. If the readings are erratic, there may be a fault in the voltage stabiliser, which will need replacing (see Chapter 12). If the fault lies in the temperature gauge alone, check it as follows.
4 If the gauge needle remains at the 'cold' end of the scale, disconnect the sender wire and earth it to the cylinder head. If the needle then deflects when the ignition is switched on, the sender unit is faulty and should be renewed. If the needle still does not move, remove the instrument panel (Chapter 12) and check the continuity of the brown/white wire between the sender unit and the gauge and the feed to the gauge unit. If continuity is shown, and the fault still exists, then the gauge is faulty and should be replaced.
5 If the gauge needle remains at the 'hot' end of the scale, disconnect the sender wire. If the needle then returns to the 'cold' end of the scale when the ignition is switched on, the sender unit is faulty and should be renewed. If the needle still does not move, check the remainder of the circuit as described previously.

Removal

6 Partially drain the cooling system, as described in Section 3, to minimise coolant spillage.
7 Disconnect the battery negative lead.
8 Disconnect the wiring from the switch, then unscrew the switch from its location.

Refitting

9 Refitting is a reversal of removal, bearing in mind the following points.
10 Coat the threads of the sender with sealant before fitting.
11 Top-up the cooling system as described in Section 3.
12 On completion, start the engine and check the operation of the temperature gauge. Also check for coolant leaks.

10.2A Coolant temperature gauge sender (arrowed) - C 16 SE model

10.2B Coolant temperature gauge sender location (arrowed) - C 20 NE model

10.2C Coolant temperature gauge sender location (arrowed) - C 20 XE model

11 Coolant level sensor - testing, removal and refitting

Testing

1 On models fitted with a coolant level sensor, the sensor is located in the coolant expansion tank, and is an integral part of the expansion tank cap.

2 To test the sensor, with the engine cold, slowly unscrew the expansion tank cap to relieve any pressure in the cooling system.

3 Fully unscrew the cap, and carefully withdraw it, complete with the sensor.

4 Hold the cap/sensor assembly vertically, clear of the coolant in the expansion tank, taking care not to strain the wiring, then have an assistant switch on the ignition (do not start the engine).

5 Have your assistant observe the check control panel on the dashboard, which should indicate 'Coolant level'.

6 Switch off the ignition, and refit the cap/sensor assembly, then switch on the ignition again, and check that the check control panel does not indicate a problem.

7 If the sensor does not operate as described, check the wiring for obvious signs of damage.

8 If the wiring appears to be intact, further fault diagnosis must be entrusted to a Vauxhall dealer. Note that if the sensor is renewed, the cap and sensor must be renewed as an assembly.

Removal

9 The engine must be cold before attempting to remove the expansion tank cap.

10 Disconnect the battery negative lead.

11 Disconnect the wiring from the terminals on top of the expansion tank cap.

12 Slowly unscrew the expansion tank cap to relieve any pressure in the cooling system, then withdraw the cap/sensor assembly.

13 Note that the sensor is an integral part of the cap, and the two cannot be separated.

Refitting

14 Refitting is a reversal of removal.

12 Coolant pump - removal and refitting

Note: *A new pump O-ring will be required when refitting. Silicone Grease (Vauxhall P/N 90167353, or equivalent) will be required to coat the pump mounting face in the cylinder block. On certain models this procedure requires the timing belt to be removed, always replace a partly worn timing belt.*

12.4 Withdrawing the coolant pump (O-ring arrowed) - C 16 NZ model

SOHC models

Removal

1 Drain the cooling system, detailed in Section 3.

2 On 1.4 and 1.6 litre models, remove the rear timing belt cover as described in Chapter 2A. On 1.8 and 2.0 litre remove the timing belt and tension roller, referring to Chapter 2B.

3 Unscrew and remove the three coolant pump securing bolts.

4 Withdraw the coolant pump from the cylinder block, and recover the O-ring **(see illustration)**. It may be necessary to tap the pump lightly with a soft-faced hammer to free it from the cylinder block.

5 No overhaul of the pump is possible, and if faulty, the unit must be renewed.

Refitting

6 If the original pump is being refitted, ensure that the sealing surfaces are clean. Smear the pump mounting face in the cylinder block with a Silicone Grease (Vauxhall P/N 90167353, or equivalent).

7 Fit the pump using a new O-ring, but do not fully tighten the pump securing bolts until the timing belt has been fitted and tensioned (Chapter 2A).

8 Refit the rear timing belt cover, timing belt and tension roller (as applicable), referring to Chapter 2A or 2B.

9 Refill the cooling system as described in Section 3.

DOHC models

Removal

10 Drain the cooling system with reference to Section 3.

11 Remove the timing belt and rear cover, as described in Chapter 2B.

12 Unbolt the three coolant pump securing bolts.

13 Withdraw the coolant pump from the cylinder block, and remove the O-ring. It may be necessary to tap the pump lightly with a soft-faced hammer to free it from the cylinder block.

14 The timing belt rear cover can be removed from the pump by rotating the cover to release it from the flange on the pump.

12.17 Lugs (arrowed) on coolant pump and cylinder block must be aligned - C 20 XE model

15 No overhaul of the pump is possible, and if faulty, the unit must be renewed.

Refitting

16 If the original pump is being refitted, ensure that the sealing surfaces are clean. Smear the pump mounting face in the cylinder block with a Silicone Grease (Vauxhall P/N 90167353, or equivalent).

17 Fit the pump using a new O-ring. Ensure that the lugs on the pump and the cylinder block are aligned before tightening the pump securing bolts **(see illustration)**.

18 Refit the timing belt rear cover, as described in Chapter 2B.

19 Fit the timing belt, as described in Chapter 2B.

20 Refill the cooling system as described in Section 3.

13 Heating and ventilation system - general

1 The heating/ventilation system consists of a pollen filter, a three (or four), speed blower motor (housed in the engine compartment), face-level vents in the centre and at each end of the facia, and air ducts to the front and rear footwells **(see illustrations)**. During 1994 models were fitted with additional side vents to improve ventilation of the side windows.

2 The control unit is located in the facia, and the controls operate flap valves to deflect and mix the air flowing through the various parts of the heating/ventilation system. The flap valves are contained in the air distribution housing, which acts as a central distribution unit, passing air to the various ducts and vents.

3 Cold air enters the system through the grille at the rear of the engine compartment, and passes through the pollen filter. If required, the airflow is boosted by the blower, and then flows through the various ducts, according to the settings of the

3

13.1A View of heating/ventilation system airflow

13.1B Heating/ventilation system components (left-hand-drive model shown)

1 Air distribution housing	8 Passenger's side ventilation nozzle housing
2 Heater matrix	9 Heater blower motor assembly
3 Heater matrix lower cover	10 Driver's side air duct
4 Facia centre panel assembly	11 Centre air duct
5 Heater/ventilation control unit	12 Water drain tube
6 Pollen filter	13 Water deflector
7 Pollen filter housing	14 Windscreen cowl panel

controls. Stale air is expelled through ducts behind the rear bumper. If warm air is required, the cold air is passed over the heater matrix, which is heated by the engine coolant.

4 A recirculation switch enables the outside air supply to be closed off, while the air inside the vehicle is recirculated. This can be useful to prevent unpleasant odours entering from outside the vehicle, but should only be used briefly, as the recirculated air inside the vehicle will soon deteriorate.

5 Certain models may be fitted with heated front seats. The heat is produced by electrically-heated mats in the seat and backrest cushions. The temperature is regulated automatically by a thermostat, and cannot be adjusted.

14 Control unit, heater and ventilation - removal and refitting

Removal

1 Remove the facia centre panel assembly, as described in Chapter 11.

2 Carefully pull the heater/ventilation control unit forwards from the facia, taking care not to strain the control cables and wiring.

3 Release the securing clips, and disconnect the control cables from the air distribution and temperature control switches (two cables on the air distribution switch, one cable on the temperature switch), noting their locations **(see illustration)**.

4 Disconnect the wiring plug from the rear of the unit.

5 Disconnect the vacuum pipes from the rear of the air recirculation switch, noting their locations.

6 The heater/ventilation control unit can now be withdrawn from the vehicle.

7 The control unit illumination bulbs can be renewed by disconnecting the wires, and pulling the bulbholder from the rear of the

14.3 Heater/ventilation control unit connections

1 Cable end connection
2 Securing clip

14.7 Pulling the heater control switch illumination bulbholder from the rear of the control unit

control unit (see illustration). The bulbs are push-fits in the holders.

Refitting

8 Refitting is a reversal of removal, bearing in mind the following points.
9 Ensure that the control cables are securely reconnected in their correct locations, and that the cable runs are free from kinks and obstructions. Check the operation of the controls before finally refitting the facia centre panel assembly.
10 Refit the facia centre panel assembly as described in Chapter 11.

15 Control cables, heater and ventilation - removal and refitting

Lower air distribution control cable

Removal

1 Pull the heater/ventilation control unit forwards from the facia, as described in Section 14.
2 Release the securing clips, and disconnect the cable from the rear of the control unit.
3 Follow the run of the cable behind the facia, taking note of its routing, and disconnect the cable from the lever on the air distribution housing. The method of fastening is the same as that used at the control unit.

Refitting

4 Fit the new cable using a reversal of the removal procedure, noting the following points.
5 Ensure that the cable is correctly routed, and free from kinks and obstructions, and make sure that the cable securing clips are fastened correctly.
6 Refit the control unit as described in Section 14.

Upper air distribution control cable

Removal

7 Remove the instrument panel, as described in Chapter 12.

8 Disconnect the lower cable, as described earlier.
9 Follow the run of the cable behind the facia, taking note of its routing, and working through the instrument panel aperture, disconnect the end of the cable from the lever on the air distribution housing. Note that the method of fastening is the same as that used at the control unit.

Refitting

10 Refit lower cable, as described earlier.
11 Refit the instrument panel as described in Chapter 12.

Air temperature control cable

Removal

12 Release the securing clips, and remove the lower cover panel from under the passenger's side facia.
13 Where applicable, remove the securing screws, and withdraw the oddments tray from under the glovebox.
14 Disconnect the lower cable, as described earlier.
15 Follow the run of the cable behind the facia, taking note of its routing, and working up behind the passenger's footwell, disconnect the end of the cable from the lever on the air distribution housing. Note that the method of fastening is the same as that used at the control unit.

16.5 Disconnecting the heater blower motor wiring plug

16.7A Pollen filter housing assembly securing bolts (arrowed)

Refitting

16 Refit lower cable, as described earlier.
17 Refit the glovebox and the facia lower cover panel using a reversal of the removal procedure.

16 Heater blower motor - removal and refitting

Removal

1 Disconnect the battery negative lead.
2 Remove the pollen filter, as described in Chapter 1.
3 Remove the windscreen wiper arms, with reference to Chapter 12 if necessary.
4 Remove the windscreen cowl panel, as described in Chapter 11.
5 Disconnect the blower motor wiring plug, then prise the wiring grommet from the pollen filter housing, and pull the wiring through the aperture in the housing (see illustration).
6 Similarly, disconnect the vacuum pipes from the connector at the front of the housing, noting their routing (see illustration).
7 Unscrew the four securing bolts (two at the front, and two at the rear), and manipulate the pollen filter housing assembly from the scuttle (see illustrations).
8 Release the two securing clips, and remove

16.6 Disconnecting a vacuum pipe from the connector in the blower motor housing

16.7B Withdrawing the pollen filter housing assembly from the scuttle

 3

16.8 Removing the blower motor upper cover

16.9 Heater blower motor fixings

1 Wires   2 Motor securing screw

17.2A Heater blower motor wiring

1 Resistor securing screw   2 Wiring plugs

the blower motor upper cover **(see illustration)**.

9 Disconnect the two blower motor wires from the blower motor resistor, then remove the two blower motor securing screws, and carefully withdraw the motor assembly from its location **(see illustration)**.

Refitting

10 Refitting is a reversal of removal, bearing in mind the following points.

11 Ensure that the wiring and the vacuum pipes are securely reconnected and correctly routed.

12 Ensure that all panels are securely refitted, and that the weatherstrips are correctly engaged with the panels.

17.2B Removing the heater blower motor resistor

13 Refit the windscreen wiper arms with reference to Chapter 12.

17 Resistor, heater blower motor - removal and refitting

Removal

1 Remove the pollen filter, as described in Chapter 1, to expose the resistor.

2 Remove the single securing screw, then disconnect the wiring, and remove the resistor **(see illustrations)**.

Refitting

3 Refitting is a reversal of removal.

18.4 Detach the two tubes (arrowed) from the bottom of the air ducts

18 Heater matrix - removal and refitting

Removal

1 Either drain the cooling system as described in Section 3, or clamp the heater hoses (working in the engine compartment) at the bulkhead to reduce coolant loss when the hoses are disconnected.

2 Place a container beneath the heater hoses, then disconnect the hoses from the heater matrix stubs. Allow the coolant to drain into the container.

3 Remove the centre console, as described in Chapter 11.

4 Carefully detach the two tubes from the bottom of the air ducts in front of the heater matrix housing **(see illustration)**.

5 Remove the five screws securing the heater matrix lower cover (the front screw also secures the air ducts), then lift up the air ducts to enable the lower cover to be withdrawn **(see illustrations)**.

6 At this stage, it is advisable to lay a piece of plastic sheeting or similar under the heater matrix to prevent any coolant which may be released as the matrix is withdrawn from damaging the carpet.

7 Carefully withdraw the heater matrix from its housing (noting that the metal fins are

18.5A Remove the front . . .

18.5B . . . and rear heater matrix lower cover securing screws . . .

18.5C . . . and lower the cover

18.7 Withdraw the heater matrix (arrowed) from its housing

19.2 Air recirculation vacuum unit

20.1 Removing a facia ventilation nozzle

sharp, and can easily be damaged), and withdraw it from the vehicle **(see illustration)**.

Refitting

8 Refitting is a reversal of removal, noting the following points.

9 Make sure that the tubes are securely refitted to the air ducts.

10 Ensure that the coolant hoses are securely reconnected to the heater matrix stubs.

11 On completion, where applicable, refill the cooling system as described in Section 3.

---

19 Vacuum unit, air recirculation -
removal and refitting

Removal

1 Remove the glove compartment, as described in Chapter 11.

2 Reach up behind the facia, and locate the vacuum unit **(see illustration)**; access is limited.

3 Unclip the actuating rod from the end of the unit, and disconnect the vacuum hose.

4 Unclip the vacuum unit from its mounting.

Refitting

5 Refitting is a reversal of removal.

---

20 Vents, heater and ventilation -
removal and refitting

Ventilation nozzles

Removal

1 Carefully release the relevant nozzle from the facia, using a screwdriver with a piece of card under the blade, to avoid damage to the facia trim, then withdraw the nozzle **(see illustration)**.

Refitting

2 Simply push the nozzle into its housing in the facia until the securing lugs click into place.

Driver's side ventilation nozzle housing

Removal

3 Remove the steering column shrouds, as described in Chapter 11.

4 Remove the instrument panel surround, as described in Chapter 11.

5 Remove the ventilation nozzle, as described previously in this Section.

6 Remove the lighting rotary switch, as described in Chapter 12.

7 Remove the upper nozzle housing securing screw (located at the top of the nozzle aperture), and the lower securing screw (located at the bottom of the lighting switch aperture) **(see illustration)**.

8 Carefully pull out the housing securing clip, accessible from behind the left-hand side (right-hand-drive models), or the right-hand side (left-hand-drive models) of the housing, as applicable **(see illustration)**.

9 Carefully withdraw the housing from the facia, and unclip the wiring plugs from the rear of the housing **(see illustration)**.

10 The remaining switches can be removed from the housing by carefully pushing them out through the front of the housing from behind **(see illustration)**.

Refitting

11 Refitting is a reversal of removal, but ensure that the housing engages correctly with the air duct in the facia.

20.7 Removing the driver's side ventilation nozzle housing upper securing screw

20.8 Removing the ventilation nozzle housing securing clip

20.9 Withdrawing the ventilation nozzle housing from the facia

20.10 Levering the headlight aim adjustment switch from the ventilation nozzle housing

3

Passenger's side ventilation nozzle housing

Removal

12 Remove the glovebox, as described in Chapter 11.

13 Remove the ventilation nozzle, as described previously in this Section.

14 Remove the upper housing securing screw (located at the top of the nozzle aperture), and the lower securing screw

21.2 Hooked tool used to remove front seat heater switches

(located at the bottom of the housing, in the glovebox aperture), then carefully withdraw the housing from the facia.

Refitting

15 Refitting is a reversal of removal, but ensure that the housing engages correctly with the air duct in the facia.

21 Heated front seat components - removal and refitting

Heater switch

Removal

1 Disconnect the battery negative lead.

2 Using a length of wire, make up a hooked tool similar to that shown **(see illustration)**.

3 Carefully slide the tool round the top edge of the switch to release the securing lugs, then pull the switch forwards from the centre console.

4 Disconnect the wiring plug from the rear of the switch, and remove the switch.

Refitting

5 Refitting is a reversal of removal.

Heater mat

General

6 For access to the heater mats, the seat must be dismantled, and the upholstery must be removed (by unstitching). The procedure for this involves removing the seat back, which is secured by rivets.

7 Due to the difficulty involved in removing the upholstery, and the possible risk of injury to the vehicle occupants, should the seat be reassembled incorrectly, this task is considered to be beyond the scope of this manual.

22 Heater blower and heated rear screen switch - removal and refitting

Removal

1 Carefully remove the switches knob using a small screwdriver.

2 Remove the switches retaining clips and remove the switch.

3 The illumination bulb can now be replaced, if necessary.

Refitting

4 Refitting is a reversal of removal.

Chapter 4 Part A
Fuel system - carburettor models

Contents

Degrees of difficulty

Easy, suitable for novice with little experience 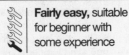	**Fairly easy,** suitable for beginner with some experience	**Fairly difficult,** suitable for competent DIY mechanic	**Difficult,** suitable for experienced DIY mechanic	**Very difficult,** suitable for expert DIY or professional

Specifications

System type

Carburettor type	Pierburg 2E3
Application *	14 NV model
Choke type	Automatic

* For details of engine code location, see 'Buying spare parts and vehicle identification numbers'.

Fuel pump

Type	Mechanical, camshaft driven

Carburettor data

Idle speed	925 ± 25 rpm	
Idle mixture CO content	$1.0 \pm 0.5\%$	
Fast idle speed	2200 to 2600 rpm	
Choke valve gap	1.5 to 3.5 mm	
Choke pull-down gap:		
'Small'	1.7 to 2.1 mm	
'Large'	2.5 to 2.9 mm	
Idle fuel jet	45	
Idle air bleed	130	
	Primary	**Secondary**
Venturi diameter	20.0 mm	24.0 mm
Main jet	X95	X110

Torque wrench settings

	Nm	lbf ft
Exhaust downpipe to manifold	25	18
Exhaust manifold	22	16
Fuel pump	18	13
Fuel tank mounting strap	20	15
Inlet manifold	22	16

1 System information and precautions - general

General

1 The fuel system on carburettor models comprises a fuel tank, a fuel pump, a vapour separator (not fitted to all models), a downdraught carburettor, and a thermostatically-controlled air cleaner.

2 The fuel tank is mounted under the rear of the vehicle, forward of the rear suspension. The tank is ventilated to the atmosphere, and is filled from the right-hand side of the vehicle through a simple filler pipe. The fuel gauge sender unit is mounted inside the tank.

3 The fuel pump is a mechanical diaphragm type, operated by a pushrod which is in turn actuated by a lobe on the camshaft.

4 The fuel vapour separator (where fitted) is used to stabilise the fuel supply to the carburettor. Vapour is purged from the carburettor fuel supply, thus improving hot starting qualities.

5 The carburettor is a Pierburg 2E3 type, a full description of which is given in Section 12.

6 The air cleaner has a vacuum-controlled air intake, supplying a blend of hot and cold air to suit the prevailing engine operating conditions.

Precautions

7 Certain adjustment points in the fuel system are protected by tamperproof caps, plugs or seals. In some territories, it is an offence to drive a vehicle with broken of missing tamperproof seals. Before disturbing a tamperproof seal, check that no local or national laws will be broken by doing so, and fit a new tamperproof seal after adjustment is complete where this is required by law. Do not break tamperproof seals on a vehicle which is still under warranty.

8 When working on fuel system components, scrupulous cleanliness must be observed, and care must be taken not to introduce any foreign matter into fuel lines or components. Carburettors in particular are delicate instruments, and care should be taken not to disturb any components unnecessarily. Before attempting work on a carburettor, ensure that the relevant spares are available. If the problems persist, it is recommended that the advice of a Vauxhall dealer or carburettor specialist is sought. Most dealers will be able to provide carburettor re-jetting and servicing facilities, and if necessary it should be possible to buy a reconditioned carburettor.

9 Refer to Chapter 5 for precautions to be observed when working on vehicles fitted with electronic control units.

 Warning: Many of the procedures in this Chapter require the removal of fuel lines and connections which may result in some fuel spillage. Before carrying out any operation on the fuel system refer to the precautions given in 'Safety first!' at the beginning of this manual, and follow them implicitly. Petrol is a highly dangerous and volatile liquid and the precautions necessary when handling it cannot be overstressed.

2 Unleaded petrol - general information and usage

Note: *The information given in this Section is correct at the time of writing, and applies only to petrol currently available in the EC. If in any doubt as to the suitability of petrol or if using the vehicle outside the EC, consult a Vauxhall dealer or one of the motoring organisations for advice on the petrol available, and their suitability for your vehicle.*

1 Vauxhall recommend the use of 95 RON (Premium) unleaded petrol in carburettor models; 98 RON (Super or 'Super Plus') unleaded petrol can be used without modification.

2 97 or 98 RON leaded (4-star) petrol can be used without modification in carburettor models not equipped with a catalytic converter. **Do not** use leaded petrol in models equipped with a catalytic converter, or the (expensive) catalyst unit will be ruined.

3 Air cleaner intake air temperature control system - testing

1 The air cleaner is thermostatically-controlled, to provide air at the most suitable temperature for combustion with minimum exhaust emission levels.

2 The optimum air temperature is achieved by drawing in cold air from an air intake at the front of the vehicle, and blending it with hot air from a shroud on the exhaust manifold. The proportion of hot air and cold air is varied by the position of a flap valve in the air cleaner intake spout, which is controlled by a vacuum diaphragm unit. The vacuum applied to the diaphragm type is regulated by a heat sensor located within the air cleaner body.

3 To check the operation of the air temperature control, the engine must be cold. First check the position of the flap valve. Disconnect the hot air tube from the air cleaner spout, and check (by probing with a finger) that the flap is closed to admit only cold air from outside the vehicle **(see illustrations)**. Start the engine, and check that the flap now opens to admit only hot air from the exhaust manifold.

4 Temporarily reconnect the hot air tube to the air cleaner spout.

5 Run the engine until it reaches normal operating temperature.

6 Disconnect the hot air tube again, and check that the flap is now closed to admit only cold air from outside the vehicle, or in hot weather, a mixture of hot and cold air. Reconnect the hot air tube after making the check.

7 If the flap does not function correctly, the air cleaner must be renewed, as parts are not available individually.

4 Air cleaner housing assembly - removal and refitting

Removal

1 Disconnect the air hose from the airbox on the carburettor.

2 Remove the air cleaner filter element, as described in Chapter 1.

3 Slacken the air cleaner housing assembly securing nuts (one front and one rear), and pull the assembly from the body panel.

Refitting

4 Refitting is a reversal of removal.

3.3A Exhaust manifold-to-air cleaner hot air tube

3.3B Checking the operation of the air cleaner flap valve

5.7 Disconnecting a fuel hose from the fuel pump

5.8 Withdrawing the fuel pump and plastic insulating block

Refitting

11 Refitting is a reversal of removal, remembering the following points.
12 Examine the condition of the sealing ring and renew if necessary.
13 Ensure that the marks made on the sender unit and fuel tank before removal are aligned.
14 Ensure that the hoses are reconnected to their correct locations as noted during removal.
15 On completion, fill the fuel tank, then run the engine and check for leaks. Also check that the fuel gauge reads correctly. If leakage is evident, stop the engine immediately and rectify the problem without delay. Note that the engine may take a longer time than usual to start when the sender unit has lbeen removed, as the fuel pump refills with fuel.

5 Fuel pump - testing, removal and refitting

Note: *Refer to the warning note in Section 1 before proceeding.*

Testing

1 Disconnect the ignition coil HT lead.
2 Place a wad of clean rag under the pump outlet, then disconnect the pump outlet hose. Be prepared for fuel spillage, and take adequate fire precautions.
3 Have an assistant crank the engine on the starter. Well-defined spurts of fuel should be ejected from the pump outlet - if not, the pump is probably faulty (or the tank is empty). Dispose of the fuel-soaked rag safely.
4 No spare parts are available for the pump, and if faulty, the unit must be renewed.

Removal

5 The fuel pump is located at the right-hand end of the camshaft housing.
6 Disconnect the battery negative lead.
7 Disconnect the fuel hoses from the pump **(see illustration)**. If necessary, label the hoses so that they can be reconnected to their original locations. Be prepared for fuel spillage, and take adequate fire precautions. Plug the open ends of the hoses to prevent dirt ingress and further fuel spillage.
8 Unscrew the two securing bolts, and withdraw the pump from the camshaft housing **(see illustration)**.
9 Recover the plastic insulating block.

Refitting

10 Refitting is a reversal of removal, but ensure that the fuel hoses are reconnected to their correct locations as noted during removal, and tighten the securing bolts to the specified torque.
11 Run the engine and check for leaks on completion. If leakage is evident, stop the engine immediately and rectify the problem without delay. Note that the engine may take a longer time than usual to start when the pump has been removed as the pump refills with fuel.

6 Fuel gauge sender unit - removal and refitting

Note: *Refer to the warning in Section 1 before proceeding.*

Removal

1 Disconnect the battery negative lead.
2 Siphon out any remaining fuel in the tank through the filler pipe. Siphon the fuel into a clean metal container that can be sealed.
3 Chock the front wheels, then jack up the rear of the vehicle and support securely on axle stands.
4 The sender unit is located in the front face of the fuel tank.
5 Make alignment marks on the sender unit and the fuel tank so that the unit can be refitted in its original position.
6 Disconnect the wiring plug from the sender unit **(see illustration)**.
7 Pull back the plastic cover **(see illustration)**, then disconnect the fuel hose(s) from the sender unit. Be prepared for fuel spillage, and take adequate fire precautions. Plug the open end(s) of the hose(s) to prevent dirt ingress and further fuel loss.
8 To remove the sender unit, engage a flat piece of metal as a lever between two of the slots on the sender unit rim, and turn the sender unit anti-clockwise.
9 Withdraw the unit carefully, to avoid bending the float arm.
10 Remove the sealing ring.

6.6 Disconnecting the wiring plug from the fuel gauge sender unit

7 Fuel vapour separator - removal and refitting

Note: *Refer to the warning in Section 1 before proceeding.*

Removal

1 Where fitted, the vapour separator is located on a bracket attached to the side of the carburettor.
2 Note the locations of the three fuel hoses, labelling them if necessary to aid refitting, then disconnect the hoses from the vapour separator. Be prepared for fuel spillage, and take adequate fire precautions. Clamp or plug the open ends of the hoses, to prevent dirt ingress and further fuel spillage.
3 Remove the two securing screws, and lift the vapour separator from its bracket.

Refitting

4 Check the body of the separator for cracks or leaks before refitting, and renew if necessary.
5 Refitting is a reversal of removal, but ensure that the three fuel hoses are connected to their correct locations as noted during removal.

 4A

6.7 Pulling the plastic cover from the fuel gauge sender unit

8.5 Removing the fuel filter from the carburettor fuel inlet pipe

8 Fuel filter - removal and refitting

Removal

1 The fuel filter is located in the carburettor fuel inlet pipe.

2 Disconnect the trunking from the air cleaner, then disconnect the vacuum pipe and breather hose from the airbox. Extract the three securing screws and lift off the airbox, complete with air trunking.

3 Place a wad of rag under the fuel inlet pipe at the carburettor to catch any fuel that may be spilled during the procedure.

4 Disconnect the fuel inlet hose from the carburettor. Be prepared for fuel spillage, and clamp or plug the end of the hose to reduce unnecessary fuel loss. Take adequate fire precautions.

5 To remove the filter, carefully screw an M3 bolt approximately 5.0 mm into the end of the filter, and pull on the bolt to withdraw the filter from the end of the inlet pipe **(see illustration)**.

Refitting

6 Push the new filter into the inlet pipe, ensuring that it engages securely, then reconnect the fuel inlet hose, and refit the airbox.

9 Fuel tank - removal and refitting

Note: *Refer to the warning in Section 1 before proceeding.*

Saloon and Hatchback models

Removal

1 Disconnect the battery negative lead.

2 Proceed as described in Section 6, paragraphs 1 to 3 inclusive.

3 Disconnect the exhaust system front flexible joint (see Chapter 4C). Suspend the front section of the exhaust system with wire or string from the underbody.

4 Disconnect the rear section of the exhaust system from its rubber mountings, and allow it to rest on the rear suspension torsion beam. It is advisable to support the centre section of the exhaust system with wire or string from the underbody to avoid straining the system.

5 Release the handbrake cables from the clips on the tank (right-hand cable) and tank securing strap (left-hand cable), and move them clear of the tank **(see illustration)**. On certain models, it may be necessary to slacken the cable adjuster to enable the cables to be moved clear of the tank (see Chapter 9).

6 Where applicable, remove the fuel filter from the side of the fuel tank. Refer to Section 8.

7 Clamp the fuel hose(s) running to the fuel gauge sender unit. This is located in the right-hand side of the tank. Then position a container under the sender unit to catch the fuel which will be released as the hose(s) are disconnected.

8 Pull back the plastic cover, then disconnect the hose(s) from the sender unit. Be prepared for fuel spillage, and take adequate fire precautions.

9 Disconnect the wiring plug from the fuel gauge sender unit. Disconnect the hose and wiring from the fuel pump, if applicable.

10 Disconnect the filler and vent hoses from the rear of the fuel tank **(see illustration)**.

11 Support the weight of the fuel tank on a jack with interposed block of wood.

12 Unscrew the securing nuts from the tank mounting straps **(see illustration)**, then remove the straps and lower the tank sufficiently to enable the disconnection of the remaining vent hose(s).

13 With the aid of an assistant, carefully lower the tank, and withdraw it from under the vehicle. Note that as the tank is withdrawn, some residual fuel may be released.

Refitting

14 If the tank contains sediment or water, it may be cleaned out using two or three rinses with clean fuel. Shake vigorously using several changes of fuel, but before doing so, remove the fuel gauge sender unit, as described in Section 6. *This procedure should be carried out in a well-ventilated area, and it is vital to take adequate fire precautions.*

15 Any repairs to the fuel tank should be carried out by a professional. **Do not** under any circumstances attempt to weld or solder a fuel tank. Removal of all residual fuel vapours requires several hours of specialist cleaning.

16 Refitting is a reversal of removal, remembering the following points.

17 Ensure that all hoses and pipes are securely reconnected to their correct locations, as noted before removal.

18 Where applicable, refit the fuel filter. Refer to Section 8.

19 If the handbrake cable adjuster has been slackened, adjust the handbrake cables as described in Chapter 9.

20 On completion, fill the fuel tank, then run the engine and check for leaks. If leakage is evident, stop the engine immediately and rectify the problem without delay. Note that the engine may take a longer time than usual to start, as the pump refills with fuel.

Estate and Van models

Removal

21 Proceed as described in Section 6, paragraphs 1 to 3 inclusive.

22 Disconnect the filler and vent hoses from the side of the tank.

9.5 Handbrake cables (arrowed) clipped to fuel tank and tank securing strap - Saloon and Hatchback models

9.10 Filler and vent hose connections at rear of fuel tank - Hatchback model

9.12 Fuel tank mounting strap nut

9.23 Disconnect the hoses (1 and 2) from the fuel filler assembly - Estate and Van models

10.2 Removing an airbox securing screw

10.3A Extract the throttle cable end clip . . .

23 Disconnect the hoses shown **(see illustration)** from the fuel filler assembly.
24 Support the weight of the fuel tank on a jack with interposed block of wood.
25 Unscrew the securing bolts from the tank mounting straps, then remove the straps, and with the aid of an assistant, carefully lower the tank and withdraw it from under the vehicle. Note that as the tank is withdrawn, some residual fuel may be released.

Refitting

26 Refer to paragraphs 14 and 15.
27 Refitting is a reversal of removal, but ensure that all hoses and pipes are securely reconnected to their correct locations, as noted before removal.
28 On completion, fill the fuel tank, then run the engine and check for leaks. If leakage is evident, stop the engine immediately and rectify the problem without delay. Note that the engine may take a longer time than usual to start, as the pump refills with fuel.

10 Throttle cable - removal, refitting and adjustment

Removal

1 Disconnect the air trunking from the air cleaner, then disconnect the vacuum pipe and breather hose from the airbox.

2 Extract the three securing screws **(see illustration)** and lift off the airbox, complete with the air trunking.
3 Extract the clip from the cable end fitting at the bracket on the carburettor, then slide the cable end grommet from the bracket **(see illustrations)**.
4 Slide the cable end from the throttle valve lever on the carburettor.
5 Working inside the vehicle, release the securing clips, and remove the lower trim panel from the driver's footwell **(see illustration)**.
6 Pull the cable retainer from the top of the pedal, and disconnect the cable end from the pedal.
7 Make a careful note of the cable routing, then withdraw the cable through the bulkhead into the engine compartment.

Refitting

8 Refitting is a reversal of removal, remembering the following points.
9 Ensure that the cable is correctly routed, as noted before removal.
10 Ensure that the bulkhead grommet is correctly seated in its aperture.
11 On completion, check the throttle mechanism for satisfactory operation, and if necessary adjust the cable, as described in the following paragraphs.

Adjustment

12 Two points of cable adjustment are provided. A stop screw is located on the pedal arm to control the fully released position of the pedal stop. A clip is located on a threaded section of the cable sheath at the bracket on the carburettor, to adjust the cable free play **(see illustration)**.
13 The cable should be adjusted so that when the throttle pedal is released, there is very slight free play in the cable at the carburettor end.
14 Check that when the throttle pedal is fully depressed, the throttle valve is fully open. Adjust the position of the clip on the cable sheath and the pedal stop screw, as necessary.

11 Throttle pedal - removal and refitting

Removal

1 Working inside the vehicle, release the securing clips, and remove the lower trim panel from the driver's footwell.
2 Pull the cable retainer from the top of the pedal, and disconnect the cable end from the pedal.

4A

10.3B . . . and slide the grommet from the bracket

10.5 Removing the lower trim panel from the driver's footwell

10.12 Throttle pedal stop screw

11.3 Throttle pedal pivot assembly - circlip arrowed

3 Extract the circlip from the right-hand end of the pedal pivot shaft, then slide out the pivot shaft from the left-hand side of the pedal pivot bracket **(see illustration)**. Recover the pivot bushes and the pedal return spring.

Refitting

4 Before refitting the pedal components, examine the pivot bushes for wear, and renew if necessary.
5 Refitting is a reversal of removal, but on completion check the throttle mechanism for satisfactory operation, and check the throttle cable adjustment, as described in Section 10.

12.1A Side view of carburettor

1 Accelerator pump
2 Main choke pull-down diaphragm unit

12.1B Side view of carburettor

1 Automatic choke housing
2 Vapour separator
3 Secondary throttle valve

12 Carburettor - general information

1 The Pierburg 2E3 carburettor is of twin-venturi, fixed-jet sequential throttle type **(see illustrations)**. The primary throttle valve operates alone except at high speeds and loads, when the secondary throttle valve is operated, until at full-throttle, both are fully open. This arrangement allows good fuel economy during light acceleration and cruising, but also gives maximum power at full-throttle. The secondary throttle valve is vacuum-operated, according to the vacuum produced in the primary venturi. The primary throttle barrel and venturi diameters are smaller than their secondary counterparts. The carburettor is a complicated instrument, with various refinements and sub-systems added to achieve improved driveability, economy and exhaust emission levels.
2 A separate idle system operates independently from the main jet system, supplying fuel controlled by a mixture control screw.
3 The main jets are calibrated to suit engine requirements at mid-range throttle openings. To provide the necessary fuel enrichment at full-throttle, a vacuum-operated power valve is used. The valve provides extra fuel under the low vacuum conditions associated with wide throttle openings.
4 To provide an enriched mixture during acceleration, an accelerator pump delivers extra fuel to the primary main venturi. The accelerator pump is operated mechanically by a cam on the throttle linkage.
5 A fully automatic choke is fitted, operated by a coolant and electrically heated bi-metal coil. When the engine is cold, the bi-metal coil is fully wound up, holding the choke plate (fitted to the primary barrel) closed. As the engine warms up, the bi-metal coil is heated and therefore unwinds, progressively opening the choke plate. A vacuum-operated pull-down system is employed, whereby, if the engine is under choke but is only cruising (i.e.

12.1C Side view of carburettor

1 Secondary choke pull-down solenoid
2 Power valve

not under heavy load), the choke plate is opened against the action of the bi-metal coil. The pull-down system prevents an over-rich mixture, which would otherwise reduce fuel economy and may cause unnecessary engine wear when the engine is cold. A secondary pull-down solenoid is fitted, which operates in conjunction with the main diaphragm unit to modify the pull-down characteristics, improving fuel economy.
6 An unusual feature of the Pierburg carburettor is that the float level is set in production, and cannot be adjusted.

13 Carburettor - removal and refitting

Note: *Refer to the warning in Section 1 before proceeding. New gasket(s) must be used when refitting the carburettor.*

Removal

1 Disconnect the battery negative lead.
2 Disconnect the trunking from the air cleaner, then disconnect the vacuum pipe and breather hose from the airbox. Extract the three securing screws and lift off the airbox, complete with air trunking.
3 Disconnect the fuel supply hose from the carburettor, or disconnect the fuel supply and return hoses from the vapour separator, as applicable. Be prepared for fuel spillage, and take adequate fire precautions. Clamp or plug the end of the hose(s), to prevent dirt ingress and further fuel spillage.
4 Extract the clip from the throttle cable end fitting at the bracket on the carburettor, then slide the cable end grommet from the bracket, and slide the cable end from the throttle valve lever.
5 Disconnect the coolant hoses from the automatic choke housing, noting their locations as an aid to refitting **(see illustration)**. Be prepared for coolant spillage, and clamp or plug the hoses, or secure them with their ends facing upwards, to prevent further coolant loss.
6 Disconnect the two vacuum pipes from the

13.5 Disconnecting the coolant hoses from the automatic choke housing

13.6 Disconnecting a vacuum pipe from the front of the carburettor

13.7 Disconnecting the choke heater wiring plug

13.8 Carburettor securing nuts (A) and top cover securing screws (B)

front of the carburettor, noting their locations and routing for use when refitting **(see illustration)**.

7 Disconnect the choke heater wiring plug **(see illustration)**.

8 Unscrew the three securing nuts, and withdraw the carburettor from the inlet manifold studs **(see illustration)**.

9 Recover the gasket(s) and insulator block which fit between the carburettor and the inlet manifold.

Refitting

10 Refitting is a reversal of removal, but renew the gasket(s).

11 On completion, carry out the following checks and adjustments.

12 Check the throttle cable free play and adjust if necessary, as described in Section 10.

13 Check and if necessary top-up the coolant level, as described in Chapter 3.

14 Check and if necessary adjust the idle speed and mixture, as described in Chapter 1.

14 Carburettor - fault diagnosis, overhaul and adjustments

Note: *Refer to the warning in Section 1 before proceeding. All gaskets and seals should be renewed on reassembly.*

Fault diagnosis

1 Faults with the carburettor are usually associated with dirt entering the float chamber and blocking the jets, causing a weak mixture or power failure within a certain engine speed range. If this is the case, then a thorough clean will normally cure the problem. If the carburettor is well worn, uneven running may be caused by air entering through the throttle valve spindle bearings.

2 If a carburettor fault is suspected, always check first (where possible) that the ignition timing is correct, and that the spark plugs are in good condition and correctly gapped. Also check that the throttle cable is correctly

adjusted, and that the air cleaner filter element is clean. Remember that it is possible that one of the hydraulic valve lifters may be faulty, resulting in an incorrect valve clearance.

3 If careful checking of all the preceding points produces no improvement, the carburettor should be removed for cleaning and overhaul.

Overhaul and adjustments

4 The following paragraphs describe cleaning and adjustment procedures which can be carried out by the home mechanic after the carburettor has been removed from the inlet manifold (see Section 13). If the carburettor is worn or damaged, it should either be renewed or overhauled by a specialist, who will be able to restore the carburettor to its original calibration.

5 With the carburettor removed, clean all external dirt from the carburettor, then remove the four carburettor top cover securing screws, noting their locations, as two lengths of screw are used.

6 Lift off the top cover, and recover the gasket.

7 Access to the carburettor jets in the top cover can now be obtained **(see illustration)**.

8 Blow through the jets and drillings with compressed air (wear eye protection), or air from a foot pump - do not probe them with wire. If the jets are to be removed, unscrew them carefully using tools of the correct size.

9 Remove the fuel filter from the inlet pipe by carefully screwing an M3 bolt approximately 5.0 mm into the end of the filter, and pulling on the bolt to withdraw the filter from the end of the inlet pipe. Push a new filter into the inlet pipe, ensuring that it engages securely.

10 Carefully clean any foreign matter from the float chamber.

11 Removal and refitting of the float and automatic choke unit, and renewal of the various diaphragm units, is described in the following Sections.

12 Further dismantling is not recommended.

13 Reassemble in the reverse order to dismantling. Use new gaskets and seals throughout.

14 Refit the carburettor as described in Section 13.

15 Needle valve and float - removal, inspection and refitting

Note: *Refer to the warning in Section 1 before proceeding. A new carburettor top cover gasket should be used on refitting. A tachometer and an exhaust gas analyser will be required to check the idle speed and mixture on completion.*

Removal

1 Disconnect the battery negative lead.

2 Disconnect the air trunking from the air cleaner, then disconnect the vacuum pipe and breather hose from the airbox.

3 Extract the three securing screws and lift off the airbox, complete with the air trunking.

4 Thoroughly clean all external dirt from the carburettor.

5 Disconnect the fuel supply hose at the carburettor. Be prepared for fuel spillage, and take adequate fire precautions. Plug the end of hose, to prevent dirt ingress and further fuel spillage.

6 Identify the automatic choke coolant hose locations as an aid to refitting, then disconnect the hoses. Be prepared for coolant spillage, and clamp or plug the hoses, or secure them with their ends facing upwards to prevent further coolant loss.

7 Disconnect the choke heater wiring plug.

8 Disconnect the two vacuum hoses from the choke pull-down unit.

14.7 Main jets in top cover

1 Primary main jet   2 Secondary main jet

4A

15.11 Float assembly in top cover

1 Float retaining pin   3 Needle valve
2 Float

16.6 Secondary throttle valve vacuum
diaphragm unit

1 Bracket   2 Diaphragm unit

17.4 Power valve components

1 Cover   3 Diaphragm assembly
2 Spring

9 Remove the four carburettor top cover securing screws, noting their locations, as two lengths of screw are used.
10 Lift off the top cover, and recover the gasket.
11 Using a pin punch, tap the float retaining pin from the base of the top cover, and lift out the float and needle valve **(see illustration)**.

Inspection

12 Inspect the components for damage, and renew as necessary. Check the needle valve for wear, and check the float for leaks by shaking it to see if it contains petrol.

Refitting

13 Clean the mating faces of the carburettor body and top cover.
14 Refitting is a reversal of removal, remembering the following points.
15 After refitting, check the float and needle valve for full and free movement. Note that no adjustment of the float is possible.
16 Use a new gasket between the top cover and the carburettor body.
17 Ensure that all hoses, pipes and wires are correctly reconnected.
18 On completion, check and if necessary top-up the coolant level, as described in Chapter 3, and check and if necessary adjust the idle speed and mixture, as described in Chapter 1.

16 Secondary throttle valve vacuum diaphragm -
removal and refitting

Note: *The diaphragm unit must be renewed in its entirety, as no spares are available.*

Removal

1 Proceed as described in Section 15, paragraphs 2 and 3.
2 Disconnect the diaphragm unit vacuum pipe from the carburettor.
3 Prise the diaphragm operating rod balljoint from the secondary throttle valve linkage.
4 Where applicable, remove the two securing screws and lift the vapour separator from the

bracket. Move the vapour separator to one side, taking care not to strain the fuel hoses.
5 If necessary, for improved access, remove the choke housing as described in Section 19, paragraphs 2 and 3.
6 Remove the four securing screws, and withdraw the diaphragm unit, complete with its bracket from the carburettor body **(see illustration)**.

Refitting

7 Fit the new diaphragm using a reversal of the removal procedure.
8 Where applicable, when refitting the choke bi-metal housing, ensure that the bi-metal spring is correctly engaged with the choke lever, and align the marks on the bi-metal housing and choke housing as noted before removal

17 Power valve diaphragm -
removal and refitting

Note: *Refer to the warning in Section 1 before proceeding.*

Removal

1 Disconnect the battery negative lead.
2 Proceed as described in Section 15, paragraphs 2 and 3.
3 Thoroughly clean all external dirt from the area around the power valve housing.
4 Remove the two securing screws, and lift off the power valve cover, spring, and diaphragm assembly **(see illustration)**.
5 Clean the mating faces of the cover and housing.

Refitting

6 Fit the new diaphragm as follows.
7 Locate the spring on the cover and diaphragm assembly, ensuring that it is correctly seated, then press the diaphragm assembly and cover together. Note that the vacuum hole in the diaphragm must align with the corresponding holes in the housing flange and cover.
8 Further fitting is a reversal of removal, but ensure that the diaphragm is correctly seated.

18 Accelerator pump diaphragm -
removal and refitting

Note: *Refer to the warning in Section 1 before proceeding.*

Removal

1 Proceed as described in Section 15, paragraphs 1 to 3.
2 Thoroughly clean all external dirt from the area around the accelerator pump housing.
3 Remove the four securing screws, and lift off the accelerator pump cover. Recover the diaphragm, spring, valve retainer and valve **(see illustration)**. Note the orientation of the valve retainer.
4 Clean the mating faces of the cover and housing.

Refitting

5 Check the condition of the valve, and renew if necessary.
6 Begin fitting of the new diaphragm by locating the valve, valve retainer and spring in the housing. Note that the valve retainer can only be fitted in one position. The larger diameter of the spring should rest against the valve retainer.

18.3 Accelerator pump components

1 Cover with   3 Spring
  operating lever   4 Valve
2 Diaphragm   5 Air passage

7 Locate the diaphragm on the housing, ensuring that the spring is correctly seated, and refit the cover. Tighten the cover securing screws progressively to avoid distorting the diaphragm.

8 Further fitting is a reversal of removal.

19 Automatic choke unit - removal, refitting and adjustment

Note: *Refer to the warning in Section 1 before proceeding. A tachometer and an exhaust gas analyser will be required to check the idle speed and mixture on completion. If the coolant housing is removed, new O-rings must be used on refitting.*

Removal

1 Proceed as described in Section 15, paragraphs 1 to 3.

2 Note the position of the bi-metal housing alignment marks as an aid to refitting, if necessary making additional marks for clarity **(see illustration)**. Then remove the three securing screws and lift off the bi-metal housing. Place the housing to one side, taking care not to strain the coolant hoses or electric choke heater wiring.

3 Remove the three screws securing the choke housing to the carburettor body, and withdraw the choke assembly, taking care not to bend the choke operating rod.

4 If it is necessary to remove the bi-metal housing for renewal, continue as follows; otherwise go on to paragraph 8.

5 Identify the automatic choke coolant hose locations as an aid to refitting, then disconnect the hoses. Be prepared for coolant spillage, and clamp or plug the hoses, or secure them with their ends facing upwards, to prevent further loss of coolant.

6 Disconnect the wiring from the electric choke heater, and withdraw the bi-metal housing.

7 The coolant housing can be separated from the bi-metal housing by unscrewing the central securing bolt. Recover the O-rings from under the bolt head, and from the rim of the coolant housing.

Refitting

8 Begin refitting by locating the choke assembly on the carburettor body, ensuring that the lever on the choke assembly engages with the choke operating rod. Tighten the three securing screws.

9 Check and if necessary adjust the choke valve gap and the fast idle cam position, as described later in this Section.

10 Connect the bi-metal spring to the choke lever, position the bi-metal housing and the choke housing as noted during removal, then tighten the securing screws.

11 Where applicable, refit the coolant housing to the bi-metal housing, using new O-rings if necessary, and reconnect the coolant hoses and the electric choke heater wiring.

19.2 Automatic choke bi-metal housing alignment marks (circled)

12 Further refitting is a reversal of removal, remembering the following points.

13 If the coolant hoses have been disconnected, check the coolant level, as described in Chapter 3.

14 Check and if necessary adjust the fast idle speed, as described later in this Section.

Adjustment

Choke valve gap

15 With the bi-metal housing removed as described previously in this Section, continue as follows.

16 Press the choke operating lever fully clockwise, and retain it in position with a rubber band.

17 Move the throttle lever to the fully open position, and measure the choke valve gap between the lower side of the choke plate and the wall of the primary barrel. Check that the gap is as given in the Specifications.

18 If necessary, adjust the choke valve gap by bending the segment (2), **(see illustration)**. If the gap is too small, enlarge the gap (B), by levering with a screwdriver. If the gap is too large, decrease gap (B) using a pair of pliers.

19 If no further adjustments are to be carried out, refit the bi-metal housing as described previously in this Section.

Fast idle cam position

20 With the bi-metal housing removed, and the choke valve gap 'A', **(see illustration)** correctly set as described previously in this Section, continue as follows.

19.20 Fast idle cam adjustment

1 Fast idle cam
2 Adjustment lever
3 Choke drive lever

4 Fast idle speed adjustment screw
A Choke valve gap

19.18 Choke valve gap adjustment

1 Choke operating lever   B Choke valve gap
2 Adjuster segment

21 Open the throttle valve, then close the choke valve using light finger pressure on the choke drive lever. Close the throttle valve.

22 Check that the fast idle speed adjustment screw is resting against the stop on the second-highest step of the fast idle cam.

23 If adjustment is required, first check that the choke return spring is correctly positioned, then adjust by bending the lever (2).

24 Refit the bi-metal housing as described previously in this Section.

Fast idle speed adjustment

Note: *To carry out the adjustment, an accurate tachometer and an exhaust gas analyser will be required.*

25 Check the idle speed and mixture, as described in Chapter 1. The idle speed **must** be correct before attempting to check or adjust the fast idle speed.

26 With the engine at normal operating temperature, and a tachometer connected according to the equipment manufacturer's instructions, continue as follows.

27 Position the fast idle speed adjustment screw on the second-highest step of the cam **(see illustration)**.

19.27 Fast idle speed adjustment

3 Fast idle speed adjustment screw
4 Fast idle cam - screw positioned on second-highest step

4A

19.29 Tamperproof cap (arrowed) covering fast idle speed adjustment screw

20.11 Secondary choke pull-down solenoid securing screw and earth lead

20.17 Checking the vacuum pull-down gap using a twist drill

28 Start the engine without touching the throttle pedal, and check that the fast idle speed is as specified. If adjustment is required, stop the engine, and continue as follows.

29 Remove the tamperproof cap from the fast idle speed adjustment screw - ensure that no local or national laws are being broken by doing so **(see illustration)**.

30 Ensure that the adjustment screw is still resting on the second-highest step of the fast idle cam, then start the engine, again without touching the throttle pedal.

31 Turn the adjustment screw using a screwdriver, until the specified fast idle speed is obtained.

32 If the cooling fan cuts in during the adjustment procedure, stop the adjustments, and continue when the cooling fan stops.

33 On completion of adjustment, stop the engine and disconnect the tachometer.

34 Fit a new tamperproof cap to the fast idle speed adjustment screw, where this is required by law.

20 Automatic choke vacuum pull-down units - removal, refitting and adjustment

Note: *Refer to the warning in Section 1 before proceeding. If the main diaphragm unit is removed, a new star clip (securing the main diaphragm unit to the carburettor top cover) will be required on refitting.*

Main diaphragm unit

Removal

1 Proceed as described in Section 15, paragraphs 1 to 3.

2 Disconnect the diaphragm unit vacuum pipes.

3 Using a pin punch, tap out the roll pin securing the diaphragm unit to the carburettor top cover.

4 Note the position of the bi-metal housing alignment marks as an aid to refitting (if necessary making additional marks for clarity) then remove the three securing screws, and lift off the bi-metal housing. Place the housing to one side, taking care not to strain the coolant hoses or electric choke heater wiring.

5 Remove the three securing screws securing the choke assembly to the carburettor body. Allow the choke assembly to drop down, but do not disconnect the choke linkage.

6 Remove the star clip which secures the diaphragm unit to the carburettor top cover, and withdraw the diaphragm unit.

Refitting

7 Refitting is a reversal of removal, but use a new star clip to secure the diaphragm unit to the carburettor top cover. Before refitting the airbox to the top of the carburettor, check and if necessary adjust the choke pull-down as described later in this Section.

Secondary pull-down solenoid

Removal

8 This unit operates in conjunction with the main diaphragm unit.

9 To remove the solenoid unit, first continue as described in Section 15, paragraphs 1 to 3.

10 Disconnect the diaphragm unit vacuum pipe.

11 Disconnect the wiring plug, then unscrew the securing screw, and withdraw the solenoid unit and its mounting bracket from the carburettor. Note that the securing screw also secures the wiring plug earth lead **(see illustration)**.

Refitting

12 Refitting is a reversal of removal, but ensure that the wiring plug earth lead is in place under the solenoid bracket securing screw.

Vacuum pull-down adjustment

13 With the airbox removed from the top of the carburettor as described in Section 15,

paragraphs 2 and 3, continue as follows.

14 Note the position of the bi-metal housing alignment marks as an aid to refitting (if necessary making additional marks for clarity) then remove the three securing screws, and lift off the bi-metal housing. Place the housing to one side, taking care not to strain the coolant hoses or electric choke heater wiring.

15 Position the fast idle speed adjustment screw on the highest step of the fast idle cam, and check that the choke valve is closed.

16 Move the pull-down arm towards the diaphragm unit by pushing on the adjustment screw until resistance is felt. Hold the arm in this position.

17 Using a drill shank of appropriate diameter, or a similar item, measure the clearance between the lower side of the choke plate and the wall of the primary barrel **(see illustration)**. Check that the clearance is as given for the 'small' choke pull-down gap in the Specifications.

18 If adjustment is necessary, turn the adjustment screw in the appropriate direction, using an Allen key, until the clearance is correct.

19 Now push the pull-down arm towards the diaphragm unit as far as its stop, and hold the arm in this position.

20 As before, measure the clearance between the lower side of the choke plate and the wall of the primary barrel. Check that the clearance is as given for the 'large' choke pull-down gap in the Specifications.

21 If adjustment is necessary, turn the adjustment screw in the appropriate direction until the clearance is correct.

22 Connect the bi-metal spring to the choke lever, position the bi-metal housing on the choke housing, and loosely fit the securing screws. Align the marks on the bi-metal housing and the choke housing as noted during removal, then tighten the securing screws.

23 Refit the airbox to the top of the carburettor on completion.

Chapter 4 Part B
Fuel system - fuel injection models

Contents

Degrees of difficulty

Easy, suitable for novice with little experience	**Fairly easy,** suitable for beginner with some experience	**Fairly difficult,** suitable for competent DIY mechanic	**Difficult,** suitable for experienced DIY mechanic	**Very difficult,** suitable for expert DIY or professional 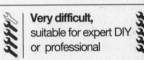

4B

Specifications

General

Injection system type *

C 14 NZ, C 16 NZ, X 16 SZ and C 18 NZ	Multec Central Fuel Injection (CFi)
14 SE, C 14 SE and C 16 SE	Multec M, Multi-Point Injection (MPi)
X 16 XEL	Multec-S, (MPi)
C 18 XE	Simtec 56.0 (MPi)
C 18 XEL and X 20 XEV	Simtec 56.1 (MPi)
C 20 NE	Motronic M 1.5 (MPi)
C 20 XE (up to 1993)	Motronic M 2.5 (MPi)
C 20 XE (from 1993)	Motronic M 2.8 (MPi)

* For details of engine code location, see 'Buying spare parts and vehicle identification numbers'.

Fuel octane rating *

Leaded	98 RON (4-star)
Unleaded (refer to Chapter 5) *	95 RON (Premium)

* Models fitted with a catalytic converter (engine code prefixed by 'C' or 'X'), must only be operated on unleaded fuel.

Fuel pump

Type	Electric, mounted in fuel tank
Delivery quantity	85.0 litres/hour at 12 volts

Fuel pressure

Note: *Pressure regulator vacuum hose connected.*

Multec (CFi)	0.76 bars
Multec (MPi) and Motronic (MPi)	3.0 bars
Multec-S and Simtec (MPi)	not available

Torque wrench settings

	Nm	lbf ft
Accelerator cable bracket to throttle body:		
Multec-S and Motronic 2.5	8	6
Bracket screw to throttle valve housing:		
Multec CFi (refer to text)	3	2
Camshaft sensor:		
Multec-S	5	4
Motronic 2.8 and Simtec	6	5
Camshaft sensor housing:		
Motronic 2.8	15	11
Controlled canister purge valve:		
Motronic 1.5	10	7
Multec-S and Simtec	8	6
DIS coil:		
Multec CFi, MPi, Multec-S and Simtec	8	6
Distributor clamp plate fastening nut:		
Multec CFi and MPi	8	6
Distributor (high voltage) to cylinder head:		
Motronic 2.5	15	11
EGR valve to intake pipe:		
Multec CFi	20	15
Fuel distribution pipe to intake pipe:		
Multec MPi	9	7
Motronic 1.5, 2.8, Multec-S and Simtec	8	6
Fuel pressure regulator to housing:		
Multec CFi	2.5	2
Fuel pressure regulator to distribution pipe:		
Multec MPi and Multec-S	8	6
Motronic 2.5	4	3
Idle air stepper motor to housing:		
Multec CFi	2.5	2
Intake air temperature sensor to intake pipe:		
Multec MPi	27	20
Knock sensor:		
Multec CFi and Multec-S	13	10
Motronic 2.5 and Simtec	20	15
Oxygen sensor (refer to text)	30	22
Pulse pick-up:		
Multec CFi, MPi and Motronic 1.5	6	5
Multec-S, Motronic 2.5, 2.8 and Simtec	8	6
Throttle body:		
Multec-S	8	6
Motronic 2.5 and Simtec	9	7
Throttle valve housing to intake pipe:		
Multec CFi (refer to text)	22	16
Multec MPi, Motronic 1.5 and Simtec	9	7
Throttle valve potentiometer to housing:		
Multec CFi (refer to text)	2	1.5
Multec MPi	3	2
Throttle valve housing, upper to lower:		
Multec Cfi (refer to text)	6	5

1 Precautions and warnings - general

1 There are four basic types of fuel injection system used in the Astra range. They are the Multec CFi (CFi), Multec MPi (MPi), Bosch Motronic and the Simtec. Both the Motronic and Simtec systems are of multi-point design. The systems are described in further detail in Section 2.

2 Fuel is supplied from a tank mounted under the rear of the vehicle, by an electric fuel pump mounted in the tank. The fuel passes through a filter, to the fuel injection system, which incorporates various sensors, actuators, and an ECU.

3 The inducted air passes through an air cleaner, which incorporates a paper filter element to filter out potentially harmful particles. Serious internal engine damage can be caused if foreign particles enter through the air intake system. On CFi models, the air cleaner has a vacuum-controlled air intake, supplying a blend of hot and cold air to suit the engine operating conditions.

4 The ECU controls both the fuel injection system and the ignition system. Combining the two into a complete engine management system. Refer to Chapter 5 for details of the ignition side of the system.

5 The exhaust system is similar to that described for carburettor models in Chapter 2A, but a catalytic converter is incorporated to reduce exhaust gas emissions.

6 Refer to the precautions and warning given in Chapter 2A. The fuel injection system is pressurised. Extra care must be taken when disconnecting the fuel lines. When disconnecting a fuel line union or hose, loosen the union or clamp screw slowly, to avoid a sudden release of pressure which may cause the fuel to spray out.

7 On CFi models, before disconnecting any

fuel lines, the system must be depressurised by removing the fuel pump relay (see Chapter 12), and cranking the engine on the starter motor for at least 5 seconds.

8 After carrying out any work involving disconnection of fuel lines, it is advisable to check the connections for leaks, pressurising the system by switching the ignition on and off several times.

9 ECUs are very sensitive components. Take the following precautions, to avoid damage to the unit when working on a vehicle equipped with an engine management system.

10 When carrying out welding operations on the vehicle using electric welding equipment, the battery and alternator should be disconnected.

11 Although the underbonnet-mounted modules will tolerate normal underbonnet conditions, they can be adversely affected by excess heat or moisture. If using welding equipment or pressure-washing equipment near an electronic module, take care not to direct heat, or jets of water or steam, at the module. If this cannot be avoided, remove the module from the vehicle and protect its wiring plug with a plastic bag.

12 Before disconnecting any wiring, or removing components, always ensure that the ignition is switched off.

13 Do not attempt fault diagnosis procedures using a test light or multimeter, as you may damage the module. Modules, generally are expensive to replace.

14 After working on fuel injection or engine management system components, ensure that all wiring is correctly reconnected before reconnecting the battery or switching on the ignition.

2 System descriptions - general

Multec CFi

1 The injection system is under the overall control of the Multec engine management system, that also controls the ignition system (see Chapter 5).

2 Fuel is supplied from the rear-mounted fuel tank by an electric pump mounted in the tank, through a fuel filter to the Multec injection unit. A fuel pressure regulator mounted on the injection unit maintains a constant fuel pressure to the fuel injector. Excess fuel is returned from the regulator to the tank.

3 The fuel injection unit (resembling a carburettor) houses the throttle valve, idle speed control motor, throttle valve potentiometer, fuel injector and a pressure regulator.

4 The duration of the electrical pulse, supplied to the fuel injector, determines the quantity of fuel injected. The pulse duration is computed by the ECU, based on the information received from the various sensors, motors and valves **(see illustration):**

a) Intake manifold pressure (MAP) sensor (C 14 NZ, C 16 NZ and C 18 NZ) - located on the engine compartment bulkhead, it informs the ECU of the engine load. This senses the amount of inlet manifold vacuum.

b) Throttle valve potentiometer (C 14 NZ, C 16 NZ and C 18 NZ) - housed on the fuel injection unit, it sends the ECU details on the throttle position, as well as the rate of opening and closing.

c) Exhaust gas recirculation (EGR) valve (C 16 NZ, X 16 SZ and C 18 NZ) - Refer to Chapter 4C for details.

d) Distributor (C 14 NZ and C 16 NZ) - sends crankshaft speed and position information to the ECU.

e) Oxygen sensor - informs the ECU on how much oxygen is in the exhaust gases.

f) Idle air control stepper motor (C 14 NZ, C 16 NZ and C 18 NZ) - this controls the idle speed. This regulates the amount of air bypassing the throttle valve.

g) Inductive pulse pick-up (X 16 SZ and C 18 NZ) - on C 18 NZ, this is mounted in the block, sends crankshaft speed and position to the ECU. The X 16 SZ is fitted with a sensor that reads the speed and position of the crankshaft from a sensor wheel located behind the crankshaft pulley.

h) Controlled canister purge valve (X 16 SZ) - feeds collected vapours from a charcoal canister into the inlet tracts for normal combustion. It is located on the camshaft housing.

i) Knock sensor (X 16 SZ) - detects pre-ignition (pinking). Refer to Chapter 5.

j) Coolant temperature sensor - this sends readings direct to the ECU, unlike the temperature sender, which is linked to the temperature gauge.

2.4 Multec single-point fuel injection (CFi) system - C 14 NZ, C 16 NZ and X 16 SZ models

1 Electronic control unit (in right-hand footwell)
2 Manifold absolute pressure (MAP) sensor
3 Fuel injector
4 Throttle position sensor
5 Exhaust gas recirculation valve (1.6 litre model only)
6 Octane rating plug (see Chapter 5)
7 Ignition coil
8 Distributor
9 Exhaust gas oxygen sensor
10 Idle speed control motor

4B

2.9 Multec multi-point fuel injection (MPi) system - C 14 SE model

1 *Electronic control unit (in right-hand footwell)*	5 *Idle speed control motor*	10 *Intake air temperature sensor*
2 *Manifold absolute pressure (MAP) sensor*	6 *Octane rating plug*	11 *Exhaust gas oxygen sensor*
	7 *Fuel pressure regulator*	12 *Crankshaft speed/position sensor (Inductive pulse pick-up)*
3 *Fuel tank vent valve*	8 *Fuel injectors*	
4 *Throttle position sensor*	9 *Distributor*	

5 A catalytic converter is fitted, to reduce harmful exhaust gas emissions.

Multec MPi

6 The injection system is under the overall control of the Multec engine management system, which also controls the ignition system (see Chapter 5).

7 Fuel is supplied from the rear-mounted fuel tank, through a fuel filter and a pressure regulator, to the fuel rail. Excess fuel is returned from the regulator to the tank.

8 A fuel rail acts as a reservoir for the four fuel injectors. Fuel is then injected into the cylinder inlet tracts, upstream of the inlet valves. The fuel injectors operate in pairs. The injectors for cylinder Nos 1 and 2 operate simultaneously and similarly the injectors for cylinder Nos 3 and 4 operate simultaneously.

9 The duration of the electrical pulses to the fuel injectors determines the quantity of fuel injected. The pulse duration is computed by the ECU, based on the information received from the various sensors, motors and valves **(see illustration):**

a) *Intake manifold pressure (MAP) sensor - located on the engine compartment bulkhead, it informs the ECU of the engine load. This senses the amount of inlet manifold vacuum.*

b) *Controlled canister purge valve (C 14 SE) - feeds collected vapours from a charcoal canister into the inlet tracts for normal combustion. It is located on the camshaft housing.*

c) *Throttle valve potentiometer (14 SE and pre-1993 C 14 SE) - housed on the throttle body, it sends the ECU details on the throttle position, as well as the rate of opening and closing.*

d) *Idle air control stepper motor - this*

controls the idle speed. This regulates the amount of air bypassing the throttle valve.

e) *Distributor (14 SE and pre-1993 C 14 SE) - sends crankshaft speed and position information to the ECU.*

f) *Intake air temperature sensor - senses the temperature of the air passing through the intake ducting and sends the reading to the ECU.*

g) *Oxygen sensor (except 14 SE) - informs the ECU about how much oxygen is in the exhaust gases.*

h) *Inductive pulse pick-up (1993-on C 14 SE and C 16 SE) - a sensor that reads the speed and position of the crankshaft from a sensor wheel located behind the crankshaft pulley.*

i) *Coolant temperature sensor - this sends readings direct to the ECU, unlike the temperature sender, which is linked to the temperature gauge.*

10 Information from the throttle valve potentiometer is also used to cut off the fuel supply on the overrun, thus improving fuel economy and reducing exhaust gas emissions.

11 There is no provision for the direct adjustment of idle speed.

12 A catalytic converter is fitted (not 14 SE), to reduce harmful exhaust gas emissions.

Multec-S

13 Apart from the location of the components, this system is basically the same as the previously described, Multec MPi. The main difference is that each injector is triggered individually, in sequence, just before the inlet valves open.

14 Besides the components listed previously, it also has a knock sensor, that detects pre-ignition (pinking).

Motronic

15 The Bosch Motronic system is available in three versions, depending on model. The Motronic M 1.5 system is used on C 20 NE models, the M 2.5 system is used on C 20 XE pre-1993 models and the M 2.8 used on C 20 XE models from 1993. The system is under the overall control of the Motronic engine management system, which also controls the ignition system (see Chapter 5).

16 Fuel is supplied from the rear-mounted fuel tank by an electric pump, mounted in the tank, through a fuel filter and a fuel pressure regulator, to a fuel rail. Excess fuel is returned from the regulator to the tank. The fuel rail acts as a reservoir for the four fuel injectors, which inject fuel into the cylinder inlet tracts, upstream of the inlet valves. On C 20 NE models, the fuel injectors receive an electrical pulse once per crankshaft revolution, which operates all four injectors simultaneously. On C 20 XE models, sequential fuel injection is used. Each injector receives an individual electrical pulse, allowing the four injectors to operate independently, that enables finer control of the fuel supply to each cylinder. The duration of the electrical pulse determines the quantity of fuel injected and pulse duration is computed by the Motronic module, based on the information received from the various sensors **(see illustrations)**:

a) *Hot film mass air flow meter (C 20 NE and C 20 XE) - this has a thin electrically heated element (or film), that is maintained at a constant temperature by the ECU. As passing air increases, the film cools. Therefore requiring more electric current to maintain temperature. The earlier M 2.5 system, uses a wire instead of a 'film' type element.*

b) *Intake air temperature sensor - senses the temperature of the air passing through the intake ducting and sends the reading to the ECU.*

c) *Throttle valve potentiometer (C 20 NE and C 20 XE) - housed on the throttle body, it sends the ECU details on the throttle position, as well as the rate of opening and closing. Pre-1993 C 20 XE models use a throttle valve sensor that only senses the position of the valve.*

d) *Idle speed adjuster - the idle speed is controlled by a solenoid, that receives it's instructions from the ECU.*

e) *Controlled canister purge valve (C 20 NE and pre-1993 C 20 XE) - feeds collected vapours from a charcoal canister into the inlet tracts for normal combustion. It is located on the camshaft housing.*

2.16A Motronic M 1.5 fuel injection system components

1	Air flow meter (hot film mass)	3	Throttle position sensor	6	Fuel tank vent valve
2	Intake air temperature sensor	4	Idle speed control valve	7	Coolant temperature sensor
		5	Distributor		

4B

2.16B Motronic M 2.5 fuel injection system components

1 *Electronic control unit (in right-hand footwell)*
2 *Air flow meter (hot wire mass)*
3 *Fuel pressure regulator*
4 *Throttle body*
5 *Fuel tank vent valve*
6 *Fuel injection wiring harness housing*
7 *Coolant temperature sensor*
8 *Knock sensor*
9 *Idle speed control valve*
10 *Crankshaft speed/position sensor (inductive pulse pick-up)*

f) Coolant temperature sensor - this sends readings direct to the ECU, unlike the temperature sender, which is linked to the temperature gauge.

g) Knock sensor (C 20 XE) - detects pre-ignition (pinking). Refer to Chapter 5.

h) Inductive pulse pick-up (pre-1993 C 20 XE) - this is mounted in the block and sends crankshaft speed and position to the ECU.

i) Intake air temperature sensor (1993-on C 20 XE) - a more precise method of sensing intake air temperature. It is located between the air filter and the hot film air flow meter and with the coolant temperature sensor, assists in starting a hot engine.

j) Camshaft sensor (1993-on C 20 XE models) - this replaces the earlier high voltage distributor, as the system uses a Direct Ignition System (DIS).

k) Oxygen sensor - informs the ECU about how much oxygen is in the exhaust gases.

l) Trigger box - used for the ignition final stage, this unit is bolted on to a heatsink (cooling plate) and attached to the inner wing. refer to Chapter 5.

17 Some models are fitted with traction control (TC), or electronic traction control (ETC) as it was known as on earlier models. It operates by reducing the throttle and operates independently from the Motronic system. Further details can be found in Chapter 9.

18 A catalytic converter is fitted, to reduce harmful exhaust gas emissions.

19 All engines must be operated on unleaded petrol, and leaded petrol **must not** be used, as it will damage the catalyst.

Simtec

20 The fuel is supplied to the engine in the same way as described for Motronic systems. However, an increased amount of electronic components are used instead of mechanical parts as sensors and actuators with the Simtec system. This provides more precise operating data as well as greater problem free motoring. Two versions have been fitted to date. The 56.0 version controlled C 18 XE models. While an uprated 56.1 version was fitted to both the C 18 XEL and X 20 XEV 'Ecotec' models.

21 The ECU is equipped with electronic ignition control. Called 'Microprocessor Spark Timing System, inductive triggered' (or MSTS-i), and means that the mechanical high voltage distributor is no longer needed. The ECU is feed and sends information to the following sensors and valves.

a) Controlled canister purge valve - feeds collected vapours from a charcoal canister into the inlet tracts for normal combustion. It is located on the camshaft housing and works with the oxygen sensor, when sending signals to the ECU.

b) Throttle valve potentiometer - housed on the throttle body, it sends the ECU details

on the throttle position, as well as the rate of opening and closing.

c) Knock sensor - detects pre-ignition (pinking). Refer to Chapter 5.

d) Dual spark ignition coil (DIS) - this is switched directly by the output stages in the ECU and replaces the previous type of coil.

e) Coolant temperature sensor - this sends readings direct to the ECU, unlike the temperature sender, which is linked to the temperature gauge.

f) Idle air stepper motor - varies the air throughput, dependant on the information received from the ECU, when the engine is idling.

g) Intake air temperature sensor - a more precise method of sensing intake air temperature. It is located between the air filter and the hot film air flow meter and with the coolant temperature sensor, assists in starting a hot engine.

h) Hot film mass air flow meter - this has a thin electrically heated element (or film), that is maintained at a constant temperature by the ECU. As passing air increases, the film cools. Therefore requiring more electric current to maintain temperature.

i) Oxygen sensor - informs the ECU about how much oxygen is in the exhaust gases.

j) Inductive pulse pick-up - this is mounted in the block and sends crankshaft speed and position to the ECU.

k) Camshaft sensor - a back-up if the inductive pulse pick-up fails. Both sensor work together to calculate 'Top Dead Centre', TDC, crankshaft angle and engine speed. The ECU uses these signals to calculate fuel injection and the ignition point.

22 On the 56.1 version, the injectors and fuel pump are actuated through a relay.

23 This engine is also fitted with an exhaust gas recirculation (EGR) system and secondary air injection (AIR - Air Injection Reactor), to conform to the latest European exhaust emission limits (as from 1996). Refer to Chapter 4C, for details.

24 Like previous systems a catalytic converter is fitted to these models, therefore must only be used with unleaded petrol.

---

3 Fuel injection system components - testing

1 Apart from the basic electrical tests outlined in Chapter 12, and the ignition system checks given in Chapter 5, the individual fuel system components cannot easily be tested by the home mechanic,

2 In most cases, if a fault does occur, the ECU will allow the engine to run. It will use a back-up programme of stored values to keep the engine running, albeit at reduced efficiency and possible driveability. While the

fault might be evident to the driver, it could easily be masked by the back-up programme in such a way that fault diagnosis becomes very difficult.

3 The ECUs have a self-analysis function, which stores fault codes in the module memory, and these fault codes can be decoded using specialist test equipment, that is used by the dealer.

4 If a fault occurs (which may be indicated by the illumination of the engine warning light on the instrument panel), and the cause is not immediately obvious, it is worth carrying out the checks described in the following paragraphs. If these checks do not resolve the problem, the best course of action is to have the complete system checked by a Vauxhall dealer using the specialist diagnostic equipment.

5 If a fault arises, first check that it is not due to poor maintenance. Check that the air cleaner element is clean and that the spark plugs are in good condition and correctly gapped. Ensure also that the crankcase ventilation system hoses are clear of obstructions and undamaged (see Chapter 4C) and that the throttle cable is correctly adjusted (see Section 38).

6 If the engine is running very roughly, carry out a compression test (see Chapter 2A) and remember that one of the hydraulic valve lifters may be faulty, producing an incorrect valve clearance.

7 If the problem is thought to be due to a dirty or blocked fuel injector, try using a fuel injector cleaning product (which is normally added to the contents of the fuel tank) according to the product manufacturer's instructions.

8 If the fault persists, check the ignition system components (as far as possible), as described in Chapter 5.

9 If the fault is still not eliminated, work methodically through the system, checking all fuses, wiring connectors, wiring, vacuum hoses, looking for any signs of poor connections, damage, dirt, leaks or other faults.

10 Once the system components have been checked for signs of obvious faults, take the vehicle to a suitably equipped Vauxhall dealer for the full system to be checked using the specialist diagnostic equipment.

11 Do not attempt to check any of the components, particularly the ECU, using anything other than the correct test equipment, as serious (and possibly expensive!) damage to the components could result.

---

4 Unleaded petrol - general

Note: *The information given in this Section is correct at the time of writing, and applies only to petrol's currently available in the EC. If in any doubt as to the suitability of petrol, or if using the vehicle outside the EC, consult a Vauxhall dealer or one of the motoring*

4.2 Octane coding plug - shown set for 95 RON petrol

organisations for advice on the petrols available, and their suitability for your vehicle.

1 Vauxhall recommend the use of 95 RON ('Premium') unleaded petrol for all fuel injection models.

2 Certain models (see Specifications) can also be operated on 98 RON ('Super' or 'Super Plus') unleaded petrol, by reversing the position of the octane coding plug in its connector on the battery tray **(see illustration)**. Where applicable, the plug is marked '95' on one side, which corresponds to the position for use with 95 RON (Premium) unleaded petrol, and '98' on the other side, which corresponds to the position for use with 98 RON ('Super' or 'Super Plus') unleaded petrol.

3 If necessary (for example, when travelling in territories where 95 RON unleaded petrol is not available), certain models (see Specifications) can be operated on 91 RON unleaded petrol by using a special octane coding plug available from Vauxhall dealers.

4 Leaded petrol **must not** be used in fuel injection models, as irreparable (and expensive) damage will be caused to the catalytic converter.

5 ECU - removal and refitting

Note: On earlier models, the control unit consists of two components, the basic control unit, and the programme memory, which clips

into a circuit board in the control unit. The two components can be renewed independently, if a fault is suspected, but the source of the fault can only be established using specialist test equipment available to a Vauxhall dealer. On C 14 NZ models, the two components cannot be separated, and the complete unit must be renewed if a fault is suspected.

Removal

1 The control unit is located behind the right-hand footwell side panel.

2 Disconnect the battery negative lead.

3 Remove the footwell side/sill trim panel, as described in Chapter 11.

4 Where applicable, unscrew the two securing nuts (bolts), and pull the wiring plug bracket from the footwell to allow sufficient access to enable the control unit to be withdrawn **(see illustration)**.

5 On Simtec models, remove the fuel pump relay.

6 On certain left-hand-drive models, it may be necessary to remove the glovebox (see Chapter 11) to allow access to the control unit.

7 Reach up into the footwell and locate the control unit.

8 Unscrew or unclip (as applicable) the control unit bracket, then lower the bracket, and disconnect the wiring plug(s) from the control unit. Take care not to touch plug contacts.

9 Unclip the control unit from the bracket, noting its orientation.

10 On C 16 NZ and C 18 NZ models, the programme memory can be unclipped from its circuit board in the control unit, after removing the cover from the rear of the control unit. The cover is secured by two screws **(see illustrations)**.

Refitting

Except Multec-S

11 Refitting is a reversal of removal. Ensure that the wiring plugs are firmly secured.

Multec-S

12 Replacement units come without the separate, program memory and knock modules, that are secured behind a panel in the ECU.

13 These modules must be carefully transferred from the original to the replacement ECU.

14 Do not try to open the individual modules or touch the plug contacts.

15 After refitting the modules, transfer part and code number information from the old ECU to the new, for future reference.

16 Refitting is a reversal of removal. Ensure that the wiring plugs are firmly secured. Remember to replace the fuel pump relay.

6 Airbox - removal and refitting

Multec CFi

Removal

1 Disconnect the breather hose from the airbox.

2 Disconnect the two vacuum pipes from the airbox, noting their locations.

3 Loosen the clamp screw, and disconnect the air trunking from the end of the airbox.

4 Remove the two securing screws, and lift the airbox from the fuel injection unit. Recover the sealing ring.

Refitting

5 Refitting is a reversal of removal, remembering the following points.

6 Inspect the sealing ring for damage or deterioration, and renew if necessary. Ensure that the sealing ring locates correctly in the groove in the base of the airbox.

7 Reconnect the vacuum pipes as noted before removal.

Motronic

Note: Sealing Cement (Vauxhall P/N 90293725) will be required to coat the sealing ring seating area in the airbox on refitting.

Removal

8 Loosen the clamp screw securing the air trunking to the left-hand side of the air flow meter.

9 Using an Allen key or hexagon bit, unscrew

4B

5.4 Lowering the fuel injection control unit and bracket assembly from the footwell

5.10A Remove the control unit rear cover . . .

5.10B . . . for access to the programme memory

6.9 Unscrewing an airbox securing bolt - Motronic M 2.5 models

6.10 Disconnecting the hose from the airbox - Motronic M 2.5 models

6.12 Removing the sealing ring from the base of the airbox - Motronic M 2.5 models

the four bolts securing the airbox to the throttle body **(see illustration)**.
10 Lift the airbox from the top of the throttle body, and disconnect the hose from the base of the airbox **(see illustration)**.
11 Withdraw the airbox, and recover the sealing ring from the base of the airbox if it is loose.

Refitting

12 Before beginning refitting, remove the sealing ring from the base of the airbox, if not already done **(see illustration)**.
13 Examine the sealing ring, and if it is worn or damaged, renew it.
14 Thoroughly clean the sealing ring seating area in the airbox, then liberally coat the seating face with a Cement (Vauxhall P/N 90293725, or equivalent).
15 Fit the sealing ring to the airbox, ensuring that it is correctly seated, then refit the assembly using a reversal of the removal procedure.

7 Air cleaner assembly - removal and refitting
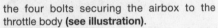

Removal

1 Disconnect the battery negative lead.
2 Disconnect the wiring from the air flow meter, if applicable.
3 Remove the air intake hose from the air cleaner housing.

4 Unclip the retaining clamps from the top cover.
5 Unscrew the two housing securing nuts and release the air flow guide hose.
6 The lower part of the housing can now be removed, complete with it's rubber support.

Refitting

6 Refitting is a reversal of removal.

8 Resonator, air cleaner - removal and refitting

Removal

1 On certain models, the base of the air cleaner housing clips into a resonator box mounted under the front wing.
2 Remove the air filter assembly as described in Section 7.
3 For easier access, remove the front wheel arch liner, as described in Chapter 11.
4 Remove the single securing screw, and lower the resonator box from the wheel arch **(see illustration)**.

Refitting

6 Refitting is a reversal of removal. However, ensure that there is a firm connection between the resonator and the lower part of the air cleaner housing.

9 Fuel injection unit (Multec CFi) - removal and refitting

Note: *Refer to the precautions given in Section 1 before starting work. All gaskets and seals must be renewed on refitting, and Locking Compound will be required to coat the fuel injection unit securing nut threads.*

Removal

1 Depressurise the fuel system by removing the fuel pump relay (see Chapter 12), and cranking the engine on the starter motor for a minimum of 5 seconds.
2 Disconnect the battery negative lead.
3 Remove the airbox from the top of the fuel injection unit, as described in Section 6.
4 Release the securing lugs, and disconnect the wiring plug from the fuel injector **(see illustration)**.
5 Remove the rubber seal from the top of the fuel injection unit (if not already done), then slide the fuel injector wiring rubber grommet from the slot in the side of the fuel injection unit **(see illustration)**. Move the wiring to one side.
6 Disconnect the wiring plugs from the idle speed control motor and the throttle position sensor.
7 Disconnect the fuel feed and return hoses from the fuel injection unit, noting their locations to aid refitting. Be prepared for fuel

8.4 Withdrawing the air cleaner resonator box from under the wheel arch

9.4 Releasing the fuel injector wiring plug retaining lugs - CFi models

9.5 Sliding the fuel injector wiring rubber grommet from the fuel injection unit

9.9 Disconnecting the MAP sensor hose from the fuel injection unit - CFi models

9.10 Disconnecting the operating rod (arrowed) from the throttle valve lever- CFi models

9.12A Recover the sleeves which fit over the manifold studs - CFi models

spillage, and take adequate fire precautions. Clamp or plug the open ends of the hoses to minimise further fuel loss.

8 Disconnect the vacuum hoses from the fuel injection unit, noting their locations and routing to ensure correct refitting.

9 Disconnect the MAP sensor hose from the rear of the fuel injection unit **(see illustration)**.

10 Disconnect the operating rod from the throttle valve lever **(see illustration)**.

11 Make a final check to ensure that all relevant hoses and wires have been disconnected to facilitate removal of the fuel injection unit.

12 Unscrew the two securing nuts and recover the washers, and recover the sleeves that fit over the manifold studs, then carefully lift the fuel injection unit from the inlet manifold **(see illustrations)**. Recover the gasket.

13 The fuel injection unit may now be split into its upper and lower sections by removing the two securing screws **(see illustration)**. The vacuum hose flange and the fuel hose unions can also be removed.

Refitting

14 Refitting is a reversal of removal, remembering the following points.

15 Where applicable, when reassembling the

9.17 Vacuum hose connections at fuel injection unit - CFi models

A Intake air temperature control
B Exhaust gas recirculation (where applicable)
C Fuel tank vent valve (where applicable)

two sections of the fuel injection unit, use a new gasket. Similarly, where applicable use a new gasket when refitting the vacuum hose flange. If the fuel hose unions have been removed, make sure that the washers are in place when refitting.

16 Refit the fuel injection unit to the manifold using a new gasket, ensuring that the sleeves are in place over the manifold studs. Coat the threads of the securing nuts with a thread-locking compound before fitting. Ensure that the washers are in place under the nuts.

17 Ensure that all hoses are reconnected and routed correctly, as noted before removal. Note that the vacuum hoses should be connected as shown **(see illustration)**.

18 On completion, check and if necessary adjust the throttle cable free play as described in Section 38.

9.12B Lifting the fuel injection unit from the inlet manifold

10.2 Loosening an air trunking clamp screw

10 Throttle body (Multec MPi) - removal and refitting

Note: *A new gasket must be used on refitting.*

Removal

1 Disconnect the battery negative lead.

2 Loosen the clamp screws securing the air trunking to the throttle body and the air cleaner cover, then withdraw the air trunking **(see illustration)**.

3 Disconnect the camshaft cover breather hoses from the throttle body **(see illustration)**.

4B

9.13 Removing a fuel injection unit upper-to-lower section securing screw - CFi models

10.3 Disconnecting a camshaft cover breather hose from the throttle body - Multec MPi models

10.4 Disconnecting the fuel tank vent valve vacuum hose from the throttle body - Multec MPi models

4 Disconnect the fuel tank vent valve vacuum hose from the throttle body **(see illustration)**.

5 Disconnect the manifold absolute pressure (MAP) sensor vacuum hose from the throttle body.

6 Disconnect the coolant hoses from the throttle body. Be prepared for coolant spillage, and clamp or plug the open ends of the hoses, to prevent further coolant loss.

7 Disconnect the wiring plugs from the throttle position sensor and the idle speed control motor.

8 Release the securing clip, then disconnect the throttle cable end balljoint from the throttle valve lever.

9 Slide the throttle cable grommet from the bracket on the inlet manifold, then unhook the throttle return spring from the bracket. If necessary, unhook the spring from the grommet in the throttle valve linkage, and lay the spring to one side out of the way (in this case, note the orientation of the spring to enable correct refitting), **(see illustration)**.

10 Make a final check to ensure that all relevant hoses and wires have been disconnected to facilitate removal of the throttle body.

11 Unscrew the four securing nuts, and withdraw the throttle body from the inlet manifold.

12 Recover the gasket.

13 The throttle position sensor and the idle speed control motor can be removed from the throttle body. Described in Sections 22 and 24.

Refitting

14 Refitting is a reversal of removal, remembering the following points.

15 Where applicable, refit the throttle position sensor and/or the idle speed control motor.

16 Thoroughly clean the mating faces of the throttle body and inlet manifold, and refit the throttle body using a new gasket.

17 Ensure that all wires and hoses are correctly reconnected and routed.

18 Check and if necessary top-up the coolant level, as described in Chapter 1.

19 On completion, check and if necessary

10.9 Throttle linkage - Multec MPi models

1 Cable end balljoint
2 Cable grommet
3 Throttle return spring (note orientation)

adjust the throttle cable free play as described in Section 38.

11 Throttle body (Multec-S) - removal and refitting

Note: *Refer to the precautions given in Section 1 before starting work. A new throttle body mounting gasket will be required on refitting*

Removal

1 Depressurise the fuel system by removing the fuel pump relay (see Chapter 12), and cranking the engine on the starter motor for a minimum of 5 seconds.

2 Disconnect the battery negative lead.

3 Remove the oil filler cap and the engine cover.

4 Place clean cloth around the fuel pressure check connector and be prepared for spillage. Remove the cap and slowly release any pressure left in the system.

5 Disconnect the wiring plugs for the following:
a) Engine multiplugs (2 and 3 pin)
b) Knock sensor
c) Earth leads (2)
d) EGR valve
e) Crankshaft pulse pick-up

11.10 Wiring trough securing bolts (arrowed) - Multec-S models

f) Controlled canister purge valve
g) Oxygen sensor
h) DIS ignition module
i) Camshaft sensor

6 Remove the wiring trough and secure to one side.

7 Disconnect the controlled canister purge valve from it's bracket from the upper part of the inlet manifold.

8 Remove the vacuum hose from the purge valve.

9 Remove the brake servo and the inlet manifold pressure sensor vacuum hoses from the manifold.

10 Remove the wiring trough from the throttle body and support bracket and place upside down to one side **(see illustration)**.

11 Disconnect the AIR switchover valve vacuum hose.

12 Undo the two bolts securing accelerator cable bracket to the throttle body.

13 Remove the accelerator cable and secure to one side.

14 Note that the plug leads should have cylinder numbers printed on them, that match the numbers on the module.

15 Remove the DIS module from it's bracket and secure to one side **(see illustration)**.

16 Undo the two fastening bolts from the air intake pipe support and remove.

17 Separate the pipe from the bracket.

18 Disconnect the intake air temperature sensor.

19 Detach the intake pipe from the air cleaner housing.

20 Place a clean cloth in the intake opening, to prevent dirt from entering into the engine.

21 Unbolt the four securing bolts from the throttle body.

22 Carefully remove the throttle body gasket.

23 Disconnect the wiring plug from the idle speed stepper motor and the potentiometer.

24 Remove both fuel hoses from the fuel rail and pressure regulator. Be prepared to catch any spilt fuel with clean cloth. Secure hoses to one side.

25 Unclip the cover from wiring trough. Note the position of the wiring, before removing and placing to one side.

26 Slowly remove cooling hose from below the trough. Be ready to collect any coolant that drains out.

11.15 Removing the three bolts from the DIS module - Multec-S models

27 Before removing the wiring trough note it's location.
28 Remove air intake pipe from throttle body.
29 Remove the coolant hose from the throttle body, again be ready to collect any coolant that drains out.
30 The throttle body can now be removed.

Refitting

31 Ensure that the sealing surfaces of both the throttle body and the intermediate flange are clean.
32 Refitting is a reversal of the removal procedure. Replace the throttle body with a new gasket, to the flange.
33 After refitting, top cooling system as described Chapter 3.

12 Throttle body (Motronic M 1.5) - removal and refitting
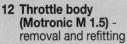

Note: *A new gasket must be used on refitting.*
Removal

1 Disconnect the battery negative lead.
2 Release the securing clip, and disconnect the wiring plug from the intake air temperature sensor (mounted in the air trunking). Pull on the plug, not on the wiring.
3 Loosen the clamp screws securing the air trunking to the throttle body and the air flow meter, then withdraw the air trunking.
4 Disconnect the idle speed control valve hose from the throttle body.
5 Disconnect the camshaft cover breather hose from the throttle body.
6 Disconnect the fuel tank vent valve vacuum hose from the throttle body.
7 Disconnect the coolant hoses from the throttle body. Be prepared for coolant spillage, and clamp or plug the open ends of the hoses, to prevent further coolant loss.
8 Release the securing clip, and disconnect the wiring plug from the throttle position sensor.
9 Release the securing clip, then disconnect the throttle cable end balljoint from the throttle valve lever.
10 Slide the throttle cable grommet from the bracket on the inlet manifold, then unhook the

12.10 Unhooking the throttle return spring from the bracket on the inlet manifold - Motronic M 1.5 models

throttle return spring from the bracket. If necessary, unhook the spring from the grommet in the throttle valve linkage, and lay the spring to one side out of the way (in this case, note the orientation of the spring to enable correct refitting), **(see illustration)**.
11 Make a final check to ensure that all relevant hoses and wires have been disconnected to facilitate removal of the throttle body.
12 Unscrew the four securing nuts **(see illustration)**, and withdraw the throttle body from the inlet manifold. Access to the lower nuts may be restricted by the two fuel hoses, and it may be necessary to move the hoses to one side to improve access. Take care not to strain the hoses.
13 Recover the gasket.
14 The throttle position sensor can be removed from the throttle body, as described in Section 22.

Refitting

15 Refitting is a reversal of removal, remembering the following points.
16 Where applicable, refit the throttle position sensor.
17 Thoroughly clean the mating faces of the throttle body and inlet manifold, and refit the throttle body using a new gasket.
18 Ensure that all wires and hoses are correctly reconnected and routed.
19 Check and if necessary top-up the coolant level, as described in Chapter 1.

12.12 Unscrewing a throttle body securing nut (arrowed) - Motronic M 1.5 models

20 On completion, check and if necessary adjust the throttle cable free play, as described in Section 38.

13 Throttle body (Motronic M 2.5 and M 2.8) - removal and refitting

Note: *A new gasket must be used on refitting. On vehicles with Traction Control refer also to Chapter 9.*

Removal

1 Disconnect the battery negative lead.
2 Remove the airbox assembly from the top of the throttle body, as described in Section 6.
3 Release the securing clip, and disconnect the wiring plug from the throttle position sensor (or potentiometer, as applicable). Pull on the plug, not on the wiring.
4 Unscrew the retaining nut, and detach the fuel hose bracket from the left-hand side of the throttle body.
5 Slide the throttle cable end from the throttle valve lever **(see illustration)**.
6 Disconnect the breather hose from the front of the throttle body **(see illustration)**.
7 Make a final check to ensure that all relevant hoses, pipes and wires have been disconnected and moved clear of the throttle body.
8 Unscrew the four securing nuts, and remove the throttle body from the inlet manifold **(see illustration)**. Recover the gasket.

4B

13.5 Disconnecting the throttle cable from the throttle valve lever - Motronic M 2.5 models

13.6 Disconnect the breather hose (arrowed) from the throttle body - Motronic M 2.5 models

13.8 Two of the main throttle body securing nuts (arrowed) - Motronic M 2.5 models

15.5A Remove the securing screw . . .

15.5B . . . and withdraw the injector clamp bracket - CFi models

15.6 Removing the fuel injector. Note O-rings (arrowed) - CFi models

9 The throttle position sensor can be removed from the throttle body.
10 Do not under any circumstances attempt to adjust the throttle valve linkage. It the throttle valve linkage is faulty, refer the problem to a Vauxhall dealer.

Refitting

11 Refitting is a reversal of removal, remembering the following points.
12 Before refitting the throttle body, check the adjustment of the throttle position sensor. Refer to the refitting procedure in Section 22.
13 Thoroughly clean the mating faces of the throttle body and the traction control (TC) throttle housing (if applicable). Refit the throttle body using a new gasket.
14 Ensure that all hoses, pipes and wires are correctly reconnected and routed.
15 Refit the airbox as described in Section 6.
16 On completion, check and if necessary adjust the throttle cable free play, as described in Section 38.

14 Throttle body (Simtec) - removal and refitting

Removal

1 Disconnect the battery negative lead.
2 Disconnect the wiring for the potentiometer.
3 Drain the cooling system, as described in Chapter 3.

4 Disconnect the coolant and vacuum hoses from the throttle body.
5 Remove both the crankcase vent hose and the air intake hose from the cylinder head cover.
6 Remove the throttle cable from the body and secure to one side.
7 Remove the idle air stepper motor's wiring.
8 Undo all four securing nuts from the housing.
9 Remove the housing from the intake pipe.
10 Place a clean cloth in the intake pipe opening to prevent dirt or dust from entering into the engine.

Refitting

11 Clean the mounting surfaces of the body and the intake pipe. Take care not to damage the surfaces.
12 Remainder of the refitting is a reversal of the removal procedure.
13 Finally, top up the cooling system as described in Chapter 3.

15 Fuel injector (Multec CFi) - removal and refitting

Note: *Refer to the precautions given in Section 1 before starting work. If the original injector is being refitted, new O-rings must be used. Locking Compound will be required to coat the clamp bracket screw threads.*

Removal

1 Depressurise the fuel system by removing the fuel pump relay (see Chapter 12), and cranking the engine on the starter motor for a minimum of 5 seconds.
2 Disconnect the battery negative lead.
3 Remove the airbox from the top of the fuel injection unit, as described in Section 6.
4 Squeeze the securing lugs, and disconnect the wiring plug from the fuel injector.
5 Remove the Torx type securing screw, and withdraw the injector clamp bracket **(see illustrations)**.
6 Carefully withdraw the injector from the fuel injection unit **(see illustration)**.

Refitting

7 If the original injector is to be refitted, renew the two O-rings at the base of the injector.
8 Carefully install the injector in the fuel injection unit, with the wiring socket pointing towards the clamp bracket screw hole.
9 Refit the injector clamp bracket, ensuring that it engages correctly with the injector (the bracket should engage with the slot below the wiring socket in the injector).
10 Coat the threads of the clamp bracket screw with a thread-locking compound, then refit and tighten the screw **(see illustration)**.
11 Reconnect the injector wiring plug, and reconnect the battery negative lead.

16 Fuel Injectors (Multec MPi) - removal and refitting

Note: *Refer to the precautions given in Section 1 before starting work. The seals at both ends of the fuel injector(s) must be renewed on refitting.*

Removal

1 Depressurise the fuel system by removing the fuel pump relay (see Chapter 12), and cranking the engine on the starter motor for a minimum of 5 seconds.
2 Disconnect the battery negative lead.
3 Place a wad of rag beneath the fuel pipe union at the fuel pressure regulator and then further depressurise the fuel system by slowly loosening the fuel pipe union. Two open-ended

15.10 Coat the fuel injector clamp bracket screw with Locking compound - CFi models

16.4 Disconnecting a fuel injector wiring plug - Multec MPi models

16.6A Fuel rail securing bolts (arrowed) -
Multec MPi models

16.6B Lifting the fuel rail from the inlet
manifold - Multec MPi models

16.7A Removing a fuel injector securing
clip - Multec MPi models

spanners will be required so one can be used to counterhold the regulator as the union is loosened. Be prepared for fuel spillage, and take adequate fire precautions. Tighten the union when the pressure has been released.

4 Disconnect the wiring plugs from the fuel injectors, then move the wiring clear of the fuel rail **(see illustration)**.

5 Disconnect the vacuum pipe from the end of the fuel pressure regulator.

6 Remove the two fuel rail securing bolts, then lift the fuel rail complete with fuel injectors sufficiently to enable the injector(s) to be removed **(see illustrations)**. Take care not to strain the fuel hoses which run under the fuel rail. Be prepared for fuel spillage, and take adequate fire precautions.

7 To remove an injector from the fuel rail, prise out the metal securing clip using a screwdriver or a pair of pliers, then pull the injector from the fuel rail **(see illustrations)**.

8 Overhaul of the fuel injectors is not possible, as no spares are available. If faulty, an injector must be renewed.

9 The fuel rail assembly can be removed from the vehicle, after disconnecting the two fuel hoses, which are connected to fuel supply and return pipes under the fuel rail. Access to the two hoses is most easily obtained from under the vehicle. Mark the hoses for position before disconnecting them, to ensure that they are reconnected correctly.

Refitting

10 Begin refitting by fitting new seals to both ends of the fuel injector(s).

11 Refitting is a reversal of removal, ensuring that all pipes and wires are correctly reconnected.

17 Fuel injectors (Multec-S) - removal and refitting

Note: *Refer to the precautions given in Section 1 before starting work.*

Removal

1 Follow removal procedure as described in Section 11, paragraphs 1 to 19.

2 Remove the upper part of the inlet manifold, by undoing the nuts and bolts.

3 Carefully place clean cloth in the inlet ports, to prevent dirt from entering into the engine.

4 Clean the sealing surfaces of the upper and lower parts of the inlet manifold.

5 Unclip the wiring from the fuel rail.

6 Disconnect the four wiring plugs from the injectors.

7 Remove the wiring plug for the inductive pulse pick-up from the bracket **(see illustration)**.

8 Place clean cloth around the fuel pressure check connector, remove the cap and release any pressure left in the system. Be prepared for fuel spillage.

9 Remove the three bolts securing the fuel rail. Carefully remove the fuel rail complete with the injectors, from the inlet manifold.

10 Carefully place pieces of clean cloth in the

openings, to prevent dirt from entering the engine.

11 Remove the spring clip on each injector, so that they can be carefully removed from the fuel rail.

Refitting

12 Before refitting injectors, coat each seal ring with clean engine oil.

13 Note the correct position of the injectors **(see illustration)**.

14 Refitting remaining components is a reversal of the removal procedure.

18 Fuel injectors (Motronic M 1.5) - removal and refitting

Note: *Refer to the precautions, given in Section 1, before starting work. The seals at both ends of the fuel injector/s) must be renewed on refitting.*

Removal

1 Disconnect the battery negative lead.

2 Unscrew the union nut, and disconnect the brake servo vacuum hose from the inlet manifold.

3 Remove the idle speed control valve, complete with hoses, as described in Section 25.

4 Disconnect the vacuum hose from the top of the fuel pressure regulator.

5 Disconnect the wiring harness housing from the fuel injectors, and move it to one side,

4B

16.7B Removing a fuel injector from the
fuel rail. O-rings arrowed - Multec MPi
models

17.7 Inductive pulse pick-up wiring plug
bracket - Multec-S models

17.13 Correct position of fuel injectors -
Multec-S models

18.10 Fitting a new O-ring to a fuel injector – Motronic M 1.5 models

19.4 Disconnecting the fuel supply hose from the fuel rail – Motronic M 2.5 models

19.11 Lifting the wiring harness housing from the fuel injectors – Motronic M 2.5 models

taking care not to strain the wiring. Pull up on the wiring harness housing, and compress the wiring plug securing clips to release the harness housing from the injectors.

6 Place a wad of rag beneath the fuel pressure regulator, then depressurise the fuel system by slowly loosening the clamp screws securing the fuel supply hose to the pressure regulator. Be prepared for fuel spillage, and take adequate fire precautions.

7 Remove the four bolts from the brackets securing the fuel rail to the inlet manifold, then lift the fuel rail complete with fuel injectors sufficiently to enable the injector(s) to be removed. Take care not to strain the fuel hoses. Be prepared for fuel spillage, and take adequate fire precautions.

8 To remove an injector from the fuel rail, prise out the metal securing clip using a screwdriver, then pull the injector from the fuel rail.

9 Overhaul of the fuel injectors is not possible, as no spares are available. If faulty, an injector must be renewed.

Refitting

10 Begin refitting by fitting new seals to both ends of the fuel injector(s) **(see illustration)**.

11 Refitting is a reversal of removal, ensuring that all hoses, pipes and wires are correctly reconnected.

19 Fuel injectors (Motronic M 2.5 and M 2.8) – removal and refitting

Note: *Refer to the precautions given in Section 1 before starting work. The seals at both ends of the fuel injector(s) must be renewed on refitting.*

Removal

1 Disconnect the battery negative lead.
2 Remove the airbox, as described in Section 6.
3 Position rag beneath one of the fuel hose unions on the fuel rail, to absorb the fuel which will be released as the union is disconnected.
4 Slowly loosen the fuel hose union to relieve the pressure in the fuel line, then disconnect the hose from the fuel rail **(see illustration)**. Be prepared for fuel spillage, and take adequate fire precautions. Clamp or plug the end of the fuel hose, to prevent dirt ingress and further fuel spillage.
5 Repeat paragraphs 3 and 4 for the remaining fuel unions.
6 Disconnect the two breather hoses from the rear of the camshaft cover. Disconnect the larger hose from the throttle body, and remove the hose completely.
7 Disconnect the vacuum pipe from the top of the fuel pressure regulator.
8 Disconnect the wiring plug from the air flow meter. Recover the sealing ring.

9 Disconnect the wiring plug from the throttle position sensor.
10 Slide the end of the throttle cable from the throttle valve lever on the throttle body, then unbolt the cable bracket from the inlet manifold, and move it to one side.
11 Disconnect the wiring harness from the fuel injectors, and move it to one side, taking care not to strain the wiring. Pull up on the wiring harness housing, and compress the wiring plug retaining clips to release the housing from the injectors **(see illustration)**.
12 Unscrew and remove the two fuel rail securing nuts, and withdraw the fuel rail complete with fuel injectors from the inlet manifold. Note the position of the earth leads on the fuel rail securing studs **(see illustration)**.
13 To remove an injector from the fuel rail, prise out the metal securing clip, then pull the injector from the fuel rail **(see illustrations)**.
14 Overhaul of the fuel injectors is not possible, as no spares are available. If faulty, an injector must be renewed.

Refitting

15 Begin refitting by fitting new seals to both ends of the fuel injector(s).
16 Further refitting is a reversal of removal, remembering the following points.
17 Where applicable, the plug strip for the injectors must firmly 'snap' into place.
18 Ensure that all hoses, pipes and wires are correctly reconnected.

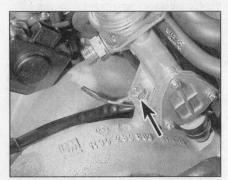

19.12 Fuel rail securing nut (arrowed). Note position of earth lead – Motronic M 2.5 models

19.13A Prise out the metal securing clip . . .

19.13B . . . and pull the injector from the fuel rail – Motronic M 2.5 models

20.10 Releasing the fuel rail - Simtec models

1 Securing pin   2 Securing bolt

19 Refit the airbox as described in Section 6.

20 On completion, check and if necessary adjust the throttle cable free play, as described in Section 38.

20 Fuel injectors (Simtec) - removal and refitting

Note: *Refer to the precautions given in Section 1 before starting work. New injector seals will be required.*

Removal

1 Depressurise the fuel system by removing the fuel pump relay (see Chapter 12), and cranking the engine on the starter motor for a minimum of 5 seconds. Disconnect the battery negative lead.

2 Remove both crankcase vent hoses from the cylinder head cover.

3 Loosen the air intake hose clamps and remove it completely.

4 Disconnect the throttle cable from the throttle valve housing and secure to side.

5 Position clean cloth around the fuel pressure check connector, to absorb any fuel that may be released.

6 Remove the cap and release any pressure left in the system.

7 Using a screwdriver, release the safety clamps for the number one and number two injectors.

8 The plug strip can now be lifted and secured to one side.

9 Disconnect the fuel pressure regulators vacuum hose and earth lead.

10 Release the pins and bolt from the fuel rail **(see illustration)**.

11 The fuel rail, complete with injectors can now be lifted upwards.

12 Release each injector from the rail, by removing the spring clamps.

Refitting

13 Refitting is a reversal of the removal procedure. However, note the following.

14 Always replace the injector seals.

15 The spring clip on the injector, must face

20.15 Fuel injector securing clip (1) - Simtec models

downwards to engage correctly in the plug strip **(see illustration)**. Ensure that each injector is securely fitted into the plug strip.

16 Make sure that all hoses are correctly seated.

21 Fuel pressure regulator - removal and refitting

Multec CFi

Note: *Refer to the precautions given in Section 1 before starting work. The pressure regulator diaphragm must be renewed whenever the regulator cover is removed. Thread-locking compound will be required to coat the regulator cover securing bolts.*

Removal

1 Depressurise the fuel system by removing the fuel pump relay (see Chapter 12), and cranking the engine on the starter motor for a minimum of 5 seconds.

2 Remove the airbox from the top of the fuel injection unit, as described in Section 6.

3 Unscrew the four Torx type pressure regulator cover securing bolts, and carefully withdraw the cover **(see illustration)**.

4 Recover the spring seat and spring assembly, and lift out the diaphragm **(see illustration)**.

21.4 Fuel pressure regulator components - CFi models

1 Diaphragm   3 Spring seat
2 Spring   4 Cover

21.3 Removing the fuel pressure regulator cover - CFi models

Refitting

5 Refitting is a reversal of removal, but ensure that the diaphragm is correctly located in the groove in the fuel injection unit, and coat the threads of the cover securing bolts with a thread locking compound before fitting.

Multec MPi

Note: *Refer to the precautions given in Section 1 before starting work. New sealing rings must be used on refitting.*

Removal

6 Disconnect the battery negative lead.

7 Disconnect the vacuum hose from the end of the pressure regulator.

8 Place a wad of rag beneath the fuel pipe union on the pressure regulator, then depressurise the fuel system by slowly loosening the union.

9 Be prepared for fuel spillage, and take adequate fire precautions. Two open-ended spanners will be required, so that one can be used to counterhold the regulator as the union is loosened **(see illustration)**. Once the pressure has been released, disconnect the fuel pipe from the pressure regulator. Plug the open end of the pipe to prevent fuel loss.

10 Unscrew the securing bolt, and pull the pressure regulator from the fuel pipe and the fuel rail **(see illustration)**.

Refitting

11 Refitting is a reversal of removal, but use new sealing rings on the regulator connections to the fuel pipe and the fuel rail.

21.9 Loosening the fuel pressure regulator fuel pipe union - Multec MPi models

4B

21.10 Removing the fuel pressure regulator - Multec MPi models

21.33 Disconnecting the vacuum pipe from the fuel pressure regulator - Motronic M 2.5 models

21.43 Fuel pressure check connector (1) - Simtec models

Multec-S

Note: *Refer to the precautions given in Section 1 before starting work.*

Removal

12 Depressurise the fuel system by removing the fuel pump relay (see Chapter 12), and cranking the engine on the starter motor for a minimum of 5 seconds.
13 Disconnect the battery negative lead.
14 Disconnect wiring plugs, as described in Section 11, paragraph 5.
15 Unclip wiring trough and secure to one side.
16 Place clean cloth around the pressure check connector, remove the cap and release any pressure left in the system. Be prepared for fuel spillage.
17 Remove vacuum hose from regulator.
18 Carefully remove the fuel hose from the regulator, collecting any spilt fuel in a container.
19 Secure fuel hose to one side.
20 Unscrew fastening bolt from regulator and remove it from the fuel rail complete with the pulse pick-up bracket.

Refitting

21 Replace the components the reverse order to which they were removed.
22 Make sure that the sealing ring is fitted between the regulator and the fuel rail.

Motronic M 1.5

Note: *Refer to the precautions given in Section 1 before starting work.*

Removal

23 Disconnect the battery negative lead.
24 For improved access, remove the idle speed control valve as described in Section 25. Then disconnect the wiring harness from the fuel injectors and move it to one side, taking care not to strain the wiring. Pull on the wiring harness housing, and compress the wiring plug retaining clips to release the harness housing from the injectors.
25 Position a wad of rag beneath the pressure regulator, to absorb any fuel which may be released as the regulator is removed.

26 Slowly loosen the clamp screws and disconnect the fuel hoses from the regulator. Be prepared for fuel spillage, and take adequate fire precautions.
27 Disconnect the vacuum hose from the top of the regulator, and withdraw the regulator.

Refitting

28 Refitting is a reversal of removal.

Motronic M 2.5 and M 2.8

Note: *Refer to the precautions given in Section 1 before starting work.*

Removal

29 Disconnect the battery negative lead.
30 Remove the airbox from the top of the throttle housing, as described in Section 6.
31 Release the retaining clip, and disconnect the wiring plug from the air flow meter. Pull on the plug, not on the wiring. Where applicable, recover the sealing ring.
32 Release the retaining clip, and disconnect the wiring plug from the throttle position sensor.
33 Disconnect the vacuum pipe from the top of the fuel pressure regulator **(see illustration)**.
34 Position a wad of rag beneath the fuel supply union on the fuel rail, then depressurise the fuel system by slowly loosening the union. Be prepared for fuel spillage, and take adequate fire precautions. Tighten the union when the pressure has been released.
35 Position a wad of rag beneath the regulator, to absorb the fuel which will be released as the regulator is removed.
36 Using a spanner or socket, and working underneath the regulator, unscrew the Torx type securing bolts, then withdraw the regulator. Be prepared for fuel spillage, and take adequate fire precautions.

Refitting

37 Refitting is a reversal of removal, remembering the following points.
38 Ensure that all wires, pipes and hoses are correctly reconnected.
39 Refit the airbox as described in Section 6.

Simtec

Note: *Refer to the precautions given in Section 1 before starting work.*

Removal

40 Depressurise the fuel system by removing the fuel pump relay (see Chapter 12), and cranking the engine on the starter motor for a minimum of 5 seconds.
41 Disconnect the battery negative lead.
42 Remove both the crankcase vent hose from the cylinder head cover and the air intake hose.
43 Place clean cloth around the pressure check connector before removing the cap and reducing any pressure **(see illustration)**. Release pressure slowly and be prepared for spillage.
44 Remove the vacuum hose from the regulator.
45 The regulator can now be unclamped and removed from the fuel rail. Note is position before removal.

Refitting

46 Replace all damaged seals and keep all parts clean.
47 Before refitting, lightly coat sealing rings with clean engine oil.
48 Refitting is a reversal of removal. Ensure that the regulator fits correctly on to the fuel rail.

22 Throttle position sensor - removal and refitting

Multec CFi

Note: *Locking Compound will be required to coat the sensor securing bolt threads on refitting.*

Removal

1 Disconnect the battery negative lead.
2 Remove the airbox from the top of the fuel injection unit, as described in Section 6.

22.3 Disconnecting the throttle position sensor wiring plug - CFi models

22.4 Removing the throttle position sensor - CFi models

22.14 Throttle position sensor (arrowed) - Motronic M 2.5 models

3 Disconnect the wiring plug from the throttle position sensor **(see illustration)**.
4 Remove the two securing screws, and withdraw the sensor from its housing in the fuel injection unit **(see illustration)**.

Refitting

5 Ensure that the throttle valve is closed, then refit the sensor to the housing, making sure that the sensor arm is correctly engaged with the throttle valve shaft.
6 Coat the sensor securing bolts with thread-locking compound, then insert and tighten them.
7 Further refitting is a reversal of removal.

Multec MPi and Motronic 1.5

Removal

8 Disconnect the battery negative lead.
9 Release the securing clips, and disconnect the wiring plug from the throttle position sensor.
10 Remove the three (two, on Motronic M 1.5 systems) securing screws, and withdraw the sensor from the throttle body.

Refitting

11 Refitting is a reversal of removal, but ensure that the sensor wiper engages correctly with the throttle valve shaft, and ensure that the sensor is correctly seated in its location on the throttle body.

Motronic M 2.5

Removal

12 Disconnect the battery negative lead.
13 Remove the airbox and the air flow meter, as described in Section 6. Note that if the connecting air trunking is left in place, the two components can be removed as an assembly.
14 Release the retaining clip, and disconnect the wiring plug from the throttle position sensor **(see illustration)**.
15 Remove the two securing screws and withdraw the sensor from the throttle body.

Refitting

16 Refit the sensor, but before tightening the securing screws, adjust the position of the sensor as follows.
17 Turn the sensor body anti-clockwise until

resistance is felt then tighten the securing screws.
18 When the throttle valve is opened, an audible click should be noticeable from the sensor, and similarly, this should be repeated as the throttle valve is closed.
19 If necessary, adjust the position of the sensor until a click is heard just as the throttle valve begins to open.
20 Refit the airbox as described in Section 6.

<hr>

23 Throttle valve potentiometer - removal and refitting

Multec-S

Note: *Refer to the precautions given in Section 1 before starting work. Locking Compound (Vauxhall P/N 90167347) will be required when refitting this component. A new throttle body mounting gasket will be required on refitting.*

Removal

1 Follow procedure as described for removing the throttle body (Section 11), from paragraph 1 to 24.
2 Undo the two fastening bolts from the potentiometer and remove.

Refitting

3 Attach the potentiometer to the throttle body.
4 Insert the securing bolts with Locking Compound (Vauxhall P/N 90167347) **(see illustration)**.
5 Remainder of refitting is a reversal of the removal procedure.
6 Ensure that all electrical, fuel and cable connections are secure.

Motronic M 2.8

Removal

7 Disconnect the battery negative lead.
8 Disconnect the wiring plug for the intake air temperature sensor and the air flow meter.
9 Remove the airbox, as described in Section 6.

10 Disconnect the wiring for the potentiometer.
11 The potentiometer can now be removed.

Refitting

12 Refitting is a reversal of removal. Ensure that the wiring plugs are firmly connected.

Simtec

Removal

13 Disconnect the battery negative lead.
14 Unplug the wiring for the potentiometer
15 The unit can now be unscrewed and removed from the throttle body.

Refitting

16 Refitting is a reversal of removal. Ensure that the wiring plugs are firmly connected.

4B

<hr>

24 Idle speed control motor - removal and refitting

Multec CFi

Note: *A new O-ring must be used on refitting, and thread-locking compound will be required to coat the motor securing bolt threads.*

Removal

1 Disconnect the battery negative lead.
2 Remove the airbox from the top of the fuel injection unit, as described in Section 6.
3 Release the securing lugs, and disconnect

23.4 Throttle valve potentiometer securing bolts - Multec-S models

24.3 Disconnecting the wiring plug from the idle speed control motor - CFi models

24.4A Remove the securing screws . . .

withdraw the motor. Where applicable, recover the O-ring seal.

Refitting

12 Before refitting the motor, examine the condition of the sealing ring, and renew if necessary.

13 Refitting is a reversal of removal, ensuring that the sealing ring is correctly located, and that the motor wiring socket faces downwards.

24.4B . . . and withdraw the idle speed control motor. Note O-ring (arrowed) - CFi models

the wiring plug from the idle speed control motor **(see illustration)**.

4 Remove the two securing screws, and withdraw the motor from the side of the fuel injection unit. Where applicable, recover the O-ring seal **(see illustrations)**.

Refitting

5 Refitting is a reversal of removal, remembering the following points.

6 To avoid damaging the housing during refitting, the distance between the end of the motor piston and the end face of the motor body flange should not be larger than 28.0 mm **(see illustration)**. Measure the distance shown, and if greater than specified, carefully push the piston into the motor body as far as its stop.

24.6 Measure the distance (A) between the end of the idle speed control motor piston and the end face of the motor body flange - CFi models

7 Refit the motor using a new O-ring seal, with the wiring socket facing downwards.

8 Coat the threads of the motor securing bolts with a thread-locking compound before fitting.

Multec MPi

Note: *A new sealing ring may be required on refitting.*

Removal

9 Disconnect the battery negative lead.

10 Release the securing clip, and disconnect the wiring plug from the idle speed control motor **(see illustration)**.

11 Remove the two securing screws, and

25 Idle speed control valve - removal and refitting

Motronic M 1.5

Removal

1 Disconnect the battery negative lead.

2 Release the retaining clip, and disconnect the wiring plug from the idle speed control valve **(see illustration)**.

3 The valve can be removed complete with its connecting hoses, or separately, leaving the hoses in place.

4 Loosen the relevant clamp screws, then disconnect the hoses and withdraw the valve **(see illustration)**.

Refitting

5 Refitting is a reversal of removal.

Motronic M 2.5 and M 2.8

Removal

6 Disconnect the battery negative lead.

7 Loosen the clamp screw, and disconnect the hose from underneath the airbox on the throttle body. Remove the clamp from the hose.

8 Apply the handbrake, then jack up the front of the vehicle, and support securely on axle stands.

9 Remove the engine undershield, if fitted, as described in Chapter 11.

10 Working underneath the vehicle, disconnect the wiring plug from the idle speed control valve, which is located underneath the

24.10 Disconnecting the idle speed control motor wiring plug - Multec MPi models

25.2 Disconnecting the wiring plug from the idle speed control valve - Motronic M 1.5 models

25.4 Withdrawing the idle speed control valve complete with hoses - Motronic M 1.5 models

25.10 Idle speed control valve (arrowed) - Motronic M 2.5 models

26.8 Idle air stepper motor maximum piston height 33.0 mm - Multec-S models

26.15 Idle air stepper motor - Simtec models

1 Motor

inlet manifold, above the starter motor **(see illustration)**.

11 Loosen the clamp screw and disconnect the remaining idle speed control valve hose from the inlet manifold, then withdraw the valve downwards, complete with the hoses.

12 If the hoses are to be removed from the valve, mark their locations before removal so that they can be correctly reconnected. Once the valve has been refitted, it is extremely difficult to swap the hose positions.

Refitting

13 Refitting is a reversal of removal, but ensure that the valve rests horizontally, with the wiring routed over the top of the coolant hose. If the wiring is routed under the coolant hose, this may cause the valve to be bent downwards, resulting in a restriction or fracture in the air hose to the inlet manifold.

26 Idle air stepper motor - removal and refitting

Multec-S

Note: *Refer to the precautions given in Section 1 before starting work. Locking Compound (Vauxhall P/N 90167347) will be required when refitting this component.*

Removal

1 Depressurise the fuel system by removing the fuel pump relay (see Chapter 12), and cranking the engine on the starter motor for a minimum of 5 seconds.

2 Disconnect the battery negative lead.

3 Remove the brake servo vacuum hose from the inlet manifold.

4 Place a clean rag around the fuel pressure test connector before removing the cap, then releasing any pressure left in the system. Be prepared for fuel spillage.

5 Detach the two fuel hoses, one from the fuel rail, the other from the regulator. Counterhold with open ended spanner.

6 Disconnect the wiring plug from the stepper motor.

7 Undo the two mounting bolts and remove the stepper motor with the sealing ring.

Refitting

8 Before refitting the motor, ensure that piston is not more than 33 mm from the face of the motor **(see illustration)**. Carefully push the piston back in, if necessary.

9 When refitting the motor, the electrical connectors should be facing downwards.

10 Replace the bolts, using Locking Compound (Vauxhall P/N 90167347).

11 Refitting the remaining components is a reversal of removal.

Simtec

Note: *A replacement mounting gasket will be needed when refitting.*

Removal

12 Disconnect the battery negative lead.

13 Remove the crankcase vent hose from the cylinder head cover and the air intake hose.

14 Disconnect the wiring plug from the stepper motor.

15 Unbolt the motor from the throttle valve housing **(see illustration)**.

Refitting

16 Clean the sealing surfaces of both the motor and the housing, but ensure that no dirt enters either component.

17 Refit the motor with a new gasket.

18 Refitting is a reversal of removal.

27 Inlet manifold pressure sensor - removal and refitting

Multec CFi

Removal

1 The sensor is located on the engine compartment bulkhead, under the edge of the water deflector **(see illustration)**.

2 Disconnect the battery negative lead.

3 Lift up the edge of the water deflector for access to the sensor.

4 Disconnect the sensor wiring plug and the vacuum pipe.

5 Pull the sensor upwards to release it from its bracket, and withdraw it from the vehicle.

Refitting

6 Refitting is a reversal of removal.

27.1 Inlet manifold pressure sensor location (water deflector lifted for access) - Multec CFi models

Multec-S

Removal

7 Disconnect the battery negative lead.

8 The sensor is located in the engine compartment, on the bulkhead.

9 Lift the rubber seal and remove the sensor, complete with bracket from the bulkhead.

10 Disconnect the wiring plug and the vacuum hose from the inlet manifold.

11 The sensor is secured in the bracket, by four plastic hook type clips **(see illustration)**. These must be carefully pushed together to release the sensor.

27.11 Inlet manifold pressure sensor - Multec-S models

1 Sensor
2 Retaining clip (note the four hooked clamps)

4B

28.1 Inductive pulse pick-up sensor location viewed from underneath vehicle (securing bolt arrowed) - Multec MPi models

28.15 Inductive pulse pick-up securing bolt (arrowed) - Multec-S models

28.20 Inductive pulse pick-up sensor gap (arrowed) - Multec-S models

12 Take great care when handling these components, as they can be easily damaged.

Refitting

13 Refitting is a reversal of removal.

28 Inductive pulse pick-up - removal and refitting

Multec MPi

Note: *A new sealing ring may be required on refitting. This sensor is also known as the crankshaft speed and position sensor.*

Removal

1 The sensor is located in a bracket bolted to the lower cylinder block, on the inlet manifold side of the engine, next to the crankshaft pulley **(see illustration)**.
2 Disconnect the battery negative lead.
3 Disconnect the sensor wiring connector, which is attached to a bracket on the camshaft cover. Release the connector from the bracket.
4 Access to the sensor is most easily obtained from under the vehicle.
5 Remove the securing screw, and withdraw the sensor from its bracket. Note the routing of the wiring to aid refitting.

Refitting

6 Examine the sensor sealing ring, and renew if necessary.
7 Refitting is a reversal of removal, ensuring that the wiring and the wiring connector are correctly located.
8 On completion, check the gap between the end face of the sensor and the toothed sensor wheel attached to the crankshaft pulley, using a feeler gauge. The gap should be as given in the Specifications. If the gap is not as specified, the sensor mounting bracket must be renewed, as no adjustment is possible.

Multec-S

Removal

9 Disconnect the battery negative lead.
10 Unclip the wiring trough from the three fastening points.
11 Disconnect the pick-up wiring plug and remove from the bracket.
12 Connect a length of cable, approximately 2.0 metres in length, to the wiring plug for the pick-up.
13 Carefully pull the cable from the pick-up so that the attached cable is pulled through the route of the original wiring.
14 Disconnect the wiring from the cable, leaving the cable in place.
15 Unbolt the single bolt from the pick-up, that is attached to the bracket on the oil pump **(see illustration)**, and remove it.

Refitting

16 Bolt the pick-up into the bracket on the oil pump.
17 Connect the pick-up's wiring to the cable. Carefully pull the cable and wiring through the original route.
18 Remove the cable and reconnect the wiring plug. Clip the plug into the bracket.
19 Replace the wiring trough.
20 Measure the gap between the pick-up and the timing disc, using a feeler gauge **(see illustration)**.
21 If the gap is not 1.0 ± 0.7 mm, replace the pick-up bracket.

C 18 NZ, Motronic M1.5 and M 2.5

Note: *A new sealing ring may be required on refitting. This sensor is also known as the crankshaft speed and position sensor.*

Removal

22 The sensor is located in the exhaust manifold side of the engine, in the lower cylinder block, behind the oil pump.
23 Disconnect the battery negative lead.
24 Where applicable, release the relevant outer timing belt cover securing clips, and unclip the sensor wiring from the timing belt cover.
25 Disconnect the sensor wiring connector, noting its location.
26 Unscrew the securing screw, and withdraw the sensor from the cylinder block **(see illustration)**.

Refitting

27 Examine the sensor sealing ring, and renew if necessary **(see illustration)**.
28 Refitting is a reversal of removal, ensuring that the sensor wiring is correctly located on the timing belt cover (where applicable), and that the wiring connector is correctly located.

Motronic M 2.8

Removal

29 Disconnect the battery negative lead.
30 Disconnect the pick-up's wiring plug, that is located between the air cleaner housing and the front suspension turret.

28.26 Unscrewing the crankshaft speed/position sensor securing screw (engine mounting bracket and power steering pump removed) - C 18 NZ models

28.27 Examine the crankshaft speed/position sensor O-ring

28.46 Inductive pulse pick-up - Simtec models

1 Support   2 Pick-up

31 Loosen the wire from the mounting straps. Note the routing for the wiring.
32 Remove the power steering pump support bracket.
33 The sensor can now be removed from the cylinder block.

Refitting

34 Refitting is a reversal of removal. Ensure that when replacing the sensor, the wiring cannot foul against any moving or hot parts, i.e. drivebelts or exhausts.

Simtec

Removal

35 Disconnect the battery negative lead.
36 Disconnect the wiring plugs from the intake air temperature sensor and the air flow meter.
37 Undo the retaining clamps and remove the meter assembly, air intake hose and temperature sensor.
38 Remove the vent hoses from the cylinder head cover.
39 Disconnect the plug strip by pressing the safety clamps, above the 1st and fourth cylinders, backwards with a screwdriver.
40 Lift the plug strip and place to one side.
41 Disconnect the wiring for the pick-up from the plug strip.
42 Remove the air cleaner assembly. Details in Section 7.
43 Remove the ribbed V-belt. Details in Chapter 5.
44 Undo the three bolts, securing the support.
45 Note the routing of the wiring, before removal.
46 The pick-up can now be removed **(see illustration)**.

Refitting

47 Re-route the wiring as it was disconnected. It should run between the cylinder block and the support.
48 Take not to squeeze or bend the wiring. Ensure that after refitting the wire can move freely, without fouling any hot or moving parts.
49 Refitting the remaining components is a

29.1A Disconnecting the coolant temperature sensor wiring plug - C 14 NZ models

reversal of the removal procedure. However take care when refitting the injector plug strip. Ensure that good contacts are made. It should snap into place.

29 Coolant temperature sensor - removal and refitting

Note: *A new sealing ring must be used on refitting. On Multec-S models, easier access to this sensor can be gained with the air cleaner assembly was removed.*

Removal

1 The sensor is located in the rear right-hand side of the inlet manifold on CFi models. On MPi models it is located in the left hand end face of the cylinder head and in the end thermostat housing on Motronic and Multec-S models **(see illustrations)**. On Simtec models it is located in the coolant flange, next to the DIS module.
2 Disconnect the battery negative lead.
3 Partially drain the cooling system, as described in Chapter 1.
4 Disconnect the sensor wiring plug **(see illustration)**.
5 Unscrew the sensor, and withdraw it. Recover the sealing ring where applicable.

Refitting

6 Refitting is a reversal of removal, but use a

29.4 Disconnecting the coolant temperature sensor wiring plug - Motronic M 1.5 models

29.1B Coolant temperature sensor and sender - Motronic M 2.5 models

1 Temperature sensor
2 Temperature sender

new sealing ring.
7 On completion, top-up the cooling system as described in Chapter 3.

30 Oxygen sensor - removal and refitting

Note: *If the original sensor is to be re-used, the threads must be lubricated with Special Grease (Vauxhall P/N 90295397) on refitting. Do not expose the sensor to fuel or silicone. This sensor is also known as the Lambda sensor.*

Removal

1 On Motronic and Simtec models, the sensor is located in the front exhaust section. Therefore it will be necessary to raise the vehicle on stands to gain access to this sensor. Refer to the Reference Chapter. Remove the engine undershield, if fitted.
2 On other models it is located on the exhaust manifold.
3 It is advisable to wear gloves, as the exhaust system will be extremely hot.
4 Start the engine, and run it until it reaches normal operating temperature. Stop the engine.
5 Disconnect the battery negative lead, then disconnect the oxygen sensor wiring plug, noting its location **(see illustration)**.

30.5 Disconnecting the oxygen sensor wiring connector. Note connector bracket location on transmission (arrowed) - C 14 NZ models

4B

30.7 Removing the exhaust gas oxygen sensor - Motronic M 2.5 models

31.3 Disconnecting the intake air temperature sensor wiring plug - Multec MPi models

31.10 Intake air temperature sensor - Multec-S models

1 Sealing ring   2 Sensor

6 Using a spanner, unscrew the sensor.

7 Withdraw the sensor and its wiring, taking care not to burn the wiring on the exhaust system **(see illustration)**. Note carefully the route of the wiring.

Refitting

8 The sensor must be refitted with the engine and exhaust system still at normal operating temperature.

9 If a new sensor is being fitted, it will be supplied with the threads coated in a special grease, to prevent the sensor seizing in the exhaust.

10 If the original sensor is being refitted, clean the threads carefully. The threads must be coated with Special Grease (Vauxhall P/N 90295397). Use only the specified grease, which consists of liquid graphite and glass beads. As the exhaust system heats up, the graphite will burn off, leaving the glass beads between the threads to prevent the sensor from seizing.

11 Refitting is a reversal of removal.

31 Intake air temperature sensor - removal and refitting

Except Multec-S

Removal

1 The sensor is located in the left-hand end of the inlet manifold plenum chamber on MPi models. On Motronic and Simtec models, the sensor is located in the air trunking between the inlet manifold and air flow meter. Take care not to damage the air trunking.

2 Disconnect the battery negative lead.

3 Disconnect the sensor wiring plug **(see illustration)**.

4 Unscrew the sensor.

Refitting

5 Refitting is a reversal of removal.

Multec-S

Removal

6 Disconnect the battery negative lead.

7 Disconnect the wiring plug from the sensor, which is located in the air intake pipe.

8 Carefully pull the sensor out of the rubber sealing ring.

9 Remove the ring from the intake pipe. Take care not to damage either component.

Refitting

10 Fit the ring on the sensor **(see illustration)**.

11 Refit the sensor, with ring, into the intake pipe.

12 Reconnect the wiring plug

32 Air flow meter - removal and refitting

Motronic M 1.5

Note: *A new sealing ring must be used on refitting, and thread-locking compound will be required to coat the securing bolts.*

Removal

1 Disconnect the battery negative lead.

2 Release the securing clip, and disconnect the wiring plug from the intake air temperature sensor (mounted in the air trunking). Pull on the plug, not on the wiring **(see illustration)**.

3 Similarly, disconnect the wiring plug from the air flow meter.

4 Loosen the clamp screws securing the air trunking to the throttle body and the air flow meter, then withdraw the air trunking.

5 Remove the air cleaner cover, complete with the air flow meter, with reference to Section 7.

6 Unscrew the two securing bolts, and remove the air flow meter from the air cleaner cover **(see illustration)**. Recover the sealing ring.

Refitting

7 Refitting is a reversal of removal, but use a new sealing ring when fitting the air flow meter to the air cleaner cover, and coat the securing bolts with a thread-locking compound.

Motronic M 2.5, M 2.8 and Simtec

Removal

8 Disconnect the battery negative lead.

9 Note the installation position of the meter assembly.

10 Release the retaining clip, and disconnect the wiring plug from the air flow meter **(see illustration)**. Pull on the plug, not on the wiring. Recover the sealing ring, where applicable.

11 Loosen the clamp screws, disconnect the air trunking from either end of the meter, then withdraw the meter.

32.2 Air flow meter (1) and intake air temperature sensor (2) - Motronic M 1.5 models

32.6 Air flow meter securing screws (arrowed) - Motronic M 1.5 models

12 Do not dismantle the meter. If faulty replace the complete assembly.

Refitting

13 Inspect the condition of the wiring plug sealing ring and renew if necessary.

14 Refitting is a reversal of removal. Ensure that the hose connections are correctly seated in the recesses of the meter.

33 Knock sensor - removal and refitting

Multec-S

Note: *A special tool (No. KM-728) is required to replace this sensor.*

Removal

1 Disconnect the battery negative lead.

2 Using the special tool **(see illustration)**, carefully unscrew the sensor from the cylinder block.

Refitting

3 Replace the sensor using the special tool.

4 The sensor torque is reached before the body of the sensor contacts the block. Do not overtighten.

5 Replace the wiring.

Motronic M 2.5 and M 2.8

Removal

6 The sensor is located on the lower inlet manifold side of the cylinder block, below the idle speed control valve, and (unless the inlet manifold has been removed) is only accessible from below the vehicle.

7 Disconnect the battery negative lead.

8 Apply the handbrake, then jack up the front of the vehicle and support securely on axle stands, as described in the Reference Chapter.

9 Remove the engine undershield, as described in Chapter 11.

10 Disconnect the sensor wiring plug.

11 Unscrew the securing bolt, and withdraw the sensor from the cylinder block.

Refitting

12 Refitting is a reversal of the removal procedure, but make sure that the sensor and its seat are perfectly clean, and that the sensor is secured firmly. Failure to observe these points could result in damage to the engine, as a poorly mounted sensor will not detect 'knocking', and the appropriate ignition correction will not be applied.

Simtec

Removal

13 Disconnect the battery negative lead.

14 Remove the hoses from the cylinder head cover.

15 Remove the injector plug strip.

16 Disconnect the knock sensor wiring from the plug strip and note it's routing through to the sensor.

17 Unbolt the sensor from the cylinder block.

32.10 Disconnecting the wiring plug from the air mass meter - Motronic M 2.5 models

Refitting

18 Before refitting, ensure that the contact surfaces of both the sensor and the block are clean. Do not use any form of washers.

19 Refitting is a reversal of removal.

34 Camshaft sensor - removal and refitting

Multec-S

Removal

1 Disconnect the battery negative lead.

2 Remove the wiring plug for the camshaft sensor from the bracket on the fuel rail.

3 Remove the air cleaner assembly, air intake pipe and air duct hose. Refer to Section 7.

4 Remove the front timing belt cover. Details in Chapter 2B.

5 Unclip the wiring for the sensor from the timing belt cover.

6 Unbolt the two bolts securing the sensor to the rear timing belt cover.

Refitting

7 Refitting is a reversal of removal.

Motronic M 2.8

Note: *A new sealing ring will be required when refitting the disc.*

34.12 Camshaft sensor location - Motronic 2.8 models

1 Camshaft sensor

33.2 Special tool (No. KM-728) for knock sensor removal - Multec-S models

Removal

8 Disconnect the battery negative lead.

9 Remove the wiring plug.

10 Place a piece of cloth below the sensor.

11 Unbolt the sensor from the end of the camshaft housing, taking care to absorb any oil that leaks.

12 Remove the sensor **(see illustration)**.

Refitting

13 Refitting is a reversal of the removal procedure. Always renew the oil seal and check the oil level after refitting.

Simtec

Removal

14 Disconnect the battery negative lead.

15 Remove the spark plug cover.

16 Disconnect the wiring plug for the sensor, that is located at the timing belt end.

17 Remove the air cleaner assembly.

18 Remove the ribbed V-belt. Refer to Chapter 5.

19 Remove the front timing belt cover, as described in Chapter 2B.

20 The camshaft sensor can now be unbolted and removed from above.

Refitting

21 Refitting is a reversal of the removal procedure. However take care not to trap the wiring for inductive pulse pick-up.

4B

35.11 Controlled canister purge valve - Motronic 2.8 models

1 Hose to canister   2 Metal securing tab

35.18 Controlled canister purge valve - Simtec models

1 Hose to canister
2 Hose to throttle valve housing

36.9 Plastic cover removed to expose fuel pump - Hatchback model

36.20 Fuel pump assembly

1 Mounting plate
2 Fuel hose
3 Pump
4 Rubber sleeve
5 Fuel filter

35 Controlled canister purge valve - removal and refitting

Note: *Refer to Chapter 4C for details on the canister.*

Multec-S

Removal

1 Disconnect the battery negative lead.
2 Disconnect the wiring plugs, as described in Section 11, paragraph 5.
3 Unclip the wiring trough and secure to one side.
4 Remove the vacuum hose from the purge valve.
5 Plug the end of the hose that goes to the canister.
6 Using a screwdriver press down the retaining clamp and remove the valve.
7 Bend the tag back into it's original position.

Refitting

8 Refitting is a reversal of the removal procedure.

Motronic M 2.8

Removal

9 Disconnect the battery negative lead.
10 Unplug the wiring for the valve.
11 Seal the hose to the canister **(see illustration).**
12 Press inwards the metal securing tab.
13 Remove the valve from it's bracket.

Refitting

14 Refitting is a reversal of the removal procedure. Ensure that the securing tab has locked on to the valve.

Simtec

Removal

15 Disconnect the battery negative lead.
16 Disconnect the wiring harness plug from the side of the DIS coil.
17 Remove the two hoses from the valve.
18 Plug the hose from carbon canister, as

shown **(see illustration),** with a bolt or similar diameter object.
19 Disconnect the wiring plug from the valve.
20 Remove the valve from it's bracket.

Refitting

21 Refitting is a reversal of the removal procedure. Make sure that the two hoses are connected correctly.

36 Fuel pump - testing, removal and refitting

Note: *Refer to the precautions given in Section 1 before starting work. A new gasket must be used on refitting the pump, and sealing compound will be required to coat the securing bolt threads.*

Testing

1 If the pump is functioning, it should be possible to hear it 'buzzing' by listening under the rear of the vehicle when the ignition is switched on. Unless the engine is started, the fuel pump should switch off after approximately one second. If the noise produced is excessive, this may be due to a faulty pump.
2 If the pump appears to have failed completely, check the wiring to the pump, and check the appropriate fuse and relay.
3 To test the performance of the pump, special equipment is required, and it is recommended that any suspected faults are referred to a Vauxhall dealer.

Saloon and Hatchback models

Removal

4 Depressurize the fuel system by removing the fuel pump relay (see Chapter 12), and cranking the engine on the starter motor for at least 5 seconds.
5 Disconnect the battery negative lead.
6 Siphon out any remaining fuel in the tank through the filler pipe. Siphon the fuel into a clean metal container that can be sealed.

7 Fold the rear sear cushions forwards.
8 Lift the carpet panel on the right-hand side of the floor to expose the plastic fuel pump cover.
9 Carefully prise the plastic cover from the floor to expose the fuel pump **(see illustration).**
10 Disconnect the pump wiring plug.
11 Release the hose clip, and carefully disconnect the fuel hose from the top of the pump. Be prepared for fuel spillage, and take adequate fire precautions. Clamp or plug the open end of the hose to prevent dirt ingress and further fuel spillage.
12 Unscrew the six securing bolts and washers, and carefully withdraw the pump assembly from the fuel tank. Again, be prepared for the release of fuel, and take precautions.
13 If required, the fuel pump can be detached from the assembly for renewal as follows.
14 Pull the fuel filter from the bottom of the pump.
15 Release the hose clip, and disconnect the fuel hose from the top of the pump.
16 Take note of the positions of the two pump wires to aid correct refitting, then using a soldering iron, de-solder the two wires from the top of the pump.
17 Carefully slide the pump from its rubber mounting sleeve.

Refitting

18 Refitting is a reversal of removal, remembering the following points.
19 If the pump has been detached from the assembly, make sure that the wires are securely soldered to the pump in their correct locations when reassembling.
20 Inspect the filter at the bottom of the pump for excessive contamination or blockage, and renew if necessary **(see illustration).**
21 Use a new pump gasket.
22 Clean the threads of the pump securing

36.24 Fuel pump location in fuel tank - Estate and Hatchback models

bolts thoroughly, and coat them with a sealing compound before refitting.

Estate and Van models

Removal

23 Chock the front wheels, then jack up the rear of the vehicle and support securely on axle stands.
24 The fuel pump is located in the front end of the fuel tank, under the vehicle (see illustration).
25 Proceed as described in paragraphs 10 to 17 inclusive.

Refitting

26 Proceed as described in paragraphs 18 to 22 inclusive.

37 Fuel filter - removal and refitting

Note: *Refer to the precautions given in Section 1 before starting work.*

Removal

1 The fuel filter is located on a bracket attached to the right-hand side of the fuel tank.
2 Clamp the fuel hoses at either end of the filter to minimise fuel loss when the hoses are disconnected, then place a container beneath the filter to catch the fuel which will be released.
3 Disconnect the fuel hoses from the filter. Be prepared for fuel spillage, and take adequate fire precautions.
4 Note the orientation of the filter (and the orientation of any flow direction markings that may appear on the filter body), then unscrew the clamp bolt, and withdraw the filter from its bracket. Note that the filter will still contain some petrol, which should be drained safely into a container.

Refitting

5 Refitting is a reversal of removal, ensuring that the filter is orientated as noted before removal.

38 Throttle cable - removal, refitting and adjustment

Removal

1 Described in Chapter 4A, but note the following.
2 Where applicable, ignore the reference to removing the airbox.
3 For 'carburettor' substitute 'throttle body' or 'fuel injection unit' as applicable, and note that the cable bracket is bolted to the inlet manifold.

Refitting

4 On some models, the throttle cable end connects to a balljoint on the throttle valve

38.4A Releasing the throttle cable balljoint clip . . .

38.4B . . . and releasing the cable grommet from its bracket - C 16 SE model

lever, and is retained by a clip. The cable is also retained by a grommet that locates in a bracket attached to the inlet manifold (see illustrations).

Adjustment

5 Described in Chapter 4A, but for 'carburettor' substitute 'throttle body' or 'fuel injection unit', as applicable.

4B

Notes

Chapter 4 Part C
Emission control and exhaust systems

Contents

Degrees of difficulty

Easy, suitable for novice with little experience		Fairly easy, suitable for beginner with some experience		Fairly difficult, suitable for competent DIY mechanic		Difficult, suitable for experienced DIY mechanic		Very difficult, suitable for expert DIY or professional	

Specifications

4C

Torque wrench settings	Nm	lbf ft
AIR combination valve to bracket	6	5
AIR metal pipe to exhaust manifold	20	15
AIR pump	10	7
AIR pump air cleaner strap	4	3
AIR pump assembly	20	.15
AIR pump insulator	10	7
AIR switchover valve	4	3
Carbon canister to wheel arch	4	3
Carbon canister strap to bracket	4	3
Exhaust downpipe to manifold	25	18
Exhaust manifold (use new nuts on DOHC models)	22	16
Inlet manifold:		
except X 16 XEL	22	16
X 16 XEL	8	6
Inlet manifold air intake shroud:		
C 18 NZ and C 20 NE	8	6

1 General information

1 All models can be operated on unleaded petrol (models with a catalytic converter can **only** be operated on unleaded petrol), but additionally, various systems may be fitted (depending on model) to reduce the emission of pollution into the atmosphere. The systems are described in more detail in the following sections. All models are fitted with a crankcase emission control system.

2 Crankcase emission control system - general

1 A crankcase ventilation system is fitted to all models, but the systems differ in detail according to model.
2 Oil fumes and blow-by gases (combustion gases that have passed by the piston rings) are drawn from the crankcase into the area of the cylinder head above the camshaft(s) through a hose. From here, the gases are drawn into the inlet manifold/throttle body (as applicable) and/or the air box on the carburettor/throttle body, where they are mixed with fresh air/fuel mixture and burnt, hence reducing harmful exhaust emissions.
3 Certain models may have a mesh filter inside the camshaft cover, which should be cleaned in paraffin if clogging is evident.

3 Exhaust emission control system - general

1 To minimise the level of exhaust gas pollutants released into the atmosphere, all fuel-injected models are fitted with a catalytic converter (see Section 4), located in the exhaust system. A 'closed loop' system is used, in which an exhaust gas oxygen sensor, mounted in the exhaust manifold or downpipe (depending on model), provides a signal to the fuel system electronic control unit. This enables it to adjust the air/fuel mixture ratio within very fine limits. This enables the catalytic converter to operate at its optimum efficiency at all times.

2 The oxygen sensor senses the level of oxygen in the exhaust gas, which is proportional to the air/fuel mixture ratio. A rich mixture produces exhaust gases with a low oxygen content, and the oxygen content rises as the mixture weakens. The catalyst operates at maximum efficiency when the air/fuel mixture ratio is at the chemically correct ratio for the complete combustion of petrol, and the output produced by the oxygen sensor allows the electronic control unit to maintain air/fuel ratio very close to the optimum value under all engine operating conditions.

4 Catalytic converter - general and precautions

General

1 All fuel-injected models are equipped with a catalytic converter, to reduce exhaust gas emissions. The catalytic converter is located in the exhaust system between the exhaust front and centre sections.

2 The purpose of the catalytic converter is to convert potentially harmful carbon monoxide gas, oxides of nitrogen, and unburnt hydrocarbons into harmless gases and water vapour before they are released into the atmosphere. The converter consists of a stainless steel canister containing a catalyst-coated honeycomb ceramic. The catalyst comprises a mixture of three precious metals; platinum, palladium and rhodium.

3 The exhaust gases pass freely through the honeycomb, where the catalyst speeds up the chemical change of the exhaust gases, without being permanently altered itself.

4 To enable the engine management system to achieve complete combustion of the fuel mixture, and thus to minimise exhaust emissions, an oxygen sensor is fitted in the exhaust gas stream. The sensor monitors the oxygen level in the exhaust gas, and sends a signal to the electronic control module. The module constantly alters the fuel/air mixture within a narrow band to reduce emissions,

and to allow the catalytic converter to operate at maximum efficiency. No adjustment of idle mixture is therefore possible on models fitted with a catalytic converter.

Precautions

5 During operation, the catalytic converter reaches very high temperatures, and this should be remembered when parking the car. Try to avoid parking the vehicle on dry grass, etc., which may present a fire hazard if the catalyst is at working temperature.

6 When carrying out any work under the vehicle, remember that the catalyst will take a considerable time to cool down from its working temperature when the engine has been running. Take precautions to avoid the possibility of burns and the risk of fire.

7 If a fault in the ignition system is suspected, rectify the problem or seek advice as soon as possible, particularly in the case of misfiring, as damage to the catalyst may result.

8 If unburnt fuel enters the catalytic converter, the fuel may burn in the catalyst, resulting in overheating and serious damage to the converter. To avoid this possibility, the following should be avoided.

(a) Frequent cold starts in succession.

(b) Operation of the starter motor for an excessively long time (fuel is injected during the starting process).

(c) Allowing the fuel level in the fuel tank to become excessively low (an irregular fuel supply may cause overheating).

(d) Starting the engine by push or tow-starting (unburnt fuel may enter the converter). Always use jump leads as an alternative.

9 To avoid damage to the catalyst, the engine must be regularly serviced, and unleaded petrol must **always** be used. Leaded petrol will 'poison' the catalyst, and **must not** be used.

5 Fuel evaporation control system - general

1 To minimise the escape into the atmosphere of unburnt hydrocarbons, a fuel evaporation control system is fitted to certain models. The fuel tank filler cap is sealed, to prevent the release of fuel vapour into the atmosphere, and a charcoal canister is mounted under the right-hand wheel arch, to collect the fuel vapours that would otherwise be released from the tank when the vehicle is parked. The vapours are stored in the canister until a fuel tank vent valve is operated by manifold vacuum, or by a purge valve controlled by the fuel system ECU (depending on model). Refer to Chapter 4B for details on the purge valve. The purge valve releases the vapours into the engine inlet tract where they are burnt during the normal combustion process.

6 Exhaust gas recirculation (EGR) system - general

1 The exhaust gas recirculation (EGR) system is designed to recirculate small quantities of exhaust gas into the inlet tract and therefore into the combustion process. This process reduces the level of oxides of nitrogen present in the final exhaust gas that is released into the atmosphere. The volume of exhaust gas recirculated is controlled by manifold vacuum through a valve mounted in the inlet manifold.

2 A tract in the cylinder head allows exhaust gas to pass from the exhaust side of the cylinder head to the exhaust gas recirculation valve in the inlet manifold.

7 Secondary air injection system - general

1 During 1995, the new 'Ecotec' models (X 16 XEL, C 18 XEL and X 20 XEV), where fitted with a secondary air injection system. It is also known as the Air Injection Reactor (AIR). An electric pump, mounted on the inner wheel arch, forces air into the exhaust manifold, during certain conditions. This increases the combustion of hydrocarbons. It also increases the exhaust temperature. This enables the catalytic converter to reach it most effective operating temperature, more quickly.

8 Emission control system - testing

1 If the system is thought to be faulty, firstly, check that the hoses are unobstructed. On high-mileage vehicles, particularly when regularly used for short journeys, a jelly-like deposit may be evident inside the crankcase emission control system hoses. If excessive deposits are present, the relevant hose(s) should be removed and cleaned.

2 Periodically inspect the system hoses for security and damage, and renew them as necessary. Note that damaged or loose hoses can cause various engine running problems (erratic idle speed, stalling, etc.) which can be difficult to trace.

3 The crankcase breather tube can be unbolted from the cylinder block after disconnecting the hose. Use a new gasket when refitting. Note that on certain engines, the dipstick tube is integral with the crankcase breather tube.

4 Certain models have a mesh filter inside the camshaft cover, which should be cleaned in paraffin if clogging is evident. For access to the filter, remove the camshaft cover as described in Chapter 2A or 2B, as applicable.

The filter can be removed from the camshaft cover for cleaning after unscrewing the securing screws.

5 The system can only be tested accurately using Vauxhall specialist diagnostic equipment. Any suspected faults should be referred to a Vauxhall dealer.

9 Fuel evaporation control system - testing

1 If the system is thought to be faulty, disconnect the hoses from the charcoal canister and vent valve, and check that the hoses are clear by blowing through them. If necessary, clean or renew the hoses.

2 If the vent valve or the charcoal canister itself are thought to be faulty, the only course of action available is renewal.

10 Charcoal canister - removal and refitting

Removal

1 Remove the wheel arch liner from the front right-hand wheel arch, as described in Chapter 11.

2 Unscrew the securing nut, and detach the clamp strap securing the canister to the bracket under the wheel arch. Withdraw the canister and disconnect the hoses (see illustrations).

Refitting

3 Refitting is a reversal of the removal procedure.

11 Fuel tank vent valve (Multec CFi and MPi models) - removal and refitting

Removal

1 The valve is located under the water deflector on the engine compartment bulkhead (see illustration).

2 To remove the valve, lift the water deflector to expose the valve, then disconnect the three hoses, noting their locations to ensure correct refitting, and withdraw the valve from the bulkhead (release the securing clip, where applicable).

Refitting

3 Refitting is a reversal of removal, ensuring that the hoses are reconnected correctly, as noted before removal.

10.2A Unscrewing the charcoal canister clamp nut

12 Fuel tank vent valve (Motronic M 1.5 models) - removal and refitting

Removal

1 The valve is located in a bracket attached to the rear of the cylinder head.

2 Disconnect the battery negative lead.

3 Disconnect the wiring plug from the fuel tank vent valve.

4 Disconnect the two hoses from the valve, noting their locations to ensure correct refitting.

5 Unclip the valve from its bracket, and withdraw it.

Refitting

6 Refitting is a reversal of removal, ensuring that the hoses are reconnected as noted before removal.

13 Fuel tank vent valve (Motronic M 2.5 models) - removal and refitting

Removal

1 The fuel tank vent valve is located at the rear left-hand side of the engine (see illustration).

2 Disconnect the battery negative lead.

3 Disconnect the wiring plug from the valve.

11.1 Fuel tank vent valve - Multec CFi model

10.2B Withdrawing the charcoal canister

4 Disconnect the two hoses from the valve, noting their locations to aid refitting.

5 Remove the securing screw, and withdraw the valve from its bracket.

Refitting

6 Refitting is a reversal of removal, ensuring that the hoses are reconnected as noted before removal.

14 EGR system - testing

1 Start the engine, and run it until it reaches normal operating temperature.

2 Stop the engine, and remove the airbox from the top of the fuel injection unit, as described in Chapter 4B.

3 Connect an accurate tachometer to the engine according to the equipment manufacturer's instructions.

4 Disconnect the vacuum hose from the valve, then start the engine and record the idle speed.

5 Disconnect the vacuum hose from the valve, then apply vacuum to the valve using a vacuum hand pump. When the vacuum is applied, the idle speed should drop by at least 100 rpm.

6 If the idle speed does not drop as described previously, firstly, check the valve vacuum hose for obstructions and leaks. Clean the hose or renew it if necessary.

7 If the hose is in good condition, and a fault

13.1 Fuel tank vent valve - Motronic M 2.5 model

4C

is still suspected, it is likely that the valve is faulty. In this case, clean and if necessary renew the valve as described in the relevant Section.

8 Disconnect the tachometer, reconnect the vacuum hose and refit the airbox on completion.

15 EGR valve - removal and refitting

Removal

1 It is recommended that the valve is cleaned as follows annually.
2 Remove the airbox from the top of the fuel injection unit, as described in Chapter 4B.
3 Disconnect the vacuum hose from the valve.
4 Unscrew the two securing bolts, and withdraw the valve from the inlet manifold. Recover the gasket.
5 Carefully clean the mating faces of the inlet manifold and the valve using a stiff brush.
6 If the original valve is to be refitted, clean all deposits from the valve seat using a brush or a pointed tool. Take great care not to damage the valve seat.

Refitting

7 Refit the valve using a new gasket, then refit the vacuum hose and the airbox.

16 AIR pump assembly - removal and refitting

Removal

1 Chock the rear wheels, jack up the front of the vehicle and support it on axle stands placed under the body side members.
2 Remove the left hand front wheel and inner wheel arch lining.
3 Loosen the hose clamp and remove the air duct hose from the pump.
4 Disconnect the battery negative lead.
5 Undo the securing nuts and remove the pump assembly from its location. Disconnect the wiring plug.
6 Remove the wiring plug from the pump's bracket.
7 Mark the position of the pump on it's bracket before separating.
8 Remove the fixing bolts and disconnect the pump from it's insulator.
9 The insulator can also be checked by removing the nuts, securing the protective shield. Before removing, mark the shield and insulator. Replace if necessary.
10 Check the pump's air cleaner for damage.

Refitting

11 Refitting is a reversal of removal. Ensure correct alignment of the components.

17.5 AIR switchover valve

1 Servo hose connection
2 AIR combination valve connection

17 AIR switchover valve - removal and refitting

Removal

1 Disconnect the battery negative lead.
2 Disconnect wiring plug from the valve.
3 Mark the location of the vacuum hoses before removing them from the valve.
4 After disconnecting the hoses undo the two bolts, and remove the from its bracket.

Refitting

5 Refitting is a reversal of removal. Ensure hoses are fitted correctly **(see illustration)**.

18 AIR pipe and combination valve - removal and refitting

Note: *The gasket should be renewed when refitting the valve.*

Removal

1 Remove the combination valve air duct and vacuum hose.
2 Mark the location of the valve before removal.
3 Remove the valve from the AIR metal pipe **(see illustration)**.
4 Remove the pipe support bracket by releasing its bolts.

19.4 Disconnecting the coolant hose . . .

18.3 AIR metal pipe and combination valve

5 Remove the heat shield that is secured by two bolts.
6 The air pipe can now be removed by releasing the two securing bolts.

Refitting

7 Secure the pipe in the exhaust manifold, coating the bolts with Assembly Paste (Vauxhall P/N 90513210).
8 Using a new gasket, refitting is a reversal of removal. Retighten to correct torque as shown in Specifications.

19 Inlet manifold (14 NV models) - removal and refitting

Note: *Refer to the warning in Chapter 4A, before starting work. A new manifold gasket must be used on refitting.*

Removal

1 Disconnect the battery negative lead.
2 Drain the cooling system as described in Chapter 3.
3 Remove the carburettor as described in Chapter 4A, ignoring the reference to coolant spillage.
4 Disconnect the coolant hose from the rear of the manifold **(see illustration)**.
5 Where applicable, disconnect the camshaft cover breather hose from the rear of the manifold **(see illustration)**.

19.5 . . . and the camshaft cover breather hose (arrowed) from the inlet manifold

19.11 Withdrawing the inlet manifold

20.3 Brake servo hose union nut (1) and wiring connector (2) attached to left-hand end of inlet manifold - Multec CFi model

20.9 Earth wire (arrowed) attached to upper alternator mounting - Multec CFi model

6 Unscrew the union and disconnect the brake servo vacuum hose from the manifold.

7 Disconnect the wiring from the temperature gauge sender.

8 Unscrew and remove the top alternator mounting nut and bolt.

9 Disconnect and remove the stub hose that connects the crankcase breather tube to the rear of the camshaft housing.

10 Make a final check to ensure that all relevant hoses, pipes and wires have been disconnected.

11 Unscrew the securing nuts, and withdraw the manifold from the cylinder head **(see illustration)**. Note the position of the rear engine lifting bracket, which is secured by one of the manifold nuts, and recover the manifold gasket.

12 It is possible that some of the manifold studs may be unscrewed from the cylinder head when the manifold securing nuts are unscrewed. In this event, the studs should be screwed back into the cylinder head once the manifold has been removed, using two manifold nuts locked together.

13 The carburettor can be removed from the manifold.

Refitting

14 Refitting is a reversal of removal, remembering the following points.

15 If the carburettor has been removed from the manifold, refit it using a new gasket.

16 If the alternator mounting bracket has been unbolted from the manifold, refit it before refitting the manifold, as access to the securing bolt is limited once the manifold is in place.

17 Refit the manifold using a new gasket, and ensure that the engine lifting bracket is in place under the relevant manifold nut.

18 Ensure that all relevant hoses, pipes and wires are correctly reconnected.

19 Refill the cooling system as described in Chapter 3.

20 Check the throttle cable free play and adjust if necessary, as described in Chapter 4A.

21 If the carburettor has been disturbed, check and if necessary, adjust the idle speed and mixture, as described in Chapter 1.

20 Inlet manifold (Multec CFi models) - removal and refitting

Note: *Refer to the precautions given in 4B before starting work. A new gasket must be used on refitting.*

Removal

1 Remove the fuel injection unit as described in Chapter 4B.

2 Release the securing clip, then disconnect the throttle cable end balljoint from the throttle valve lever. Slide the throttle cable grommet from the bracket on the inlet manifold, and move the throttle cable to one side out of the way.

3 Unscrew the union nut, and disconnect the brake servo vacuum hose from the inlet manifold **(see illustration)**.

4 Where applicable, disconnect the hose from the EGR valve.

5 Disconnect the wiring from the temperature gauge sender.

6 Where applicable, disconnect the wiring from the coolant temperature sensor.

7 Separate the two halves of the wiring connector located in the bracket attached to the left-hand end of the inlet manifold. Unclip the connector from the bracket.

8 Partially drain the cooling system as described in Chapter 3. Then disconnect the coolant hose from the rear of the inlet manifold. Be prepared for coolant spillage, and plug the open end of the hose to reduce coolant loss.

9 Unscrew and remove the top alternator mounting nut and bolt, noting the location of the earth wire on the bolt **(see illustration)**.

10 Make a final check to ensure that all relevant hoses, pipes and wires have been disconnected.

11 Unscrew the securing nuts, and withdraw the manifold from the cylinder head. Recover the gasket.

12 It is possible that some of the manifold studs may be unscrewed from the cylinder head when the manifold securing nuts are

unscrewed. In this event, the studs should be screwed back into the cylinder head once the manifold has been removed, using two manifold nuts locked together.

13 Ancillary components can be removed from the manifold with reference to the relevant Sections of Chapter 4B.

Refitting

14 Refitting is a reversal of removal, remembering the following points.

15 Where applicable, refit any ancillary components to the manifold, referring to Chapter 4B for details.

16 If the alternator mounting bracket has been unbolted from the manifold, refit it before refitting the manifold, as access is limited once the manifold is in place.

17 Refit the manifold using a new gasket, and tighten the securing nuts to the specified torque.

18 Ensure that all relevant hoses, pipes and wires are correctly reconnected and routed.

19 On completion, check and if necessary top-up the coolant level, as described in Chapter 3.

20 Check and if necessary, adjust the throttle cable free play, as described in Chapter 4B.

21 Inlet manifold (Multec MPi models) - removal and refitting

Note: *Refer to the precautions given in Chapter 4B, before starting work. New gaskets will be required on refitting.*

Removal

1 Disconnect the battery negative lead.

2 Release the securing clip, then disconnect the throttle cable end balljoint from the throttle valve lever. Slide the throttle cable grommet from the bracket on the inlet manifold, and move the throttle cable to one side out of the way.

3 Loosen the clamp screw, and disconnect the air trunking from the throttle body.

4C

21.4 Brake servo hose union nut (arrowed) - Multec MPi model

21.9 Earth lead securing bolts (arrowed) at right-hand end of cylinder head - Multec MPi model

21.14A Fuel pipe connections (arrowed) under inlet manifold (viewed from underneath vehicle) - Multec MPi model

4 Unscrew the union nut, and disconnect the brake servo vacuum hose from the inlet manifold **(see illustration)**.

5 Disconnect the camshaft cover breather hoses from the throttle body.

6 Disconnect the vacuum hoses from the throttle body, noting their locations to aid refitting.

7 Disconnect the coolant hoses from the throttle body (two hoses) and the inlet manifold (one hose), noting their locations to aid refitting. Be prepared for coolant spillage, and clamp or plug the open ends of the hoses, to prevent further coolant loss. Where applicable, unclip the coolant hose from the rear of the manifold.

8 Disconnect the wiring plugs from the throttle position sensor and the idle speed control motor in the throttle housing, and from the intake air temperature sensor in the inlet manifold plenum chamber.

9 Unscrew the two securing bolts, and disconnect the two earth leads from the right-hand end of the cylinder head **(see illustration)**.

10 Disconnect the earth lead from the engine lifting eye bolt at the left-hand end of the inlet manifold.

11 Disconnect the wiring from the coolant temperature gauge sender in the inlet manifold.

12 Disconnect the wiring plugs from the fuel injectors.

13 Separate the two halves of the wiring

connector located in the bracket attached to the upper left-hand inlet manifold stud.

14 Disconnect the fuel hoses from the fuel pipes under the fuel rail, noting their locations to ensure correct refitting. Access is most easily obtained from under the vehicle. Loosen the clamp screws slowly, to release the pressure in the system. Be prepared for fuel spillage, and take adequate fire precautions. Clamp or plug the open ends of the hoses to prevent dirt ingress and further fuel leakage **(see illustrations)**.

15 Unscrew and remove the top alternator mounting nut and bolt.

16 Make a final check to ensure that all relevant hoses, pipes and wires have been disconnected.

17 Unscrew the securing nuts, and withdraw the manifold from the cylinder head **(see illustration)**. Recover the gasket.

18 It is possible that some of the manifold studs may be unscrewed from the cylinder head when the manifold securing nuts are unscrewed. In this event, the studs should be screwed back into the cylinder head once the manifold has been removed, using two manifold nuts locked together.

19 Ancillary components can be removed from the manifold with reference to the relevant Sections of Chapter 4B.

Refitting

20 Refitting is as described for Multec CFi models, in Section 20.

22 Inlet manifold, upper (Multec-S models) - removal and refitting

Note: Refer to the precautions given in Chapter 4B, before starting work. New gaskets will be required on refitting.

Removal

1 Depressurise the fuel system by removing the fuel pump relay (see Chapter 12), and cranking the engine on the starter motor for a minimum of 5 seconds.

2 Disconnect the battery negative lead.

3 Remove the oil filler cap and the engine cover.

4 Place clean cloth around the fuel pressure check connector and be prepared for spillage. Remove the cap and slowly release any pressure left in the system.

5 Disconnect the wiring plugs for the following:

a) *Engine multiplugs (2 and 3 pin)*
b) *Knock sensor*
c) *Earth leads (2)*
d) *EGR valve*
e) *Crankshaft pulse pick-up*
f) *Controlled canister purge valve*
g) *Oxygen sensor*
h) *DIS ignition module*
i) *Camshaft sensor*

6 Remove the wiring trough and secure to one side.

7 Disconnect the controlled canister purge valve from it's bracket from the upper part of the inlet manifold.

8 Remove the vacuum hose from the fuel pressure regulator and the crankcase vent hose from the manifold **(see illustration)**.

9 Disconnect the two vacuum hoses from manifold pressure sensor and the brake servo.

10 Loosen the air intake pipe clamp.

11 Unbolt the upper manifold from the lower manifold and cylinder head cover.

12 The upper manifold can now be carefully lifted up.

Refitting

13 Remove old gasket and clean sealing surfaces.

14 Replace components using new gaskets.

21.14B Clamp the fuel hoses (arrowed) to prevent fuel spillage

21.17 Lifting the inlet manifold from the engine - Multec MPi model

22.8 Removing crankcase vent hose and vacuum hose - Multec-S model

1 Controlled canister purge valve

15 Refitting is a reversal of the removal procedure.

16 Ensure that all wiring plugs are firmly connected.

23 Inlet manifold, lower (Multec-S models) - removal and refitting

Note: *Refer to the precautions given in Chapter 4B, before starting work. New gaskets will be required on refitting.*

Removal

1 Remove upper manifold as described in Section 22.

2 Drain cooling system as described in Chapter 3.

3 Disconnect air intake pipe from the upper part of the air cleaner housing.

4 Remove the wiring plug from the intake air temperature sensor.

5 Undo the securing bolt from the lower manifold.

6 Remove the air cleaner assembly and air duct hose. Refer to Chapter 4B, if necessary.

7 Remove the crankcase vent hose from the cylinder head cover.

8 Lift the air intake pipe with the crankcase vent hose from the throttle body.

9 Mark on the ribbed V-belt the running direction and remove it. Refer to Chapter 5, if necessary.

10 Remove the earth lead from the wiring bracket attached to the lower manifold. Then remove the bracket **(see illustration)**.

11 Remove the alternator completely or undo the mounting bolts and secure to one side. Refer to Chapter 5, if necessary.

12 Remove the coolant flange.

13 Disconnect the connector hose from the throttle body.

14 Detach the throttle cable and secure to one side.

15 With clean cloth and container to hand, disconnect slowly, the fuel pipes to the fuel rail and regulator. Be prepared for spillage and collect any escaping fuel in the container.

16 Disconnect the wiring plugs for both the idle speed stepper motor and potentiometer.

23.10 Disconnect the earth lead and removing the bracket

1 Earth lead   2 Bracket

17 Detach the wiring from the fuel rail and the injectors.

18 Lift the wiring trough from the lower inlet manifold.

19 Remove the four securing bolts from the throttle body, remove and secure the body below.

20 When removing the throttle body flange, note the bolts lengths as they vary.

21 The lower manifold can now be unbolted and removed.

Refitting

22 Remove old gasket and clean sealing surfaces.

23 Replace components using new gaskets.

24 Refitting is a reversal of the removal procedure.

25 When replacing the lower manifold use new nuts.

26 Ensure that the throttle body flange bolts are replaced in their original locations.

27 Make sure that the ribbed V-belt is correctly fitted and that all wiring plugs are firmly connected.

28 Tighten all fixings to their correct torque as shown in Specifications, Chapter 4B.

29 Replace upper manifold as described in Section 22.

30 Finally, upon completion top up cooling system as described in Chapter 3.

24 Inlet manifold (Motronic M 1.5 models) - removal and refitting

Note: *Refer to the precautions given in Chapter 4B, before starting work. New gaskets will be required on refitting.*

Removal

1 Disconnect the battery negative lead.

2 Remove the idle speed control valve and its hoses, referring to Chapter 4B, if necessary.

3 Release the securing clip, then disconnect the throttle cable and balljoint from the throttle valve lever. Slide the throttle cable grommet from the bracket on the inlet manifold, and move the cable to one side out of the way.

4 Loosen the clamp screw, and disconnect the air trunking from the throttle body.

5 Unscrew the union nut, and disconnect the brake servo vacuum hose from the inlet manifold.

6 Disconnect the camshaft cover breather hose from the throttle body.

7 Disconnect the coolant hoses from the throttle body. Be prepared for coolant spillage, and clamp or plug the open ends of the hoses to prevent further coolant loss.

8 Disconnect the wiring plug from the throttle position sensor.

9 Disconnect the vacuum pipe from the top of the fuel pressure regulator.

10 Disconnect the wiring harness housing from the fuel injectors, and move it to one side, taking care not to strain the wiring. Pull up on the wiring harness housing, and compress the wiring plug retaining clips to release the harness housing from the injectors.

11 Disconnect the fuel hoses from the fuel rail. Loosen the clamps slowly, to depressurise the fuel system. Be prepared for fuel spillage, and take adequate fire precautions. Clamp or plug the open ends of the hoses, to prevent dirt ingress and further fuel leakage.

12 Unscrew and remove the top alternator mounting nut and bolt.

13 Make a final check to ensure that all relevant hoses, pipes and wires have been disconnected.

14 Complete removal, as described in paragraphs 11 to 13 inclusive of Section 20 **(see illustrations)**.

4C

24.14A Unscrewing an inlet manifold securing nut - Motronic M 1.5 model

24.14B Removing the inlet manifold - Motronic M 1.5 model

Refitting

20 Refitting is as described for Multec CFi models, in Section 20.

25 Inlet manifold (Motronic M 2.5 and M 2.8 models) - removal and refitting

Note: *Refer to the precautions given in Chapter 4B, before starting work. New gaskets will be required on refitting.*

Removal

1 Disconnect the battery negative lead.
2 Disconnect the wiring from the air mass meter. Recover the sealing ring, where applicable.
3 Loosen the clamp screw securing the air trunking to the right-hand end of the air mass meter.
4 Using an Allen key or hexagon bit, unscrew the four bolts securing the airbox to the throttle body. Lift the airbox from the throttle body, and disconnect the hose from the base of the airbox, then withdraw the airbox/air mass meter assembly.
5 Disconnect the wiring plug from the throttle position sensor and intake air temperature sensor (if applicable).
6 Slide the throttle cable end from the throttle valve lever, then pull the cable end grommet from the bracket on the inlet manifold, and move the throttle cable to one side out of the way.
7 Disconnect the two breather hoses from the rear of the camshaft cover. Disconnect the larger hose from the main throttle body, and remove the hose completely.
8 Position a piece of cloth beneath one of the fuel hose unions on the fuel rail, to absorb the fuel that will be released as the union is disconnected.
9 Slowly loosen the fuel hose unions, to gradually relieve the pressure in the fuel feed line, then disconnect the hose from the fuel rail. Be prepared for fuel spillage, and take adequate fire precautions. Plug the end of the fuel hose, to prevent dirt ingress and further fuel leakage.
10 Repeat paragraphs 8 and 9 for the remaining fuel hose-to-fuel rail union.
11 Disconnect the vacuum pipes from the front of the traction control (TC) throttle housing, if fitted.
12 Disconnect the coolant hoses from the TC throttle valve housing, noting their locations and routing to aid correct refitting. Be prepared for coolant spillage, and clamp or plug the open ends of the hoses to minimise coolant loss.
13 Disconnect the wiring harness housing from the fuel injectors, and move it to one side, taking care not to strain the wiring. Pull up on the wiring harness housing, and compress the wiring plug retaining clips to release the housing from the injectors.

25.14 Disconnecting the brake servo hose from the inlet manifold - Motronic M 2.5 model

14 Unscrew the union nut, and disconnect the brake servo vacuum hose from the left-hand side of the inlet manifold **(see illustration)**.
15 Unscrew the retaining nut, and remove the fuel hose bracket from the left-hand side of the throttle body.
16 Unscrew the securing nuts, and disconnect the earth leads from the fuel rail securing studs at either end of the fuel rail.
17 Unscrew the securing bolt, and remove the cable/hose bracket from the left-hand end of the inlet manifold.
18 Remove the idle speed control valve, as described in Chapter 4B.
19 Remove the drive belt and unscrew and remove the top alternator mounting nut and bolt. Refer to Chapter 5 for details. On M 2.8 models, remove the alternator shackle and support bracket.
20 Make a final check to ensure that all relevant hoses, pipes and wires have been disconnected.
21 Complete removal, as described in paragraphs 11 to 13 inclusive of Section 20.

Refitting

22 Refitting is as described for Multec CFi models, in Section 20, but additionally, make sure that the TC throttle housing coolant hoses are correctly routed and reconnected, as noted before removal.

26 Inlet manifold (Simtec models) - removal and refitting

Note: *Refer to the precautions given in Chapter 4B, before starting work. New gaskets will be required on refitting.*

Removal

1 Disconnect the battery negative lead.
2 Disconnect the wiring plugs from the air temperature sensor and the air flow meter from the air intake pipe.
3 Remove the air intake hose and the air intake housing.
4 Remove the lower radiator hose and drain the cooling system as described in Chapter 3.

26.6 Remove the DIS module wiring plug - Simtec model

1 Wiring plug

5 Remove the wiring plugs from the temperature sender and sensor.
6 Disconnect the wiring plug from the DIS module **(see illustration)**. Do not disconnect the ignition leads.
7 Disconnect the engine wiring multiplug.
8 Remove the wiring and the vacuum hoses from the purge valve, noting their position.
9 Remove the crankcase vent hoses from the cylinder head cover.
10 Remove the ignition lead cover from the top of the engine.
11 Detach the earth lead from the fuel rail.
12 Disconnect the wiring plug from the idle air control and the camshaft sensor.
13 Remove the throttle cable and secure to one side.
14 Using a screwdriver push in the retaining clamps for the first and fourth cylinder injectors. Lift the plug strip and disconnect the wiring plugs for the knock sensor and the inductive pulse pick-up.
15 With clean cloth and container ready, release the fuel pressure by removing the cap from the fuel pressure test connector. Then slowly, depress the valve relieving any pressure, at the same time catch escaping fuel using the cloth.
16 Disconnect the wiring plug from the potentiometer.
17 Remove the ribbed V-belt, referring to Chapter 5, if necessary. Note the direction of rotation before removal.
18 Remove the alternator and secure to one side. Refer to Chapter 5 for details.
19 Disconnect the cooling hoses from the throttle body.
20 Remove the brake servo vacuum hose from the inlet manifold.
21 Unbolt the inlet manifold to cylinder block support brackets lower securing bolt and secure to one side.
22 Remove the inlet manifold.

Refitting

23 Remove old gasket and clean sealing surfaces.
24 Replace components using new gaskets.
25 Refitting is a reversal of the removal procedure.

27.4 Exhaust manifold hot air shroud securing bolts (arrowed) - C 16 SE model

27.8A Removing the exhaust manifold - C 16 SE model

27.8B Removing an exhaust manifold securing nut. Note position of engine lifting bracket (arrowed) - C 16 SE model

26 Make sure that the ribbed V-belt is correctly fitted and that all wiring plugs are firmly connected.

27 Tighten all fixings to their correct torque as shown in Specifications, Chapter 4B.

28 Finally, upon completion top up cooling system as described in Chapter 3.

27 Exhaust manifold - removal and refitting

Note: *New manifold-to-cylinder head and manifold-to-downpipe gaskets must be used on refitting. On DOHC models, a tubular exhaust manifold is fitted, which incorporates the front section of the exhaust system. Refer to Section 30 for details.*

Removal

1 Disconnect the battery negative lead.

2 Disconnect the HT leads from the spark plugs, if necessary labelling them to ensure refitting to their correct cylinders.

3 Loosen the clamp screw and disconnect the air cleaner hot air tube from the shroud on the manifold, if applicable.

4 Remove the securing screws and withdraw the hot air shroud from the manifold **(see illustration)**.

5 If fitted, remove the oxygen sensor as described in Chapter 4B.

6 Working under the manifold, unscrew and remove the four bolts securing the exhaust downpipe to the manifold.

7 Separate the downpipe from the manifold, and support with wire or string. Do not allow the front section of the exhaust system to hang under its own weight. Recover the gasket.

8 Unscrew the securing nuts, and withdraw the manifold from the cylinder head. Note the position of the front engine lifting bracket, which is secured by one of the manifold studs, and recover the manifold gasket **(see illustrations)**.

9 It is possible that some of the manifold studs may be unscrewed from the cylinder head when the manifold securing nuts are unscrewed. If this happens, screw the studs back into the cylinder head once the manifold has been removed, using two manifold nuts locked together.

Refitting

10 Refit the manifold using a new gasket, and ensure that the engine lifting bracket is in place under the relevant manifold nut **(see illustration)**.

11 Reconnect the exhaust downpipe to the manifold, using a new gasket.

12 Further refitting is a reversal of removal.

28 Exhaust system - general

1 Periodically, the exhaust system should be checked for signs of leaks or damage. Also inspect the system rubber mountings, and renew if necessary.

2 Small holes or cracks can be repaired using exhaust repair products, such as paste or bandage.

3 The original factory-fitted exhaust system consists of four separate sections, all of which can be renewed individually.

4 Before renewing an individual section of the exhaust system, it is wise to inspect the remaining sections. If corrosion or damage is evident on more than one section of the system, it may prove more economical to renew the entire system.

5 Individual sections of the system can be renewed as follows.

29 Exhaust system - removal and refitting

Note: *All relevant gaskets and/or sealing rings should be renewed on refitting. Some models are fitted with a flexible joint between the exhaust manifold and the front pipe.*

Front section

Removal

1 Raise the vehicle, and support securely on axle stands.

2 Remove the oxygen sensor, if fitted (refer to Chapter 4B). Unscrew the two securing bolts and disconnect the exhaust front section from the front expansion box at the joint. Remove the sealing ring and the springs **(see illustrations)**.

 4C

27.10 Fitting a new exhaust manifold gasket - DOHC model

29.2A Exhaust front section-to-manifold joint - C 14 NZ model

29.2B Exhaust front section-to-manifold joint - C 16 SE model

29.2C Use a new sealing ring when connecting the exhaust flexible joint

29.3A Exhaust front section mounting - C 16 SE model

1 Bracket   2 Sprung joint

29.3B Exhaust front section-to-cylinder block bracket - 14 NV model

3 Unbolt the exhaust front section from the bracket on the cylinder block **(see illustrations)**.

4 Unscrew and remove the bolts securing the downpipe to the exhaust manifold, and withdraw the exhaust front section. Recover the downpipe-to-manifold gasket, and where applicable, recover the springs from the bolts.

Refitting

5 Refitting is a reversal of removal, but use a new gasket when reconnecting the downpipe to the manifold, and a new sealing ring when connecting the joint **(see illustration)**.

Front expansion box or catalytic converter (as applicable) - SOHC models

Note: *Refer to Section 30 for DOHC models. The internal components of the converter are fragile - take care not to strike it during removal, and do not drop it once removed.*

Removal

6 Raise the vehicle, and support securely on axle stands.

7 Unscrew the two securing bolts, and disconnect the exhaust front section from the front expansion box (or converter), at the flexible joint. Remove the sealing ring and the springs

8 Unscrew the securing bolts (and nuts, where applicable), and disconnect the front expansion box (or converter), from the

exhaust centre section. Remove the sealing ring, gasket and, where applicable, the springs.

9 Withdraw the expansion box (or converter), from under the vehicle.

Refitting

10 Refitting is a reversal of removal, but use new sealing rings or gaskets, as applicable.

Centre section

Removal

11 Raise the vehicle, and support securely on axle stands.

12 Unscrew the clamp bolt, and disconnect the exhaust centre section from the rear section **(see illustrations)**. If necessary, tap round the joint with a hammer to break the seal, and gently prise the two sections apart. Note that the end of the centre section fits inside the rear section, to form a sleeve joint.

13 Unscrew the securing bolts (and nuts, where applicable), and disconnect the exhaust centre section from the front expansion box. Recover the sealing ring/gasket and, where applicable, the springs.

14 Release the exhaust centre section from its rubber mountings on the underbody, and withdraw it from the vehicle.

Refitting

15 Refitting is a reversal of removal, but use a new sealing ring when connecting the flexible

joint, and lubricate the pipes with exhaust assembly paste when connecting the centre section to the rear section.

Rear section

Removal

16 Remove the centre section, as described in paragraphs 11 and 12.

17 Release the exhaust rear section from its rubber mountings on the underbody, and withdraw it from the vehicle.

Refitting

18 Refitting is a reversal of removal, but lubricate the pipes with exhaust assembly paste when connecting the rear section to the centre section.

---

30 Exhaust, front section (DOHC models) -
removal and refitting

Note: *All relevant gaskets and/or sealing rings should be renewed on refitting.*

Removal

1 Disconnect the battery negative earth lead and remove the oxygen sensor as described in Chapter 4B.

2 Raise the vehicle, and support securely on axle stands.

3 Remove the engine undershield, as described in Chapter 11.

29.5 Fitting a new exhaust downpipe-to-manifold gasket - C 16 SE model

29.12A Exhaust centre section-to-catalytic converter joint - C 16 SE model

29.12B Exhaust centre section-to-rear section clamp

30.6 Unscrewing an exhaust manifold heat shield-to-cylinder head bolt - DOHC model

4 Unscrew the two securing bolts, and disconnect the exhaust front section from the catalytic converter at the flexible joint. Recover the sealing ring and springs.

5 Unbolt the exhaust front section from the bracket on the cylinder block.

6 Working in the engine compartment, remove the bolts securing the exhaust manifold heat shield to the cylinder head **(see illustration)**.

7 Unscrew the two lower exhaust manifold securing nuts that also secure the heat shield brackets, and withdraw the heat shield.

8 Unscrew the remaining manifold securing nuts, then withdraw the manifold/exhaust front section from the vehicle. Recover the manifold gasket.

9 It is possible that some of the manifold studs may be unscrewed from the cylinder head when the manifold securing nuts are unscrewed. In this event, the studs should be screwed back into the cylinder head once the manifold has been removed, using two manifold nuts locked together.

Refitting

10 Refitting is a reversal of removal, but use a new manifold gasket, and use a new sealing ring when reconnecting the flexible joint.

4C

Notes

Chapter 5
Engine electrical systems

Contents

Degrees of difficulty

Easy, suitable for novice with little experience		Fairly easy, suitable for beginner with some experience		Fairly difficult, suitable for competent DIY mechanic		Difficult, suitable for experienced DIY mechanic		Very difficult, suitable for expert DIY or professional	

Specifications

Battery
Type .... Maintenance free (sealed for life) lead acid
Capacity .... 36, 44, 66, or 70 Amp

Ignition system

Type *
14 NV .... Bosch High Energy Ignition (HEI) inductive discharge system
14 SE, C 14 SE (up to 1993), C 14 NZ and C 16 NZ .... Multec Microprocessor-controlled Spark Timing System (MSTS) with 'Hall-effect' distributor
C 14 SE (from 1993) and C 18 NZ .... Multec MSTS with crankshaft speed and position sensor
C 16 SE .... Multec MSTS with Direct Ignition System (DIS) and crankshaft speed and position sensor
X 16 SZ and X 16 XEL .... Multec MSTS with DIS
C 18 NZ .... Multec MSTS with High Voltage Distributor
C 18 XE .... Simtec 56.0 with DIS
C 20 NE .... Motronic M 1.5 with crankshaft speed and position sensor
C 20 XE .... Motronic M 2.5 with 'Hall-effect' distributor and crankshaft speed and position sensor
X 20 XEV and C 18 XEL .... Simtec 56.1 with DIS
For details of engine code location, refer to the Reference part of this manual.

Firing order
All models .... 1 - 3 - 4 - 2

Location of No 1 cylinder
All models .... Timing belt end of engine

Ignition timing (stroboscopic, at idle speed, vacuum hose disconnected) *
14 NV .... 5° BTDC
C 14 NZ, C 14 SE (pre-1993) and C 16 NZ .... 10° BTDC **
Other models .... Controlled by the ECU (Electronic Control Unit)
For details of engine code location, refer to the Reference part of this manual.
** Checking and basic adjustment only possible using special equipment.

Distributor
Direction of rotor arm rotation .... Anti-clockwise (viewed from cap)

5

Alternator

Type	Bosch or Delco-Remy
Output	55 or 70 amps, depending on model

Minimum brush length

Bosch type alternator (all except code number 0 120 488 193)	5.0 mm
Bosch type alternator (code number 0 120 488 193)	11.0 to 12.0 mm
Delco-Remy type alternator	12.0 mm overall length

Starter motor

Type	Pre-engaged Bosch, Delco-Remy or Valeo

Brush minimum length

Bosch DM type starter motor	3.0 mm
Bosch DW type starter motor	8.0 mm
Delco-Remy type starter motor (all except code number 09 000 756) .	4.0 mm
Delco-Remy type starter motor (code number 09 000 756)	8.5 mm
Valeo type starter motor	No data available at time of writing

Torque wrench setting

	Nm	lbf ft
Adjuster bracket to alternator:		
1.4 and 1.6 litre models (except X 16 XEL)	25	18
X 16 XEL	20	15
C 18 NZ and C 20 NE:		
Pre 1993 models	25	18
1993-on models	18	13
C 18 XE, C 18 XEL and C 20 XE	18	13
C 18 XE, C 18 XEL and C 20 XE (M10)	40	30
Alternator mounting (lower):		
DOHC models	35	26
Alternator to mounting bracket (SOHC models):		
M8 bolts	30	22
M10 bolts	40	29
Ribbed V-belt tension roller	20	15
Ribbed V-belt tension roller support to cylinder block:		
DOHC models	25	18
Spark plugs	25	18
Starter motor to cylinder block:		
SOHC models:		
Engine side	45	32
Transmission side	60	43
X 16 XEL	25	19
C 18 XE, C 18 XEL, C 20 XE and X 20 XEV	45	33

1 System information - general

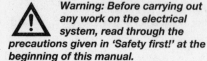

Warning: Before carrying out any work on the electrical system, read through the precautions given in 'Safety first!' at the beginning of this manual.

1 The electrical system is of the 12-volt negative earth type, and consists of a 12-volt battery, an alternator with integral voltage regulator, a starter motor and related electrical accessories, components and wiring.

2 The battery is of the 'maintenance-free' (sealed-for-life) type, and is charged by the alternator, which is belt-driven from a crankshaft-mounted pulley. From 1993 models were fitted with a flat ribbed V-belt with an automatic tension roller.

3 The starter motor is of the pre-engaged type, incorporating an integral solenoid. On starting, the solenoid moves the drive pinion into engagement with the flywheel ring gear before the starter motor is energised. Once the engine has started, a one-way clutch prevents the motor armature being driven by the engine until the pinion disengages from the flywheel.

4 Further details of the various systems are given in the relevant Sections of this Chapter. While some repair procedures are given, the usual course of action is to renew the component concerned. The owner whose interest extends beyond mere component renewal should obtain a copy of the *'Automobile Electrical & Electronic Systems Manual'* available from Haynes Publishing.

5 It is necessary to take extra care when working on the electrical system to avoid damage to semi-conductor devices (diodes and transistors), and to avoid the risk of personal injury. Along with the precautions given in *'Safety first!'* at the beginning of this manual, observe the following when working on the system.

6 *Always remove rings, watches, etc., before working on the electrical system.* Even with the battery disconnected, capacitive discharge could occur if a component's live terminal is earthed through a metal object. This could cause a shock or nasty burn.

7 *Do not reverse the battery connections.* Components such as the alternator, fuel injection/ignition system ECU (where applicable), or any other components having semi-conductor circuitry could be irreparably damaged.

8 If the engine is being started using jump leads and a slave battery, connect the batteries positive-to-positive and negative-to-negative. This also applies when connecting a battery charger.

9 Never disconnect the battery terminals, the alternator, any electrical wiring or any test instruments when the engine is running.

10 Do not allow the engine to turn the alternator when the alternator is not connected.

11 Never 'test' for alternator output by 'shorting' the output lead to earth.

12 Never use an ohmmeter of the type incorporating a hand-cranked generator for circuit or continuity testing.

13 Always ensure that the battery negative lead is disconnected when working on the electrical system.

14 Before using electric-arc welding equipment on the car, disconnect the battery, alternator and components such as the fuel injection/ignition system ECU (where applicable), to protect them from the risk of damage.

2 Precautions - general

1 Refer to the precautions to be observed when working on models fitted with an ECU, given in Chapter 4B.

 Warning: The HT voltage generated by an electronic ignition system is extremely high and, in certain circumstances, could prove fatal. Take care to avoid receiving electric shocks from the HT side of the ignition system. Do not handle HT leads, or touch the distributor or coil when the engine is running. If tracing faults in the HT circuit use well-insulated tools to manipulate live leads. Persons with surgically implanted cardiac pacemaker devices should keep well away of the Ignition circuits, components and test equipment.

3 Ignition system information - general

1 The ignition system is responsible for igniting the air/fuel mixture in each cylinder at the correct moment, in relation to engine speed and load. A number of different types of ignition systems are fitted to models within the Astra range, ranging from a basic breakerless electronic system, to a fully integrated engine management system controlling both ignition and fuel injection systems. Each system is described in further detail later in this Section.

2 The ignition system is based on feeding low-tension voltage from the battery to the coil, where it is converted into high-tension voltage. The high-tension voltage is powerful enough to jump the spark plug gap in the cylinders many times a second under high compression pressures, providing that the system is in good condition. The low-tension (or primary) circuit consists of the battery, the lead to the ignition switch, the lead from the ignition switch to the low-tension coil windings, and also to the supply terminal on the electronic module, and the lead from the low-tension coil windings to the control terminal on the electronic module. The high-tension (or secondary) circuit consists of the high-tension coil windings, the HT (high-

tension) lead from the coil to the distributor cap (where applicable), the rotor arm (where applicable), the HT leads to the spark plugs, and the spark plugs.

3 The system functions in the following manner. Current flowing through the low-tension coil windings produces a magnetic field around the high-tension windings. As the engine rotates, a sensor produces an electrical impulse that is amplified in the electronic module and used to switch off the low-tension circuit.

4 The subsequent collapse of the magnetic field over the high-tension windings produces a high-tension voltage, which is then fed to the relevant spark plug(s), either directly from the coil, or through the distributor cap and rotor arm, as applicable. The low-tension circuit is automatically switched on again by the electronic module, to allow the magnetic field to build up again before the firing of the next spark plug(s). The ignition is advanced and retarded automatically, to ensure that the spark occurs at the correct instant in relation to the engine speed and load.

HEI (High-Energy Ignition) system

5 This system comprises of a breakerless distributor and an electronic switching and amplifier module along with the coil and spark plugs.

6 The electrical impulse that is required to switch off the low-tension circuit is generated by a magnetic trigger coil in the distributor.

7 The ignition advance is a function of the distributor, and is controlled both mechanically and by a vacuum-operated system.

Multec MSTS (Microprocessor-controlled Spark Timing System) - CFi models

8 This system controls both the ignition and fuel injection systems, and comprises a 'Hall-effect' distributor (C 14 NZ and C 16 NZ models) or a crankshaft speed/position sensor (C 18 NZ), a manifold pressure sensor, a coolant temperature sensor, a throttle position sensor, an exhaust gas oxygen sensor, and the Multec ECU, along with the coil, electronic module, and spark plugs.

9 On C 14 NZ and C 16 NZ models, the electrical impulse that is required to switch off the low-tension circuit is generated by a sensor in the distributor.

10 On C 18 NZ models, the electrical impulse that is required to switch off the low-tension circuit is generated by a crankshaft speed and position sensor, which is activated by a toothed wheel on the crankshaft. The distributor consists simply of a rotor arm and distributor cap, and is used solely to distribute the HT current to the spark plugs.

11 Engine load information is supplied to the Multec control unit by a pressure sensor, which is connected to the fuel injection unit by a vacuum pipe. Additional information is supplied by a coolant temperature sensor, a

throttle position sensor, and an exhaust gas oxygen sensor.

12 The control unit selects the optimum ignition advance setting based on the information received from the sensors. The degree of advance can thus be constantly varied to suit the prevailing engine conditions. The control unit also provides outputs to control the fuel injection system, which is described in Chapter 4B.

Multec MSTS (Microprocessor-controlled Spark Timing System) - MPi models

13 The system is similar to that described previously for CFi models, but note the following differences.

14 The system comprises a crankshaft speed/position sensor, a manifold pressure sensor, a coolant temperature sensor, an intake air temperature sensor, an exhaust gas oxygen sensor, and the Multec ECU, along with the coil(s) and spark plugs.

15 The electrical impulse that is required to switch off the low-tension circuit is generated by a crankshaft speed/position sensor, similar to that described previously for C 18 NZ models.

16 On 14 SE models, the distributor consists simply of a rotor arm and distributor cap, and is used solely to distribute the HT current to the spark plugs.

17 On C 16 SE, a DIS (Direct Ignition System) module is used in place of the distributor and the coil. The DIS module is attached to the camshaft housing in the position normally occupied by the distributor, and consists of two ignition coils and an electronic control module, housed in a cast casing. Each ignition coil supplies two spark plugs with HT voltage one spark is provided in a cylinder with its piston on the compression stroke, and one spark is provided to a cylinder with its piston on the exhaust stroke. This means that a 'wasted spark' is supplied to one cylinder during each ignition cycle, but this has no detrimental effect. This system has the advantage that there are no moving parts therefore there is no wear, and the system is largely maintenance-free.

18 Additional information is supplied to the Multec ECU by an intake air temperature sensor, mounted in the inlet manifold.

Motronic M 1.5 system

19 This system controls both the ignition and fuel injection systems.

20 The Motronic ECU receives information from a crankshaft speed/position sensor (similar to that described for C 18 NZ models), an air mass meter, an engine coolant temperature sensor, a throttle position sensor, an intake air temperature sensor, and an exhaust gas oxygen sensor.

21 The electrical impulse that is required to switch off the low-tension circuit is generated by a crankshaft speed/position sensor, similar to that described previously for C 18 NZ models.

5

22 The distributor consists simply of a rotor arm and distributor cap, and is used solely to distribute the HT current to the spark plugs.

23 The control unit selects the optimum ignition advance setting, based on the information received from the sensors. The degree of advance can thus be constantly varied to suit the prevailing engine conditions. The control unit also provides outputs to control the fuel injection system, which is described in Chapter 4B.

Motronic M 2.5 system

24 The system is similar to the Motronic M 1.5 system described previously, with the following differences.

25 Besides the crankshaft speed/position sensor, a 'Hall-effect' distributor is used. The electrical impulse that is required to switch off the ignition low-tension circuit is generated by the crankshaft speed/ position sensor, and the sensor in the distributor provides a cylinder recognition signal.

26 Additionally, the electronic control module receives information from a cylinder block-mounted knock sensor (see Chapter 4B), which senses 'knocking' (or pre-ignition) just as it begins to occur, enabling the module to retard the ignition timing, thus preventing engine damage.

Motronic M 2.8 system

27 During 1993, the M 2.5 system fitted to C 20 XE models, was replaced with the Motronic M 2.8.

28 On this system a DIS module replaces the distributor. Also intake air temperature and camshaft sensors are fitted.

Simtec system

29 This system like previous Motronic types, controls both the fuel and ignition operations. However it uses more sensors and actuators than before to provide more reliable information and less maintenance.

30 It uses DIS, described previously, to provide the voltage to fire the spark plugs. The sensors include a camshaft sensor, that will provide the ECU with enough information to keep the engine running, should the crankshaft speed and position sensor (inductive pulse pick-up) fail.

31 Further information is described in Chapter 4B.

4 Ignition system (14 NV) - testing

Note: *Refer to the warning given in Section 2 before starting work.*

1 The components of the electronic ignition system are normally very reliable; most faults are far more likely to be due to loose or dirty connections or to 'tracking' of HT voltage due to dirt, dampness or damaged insulation than to the failure of any of the system components. **Always** check all wiring thoroughly before condemning an electrical component, and work methodically to eliminate all other possibilities before deciding that a particular component is faulty.

2 The practice of checking for a spark by holding the live end of a HT lead a short distance away from the engine is not recommended - not only is there a high risk of a powerful electric shock, but the coil or electronic module may be damaged.

Engine fails to start

3 If the engine either will not turn over at all, or only turns over very slowly, check the battery and starter motor. Connect a voltmeter across the battery terminals (meter positive probe to battery positive terminal), disconnect the ignition coil HT lead from the distributor cap and earth it, then note the voltage reading obtained while turning over the engine on the starter for around ten seconds (no more). If the reading obtained is less than approximately 8 volts, check the battery, starter motor and charging system.

4 If the engine turns over at normal speed, but will not start, check the HT circuit by connecting a timing light (following the equipment manufacturer's instructions) and turning the engine over on the starter motor; if the light flashes, voltage is reaching the spark plugs, so these should be checked first. If the light does not flash, check the HT leads themselves, followed by the distributor cap, carbon brush and rotor arm (see Section 17). Additionally, use an ohmmeter or continuity tester to check that there is no continuity between any of the distributor cap contacts. Similarly, check that there is no continuity between the rotor arm body and its metal contact - note that the arm has a built-in resistance.

5 If there is a spark, check the fuel system for faults (see Chapter 4A).

6 If there is still no spark, check the voltage at the ignition coil '+ ' terminal (black wires), which should be the same as the battery voltage (i.e. at least 11.5 volts). If the voltage at the coil is significantly (more than 1.0 volt) less than that at the battery, check the feed back through the fusebox and ignition switch to the battery and its earth until the fault is found.

7 If the feed to the coil is sound, check the coil windings, as described in Section 21. Renew the coil if faulty, but be careful to check carefully the condition of the LT connections themselves before doing so, to ensure that the fault is not due to dirty or loose connections.

8 If the coil is in good condition, the fault is probably within the electronic module or the distributor. To check the module and distributor, connect a test meter across the coil LT terminals, according to the equipment manufacturer's instructions. If the ignition is switched on, and the engine is turned over on the starter motor, the meter voltage readings should fluctuate each time the module triggers a HT pulse in the coil. If the meter reading fluctuates as the engine is turned over, the electronic module and the distributor are sound.

9 If the electronic module and distributor are sound, and the entire LT circuit is in good condition, the fault, if it lies in the ignition system, must be in the HT circuit components. These should be checked carefully, as outlined previously.

Engine misfires

10 An irregular misfire suggests either a loose connection or intermittent fault in the primary circuit, or a HT fault on the coil side of the rotor arm.

11 With the ignition switched off, check carefully through the system, ensuring that all connections are clean and securely fastened. If the equipment is available, check the LT circuit, as described previously in paragraphs 6 to 8 inclusive.

12 Check that the coil, the distributor cap and the HT leads are clean and dry. Check the leads themselves and the spark plugs (by substitution if necessary), then check the distributor cap, carbon brush and rotor arm.

13 Regular misfiring is almost certainly due to a fault in the distributor cap, HT leads or spark plugs. Use a timing light (see paragraph 4) to check whether HT voltage is present at all leads.

14 If HT voltage is not present on any particular lead, the fault will be in that lead or in the distributor cap. If HT voltage is present on all leads, the fault will be in the spark plugs; check and renew them if there is any doubt about their condition.

15 If no HT voltage is present, check the coil, as the secondary windings may be breaking down under load.

5 Ignition system (except 14 NV) - testing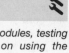

Note: *Models fitted with DIS modules, testing should only be carried out on using the appropriate test equipment available to a Vauxhall dealer.*

1 The general comments made above apply equally to the fuel injection engines, but note that extreme care should be taken when testing the system, as the ECU is very sensitive, and if damaged, it may prove very costly to renew.

2 If in any doubt as to test procedures, or if the correct equipment is not available, entrust testing and fault diagnosis to a Vauxhall dealer. It is far better to pay the labour charges involved in having the car checked by someone suitably qualified, than to risk damage to the system or yourself.

3 At the time of writing, test equipment, including ECU fault code readers, were being released by certain companies to the general public. If using such equipment, follow the manufacturers instructions carefully. A list of the fault codes should also be supplied with the equipment.

Engine fails to start

4 Check whether the fault lies in the ignition system, by following the procedure described in Section 4, paragraphs 3 and 4, and check the HT circuit as described.

5 If the HT circuit appears to be sound, the feed to the coil can be checked as described in Section 4, paragraph 6. Note that the ECU controls the coil feed. **Do not** attempt to 'test' the ECU with anything other than the appropriate test equipment, which will be available only at a suitably equipped Vauxhall dealer. If any of the wires are to be checked which run to the ECU (although this is not recommended without the correct test equipment), always first unplug the relevant connector from the control unit (with the ignition switched off) so that there is no risk of the unit being damaged by the application of incorrect voltages from the test equipment.

6 If all components have been checked for signs of obvious faults, such as dirty or loose connections, damp, or 'tracking', and have been tested as far as possible, but the system is still thought to be faulty, the vehicle must be taken to a Vauxhall dealer for testing using the appropriate equipment.

Engine misfires

7 Refer to Section 4, paragraphs 10 to 15, but note that the possible causes of partial failures that may result in a misfire are far too numerous to be eliminated without using test equipment. Once the ignition system components have been checked for signs of obvious faults, such as dirty or loose connections, damp, or 'tracking', and have been tested as far as possible, but the system is still thought to be faulty, take the vehicle to a Vauxhall dealer for the full engine management system to be tested using the appropriate equipment.

6 Battery - testing and charging

Note: *The following information refers only to the maintenance-free type battery fitted as original equipment by the manufacturers.*

Testing

1 Topping-up and testing of the electrolyte in each battery cell is not possible. The condition of the battery can therefore only be tested by observing the battery condition indicator.

2 The battery condition indicator is located in the top of the battery casing, and indicates the condition of the battery by its colour. If the indicator shows green, then the battery is in a good state of charge. If the indicator turns darker, eventually to black, then the battery requires charging, as described later in this Section. If the indicator shows clear/yellow, then the electrolyte level in the battery is too low to allow further use, and the battery

should be renewed. **Do not** attempt to charge, load or jump-start a battery when the indicator shows clear/yellow.

Charging

3 If the battery is to be charged, remove it from the vehicle and charge it as follows.

4 The maintenance-free type battery takes considerably longer to fully recharge than the standard type, the time taken being dependent on the extent of discharge.

5 A constant-voltage type charger is required; connect it up and set it to 13.9 to 14.9 volts, with a charge current below 25 amps.

6 If the battery is to be charged from a fully discharged state (less than 12.2 volts output), have it recharged by a Vauxhall dealer or a competent automotive electrician, as the charge rate is high, and constant supervision during charging is necessary.

7 Battery - removal and refitting

Removal

1 The battery is located at the front left-hand corner of the engine compartment.

2 Disconnect the negative (earth or "-") lead first, by unscrewing the retaining nut and removing the terminal clamp.

3 Disconnect the positive terminal lead in the same way.

4 Unscrew the clamp bolt sufficiently to enable the battery to be lifted from its location. Keep the battery upright, to avoid spilling electrolyte on the bodywork.

Refitting

5 Refitting is a reversal of removal, but smear petroleum jelly on the terminals when reconnecting the leads. Always reconnect the positive lead first, and the negative lead last.

8 Charging system - testing

Note: *Refer to the warnings given in 'Safety first!' and in Section 2, before starting work.*

1 If the ignition warning light fails to illuminate when the ignition is switched on, first check the alternator wiring connections for security. If satisfactory, check that the warning light bulb has not blown, and that the bulbholder is secure in its location in the instrument panel. If the light still fails to illuminate, check the continuity of the warning light feed wire from the alternator to the bulbholder. If all is satisfactory, the alternator is at fault, and should be renewed or taken to an auto-electrician for testing and repair.

2 If the ignition warning light illuminates when the engine is running, stop the engine and check that the drivebelt is correctly tensioned (Section 9) and that the alternator connections are secure. If all is so far satisfactory, check

the alternator brushes (see Section 12 or 13, as applicable). If the fault persists, the alternator should be renewed, or taken to an auto-electrician for testing and repair.

3 If the alternator output is suspect even though the warning light functions correctly, the regulated voltage may be checked as follows.

4 Connect a voltmeter across the battery terminals and start the engine.

5 Increase the engine speed until the voltmeter reading remains steady; the reading should be approximately 12 to 13 volts, and no more than 14 volts.

6 Switch on as many electrical accessories (e.g., the headlights, heated rear window and heater blower) as possible, and check that the alternator maintains the regulated voltage at around 13 to 14 volts.

7 If the regulated voltage is not as stated, the fault may be due to worn brushes, weak brush springs, a faulty voltage regulator, a faulty diode, a severed phase winding, or worn or damaged slip rings. The brushes may be checked (see Section 12 or 13), but if the fault persists, the alternator should be renewed or taken to an auto-electrician for testing and repair.

9 V-belt - removal, refitting and tensioning

Note: *During 1993 ribbed V-belts, with automatic tensioners were fitted. Refer to Section 10 for details on renewal.*

Removal

1 Disconnect the air intake trunking from the air cleaner, and from the airbox or the throttle body, as applicable, and remove it for improved access.

2 On 1.4 and 1.6 litre models with power steering, the V-belt (or drivebelt) also drives the power steering pump.

3 To remove the belt on 1.8 and 2.0 litre models, first remove the power steering pump drivebelt, as described in Chapter 10.

4 Loosen the alternator mounting nuts and bolts sufficiently to allow the alternator to be pivoted in towards the engine **(see illustration)**.

5 Slide the belt from the pulleys.

9.4 Lower alternator mounting nuts and bolts (arrowed). Viewed with top alternator mounting disconnected - Bosch type

5

10.5 Remove the engine mounting bracket (1) - DOHC models

10.7A Ribbed V-belt shown correctly fitted - C 18 XE, C 18 XEL and C 20 XE models

10.7B Ribbed V-belt shown correctly fitted - 1.4 and 1.6 litre SOHC models with power steering

Refitting

6 Fit the belt around the pulleys, ensuring that the belt is of the correct type if it is being renewed, and take up the slack in the belt by swinging the alternator away from the engine and lightly tightening the mounting nuts and bolts.

7 On 1.8 and 2.0 litre models, refit and tension the power steering pump drivebelt, as described in Chapter 10.

8 Tension the alternator drivebelt as described in the following paragraphs.

Tensioning

9 Correct tensioning of the drivebelt will ensure that it has a long life. Beware, however, of over-tightening, as this can cause excessive wear in the alternator.

10 Refer to paragraphs 1 and 2.

11 Although special tools are available for checking the belt tension, a good approximation can be achieved if the belt is tensioned so that there is approximately 13.0 mm of free movement under firm thumb pressure at the mid-point of the longest run between pulleys.

12 With the mounting bolts just holding the unit firm, lever the alternator away from the engine using a wooden lever at the mounting bracket end until the correct tension is achieved, then tighten the mounting nuts and bolts. **On no account** lever at the free end of the alternator, as serious internal damage could be caused.

13 Refit the air trunking.

14 When a new belt has been fitted, it will probably stretch slightly when it is first run,

and the tension should be rechecked and if necessary adjusted after approximately 250 miles (400 km) of running.

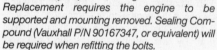

10 Ribbed V-belt - removal and refitting

Note: *The tension on these belts are automatically adjusted, using a tension roller. Replacement requires the engine to be supported and mounting removed. Sealing Compound (Vauxhall P/N 90167347, or equivalent) will be required when refitting the bolts.*

Removal

1 On models with an intake air temperature sensor, first disconnect the negative lead from the battery and then remove its wiring plug.

2 Remove the air intake pipe. On some models it may be necessary to remove the complete air cleaner assembly and engine cover. If fitted, remove the panel from behind the right hand front wheel.

3 Support the engine using hoist or a trolley jack. If using a trolley jack, place a piece of wood between the jack and the engine to prevent damaging the sump.

4 Release the tension roller, turning in a clockwise direction and remove the belt from the roller.

5 Remove the right-hand engine mounting from the chassis member. On DOHC models remove the engine mounting bracket from the support **(see illustration)**.

6 Slowly and carefully lower the engine and remove the belt, noting how is fitted.

Refitting

7 Refitting is a reversal of the removal procedure. However, locate the belt as the original was fitted **(see illustrations)**.

8 Recut the threads of the engine mounting bolts and replace using Sealing Compound (Vauxhall P/N 90167347, or equivalent).

9 Tighten the engine mountings to their correct torque. Refer to Specifications in Chapter 2A or 2B, as applicable.

11 Alternator - removal and refitting

Removal

1 Disconnect the battery leads.

2 For improved access, remove the air intake pipe and the air cleaner assembly.

3 Disconnect the wires from their terminals on the rear of the alternator, noting their locations, or disconnect the wiring plug, as applicable **(see illustration)**.

4 Mark the running direction on the belt, before removing it, as described in Section 9 or 10.

5 Unscrew the two mounting bolts and nuts, and recover any washers and insulating bushes, noting their locations. Note the earth strap attached to the top mounting bolts on certain models **(see illustration)**.

6 Withdraw the alternator **(see illustration)**, taking care not to knock or drop it, as this can cause irreparable damage.

11.3 Wiring connections (arrowed) at rear of alternator - Bosch type

11.5 Earth strap (arrowed) attached to top alternator mounting bolts

11.6 Withdrawing the alternator

12.4 Separating the drive end housing from the slip ring end housing - Delco-Remy type

12.5 Alternator slip rings (arrowed) - Delco-Remy type

12.6 Stator lead securing nuts (A) and brush holder/voltage regulator securing screws (B) - Delco-Remy type

Refitting

7 Refitting is a reversal of removal, remembering the following points.
8 Where applicable, ensure that the earth lead is in place on the top mounting bolt.
9 Refit and tension the drivebelt, as described in Section 9 or 10.

12 Alternator brushes and regulator (Delco-Remy type) - removal and refitting

Removal

1 The brush holder and voltage regulator are combined in a single assembly. For access to the assembly, the alternator must be partially dismantled as follows. If the voltage regulator is faulty, the complete assembly must be renewed.
2 Remove the alternator as described in Section 11.
3 Scribe a line across the drive end housing and the slip ring end housing, to ensure correct alignment when reassembling.
4 Unscrew the three through-bolts, and prise the drive end housing and rotor away from the slip ring end housing and stator **(see illustration)**.
5 Check the condition of the slip rings, and if necessary clean with a rag or very fine glass paper **(see illustration)**.
6 Remove the three nuts and washers

securing the stator leads to the rectifier, and lift away the stator assembly **(see illustration)**.
7 Remove the terminal screw, and lift out the diode assembly.
8 Extract the two screws securing the brush holder and voltage regulator to the slip ring end housing, and remove the brush holder assembly. Note the insulation washers under the screw heads.
9 Check that the brushes move freely in their guides, and that the brush lengths are within the limits given in the Specifications. If any doubt exists regarding the condition of the brushes, the best policy is to renew them.
10 To fit new brushes, unsolder the old brush leads from the brush holder, and solder on the new leads in exactly the same place.
11 Check that the new brushes move freely in the guides.

Refitting

12 Before refitting the brush holder assembly, retain the brushes in the retracted position using a stiff piece of wire or a twist drill.
13 Refit the brush holder assembly so that the wire or drill protrudes through the slot in the slip ring end housing, and tighten the securing screws.
14 Refit the diode assembly and the stator assembly to the housing, ensuring that the stator leads are in their correct positions, and refit the terminal screw and nuts.

15 Assemble the drive end housing and rotor to the slip ring end housing, ensuring that the previously made marks are still aligned. Insert and tighten the three through-bolts.
16 Pull the wire or drill, as applicable, from the slot in the slip ring end housing, so that the brushes rest on the rotor slip rings **(see illustration)**.
17 Refit the alternator, as described in Section 11.

13 Alternator brushes and regulator (Bosch type) - removal and refitting

Removal

1 The brush holder and voltage regulator are combined in a single assembly, which is bolted to the rear of the alternator. If the voltage regulator is faulty, the complete assembly must be renewed.
2 Disconnect the air trunking from the air cleaner, and from the airbox or throttle body, as applicable, and remove it for improved access.
3 Disconnect the battery negative lead.
4 To improve access further, the alternator can be removed, as described in Section 11.
5 Remove the two securing screws, and withdraw the brush holder/voltage regulator assembly **(see illustrations)**.

5

12.16 Removing drill bit used to hold brushes in retracted position

13.5A Remove the securing screws . . .

13.5B . . . and withdraw the brush holder/voltage regulator - Bosch type

13.6 Measuring the length of an alternator brush - Bosch type

13.11 Alternator slip rings (arrowed) - Bosch type

6 Check that the brushes move freely in their guides, and that the brush lengths are within the limits given in the Specifications **(see illustration)**. If any doubt exists regarding the condition of the brushes, the best policy is to renew them as follows.

7 Hold the brush wire with a pair of pliers, and unsolder it from the brush holder. Lift away the brush. Repeat for the remaining brush.

Refitting

8 Note that whenever new brushes are fitted, new brush springs should also be fitted.

9 With the new springs fitted to the brush holder, insert the new brushes, and check that they move freely in their guides. If they bind, lightly polish with a very fine file or glass paper.

10 Solder the brush wire ends to the brush holder, taking care not to allow solder to pass to the stranded wire.

11 Check the condition of the slip rings, and if necessary clean them with a rag or very fine glass paper **(see illustration)**.

12 Refit the brush holder/voltage regulator assembly, and tighten the securing screws.

13 Where applicable, refit the alternator, as described in Section 11.

14 Reconnect the battery leads.

15 Refit the air trunking.

14 Starting system - testing

Note: *Refer to the precautions given In 'Safety first!' and in Section 2 before starting work.*

1 If the starter motor fails to operate when the ignition key is turned to the appropriate position, the following possible causes may be to blame.

(a) The battery is faulty.

(b) The electrical connections between the switch, solenoid battery and starter motor are somewhere failing to pass the necessary current from the battery through the starter to earth.

(c) The solenoid is faulty.

(d) The starter motor Is mechanically or electrically defective.

2 To check the battery, switch on the headlights. If they dim after a few seconds, this indicates that the battery is discharged - recharge (see Section 6) or renew the battery. If the headlights glow brightly, operate the ignition switch and observe the lights. If they dim, then this indicates that current is reaching the starter motor, therefore the fault must lie in the starter motor. If the lights continue to glow brightly (and no clicking sound can be heard from the starter motor solenoid), this indicates that there is a fault in the circuit or solenoid - see following paragraphs. If the starter motor turns slowly when operated, but the battery is in good condition, then this indicates that either the starter motor is faulty, or there is considerable resistance somewhere in the circuit.

3 If a fault in the circuit is suspected, disconnect the battery leads (including the earth connection to the body), the starter/solenoid wiring and the engine/transmission earth strap. Thoroughly clean the connections, reconnect the leads and wiring, then use a voltmeter or test light to check that full battery voltage is available at the battery positive lead connection to the solenoid, and that the earth is sound. Smear petroleum jelly around the battery terminals to prevent corrosion - corroded connections are amongst the most frequent causes of electrical system faults.

4 If the battery and all connections are in good condition, check the circuit by disconnecting the wire from the solenoid blade terminal. Connect a voltmeter or test light between the wire end and a good earth (such as the battery negative terminal), and check that the wire is live when the ignition switch is turned to the 'start' position. If it is, then the circuit is sound - if not, continue on to paragraph 5.

5 The solenoid contacts can be checked by connecting a voltmeter or test light between the battery positive feed connection on the starter side of the solenoid, and earth. When the ignition switch is turned to the 'start' position, there should be a reading or lighted bulb, as applicable. If there is no reading or lighted bulb, the solenoid is faulty and should be renewed.

6 If the circuit and solenoid are proved sound, the fault must lie in the starter motor. Refer to Section 16.

15 Starter motor - removal and refitting

Removal

1 Disconnect the battery negative lead.

2 Apply the handbrake, then jack up the front of the vehicle, and support securely on axle stands.

3 Where fitted, remove the engine undershield, as described in Chapter 11.

4 Note the wiring connections on the solenoid, then disconnect them **(see illustration)**.

5 Where applicable, unscrew the bolt securing the starter motor mounting bracket to the cylinder block.

6 Unscrew the two starter motor mounting bolts, noting that the top bolt on some models is fitted from the transmission side, and also secures the wiring harness bracket **(see illustration)**. Where applicable, also note the location of the engine earth strap, which may be secured by one of the starter motor mounting bolts on certain models.

7 Withdraw the starter motor.

Refitting

8 Refitting is a reversal of removal, but where applicable, ensure that the wiring harness bracket is in place on the top mounting bolt, and tighten all bolts to the specified torque.

15.4 Starter motor solenoid wiring connections

15.6 Starter motor mounting bolt (arrowed) - viewed from above

17.4 Disconnecting the distributor wiring plug - 14 NV models

16 Starter motor overhaul - general

1 If the starter motor is thought to be suspect, it should be removed from the vehicle and taken to an auto-electrician for testing. Most auto-electricians will be able to supply and fit brushes at a reasonable cost. However, check on the cost of repairs before continuing as it may prove more economical to obtain a new or exchange motor.

17 Distributor (14 NV) - removal, overhaul and refitting

Removal

1 Disconnect the battery negative lead.
2 If necessary, identify each HT lead for position to aid correct refitting, then disconnect the leads from the spark plugs by pulling on the connectors, not on the leads. Similarly, disconnect the HT lead from the coil. Pull the leads from the clips on the camshaft cover.
3 Release the two securing clips using a screwdriver, and lift the distributor cap, complete with HT leads, from the distributor.
4 Disconnect the distributor wiring plug (see illustration).
5 Disconnect the vacuum pipe from the diaphragm unit on the side of the distributor.
6 If the original distributor is to be refitted,

17.8B . . . remove the clamp plate . . .

17.7 Timing pointer on rear timing belt cover aligned with 10° BTDC notch in crankshaft pulley - 14 NV models

make alignment marks between the distributor body and the camshaft housing, so that the distributor can be refitted in its original position.
7 Using a socket or spanner on the crankshaft pulley bolt, or by engaging top gear (manual transmission) and pushing the vehicle backwards or forwards as necessary (with the handbrake released!), turn the crankshaft to bring No 1 piston to the firing point. No 1 piston is at the firing point when:
(a) The timing pointer on the rear timing belt cover is aligned with the 10° BTDC notch in the crankshaft pulley (see illustration).
(b) The tip of the rotor arm is pointing to the position occupied by the No 1 cylinder HT lead terminal in the distributor cap.
(c) The rotor arm is aligned with the notch in the distributor body (remove the rotor arm and plastic shield, then refit the rotor arm to check the alignment with the notch).
8 Unscrew the clamp nut and remove the clamp plate, then withdraw the distributor from the camshaft housing (see illustrations).

Overhaul

9 With the distributor removed, pull off the rotor arm, and remove the plastic shield.
10 Although the top bearing plate can be removed after unscrewing the two securing screws - this is of academic interest, as other than the vacuum diaphragm unit, no spares are available for the distributor, and no adjustments are required.
11 The vacuum diaphragm unit can be removed by extracting the two securing screws and unhooking the operating arm from the distributor baseplate. Note that the screws

17.8C . . . and withdraw the distributor – 14 NV models

17.8A Unscrew the clamp nut . . .

are of differing lengths; the longer screw also secures one of the distributor cap clips.
12 The vacuum unit can be tested by applying suction to the vacuum port, and checking that the operating rod moves into the unit as suction is applied. Remove the suction, and check that the operating rod returns to its original position. If the operating rod does not move as described, renew the vacuum unit.
13 Check the distributor cap for corrosion of the segments, and for signs of tracking, indicated by a thin black line between the segments. Make sure that the carbon brush in the centre of the cap moves freely, and stands proud of the surface of the cap. Renew the cap if necessary.
14 If the metal portion of the rotor arm is badly burnt or loose, renew it. If slightly burnt or corroded, it may be cleaned with a fine file.
15 Examine the seal ring at the rear of the distributor body, and renew if necessary.
16 Reassembly is a reversal of dismantling, ensuring that the vacuum unit operating arm is correctly engaged with the peg on the baseplate several attempts may be required to reconnect it (see illustration).

17.16 Exploded view of distributor fitted to 14 NV models

1	Vacuum diaphragm unit	5	Distributor cap
2	Body	6	Rotor arm
3	Cap retaining clip	7	Plastic shield
4	Seal ring	8	Top bearing plate
		9	Abutment ring

5

18.3 Removing the distributor cap - C 14 NZ models

18.4 Disconnecting the distributor wiring plug - C 14 NZ models

18 Distributor (14 SE, C 14 NZ and C 16 NZ) - removal, overhaul and refitting

Removal

1 Start removal as described in Section 17, paragraphs 1 and 2.

2 Note that various types of distributor may be fitted, depending on model.

3 Loosen the two securing screws, or release the two securing clips using a screwdriver, as applicable, and remove the distributor cap, complete with HT leads, from the distributor **(see illustration)**.

4 Where applicable, disconnect the distributor wiring plug **(see illustration)**.

5 Continue as described in Section 17, paragraphs 6 to 8 inclusive, noting the following points **(see illustrations)**:

(a) Some distributors may already have alignment marks on the distributor body and camshaft housing.

(b) On certain distributors, No 1 piston is at the firing point when the rotor arm is aligned with the TDC arrow stamped on the distributor body (in place of a notch in the distributor body).

Overhaul

6 On some Bosch distributors, the plastic drive collar can be renewed if necessary after

Refitting

17 Begin refitting by checking that No 1 cylinder is still at the firing point (see paragraph 7). The relevant timing marks should be aligned. If the engine has been turned whilst the distributor has been removed, check that No 1 cylinder is on its firing stroke by removing No 1 cylinder spark plug and placing a finger over the plug hole. Turn the crankshaft until compression can be felt which indicates that No 1 piston is rising on its compression stroke. Continue turning the crankshaft until the relevant timing marks are in alignment.

18 Turn the rotor arm to the position noted in paragraph 7 (c), and hold the rotor arm in this position as the distributor is fitted, noting that the distributor driveshaft will only engage with the camshaft in one

position. If the original distributor is being refitted, align the marks made on the distributor body and camshaft housing before removal.

19 Refit the clamp plate and nut, but do not fully tighten the nut at this stage.

20 Remove the rotor arm, then refit the plastic shield and the rotor arm.

21 Reconnect the vacuum pipe to the diaphragm unit.

22 Reconnect the distributor wiring plug.

23 Refit the distributor cap, ensuring that the HT leads are correctly reconnected.

24 Reconnect the battery negative lead.

25 Check and if necessary adjust the ignition timing, as described in Chapter 1.

18.5A Alignment marks (circled) between distributor body and camshaft housing - C 14 NZ models

18.5B Rotor arm aligned with arrow (circled) stamped on distributor body - C 14 NZ models

18.5C Remove the plastic shield . . .

18.5D . . . and check that the rotor arm is aligned with the notch (circled) in the distributor body rim - C 14 SE models

18.5E Removing the clamp plate . . .

18.5F . . . and withdrawing the distributor - C 14 SE models

18.6 Driving out the distributor drive collar roll pin - C 14 SE models

19.3 Unscrewing a distributor cap securing screw - C 20 NE models

19.4 Removing the plastic shield from the rotor arm housing - C 20 NE models

driving out the securing roll pin **(see illustration)**, but otherwise no spare parts are available for the distributors, and if faulty, the complete unit must be renewed. The distributor cap and rotor arm can be examined as described in paragraphs 13 and 14 of Section 17.

Refitting

7 Where applicable, examine the condition of the O-ring seal at the base of the distributor, and renew if necessary.

8 The refitting procedure is, as described in Section 17, noting the points made in paragraph 5.

19 Distributor (C 18 NZ and C 20 NE) - removal, overhaul and refitting

Removal

1 The distributor consists simply of a cap, rotor arm and plastic shield, mounted on the end of the camshaft housing, which can be removed as follows.

2 Proceed as described in paragraphs 1 and 2 of Section 17.

3 Using a Torx socket, unscrew the three captive securing screws **(see illustration)**, and withdraw the distributor cap (complete with HT leads) from the distributor.

4 Withdraw the plastic shield from the rotor

arm housing. The shield is an interference fit in the housing, via an O-ring seal located in a groove in its periphery. Ease out the shield, taking care not to damage the rotor arm **(see illustration)**.

5 Using an Allen key or hexagon bit, extract the two securing screws and withdraw the rotor arm, leaving the metal rotor hub in the housing **(see illustrations)**.

Overhaul

6 Examine the distributor cap and rotor arm as described in paragraphs 13 and 14 of Section 17.

Refitting

7 Examine the O-ring on the plastic shield, and renew if necessary.

8 Refitting is a reversal of removal, noting that the rotor arm can only be fitted in one position. If necessary, turn the metal rotor hub so that the screw holes align with those in the rotor arm and the end of the camshaft. Ensure that the HT leads are correctly reconnected.

20 Distributor (early C 20 XE models) - removal, overhaul and refitting

Removal

1 Disconnect the battery negative lead.

2 Remove the securing screws and lift the

19.5A Extract the securing screws . . .

spark plug cover from the camshaft cover, then disconnect the HT leads from the spark plugs, and unclip the leads from the bracket on the end of the camshaft cover. Also disconnect the HT lead from the coil. Identify the leads for position if necessary, to aid refitting.

3 Using a Torx socket, unscrew the three captive securing screws, and withdraw the distributor cap (complete with HT leads) from the distributor.

4 Disconnect the distributor wiring plug.

5 Unscrew the two bolts securing the distributor to the cylinder head, and withdraw the distributor. Note that the offset peg on the distributor drive engages with the corresponding hole in the end of the camshaft **(see illustrations)**.

5

19.5B . . . and withdraw the rotor arm - C 20 NE models

20.5A Unscrewing a distributor securing bolt - C 20 XE models

20.5B Offset peg (A) engages with hole (B) in camshaft

21.3 Disconnecting the HT lead from the coil - C 14 SE models

21.4 Disconnecting the coil wiring plug . . .

21.5 . . . and the amplifier module wiring plug - C 14 SE models

Overhaul

6 No spare parts are available for the distributor, and if faulty, the complete unit must be renewed. The distributor cap and rotor arm can be examined as described in paragraphs 13 and 14 of Section 17.

Refitting

7 Examine the condition of the O-ring seal at the base of the distributor, and renew if necessary.

8 Refitting is a reversal of removal, noting that the distributor can only be fitted in one position.

21 Ignition coil - removal, testing and refitting

Note: *For details on the DIS module, refer to Section 22.*

Removal

1 The coil is mounted on the left-hand side of the engine compartment, in front of the suspension turret.

2 Disconnect the battery negative lead.

3 Disconnect the HT lead from the coil **(see illustration)**.

4 Disconnect the LT wires from the coil, and/or disconnect the coil wiring plug, as applicable **(see illustration)**. Note that the LT wires may be secured with spade connectors

or by nuts depending on model. Where applicable, make a note of the LT wire connections to aid refitting.

5 Where applicable, disconnect the wiring plug from the ignition amplifier module mounted under the coil **(see illustration)**.

6 Unscrew the two coil securing bolts, and withdraw the coil, complete with the amplifier module and mounting plate, where applicable **(see illustrations)**. Note that on certain models fitted with power steering, one of the coil securing bolts also secures the power steering fluid reservoir bracket. Also note the location of the coil suppressor that may be secured by one of the coil securing screws on certain models.

7 Where applicable, disengage the coil from the amplifier module mounting plate.

8 On models with a cylindrical type coil, the mounting clamp can be removed from the coil by loosening the clamp nut.

Testing

9 Connect an ohmmeter between both LT terminals, and check the primary windings for continuity. Connect the ohmmeter between the HT terminal and either LT terminal, and check the secondary windings for continuity. If there is no continuity, the coil should be renewed.

10 Using an ohmmeter or a continuity tester, check that there is no continuity between the HT terminal and the coil body. If there is continuity, the coil should be renewed.

Refitting

11 Refitting is a reversal of removal, ensuring that (where applicable) the coil suppressor is in position before fitting the coil securing bolts. Ensure that all wiring is correctly reconnected as noted before removal, and that all connections are secure.

22 DIS module - removal, testing and refitting

Removal

1 The coil is mounted on the left-hand end of the camshaft housing, in the position normally occupied by the distributor.

2 Disconnect the battery negative lead.

3 Disconnect the HT leads from the coil, noting their locations to ensure correct refitting. Note that the HT lead cylinder numbers are stamped into the coil casing **(see illustration)**.

4 Disconnect the coil wiring plug **(see illustration)**.

5 Unscrew the three Torx type securing screws, and remove the coil from its mounting plate **(see illustration)**.

Testing

6 Due to the construction of the coil, testing should be carried out using the appropriate test equipment available to a Vauxhall dealer.

21.6A Cylindrical type ignition coil mounting bolts (arrowed) - 14 NV models

21.6B Ignition coil securing bolts (arrowed) - C 14 SE models

22.3 HT lead cylinder numbers (arrowed) marked on DIS module (shown removed) - C 16 SE models

22.4 Disconnecting the DIS module wiring plug - C 16 SE models

22.5 Unscrewing a DIS module securing screw - C 16 SE models

23.3 Ignition coil (1) and amplifier module and mounting bracket (2)

Refitting

7 Refitting is a reversal of removal.

23 Ignition amplifier module - removal and refitting

Note: *This is also known as the trigger box.*

Removal

1 Where applicable, the amplifier module is located on a bracket under the ignition coil.
2 Remove the ignition coil and amplifier module mounting bracket, as described in Section 21.
3 The module can be removed from the mounting plate by unscrewing the two securing screws **(see illustration)**.

Refitting

4 Before refitting the module, special heat-sink compound should be applied to the mounting plate to improve heat dissipation. If

a new module is being fitted, it should be supplied with heat sink compound. Similar compounds can be bought from DIY electrical shops.
5 Refit the coil mounting plate and coil assembly, as described in Section 21.

24 Oil pressure warning light switch - removal and refitting

Removal

1 The switch is screwed into the end of the oil pump, on the inlet manifold side of the engine.
2 Disconnect the battery negative lead.
3 On most models, access to the switch can be obtained from above, but on some models improved access can be obtained by jacking up the front of the vehicle, and supporting securely on axle stands), then removing the right-hand roadwheel. Where fitted, remove

the access hatch from the engine undershield **(see illustration)**.
4 Disconnect the wiring from the switch.
5 Place a container under the switch to catch the oil that will be released as the switch is removed.
6 Using a spanner, unscrew the switch. Be prepared for oil spillage, and plug the hole in the oil pump to minimise oil loss and prevent dirt ingress.

Refitting

7 Refitting is a reversal of removal, but on completion check and if necessary top-up the engine oil level as described in Chapter 1.

25 Oil level sensor - removal and refitting

Removal

1 The engine oil level sensor is located in the front face of the sump **(see illustration)**.
2 Where fitted, remove the access hatch from the engine undershield.
3 Disconnect the battery negative lead, then disconnect the wiring plug from the sensor.
4 Place a container under the sump, to catch any oil that may be released as the sensor is unscrewed.
5 Unscrew the securing screws, and withdraw the sensor from the sump.
6 Recover the sealing ring.

Refitting

7 Refitting is a reversal of removal, but before refitting the sensor, examine the condition of the sealing ring, and renew if necessary.

5

24.3 Low oil pressure warning light switch viewed from underneath vehicle - C 20 XE model

25.1 Engine oil level sensor location - C 20 XE model

Notes

Chapter 6
Clutch

Contents

Degrees of difficulty

Easy, suitable for novice with little experience	Fairly easy, suitable for beginner with some experience	Fairly difficult, suitable for competent DIY mechanic	Difficult, suitable for experienced DIY mechanic	Very difficult, suitable for expert DIY or professional

Specifications

Type .... Single dry plate, operated by cable

Clutch disc

Diameter:
1.4 litre models	190.0 mm
1.6 litre models	200.0 mm
C 18 NZ, C 18 XE, C 18 XEL and C 20 NE models	216.0 mm
C 20 XE models	228.0 mm
Lining thickness (new all models)	3.5 mm

Torque wrench settings

	Nm	lbf ft
Bellhousing cover plate:		
Alloy type	6	4
Steel type	12	9
Clutch cover to flywheel	15	11
Clutch fork to release lever	35	26
Differential housing cover plate bolts:		
Except F18 and F18+ transmission models:		
Steel plate	30	22
Alloy plate	18	13
F18 and F18+ transmission models	40	30
Input shaft socket-headed screw	15	11
Transmission endplate bolts:		
M7 bolts	15	11
M8 bolts	20	15
Transmission to cylinder block	75	55

1 General information

1 All manual transmission models are fitted with a single dry plate clutch, which consists of five main components; friction disc, pressure plate, diaphragm spring, cover and release bearing.

2 The friction disc is free to slide along the splines of the transmission input shaft, and is held in position between the flywheel and the pressure plate by the pressure exerted on the pressure plate by the diaphragm spring. Friction lining material is riveted to both sides of the friction disc, and spring cushioning between the friction linings and the hub absorbs transmission shocks, and helps to ensure a smooth take-up of power as the clutch is engaged.

3 The diaphragm spring is mounted on pins, and is held in place in the cover by annular fulcrum rings.

4 The release bearing is located on a guide sleeve at the front of the transmission, and the bearing is free to slide on the sleeve, under the action of the release arm that pivots inside the clutch bellhousing.

5 The release arm is operated by the clutch pedal, by way of a cable. As wear takes place on the friction disc over a period of time, the clutch pedal will rise progressively, relative to its original position. No periodic adjustment of the clutch cable is specified by the manufacturers.

6 When the clutch pedal is depressed, the release arm is actuated by means of the cable. The release arm pushes the release bearing forwards, to bear against the centre of the diaphragm spring, thus pushing the centre of the diaphragm spring inwards. The diaphragm spring acts against the fulcrum rings in the cover. So, as the centre of the spring is pushed in, the outside of the spring is pushed out, thus allowing the pressure plate to move backwards away from the friction disc.

6

7 When the clutch pedal is released, the diaphragm spring forces the pressure plate into contact with the friction linings on the friction disc, and simultaneously pushes the friction disc forwards on its splines, forcing it against the flywheel. The friction disc is now firmly sandwiched between the pressure plate and the flywheel, and drive is taken up.

8 On certain models, the clutch assembly, release bearing and guide sleeve oil seal can be renewed without removing the engine or transmission from the vehicle.

9 During 1992, certain models were being gradually fitted with a 'pot type' flywheel **(see illustration)**. This design assists in smoother running and reduces transmission rattle. On these vehicles, the transmission must be removed, to replace the clutch.

2 Clutch cable - removal and refitting

1.9 Two different types of flywheel

1 Earlier flat flywheel   *2 'Pot-type' flywheel introduced on some models during 1992*

Removal

1 Working in the engine compartment, measure the length of the threaded rod protruding through the plastic block at the release arm end of the cable **(see illustration)**. This will enable approximate pre-setting of the cable when refitting.

2 Remove the clip from the threaded rod at the release arm, then slide the rod from the

2.1 Measuring the length of protruding threaded rod at the end of the clutch cable

release arm **(see illustration)**. Push the release arm towards the engine, and if necessary slacken the cable adjuster, to aid removal.

3 Pull the cable assembly from the lug on the clutch bellhousing **(see illustration)**.

4 Working inside the vehicle, release the securing clips, and remove the lower trim panel from the driver's footwell.

5 Unhook the return spring from the clutch pedal, and disconnect the cable end from the pedal. Note that the end of the return spring retains the cable end in the pedal. Access is limited, and it may prove easier to remove the clutch pedal, as described in Section 3, before disconnecting the cable.

6 The cable assembly can now be withdrawn into the engine compartment, by pulling it through the bulkhead. Take care not to damage the bulkhead grommet as the cable is withdrawn.

Refitting

7 Refitting is a reversal of removal, remembering the following points.

8 Position the threaded rod so that the length of thread protruding through the plastic block

is as noted before removal, then adjust the cable as described in Chapter 1.

9 Ensure that the bulkhead grommet is correctly seated.

3 Clutch pedal - removal and refitting

Removal

1 Start to remove the clutch cable, as described in Section 2, paragraphs 1 and 2.

2 Working inside the vehicle, release the securing clips, and remove the lower trim panel from the driver's footwell.

3 Remove the locking clip from the right-hand end of the pedal pivot shaft **(see illustration)**, then unscrew the pedal retaining nut and recover the washer(s).

4 Push the pivot shaft out of the pedal bracket (to the left), then lower the pedal and return spring. Note the position of any washers and/or spacers on the pivot shaft, so that they can be refitted in their original positions.

2.2 Removing the clip from the threaded rod at the release arm

2.3 Clutch cable attachment to lug on bellhousing

3.3 Clutch pedal pivot locking clip (arrowed)

3.5A Clutch pedal components assembled as when in place in vehicle. Clutch cable is retained by return spring at 'A'

3.5B Clutch pedal pivot components

4.2 Removing the cover plate from the clutch bellhousing

5 Disconnect the cable end from the pedal by releasing the return spring, and withdraw the pedal and return spring from the vehicle **(see illustrations)**.

Refitting

6 Refitting is a reversal of removal, but before inserting the pedal pivot shaft, smear the surface with a little molybdenum disulphide grease.

7 On completion, adjust the clutch cable if necessary, as described in Chapter 1.

4 Clutch assembly (models with flat flywheel) - removal, inspection and refitting

> ⚠ *Warning: Dust created by clutch wear and deposited on the clutch components may contain asbestos, which is a health hazard. DO NOT blow it out with compressed air, or inhale any of it. DO NOT use petrol (or petroleum-based solvents) to clean off the dust. Brake system cleaner or methylated spirit should be used to flush the dust into a container. After the clutch components are wiped clean with rags, dispose of the contaminated rags and cleaner in a sealed, marked container.*

Note: *During 1992, certain models have been progressively fitted with a 'pot-type' flywheel*

during production. The 'pot-type' flywheel is significantly thicker than the standard item, and consequently there is insufficient clearance between the flywheel and the clutch bellhousing to enable the clutch to be removed with the engine and transmission in the vehicle. Before attempting to remove the clutch, remove the clutch bellhousing cover plate and examine the flywheel to ascertain which type is fitted, then continue as follows, according to flywheel type. Vauxhall recommend the use of special tools for this procedure. However, an alternative method is described in the text. It is suggested that this Section is read thoroughly before work starts, so that tools can be made available as required.

Removal

1 Where applicable, remove the left-hand front wheel trim, then loosen the roadwheel bolts. Apply the handbrake, jack up the front of the vehicle, and support securely on axle stands. Remove the roadwheel for improved access. Where fitted, remove the engine undershield with reference to Chapter 11.

2 Unscrew the securing bolts, and remove the cover plate from the base of the clutch bellhousing **(see illustration)**.

3 For improved access, remove the wheel arch liner, as described in Chapter 11.

4 Unscrew the retaining nut and disconnect the earth strap from the transmission endplate, where fitted **(see illustration)**.

5 Place a container beneath the transmission endplate, to catch any escaping oil. Then unscrew the securing bolts and remove the endplate **(see illustration)**. Note the location of the bolts (including the stud for the earth strap, where applicable), as two different lengths are used.

6 Remove the gasket.

7 Extract the circlip from inside the end of the transmission input shaft, using a pair of circlip pliers **(see illustration)**.

8 Using a twelve-point splined key, unscrew the bolt from the end of the input shaft **(see illustration)**.

9 The input shaft can now be pulled from the splined hub of the clutch friction disc. The manufacturers specify the use of special tools

4.4 Earth strap on transmission endplate

4.5 Removing the transmission endplate

4.7 Extract the circlip (arrowed) from the end of the transmission input shaft

4.8 Unscrew the bolt from the end of the input shaft

6

4.9A Self-made tool for disengaging transmission input shaft from clutch

4.9B Disengaging the input shaft from the clutch using the self-made tool

4.12 Clutch pressure plate retaining clamp dimensions - in mm

for this operation (tool No's KM-556-1-A and KM-556-4), but an alternative can be made, as shown **(see illustrations)**. The tool bolts into place on the end of the transmission, using the endplate securing bolts. Tool dimensions will vary according to transmission type.

10 Alternatively, screw an M7 bolt into the end of the input shaft, and use the bolt to pull the shaft out to its stop. It is likely that the input shaft will be a very tight fit, in which case it may prove difficult to withdraw, without using the special tool previously described. In extreme cases, a slide hammer can be attached to the end of the shaft to enable it to be withdrawn. Using this method may damage transmission components, use only when absolutely necessary.

11 Before the clutch assembly can be removed, the pressure plate must be compressed against the tension of the diaphragm spring. Otherwise the assembly will be too thick to be withdrawn through the space between the flywheel and the edge of the bellhousing.

12 Three special clamps are available from the manufacturers for this purpose (tool No KM-526-A), but alternatives can be made up from strips of metal. The clamps should be U-shaped, and conform to the dimensions given below and as shown **(see illustration)**. Bevel the edges of the clamps to ease fitting, and cut a slot in one of the U-legs to clear the pressure plate rivets.

a) *Thickness of metal strip - 3.0 mm*
b) *Distance between U-legs - 15.0 mm*

13 Have an assistant depress the clutch pedal fully, then fit each clamp securely over the edge of the cover pressure plate, fitting the clamps in the slots around the rim of the cover **(see illustrations)**. Turn the crankshaft using a socket or spanner on the pulley/gear bolt, to bring each clamp location into view.

14 Once the clamps have been fitted, have the assistant release the clutch pedal.

15 Progressively loosen and remove the six bolts and spring washers that secure the clutch cover to the flywheel. As previously, turn the crankshaft to bring each bolt into view. Where applicable (and if the original clutch is to be refitted), note the position of the mark on the flywheel that aligns with the notch in the rim of the clutch cover **(see illustrations)**.

16 The clutch assembly can now be withdrawn downwards from the bellhousing **(see illustration)**. Be prepared to catch the clutch friction disc, which may drop out of the cover as it is withdrawn, and note which way round the friction disc is fitted. The flatter side faces the flywheel.

17 The pressure plate can be compressed against the tension of the diaphragm spring, in a vice fitted with soft jaw protectors, in order to remove the clamps.

Inspection

18 With the clutch assembly removed, clean off all traces of dust using a dry cloth. Although most friction discs now have

4.13A Fitting a clamp . . .

4.13B . . . to compress the clutch pressure plate prior to removal

4.15A Loosening a clutch cover to flywheel bolt

4.15B Stamped mark on flywheel (arrowed) aligned with notch in clutch cover

4.16 Withdrawing the clutch assembly from the bellhousing

asbestos-free linings, some do not, and it is wise to take precautions. Asbestos dust is harmful and must not be inhaled.

19 Examine the linings of the clutch disc for wear and loose rivets, and the disc for distortion, cracks, broken torsion springs and worn splines. The surface of the friction linings may be glazed, but as long as the friction material pattern can be clearly seen, this is satisfactory. If there is any sign of oil contamination, indicated by a continuous, or patchy, shiny black discoloration, the disc must be renewed. The source of the contamination must be traced and rectified before fitting new clutch components. Typically, a leaking crankshaft oil seal or transmission input shaft oil seal or both, may need replacing (refer to Chapters 2A or 2B and 7A, as appropriate). The disc must also be renewed if the lining thickness has worn down to, or just above, the level of the rivet heads.

20 Check the machined faces of the flywheel and pressure plate. If either is grooved, or heavily scored, renewal is necessary. The pressure plate must also be renewed if any cracks are apparent, or if the diaphragm spring is damaged or its pressure suspect.

21 With the clutch removed, check the condition of the release bearing, as described in Section 6.

Refitting

Note: *The circlip in the end of the input shaft and the transmission endplate gasket should be renewed on reassembly.*

22 Some replacement clutch assemblies are supplied with the pressure plate already compressed using the three clamps described in paragraph 12. If not, the pressure plate should be compressed against the tension of the diaphragm spring. Use a vice fitted with soft jaw protectors and the clamps used during removal.

23 It is important to ensure that no oil or grease gets onto the friction disc linings, or the pressure plate and flywheel faces. Refit the clutch assembly with clean hands. Wipe down the pressure plate and flywheel faces with a clean rag before refitting.

24 Apply a smear Longlife Grease (MoS$_2$), to the splines of the friction disc hub, then offer the disc to the flywheel, with the flatter side of the disc facing the flywheel. Hold the friction disc against the flywheel while the pressure plate assembly is fitted into position.

25 The input shaft must now be pushed through the hub of the friction disc, until its end engages in the spigot bearing in the end of the crankshaft. **Under no circumstances** must the shaft be hammered home, as transmission damage may result. If the input shaft cannot be pushed home by hand, steady pressure should be exerted on the end of the shaft. The manufacturers specify the use of a special tool for this operation (tool No KM-564), but the improvised tool used to

withdraw the shaft during the removal procedure can be used by repositioning the nut as shown.

26 With the input shaft pushed fully home, position the pressure plate assembly so that the mark on the flywheel is in alignment with the notch on the rim. Then refit and progressively tighten the six clutch cover to flywheel bolts (ensuring that the spring washers are fitted) in a diagonal sequence. Turn the crankshaft, using a socket or spanner on the pulley/gear bolt, to gain access to each bolt in turn, and finally tighten all the bolts to the specified torque.

27 Have an assistant depress the clutch pedal. Then remove the three clamps from the edge of the pressure plate, again turning the crankshaft for access to each clamp.

28 Once the clamps have been removed, have the assistant release the clutch pedal.

29 Refit the screw to the end of the transmission input shaft, then fit a new circlip.

30 Using a new gasket, refit the transmission endplate, and tighten the securing bolts to the specified torque. Where applicable, ensure that the studded bolt that retains the earth strap is fitted to its correct location, as noted during removal.

31 Where applicable, reconnect the transmission earth strap, and fit the retaining nut.

32 Refit the cover plate to the base of the clutch bellhousing, and tighten the securing bolts. Where applicable, refit the wheel arch liner.

33 Refit the roadwheel, then lower the vehicle to the ground and finally tighten the roadwheel bolts. Refit the wheel trim and undershield, as applicable.

34 Check the clutch cable adjustment, as described in Chapter 1.

35 Check and if necessary top-up the transmission oil level, as described in Chapter 1.

5 Clutch assembly (models with 'pot-type' flywheel) - removal, inspection and refitting

Removal

1 Due to the design of the 'pot-type' flywheel, there is insufficient space for the clutch to be withdrawn through the aperture in the clutch bellhousing, as described for models with a flat flywheel.

2 Unless the complete engine and transmission assembly is to be removed from the vehicle, access to the clutch can be obtained by removing the engine or (with most models) the transmission (refer to Chapters 2A or 2B and 7A).

3 With the engine or transmission removed, continue as follows.

4 Where applicable (and if the original clutch is to be refitted), note the position of the mark on the flywheel that aligns with the notch in

the rim of the clutch cover. Then progressively unscrew the six bolts and spring washers that secure the clutch cover to the flywheel.

5 With all the bolts removed, lift off the clutch assembly. Be prepared to catch the friction disc as the cover assembly is lifted from the flywheel, and note which way round the friction disc is fitted. The flatter side should face the flywheel.

Inspection

6 Inspect the clutch as described in Section 4.

Refitting

7 Start refitting, as described in Section 4, paragraphs 23 and 24.

8 Fit the clutch cover assembly, where applicable aligning the mark on the flywheel with the notch in the rim of the clutch cover. Insert the six bolts and spring washers, and tighten them finger-tight, so that the friction disc is gripped, but can still be moved.

9 The friction disc must now be centralised, so that when the engine and transmission are mated, the transmission input shaft splines will pass through the splines in the friction disc hub.

10 Centralisation can be carried out by inserting a round bar or a long screwdriver through the hole in the centre of the friction disc, so that the end of the bar rests in the spigot bearing in the centre of the crankshaft. Where possible, use a blunt instrument, but if a screwdriver is used, wrap tape around the blade to prevent damage to the bearing surface. Moving the bar sideways or up and down as necessary, move the friction disc in whichever direction is necessary to achieve centralisation. With the bar removed, view the friction disc hub in relation to the hole in the centre of the crankshaft and the circle created by the ends of the diaphragm spring fingers. When the hub appears exactly in the centre, all is correct. Alternatively, if a clutch alignment tool can be obtained, this will eliminate all the guesswork, and obviate the need for visual alignment.

11 Tighten the cover retaining bolts gradually in a diagonal sequence, to the specified torque. Remove the alignment tool.

12 Refit the engine or the transmission, as described in the relevant Chapter.

13 On completion, check the clutch cable adjustment, as described in Chapter 1.

6 Clutch release bearing - removal, inspection and refitting

Note: *Refer to the note at the beginning of Section 4 before proceeding.*

Removal

1 On models with a flat flywheel, access to the release bearing can be obtained with the engine and transmission in the vehicle, after

6.3 Unscrewing the clamp bolt securing the release fork to the release arm pivot shaft (model with a flat flywheel)

6.5 Withdrawing the clutch release bearing (model with a flat flywheel)

removing the clutch assembly, as described in Section 4. Although access is improved if the transmission is removed.

2 On models with a 'pot-type' flywheel, the transmission (on some models, the engine and transmission) must be removed for access to the release bearing. Refer to Chapters 2A or 2B and 7A.

3 Unscrew the clamp bolt securing the release fork to the release arm pivot shaft **(see illustration)**.

4 Disconnect the clutch cable (if still attached), from the release arm, by removing the clip from the threaded rod, and then sliding the threaded rod from the release arm.

5 Pull the release arm pivot shaft up and out of the bellhousing, then withdraw the release fork and the bearing **(see illustration)**. Where necessary, slide the bearing from the release fork, and where applicable, pull the bearing from the plastic collar.

6 The transmission input shaft oil seal can be renewed after removing the release bearing guide sleeve, as described in Chapter 7A.

Inspection

7 Spin the release bearing, and check it for excessive roughness. Hold the outer race, and attempt to move it laterally against the inner race. If any excessive movement or roughness is evident, renew the bearing. If a new clutch has been fitted, it is wise to renew the release bearing as a matter of course.

8 The nylon bushes supporting the release arm pivot shaft can be renewed if necessary, by tapping them from their lugs in the bellhousing using a drift. This is likely to be difficult if the transmission is still in the vehicle. Drive the new bushes into position, ensuring that their locating tabs engage with the slots in the bellhousing lugs.

Refitting

9 Refitting of the release bearing and arm is a reversal of the removal procedure, remembering the following points.

10 Lightly smear the inner surfaces of the release arm pivot bushes, and the outer surfaces of the release bearing guide sleeve, with Longlife Grease (MoS$_2$).

11 Where applicable, fit the release bearing to the plastic collar. Then fit the release bearing and fork together, and tighten the release fork clamp bolt to the specified torque.

12 Refit the clutch as described in Section 4, or refit the transmission as described in Chapter 7A, as applicable.

13 On completion, check the clutch cable adjustment as described in Chapter 1.

Chapter 7 Part A
Manual transmission

Contents

Degrees of difficulty

| **Easy,** suitable for novice with little experience | | **Fairly easy,** suitable for beginner with some experience | | **Fairly difficult,** suitable for competent DIY mechanic | 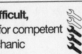 | **Difficult,** suitable for experienced DIY mechanic | | **Very difficult,** suitable for expert DIY or professional | 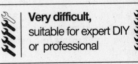 |

7A

Specifications

Type
All models . . . . Five forward speeds and one reverse, synchromesh on all forward gears. Integral differential.

Transmission codes
Note: *The transmission code is either cast into the casing, or can be found on a plate fixed to the end shield.*

		Final drive ratio
14 NV and C 14 NZ:		
Up to 1994	F 10	4.18 : 1
From 1994	F 13	4.18 : 1
14 SE and C 14 SE:		
Up to 1994	F 10	3.94/4.18 : 1
From 1994:		
Sports models	F 13 or F 15 Close Ratio (CR)	3.94 : 1
C 16 NZ	F 13	4.18/3.94/3.74 : 1
C 16 SE	F 13, F 13 CR or F 15 CR	3.94/3.74 : 1
X 16 SZ	F 13 or F 13 CR	3.74 : 1
X 16 XEL	F 15 or F 15 CR	3.55 : 1
C 18 NZ, C 18 XE, C 18 XEL and C 20 NE	F 16, F 16 CR, F 18 or F18 CR	3.55/3.57/3.72/3.74 :1
C 20 XE	F 20 CR and F 18 CR	3.42/3.45 : 1
X 20 XEV	F 18	3.45 : 1

Torque wrench settings

	Nm	lbf ft
Bearing flange, differential to transmission	25	18
Bearing support for pawl to end shield	7	5
Differential housing cover plate bolts:		
Except F 18 and F 18+:		
Steel plate	30	22
Alloy plate	18	13
F 18 and F 18+	40	30
Drive gear, speedo (driven)	4	3
Endplate to transmission:		
M7 bolts	15	11
M8 bolts	20	15
Engine support, front left mounting to chassis (refer to text) *	65	48
Engine support, front left to transmission	60	44
Engine support, rear to chassis	40	30
Gearchange lever housing to floorpan	6	4
Input shaft socket headed screw	15	11
Locking plate to differential bearing adjusting nut	9	7
Release bearing guide sleeve	5	4
Reversing light switch	20	15
Shift cover to transmission	15	11
Shift rod clamp	15	11
Sump to transmission (X 16 XEL)	40	30
Transmission to cylinder block	75	55

*Use new bolts

1 General information

1 A five-speed transmission is fitted to all models. Six different types of transmission are used, depending on the model and the power output of the engine fitted (see Specifications), but there are only minor internal differences between the transmission types.
2 Drive from the clutch is picked up by the input shaft, which runs in parallel with the mainshaft. The input shaft and mainshaft gears are in constant mesh, and selection of gears is by sliding synchromesh hubs, which lock the appropriate mainshaft gear to the mainshaft.
3 The 5th speed components are located in an extension housing at the end of the transmission.
4 Reverse gear is obtained by sliding an idler gear into mesh with two straight-cut gears on the input shaft and mainshaft.
5 All the forward gear teeth are helically-cut, to reduce noise and to improve wear characteristics.

6 The differential is mounted in the main transmission casing, and drive is transmitted to the differential by a pinion gear on the end of the mainshaft. The inboard ends of the driveshafts locate directly into the differential. The transmission and differential unit share the same lubricating oil.
7 Gear selection is by a floor-mounted gearchange lever, through a remote control linkage.

2 Transmission oil - draining and refilling

Draining

1 Where fitted, remove the engine undershield as described in Chapter 11.
2 Place a container under the differential cover plate, then unscrew the securing bolts, and withdraw the cover plate, allowing the transmission oil to drain into the container.
3 Refit the differential cover plate, and tighten the securing bolts when the oil has drained.

4 Do not refit the engine undershield until the transmission has been refilled with oil, if applicable.

Refilling

5 Proceed as described for the transmission oil level check in Chapter 1.

3 Gearchange linkage/mechanism - adjustment

Note: *A new plug should be fitted to the gear linkage adjuster hole in the gear selector cover on completion of adjustment.*
1 Working in the engine compartment, loosen the clamp bolt securing the gear selector rod to the clamp sleeve **(see illustration)**.
2 Extract the plug from the adjuster hole in the gear selector cover **(see illustration)**.
3 Looking towards the engine compartment bulkhead, grip the gear selector rod. Twist it clockwise until a 4.5 mm diameter twist drill can be inserted through the adjuster hole in the gear selector cover, to engage with the hole in the selector lever **(see illustration)**.

3.1 Gear selector rod-to-clamp sleeve clamp bolt (arrowed)

3.2 Extract the plug from the adjuster hole . . .

3.3 . . . and insert a twist drill to engage with the selector lever

4 Working inside the vehicle, pull back on the front edge of the gearchange lever gaiter, and free its lower end from the centre console, to allow access to the base of the gearchange lever.

5 The help of an assistant will now be required, to hold the gearchange lever in neutral in the 1st/2nd gear plane. The lever should be resting against the reverse stop, and the arrow and notch should be aligned as shown **(see illustration)**.

6 Without moving the gearchange lever, tighten the clamp bolt securing the gear selector rod to the clamp sleeve in the engine compartment.

7 Check that the free play between the hook (A) and the stop (B) at the base of the gearchange lever is as specified **(see illustration)**.

8 Refit the gearchange lever gaiter to the centre console.

9 Remove the twist drill from the adjuster hole in the gear selector cover, and seal the hole with a **new** plug.

10 Finally check that all gears can be engaged easily with the vehicle at rest, engine running, and clutch pedal depressed.

4 Gearchange lever - removal, overhaul and refitting

Removal

1 Ensure that the lever is in the neutral position.

2 Pull back on the front edge of the gearchange lever gaiter, and free its lower end from the centre console to allow access to the base of the lever.

3 Release the clip from the base of the lever shaft, then withdraw the pivot pin, and lift out the lever **(see illustrations)**.

Overhaul

4 To renew the gearchange lever gaiter and/or the knob, continue as follows.

5 On models with a plastic lever knob, immerse the knob in hot water (approximately 80°C) for a few minutes, then twist the knob and tap it from the lever. On models with a leather-covered lever knob, clamp the lever in

3.5 Arrow on gearchange lever aligned with notch in reverse stop

a vice fitted with soft jaw protectors, and place an open-ended spanner under the metal insert at the bottom of the knob. Then tap the knob from the lever, using the spanner as an insulator to protect the knob. There is a strong possibility that the knob will be destroyed during the removal process.

6 If renewing the gaiter, slide the old gaiter from the lever, and fit the new one. Use a little liquid detergent to aid fitting if necessary.

7 Refit the knob (or fit the new knob, as applicable). When fitting a plastic knob, preheat it in hot water, as during removal. When fitting a leather-covered knob, preheat the metal insert at the base of the knob using a hair drier or hot-air gun. Ensure that the knob is fitted the correct way round.

Refitting

8 Refitting is a reversal of removal.

5 Gearchange lever housing assembly - removal, overhaul and refitting

Removal

1 Working in the engine compartment, loosen the clamp bolt securing the gear selector rod to the clamp sleeve.

2 Remove the gearchange lever, as described previously in Section 4.

3 Remove the centre console, as described in Chapter 11.

3.7 Gearchange lever free play between hook (A) and stop (B) should be a maximum of 3.0 mm

4 Unscrew the four bolts securing the gearchange lever housing to the floorpan **(see illustration)**.

5 The housing and clamp sleeve can now be withdrawn. Pull the assembly towards the rear of the vehicle, to feed the clamp sleeve through the bulkhead. As the clamp sleeve is fed through the bulkhead, have an assistant remove the clamp from the end of the clamp sleeve in the engine compartment, to avoid damage to the rubber boot on the bulkhead.

Overhaul

6 The rubber boot can be renewed by pulling the old boot from the bulkhead, and pushing the new boot into position, ensuring that it is correctly seated.

7 The clamp sleeve bush in the gearchange lever housing can be renewed after sliding the clamp sleeve from the housing. Prise the bush insert from the front of the housing, then prise the bush from the insert. Fit the new bush using a reversal of the removal procedure, but lubricate the inside of the bush with a little silicone grease.

Refitting

8 Refitting of the assembly is a reversal of removal, but before tightening the clamp bolt, adjust the gear selector linkage as described in Section 3.

7A

4.3A Release the clip from the base of the gearchange lever shaft . . .

4.3B . . . then withdraw the pivot pin

5.4 Gear lever housing securing bolts (arrowed)

**6.3 Gear selector linkage components -
link rod arrowed**

6 Gear selector linkage -
removal, overhaul and refitting

Removal

1 Loosen the clamp bolt securing the clamp sleeve to the linkage.
2 Prise off the securing clip, then withdraw the pivot pin from the linkage universal joint.
3 Release the spring clip, the pull the bellcrank pivot pin from the bracket on the rear engine/transmission mounting **(see illustration)**.
4 Withdraw the linkage from the vehicle.

Overhaul

5 Check the linkage components for wear,

**7.2 Disconnecting the speedometer cable
from the transmission**

**7.3B . . . and withdraw the speedometer
drive assembly**

and renew as necessary. The pivot bushes can be renewed by prising out the old bushes and pressing in the new, and the link can be renewed by pulling it from the balljoints. Further dismantling is not recommended.

Refitting

6 Refitting is a reversal of removal, but before tightening the clamp bolt, adjust the gear selector linkage as described in Section 3.

7 Speedometer drive -
removal and refitting

Removal

1 Where applicable, disconnect the battery negative lead, and disconnect the wiring plug from the vehicle speed sensor.
2 Unscrew the securing sleeve, and disconnect the speedometer cable from the top of the transmission **(see illustration)**.
3 Unbolt the retaining plate, and withdraw the speedometer drive assembly **(see illustrations)**.
4 The speedometer driven gear can be withdrawn from its sleeve, in which case note the thrustwasher under the gear **(see illustration)**.

Refitting

5 If the driven gear has been removed from the sleeve, lubricate the gear shaft with a little

7.3A Unbolt the retaining plate . . .

**7.4 Withdrawing the speedometer driven
gear from its sleeve. Note thrustwasher
(arrowed)**

silicon grease, then slide the gear into the sleeve, ensuring that the thrustwasher is in place on the gear shaft.
6 Inspect the O-ring seal on the sleeve, and renew if worn or damaged.
7 Further refitting is a reversal of removal.

8 Differential side (driveshaft)
oil seals -
removal and refitting

Note: *A balljoint separator tool will be required for this operation. The driveshaft snap-ring(s) and lower arm-to-suspension strut balljoint locking pin(s) must be renewed on reassembly.*

Removal

1 Jack up the front of the vehicle, and support securely on axle stands, then remove the roadwheel.
2 Drain the transmission oil, as described in Section 2.
3 Extract the locking pin, then unscrew the castellated nut from the lower arm-to-suspension strut balljoint.
4 Using a balljoint separator tool, disconnect the lower arm-to-suspension strut balljoint.
5 A tool will now be required to release the inner end of the driveshaft from the differential. To release the right-hand driveshaft, a flat steel bar with a good chamfer on one end can be used. On certain models, the left-hand driveshaft may be more difficult to release, and a square- or rectangular-section bar will be required.
6 Lever between the driveshaft and the differential housing to release the driveshaft snap-ring from the differential. Oil will probably be released as the driveshaft is withdrawn from the differential, even though the transmission has been drained. Support the driveshaft by suspending it with wire or string, and do not allow it to hang under its own weight.
7 Prise the now-exposed oil seal from the differential, using a screwdriver or similar instrument **(see illustration)**.

8.7 Prising out a differential side oil seal

8.8 Driving a new differential side oil seal into position

9.2A Withdraw the clutch release bearing guide sleeve . . .

9.2B . . . and recover the O-ring

Refitting

8 Smear the sealing lip of the new oil seal with a little transmission oil. Then using a metal tube or socket of similar diameter, drive the new seal into the differential until the outer surface of the seal is flush with the outer surface of the differential casing **(see illustration)**.

9 Fit a new snap-ring to the inboard end of the driveshaft, then push the driveshaft into the differential as far as possible.

10 Place a screwdriver or similar tool on the weld bead of the inner driveshaft joint, **not** the metal cover, and drive the shaft into the differential until the retaining snap-ring engages positively. Pull on the **outer** circumference of the joint to check the engagement.

11 Reconnect the lower arm-to-suspension strut balljoint, then fit the castellated nut and tighten to the specified torque. Secure the nut with a new locking pin.

12 Refit the roadwheel, then lower the vehicle to the ground, and finally tighten the roadwheel bolts. Refit the wheel trim, where applicable.

13 Refill the transmission with oil, as described in Section 2.

9 Input shaft (clutch) oil seal - removal and refitting

Note: *A new clutch release bearing guide sleeve O-ring must be used on refitting.*

Removal

1 Remove the clutch release bearing and fork, as described in Chapter 6.

2 Unscrew the securing bolts, and withdraw the clutch release bearing guide sleeve from the bellhousing. Recover the O-ring that fits between the guide sleeve and the bellhousing **(see illustrations)**.

3 Drive the old oil seal from the guide sleeve **(see illustration)**, and fit a new seal using a tube or socket.

Refitting

4 Press the new seal into position do not drive it in, as the seal is easily damaged.

5 Fill the space between the lips of the new seal with lithium-based grease, then refit the guide sleeve, using a new O-ring. The O-ring should be fitted dry.

6 Refit the guide sleeve to the bellhousing, and tighten the securing bolts.

7 Refit the clutch release bearing and fork, as described in Chapter 6.

10 Reversing light switch - testing, removal and refitting

Testing

1 The reversing light circuit is operated by a plunger-type switch, mounted in the front of the transmission casing.

2 To test the switch, disconnect the wiring, and use a meter or a battery-and-bulb test circuit to check for continuity between the switch terminals. Continuity should only exist when reverse gear is selected. If this is not the case, and there are no obvious breaks or other damage to the wires, the switch is faulty and must be renewed.

Removal

3 The reversing light switch is located in the front of the transmission casing, and is accessible from the engine compartment.

4 Disconnect the battery negative lead, then

9.3 Driving the oil seal from the clutch release bearing guide sleeve

disconnect the wiring from the switch **(see illustration)**.

5 Unscrew the switch from the transmission.

Refitting

6 Refitting is a reversal of removal.

11 Transmission assembly - removal and refitting

Note: *This is an involved procedure, and it is easier in many cases to remove the transmission with the engine as an assembly, as described in Chapter 2A or 2B. If removing the transmission on its own, it is suggested that this Section is read through thoroughly before starting work. Various components must be renewed on reassembly, a hoist or similar equipment will be required to support the engine, and a special tool will be required to engage the transmission input shaft with the clutch on refitting.*

Note: *New left-hand engine/transmission mounting to body bolts, new driveshaft snap-rings, and a new transmission endplate gasket must be used on refitting.*

Removal

1 Disconnect the battery negative lead. Where fitted, remove the engine cover.

2 Working in the engine compartment, loosen the clamp bolt securing the gear selector rod to the linkage, then pull the selector tube

10.4 Reversing light switch wiring connector (arrowed)

7A

11.8 Vauxhall special tool No KM-263 used to support engine

11.23A Remove the left-hand engine/transmission mounting by unscrewing the five bolts (arrowed)

11.23B Transmission fixings - X 16 XEL models

1 Cylinder block to transmission bolts (3)
2 Sump to transmission bolts (3)

towards the engine compartment bulkhead to separate it from the linkage.

3 Remove the retaining clip, then slide the clutch cable from the release lever, pushing the release lever back towards the bulkhead if necessary, to allow the cable to be disconnected. Pull the cable support from the bracket on the transmission casing, then move the cable to one side out of the way, taking note of its routing.

4 Disconnect the wiring from the reversing light switch, which is located at the front of the transmission casing, above the left-hand mounting bracket.

5 Where applicable, disconnect the wiring from the vehicle speed sensor and oxygen sensor (if located behind the coolant expansion tank).

6 Unscrew the securing sleeve, and disconnect the speedometer cable from the top of the transmission.

7 Except for X 16 XEL models, unscrew and remove the three upper engine-to-transmission bolts, noting the locations of any brackets or clips attached to the bolts. On X 16 XEL models, the three upper bolts can only be removed after the front suspension subframe has been removed.

8 The engine must now be supported from its left-hand lifting bracket. Ideally, the engine should be supported using a strong wooden or metal beam, resting on blocks positioned securely in the channels at the sides of the engine compartment. The Vauxhall special tool designed specifically for this purpose is shown (see illustration). Alternatively, the engine can be supported using a hoist and lifting tackle. However, in this case, the hoist must be of such a design to enable the engine to be supported with the vehicle raised off the ground, leaving sufficient clearance to withdraw the transmission from under the front of the vehicle.

9 Jack up the front of the vehicle, and support securely on axle stands. Note that the vehicle must be raised sufficiently high to enable the transmission to be withdrawn from under the front of the vehicle.

10 Where fitted, remove the engine undershield, with reference to Chapter 11.

11 Ensure that the engine is adequately supported, as described in paragraph 8, then remove the front suspension subframe, as described in Chapter 10.

12 Drain the transmission oil, as described in Section 2.

13 The inner ends of the driveshafts from the differential, now need to be released. To release the right-hand driveshaft, a flat steel bar with a good chamfer on one end can be used. On certain models, the left-hand driveshaft may be more difficult to release, and a square or rectangular section bar may be required.

14 Lever between the driveshaft and the differential housing to release the driveshaft snap-ring from the differential. Oil will probably be released as the driveshaft is withdrawn from the differential, even though the transmission has been drained. Support the driveshafts by
suspending them with wire or string, and do not allow them to hang under their own weight.

15 Where applicable, unscrew the retaining nut, and disconnect the earth strap from the transmission endplate.

16 Place a container beneath the transmission endplate, to catch the oil that will be released, then unscrew the securing bolts and remove the endplate. Note the location of the bolts (including the stud for the earth strap, where applicable), as two different lengths are used.

17 Recover the gasket.

18 Extract the circlip from the end of the transmission input shaft, using a pair of circlip pliers.

19 Using a twelve-point splined key, unscrew the bolt from the end of the input shaft.

20 The input shaft can now be pulled out of engagement with the splined hub of the clutch friction disc. The manufacturers specify the use of special tools for this operation (tool Nos KM-556-1-A and KM-556-4, but an alternative can be improvised (refer to

Chapter 6 for details). The tool bolts into place on the end of the transmission, using the endplate securing bolts. Tool dimensions will vary according to transmission type.

21 Alternatively, screw an M7 bolt into the end of the input shaft, and use the bolt to pull the shaft out to its stop. It is likely that the input shaft will be a very tight fit, in which case it may prove difficult to withdraw, without using the special tool previously described. In extreme cases, a slide hammer can be attached to the end of the shaft to enable it to be withdrawn, although this is not to be recommended, as damage to the transmission components may result.

22 Support the transmission with a trolley jack, with an interposed block of wood to spread the load.

23 Remove the left-hand engine/transmission mounting completely, by unscrewing the two bolts securing the rubber mounting to the vehicle body, and the three bolts securing the mounting bracket to the transmission. On X 16 XEL models, remove the three upper transmission to engine bolts and loosen the wheel arch panel (see illustrations).

24 Except for X 16 XEL models, unscrew the securing bolts, and remove the cover plate from the base of the clutch bellhousing. On X 16 XEL models, remove the three bolts from the transmission to engine and the three from the sump.

25 Ensure that the transmission is adequately supported, then unscrew and remove the remaining engine-to-transmission bolts.

26 The transmission can now be lowered and withdrawn from under the front of the vehicle. The help of an assistant will greatly ease this operation.

Refitting

27 Before starting the refitting operations, check that the two original bolts that secured the left-hand engine/transmission mounting to the vehicle body rotate freely in their threaded bores in the body. If necessary, re-cut the threaded bores, using an M10 x 1.25 mm tap.

28 Begin refitting by positioning the transmission under the front of the vehicle, and support with a trolley jack and interposed block of wood, as during removal.

29 Raise the transmission sufficiently to enable the lower engine-to-transmission bolts to be fitted, then refit the bolts. Except X 16 XEL models, do not fully retighten at this stage.

30 Refit the left-hand engine/transmission mounting, using two new bolts to secure the rubber mounting to the vehicle body. Tighten all bolts to the specified torque.

31 Tighten the previously fitted lower engine-to-transmission bolts to the specified torque, then withdraw the trolley jack from under the transmission.

32 The transmission input shaft must now be pushed through the hub of the clutch friction disc, until its end engages in the spigot bearing in the end of the crankshaft. **Under no circumstances** must the shaft be hammered home, as transmission damage may result. If the input shaft cannot be pushed home by hand, steady pressure should be exerted on the end of the shaft. The manufacturers specify the use of a special tool for this operation (tool No KM-564), but the improvised tool used to withdraw the shaft during the removal procedure can be used by repositioning the nut (see Chapter 6).

33 Refit the bolt to the end of the input shaft, then fit a new circlip.

34 Using a new gasket, refit the transmission endplate, and tighten the securing bolts to the specified torque. Where applicable, ensure that the studded bolt that retains the earth strap is fitted to its correct location, as noted during removal.

35 Where applicable, reconnect the transmission earth strap, and fit the retaining nut.

36 Refit the cover plate to the base of the clutch bellhousing, and tighten the securing bolts.

37 Fit new snap-rings to the inboards end of the driveshafts, then push the driveshafts into the differential as far as possible.

38 Place a screwdriver or similar tool on the weld bead of each inner driveshaft joint, **not** the metal cover, and drive the shaft into the differential until the retaining snap-ring engages positively. Pull on the **outer** circumference of the joint to check the engagement.

39 Refit the front suspension subframe, as described in Chapter 10.

40 Refit the front wheels.

41 If a hoist and lifting tackle has been used to support the engine, either disconnect the lifting tackle, or lower the hoist sufficiently to enable the vehicle to be lowered to the ground.

42 Lower the vehicle to the ground, and remove or disconnect the equipment used to support the engine, if not already done.

43 Refit the three upper engine-to-transmission bolts, and tighten them to the specified torque.

44 Reconnect the speedometer cable, and tighten the securing sleeve.

45 Where applicable, reconnect the wiring to the vehicle speed sensor.

46 Reconnect the reversing light switch wiring.

47 Refit the clutch cable support to the bracket on the transmission casing, then reconnect the cable to the release lever, and adjust the cable as described in Chapter 1. Ensure that the cable is routed as noted during removal.

48 Reconnect the gear selector rod to the linkage, then adjust the linkage as described in Section 3, before tightening the clamp bolt.

49 Refill the transmission with oil, as described in Chapter 1.

50 Reconnect the battery negative lead.

12 Transmission overhaul - general

1 The complete overhaul of a manual transmission is a complicated task, requiring a number of special tools. Previous experience is a great help. It is therefore recommended that owners remove the transmission themselves, if wished, but then either fit a new or reconditioned unit, or have the existing unit overhauled by a Vauxhall dealer or transmission specialist.

2 The dismantling of the transmission into its major assemblies is a reasonably straight-forward operation, and can be carried out to enable an assessment of wear or damage to be made (exploded views of the transmissions are provided to assist owners who wish to undertake this). From this assessment, a decision can be taken as to whether or not to proceed with a full overhaul. Note however that any overhaul work will require the dismantling and reassembly of many small and intricate assemblies, as well as the taking of certain measurements to assess wear.

3 This will require a number of special tools, and previous experience will prove invaluable. As a minimum, the following tools will be required:

a) *Internal and external circlip pliers*
b) *A selection of pin punches*
c) *A selection of Torx and splined bits*
d) *A bearing puller*
e) *A hydraulic press*
f) *A slide hammer*
g) *A selection of heat-sensitive marker pencils*

4 While the *'Fault finding'*, part of this manual should help to isolate most transmission faults to enable a decision to be taken on what course of action to follow, remember that economic considerations may rule out an apparently-simple repair. For example, a common reason for transmission dismantling is to renew the synchromesh units, wear or faults in these assemblies being indicated by noise when changing gear. Jumping out of gear or similar gear selection faults may be due to worn selector forks, or synchro-sleeves. General noise during operation may be due to worn bearings, shafts or gears. The cumulative cost of renewing all worn components may make it more economical to renew the transmission complete.

5 To establish whether transmission overhaul is economically viable, first establish the cost of a complete replacement transmission, comparing the cost of a new unit with that of an exchange reconditioned unit (if available), or even a good second-hand unit (with a guarantee) from a vehicle breaker. Compare these costs with the likely cost of the replacement parts which will be required if the existing transmission is overhauled; do not forget to include all items that must be renewed when they are disturbed, such as oil seals, O-rings, roll pins, circlips, snap-rings, etc.

7A

Notes

Chapter 7 Part B
Automatic transmission

Contents

Degrees of difficulty

Easy, suitable for novice with little experience	Fairly easy, suitable for beginner with some experience	Fairly difficult, suitable for competent DIY mechanic	Difficult, suitable for experienced DIY mechanic	Very difficult, suitable for expert DIY or professional 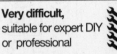

Specifications

Type

All models .... Hydrodynamic torque converter with electronically controlled mechanical lock-up system, two epicyclic gearsets giving four forward speeds and reverse, integral final drive. Gear changing under full electronic control, with three 'driving modes' selectable

Transmission code

Except C 18 NZ and X 20 XEV .... AF 13
C 18 NZ and X 20 XEV .... AF 20

Torque wrench settings

	Nm	lbf ft
Actuating lever to selector lever shaft	16	12
Converter bellhousing cover plate bolts	7	5
Cooler pipe unions	22	16
Dipstick and filler tube nut	20	15
Drain plug	35	26
Engine bracket, front left to transmission	60	44
Mounting to front chassis *	65	48
Temperature sensor	25	18
Temperature sensor cover plate to transmission	25	18
Torque converter to driveplate (refer to text) *	50	37
Transmission to engine	75	55
Selector cable clamp bolt	6	4
Speed sensor	6	4
Starter inhibitor/reversing light switch securing nut	25	18
Starter inhibitor switch/reversing light switch to selector lever shaft nut	8	6

Use new bolts

1 Description - general

1 A 4-speed fully automatic transmission is available as an option on certain models. The transmission consists of a torque converter, an epicyclic geartrain and hydraulically operated clutches and brakes. The differential is integral with the transmission, and is similar to that used in manual transmission models.

2 The torque converter provides a fluid coupling between the engine and transmission that acts as an automatic 'clutch', and provides a degree of torque multiplication when accelerating.

3 The epicyclic geartrain provides either one of the four forward gear ratios, or reverse gear, according to which of its component parts are held stationary or allowed to turn. The components of the geartrain are held or released by brakes and clutches, which are activated by a hydraulic control unit. A fluid pump within the transmission provides the necessary hydraulic pressure to operate the brakes and clutches.

7B

1 Distributor
2 Transmission fluid temperature sensor
3 Starter inhibitor/reversing light switch
4 Connection for pressure-regulating solenoids
5 Transmission input speed sensor
6 Transmission output sensor
7 Speedometer cable connection
8 Throttle position sensor
9 Engine electronic control unit
10 Automatic transmission electronic control unit
11 'Winter' mode switch
12 'Economy/Sport' mode switch
13 Kickdown switch
14 Brake light switch

1.4A Electronic control system - AF 20 models

4 The transmission is electronically controlled, and three driving modes; 'Economy', 'Sport' and 'Winter' are provided. The transmission electronic control unit operates in conjunction with the engine electronic control unit to control the gearchanges. The electronic control unit receives information on transmission fluid temperature, throttle position, engine coolant temperature, and input versus output speed. The control unit controls the hydraulically operated clutches and brakes through four solenoids. The control system can also retard the engine ignition timing, by way of the engine electronic control unit, to allow smoother gearchanges **(see illustrations)**.

5 During 1993, the AF 13 transmission was introduced. Although based on the AF 20 unit, it is more compact and includes an electronic reverse pawl. This prevents reverse gear being selected, if the forward motion is greater than 5 mph.

6 Due to the complexity of the automatic transmission, any repair or overhaul work must be entrusted to a Vauxhall dealer, with the necessary specialist equipment and knowledge for fault diagnosis and repair. Refer to the 'Fault finding' part of this manual.

7 Never tow an automatic model backwards. If the transmission appears to be in working order, the vehicle can be towed for a maximum distance of 62 miles (100 km) at no more than 50 mph (80 km/h). The vehicle can be towed greater distances with the front wheels raised.

1.4B External electrical components - AF 13 models

1 Selector lever position switch
2 Solenoid valves wiring harness
3 Transmission vent
4 Input speed sensor
5 Valve body cover
6 Output speed sensor

2.6 Automatic transmission selector cable connection at selector lever

1 Cable clamp bolt   3 Lever pivot nut
2 Cable locknut

2 Selector cable - removal, refitting and adjustment

Removal

1 Apply the handbrake, and ensure that the transmission selector lever is in position 'P'.
2 Disconnect the battery negative lead.
3 Remove the retaining clamp and the washer, and disconnect the selector cable from the actuating lever on the transmission.
4 Unscrew the securing nuts, and withdraw the cable mounting bracket from the transmission.
5 Remove the centre console, as described in Chapter 11.
6 Slacken the cable clamp bolt and unscrew the cable locknut, items 1 and 2 **(see illustration)**, then withdraw the cable, and pull it through the bulkhead into the engine compartment, prising out the bulkhead grommet where necessary.

Refitting

7 Refitting is a reversal of the removal procedure, but make sure that the bulkhead grommet is correctly located, and before tightening the cable clamp bolt and refitting the selector cover, adjust the cable as described in the following paragraphs.

Adjustment

8 Working in the engine compartment, check that the actuating lever on the transmission moves to the appropriate position, while an assistant moves the selector lever inside the vehicle through the full range of positions. Note that positions 'P' and 'N' are marked on the transmission, but the remaining positions are unmarked.
9 If adjustment is required, move the selector lever to position 'P'. Check that the lever is locked in position 'P' by attempting to move the lever backwards and forwards without lifting the lever knob.
10 Working inside the vehicle, release the transmission selector cover from the centre

2.11 Automatic transmission selector cable adjustment

1 Long-reach socket can be inserted through aperture to slacken cable clamp bolt
Selector cover clips arrowed

console (the cover is secured by clips on either side), then rotate the cover until the cable clamp bolt aperture is visible.
11 Using a long reach socket, slacken the cable clamp bolt **(see illustration)**.
12 Again working in the engine compartment, turn the actuating lever on the transmission to the right (i.e., towards the battery holder), until it reaches its stop.
13 Attempt to turn the front roadwheels, and check that the parking pawl engages, locking the wheels in position.
14 Have the assistant hold the actuating lever against the stop, while the cable clamp bolt inside the vehicle is tightened to the specified torque.
15 Recheck the selector operation, as described in paragraph 1.
16 Refit the selector cover on completion.

3 Selector lever assembly - removal and refitting

Removal

1 Apply the handbrake, and ensure that the transmission selector lever is in position 'P'.
2 Disconnect the battery negative lead.
3 Release the transmission selector cover from the centre console (the cover is secured by clips at either side). Pull the illumination light bulb holder from the selector cover, and disconnect the transmission 'Winter' mode switch wiring connector.
4 Slacken the selector cable clamp bolt and unscrew the cable locknut, items 1 and 2 (refer to Section 2). Then disconnect the cable from the selector lever assembly.
5 Disconnect the transmission 'Economy/Sport' mode switch wiring connector.
6 Unscrew the securing nut, and slide the selector lever from the end of the pivot shaft, then withdraw the assembly.

4.1 Automatic transmission fluid draining

1 Drain plug

7 No attempt should be made to dismantle the assembly.

Refitting

8 Refitting is a reversal of removal, but on completion, adjust the cable as described in Section 2.

4 Differential side (driveshaft) oil seals - renewal

1 The procedure is as described for the manual transmission in Chapter 7A, remembering the following points.
(a) *Drain the transmission fluid into a container by removing the drain plug located at the lower right-hand side of the transmission housing* **(see illustration)**.
(b) *Smear the sealing ring of the new oil seal with transmission fluid.*
(c) *On completion, refill the transmission through the dipstick tube with the correct quantity and type of fluid, and check the level as described in Chapter 1.*

5 Oil cooler information - general

1 The transmission oil cooler is an integral part of the radiator assembly, and removal and refitting is described in Chapter 3.
2 The hoses running from the transmission to the cooler should be checked at regular intervals, and renewed if there is any doubt about their condition.
3 Always take note of the pipe and hose connections before disturbing them, and take note of the hose routing.
4 To minimise the loss of fluid, and to prevent the entry of dirt into the system, clamp the hoses before disconnecting them, and plug the unions once the hoses have been disconnected.
5 When reconnecting the hoses, ensure that they are connected to their original locations, and route them so that they are not kinked or

7B

twisted. Also allow for the movement of the engine on its mountings, ensuring that the hoses will not be stretched or fouled by surrounding components.

6 Always renew the sealing washers if the banjo union bolts are disturbed, and tighten the bolts to their specified torque wrench setting. Be particularly careful when tightening the cooler unions.

6 Kickdown switch - removal, refitting and adjustment

Removal

1 Disconnect the battery negative lead.

2 Release the carpet from the retainer under the throttle pedal, and lift the carpet to expose the switch mounting.

3 Disconnect the switch wiring, then unclip the switch from its retainer.

Refitting

4 Refitting is a reversal of removal, but push the switch into the retainer as far as the stop, and check the switch adjustment as described in the following paragraphs.

Adjustment

5 Working in the engine compartment, where applicable, remove the airbox from the top of the fuel injection unit, to enable the throttle valve to be observed.

6 Have an assistant depress the throttle pedal until it contacts the switch on the vehicle floor, then check that the throttle valve is fully open, and that the pedal acts squarely on the centre of the switch button.

7 If the pedal/switch button contact point requires adjustment, this must be carried out by resetting the throttle stop screw and then adjusting the cable free play - see Chapter 4.

7 Starter inhibitor/reversing light switch - removal, refitting and adjustment

Note: *The dipstick tube O-ring must be renewed on refitting.*

Removal

1 Apply the handbrake and select position 'N' with the gear selector lever.

2 Disconnect the battery negative lead.

3 Working in the engine compartment, unscrew the securing nut from the starter inhibitor/reversing light switch mounting stud, and withdraw the dipstick tube upwards from the transmission.

4 Remove the retaining clamp and the washer, and disconnect the selector cable from the actuating lever on the transmission.

5 Disconnect the wiring from the switch.

6 Using pliers to counterhold the shaft, unscrew the nut securing the actuating lever to the selector lever shaft, then remove the locking plate and unscrew the large nut and washer securing the switch to the shaft **(see illustration)**.

7 Unscrew the nut securing the switch to the transmission, and withdraw the switch.

Refitting

8 Ensure that the selector lever shaft is in position 'N' (the third detent from the front). Lower the switch onto the shaft and rotate it until the shaft's flattened surface is aligned with the groove in the switch housing. Then refit the nut that secures the switch to the transmission, and tighten it to the specified torque.

9 Refit the washer, then refit and tighten the large nut securing the switch to the selector lever shaft. Tighten the nut to the specified torque wrench setting, then refit the locking plate.

10 Refit the nut securing the actuating lever to the selector lever shaft. Use pliers to counterhold the shaft as the nut is tightened, as during removal.

11 Refit the dipstick tube, using a new O-ring, then refit and tighten the securing nut.

12 Reconnect the switch wiring, and the battery negative lead.

13 Reconnect the selector cable to the actuating lever on the transmission, and adjust the cable as described in Section 2.

Adjustment

14 Remove the retaining clamp and the washer, and disconnect the selector cable from the actuating lever on the transmission.

15 Move the actuating lever fully to the right against the stop, then turn the lever back two notches to position 'N' **(see illustration)**.

16 Observe the end of the selector lever shaft. The shaft's flattened surface should be aligned with the groove in the switch housing. If necessary, loosen the nut securing the switch to the transmission, and turn the switch until the alignment is correct.

17 On completion of adjustment, tighten the switch securing nut to the specified torque.

18 Reconnect the selector cable to the actuating lever on the transmission, and adjust the cable as described in Section 2.

8 Transmission 'mode' switches - removal and refitting

'Economy'/'Sport' mode switch
Removal

1 Remove the selector lever assembly as described in Section 3.

2 Using a length of welding rod or a similar tool inserted through the lower end of the selector lever, push out the switch **(see illustration)**.

3 Note the wiring connections, then carefully unsolder the wires from the switch.

7.6 Starter inhibitor/reversing light switch

1 Large nut
2 Selector lever shaft
3 Actuating lever
Arrows indicate switch mountings

7.15 Starter inhibitor/reversing light switch adjustment

1 Selector lever shaft
2 Groove switch housing
3 Switch securing nut
Arrows show shaft in alignment with groove in switch housing

8.2 Removing the transmission mode switches

1 Welding rod
2 Soldered switch connectors

9.2 Removing the temperature sensor

1 Temperature sensor
Shield securing bolts arrowed

10.1 Speed sensor locations

1 Input speed sensor   2 Output speed
Securing screws arrowed

**11.1 Automatic transmission electronic
control unit location**

1 Wiring plug
2 Control unit-to-bracket clip

Refitting

4 Refitting is a reversal of removal, but ensure that the wiring connections are correct, as noted before removal, and refit the selector lever assembly as described in Section 3.

'Winter' mode switch

Removal

5 Disconnect the battery negative lead.
6 Release the transmission selector cover from the centre console (the cover is secured by clips on either side), then carefully push the switch from the selector cover, and disconnect the wiring plug.

Refitting

7 Refitting is a reversal of removal.

9 Temperature sensor - removal and refitting

Note: *A new sensor sealing ring must be used on refitting.*

Removal

1 Disconnect the battery negative lead.
2 Unscrew the two securing nuts, and remove the sensor shield from the front of the transmission **(see illustration)**.
3 Disconnect the sensor wiring connector.
4 Unscrew the sensor, and withdraw it from the transmission. Be prepared for fluid spillage, and plug the aperture in the transmission to prevent dirt ingress and minimise fluid loss. Recover the sealing ring.

Refitting

5 Refitting is a reversal of removal, using a new sealing ring. On completion, check the fluid level and top-up if necessary as described in Chapter 1.

10 Speed sensors - removal and refitting

Note: *A new sensor sealing ring must be used on refitting.*

Removal

1 The speed sensors are located in the upper face of the transmission casing. The input speed sensor is nearest to the left-hand end of the transmission **(see illustration)**.
2 Disconnect the battery negative lead.
3 Disconnect the relevant wiring connector.
4 Unscrew the sensor securing screw, and withdraw the sensor from the transmission. Be prepared for fluid spillage, and plug the aperture in the transmission to prevent dirt ingress and minimise fluid loss. Recover the sealing ring.

Refitting

5 Refitting is a reversal of removal, using a new sealing ring. On completion, check the fluid level and top-up if necessary, as described in Chapter 1.

11 Electronic control unit - removal and refitting

Removal

1 The electronic control unit is located behind the glovebox on the passenger's side of the facia **(see illustration)**.
2 Disconnect the battery negative lead.
3 Remove the glovebox as described in Chapter 11.
4 Disconnect the wiring plug from the control unit.
5 Release the control unit from its securing bracket, and withdraw it from the facia.

Refitting

6 Refitting is a reversal of removal.

12 Transmission assembly - removal and refitting

Note: *This is an involved procedure, and it is easier in many cases to remove the transmission with the engine as an assembly, as described in Chapter 2A or 2B. If removing the transmission on its own, it is suggested that this Section is read through thoroughly before starting work. Various components must be renewed on reassembly and an engine hoist, or equivalent will be required to support the engine.*

Removal

1 Disconnect the battery negative lead.
2 Working in the engine compartment, remove the retaining clamp and the washer, and disconnect the selector cable from the actuating lever on the transmission.
3 Disconnect the vent hose from the transmission (the vent hose is located below the battery tray).
4 Disconnect the transmission wiring harness plug, and unbolt the wiring harness bracket(s) from the transmission, if fitted.
5 Unscrew the securing sleeve, and disconnect the speedometer cable from the top of the transmission.
6 Unscrew and remove the three upper engine to transmission bolts, noting the locations of any brackets or clips attached to the bolts. Remove the oxygen sensor (located behind the coolant expansion tank), if fitted.
7 Proceed as described in Chapter 7A, Section 11, paragraphs 8 to 14, noting the following. Drain the transmission fluid by removing the drain plug located at the lower right-hand side of the transmission housing.
8 Clamp the transmission fluid cooler hoses, then disconnect them from the transmission, noting their locations. Some AF 13 models

7B

12.8 Cooling hose connections - AF 13 models

1 Cooling hose   3 Union
2 Retaining clip

12.16 Torque converter-to-driveplate bolt threads (arrowed) must be recut on refitting

are fitted with 'quick release sockets' **(see illustration)**. These can be released using a small screwdriver. In either case, be prepared for fluid spillage, and plug the open ends of the hoses and transmission to minimise fluid loss and prevent dirt ingress.

9 Unbolt and remove the transmission bellhousing cover plate.

10 If the original torque converter and driveplate are to be refitted, make alignment marks between the torque converter and the driveplate, to ensure that the components are reassembled in their original positions.

11 Working through the bottom of the bellhousing, unscrew the three torque converter to driveplate bolts. It will be necessary to turn the crankshaft using a spanner or socket on the crankshaft pulley or gear bolt (as applicable), to gain access to each bolt in turn through the aperture. Use a screwdriver or a similar tool to jam the driveplate ring gear, preventing the driveplate from rotating as the bolts are loosened. Discard the bolts.

12 Support the transmission with a trolley jack, with an interposed block of wood to spread the load.

13 Remove the left-hand engine/transmission mounting completely, by unscrewing the two bolts securing the rubber mounting to the vehicle body, and the three bolts securing the mounting bracket to the transmission.

14 Ensure that the transmission is adequately supported, then unscrew and remove the remaining engine to transmission bolts. Ensure that the torque converter is held firmly in place in the transmission casing as the engine and transmission are separated, otherwise it could fall out, resulting in fluid spillage and possible damage. Retain the torque converter while the transmission is

removed by bolting a strip of metal across the transmission bellhousing end face.

15 The transmission can now be lowered and withdrawn from under the front of the vehicle. The help of an assistant will greatly ease this operation.

Refitting

Note: *New torque converter to driveplate bolts must be used on refitting, and if the original torque converter is being used, an M10 x 1.25 mm tap will be required. New left-hand engine/transmission mounting to body bolts, and new driveshaft snap-rings, must be used on refitting.*

16 If the original torque converter is being refitted, begin refitting by recutting the torque converter to driveplate bolt threads in the torque converter using an M10 x 1.25 mm tap **(see illustration)**.

17 If a new transmission is being fitted, the manufacturers recommend that the radiator fluid cooler passages are flushed clean before the new transmission is installed. Ideally, compressed air should be used (in which case, ensure that adequate safety precautions are taken), but alternatively, the cooler can be flushed with clean automatic transmission fluid until all the old fluid has been expelled, and fresh fluid runs clear from the cooler outlet.

18 Begin refitting by positioning the transmission under the front of the vehicle, and support with a trolley jack and interposed block of wood, as during removal.

19 Where applicable, remove the strip of metal retaining the torque converter in the transmission, and hold the torque converter in position as the transmission is mated to the engine.

20 Raise the transmission sufficiently to enable the upper and lower engine to

transmission bolts to be fitted, but do not tighten them fully at this stage. Ensure that any brackets or clips noted during removal are in place on the bolts.

21 Refit the left-hand engine/transmission mounting, using two new bolts to secure the rubber mounting to the vehicle body. Tighten all bolts to the specified torque.

22 Tighten the previously fitted engine to transmission bolts to the specified torque, then withdraw the trolley jack from under the transmission.

23 If the original torque converter and driveplate have been refitted, carefully turn the crankshaft to align the marks made before removal, before fitting the torque converter to driveplate bolts.

24 Fit **new** torque converter to driveplate bolts, and tighten them to the specified torque. Turn the crankshaft for access to each bolt in turn, and prevent the driveplate from turning as during removal.

25 Refit the transmission bellhousing cover plate.

26 Proceed as described in Chapter 7A, Section 11, paragraphs 37 to 42 inclusive.

27 Reconnect the transmission fluid cooler hoses to the transmission, using new sealing washers.

28 Reconnect the speedometer drive cable to the transmission.

29 Refit the transmission harness brackets, and reconnect the wiring harness plug.

30 Reconnect the transmission vent hose.

31 Reconnect the selector cable to the actuating lever on the transmission, and adjust the cable as described in Section 2.

32 Refill the transmission with the specified type and quantity of fluid through the dipstick tube.

33 Reconnect the battery negative lead.

34 On completion, check the transmission fluid level and top-up if necessary, as described in Chapter 1.

13 Transmission overhaul - general

1 If a fault develops in the transmission, it is first necessary to determine whether it is of an electrical, mechanical or hydraulic nature, and to achieve this, special test equipment is required. It is therefore essential to have the work carried out by a Vauxhall dealer if a transmission fault is suspected.

2 Do not remove the transmission from the car for possible repair before professional fault diagnosis has been carried out, since most tests require the transmission to be in the vehicle.

Chapter 8
Driveshafts

Contents

Degrees of difficulty

Easy, suitable for novice with little experience	Fairly easy, suitable for beginner with some experience	Fairly difficult, suitable for competent DIY mechanic	Difficult, suitable for experienced DIY mechanic	Very difficult, suitable for expert DIY or professional

Specifications

Type .... Unequal-length open shafts, with constant velocity joint at each end. Certain models have vibration damper fitted to right-hand shaft

Driveshaft joint grease specification .... Special Grease (Vauxhall P/N 90094176)

Torque wrench settings	**Nm**	**lbf ft**
Front hub (refer to text):		
Stage 1	100	74
Stage 2	Loosen nut fully	
Stage 3	20	15
Stage 4	Angle-tighten by a further 80° (plus up to 9° if necessary)	
Lower arm-to-suspension strut balljoint	70	52
Wheel	110	81

1 Description - general

1 Drive from the differential is taken to the roadwheels by two open driveshafts with a constant velocity joint at each end. The driveshafts are splined at both ends.

2 The inner ends fit into the differential, and are retained by snap-rings, while the outer ends fit into the front hubs, and are retained by the front hub nuts.

3 The right-hand driveshaft is longer than the left-hand one, due to the position of the differential. Certain models have a two-piece vibration damper fitted to the right-hand driveshaft.

2 Driveshafts - removal and refitting

Note: *A balljoint separator tool will be required for this operation. The following components must be renewed when refitting the driveshaft: hub nut, washer and split pin, driveshaft retaining snap-ring, and lower arm-to-suspension strut balljoint nut locking pin.*

Removal

1 Jack up the front of the vehicle and support securely on axle stands. Remove the relevant roadwheel.
2 Extract the split pin from the castellated hub nut on the end of the driveshaft.
3 The hub nut must now be loosened. The nut is extremely tight, and an extension bar will be required to loosen it. To prevent the driveshaft from turning, insert two roadwheel bolts, and insert a metal bar between them to counterhold the hub.
4 Remove the hub nut and washer from the driveshaft **(see illustration)**.

2.4 Removing the hub nut and washer from the driveshaft

8

2.5A Extract the locking pin (arrowed) . . .

2.5B . . . then remove the balljoint castellated nut

2.6 Using a balljoint separator tool to disconnect the balljoint

5 Extract the locking pin, then unscrew the castellated nut from the lower arm-to-suspension strut balljoint **(see illustrations)**.

6 Using a balljoint separator tool, disconnect the lower arm-to-suspension strut balljoint **(see illustration)**.

7 Where fitted, remove the undershield, as described in Chapter 11.

8 To release the right-hand driveshaft, a flat steel bar with a good chamfer on one end can be used. The left-hand driveshaft may prove more difficult to release, and a square or rectangular section bar may be required.

9 Lever between the driveshaft and the differential housing to release the driveshaft snap-ring from the differential **(see**

illustration**)**. Have a container available, to catch the oil that will be released as the driveshaft is withdrawn from the differential. Support the driveshaft by suspending it with wire or string, and do not allow it to hang under its own weight.

10 Plug the opening in the differential, to prevent further oil loss and dirt ingress.

11 Withdraw the outer end of the driveshaft from the hub, and remove the driveshaft from the vehicle **(see illustration)**. It should be possible to pull the driveshaft from the hub by hand, but if necessary tap the end of the shaft with a soft-faced mallet to release it. **Do not** *use heavy blows, as damage to the driveshaft joints may result.*

12 Do not *allow the vehicle to rest on its wheels with one or both driveshaft(s) removed, as damage to the wheel bearing(s) may result.* If moving the vehicle is unavoidable, temporarily insert the outer end of the driveshaft(s) in the hub(s) and tighten the hub nut(s). In this case, the inner end(s) of the driveshaft(s) must be supported, for example by suspending with string from the vehicle underbody. **Do not** *allow the driveshaft to hang down under its own weight.*

13 Certain models have a two-piece vibration damper fitted to the right-hand driveshaft. If the damper is removed for any reason, it is important to refit it so that the distance between the inner end of the outer joint gaiter and the outer face of the damper is as shown **(see illustrations)**.

Refitting

14 Before refitting a driveshaft, make sure that the contact faces of the shaft and the wheel bearing are absolutely clean **(see illustration)**.

15 Begin refitting by applying a little

2.9 Using a steel bar to release the end of the driveshaft from the differential

2.11 Withdrawing the outer end of the driveshaft from the hub

2.14 Sectional view of front hub assembly

Clean the contact faces (arrowed) of the driveshaft and wheel bearing

2.13A Driveshaft vibration damper (arrowed) - DOHC model viewed through right-hand wheel arch

2.13B Driveshaft damper weight distance from outer joint gaiter (2)

1 = 268.0 to 270.0 mm

2.16 Always renew driveshaft retaining snap-ring on refitting

2.19A Tighten the hub nut to the specified torque . . .

2.19B . . . then through the specified angle (see Specifications)

molybdenum disulphide grease to the driveshaft splines, then insert the outer end of the shaft into the hub. Fit a new washer, and screw on a new hub nut finger-tight.

16 Fit a new snap-ring to the inboard end of the driveshaft **(see illustration)**, then remove the plug from the opening in the differential, and push the driveshaft into the differential as far as possible.

17 Place a screwdriver or similar tool on the weld bead of the inner driveshaft joint, **not** the metal cover, and drive the shaft into the differential until the retaining snap-ring engages positively. Pull on the **outer** circumference of the joint to check the engagement.

18 Reconnect the lower arm-to-suspension strut balljoint, then fit the castellated nut, and tighten to the specified torque. Secure the nut with a new locking pin.

19 Tighten the new hub nut to the specified torque, in the stages given in the Specifications. Prevent the driveshaft from turning as during removal **(see illustrations)**. If the holes in the driveshaft for the split pin do not line up with any of the slots in the nut, loosen (**do not** tighten) the nut, until the holes line up with the nearest slots to enable the split pin to be fitted. Use a new split pin, bending over the ends of the pin to secure it.

20 Refit the roadwheel, then lower the vehicle to the ground.

21 Check and if necessary top-up the gearbox oil/transmission fluid level, as described in Chapter 1.

22 Where applicable, refit the engine undershield.

3 Driveshaft joint - removal and refitting

Note: *Check to ensure that a new securing circlip is supplied when ordering a new driveshaft joint.*

Removal

1 A worn driveshaft joint must be renewed, as it cannot be overhauled. If driveshaft joint

wear is apparent on a vehicle in which the driveshaft has covered more than 48 000 miles (80 000 km), the manufacturers recommend that the complete driveshaft is renewed.

2 With the driveshaft removed as described in Section 2, release the metal securing band, and slide the rubber gaiter from the worn joint.

3 Using circlip pliers, expand the circlip that secures the joint to the driveshaft **(see illustration)**.

4 Using a soft-faced mallet, tap the joint from the driveshaft **(see illustration)**.

Refitting

5 Ensure that a new circlip is fitted to the new joint, then tap the new joint onto the driveshaft until the circlip engages in its groove.

6 Pack the joint with the Special Grease.

7 Refit the rubber gaiter to the new joint, with reference to Section 4.

8 Refit the driveshaft to the vehicle, as described in Section 2.

4 Driveshaft joint gaiter - removal and refitting

Removal

1 With the driveshaft removed as described

in Section 2, remove the relevant joint as described in Section 3. Note that if both gaiters on a driveshaft are to be renewed, it is only necessary to remove one joint.

2 Release the remaining securing band, and slide the gaiter from the driveshaft.

Refitting

3 Clean the old grease from the joint, then repack the joint with the Special Grease. If excessively worn or damaged, the driveshaft joint should be renewed, with reference to Section 3 if necessary.

4 Slide the new gaiter onto the driveshaft so that the smaller diameter opening is located in the groove in the driveshaft.

5 Refit the joint, using a new securing circlip. Tap the joint onto the driveshaft until the circlip engages in its groove.

6 Slide the gaiter over the joint, then squeeze the gaiter to expel as much air as possible.

7 Secure the gaiter using new securing bands. To fit a securing band, wrap it around the gaiter, and while pulling on the band as tight as possible, engage the lug on the end of the band with one of the slots. Use a screwdriver if necessary to push the band as tight as possible before engaging the lug and slot. Finally tighten the band by compressing the raised square portion of the band with pliers.

8

3.3 Driveshaft joint retaining circlip (arrowed)

3.4 Tapping joint from driveshaft

5 Driveshaft overhaul - general

1 If any of the checks in Chapter 1 reveal wear in any driveshaft joint, first remove the roadwheel trim or wheel centre cap, as applicable. If the driveshaft nut staking is still effective, the nut should be correctly tightened. If in doubt, use a torque wrench to check that the nut is securely fastened and re-stake it (see Section 2), then refit the wheel trim or centre cap, as applicable. Repeat this check on the remaining driveshaft nut.

2 Road test the vehicle, and listen for a metallic clicking from the front as the vehicle is driven slowly in a circle on full steering lock. If a clicking noise is heard, this indicates wear in the outer constant velocity joint. This means that the joint must be renewed, as overhaul is not possible (see Section 3).

3 If vibration, consistent with road speed, is felt through the vehicle when accelerating, there is a possibility of wear in the inner constant velocity joints.

Chapter 9
Braking system

Contents

Degrees of difficulty

| Easy, suitable for novice with little experience | | Fairly easy, suitable for beginner with some experience | | Fairly difficult, suitable for competent DIY mechanic | | Difficult, suitable for experienced DIY mechanic | | Very difficult, suitable for expert DIY or professional | |

Specifications

System type

Conventional braking system .... Front discs and rear drums, with vacuum servo assistance, dual hydraulic circuit split diagonally, pressure-regulating valves in rear hydraulic circuits. Cable-operated handbrake on rear wheels

ABS (Anti-lock Braking System) .... Front discs and rear discs or drums, with vacuum servo assistance, operated via hydraulic modulator, dual hydraulic circuit split front/rear, pressure-regulating valves in rear hydraulic circuit. Cable-operated handbrake on rear wheels

Front brakes

Type
14 NV, 14 SE (Manual transmission (MT)), C 14 NZ, C 14 SE (MT),
C 16 NZ and X 16 SZ (MT) .... Solid discs with floating calipers
Other models .... Ventilated discs with floating calipers

Disc diameter
Solid discs models .... 236.0 mm
Vented disc models .... 256.0 mm

Front brakes (continued)
Disc thickness
New:
Solid disc models .... 12.7 mm
    Vented disc models:
       14 SE (Automatic transmission (AT)), C 14 SE (AT), C 16 SE,
       X 16 SZ (AT) and C 18 NZ .... 20.0 mm
       X 16 XEL, C 18 XE, C 18 XEL, C 20 NE, C 20 XE and X 20 XEV .. 24.0 mm
Minimum permissible thickness after machining: *
Solid disc models .... 10.7 mm
    Vented disc models:
       14 SE (AT), C 14 SE (AT), C 16 SE, X 16 SZ (AT) and C 18 NZ ... 18.0 mm
       X 16 XEL, C 18 XE, C 18 XEL, C 20 NE, C 20 XE and X 20 XEV .. 22.0 mm
Minimum permissible thickness (at which point discs must be renewed):
Solid disc models .... 9.7 mm
    Vented disc models:
       14 SE (AT), C 14 SE (AT), C 16 SE, X 16 SZ (AT) and C 18 NZ ... 17.0 mm
       X 16 XEL, C 18 XE, C 18 XEL, C 20 NE, C 20 XE and X 20 XEV .. 21.0 mm
Maximum disc run-out .... 0.1 mm
When this dimension is reached, only one further new set of pads is permissible, then renew the discs.

Rear brakes
Type
Non-ABS models .... Drums
ABS models .... Solid discs or drums
Drum brakes
Drum internal width:
    Saloon models:
       14 NV, C 14 NZ, 14 SE, C 14 SE, C 16 NZ and X 16 SZ .... 28.0 mm
    All other models .... 45.0 mm
Drum internal diameter:
    New .... 200.0 mm
    Maximum permissible diameter after machining .... 201.0 mm
Disc brakes
Disc diameter .... 260.0 mm
Disc thickness:
    New .... 10.0 mm
    Minimum permissible thickness after machining * .... 8.0 mm
    Minimum permissible thickness (at which point discs must
    be renewed) .... 7.0 mm
Maximum disc run-out .... 0.1 mm
When this dimension is reached, only one further new set of pads is permissible, then renew the discs.

Torque wrench settings

	Nm	lbf ft
ABS hydraulic modulator securing nuts	8	6
ABS wheel sensor securing bolt	8	6
Bleed nipples	6	4
Brake drum securing screw	4	3
Brake fluid pipe union nuts	16	12
Brake hose to caliper	40	30
Caliper guide bolt	30	22
Caliper, front to steering knuckle	95	70
Brake master cylinder to servo	22	16
Front brake disc securing screw	4	3
Front brake disc shield screws	4	3
Handbrake lever securing bolts	20	15
Master cylinder, ATE type stop-screw	6	4
Pressure regulating valve securing screws (Estate and Van models) ..	20	15
Rear brake backplate/hub unit securing nuts: *		
Stage 1	50	37
Stage 2	Angle-tighten by a further 30 to 45°	
Rear brake disc securing screw	8	6
Rear caliper mounting	80	59
Rear wheel cylinder bolts	9	7
Servo with bracket to bulkhead	22	16
Servo to bracket	20	15
TC motor to body	7	6

Use new nuts

1 System description - general and precautions

General

1 The footbrake operates on all four wheels. Solid or ventilated disc brakes are fitted at the front, and self-adjusting drum or solid disc brakes are fitted at the rear, depending on model. Actuation is hydraulic, with vacuum servo assistance. The handbrake is cable-operated, and acts on the rear wheels only.

2 The hydraulic system is split into two circuits. On non-ABS (Anti-lock Braking System) models, the system is split diagonally, and on ABS models, the system is split front and rear. If there is a brake fluid leak in one circuit, the remaining circuit will still function, so that some braking capability remains.

3 The brake fluid supply to the rear brakes is regulated so that the front brakes always lock first under heavy braking (this reduces the danger of the car spinning). On Saloon and Hatchback models, the fluid pressure to the rear brakes is controlled by two valves, one for each brake, which are mounted on the rear underbody of the vehicle. On Estate and Van models, the fluid pressure to the rear brakes is controlled by a single load-dependent valve, which acts depending on the loading of the rear suspension.

4 The brake servo is of the direct-acting type, fitted between the pedal and the master cylinder. The servo is powered by vacuum developed in the inlet manifold. Should the servo fail, the brakes will still operate, but increased pedal pressure will be required.

Precautions

5 When working on any part of the system, work carefully and methodically; also observe scrupulous cleanliness when overhauling any part of the hydraulic system. Always renew components (in axle sets, not just on one wheel, where applicable) if in doubt about their condition, and use only Vauxhall replacement parts, or at least those of known good quality. Note the warnings given in 'Safety first' and at the relevant points in this Chapter concerning the dangers of asbestos dust and brake fluid.

2 ABS (Anti-lock Braking System) - general

1 ABS (Anti-lock Braking System) is fitted as standard on certain models, and is available as an option for all others.

2 The system comprises an electronic control unit, roadwheel sensors, hydraulic modulator, and the necessary valves and relays. The purpose of the system is to prevent wheel(s) locking during heavy brake applications. This

is achieved by automatic release of the brake on the locked wheel, followed by reapplication of the brake. This procedure is carried out several times a second by the hydraulic modulator. The modulator is controlled by the electronic control unit, which itself receives signals from the wheel sensors, which monitor the locked or unlocked state of the wheels. The two front brakes are modulated separately, but the two rear brakes are modulated together. The ABS unit is fitted between the brake master cylinder and the brakes, the vacuum servo and master cylinder being of similar type for both non-ABS and ABS models.

3 The front wheel sensors are mounted on the hub carriers, and monitor the rotation of the wheels through toothed discs on the driveshafts. The rear wheel sensors are integral with the rear hub units.

4 If the ABS develops a fault, the complete system should be tested by a Vauxhall dealer, who will have the necessary specialist equipment to make a quick and accurate diagnosis of the problem. Due to the special equipment required, it is not practical for the DIY mechanic to carry out the test procedure.

5 To prevent possible damage to the electronic control unit, always disconnect the control unit wiring plug before carrying out electrical welding work.

6 It is recommended that the control unit is removed if the vehicle is to be subjected to

high temperatures, as may be encountered (for instance) during certain paint-drying processes.

7 If using steam-cleaning equipment, do not aim the water/steam jet directly at the control unit.

8 Do not disconnect the control unit wiring plug with the ignition switched on.

9 Do not use a battery booster to start the engine.

10 After working on the ABS system components, ensure that all wiring plugs are correctly reconnected, and have the complete system tested by a Vauxhall dealer using the dedicated ABS test equipment, at the earliest opportunity.

11 On some models, the ABS wheel sensors also send signals to the traction control system.

3 Traction control (TC) system - general

1 A traction control (TC) system is fitted to certain models. It monitors the traction provided by the driven (front) wheels, preventing the wheels from spinning, regardless of the road conditions and the grip of the tyres. This is particularly beneficial in helping to increase traction when driving on slippery roads due to rain, snow, or ice.

2 The TC system is controlled by control unit.

1 Throttle housing
2 Throttle valve control motor
3 Front wheel ABS sensor
4 Rear wheel ABS sensor (see Chapter 10)
5 Electronic control unit
6 Control button
7 ABS hydraulic modulator
8 Warning light

3.2 Traction control (TC) system

9

This receives information from the engine and ABS system ECUs. The four ABS wheel sensors continuously monitor the traction of the front wheels by comparing the speeds of the front wheels with those of the rear wheels. Immediately a difference in speed is registered between the front and rear wheels, a signal is fed to the TC control unit. The TC control unit activates an auxiliary throttle valve, which reduces the engine speed (and thus torque) to optimum levels in relation to the rotation of the wheels, even though the driver may be applying full-throttle. In exceptional circumstances, such as when driving away from rest using full-throttle on an icy surface, the TC control unit supplies a signal to the engine ECU to interrupt the fuel injection and ignition systems intermittently, reducing engine torque more rapid **(see illustration)**. Refer to Chapters 4B and 5, for further details.

3 The TC system throttle valve is mounted in a housing fitted between the main throttle body and the inlet manifold. The throttle valve is actuated by a control motor, through a coupling rod. A potentiometer is incorporated in the control motor to provide the TC control unit with information on the TC throttle valve position.

4 The system can be switched off by using a button mounted in the centre console. This may be beneficial in certain circumstances such as when driving in deep snow, or when 'digging' the vehicle out of soft ground.

4 Hydraulic system - general and bleeding

Note: *Brake fluid is poisonous. Wash off skin immediately and seek immediate medical advice if any is swallowed or gets into the eyes. Certain types of brake fluid are inflammable and may ignite on contact with hot components. When servicing any hydraulic system, it is safest to assume that the fluid IS inflammable, and to take precautions against the risk of fire as when handling petrol. Brake fluid is also an effective paint stripper and will attack certain plastics. If any is spilt, it should be washed off immediately using plenty of clean water. Finally, it absorbs moisture from the air. When topping-up or renewing the fluid always use the recommended type and ensure that it comes from a freshly opened, sealed container.*

General

1 The efficient operation of any hydraulic system is only possible after removing all air from the components and circuit. If any of the hydraulic components in the braking system have been removed or disconnected, or if the fluid level has been allowed to fall appreciably, it is inevitable that air will have been introduced into the system. The removal

of all this air from the hydraulic system is essential if the brakes are to function correctly, and the process of removing it is known as 'bleeding'.

2 During the bleeding procedure, add only clean, unused brake fluid of the recommended type; never re-use fluid that has already been bled from the system. Ensure that sufficient fluid is available before starting work.

3 If there is any possibility of incorrect fluid already being present in the system, the complete hydraulic circuit must be flushed with fresh fluid of the correct type, and new fluid seals should be fitted to all the components.

4 If brake fluid has been lost from the system, or air has entered due to a leak, ensure that the fault is rectified before continuing further.

5 Park the vehicle on level ground, stop the engine, and select first or reverse gear on manual gearbox models (or 'P' on models with automatic transmission) then chock the wheels and release the handbrake.

6 Check that all pipes and hoses are secure, unions tight and bleed nipples closed. Clean any dirt from around the bleed nipples.

7 Top-up the brake fluid reservoir to the 'MAX' level line. Refit the cap loosely and maintain the fluid level above the 'MIN' level line throughout the procedure, or there is a risk of further air entering the system through the reservoir.

8 There are a number of one-man, do-it-yourself brake bleeding kits currently available from motor accessory shops. It is recommended that one of these kits is used whenever possible, as they greatly simplify the bleeding operation, and also reduce the risk of expelled air and fluid being drawn back into the system. If such a kit is not available, the basic (two-man) method must be used, which is described in detail later in this Section. Note that Vauxhall recommend the use of a pressure-bleeding kit when bleeding the braking system.

9 If a kit is to be used, prepare the car as described previously, and follow the kit manufacturer's instructions, as the procedure may vary slightly according to the type being used. Generally, instructions for using a kit will

be as outlined below in the relevant sub-Section.

10 Whichever method is used, if the complete system is to be bled, the same sequence must be followed (paragraphs 11 and 12) to ensure the removal of all air from the system.

Bleeding

11 Where an operation has only affected one circuit of the hydraulic system (the system is split diagonally on non-ABS models, and front and rear on models with ABS), then it will only be necessary to bleed the relevant circuit. If the master cylinder has been disconnected and reconnected, or the fluid level has been allowed to fall appreciably, then the complete system must be bled.

12 If the complete system is to be bled, models with ABS should have the front brake circuits bled first.

Bleeding - basic (two-man) method

13 Gather together a clean glass jar, a length of plastic or rubber tubing that will fit the bleed nipples tightly, and a ring spanner to fit the nipples. The help of an assistant will also be required.

14 Remove the dust cap from the first nipple in the sequence **(see illustrations)**. Fit the spanner and tube to the nipple, place the other end of the tube in the jar, and pour in sufficient fluid to cover the end of the tube.

15 Ensure that the brake fluid reservoir level is maintained at least above the 'MIN' level mark throughout this procedure.

16 Have the assistant fully depress the brake pedal several times to build up pressure, then maintain it on the final stroke.

17 While pedal pressure is maintained, unscrew the bleed nipple (approximately one turn) and allow the fluid to flow into the jar. The assistant should maintain pedal pressure, pushing the pedal down to the floor if necessary, and should not release the pedal until instructed to do so. When the flow stops, tighten the bleed nipple again, instruct the assistant to release the pedal slowly, and recheck the reservoir fluid level.

18 Repeat the steps given in paragraphs 16 and 17 until the fluid emerging from the bleed nipple is free from air bubbles.

4.14A Removing the dust cap from a front brake caliper bleed nipple

4.14B Removing the dust cap from a rear wheel cylinder bleed nipple - model with rear drum brakes

4.21 Bleeding the brake hydraulic system using a typical one-way valve kit

5.4 Using a brake hose clamp will minimise fluid loss when brake flexible hoses are disconnected

5.6 Typical brake pipe-to-flexible hose union

19 When no more air bubbles appear, tighten the bleed nipple securely, remove the tube and spanner, and refit the dust cap. Do not overtighten the bleed nipple.

20 Repeat the procedure on the remaining nipples in the sequence, until all air is removed from the system and the brake pedal feels firm again.

Bleeding - using a one-way valve kit

21 As the name implies, these kits consist of a length of tubing with a one-way valve fitted to prevent expelled air and fluid being drawn back into the system. Some kits include a clear container that can be positioned so that the air bubbles can be more easily seen flowing from the end of the tube (see illustration).

22 The kit is connected to the bleed nipple, which is then opened. The user returns to the driver's seat and depresses the brake pedal with a smooth, steady stroke and slowly releases it. This is repeated until the expelled fluid is free from air bubbles.

23 Note that although these kits simplify the work, it is easy to forget the brake fluid reservoir fluid level. Ensure that the level is maintained above the 'MIN' level mark at all times, or more air will be drawn into the system.

Bleeding - using a pressure-bleeding kit

24 These kits are usually operated by the pressurised air contained in the spare tyre. Although note that it will probably be necessary to reduce the pressure to a lower limit than normal. Refer to the instructions supplied with the kit.

25 By connecting a pressurised, fluid-filled container to the brake fluid reservoir, bleeding can be carried out simply by opening each nipple in turn (in the specified sequence) and allowing the fluid to flow out until no more air bubbles can be seen in the expelled fluid.

26 This method has the advantage that the large reservoir of fluid provides an additional safeguard against air being drawn into the system during bleeding.

27 Pressure-bleeding is particularly effective

when bleeding 'difficult' systems, or when bleeding the complete system at the time of routine fluid renewal.

All methods

28 When bleeding is complete, and firm pedal feel is restored, wash off any spilt fluid, tighten the bleed nipples securely and refit their dust caps. Do not overtighten the bleed nipples.

29 Check the brake fluid level, and top-up if necessary.

30 Discard any brake fluid that has been bled from the system; it will not be fit for re-use.

31 Depress the brake pedal in the normal way to check its 'feel'. If it feels at all spongy, air must still be present in the system, and further bleeding is required. Failure to bleed satisfactorily after a reasonable repetition of the bleeding procedure may be due to worn master cylinder seals.

5 Hydraulic pipes and hoses - inspection, removal and refitting

Note: *Refer to the note at the beginning of Section 4 before proceeding.*

Inspection

1 The brake fluid pipes, hoses, hose connections and pipe unions should be regularly examined.

2 First check for signs of leakage at the pipe unions, then examine the flexible hoses for signs of cracking, chafing and fraying.

3 The rigid brake pipes should be examined carefully for signs of dents, corrosion or other damage. Corrosion should be scraped off, and if the depth of pitting is significant, the pipes should be renewed. This is particularly likely in those areas underneath the vehicle body where the pipes are exposed and unprotected.

Removal

4 If any section of pipe or hose is to be removed, the loss of fluid may be reduced by removing the brake fluid reservoir filler cap,

placing a piece of polythene over the filler neck and securing it tightly with an elastic band. If a section of pipe is to be disconnected from the master cylinder, the reservoir should be emptied by syphoning out the fluid or drawing out the fluid with a pipette. Alternatively, flexible hoses can be sealed, if required, using a brake hose clamp (see illustration), while metal pipe unions can be plugged (if care is taken not to allow dirt into the system), or capped immediately they are disconnected.

5 To remove a section of pipe, unscrew the union nuts at each end of the pipe, and release the pipe from the clips attaching it to the body. Some union nuts can be very tight, particularly if they are exposed to road dirt, etc., under the vehicle. If an open-ended spanner is used, burring of the flats on the nuts is not uncommon, and for this reason it is preferable to use a split ring spanner that will engage all the flats. If such a spanner is not available, self-locking grips may be used, although this is NOT recommended.

6 To remove a flexible hose, first clean the ends of the hose and the surrounding area, then unscrew the union nut(s)/bolt(s), as applicable, from the hose end(s). Where applicable, unclip the hose from its mounting bracket, and withdraw the hose (see illustration).

7 Brake pipes with flared ends and union nuts in place can be obtained individually or in sets, from Vauxhall dealers or accessory shops. The pipe is then bent to shape, using the old pipe as a guide, and is ready for fitting to the car.

Refitting

8 Refitting the pipes and hoses is a reversal of removal. Make sure that brake pipes are securely supported in their clips, and ensure that the hoses are not kinked. Check also that the hoses are clear of all suspension components and underbody fittings, and will remain clear during movement of the suspension and steering. After refitting, remove the polythene from the reservoir, and bleed the brake hydraulic system as described in Section 4.

9

6.2 Pad wear sensor (and ABS wheel sensor) wiring connectors (arrowed) under front wheel arch

6.3 Removing the pad retaining clip from the edge of the caliper

6.4A Prise out the dust caps . . .

6 Front brake pads - removal and refitting

⚠ *Warning: Renew both sets of front brake pads at the same time. Never renew the pads on only one wheel, as the vehicle may pull to one side when braking. Note that the dust created by wear of the pads may contain asbestos, which is a health hazard. Never blow it out with compressed air, and do not inhale it. A filter mask should be worn when working on the brakes. DO NOT use petroleum-based solvents to clean brake parts - use brake cleaner or methylated spirit only.*

Removal

1 Apply the handbrake, then jack up the front of the vehicle, and support securely on axle stands.

2 Where applicable, pull the pad wear sensor from the inboard pad, and disconnect the wiring at the connector under the wheel arch, next to the suspension strut **(see illustration)**. Note the wire routing.

3 Using a screwdriver, prise the pad retaining clip from the outboard edge of the caliper, noting how it is located **(see illustration)**.

4 Prise out the two guide bolt dust caps from the inboard edge of the caliper, then using an Allen key or hexagon bit, unscrew the guide bolts, and lift the caliper and inboard pad from the bracket **(see illustrations)**. Recover the outboard brake pad. Suspend the caliper

body with wire or string, to avoid straining the brake fluid hose.

5 Pull the inboard pad from the caliper piston, noting that it is retained by a clip attached to the pad backing plate **(see illustration)**.

Refitting

6 Brush the dirt and dust from the caliper, but take care not to inhale it. Carefully remove any rust from the edge of the brake disc.

7 To accommodate the new thicker pads, the caliper piston must be depressed fully into its cylinder bore, using a flat metal bar such as a tyre lever. Do not lever between the piston and disc to depress the piston. The action of depressing the piston will cause the fluid level in the reservoir to rise, so to avoid spillage, syphon out some fluid using a (clean) old battery hydrometer or a pipette.

8 Check that the cutaway recesses in the piston are positioned vertically. If necessary, carefully turn the piston to its correct position.

9 Apply a little brake grease to the contact surfaces of the new brake pads.

10 Fit the new inboard pad to the caliper piston, ensuring that the clip is correctly located.

11 Locate the outboard pad on the caliper bracket, with the friction material facing the disc.

12 Refit the caliper to the bracket, and tighten the guide bolts to the specified torque **(see illustration)**.

13 Refit the guide bolt dust caps.

14 Refit the pad retaining clip, locating it as noted before removal **(see illustration)**.

6.4B . . . then remove the caliper guide bolts . . .

6.4C . . . and withdraw the caliper and inboard pad

6.5 Pulling the inboard pad from the caliper piston

6.12 Tightening a caliper guide bolt

6.14 Pad retaining clip correctly positioned on caliper

7.6 Caliper bracket securing bolts (arrowed)

7.11 Prising the seal from the groove in the front caliper piston bore

8.2 Refit a wheel bolt and spacer (arrowed) opposite the disc securing screw (A) before checking brake disc run-out

15 Where applicable, fit a new pad wear sensor to the inboard pad, and connect the wiring at the connector under the wheel arch. Route the wiring as noted during removal.
16 Repeat the operations on the remaining side of the vehicle.
17 Refit the roadwheels and lower the vehicle to the ground.
18 Apply the footbrake several times to position the pads against the discs.
19 Check and if necessary top-up the brake fluid level.
20 New pads should be carefully bedded-in and, where possible, heavy braking should be avoided during the first 100 miles (160 km) or so after fitting new pads.

7 Front brake caliper - removal, overhaul and refitting

Note: *Refer to the note at the beginning of Section 4, and the warning concerning brake dust at the beginning of Section 6 before proceeding. Before dismantling a caliper, check that replacement parts can be obtained, and retain the old components to compare them with the new ones. New sealing rings must be used on the fluid hose union bolt on refitting.*

Removal

1 Apply the handbrake, then jack up the front of the vehicle, and support securely on axle stands.
2 Remove the brake pads, as described in Section 6.
3 Working under the bonnet, remove the brake fluid reservoir cap, and secure a piece of polythene over the filler neck with a rubber band, or by refitting the cap. This will reduce the loss of fluid during the following procedure.
4 Unscrew the brake fluid hose union bolt from the rear of the caliper, and disconnect the hose. Recover the two sealing rings from the union bolt (one either side of the hose end fitting). Be prepared for fluid spillage, and plug the open ends to prevent dirt ingress and further fluid loss.

5 Withdraw the caliper body from the vehicle.
6 The caliper bracket can be removed from the hub carrier by unscrewing the two securing bolts **(see illustration)**.

Overhaul

7 Brush the dirt from the caliper, but take care not to inhale it.
8 Using a screwdriver, carefully prise the dust seal from the end of the piston and the caliper body, and remove it.
9 Place a thin piece of wood in front of the piston to prevent it from falling out of its bore and sustaining damage. Then apply low air pressure - e.g. from a foot pump - to the brake fluid union hole in the rear of the caliper body, to eject the piston from its bore.
10 Remove the wood, and carefully withdraw the piston.
11 Carefully prise the seal from the groove in the caliper piston bore, using a plastic or wooden instrument **(see illustration)**.
12 Inspect the surfaces of the piston and its bore in the caliper for scoring, or evidence of metal-to-metal contact. If evident, renew the complete caliper assembly.
13 If the piston and bore are in good condition, discard the seals and obtain a repair kit, which will contain all the necessary renewable items.
14 Clean the piston and cylinder bore with brake fluid or methylated spirit nothing else.
15 Begin reassembly by fitting the dust seal into the caliper bore.
16 Locate the dust seal in its groove in the piston. Dip the piston in clean brake fluid, and insert it squarely into the cylinder. Check that the cutaway recesses in the piston are positioned vertically. If necessary, carefully turn the piston to its correct position.
17 When the piston has been partially depressed, engage the dust seal with the rim of the caliper bore.
18 Push the piston further into its bore, but not as far as the stop, ensuring that it does not jam.
19 The guide bolt sleeves can be renewed. Extract the nylon compression sleeve from within each rubber, then carefully compress the rubber shoulder, and push the rubber

through the hole in the caliper body to remove it from the inboard end.
20 Fit the new sleeves using a reversal of the removal procedure.

Refitting

21 Where applicable, refit the caliper bracket to the hub carrier, and tighten the securing bolts to the specified torque.
22 Reconnect the brake fluid hose union, using new sealing rings on the union bolt.
23 Refit the brake pads, as described in Section 6.
24 Remove the polythene from the brake fluid reservoir filler neck, and bleed the relevant brake hydraulic circuit, as described in Section 4.
25 Refit the roadwheel and lower the vehicle to the ground.

8 Brake disc - inspection, removal and refitting

Note: *Refer to the warning concerning brake dust at the beginning of Section 6 before proceeding.*

Inspection

1 If checking a front disc, apply the handbrake, and if checking a rear disc, chock the front wheels, then jack up the relevant end of the vehicle, and support securely on axle stands.
2 Check that the brake disc securing screw is tight, then fit a spacer approximately 10.0 mm thick to one of the roadwheel bolts, and refit and tighten the bolt in the hole opposite the disc securing screw **(see illustration)**.
3 Rotate the brake disc, and examine it for deep scoring or grooving. Light scoring is normal, but if excessive, the disc should be removed and either renewed or machined (within the specified limits) by an engineering works.
4 Using a dial gauge, or a flat metal block and feeler gauges, check that the disc run-out

9

8.11 Unscrewing a front brake disc securing screw

8.15 Removing a rear brake disc

9.5 Cutting a section of metal from a new front brake disc shield prior to fitting

does not exceed the figure given in the Specifications.

5 If the disc run-out is excessive, remove the disc as described later in this Section, and check that the disc-to-hub surfaces are perfectly clean.

6 With the disc removed, check the hub run-out. If the run-out exceeds the maximum specified for disc run-out, it is likely that the hub bearings are severely worn or damaged. Refer to Chapter 10 for details of renewal.

7 Refit the disc, and check the disc run-out again. If the hub bearings are in good condition, the fault must lie with the disc, which should be renewed.

Removal

Front disc

8 Where applicable, remove the roadwheel bolt and spacer used when checking the disc.
9 Remove the brake pads, as described in Section 6.
10 Unscrew the two securing bolts, and remove the caliper bracket.
11 Remove the securing screw **(see illustration)**, and withdraw the disc from the hub.

Rear disc

12 Where applicable, remove the roadwheel bolt and spacer used when checking the disc.
13 Remove the brake pads, as described in Section 13.
14 Remove the brake caliper with reference to Section 14, but leave the hydraulic pipe connected. Move the caliper to one side, and suspend it using wire or string to avoid straining the pipe.
15 Remove the securing screw, and withdraw the disc from the hub **(see illustration)**. If the disc is tight, collapse the handbrake shoes by inserting a screwdriver through the adjuster hole in the disc and turning the adjuster wheel.

Refitting

16 Refitting is a reversal of removal, but make sure that the mating faces of the disc and hub are perfectly clean. Refit the brake pads as described in Section 6 or 13, as applicable.

9 Front brake disc shield - removal and refitting

Note: *Refer to the warning concerning brake dust at the beginning of Section 6 before proceeding.*

Removal

1 Apply the handbrake, then jack up the front of the vehicle, and support securely on axle stands. Remove the relevant roadwheel.
2 Remove the brake disc, as described in Section 8.
3 Using a screwdriver inserted through the holes in the hub flange, extract the three screws securing the disc shield to the hub carrier.
4 Using plate shears or an alternative tool, cut a section of metal from the rear edge of the shield to enable the shield to be withdrawn over the hub, then remove the shield.

Refitting

5 If a new shield is to be fitted, cut out a section of metal, as during removal of the old shield, to enable the shield to be fitted **(see illustration)**. De-burr the cut edges, and coat them with anti-corrosion paint.
6 Further refitting is a reversal of removal; refit the brake disc as described in Section 8.

10 Rear brake shoes - removal and refitting

Note: *Renew both sets of rear brake shoes at the same time - never renew the shoes on one wheel, as uneven braking may result. Refer to the warning concerning brake dust at the beginning of Section 6 before proceeding.*

Removal

1 Chock the front wheels, then jack up the rear of the vehicle and support securely on axle stands. Remove the rear roadwheels.
2 Working on one side of the vehicle, remove the brake drum, as described in Section 11.
3 Note the location and orientation of all

components before dismantling, as an aid to reassembly.
4 Clean the dust and dirt from the drum and shoes, but take care not to inhale it.
5 Remove the shoe hold-down pins, springs and cups by depressing the cups and turning them through 90° using a pair of pliers **(see illustrations)**. Note that the hold-down pins are removed through the rear of the backplate.
6 Disconnect the handbrake cable from the operating lever **(see illustration)**.
7 The upper and lower return springs may now be unhooked and the shoes removed separately, or the assembly of shoes, adjuster strut and springs may be removed together. The second course of action is particularly easy if the hub is removed - see Chapter 10.

10.5A Release the shoe hold-down cup ...

10.5B ... and withdraw the cup and spring

10.6 Disconnecting the handbrake cable from the operating lever (hub removed for clarity)

10.8 Rubber band fitted to wheel cylinder to retain pistons

10.15 Right-hand brake shoe adjuster components - thermo-clip arrowed

Take care not to damage the wheel cylinder rubber boots. Before removing the return springs, note the position and orientation of the springs and adjuster strut.

8 If the shoes are to be removed for some time, fit a stout rubber band or a spring clip to the wheel cylinder, to prevent the pistons from being pushed out of their bores **(see illustration)**. In any event, **do not** press the brake pedal while the drum is removed.

Refitting

9 Clean the dust and dirt from the brake backplate, but take care not to inhale it.
10 Apply a small amount of brake grease to the shoe rubbing areas on the backplate.
11 If the linings removed were contaminated with brake fluid or grease, investigate and rectify any source of contamination before fitting new linings (wheel cylinder or hub bearing oil seal leaking).
12 Although linings are available separately (without shoes), renewal of the shoes complete with linings is to be preferred, unless the necessary skills and equipment are available to fit new linings to the old shoes.
13 If not already done, dismantle the shoes, strut and springs. Note the position and orientation of the components.
14 If both brake assemblies are dismantled at the same time, take care not to mix up the components. Note that the left-hand and right-hand adjuster components are marked; the threaded rod is marked 'L' or 'R', and the other 'handed' components are colour-coded black for the left-hand side, and silver for the right-hand side.
15 Dismantle and clean the adjuster strut. Apply a smear of silicone-based grease to the adjuster threads. If new brake linings or shoes are to be fitted, the thermo-clip on the adjuster strut must also be renewed **(see illustration)**.
16 Examine the return springs. If they are distorted, or if they have seen extensive service, renewal is advisable. Weak springs may cause the brakes to bind.
17 If a new handbrake operating lever was not supplied with the new shoes (where applicable), transfer the lever from the old shoes. The lever may be secured with a pin

and circlip, or by a rivet, which will have to be drilled out.
18 If the components are to be refitted as an assembly, assemble the new shoes, springs and adjuster components. Expand the adjuster strut to ease fitting.
19 Offer the shoes to the brake backplate. Be careful not to damage the wheel cylinder boots, or to displace the pistons. Remember to remove the rubber band or spring clip from the wheel cylinder, where applicable.
20 When the shoes are in position, insert the hold-down pins and secure them with the springs and cups.
21 Reconnect the handbrake cable, then refit the hub, where applicable.
22 If fitting the shoes and springs together as an assembly is found too difficult, it is possible to fit the shoes and secure them with the hold-down pins. Then to fit the adjuster strut and fit the return springs and adjuster.
23 Back off the adjuster wheel to reduce the length of the strut, until the brake drum will pass over the shoes.
24 Make sure that the handbrake operating lever is correctly positioned, with the pin on the edge of the shoe web, not riding on top of it, then refit and secure the brake drum **(see illustration)**.
25 Repeat the operations on the remaining side of the vehicle.
26 Adjust the brakes by operating the footbrake at least fifteen times. A clicking

noise will be heard at the drums, as the automatic adjusters operate. When the clicking stops, adjustment is complete.
27 Check the handbrake cable adjustment, as described in Section 21.
28 Refit the roadwheels, and lower the vehicle to the ground.
29 New brake linings should be carefully bedded-in and, where possible, heavy braking should be avoided during the first 100 miles (160 km) or so after fitting new linings.

---

11 Rear brake drum - removal, inspection and refitting

Note: *Refer to the warning concerning brake dust at the beginning of Section 6 before proceeding.*

Removal

1 Chock the front wheels, then jack up the rear of the vehicle and support securely on axle stands.
2 Fully release the handbrake.
3 Extract the drum securing screw **(see illustration)**, and remove the drum. If the drum is tight, remove the plug from the inspection hole in the brake backplate, and push the handbrake operating lever towards the brake shoe to move the shoes away from the drums. If necessary, slacken the handbrake cable adjuster (see Section 21).

10.24 Rear drum brake components correctly assembled. Hub removed for clarity

11.3 Removing a brake drum securing screw

9

12.5 Unscrewing the fluid pipe union nut from the rear wheel cylinder

Inspection

4 Brush the dirt and dust from the drum, taking care not to inhale it.

5 Examine the internal friction surfaces of the drum. If they are deeply scored, or so worn that the drum has become ridged to the width of the shoes, then both drums must be renewed.

6 Regrinding of the friction surface is not recommended, since the internal diameter of the drum will no longer be compatible with the shoe friction material contact diameter.

Refitting

7 Refit the brake drum and tighten the securing screw. If necessary, back off the adjuster wheel until the drum will pass over the shoes.

8 Adjust the brakes by operating the footbrake a number of times. A clicking noise will be heard at the drum as the automatic adjuster operates. When the clicking stops, adjustment is complete.

9 Refit the roadwheel and lower the vehicle to the ground.

12 Rear wheel cylinder - removal, overhaul and refitting

Note: *Refer to the note at the beginning of Section 4, and the warning concerning brake dust at the beginning of Section 6 before proceeding. Before dismantling a wheel cylinder, check that replacement parts can be obtained, and retain the old components to compare them with the new ones.*

Removal

1 Chock the front wheels, then jack up the front of the vehicle and support securely on axle stands. Remove the relevant roadwheel.

2 Remove the brake drum, as described in Section 11.

3 Using a pair of pliers, unhook the upper return spring from the brake shoes, noting its orientation, then push the upper ends of the shoes apart until they are clear of the wheel cylinder.

4 Working under the bonnet, remove the brake fluid reservoir cap, and secure a piece

12.11 Exploded view of a rear brake wheel cylinder

1 Dust cap
2 Bleed nipple
3 Cylinder body
4 Dust seal
5 Piston
6 Piston seal
7 Spring

of polythene over the filler neck with a rubber band, or by refitting the cap. This will reduce the loss of fluid during the following procedure.

5 Unscrew the brake fluid pipe union nut from the rear of the wheel cylinder, and disconnect the pipe **(see illustration)**. Take care not to strain the pipe. Be prepared for fluid spillage, and plug the open ends to prevent dirt ingress and further fluid loss.

6 Unscrew the two securing bolts from the rear of the brake backplate, and withdraw the wheel cylinder.

Overhaul

7 Brush the dirt and dust from the wheel cylinder, but take care not to inhale it.

8 Pull the rubber dust seals from the ends of the cylinder body.

9 The pistons will normally be ejected by the pressure of the coil spring, but if they are not, tap the end of the cylinder body on a piece of wood, or apply low air pressure - e.g., from a foot pump - to the brake fluid union hole in the rear of the cylinder body, to eject the pistons from their bores.

10 Inspect the surfaces of the pistons and their bores in the cylinder body for scoring, or evidence of metal-to-metal contact. If evident, renew the complete wheel cylinder assembly.

11 If the pistons and bores are in good

condition, discard the seals and obtain a repair kit, which will contain all the necessary renewable items **(see illustration)**.

12 Lubricate the piston seals with clean brake fluid, and insert them into the cylinder bores, with the spring between them, using finger pressure only.

13 Dip the pistons in clean brake fluid, and insert them into the cylinder bores.

14 Fit the dust seals, and check that the pistons can move freely in their bores.

Refitting

15 Refit the wheel cylinder to the backplate, and tighten the securing bolts.

16 Reconnect the brake fluid pipe to the cylinder, and tighten the union nut.

17 Push the brake shoes against the pistons, then refit the upper return spring as noted before removal.

18 Refit the brake drum, and tighten the securing screw. If necessary, back off the adjuster wheel until the drum will pass over the shoes.

19 Remove the polythene from the brake fluid reservoir filler neck, and bleed the relevant brake hydraulic circuit, as described in Section 4.

20 Adjust the brakes by operating the footbrake a number of times. A clicking noise will be heard at the drum as the automatic adjuster operates. When the clicking stops, adjustment is complete.

21 Refit the roadwheel and lower the vehicle to the ground.

13 Rear brake pads (models with rear disc brakes) - removal and refitting

Note: *Refer to the warning concerning brake dust at the beginning of Section 6 before proceeding.*

Removal

1 Chock the front wheels, then jack up the rear of the vehicle and support securely on axle stands.

2 Note how the anti-rattle spring is located, then drive out the upper and lower pad retaining pins from the outside of the caliper using a pin punch **(see illustrations)**.

13.2A Rear brake pad anti-rattle spring correctly located. Note lower pad retaining pin has been partially removed

13.2B Driving out the upper pad retaining pin

13.5 Removing the rear inboard brake pad

13.8 Checking a rear caliper piston cutaway recess angle with a card template

14.5 Rear brake caliper mounting bolts (arrowed)

3 Remove the anti-rattle spring.
4 Push the pads away from the disc slightly then, using a pair of pliers, withdraw the outboard pad and, where applicable, the anti-squeal shim that fits between the pad and the caliper body.
5 Withdraw the inboard pad **(see illustration)** and, where applicable, the anti-squeal shim.
6 Brush the dust and dirt from the caliper, but take care not to inhale it. Carefully remove any rust from the edge of the brake disc.

Refitting

7 To accommodate the new thicker pads, the caliper piston must be depressed fully into its cylinder bore, using a flat metal bar such as a tyre lever. Do not lever between the piston and the disc to depress the piston. The action of depressing the piston will cause the fluid level in the reservoir to rise, so to avoid spillage, syphon out some fluid using a (clean) old battery hydrometer or a teat pipette.
8 Check that the cutaway recesses in the pistons are positioned downwards, at approximately 23° to the horizontal. A template made of card may be used to check the setting **(see illustration)**. If necessary, carefully turn the pistons to their correct positions.
9 Apply a little brake grease to the top and bottom edges of the backplates on the new brake pads.
10 Locate the new pads and the anti-squeal shims in the caliper. Ensure that the friction material faces the disc, and check that the pads are free to move slightly.
11 Locate the anti-rattle spring on the pads, then insert the pad retaining pins from the inside edge of the caliper, while depressing the spring. Tap the pins firmly into the caliper.
12 Repeat the operations on the remaining side of the vehicle.
13 Refit the roadwheels, and lower the vehicle to the ground.
14 Apply the footbrake hard several times to position the pads against the discs.
15 Check and if necessary top-up the brake fluid level.
16 New brake pads should be carefully

bedded-in and, where possible, heavy braking should be avoided during the first 100 miles (160 km) or so after fitting new pads.

14 Rear brake caliper (models with rear disc brakes) - removal, overhaul and refitting

Note: *Refer to the note at the beginning of Section 4, and the warning concerning brake dust at the beginning of Section 6 before proceeding. Before dismantling a caliper, check that replacement parts can be obtained, and retain the old components to compare them with the new ones.*

Removal

1 Chock the front wheels, then jack up the rear of the vehicle and support securely on axle stands. Remove the relevant roadwheel.
2 Remove the brake pads, as described in Section 13.
3 Working under the bonnet, remove the brake fluid reservoir cap, and secure a piece of polythene over the filler neck with a rubber band, or by refitting the cap. This will reduce the loss of fluid during the following procedure.
4 Unscrew the brake fluid pipe union nut from the rear of the caliper, and disconnect the pipe. Take care not to strain the pipe. Be prepared for fluid spillage, and plug the open ends to prevent dirt ingress and further fluid loss.
5 Unscrew the two mounting bolts and withdraw the caliper from the vehicle **(see illustration)**.

Overhaul

6 Brush the dirt and dust from the caliper, but take care not to inhale it.
7 Note that no attempt must be made to separate the two halves of the caliper.
8 Using a screwdriver, prise the dust seal retaining clips from the piston dust seals, then carefully prise off the dust seals.
9 Using a clamp, clamp one of the pistons in its fully retracted position. Then apply low air pressure - e.g. from a foot pump - to the brake fluid union hole in the rear of the caliper

body, to eject the remaining piston from its bore. Take care not to drop the piston, as it may result in damage.
10 Temporarily close off the bore of the removed piston, using a flat piece of wood or similar improvised tool. Then remove the clamp from the remaining piston, and again apply air pressure to the caliper union to eject the piston.
11 Carefully prise the seals from the grooves in the caliper piston bores, using a plastic or wooden instrument.
12 Inspect the surfaces of the pistons and their bores in the caliper for scoring, or evidence of metal-to-metal contact. If evident, renew the complete caliper assembly.
13 If the pistons and bores are in good condition, discard the seals, and obtain a repair kit, which will contain all the necessary renewable items. Also obtain a tube of brake cylinder paste.
14 Clean the piston and cylinder bore with brake fluid or methylated spirit - nothing else.
15 Apply a little brake cylinder paste to the pistons, cylinder bores, and piston seals.
16 Begin reassembly by fitting the seals to the grooves in the caliper bores.
17 Locate the dust seals in their grooves in the pistons, then insert the pistons carefully into their bores until they enter the seals. It may be necessary to rotate the pistons to prevent them from jamming in the seals.
18 When the pistons have been partially depressed, engage the dust seals with the rims of the caliper bores, and refit the retaining clips.

Refitting

19 Refit the caliper, and tighten the securing bolts to the specified torque.
20 Reconnect the brake fluid pipe to the caliper, and tighten the union nut.
21 Refit the brake pads, as described in Section 13.
22 Refit the roadwheel, and lower the vehicle to the ground.
23 Remove the polythene from the brake fluid reservoir filler neck, and bleed the relevant brake hydraulic circuit, as described in Section 4.

9

15.4 Handbrake cable and return spring connection to handbrake operating lever - model with rear disc brakes

15 Handbrake shoes (models with rear disc brakes) - removal and refitting

Note: *Refer to the warning concerning brake dust at the beginning of Section 6 before proceeding.*

Removal

1 Jack up the vehicle, and support on axle stands positioned under the body side members.
2 Remove the brake disc, as described in Section 8.
3 Clean the dust and dirt from the various components, but take care not to inhale it.
4 Disconnect the handbrake cable and the return spring from the handbrake operating lever at the brake backplate (see illustration). If necessary, slacken the handbrake cable adjustment, with reference to Section 21.
5 Remove the shoe hold-down pins, springs and cups by depressing the cups and turning them through 90° using a pair of pliers. Note that the hold-down pins are removed through the rear of the brake backplate.
6 The shoes, adjuster, handbrake operating lever and return springs can now be removed together as an assembly.
7 Note the position and orientation of all components, then unhook the upper and lower return springs from the shoes, and recover the handbrake operating lever and the adjuster (see illustration).

Refitting

8 Apply a little brake grease to the threads of the adjuster, then screw it together to its minimum length. Also apply a little brake grease to the shoe rubbing areas on the backplate.
9 Fit one of the new brake shoes, and secure it to the backplate with the hold-down pin, spring and cup.
10 Locate the handbrake operating lever in position.
11 Fit the remaining brake shoe, and secure with the hold-down pin, spring and cup.
12 Hook the upper return spring onto the shoes.

1 Brake shoes
2 Upper return spring
3 Handbrake operating lever
4 Adjuster
5 Lower return spring
6 Hold-down pin
7 Hold-down spring
8 Hold-down clip

H.22799

15.7 Rear handbrake shoe components - models with rear disc brakes

13 Fit the adjuster between the lower ends of the shoes, as noted before dismantling, then fit the lower return spring.
14 Reconnect the handbrake cable and the return spring to the handbrake operating lever.
15 Refit the brake disc, as described in Section 8, but do not refit the roadwheel at this stage.
16 Repeat the operations on the remaining side of the vehicle.
17 Check the handbrake cable adjustment, as described in Section 21.
18 Refit the roadwheels, and lower the vehicle to the ground.

16 Rear brake backplate - removal and refitting

Models with rear drum brakes

Removal

1 Chock the front wheels, then jack up the rear of the vehicle, and support securely on axle. Remove the relevant roadwheel.
2 Remove the brake shoes, as described in Section 10.
3 Remove the rear wheel cylinder, as described in Section 12.
4 Using a pair of pliers, prise out the clip securing the handbrake cable to the backplate.
5 Remove the rear hub unit, as described in Chapter 10, and withdraw the backplate.

Refitting

6 Fit the backplate and the rear hub unit, with reference to Chapter 10, using new nuts

tightened in the three stages given in the Specifications.
7 Locate the handbrake cable in the backplate, and refit the securing clip.
8 Refit the rear wheel cylinder, as described in Section 12.
9 Refit the brake shoes, as described in Section 10.
10 Before refitting the roadwheel and lowering the vehicle to the ground, check and if necessary adjust the handbrake, as described in Section 21.
11 Bleed the relevant brake hydraulic circuit, as described in Section 4.

Models with rear disc brakes

Removal

12 Chock the front wheels, then jack up the rear of the vehicle, and support securely on axle. Remove the relevant roadwheel.
13 Remove the brake disc, as described in Section 8.
14 Remove the handbrake shoes, as described in Section 15.
15 Remove the rear hub unit, as described in Chapter 10, and withdraw the brake backplate.

Refitting

16 Fit the backplate and the rear hub unit, with reference to Chapter 10, using new nuts tightened in the three stages given in the Specifications.
17 Refit the handbrake shoes, as described in Section 15.
18 Refit the brake disc, as described in Section 8.
19 Before refitting the roadwheel and lowering the vehicle to the ground, check and if necessary adjust the handbrake, as described in Section 21.

17.4 Brake servo fork-to-pedal pivot pin spring clip (arrowed)

17 Brake pedal -
removal and refitting

Removal

1 Disconnect the battery negative lead.
2 Remove the lower trim panel from the driver's footwell.
3 Disconnect the wiring plug from the brake light switch, then twist the switch anticlockwise and remove it from its bracket.
4 Pull the spring clip from the right-hand end of the servo fork-to-pedal pivot pin **(see illustration)**.
5 Using a pair of pliers, pull back the end of the pedal return spring from the pedal, to enable the servo fork-to-pedal pivot pin to be removed. Withdraw the pivot pin **(see illustration)**.
6 Pull the locking clip from the left-hand end of the pedal pivot pin.
7 Unscrew the nut from the left-hand end of the pivot pin, then slide the pivot pin from the right-hand end of the pedal mounting bracket. If necessary, tap the end of the pivot pin with a soft-faced hammer to free the splines from the mounting bracket. Recover any washers that may be positioned on the pivot pin, noting their locations.
8 Withdraw the pedal and return spring.

Refitting

9 Refitting is a reversal of removal, remembering the following points.
10 Ensure that the pedal return spring is correctly located on the pedal before refitting.

17.5 Brake pedal assembly removed from vehicle

1 Locking clip
2 Pedal return spring
3 Pedal pivot pin

11 Coat the pedal pivot pin with a little molybdenum disulphide grease.
12 Ensure that any washers on the pedal pivot pin are positioned as noted before removal.

18 Servo unit -
testing, removal and refitting

Note: *When refitting, some Sealing Compound (Vauxhall P/N 90485251, or equivalent) will be required to coat the mating faces of the servo mounting bracket, and thread-locking compound will be required to coat the servo securing bolts.*

Right-hand-drive models
Testing

1 To test the operation of the servo unit, depress the footbrake four or five times to exhaust the vacuum, then start the engine while keeping the footbrake depressed. As the engine starts, there should be a noticeable 'give' in the brake pedal as vacuum builds up. Allow the engine to run for at least two minutes, and then switch it off. If the brake pedal is now depressed again, it should be possible to detect a hiss from the servo when the pedal is depressed. After about four or five applications, no further hissing will be heard, and the pedal will feel considerably firmer.

Removal
2 Disconnect the battery negative lead.

3 Working inside the vehicle, release the securing clips, and remove the lower trim panel from the driver's footwell.
4 Disconnect the wiring plug from the brake light switch, then twist the switch anticlockwise and remove it from its bracket.
5 Pull the spring clip from right-hand end of the servo fork-to-pedal pivot pin.
6 Using a pair of pliers, pull back the end of the pedal return spring from the pedal, to enable the servo fork-to-pedal pin to be removed. Withdraw the pivot pin.
7 Remove the windscreen cowl trim panel, as described in Chapter 11, then remove the windscreen wiper motor and linkage, as described in Chapter 12.
8 Remove the washer fluid reservoir, as described in Chapter 12.
9 Disconnect the vacuum pipe from the brake servo.
10 Unscrew the two securing nuts, and carefully withdaw the brake master cylinder from the studs on the servo. Move the master cylinder forwards slightly, taking care not to strain the brake pipes.
11 Remove the two plugs covering the servo securing bolts from the cowl panel **(see illustration)**.
12 Using an Allen key or hexagon bit, unscrew the servo securing bolts and remove them completely **(see illustration)**, then lift the servo complete with mounting bracket from the bulkhead. Note that the bracket may stick to the bulkhead, as it is fitted with sealing compound.
13 The mounting bracket can be removed from the servo by unscrewing the four securing nuts. Note that the bracket will stick to the servo, as it is fitted with sealing compound.
14 The servo cannot be overhauled, and if faulty, the complete unit must be renewed.

Refitting
15 Before refitting the servo, check that the operating fork dimension is correct, as follows.
16 Measure the distance from the end face of the servo casing to the centre of the pivot pin hole in the end of the operating fork. The distance should be 147.70 mm. To make accurate measurement easier, insert a bolt or bar of diameter through the pivot pin hole, and measure to the centre of the bolt or bar **(see illustration)**.

9

18.11 Plug removed from cowl panel to expose brake servo securing bolt

18.12 Unscrewing a brake servo securing bolt

18.16 Measuring the servo operating fork dimension using a bolt inserted through the pivot pin hole

18.30 Brake servo and mounting bracket removed showing securing nut locations (arrowed) - left-hand-drive models

18.32 Prising out the securing clip to remove the operating fork from the servo operating rod sleeve - left-hand-drive models

18.34 Brake servo operating fork dimension (1) left-hand-drive models

17 If adjustment is necessary, slacken the locknut, turn the fork to give the specified dimension, then tighten the locknut.

18 Coat the mating surfaces of the mounting bracket with sealing compound (Vauxhall P/N 90485251, or equivalent), then refit the bracket to the servo.

19 Coat the threads of the servo securing bolts with thread-locking fluid, then fit the servo to the bulkhead and tighten the securing bolts.

20 Refit the securing bolt cover plugs to the cowl panel.

21 Refit the master cylinder to the servo, and tighten the securing nuts to the specified torque.

22 Reconnect the vacuum pipe to the servo.

23 Refit the washer fluid reservoir.

24 Refit the windscreen wiper motor and linkage, as described in Chapter 12, then refit the windscreen cowl trim panel.

25 Further refitting is a reversal of removal. On completion, check the operation of the servo, as described in paragraph 16.

Left-hand-drive models

Note: *New self-locking nuts will be required when refitting the servo mounting bracket to the bulkhead.*

Testing

26 Refer to paragraph 1.

Removal

27 Proceed as described in paragraphs 2 to 6 inclusive.

28 Disconnect the vacuum pipe from the brake servo.

29 Unscrew the two securing nuts, and carefully withdraw the brake master cylinder from the studs on the servo. Move the master cylinder forwards slightly, taking care not to strain the brake pipes.

30 Unscrew the four servo bracket securing nuts from the bulkhead (a flexible socket coupling will be required to reach the lower

bolt), then tilt the servo/bracket assembly, and withdraw it upwards from the engine compartment **(see illustration)**.

31 The mounting bracket can be removed from the servo by unscrewing the four securing nuts. The rubber sleeve can now be removed from the brake servo.

32 To remove the operating fork from the servo operating rod sleeve, prise out the securing clip **(see illustration)**.

Refitting

33 Before refitting the servo, check that the operating fork dimension is correct, as follows.

34 Measure the distance from the end face of the servo casing to the centre of the pivot pin hole in the end of the operating fork. The distance should be 255.5 mm **(see illustration)**. To make accurate measurement easier, insert a bolt or bar of diameter through the pivot pin hole, and measure to the centre of the bolt or bar.

35 If adjustment is necessary, slacken the locknut on the operating rod sleeve, turn the fork to give the specified dimension, then tighten the locknut.

36 Where applicable, refit the rubber sleeve, and refit the servo to the mounting bracket. Tighten the servo-to-mounting bracket nuts to the specified torque.

37 Lower the servo and mounting bracket and servo assembly into position, then refit the assembly to the bulkhead, using new self-locking nuts, and tighten the nuts to the specified torque.

38 Refit the master cylinder to the servo, and tighten the securing nuts to the specified torque.

39 Reconnect the vacuum pipe to the servo.

40 Further refitting is a reversal of removal. On completion, check the operation of the servo, as described in paragraph 1.

19 Non-return valve (servo) - testing, removal and refitting

Testing

1 The function of the valve is to allow air to flow in one direction only, out of the servo unit. If the valve allows air to flow in both directions, it is faulty, and must be renewed.

2 To test the valve, first remove the hose/valve assembly, as described later in this Section.

3 Blow through the hose on the servo side of the valve; air should pass freely through the valve.

4 Now blow through the hose on the inlet manifold side of the valve; no air should pass through.

5 If the valve is faulty, it must be renewed.

Removal

6 The plastic valve is located in the vacuum hose running from the inlet manifold to the brake servo.

7 Although the valve is available separately from the hoses, to remove the valve, the hoses must be cut, and therefore renewed on reassembly. If the valve is to be renewed, it is therefore easier to remove the complete hose/valve assembly, and renew it complete.

8 To remove the assembly, carefully unplug the hose adaptor from the vacuum servo unit, then unscrew the hose union from the inlet manifold, and withdraw the assembly.

Refitting

9 Refitting is a reversal of removal, but when reconnecting the hose adaptor to the servo, take care not to damage or distort the sealing grommet, and on completion, start the engine and check for air leaks.

20 Master cylinder - removal, overhaul and refitting

Note: *Refer to the note at the beginning of Section 4 before proceeding. Check availability of parts before overhauling the master cylinder. Compare the new parts with the old ones before fitting.*

Removal

1 Disconnect the battery negative lead.
2 Depress the footbrake pedal several times to dissipate the vacuum in the servo unit.
3 Disconnect the wiring plug from the brake fluid level sensor in the reservoir filler cap.
4 If possible, use a pipette or a (clean) old battery hydrometer to remove the brake fluid from the reservoir. This will reduce the loss of fluid later in the procedure.
5 Position a container beneath the master cylinder, to catch the brake fluid that will be released.
6 Identify the brake fluid pipes for position, then unscrew the union nuts and disconnect the pipes from the master cylinder.
7 Unscrew the two securing nuts, and withdraw the master cylinder from the studs on the vacuum servo unit.
8 Clean the external surfaces of the cylinder, then using a screwdriver, carefully prise the fluid reservoir and its seals from the top of the cylinder.

Overhaul

9 On models with a conventional (non-ABS) braking system, the master cylinder can be overhauled, as described in the following paragraphs. No overhaul of the master cylinder is possible on models with ABS.
10 With the master cylinder removed, continue as follows, according to type.

GMF type master cylinder

11 Clamp the master cylinder in a soft-jawed vice.
12 Carefully prise out the sealing ring from the end of the cylinder bore.
13 Depress the primary piston slightly using a piece of wood or plastic. Then hold the piston in the depressed position by inserting a smooth pin or rod of 3.0 mm diameter through the primary fluid reservoir port in the cylinder **(see illustration)**.
14 Extract the circlip from the end of the cylinder bore using a screwdriver. Take care not to damage the piston or cylinder bore.
15 Withdraw the pin or rod retaining the piston.
16 Withdraw the primary piston assembly from the cylinder, if necessary tapping the cylinder on a wooden block to free the piston from the bore.
17 Apply low air pressure - e.g. from a foot

20.13 Holding the primary piston depressed while extracting the circlip from the cylinder body - GMF type master cylinder

pump - to the front fluid reservoir port in the cylinder, to eject the secondary piston assembly.
18 Clean all the components, in clean brake fluid or methylated spirit only, and examine them for wear and damage. In particular, check the surfaces of the pistons and cylinder bore for scoring and corrosion **(see illustration)**. If the bore shows signs of wear, renew the complete master cylinder assembly.
19 If the cylinder bore is in good condition, obtain a repair kit, which will contain all the necessary renewable items. A Vauxhall dealer will be able to supply a pre-assembled kit of parts, which should be fitted as follows.
20 Lubricate the cylinder bore with clean brake fluid or brake grease, then clamp the cylinder in a soft-jawed vice, with the bore horizontal.
21 Remove the plug from the end of the assembly tube, and insert the short part of the tube into the cylinder bore as far as the shoulder on the tube.
22 Use a piece of wood or plastic to push the components out of the tube and into the cylinder bore. Then hold the primary piston in the depressed position by inserting the pin or rod used during dismantling through the cylinder primary fluid reservoir port.
23 Fit a new circlip to the end of the cylinder bore, ensuring that it seats correctly, and that the piston is free to move.
24 Depress the primary piston, and withdraw the pin or rod from the fluid reservoir port.
25 Fit a new sealing ring to the end of the cylinder bore.

ATE type master cylinder

26 Clamp the master cylinder in a soft-jawed vice.
27 Carefully prise out the sealing ring from the end of the cylinder bore.
28 Depress the primary piston slightly using a piece of wood or plastic, then extract the circlip from the end of the cylinder bore.
29 Withdraw the primary piston assembly, noting the location of the stopwashers.
30 Depress the secondary piston, again

20.18 Exploded view of GMF type master cylinder

1 Filler cap (standard)
2 Filler cap (with fluid level sensor)
3 Fluid reservoir
4 Fluid reservoir retaining clips
5 Fluid reservoir seals
6 Cylinder body
7 Secondary piston and springs
8 Primary piston
9 Circlip
10 Sealing ring

using a piece of wood or plastic, and withdraw the stop-screw from the end of cylinder body **(see illustration)**.
31 Withdraw the secondary piston assembly from the cylinder, if necessary tapping the cylinder on a wooden block to free the piston from the bore.
32 Clean all the components, using clean brake fluid or methylated spirit only, and examine them for wear and damage. In particular, check the surfaces of the pistons and cylinder bores for scoring and corrosion

20.30 Depressing the secondary piston while extracting the stop-screw - ATE type master cylinder

9

20.32 Exploded view of ATE type master cylinder

1 Filler cap (standard)
2 Strainer
3 Filler cap (with fluid level sensor)
4 Guide sleeve for float
5 Fluid reservoir
6 Cylinder body
7 Sealing ring
8 Fluid reservoir seals
9 Stop-screw
10 Repair kit assembly

(see illustration). If the bore shows signs of wear, renew the complete master cylinder assembly.

33 If the cylinder bore is in good condition, obtain a repair kit, which will contain all the necessary renewable items. A Vauxhall dealer will supply a pre-assembled kit of parts, which should be fitted as follows.

34 Lubricate the cylinder bore with clean brake fluid or brake grease, then clamp the cylinder in a soft-jawed vice, with the bore horizontal.

35 Fit a new sealing ring to the stop-screw, then screw it into the cylinder body a little way, but not so far that it protrudes into the bore.

36 Remove the plugs from the ends of the assembly tube, then remove all the components from the short part of the tube, and push the short part into the long part until they are flush.

37 Insert the assembly tube into the cylinder bore as far as the collar on the short sleeve. Then use a piece of wood or plastic to push the secondary piston assembly into the bore until it contacts the end of the cylinder.

38 Lightly tighten the stop-screw, then withdraw the piece of wood or plastic and the

assembly tube, and fully tighten the stop-screw.

39 Reposition the master cylinder in the vice, with the bore facing upwards.

40 Smear the primary piston skirt and the seal grooves with the special grease provided in the repair kit. Fit the stop-washer to the piston.

41 Adjust the assembly tube so that the end of the long part is flush with the inner shoulder of the short part.

42 Fit the front seal to the primary piston, with the open end of the seal facing the front of the master cylinder.

43 Place the assembly tube over the cylinder to compress the seal, insert the piston and tube part way into the bore, and withdraw the tube.

44 Place the intermediate ring on the primary piston, then fit the remaining seal using the assembly tube as described previously.

45 Place the stop-washer on the primary piston, then depress the piston slightly using a piece of wood or plastic, and fit a new circlip to the end of the cylinder bore. Ensure that the circlip is correctly seated, and that the piston is free to move.

46 Fit a new sealing ring to the end of the cylinder bore.

Refitting

47 Refitting is a reversal of removal, but on completion, bleed the complete brake hydraulic system, as described in Section 4.

21 Handbrake - adjustment

Models with rear drum brakes

1 The handbrake will normally be kept in correct adjustment by the self-adjusting action of the rear brake shoes. However, due to cable stretch over a period of time, the travel of the handbrake lever may become excessive, in which case the following operations should be carried out.

2 Chock the front wheels, then jack up the rear of the vehicle, and support securely on axle. Remove the rear roadwheels.

21.5 Handbrake cable adjuster nut (arrowed)

3 Fully release the handbrake.

4 On models with a catalytic converter, unscrew the securing nuts, and withdraw the exhaust centre box heat shield by carefully sliding it round the centre box.

5 Turn the adjuster nut on the now-exposed cable adjuster **(see illustration)**, until the brake shoes can just be heard to rub when the rear wheels are turned by hand in the normal direction of rotation.

6 Loosen the adjuster nut until the wheels are just free to turn.

7 The handbrake must start to operate with the lever on the second notch of the ratchet.

8 On completion of adjustment, check the handbrake cables for free movement, and apply a little grease to the adjuster threads to prevent corrosion.

9 Where applicable, refit the exhaust heat shield.

10 Refit the roadwheels, and lower the vehicle to the ground.

Models with rear disc brakes

11 Chock the front wheels, then jack up the rear of the vehicle, and support securely on axle stands. Remove the rear roadwheels.

12 Pull the handbrake lever as far as the second notch on the ratchet.

13 On models with a catalytic converter, unscrew the securing nuts, and withdraw the exhaust centre box heat shield by carefully sliding it round the centre box.

14 Loosen the nut on the now-exposed cable adjuster.

15 Using a screwdriver inserted through the adjuster hole in one of the discs, turn the adjuster wheel until the brake shoes can just be heard to rub when the disc is turned by hand in the normal direction of rotation **(see illustration)**.

16 Turn the adjuster wheel back until the disc is just free to turn.

17 Repeat paragraphs 15 and 16 on the remaining side of the vehicle.

18 Tighten the nut on the cable adjuster until the brake shoes just begin to operate. Check that the shoes operate equally on both wheels.

21.15 Using a screwdriver to turn the handbrake adjuster wheel - models with rear disc brakes

22.8 Carpet pulled back to expose handbrake lever securing bolts (arrowed)

22.12 Driving out the handbrake lever ratchet segment securing sleeve

22.13 Drilling out the handbrake lever pawl pivot pin

19 Fully release the handbrake, then apply it again.
20 The discs must lock when the handbrake lever reaches the sixth notch on the ratchet. If necessary, turn the nut on the adjuster to achieve this.
21 Where applicable, refit the exhaust heat shield.
22 Refit the roadwheels, and lower the vehicle to the ground.

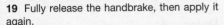

22 Handbrake lever - removal, overhaul and refitting

Note: A new self-locking nut must be used to secure the handbrake cable to the operating rod on refitting.

Removal

1 Disconnect the battery negative lead.
2 Jack up the vehicle, and support on axle stands positioned under the body side members.
3 On models with a catalytic converter, unscrew the securing nuts, and withdraw the exhaust centre box heat shield by carefully sliding it round the centre box.
4 Note the length of exposed thread on the now-exposed handbrake cable adjuster, then remove the adjuster nut to enable the cable bracket to be disconnected from the handbrake lever operating rod.
5 Disconnect the cable bracket from the operating rod, and slide the rubber sealing grommet from the underbody and the operating rod.
6 Remove the passenger's seat on right-hand-drive models, or the driver's seat on left-hand-drive models (as applicable), as described in Chapter 11. Pay particular attention to the warning given regarding the seat belt tensioner mechanism.
7 Remove the centre console, as described in Chapter 11.
8 Carefully lift up the carpet around the handbrake lever housing, to expose the two handbrake lever securing bolts **(see illustration)**. Alternatively, slits can be cut in the carpet for access to the bolts.

9 Unscrew the securing bolts, and withdraw the handbrake lever sufficiently to disconnect the handbrake 'on' warning light switch wiring.
10 Disconnect the wiring, and withdraw the handbrake lever and operating rod from the vehicle.

Overhaul

11 A worn ratchet segment can be renewed by driving the securing sleeve from the handbrake lever, using a metal rod or a bolt of diameter.
12 Drive the new sleeve supplied with the new segment into the lever to permit a little play between the segment and lever **(see illustration)**.
13 A new pawl can be fitted if the original pivot rivet is drilled out **(see illustration)**.
14 Rivet the new pawl so that it is still free to move.
15 The handbrake 'on' warning light switch can be removed from the lever assembly after unscrewing the securing bolt.

Refitting

16 Refitting is a reversal of removal, remembering the following points.
17 Refit the seat as described in Chapter 11.
18 Use a new self-locking nut to secure the handbrake cable bracket to the operating rod, and screw the nut onto the rod to the position noted before removal.
19 Before lowering the vehicle to the ground, adjust the handbrake, as described in Section 21.

23 Handbrake cables - removal and refitting

Note: A new self-locking nut must be used to secure the handbrake cable to the operating rod on refitting.

Models with rear drum brakes
Removal

1 The handbrake cable assembly consists of two cables (one running to each rear brake assembly), attached to a bracket on the

handbrake lever operating rod. The two cables cannot be removed separately, and the complete cable assembly must therefore be removed as a unit.
2 Jack up the vehicle, and support on axle stands positioned under the body side members.
3 On models with a catalytic converter, unscrew the securing nuts, and withdraw the exhaust centre box heat shield by carefully sliding it round the centre box.
4 Note the length of exposed thread on the now-exposed handbrake cable adjuster, then remove the adjuster nut to enable the cable bracket to be disconnected from the handbrake lever operating rod.
5 Disconnect the cable bracket from the operating rod.
6 Remove the brake shoes, and disconnect the handbrake cables from the shoes, as described in Section 10.
7 Using a pair of pliers, prise out the clips (one for each cable) which secure the handbrake cables to the brake backplates **(see illustration)**.
8 Detach the cables from the guides on the underbody and rear suspension. Note that the cables can be fed through certain guides, but in some cases, the guide brackets must be bent away from the underbody to allow the cable to be withdrawn.
9 Withdraw the cable assembly from the vehicle.

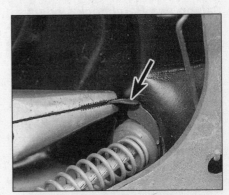

23.7 Removing a handbrake cable securing clip (arrowed) from the brake backplate - model with rear drum brakes

9

Refitting

10 Refitting is a reversal of removal, remembering the following points.

11 Ensure that the cables are routed as noted before removal.

12 Refit the brake shoes, as described in Section 10.

13 Use a new self-locking nut to secure the handbrake cable bracket to the operating rod, and screw the nut onto the rod to the position noted before removal.

14 Before refitting the roadwheels and lowering the vehicle to the ground, adjust the handbrake, as described in Section 21.

Models with rear disc brakes

Removal

15 The procedure is as described for models with rear drum brakes, remembering the following points.

16 Ignore the references to removal and refitting of the brake drum.

17 Note that there is no lockplate securing the handbrake cable to the brake backplate, but the return spring must be unhooked from the cable end.

Refitting

18 Refitting is a reversal of removal, remembering the following points.

19 Ensure that the cables are routed as noted before removal.

20 Use a new self-locking nut to secure the handbrake cable bracket to the operating rod, and screw the nut onto the rod to the position noted before removal.

21 Before refitting the roadwheels and lowering the vehicle to the ground, adjust the handbrake, as described in Section 21.

24 Rear brake pressure-regulating valve - removal, refitting and adjustment

Note: *Refer to the note at the beginning of Section 4 before proceeding. Note also that the valves must only be renewed in pairs, and both valves must be of the same calibration.*

Saloon and Hatchback models

Removal

1 Two valves are fitted, one for each hydraulic circuit, located under the rear of the vehicle **(see illustration)**.

2 Chock the front wheels, then jack up the rear of the car and support securely on axle stands.

3 Working under the bonnet, remove the brake fluid reservoir cap, and secure a piece of polythene over the filler neck with a rubber band, or by refitting the cap. This will reduce the loss of fluid during the following procedure.

4 Working under the rear of the vehicle, unscrew the union nut, and disconnect the brake pipe from one of the valves. Be

prepared for fluid spillage, and plug the open end of the pipe to prevent dirt ingress and further fluid spillage.

5 Similarly, disconnect the flexible hose from the valve.

6 Pull the valve retaining clip from the bracket on the underbody, noting that on certain models, the retaining clip also secures the ABS sensor wiring, and withdraw the valve.

7 Repeat the procedure for the remaining valve.

Refitting

8 Refitting is a reversal of removal, but on completion, remove the polythene from the brake fluid reservoir filler neck, and bleed the complete hydraulic system, as described in Section 4.

Adjustment

9 The valves are calibrated at the factory, and no adjustment is possible.

Estate and Van models

Removal

10 A single tandem valve is used, which is located under the rear of the vehicle, above the rear suspension torsion beam.

11 Proceed as described in paragraphs 2 and 3.

12 Unhook the spring from the valve operating lever.

13 Unscrew the union nuts, and disconnect the brake pipes from the valve. Be prepared for fluid spillage, and plug the open ends of the pipes to prevent dirt ingress and further fluid spillage. Note that the union nuts differ in size, to ensure correct reconnection.

14 Remove the two securing screws, and withdraw the valve from its bracket on the underbody.

15 If the valve is to be renewed, the protective shield should be removed from the old valve and transferred to the new valve. The shield is secured by a single nut.

Refitting

16 Fit the valve to the bracket on the underbody, and tighten the two securing bolts.

17 Reconnect the two brake pipes to the valve, and tighten the union nuts. Note that

24.1 Rear brake pressure-regulating valve (arrowed) - Hatchback model

the two union nuts differ in size; also take care not to overtighten the nuts.

18 Reconnect the spring to the valve operating lever.

19 Refit the roadwheels, and lower the vehicle to the ground.

20 Bleed the complete hydraulic system, as described in Section 4, then refer to Chapter 1 and adjust the valve.

Adjustment

21 Refer to Chapter 1.

25 Brake light switch - removal and refitting

Removal

1 Disconnect the battery negative lead.

2 Release the securing clips, and remove the lower trim panel from under the driver's side facia.

3 Disconnect the wiring plug from the brake light switch, then twist the switch anti-clockwise and remove it from its bracket **(see illustration)**.

4 No adjustment of the switch is possible, except by bending the bracket, which is not recommended.

Refitting

5 Refitting is a reversal of removal.

26 Braking system warning lights - general

Brake lights

1 The brake light circuit is controlled by a plunger-type switch mounted on the brake pedal bracket.

2 If the switch is thought to be faulty, it can be tested by disconnecting the wires and connecting either a multi-meter (set to the resistance function) or a battery-and-bulb test circuit, across the switch terminals. The switch should allow current to flow only when

H.22804

25.3 Twist the brake light switch anti-clockwise to remove it from its bracket

27.3 Withdrawing the plastic cover from the ABS hydraulic modulator

27.4A Removing the ABS control unit wiring plug securing screw

27.4B Disconnecting the ABS solenoid valve wiring plug

its plunger is extended. If the switch is faulty, it must be renewed.
3 Details for removal and refitting of the switch are given in Section 25.

Low fluid level warning light

4 The warning light circuit is activated by a float-type sensor attached to the brake fluid reservoir filler cap.
5 If the sensor is thought to be faulty, unscrew the filler cap, and connect the test equipment described in paragraph 2 across the sensor terminals on the cap. The sensor should allow current to flow only when the float is hanging at the bottom of its travel. If the sensor is faulty, the complete filler cap/sensor assembly must be renewed.

Handbrake 'on' warning light

6 The warning light is activated by a plunger-type switch mounted at the base of the handbrake lever.
7 The switch should illuminate whenever the handbrake is applied, and should extinguish when the handbrake is released.
8 If the switch is thought to be faulty, remove it as described in Section 22, and connect the test equipment described previously in paragraph 2. The switch should only allow current to flow only when the plunger is fully extended. If the switch is faulty, it must be renewed.

ABS warning light

9 The ABS warning light will illuminate when the ignition is first switched on, and should extinguish after a few seconds. If the warning light stays on, or comes on whilst driving, this indicates a fault in the system. The vehicle is still safe to drive (the conventional braking system will still be effective); however, at the earliest opportunity, take the vehicle to a Vauxhall dealer, and have the complete system tested using the dedicated test equipment.

Check control unit warnings

10 On models fitted with a check control system, warnings are provided to indicate front disc pad wear, and brake light bulb failure. Further details of this system can be found in Chapter 12.

27 ABS modulator - removal and refitting

Note: *Refer to the note at the beginning of Section 4 before proceeding.*

Removal

1 Disconnect the battery negative lead.
2 Remove the brake fluid reservoir cap, and secure a piece of polythene over the filler neck with a rubber band, or by refitting the cap. This will reduce the loss of fluid during the following procedure.
3 Remove the securing screw, and withdraw the plastic cover from the hydraulic modulator **(see illustration)**.
4 Disconnect the control unit wiring plug, and the solenoid valve wiring plug. Note that the control unit wiring plug is secured by a screw **(see illustrations)**.
5 Unscrew the brake fluid pipe union nuts, and disconnect the pipes from the modulator. Be prepared for fluid spillage, and plug the open ends to prevent dirt ingress and further fluid loss. Move the pipes just clear of the modulator, taking care not to strain them.
6 Unscrew the three securing nuts. Then tilt the modulator slightly, and withdraw it upwards from its bracket, sufficiently to gain access to the earth lead securing nut at the lower front edge of the modulator **(see illustrations)**.

7 Unscrew the securing nut and disconnect the earth lead, then withdraw the modulator from the vehicle, taking care not to spill brake fluid on the vehicle paintwork.
8 If a new modulator is to be fitted, pull the two relays from the top of the old modulator, and transfer them to the new unit. No attempt must be made to dismantle the modulator.

Refitting

9 Before refitting the modulator, check that the bolts securing the mounting bracket to the body panel are tight, and that the modulator rubber mountings are in good condition. Renew the rubber mountings if necessary.
10 Refitting is a reversal of removal, remembering the following points.
11 Make sure that the earth lead is reconnected before fitting the modulator to its mounting bracket.
12 On completion, remove the polythene sheet from the brake fluid reservoir filler neck, and bleed the complete hydraulic system, as described in Section 4.
13 Check that the ABS warning light extinguishes when first starting the engine after the modulator has been removed. At the earliest opportunity, take the vehicle to a Vauxhall dealer, and have the complete system tested using the dedicated test equipment.

27.6A ABS hydraulic modulator earth lead and securing nut

27.6B ABS hydraulic modulator securing nuts (arrowed)

9

28.4 ABS front wheel sensor securing bolt (arrowed)

29.4 ABS electronic control unit

1 Wiring plug   *2 Securing screws*

30.1 ABS relays (arrowed)

28 ABS front wheel sensor - removal and refitting

Note: *Refer to Chapter 10, for details of the rear wheel sensors, that are integral with the rear hub assembly.*

Removal

1 Disconnect the battery negative lead.
2 Apply the handbrake, then jack up the front of the vehicle, and support securely on axle stands.
3 Unclip the sensor wiring connector from the retaining clip under the wheel arch, then separate the two halves of the wiring connector, prising them apart with a screwdriver if necessary.
4 Using an Allen key or hexagon bit, unscrew the bolt securing the wheel sensor to the mounting bracket **(see illustration)**, then carefully lever the sensor from the bracket using a screwdriver. Recover the sealing ring.

Refitting

5 Examine the condition of the sealing ring, and renew if necessary.
6 Refitting is a reversal of removal, remembering the following points.
7 Smear a little grease on the sensor casing before fitting it to the bracket.
8 Check that the ABS warning light extinguishes when first starting the engine. At the earliest opportunity, take the vehicle to a Vauxhall dealer, and have the complete system tested using the dedicated test equipment.

29 ABS electronic control unit - removal and refitting

Note: *Refer to the precautions concerning the ABS system given in Section 2 before proceeding.*

Removal

1 Ensure that the ignition is switched off, then disconnect the battery negative lead.

2 The module is attached to the hydraulic modulator assembly in the engine compartment.
3 Remove the securing screw, and withdraw the plastic cover from the hydraulic modulator.
4 Disconnect the control unit wiring plug, and the solenoid valve wiring plug **(see illustration)**.
5 Remove the two relays from the top of the assembly.
6 Disconnect the remaining wiring plug from the control unit.
7 Unscrew the seven securing screws, and withdraw the control unit from the modulator assembly.

Refitting

8 Refitting is a reversal of removal, but take care not to overtighten the control unit securing screws.

30 ABS relays - removal and refitting

Removal

1 Two relays are used, one for the solenoid valve, and one for the pump motor; both relays are mounted on the control unit **(see illustration)**.
2 Disconnect the battery negative lead.
3 Remove the securing screw, and withdraw the plastic cover from the hydraulic modulator.
4 Pull out the appropriate relay.

Refitting

5 Refitting is a reversal of removal.
6 Check that the ABS warning light extinguishes when first starting the engine. At the earliest opportunity, take the vehicle to a Vauxhall dealer, and have the complete system tested using the dedicated test equipment.

31 Throttle housing (TC) - removal and refitting

Note: *New gaskets must be used on refitting.*

Removal

1 Disconnect the battery negative lead.
2 Remove the main throttle body, as described in Chapter 4B.
3 Disconnect the camshaft cover breather hose from the right-hand side of the TC throttle valve housing.
4 Disconnect the coolant hoses from the TC throttle valve housing, noting their locations and routing to aid correct refitting. Be prepared for coolant spillage, and clamp or plug the open ends of the hoses to minimise coolant loss.
5 Unscrew and remove the two bolts securing the throttle valve control motor to the throttle valve housing.
6 Disconnect the two vacuum hoses from the front of the throttle valve housing, noting their locations to aid refitting.
7 Disconnect the throttle valve actuating rod from the lever on the side of the throttle valve housing.
8 Lift the TC throttle valve housing from the inlet manifold. Recover the gasket.

Refitting

9 Before starting refitting, thoroughly clean the mating surfaces of the TC throttle valve housing and the inlet manifold.
10 Fit the TC throttle valve housing to the inlet manifold, using a new gasket.
11 Further refitting is a reversal of removal, remembering the following points.
12 Ensure that the coolant hoses are correctly reconnected and routed, as noted before removal.
13 When reconnecting the throttle valve actuating rod to the lever on the throttle valve housing, ensure that the retaining clip engages.
14 When reconnecting the vacuum hoses to the throttle valve housing, ensure that they are correctly positioned as noted previously.

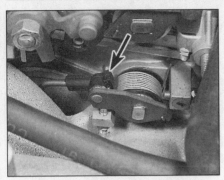

32.7 Throttle valve operating rod connection (arrowed) to TC throttle valve

15 Refit the main throttle body, using a new gasket, as described in Chapter 4B.
16 On completion, check the coolant level and top-up if necessary, as described in Chapter 3.

32 Throttle valve control motor (TC) - removal and refitting

Removal

1 Disconnect the battery negative lead.
2 Remove the airbox from the top of the throttle body, as described in Chapter 4B.
3 Disconnect the crankcase ventilation hose from the main throttle body.
4 Loosen the alternator mounting bolts, then remove the top mounting bolt, slip the drivebelt from the alternator pulley, and swing the alternator to one side, away from the engine.
5 Unscrew the two securing screws, and detach the throttle cable bracket from the inlet manifold.
6 Disconnect the throttle valve control motor wiring plug, which is accessible from the alternator side of the throttle housing.
7 Disconnect the TC throttle valve operating rod from the throttle valve **(see illustration)**.
8 Unscrew and remove the two bolts securing the throttle valve control motor to the TC throttle valve housing, then carefully withdraw the motor assembly **(see illustration)**.
9 If the throttle valve operating rod is disconnected from the motor, take careful note of the orientation of the rod, to enable correct refitting **(see illustration)**.

Refitting

10 Refitting is a reversal of removal, remembering the following points.
11 Where applicable, ensure that the throttle

32.8 TC throttle valve control motor

1 Securing screws
2 Throttle cable bracket

valve operating rod is correctly orientated, as noted before removal.
12 Before tightening the alternator mounting bolts, tension the drivebelt as described in Chapter 5.
13 Refit the airbox as described in Chapter 4B.

33 Control unit (TC) - removal and refitting

Removal

1 The TC control unit is located inside the vehicle, next to the left-hand front seat, beneath a cover in the sill.
2 Ensure that the ignition is switched off, then disconnect the battery negative lead.
3 Prise up the two flaps that conceal the control unit cover securing nuts, then remove the securing nuts **(see illustration)**.
4 Carefully withdraw the control unit cover, noting that it clips into the seat runner cover panel.

33.3 TC electronic control unit cover securing nuts

32.9 TC throttle valve control motor assembly

5 Pull the control unit from its location, then remove the wiring plug securing screw, release the clips to disconnect the wiring plug, and withdraw the unit **(see illustration)**.

Refitting

6 Refitting is a reversal of removal, ensuring that the cover engages correctly with the seat runner cover panel.

34 Manual override switch (TC) - removal and refitting

Removal

1 The switch is located in the centre console.
2 Disconnect the battery negative lead.
3 Carefully prise the central storage tray from the centre console.
4 Disconnect the wiring from the switch.
5 Carefully push the switch out through the top of the centre console.

Refitting

6 Refitting is a reversal of removal.

33.5 Withdrawing the TC electronic control unit

9

Notes

Chapter 10
Suspension and steering

Contents

Degrees of difficulty

| Easy, suitable for novice with little experience | | Fairly easy, suitable for beginner with some experience | | Fairly difficult, suitable for competent DIY mechanic | | Difficult, suitable for experienced DIY mechanic | | Very difficult, suitable for expert DIY or professional | |

Specifications

Front suspension
Type .... Independent, with MacPherson struts and anti-roll bar

Rear suspension
Type .... Semi-independent torsion beam, with trailing arms, coil springs and telescopic shock absorbers. Anti-roll bar on certain models. Twin anti-roll bars on DOHC models. Manual level control system standard on certain models, optional on others
Rear wheel toe setting (not adjustable) .... 10' toe-out to 40' toe-in
Rear wheel camber angle (not adjustable) .... 2°10' negative to 1°10' negative

Roadwheels
Type .... Steel or alloy
Size .... 5½J x 13, 5½J x 14 or 6J x 15

Tyres
Size:
   5½J x 13 wheels .... 155 R13 78S/T or 175/70 R13 82T/H
   5½J x 14 wheels .... 175/65 R14 82T/H, 175/70 R14 84T, 185/60 R14 82 H, 185/60 R14 82T/H or 195/60 R14 85H/V *
   6J x 15 wheels .... 195/55 R15 84 H/V or 205/50 R15 85V
* Only permissible for use with Vauxhall snow chains
Tyre pressures .... Refer to 'Weekly Checks'

10

Steering

Type
All models . . . .   Rack-and-pinion. Power assistance standard on certain models, optional on others

Turns lock-to-lock
Manual steering 4.11
Power steering 3.43

Camber angle (laden * - not adjustable)
All models . . . .   1°50' negative to 0°20' negative

Maximum camber variation between sides
All models . . . .   1° 00'

Castor angle (laden * not adjustable)
Saloon and Hatchback models . . . .   1°15' positive to 3°15' positive
Estate and Van models . . . .   0°30' positive to 2°30' positive

Maximum castor variation between sides
All models   10

Toe setting
All models . . . .   0° 25' toe-out to 0° 5' toe-out

For the purposes of these figures, a vehicle is considered to be 'laden' when it has a load equivalent to 70.0 kg in each front seat.

Torque wrench settings

	Nm	lbf ft
Front suspension		
Anti-roll bar-to-lower arm locknuts *	20	15
Anti-roll bar-to-subframe bolts	20	15
Balljoint-to-lower arm nuts	60	44
Front hub nut (refer to text): *		
Stage 1	100	74
Stage 2	Loosen nut fully	
Stage 3	20	15
Stage 4	Angle-tighten by a further 80° (plus another 9° if necessary)	
Lower arm damper weight bolts (where applicable)	20	15
Lower arm-to-front subframe (horizontal) pivot bolt	110	81
Lower arm-to-suspension strut balljoint nut *	70	52
Suspension strut piston rod nut	55	
Suspension strut ring nut	200	148
Suspension strut upper mounting nuts	30	22
Subframe-to-underbody bolts: *		
Front bolts (not applicable to certain early left-hand-drive models - refer to text)	115	85
Centre bolts (front bolts on early left-hand-drive models - refer to text)	170	125
Rear bolts:		
Stage 1	100	74
Stage 2	Angle-tighten by a further 75°	
Stage 3	Angle-tighten by a further 15°	
Rear suspension		
Additional anti-roll bar securing bolts (if fitted): *		
Stage 1	60	44
Stage 2	Angle-tighten a further 60°	
Stage 3	Angle-tighten a further 15°	
Main anti-roll bar securing bolts: *		
Stage 1	30	22
Stage 2	Angle-tighten a further 30°	
Stage 3	Angle-tighten a further 15°	
Rear hub unit securing nuts (refer to text): *		
Stage 1	50	37
Stage 2	Angle-tighten by a further 30°	
Stage 3	Angle-tighten by a further 15°	
Shock absorber lower mounting bolt (Saloon and Hatchback models)	70	52
Shock absorber lower mounting nut (Estate and Van models)	12	9
Shock absorber top mounting nut (Saloon and Hatchback models)	20	15
Shock absorber upper mounting bolt	70	52
Trailing arm-to-underbody fixings	105	77

Steering	Nm	lbf ft
Power steering fluid pipe unions	28	21
Power steering pump mounting bolts:		
SOHC models:		
with V-belts	30	22
with ribbed V-belts	20	15
DOHC models:		
with V-belts	30	22
Bolts 'A' and 'C' (refer to text)	25	18
Bolt 'B' (refer to text)	40	30
with ribbed V-belts	20	15
Bolts 'A' and 'C' (refer to text)	25	18
Bolt 'B' (refer to text)	18	13
Power steering pump pulley bolts (1.4 and 1.6 litre, V-belt models) . . .	25	18
Steering column fixings	22	16
Steering gear damper adjuster locknut	60	44
Steering gear pinion nut	40	30
Steering gear pinion-to-rubber coupling pinch-bolt	22	16
Steering gear-to-bulkhead fixings	22	16
Steering shaft-to-rubber coupling pinch-bolt	22	16
Steering wheel retaining nut	25	18
Tie-rod end clamp bolts	20	15
Tie-rod-to-steering gear bolts	95	70
Tie-rod end-to-suspension strut balljoint nut	60	44
Roadwheels		
Roadwheel bolts	110	81

* Use new bolts/nuts, as applicable.

1 System description - general

1 The front suspension consists of MacPherson struts, lower arms, and an anti-roll bar. The lower arms and the anti-roll bar are mounted on a detachable U-shaped front subframe, which also carries the rear engine/transmission mounting **(see illustration)**.

2 Each lower arm is attached to the subframe by a horizontal front bush and a vertical rear bush.

3 The hub carriers are mounted between the lower ends of the MacPherson struts and the lower arms, and carry the double-row ball type wheel bearings and the brake assemblies.

4 The rear suspension is of semi-independent type, consisting of a torsion beam and trailing arms, with double-conical coil springs and telescopic shock absorbers, and (on certain models) an anti-roll bar. The front ends of the trailing arms are attached to the vehicle underbody by horizontal bushes, and the rear ends are located by the shock absorbers, which are bolted to the underbody at their upper ends. The coil springs are mounted independently of the shock absorbers, and act directly between the trailing arms and the underbody. Certain models are fitted with an anti-roll bar, which is mounted between the torsion beam and the trailing arms. DOHC models are fitted with twin rear anti-roll bars. On all models, each rear wheel bearing, hub

1.1 Front suspension layout

A Early left-hand-drive models (see Section 10)
B Later left-hand-drive and all right-hand-drive models

10

1.4A Rear suspension layout - Saloon and Hatchback models with rear disc brakes

1.4B Rear suspension layout - Estate and Van models with rear drum brakes

and stub axle assembly is manufactured as a sealed unit, which cannot be dismantled **(see illustrations)**.

5 From 1995 on, all models were fitted with gas filled shock absorbers.

6 A manual rear suspension level control system is available on Estate and Van models. The system operates using compressed air-filled shock absorbers. The rear suspension level is adjusted by altering the air pressure in the shock absorbers, through a valve located in the luggage compartment.

7 The steering gear is of rack-and-pinion type. Movement is transmitted to the front wheels through tie-rods, which are connected to the rack through a sliding sleeve at their inner ends, and to the suspension struts through balljoints at their outer ends.

8 The steering column consists of an outer column that incorporates a collapsible section, and a shaft connected to a flexible coupling at its lower end.

9 Power steering is fitted as standard to certain models, and is available as an option on others. The power steering is hydraulically operated, and pressure is supplied by a fluid pump driven by way of a drivebelt from the engine crankshaft. On 1.8 and 2.0 litre models, fluid cooler pipes are mounted

beneath the radiator to keep the temperature of the hydraulic fluid within operating limits.

10 Refer to Chapter 1, for routine checking procedures.

2 Front suspension strut - removal and refitting

Note: *A balljoint separator tool will be required during this procedure. The tie-rod end balljoint nut, lower arm-to-suspension strut balljoint nut locking pin, and the hub nut, washer and split pin, must be renewed on refitting.*

Removal

1 Apply the handbrake, then jack up the front of the vehicle and support securely on axle stands. Remove the relevant roadwheel.

2 Where applicable, remove the ABS wheel sensor from the hub carrier, referring to Chapter 9 if necessary, and disconnect the wiring from the strut.

3 Remove the brake caliper from the hub carrier, as described in Chapter 9. The caliper can be suspended out of the way, using wire or string, to avoid the need to disconnect the hydraulic fluid hose.

4 Unscrew and remove the self-locking nut from the tie-rod end-to-suspension strut balljoint.

5 Using a balljoint separator tool, disconnect the tie-rod end-to-suspension strut balljoint.

6 Extract the split pin from the castellated hub nut on the end of the driveshaft.

7 The hub nut must now be loosened. The nut is extremely tight, and an extension bar will be required to loosen it. To prevent the driveshaft from turning, insert two roadwheel bolts, and insert a metal bar between them to counterhold the hub.

8 Remove the hub nut and washer from the driveshaft.

9 Extract the locking pin, then unscrew the castellated nut from the lower arm-to-suspension strut balljoint.

10 Using a balljoint separator tool, disconnect the lower arm-to-suspension strut balljoint.

11 Withdraw the outer end of the driveshaft from the hub. It should be possible to pull the driveshaft from the hub by hand, but if necessary tap the end of the shaft with a soft-faced mallet to release it. **Do not** *use heavy blows, as damage to the driveshaft joints may result.* Support the driveshaft by suspending it with wire or string - **do not** allow the driveshaft to hang down under its own weight.

12 Working in the engine compartment, unscrew the two nuts securing the suspension strut to the suspension turret **(see illustration)**. Support the suspension strut as the nuts are unscrewed, as once the nuts have been removed, the strut is free to drop from the vehicle.

13 Withdraw the suspension strut/hub carrier assembly from the vehicle **(see illustration)**.

Refitting

14 Locate the top end of the strut in the suspension turret, then refit the securing nuts and tighten them to the specified torque.

15 Apply a little molybdenum disulphide

2.12 Suspension strut securing nuts (arrowed)

2.13 Withdrawing the suspension strut/hub carrier assembly

grease to the driveshaft splines, then insert the outer end of the shaft into the hub. Fit a new washer, and screw on a new hub nut finger-tight.

16 Reconnect the lower arm-to-suspension strut balljoint, then fit the castellated nut, and tighten to the specified torque. Secure the nut with a new locking pin.

17 Tighten the new hub nut to the specified torque, in the stages given in the Specifications. Prevent the driveshaft from turning as during removal. If the holes in the driveshaft for the split pin do not line up with any of the slots in the nut, tighten the nut a further 9∞ (no more), until the holes line up with the nearest slots to enable the split pin to be fitted. Use a new split pin, bending over the ends of the pin to secure it.

18 Reconnect the tie-rod balljoint to the suspension strut, and tighten a new self-locking nut to the specified torque.

19 Refit the brake caliper to the hub carrier, as described in Chapter 9.

20 Where applicable, refit the ABS wheel sensor to the hub carrier, referring to Chapter 9 if necessary, and reconnect the wiring to the strut.

21 Refit the roadwheel, and lower the vehicle to the ground.

22 On completion, check and if necessary adjust the front wheel alignment, as described in Section 35.

3 Front suspension strut - overhaul

Note: *A spring compressor tool will be required for this operation.*

1 With the strut removed as described in Section 2, continue as follows.

2 The hub, wheel bearing and brake disc shield can be removed, as described in Section 4.

3 With the suspension strut resting on a bench or clamped in a vice, fit a spring compressor tool, and compress the coil spring to relieve the pressure on the upper spring seat. Ensure that the compressor tool

3.3 Vauxhall spring compressor tool components in position on front suspension strut

is securely located on the spring according to the tool manufacturer's instructions (see illustration).

4 Prise out the plastic cover from the top of the strut.

5 Hold the strut piston rod with a socket, and unscrew the piston rod nut.

6 Lift off the strut upper mounting rubber and the bearing.

7 Lift off the upper spring seat and damper ring, then carefully release the spring compressor and remove the spring. Note which way round the spring is fitted.

8 Slide the bellows, and the rubber buffer that fits inside the bellows, from the strut.

9 To remove the shock absorber cartridge, the ring nut must be unscrewed from the top of the strut tube. This nut is extremely tight. One method that can be used to unscrew the nut is to invert the strut and clamp the nut in a vice. Then lever the strut round using a long bar and a bolt passed through the tie-rod bracket (see illustrations).

10 With the ring nut removed, the shock absorber cartridge can be withdrawn (see illustration).

11 The shock absorber can be tested by clamping the lower end in a vice, then fully extending and contracting the shock absorber several times. Any evidence of jerky movement or lack of resistance indicates the need for renewal.

12 Examine all components for wear or damage, and renew as necessary. Pay

3.9A One method of unscrewing the suspension strut ring nut

particular attention to the mounting rubber and the bearing (see illustration).

13 Begin reassembly by sliding the shock absorber cartridge into the strut and refitting the ring nut. Do not remove the wax coating from the nut.

14 Clamp the strut in a vice, and tighten the ring nut to the specified torque, using a large long-reach socket.

15 Refit and compress the coil spring, ensuring that the lower end of the spring rests against the lug on the lower spring seat.

16 Refit the rubber buffer and the bellows.

17 Refit the upper spring seat and the damper ring.

18 Lubricate the bearing with a little grease, then refit it with the visible part of the bearing race uppermost.

19 Refit the strut upper mounting rubber.

20 Counterhold the strut piston rod, and tighten the piston rod nut to the specified torque. This can be achieved by holding the piston rod using a splined key fitted to a torque wrench, and tightening the nut using a spanner until the specified torque is reached.

21 Carefully release and remove the spring compressor tool, ensuring that the spring

3.12 Front suspension strut components

1 *Upper mounting rubber assembly*
2 *Bearing*
3 *Upper spring seat and damper ring*
4 *Bellows and rubber buffer*
5 *Spring*
6 *Lower spring seat*

3.9B Removing the ring nut . . .

3.10 . . . and withdrawing the shock absorber cartridge

4.3 Pressing the front hub from the wheel bearing

4.4 Removing the half inner bearing race from the hub

4.5 Removing a brake disc shield securing screw

seats correctly at top and bottom. Ensure that the lower end of the spring still rests against the lug on the lower spring seat.

22 Refit the strut, as described in Section 2.

4 Front hub bearing - removal and refitting

Note: *The bearing will probably be destroyed during the removal operation. The use of a puller will greatly ease the procedure.*

4.6A Extracting the outer bearing retaining circlip

4.6B Cross-sectional view of front wheel bearing/hub assembly

A Outer bearing retaining circlip
B Inner bearing retaining circlip

Removal

1 Remove the relevant suspension strut/hub carrier assembly, as described in Section 2.

2 Unscrew the securing screw, and remove the brake disc from the hub.

3 Support the hub carrier on two metal bars positioned as shown (see illustration). Then, using a metal bar, press or drive the hub from the wheel bearing. Alternatively, screw two roadwheel bolts into the hub and, using progressively thicker packing pieces, tighten the bolts to force the hub from the bearing. Note that one half of the inner bearing race will remain on the hub .

4 Using a puller, pull the half inner bearing race from the hub (see illustration). Alternatively, support the bearing race on thin metal bars, and press or drive the hub from the bearing race.

5 Remove the three securing screws (see illustration), and lift the brake disc shield from the hub carrier.

6 Extract the inner and outer bearing retaining circlips (see illustrations).

7 Using a puller, pull the bearing from the hub carrier, applying pressure to the outer race. Alternatively, support the hub carrier, and press or drive out the bearing.

Refitting

8 Before installing the new bearing, thoroughly clean the bearing location in the hub carrier, and fit the outer bearing retaining circlip 'A' (see illustration 4.6B). Note that

the circlip tabs should be positioned towards the bottom of the hub carrier.

9 Press or drive the new bearing into position until it contacts the outer circlip, applying pressure to the outer race (see illustration).

10 Fit the inner bearing retaining circlip, with the tabs positioned towards the bottom of the hub carrier.

11 Fit the brake disc shield.

12 Press or draw the hub into the bearing. The bearing inner track **must** be supported during this operation. This can be achieved using a socket, long bolt, washer, and a length of bar as shown (see illustration).

13 Refit the brake disc.

14 Refit the suspension strut/hub carrier assembly, as described in Section 2.

5 Front suspension lower arm - removal and refitting

Note: *A balljoint separator tool will be required for this operation. The lower arm rear pivot bolt, lower arm-to-suspension strut balljoint nut locking pin, and anti-roll bar-to-lower arm securing nuts and locknuts must be renewed on refitting.*

Removal

1 Apply the handbrake, then jack up the front of the vehicle, and support securely on axle stands. Remove the relevant roadwheel.

4.9 Fitting a new front wheel bearing using a socket, nut, bolt, washers, and a length of bar

4.12 Drawing the hub into the bearing using improvised tools

5.5 Lower arm front pivot bolt (arrowed)

2 Unscrew and discard the nuts securing the end of the anti-roll bar to the lower arm. Note that the nut that rests against the dished washer is a conventional nut, and the second nut is a locknut. Recover the dished washers and the mounting rubbers.

3 Extract the locking pin, then unscrew the castellated nut from the lower arm-to-suspension strut balljoint.

4 Using a balljoint separator tool, disconnect the lower arm-to-suspension strut balljoint.

5 Unscrew and remove the two pivot bolts securing the lower arm to the subframe **(see illustration)**. Note that the rear pivot bolt also secures the subframe to the underbody. Both bolts are very tight, and an extension bar will probably be required to loosen them.

6 Pull the lower arm from the subframe, and withdraw it from the vehicle.

Refitting

7 Note that on certain models, a damper weight may be bolted to the right-hand lower arm. If the right-hand lower arm is to be renewed on such a vehicle, it is important to ensure that the damper weight is transferred to the new arm.

8 Note that the metal sleeves in the rear mounting bush can be discarded when refitting the lower arm.

9 Begin refitting by pushing the lower arm into position in the subframe.

10 Fit the two pivot bolts, then hold the lower arm in a horizontal position, and tighten the bolts to the specified torque. Note that a new rear pivot bolt must be used, and the new bolt must be tightened to the specified torque in the three stages given in the Specifications.

11 Reconnect the lower arm-to-suspension strut balljoint, and tighten the castellated nut to the specified torque. Secure the nut with a new locking pin.

12 Reconnect the end of the anti-roll bar to the lower arm, noting that the dished washers that retain the mounting rubbers should be fitted with their concave sides facing towards the lower arm.

13 Fit a new anti-roll bar-to-lower arm securing nut, and tighten it to give the specified rubber bush compression shown **(see illustration)**. If necessary, renew the rubber bushes.

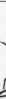

5.13 Front anti-roll bar rubber bush compression (1) should be 38.0 to 39.0 mm

14 Fit a new anti-roll bar-to-lower arm locknut, and tighten it to the specified torque.

15 Refit the roadwheel and lower the vehicle to the ground.

16 On completion, check and if necessary adjust the front wheel alignment, as described in Section 35.

6 Front suspension lower arm bushes - removal and refitting

Removal

1 Remove the lower arm, as described in Section 5.

2 The bushes are a tight fit in the lower arm, and must be pressed out.

3 If a press is not available, the bushes can be drawn out using a long bolt, nut, washers and a socket or length of metal tubing.

4 The vertical bush should be pressed out through the top of the lower arm, from below, and the horizontal bush should pressed out towards the front of the lower arm, from the rear.

Refitting

5 Lubricate the new bushes using soapy water, then fit them to the lower arm, using the method described in paragraph 3.

6 The new vertical bush should be pressed into the lower arm from below, and the new horizontal bush should be pressed into the lower arm from front to rear. The horizontal bush should project from the lower arm equally at both ends.

7 Refit the lower arm, as described in Section 5.

7 Front suspension lower arm balljoint - removal and refitting

Note: *Three special bolts, spring washers and nuts (available from Vauxhall dealers) will be required when fitting the new balljoint.*

Removal

1 Remove the lower arm, as described in Section 5.

2 Mount the lower arm in a vice, then drill the heads from the three rivets that secure the balljoint to the lower arm, using a 12.0 mm diameter drill.

3 If necessary, tap the rivets from the lower arm, then remove the balljoint.

Refitting

4 The new balljoint should be fitted using three special bolts, spring washers and nuts, available from a Vauxhall parts centre.

5 Ensure that the balljoint is fitted the correct way up, noting that the securing nuts should be positioned on the underside of the lower arm.

6 Tighten the balljoint-to-lower arm nuts to the specified torque.

7 Refit the lower arm, as described in Section 5.

8 Front anti-roll bar - removal and refitting

Note: *A hoist or similar lifting equipment will be required to support the engine during this procedure. The rear subframe securing bolts, and the anti-roll bar-to-lower arm securing nuts and locknuts, must be renewed on refitting.*

Removal

1 Before removing the anti-roll bar, the engine must be supported from its left-hand lifting bracket. Ideally, the engine should be supported using a strong wooden or metal beam resting on blocks positioned securely in the channels at the sides of the engine compartment. The Vauxhall special tool designed specifically for this purpose is shown Chapter 7A or 7B. Alternatively, the engine can be supported using a hoist and lifting tackle. However, in this case, the hoist must be of such a design as to enable the engine to be supported with the vehicle raised off the ground, leaving sufficient clearance to lower the front subframe.

2 Apply the handbrake, then jack up the front of the vehicle, and support securely on axle stands. Remove the front roadwheels.

3 If fitted, remove the engine undershield, as described in Chapter 11.

4 For improved access, remove the front section of the exhaust system, as described in Chapter 4C.

10

8.5 Front anti-roll bar-to-lower arm securing nuts (arrowed)

5 Working under the vehicle, unscrew and remove the nuts securing the ends of the anti-roll bar to the lower arms. Recover the dished washers and mounting rubbers **(see illustration)**.

6 Ensure that the engine is adequately supported, then unscrew and remove the two nuts and washers securing the engine/transmission rear mounting to the subframe.

7 Support the subframe on a trolley jack, with an interposed wooden beam to spread the load.

8 Unscrew and remove the two rear and two centre bolts securing the subframe to the vehicle underbody. Note that the rear bolts also secure the lower arms to the subframe. The bolts are very tight, and an extension bar will probably be required to loosen them. On certain early left-hand-drive models, a short front subframe was used, which was secured by four bolts instead of six. On these models, remove all four subframe securing bolts, and lower the complete subframe from the vehicle.

9 Loosen, but do not remove, the two front subframe-to-underbody securing bolts (not applicable to certain early left-hand-drive models - see paragraph 8).

10 Carefully lower the subframe until the anti-roll bar-to-subframe bolts are accessible, then unscrew and remove the bolts.

11 Lift the anti-roll bar from the subframe and the lower arms, and withdraw it from the vehicle.

Refitting

12 The anti-roll bar mounting bushes can be renewed, as described in Section 9.

13 Refitting is a reversal of removal, remembering the following points.

14 When refitting the subframe to the underbody, use new rear securing bolts, and tighten them to the specified torque in the three stages given in the Specifications.

15 Reconnect the ends of the anti-roll bar to the lower arms, noting that the dished washers that retain the mounting rubbers should be fitted with their concave sides facing towards the lower arm.

16 Fit new anti-roll bar-to-lower arm securing nuts, and tighten them to give the specified rubber bush compression as described in

paragraph 13 of Section 5. If necessary, renew the rubber bushes.

17 Fit new anti-roll bar-to-lower arm locknuts, and tighten them to the specified torque.

18 Tighten all nuts and bolts to the specified torques.

19 Where applicable, refit the front section of the exhaust system, referring to Chapter 4C.

9 Front anti-roll bar bushes - removal and refitting

Note: *The use of a balljoint separator tool will greatly ease this procedure.*

Removal

1 Remove the anti-roll bar, as described in Section 8.

2 If an anti-roll bar end link bush (between the end link and the anti-roll bar) requires renewal, the complete end link must be renewed.

3 To remove an end link, mount the anti-roll bar in a vice, then, using a balljoint separator tool and progressively thicker packing pieces, remove the end link from the end of the anti-roll bar. Alternatively, the end link can be removed by driving it from the anti-roll bar using light hammer blows on a drift, although this is likely to cause damage to the end link unless carried out with extreme care.

4 If necessary, repeat the procedure on the remaining end link.

5 With either end link removed, the anti-roll bar-to-subframe mounting bushes can be renewed, by sliding the bushes along the bar and manipulating them until they can be withdrawn from the end of the bar. Fit the new bushes in a similar way.

6 Press or drive the end link(s) onto the anti-roll bar, to the position shown **(see illustration)**. Use a metal tube or socket to avoid damage to the end link(s).

9.6 Correct position of end link on front anti-roll bar

Dimensions in mm

Refitting

7 Before refitting the anti-roll bar, examine the anti-roll bar-to-lower arm bushes, and renew if necessary.

8 Refit the anti-roll bar, as described in Section 8.

10 Front suspension subframe - removal and refitting

Note: *A hoist or similar lifting equipment will be required to support the engine during this procedure; a balljoint separator tool will also be required. The subframe securing bolts, and the lower arm-to-suspension strut balljoint nut locking pins, must be renewed on refitting.*

Removal

1 The subframe is removed complete with the lower arms and the anti-roll bar, as an assembly.

2 Before removing the subframe, the engine must be supported from its left-hand lifting bracket. Ideally, the engine should be supported using a strong wooden or metal beam resting on blocks positioned securely in the channels at the sides of the engine compartment. The Vauxhall special tool designed specifically for this purpose is shown in Chapter 7A. Alternatively, the engine can be supported using a hoist and lifting tackle. However, in this case, the hoist must be of such a design as to enable the engine to be supported with the vehicle raised off the ground, leaving sufficient clearance to withdraw the subframe from under the front of the vehicle.

3 Apply the handbrake, then jack up the front of the vehicle and support securely on axle stands. Remove the front roadwheels.

4 If fitted, remove the engine undershield, as described in Chapter 11.

5 Remove the front section of the exhaust system, referring to Chapter 4C. Where applicable, unbolt the oil cooler hose bracket from the right-hand side of the subframe.

6 Working on one side of the vehicle, extract the locking pin, then unscrew the castellated nut from the lower arm-to-suspension strut balljoint.

7 Using a balljoint separator tool, disconnect the lower arm-to-suspension strut balljoint.

8 Repeat paragraphs 6 and 7 for the remaining lower arm.

9 Ensure that the engine is adequately supported, then unscrew and remove the two nuts and washers securing the rear engine/transmission mounting to the subframe.

10 Support the subframe on a trolley jack, with an interposed wooden beam to prevent the subframe from tipping as it is withdrawn.

11 Unscrew and remove the six bolts securing the subframe to the vehicle underbody. *Note that on certain early left-*

10.11A Front subframe front securing bolt (arrowed)

10.11B Front subframe centre and rear securing bolts (arrowed)

11.6A Rear hub securing nuts (arrowed) - model with rear drum brakes

hand-drive models, a short front subframe was used, which was secured by four bolts instead of six. On these models, remove all four subframe securing bolts. Note that the rear bolts also secure the lower arms to the subframe **(see illustrations)**. The bolts are very tight, and an extension bar will probably be required to loosen them.

12 Lower the jack supporting the subframe, and withdraw the assembly from under the front of the vehicle.

13 The anti-roll bar and/or the lower arms can be removed from the subframe, referring to Section 8 and/or Section 5, as applicable.

Refitting

14 Refitting is a reversal of removal, remembering the following points.

15 If the anti-roll bar and/or the lower arms have been removed from the subframe, refit them referring to Sections 8 and/or Section 5, as applicable.

16 Fit new subframe securing bolts, and tighten them to the specified torque given in the Specifications. Note that the rear subframe/lower arm securing bolts must be tightened in three stages.

17 Secure the lower arm-to-suspension strut balljoint nuts with new locking pins.

18 Refit the front section of the exhaust system, referring to Chapter 4C and, where applicable, refit the oil cooler bracket to the subframe, followed by the engine undershield.

11 Rear hub -
removal and refitting

Note: The hub unit securing nuts must be renewed on refitting.

Removal

1 Chock the front wheels, then jack up the rear of the vehicle and support securely on axle stands. Remove the relevant roadwheel.

2 On models with rear drum brakes, remove the brake drum, as described in Chapter 9.

3 On models with rear disc brakes, remove the brake caliper and the brake disc, as described in Chapter 9. The caliper can be suspended out of the way, using wire or string, to avoid the need to disconnect the hydraulic fluid pipe.

4 On models with rear disc brakes, disconnect the return spring from the handbrake shoe lever and the brake backplate.

5 On models with ABS, disconnect the ABS sensor wiring plug at the rear of the hub assembly.

6 Unscrew the four securing nuts, and

withdraw the hub assembly **(see illustrations)**. On models with rear disc brakes, the hub assembly can be withdrawn complete with the brake backplate, in which case, detach the handbrake cable from the handbrake shoe lever as the hub assembly is withdrawn. On models with rear drum brakes, the brake backplate can be left attached to the rear suspension torsion beam.

Refitting

7 Refitting is a reversal of removal, remembering the following points.

8 New hub unit securing nuts must be used, and they must be tightened in the three stages given in the Specifications. Note that a socket extension and a universal joint may be required, to enable the use of an angle gauge **(see illustration)**.

9 On models with rear disc brakes, where applicable, make sure that the handbrake cable and the return spring are correctly reconnected.

10 On models with rear disc brakes, refit the brake disc and the brake caliper as described in Chapter 9.

11 On models with rear drum brakes, refit the brake drum as described in Chapter 9.

12 Before refitting the roadwheel and lowering the vehicle to the ground, check the handbrake cable adjustment, as described in Chapter 9.

11.6B Removing a rear hub - model with rear drum brakes

11.6C Sectional view of rear hub assembly

1	Hub	5	Bearings
2	Stub axle	6	Oil seal
3	Threaded bolt		
4	Dust cap with integral ABS wheel sensor		

11.8 Tightening a rear hub nut using an angle gauge

10

12.2 Unscrewing a rear shock absorber top mounting nut while counter-holding the piston rod - Hatchback model

12.4 Rear shock absorber lower securing bolt - Hatchback model

12.14 Rear shock absorber mountings - Estate and Van models

1 Lower mounting
2 Upper mounting

12 Rear shock absorber - removal, inspection and refitting

Note: *Only one shock absorber should be removed at a time. Shock absorbers should be renewed in pairs.*

Saloon and Hatchback models

Removal

1 Working in the luggage compartment, pull the plastic cover from the shock absorber top mounting.
2 Counterhold the shock absorber piston rod, and unscrew the shock absorber top mounting nut **(see illustration)**. Remove the washer and the upper mounting rubber.
3 For improved access, drive the rear of the vehicle up onto ramps, and chock the front wheels. Alternatively, chock the front wheels, then jack up the rear of the vehicle, and support securely on axle stands. If the vehicle is jacked up, the relevant trailing arm **must be** supported with a jack as the vehicle is raised, to prevent the trailing arm being forced down by the coil spring.
4 Unscrew and remove the bolt securing the lower end of the shock absorber to the trailing arm **(see illustration)**.
5 Compress the shock absorber by hand, if necessary prising the lower end to free it from the trailing arm.
6 Withdraw the shock absorber from under the vehicle, and recover the remaining mounting rubber and the spacer sleeve from the top of the shock absorber.

Inspection

7 Examine the shock absorber mounting rubbers for wear or damage, and renew if necessary.
8 The shock absorber can be tested by clamping the lower mounting eye in a vice, then fully extending and compressing the shock absorber several times. Any evidence of jerky movement or lack of resistance indicates the need for renewal.

Refitting

9 Refitting is a reversal of removal, but tighten the shock absorber lower mounting bolt to the specified torque.

Estate and Van models

Removal

10 On models with manual rear suspension level control, depressurise the system by releasing the air through the valve in the luggage compartment.
11 Proceed as described in paragraph 3.
12 Where applicable, disconnect the manual suspension level control air line from the shock absorber.
13 Counterhold the shock absorber piston rod, and unscrew the shock absorber lower mounting nut from the trailing arm. Remove the washer and the upper mounting rubber.
14 Unscrew and remove the bolt securing the upper end of the shock absorber to the vehicle underbody **(see illustration)**.
15 Compress the shock absorber by hand, if necessary prising the upper end to free it from the body.
16 Withdraw the shock absorber from under the vehicle, and recover the remaining mounting rubber and the spacer sleeve from the lower end of the shock absorber.

Inspection

17 Proceed as described in paragraphs 7 and 8, but clamp the upper mounting eye in the vice when testing the shock absorber.

Refitting

18 Refitting is a reversal of removal, remembering the following points.
19 Where applicable, ensure that the shock absorber is fitted with the air line union facing the correct way round.
20 Tighten the shock absorber upper mounting bolt to the specified torque.
21 On models with manual rear suspension level control, pressurise the system to 0.8 bars, and check for air leaks.

13 Rear shock absorber mounting rubbers - removal and refitting

Note: *Only one shock absorber should be disconnected at a time.*

Saloon and Hatchback models

Removal

1 The mounting bush in the shock absorber lower eye is not available separately, and if worn or damaged, the complete shock absorber must be renewed.
2 The shock absorber upper mounting rubbers can be renewed without removing the shock absorber as follows.
3 Proceed as described in Section 12, paragraphs 1 and 2.
4 With the roadwheels resting on the ground, jack up the rear of the vehicle slightly, to enable the shock absorber to be compressed sufficiently by hand to release the top mounting from the body.
5 Remove the remaining mounting rubber from the top of the shock absorber.

Refitting

6 Fit the new mounting rubbers using a reversal of the removal procedure.

Estate and Van models

Removal

7 The mounting bush in the shock absorber upper eye is not available separately, and if worn or damaged, the complete shock absorber must be renewed.
8 The shock absorber lower mounting rubbers can be renewed without removing the shock absorber as follows.
9 On models with manual rear suspension level control, depressurise the system by releasing the air through the valve in the luggage compartment.
10 Counterhold the shock absorber piston rod, and unscrew the shock absorber lower

mounting nut from the trailing arm. Remove the washer and mounting rubber.
11 Compress the shock absorber by hand sufficiently to release the lower end from the trailing arm.
12 Remove the remaining mounting rubber and the spacer sleeve from the lower end of the shock absorber.

Refitting

13 Fit the new mounting rubbers using a reversal of the removal procedure.
14 On models with manual rear suspension level control, pressurise the system to 0.8 bars on completion.

14 Rear suspension coil spring - removal and refitting
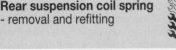

Note: *Due to the design of the rear suspension, it is important to note that only one coil spring should be removed at a time. Note that the rear springs should be renewed in pairs, and if the springs are to be renewed, it is advisable to renew the spring damping rubbers at the same time.*

Removal

1 On models with manual rear suspension level control, depressurise the system by releasing the air through the valve in the luggage compartment.
2 Chock the front wheels, then jack up the rear of the vehicle, and support securely on axle stands.
3 Raise the relevant trailing arm slightly using a jack.
4 Unscrew and remove the bolt and washer securing the lower end of the shock absorber to the trailing arm, and free the lower end of the shock absorber.
5 Carefully lower the jack supporting the trailing arm, and remove the coil spring and its damping rubbers. Lever the trailing arm downwards slightly if necessary to remove the spring.

Refitting

6 Refitting is a reversal of removal, remembering the following points.

7 Ensure that the spring locates correctly on the trailing arm and the underbody.
8 Tighten the shock absorber lower mounting bolt to the specified torque.
9 If the springs are to be renewed, repeat the procedure on the remaining side of the vehicle.
10 On models with manual rear suspension level control, pressurise the system to 0.8 bars on completion.

15 Rear anti-roll bar(s) - removal and refitting

Note: *New anti-roll bar securing nuts and bolts must be used on refitting.*

Main anti-roll bar

Removal

1 On all models fitted with a rear anti-roll bar, the anti-roll bar is located inside the rear suspension torsion beam. On some models, an additional rear anti-roll bar is fitted, which is bolted to the exterior of the torsion beam removal and refitting is described in the following sub-Section.
2 Chock the front wheels, then jack up the rear of the vehicle, and support securely on axle stands. Remove one of the rear roadwheels.
3 Working at one end of the anti-roll bar, counterhold the securing bolt, while unscrewing the securing nut **(see illustration)**.
4 Repeat the procedure for the remaining securing nut at the other end of the anti-roll bar.
5 Prise the anti-roll bar insulation rubber from the centre of the torsion beam **(see illustration)**.
6 Working at the side of the vehicle from which the wheel has been removed, draw the anti-roll bar out through the end of the torsion beam.

Refitting

7 Refitting is a reversal of removal, remembering the following points.

8 To ease refitting, lightly coat the anti-roll bar with a lubricant, such as light oil.
9 Ensure that the insulation rubber is correctly refitted to the centre of the torsion beam.
10 Use new anti-roll bar securing nuts and bolts. Counterhold the securing nuts, while tightening the bolts in the three stages given in the Specifications.

Additional anti-roll bar (if fitted)

Removal

11 To improve access, chock the front wheels, then jack up the rear of the vehicle, and support securely on axle stands.
12 Unscrew the four securing bolts - two at each end of the anti-roll bar **(see illustration)** while counter-holding the nuts, and lower the anti-roll bar from the torsion beam.

Refitting

13 Refitting is a reversal of removal, but use new securing nuts and bolts. Counterhold the securing nuts, while tightening the bolts in the three stages given in the Specifications.

16 Rear suspension torsion beam/trailing arms assembly - removal and refitting

Removal

1 Chock the front wheels, then jack up the rear of the vehicle, and support securely on axle stands. Remove the rear roadwheels.
2 On models with manual rear suspension level control, depressurise the system by releasing the air through the valve in the luggage compartment.
3 On models with a catalytic converter, unbolt and remove the exhaust centre box heat shield.
4 Note the length of exposed thread on the now-exposed handbrake cable adjuster, then remove the adjuster nut to enable the cable bracket to be disconnected from the handbrake lever operating rod.
5 Release the handbrake cables from the brackets on the underbody.
6 Working in the engine compartment,

15.3 Rear anti-roll bar securing nut and bolt

15.5 Rear anti-roll bar insulation rubber (arrowed)

15.12 Additional rear anti-roll bar securing bolts (arrowed) - C 20 XE model

10

16.10 Trailing arm-to-underbody securing nut (arrowed) viewed through rear wheel arch

remove the filler cap from the brake hydraulic fluid reservoir, then place a piece of polythene across the top of the reservoir filler hole, and refit the filler cap. This will minimise fluid loss when the brake lines are disconnected.

7 Disconnect the flexible hoses from the rigid brake pipes at the front edge of each trailing arm. Be prepared for fluid loss, and plug the open ends of the pipes and hoses, to prevent dirt ingress and further fluid loss.

8 Where applicable, disconnect the wiring plugs from the ABS wheel sensors, and release the wiring from the brackets on the trailing arms.

9 On Estate and Van models, disconnect the brake pressure-regulating valve spring from the bracket on the torsion beam.

10 Loosen, but **do not** remove, the nuts and bolts securing the front ends of the trailing arms to the vehicle underbody **(see illustration)**.

11 Support the torsion beam with a trolley jack and interposed block of wood. Position the jack securely under the centre of the torsion beam.

12 On Saloon and Hatchback models, unscrew and remove the bolts securing the lower ends of the shock absorbers to the trailing arms.

13 On Estate and Van models, counterhold the shock absorber piston rods, and unscrew the nuts securing the lower ends of the shock absorbers to the trailing arms.

14 Gently lower the jack supporting the torsion beam, until the coil springs can be removed. Remove the coil springs, referring to Section 14 if necessary.

15 Ensure that the torsion beam is adequately supported, then remove the nuts and bolts securing the front ends of the trailing arms to the vehicle underbody. The help of an assistant will greatly ease this task - ensure that the torsion beam does not slip off the jack.

16 Withdraw the torsion beam/trailing arms assembly from under the rear of the vehicle.

17 The brake components can be removed from the trailing arms, referring to the relevant Sections of Chapter 9. The hub units can be removed referring to Section 11, and where

applicable, the anti-roll bar(s) can be removed referring to Section 15.

18 If necessary, the trailing arm bushes can be renewed, referring to Section 17.

Refitting

19 Start reassembly by refitting any components that were removed from the torsion beam/trailing arms assembly, referring to the relevant Sections of this Chapter and/or Chapter 9, as applicable.

20 Support the torsion beam/trailing arms assembly on the trolley jack, and position the assembly under the rear of the vehicle.

21 Raise the jack, and fit the bolts and nuts that secure the front ends of the trailing arms to the underbody. Do not fully tighten the fixings at this stage.

22 Refit the coil springs, referring to Section 14 if necessary.

23 Raise the rear ends of the trailing arms, and refit the bolts or nuts, as applicable, securing the lower ends of the shock absorbers to the trailing arms. Tighten the fixings to the specified torque, counter-holding the shock absorber piston rod on Estate and Van models. Withdraw the jack from under the rear of the vehicle.

24 Where applicable, reconnect the ABS wheel sensor wiring, and refit the wiring to the brackets on the trailing arms.

25 Remove the plugs from the brake pipes and hoses, and reconnect the unions.

26 Refit the handbrake cables to the brackets on the underbody, then reconnect the handbrake cable bracket to the handbrake lever operating rod.

27 Fit a new handbrake cable adjuster nut, and screw the nut onto the rod to the position noted before removal. Check the handbrake adjustment, as described in Chapter 9.

28 On models with a catalytic converter, refit the exhaust centre box heat shield.

29 On Estate and Van models, reconnect the brake pressure-regulating valve spring to the bracket on the torsion beam.

30 Refit the roadwheels, and lower the vehicle to the ground.

31 On models with manual rear suspension level control, pressurise the system to 0.8 bars.

32 Remove the chocks from the front wheels.

33 Ensure that the vehicle is parked on level ground, then with the equivalent of a load of 70.0 kg in each front seat, 'bounce' the vehicle to settle the suspension.

34 Without disturbing the position of the vehicle, place chocks at the front and rear edges of the front wheels, to prevent the vehicle from moving.

35 Working under the rear of the vehicle, tighten the fixings securing the front ends of the trailing arms to the underbody to the specified torque.

36 Finally, recheck the handbrake cable adjustment, then remove the polythene from beneath the brake hydraulic fluid reservoir cap, and bleed the complete brake hydraulic system, as described in Chapter 9.

37 On Estate and Van models, check the adjustment of the brake pressure-regulating valve, as described in Chapter 1.

17 Rear suspension trailing arm bushes - removal and refitting

Note: *Trailing arm bushes should always be renewed in pairs - i.e., on both sides of the vehicle.*

Removal

1 The trailing arm bushes can be renewed without removing the torsion beam/trailing arms assembly from the vehicle, as follows.

2 Chock the front wheels, then jack up the rear of the vehicle, and support securely on axle stands. Remove the rear roadwheels.

3 On models with manual rear suspension level control, depressurise the system by releasing the air through the valve in the luggage compartment.

4 On Estate and Van models, disconnect the brake pressure-regulating valve spring from the bracket on the torsion beam.

5 Unclip the flexible hoses and the rear ends of the rigid brake pipes from the vehicle underbody. Also unclip the handbrake cables and ABS sensor wiring, where applicable.

6 Support the torsion beam with a trolley jack and interposed block of wood. Position the jack under the centre of the torsion beam.

7 Unscrew and remove the nuts and bolts securing the trailing arms to the underbody.

8 Gently lower the jack until the trailing arm bushes are accessible, then support the torsion beam on axle stands. Take care not to strain the brake pipes.

9 A special Vauxhall tool is available for removal and refitting of the bushes, but an alternative can be improvised using a long bolt, nut, washers, and a length of metal tubing or a socket.

10 Where applicable, before removing a bush, cut the flange from the inner end of the bush using a sharp knife **(see illustration)**.

11 Removal of the bush will be made easier if the bush housing in the trailing arm is heated to approximately 70°C using a heat gun or a hairdryer. Do not use a naked flame, due to the close proximity of the fuel tank.

17.10 Cutting the inner flange from a trailing arm bush

12 Draw the bush from the trailing arm using the tool described in paragraph 9.

Refitting

13 Lubricate the new bush with a little soapy water, then draw it into position, ensuring that the narrow part of the bush points upwards.
14 Repeat the procedure on the remaining trailing arm.
15 Raise the torsion beam using the jack, and fit the bolts and nuts that secure the front ends of the trailing arms to the underbody. Do not fully tighten the fixings at this stage. Withdraw the axle stands.
16 Clip the rigid brake pipes and the flexible hoses to the vehicle underbody.
17 On Estate and Van models, reconnect the brake pressure-regulating valve spring to the bracket on the torsion beam.
18 Proceed as described in Section 16, paragraphs 30 to 35 inclusive.
19 On Estate and Van models, check the adjustment of the brake pressure-regulating valve, as described in Chapter 1.

18 Rear suspension level control system - general

1 The suspension level control system is manually operated, and the level is adjusted by altering the air pressure in the rear shock absorbers, through a valve located in the luggage compartment.
2 For safety reasons, if the vehicle is to be driven fully loaded, the level control system must not be fully pressurised with the vehicle in the unladen condition.
3 To adjust the system, continue as follows.
4 With the vehicle unladen, use a tyre pressure gauge on the air valve to check that the system pressure is 0.8 bars. Adjust if necessary.
5 With the vehicle standing on a level surface, measure the distance from the centre of the rear bumper to the ground. Subtract 50.0 mm from the distance measured, and note the new value.
6 Load the vehicle, and if necessary increase the pressure in the system until the noted value for the bumper height is reached. Do not exceed a pressure of 5.0 bars.
7 After unloading the vehicle, depressurise the system to the minimum pressure of 0.8 bars.
8 Do not drive an unladen vehicle with the system fully pressurised.

19 Rear suspension level control system components - removal and refitting

Air valve

Removal
1 Working in the luggage compartment, pull back the floor covering for access to the air valve.
2 Fully depressurise the system.

3 Remove the cap and retaining sleeve from the valve, then compress the retaining lugs and push the valve downwards, taking care not to damage the air lines **(see illustration)**.
4 Unscrew the air line unions from the valve, and then withdraw the valve from the vehicle.

Refitting
5 Refitting is a reversal of removal, but on completion, pressurise the system and check for air leaks.

Air lines

Removal
6 To remove an air line, first fully depressurise the system.
7 Unscrew the unions at the shock absorber and air valve, then release the air line from the clips on the vehicle underbody.

Refitting
8 Refitting is a reversal of removal, but on completion, pressurise the system and check for air leaks.

20 Steering wheel - removal and refitting

Note: *A two-legged puller will be required for this operation.*

⚠ **Warning: If an airbag is fitted, read the warning in Chapter 12, before starting work.**

Removal
1 Disconnect the battery negative lead.
2 Set the front wheels in the straight-ahead position, and unless it is unavoidable, do not move them until the steering wheel has been refitted.
3 Prise the horn push pad from the centre of the steering wheel, and disconnect the wiring.
4 Using a screwdriver, prise back the tabs on the lockwasher securing the steering wheel retaining nut.
5 Unscrew and remove the steering wheel retaining nut and the lockwasher.
6 Make alignment marks between the steering wheel and the end of the column shaft.
7 A small two-legged puller must now be

19.3 Rear suspension level control system air valve. Compress retaining lugs (arrowed) to remove valve

fitted to the steering wheel to pull it from the column shaft. Note that the steering wheel is a very tight fit on the shaft.

Refitting
8 Begin refitting by gently tapping the steering wheel into position on the column shaft, using a metal tube or socket, and ensuring that the marks made before removal are aligned. Before tapping the wheel fully home, check the centralisation, as described in Section 21.
9 Refit the lockwasher and the steering wheel retaining nut, and tighten the nut to the specified torque. Bend up the lockwasher tabs to secure the nut.
10 Refit the horn push pad, ensuring that the wiring is securely connected, and reconnect the battery negative lead.

21 Steering wheel - centralising

1 The steering straight-ahead position is achieved when the reference dimension between the centre of the tie-rod-to-steering gear bolt locking plate(s), and the centre of the rib on the right-hand steering gear mounting clamp (right-hand-drive models), or the left-hand steering gear mounting clamp (left-hand-drive models), as applicable, is as shown. In this position, the flexible rubber coupling upper pinch-bolt should lie horizontally on top of the steering shaft **(see illustrations)**.

21.1A Steering gear centralised for setting of steering wheel straight-ahead position - right-hand-drive shown

1 = 325.0 mm

21.1B Flexible coupling upper pinch-bolt alignment (arrowed) with steering gear centralised - right-hand-drive shown

10

22.4 Removing the steering column lock cylinder

2 Check that the steering wheel is centralised.

3 If the steering wheel is off-centre by more than 5°, it should be removed, then moved the required number of splines on the column shaft to achieve centralisation, and refitted as described in Section 20.

22 Steering column lock - removal and refitting

Removal

1 Disconnect the battery negative lead.

2 Remove the steering column shrouds, as described in Chapter 11.

3 Insert the ignition key into the ignition switch, and turn it to position 'II'.

4 Insert a thin rod into the hole in the lock housing, then press the rod to release the detent spring, and pull out the lock cylinder using the key **(see illustration)**.

5 Removal and refitting of the lock housing is described in Section 24 as part of the steering column dismantling and reassembly procedure.

Refitting

6 Where applicable refit the lock housing as described in Section 24.

7 Refit the lock cylinder, with the key in position 'II' by simply pushing it into position

in the housing. Turn the key back to position '0', and remove it.

8 Further refitting is a reversal of removal.

23 Steering column - removal and refitting

Note: *A bolt/stud extractor will be required for this operation. A new shear-head bolt must be used on refitting.*

Removal

1 Disconnect the battery negative lead.

2 Set the front wheels in the straight-ahead position.

3 Working in the drivers footwell, release the securing clips and remove the lower trim panel.

4 Remove the steering wheel as described in Section 20, for improved access.

5 Remove the steering column lock as described in Section 22.

6 Depress the retaining clips release the two stalk switches from the steering column, then disconnect the wiring plugs and withdraw the switches.

7 Unclip the fusebox cover and unclip the blanking cover from the aperture in the facia panel below the steering column.

8 Working at the lower end of the steering shaft, unscrew and remove the upper pinch-bolt securing the steering shaft to the flexible rubber coupling **(see illustration)**.

9 Locate the plastic disc that should be fitted loosely to the lower end of the steering shaft and push it up the shaft until it engages with the steering column tube.

10 Using a socket and extension bar, unscrew the bolt securing the steering column to the facia bracket **(see illustration)**.

11 Two fixings must now be extracted from the column upper mounting bracket. A conventional nut is used on one side of the column (the left-hand side on right-hand-drive models, or the right-hand side on left-hand-drive models) and a shear-head type bolt is used on the remaining side.

12 The shear-head type bolt must be removed by centre-punching, drilling off the head and then using a bolt/stud extractor (sometimes called 'easy-outs'). When drilling the bolt take care not to damage the facia panel **(see illustration)**.

13 Withdraw the column assembly into the vehicle interior and then remove it from the vehicle. Handle the column carefully avoiding knocks or impact of any kind, which may damage the collapsible section of the column.

14 The column can be dismantled as described in Section 24.

Refitting

15 Begin refitting by ensuring that the roadwheels are still in the straight-ahead position and that the plastic disc on the steering shaft is engaged with the column tube.

16 The flexible coupling should be positioned so that the upper pinch-bolt will be horizontal on top of the steering shaft.

17 Offer the column into position and reconnect the flexible coupling. Refit the pinch-bolt, but do not fully tighten it at this stage.

18 Loosely fit the upper mounting fixings using a new shear-head bolt.

19 Refit the bolt securing the steering column to the facia bracket and tighten to the specified torque.

20 Tighten the upper mounting fixings. The shear-head bolt should be tightened until the head breaks off and the conventional nut should be tightened to the specified torque.

21 Pull upwards on the steering shaft until the shaft contacts the bearing stop then tighten the flexible coupling upper pinch-bolt.

22 Prise the plastic centring disc from the base of the column tube and leave it loose on the steering shaft.

23 Further refitting is a reversal of the removal procedure. Refit the steering wheel as described in Section 20.

24 On completion, first manoeuvre the vehicle at low speed, then carry out a test drive along a route with several corners and check that the steering mechanism operates smoothly.

23.8 Steering shaft flexible rubber coupling pinch-bolt (1) and plastic disc (2)

23.10 Steering column-to-facia bracket securing bolt (arrowed) viewed through instrument panel aperture

23.12 Drilling out the steering column shear-head bolt - right-hand-drive model

24.3 Exploded view of steering column and associated components

1 Horn push pad
2 Steering wheel
3 Cam assembly
4 Spring
5 Lighting switch
6 Wash/wipe switch

7 Switch housing
8 Bearing
9 Lower column shroud
10 Steering shaft
11 Centralising plastic disc
12 Column tube

13 Lock barrel
14 Lock barrel
15 Lock housing
16 Switch housing safety
   plugs
17 Upper column shroud

24 Steering column -
dismantling and reassembly

Dismantling

1 If the steering column is in position in the vehicle, continue as described in Section 22 paragraphs 1 to 4 inclusive.
2 Prise out the ignition switch housing safety plugs, then turn the housing anti-clockwise, and pull it from the steering column.
3 The bearing can be removed from the ignition switch housing by prising apart the two bearing fixing catches, and pressing or driving out the bearing with a piece of tubing on the bearing outer race. When pressing in the new bearing, make sure that the thrustwasher and contact springs are correctly located **(see illustration)**.
4 The ignition switch is secured to the lock housing by two grub screws. Remove the screws to extract the switch. It is recommended that the switch and the lock cylinder are not both removed at the same time, otherwise their mutual alignment will be lost **(see illustration)**.
5 If the steering column is in position in the vehicle, unscrew and remove the upper pinch-bolt from the steering shaft flexible

coupling in the driver's footwell.
6 Withdraw the steering shaft from the steering column tube.

Reassembly

7 Begin reassembly by fitting the plastic centring disc, which will be supplied with a new column or steering shaft, into the base of the column tube.
8 Insert the shaft into the column tube, and if the column is in position in the vehicle, engage the bottom end of the shaft with the flexible coupling and refit the upper pinch-bolt, but do not tighten it at this stage.

24.4 Sectional view of ignition switch housing

A Thrustwasher   B Contact springs

9 Where applicable, refit the ignition switch, and tighten the grub screws.
10 Refit the ignition switch housing, using new safety plugs.
11 If the column is in position in the vehicle, pull upwards on the steering shaft until the shaft contacts the bearing stop, then tighten the flexible coupling upper pinch-bolt. Ensure that the roadwheels are in the straight-ahead position, and that the flexible coupling is positioned so that the upper pinch-bolt is horizontal on top of the steering shaft.
12 Where applicable, further reassembly is a reversal of dismantling. Refit the steering wheel, as described in Section 20.
13 On completion, first manoeuvre the vehicle at low speed, then carry out a test drive along a route with several corners, and check that the steering mechanism operates smoothly.

25 Steering shaft flexible rubber coupling -
removal and refitting

Removal

1 Set the front wheels in the straight-ahead position.
2 Working in the driver's footwell, release the securing clips, and remove the lower trim panel.
3 Unscrew and remove the two pinch-bolts securing the rubber coupling to the steering shaft and the steering gear pinion shaft **(see illustration)**.
4 Unscrew the bolts securing the steering gear to the bulkhead in the engine compartment, then move the steering gear away from the bulkhead sufficiently to disconnect the coupling from the steering gear pinion.
5 Pull the coupling from the steering shaft, noting which way round it is fitted.

Refitting

6 Check that the steering wheel and the front wheels are still in the straight-ahead position.
7 Fit the coupling to the steering gear pinion, and tighten the clamp bolt.

25.3 Steering shaft flexible rubber coupling pinch-bolts (arrowed)

10

8 Push the steering gear back into position on the bulkhead, ensure that the steering shaft engages with the coupling, then tighten the steering gear securing bolts to the specified torque.

9 Pull upwards on the steering shaft until the shaft contacts the bearing stop, then tighten the flexible coupling upper pinch-bolt.

10 Check that the steering wheel is centralised, as described in Section 21.

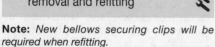

26 Steering gear rubber bellows - removal and refitting

Note: *New bellows securing clips will be required when refitting.*

Removal

1 Remove the steering gear, as described in Section 27.

2 Remove the mounting clamp and rubber from the left-hand end of the steering gear on right-hand-drive models, or from the right-hand end of the steering gear on left-hand-drive models, as applicable.

3 On power steering gear, disconnect the fluid pipe unions from the left-hand end of the steering gear (right-hand-drive models), or the right-hand end of the steering gear (left-hand-drive models).

4 Remove the outer bellows securing clips from each end of the steering gear, then slide off the bellows/tube assembly.

5 Remove the inner bellows securing clips, and separate the bellows from the tube.

Refitting

6 Fit the new bellows to the tube, using new clips. The clips should be positioned so that when the steering gear is fitted to the vehicle, the ends of the clips point upwards.

7 Fit the bellows/tube assembly to the steering gear, and secure with new clips, again positioned with the ends of the clips pointing upwards. Ensure that the bellows are not twisted.

8 On power steering gear, reconnect the fluid pipe unions, using new O-rings.

9 Refit the mounting clamp and rubber, then refit the steering gear, as described in Section 27.

27 Steering gear - removal and refitting

Note: *New steering gear-to-bulkhead bolts, and a new tie-rod-to-steering gear locking plate must be used on refitting. On models with power steering, the fluid hose-to-pipe O-ring(s) must be renewed on refitting.*

Removal

1 Disconnect the battery negative lead.

2 Set the front wheels in the straight-ahead position.

3 Where applicable, remove the airbox from the top of the carburettor or throttle body (see Chapter 4A or 4B, as applicable).

4 Remove the coolant expansion tank, as described in Chapter 3. On certain models, it may be possible to move the expansion tank sufficiently to allow access for removal of the steering gear without disconnecting the hoses.

5 Where applicable, disconnect the wiring harness from the anti-theft alarm switch on the left-hand suspension turret, and move the harness clear of the steering gear. Alternatively, the switch can be removed.

6 Prise the locking plate from the tie-rod-to-steering gear bolts, then unscrew and remove the bolts, and recover the washers and spacer plate **(see illustration)**.

7 On models with power steering, disconnect the fluid hoses from the pipes at the left-hand side of the engine compartment (next to the coolant expansion tank location). Recover the O-ring(s) where applicable. Be prepared for fluid spillage, and plug the open ends of the pipes and hoses to prevent dirt ingress and further fluid loss.

8 Working in the driver's footwell, release the securing clips, and remove the lower trim panel.

9 Unscrew and remove the upper pinch-bolt securing the steering shaft to the flexible rubber coupling.

10 Working in the engine compartment, unbolt the two clamps securing the steering gear to the bulkhead **(see illustration)**. Then push the right-hand end of the steering gear through the large rubber grommet in the right-hand wheel arch, and manipulate the steering gear upwards out of the engine compartment. The help of an assistant may be required to release the flexible rubber coupling from the steering shaft as the steering gear is withdrawn. Note that on some models, various wires and hoses may be secured to the steering gear with cable ties - ensure that, where applicable, all wires and hoses are freed before the steering gear is removed.

Refitting

11 Refitting is a reversal of removal, remembering the following points.

12 Use new mounting bolts to secure the steering gear clamps to the bulkhead.

13 Reconnect the flexible rubber-coupling to the steering shaft (with the rack and steering wheel centralised) so that the upper pinch-bolt lies horizontally on top of the steering shaft **(see illustration 21.1B)**.

14 On models with power steering, renew the O-ring(s) when reconnecting the fluid hoses to the pipes.

15 The tie-rod-to-steering gear locking plate must be renewed on refitting.

16 Where applicable, after refitting the expansion tank, top-up the coolant level as described in Chapter 3.

17 On models with power steering, on completion, bleed the hydraulic system, as described in Section 29.

18 On completion, check the steering wheel centralisation, as described in Section 21.

28 Steering gear - overhaul

Manual steering gear

1 Examine the steering gear assembly for signs of wear or damage. Check that the rack moves freely throughout the full length of its travel, with no signs of roughness or excessive free play between the steering gear pinion and rack. It is possible to overhaul the steering gear assembly housing components, but this task should be entrusted to a Vauxhall dealer.

2 The only components that can be renewed easily by the home mechanic are the steering gear gaiters, the track rod balljoints and the track rods.

Power steering gear

3 Overhaul of the power steering gear is not recommended by the manufacturers.

4 Fluid leaks from the hydraulic fluid pipe unions can normally be corrected by renewing the union seals with the rack installed.

5 Bellows renewal is covered in Section 26.

6 Adjustment of the power steering gear should not be attempted.

7 Any faults with the steering gear should be referred to a Vauxhall dealer, although renewal of the complete assembly will probably be the only course of action available.

27.6 Tie-rod-to-steering gear bolts (1), locking plate (2) and spacer plate (3)

27.10 Steering gear clamp bolt (arrowed) - model with power steering

29 Power steering hydraulic system - bleeding

1 With the engine stopped, initially fill the reservoir to the level of the 'MAX' mark on the dipstick attached to the reservoir filler cap.

2 Start the engine, and immediately top-up the fluid level to the 'MIN' mark on the dipstick. **Do not** allow the reservoir to run dry at any time. The help of an assistant will ease this operation.

3 With the engine running at idle speed, turn the steering wheel slowly two or three times approximately 45° to the left and right of the centre, then turn the wheel twice from lock to lock. Do not hold the wheel on either lock, as this imposes strain on the hydraulic system.

4 Stop the engine, and check the fluid level. With the fluid at operating temperature (80°C), the level should be on the 'MAX' mark, and with the fluid cold (20°C), the level should be on the 'MIN' mark. Top-up if necessary.

30 Power steering pump - removal and refitting

Note: *A new fluid pipe union O-ring must be used on refitting.*

1.4 and 1.6 litre models, with V-belt

Removal

1 For improved access, remove the air cleaner casing from the right-hand front wing, as described in Chapter 4A or 4B, as applicable.

2 Remove the alternator/power steering pump drivebelt, as described in Chapter 5.

3 Counterhold the power steering pump pulley, using an old drivebelt, then unscrew the three pulley securing bolts, and remove the pulley (see illustration).

4 To improve access, remove the upper outer timing belt cover, as described in Chapter 2A or 2B.

5 Disconnect the fluid pipe union and the

30.3 Removing the power steering pump pulley - C 16 SE model

flexible fluid hose from the pump. Be prepared for fluid spillage, and plug or cover the open ends of the pump, pipe and hose, to prevent dirt ingress and further fluid loss (see illustrations).

6 Carefully manipulate the pump from its location and withdraw it from the engine compartment. Take care not to damage the bodywork, as there is very little clearance to withdraw the pump (see illustration).

7 No overhaul of the pump is possible, and if faulty, a new unit must be fitted.

Refitting

8 Refitting is a reversal of removal, but renew the O-ring when reconnecting the fluid pipe union (see illustration), and tension the alternator/ power steering pump drivebelt, as described in Chapter 5.

9 On completion, top-up the fluid level, and bleed the fluid circuit as described in Section 29.

Ribbed V-belt models

Removal

10 Remove the power steering pump drivebelt, as described in Chapter 1. On DOHC models remove the air cleaner box. Refer to Chapter 4B.

11 Disconnect the fluid pipe union and the flexible fluid hose from the pump. Be prepared for fluid spillage, and plug the open ends of the pump, pipe and hose, to prevent dirt ingress and further fluid loss.

30.5A Unscrewing the power steering pump fluid pipe union (arrowed) - C 16 NZ model

30.5B Power steering pump fluid pipe and hose ends covered to prevent dirt ingress and fluid loss

12 Unscrew and remove the four mounting bolts shown (see illustration). Recover the nuts, and take care not to lose the rubber insulators that fit into the mounting bracket.

13 Withdraw the pump from the vehicle.

14 No overhaul of the pump is possible, and if faulty, a new unit must be fitted.

Refitting

15 Refitting is a reversal of removal, but renew the O-ring when reconnecting the fluid pipe union, and before finally tightening the pump mounting bolts, tension the drivebelt, as described in Chapter 1.

16 On completion, top-up the fluid level, and bleed the fluid circuit as described in Section 29.

30.6 Removing the power steering pump - C 16 NZ model

30.8 Renew the power steering pump fluid pipe O-ring (arrowed) on refitting

30.12 Power steering pump mounting bolts (arrowed) - SOHC ribbed V-belt model

10

32.3 Power steering fluid cooler pipes (arrowed) viewed from underneath vehicle

31 Power steering fluid reservoir - removal and refitting

Removal

1 The reservoir can be removed from the mounting bracket by unscrewing the clamp screw and removing the clamp.
2 Have a container ready to catch the fluid, then disconnect the fluid hoses from the reservoir, and drain the fluid. Plug the open ends of the hoses, to prevent dirt ingress and further fluid loss.
3 The mounting bracket can be unbolted from the body panel, but note that on certain models, the bolts securing the bracket also secure the ignition coil and suppressor - refer to Chapter 3 if necessary. Where applicable, unclip the brake fluid pipes and any wiring from the bracket before removal.

Refitting

4 Refitting is a reversal of removal, but on completion, bleed the fluid circuit, as described in Section 29.

32 Power steering fluid cooler pipes - removal and refitting

Note: *New fluid pipe union O-rings must be used on refitting.*

Removal

1 For improved access, apply the handbrake, then jack up the front of the vehicle, and support securely on axle stands.
2 If fitted, remove the engine undershield, as described in Chapter 11.
3 Disconnect the fluid cooler pipe unions **(see illustration)**. Be prepared for fluid spillage, and plug the open ends of the pipes, to prevent dirt ingress and further fluid loss. Recover the O-rings.
4 Release the three plastic clips securing the pipes to the lower body panel **(see illustration)**, then manipulate the pipes from the engine compartment.

32.4 Releasing a power steering fluid cooler pipe securing clip (viewed from above with radiator removed)

Refitting

5 Refitting is a reversal of removal, but renew the O-rings when reconnecting the fluid pipe unions.
6 On completion, top-up the fluid level, and bleed the fluid circuit as described in Section 29.

33 Tie-rod end/balljoint - removal and refitting

Note: *A balljoint separator tool will be required for this operation. A new tie-rod end balljoint nut must be used on refitting.*

Removal

1 Apply the handbrake, then jack up the front of the vehicle and support securely on axle stands. Remove the relevant front roadwheel.
2 Loosen the tie-rod end clamp bolt, which secures the tie-rod end to the threaded adjuster pin on the tie-rod **(see illustration)**.
3 Unscrew the self-locking nut from the tie-rod end-to-suspension strut balljoint.
4 Using a balljoint separator tool, disconnect the tie-rod end-to-suspension strut balljoint **(see illustration)**.
5 Note the position of the tie-rod end on the adjuster pin, either by marking the pin with paint or tape, or by counting the number of

33.2 Tie-rod end viewed from underneath

1 Tie-rod end clamp bolt
2 Threaded adjuster pin
3 Tie-rod clamp bolt

threads exposed, then unscrew the tie-rod end from the tie-rod.
6 Note that the tie-rod ends are 'handed'. The right-hand tie-rod end is marked 'R', but the left-hand tie-rod end has no marking.

Refitting

7 Begin refitting by screwing the tie-rod end onto the adjuster pin to approximately the same position as was noted during removal.
8 Reconnect the tie-rod end balljoint to the suspension strut, and tighten a new self-locking nut to the specified torque.
9 Tighten the tie-rod end clamp bolt.
10 Refit the roadwheel and lower the vehicle to the ground.
11 Check the front wheel alignment, as described in Section 35, and adjust if necessary. No harm will result from driving the vehicle a short distance to have the alignment checked.

34 Tie-rod - removal and refitting

Note: *A new tie-rod end-to-steering gear locking plate, and where applicable, a new tie-rod end balljoint nut, must be used on refitting.*

Removal

1 The tie-rod can either be removed leaving the tie-rod end in place, or as an assembly with the tie-rod end.
2 Apply the handbrake, then jack up the front of the vehicle and support securely on axle stands. Remove the relevant front roadwheel.
3 If the tie-rod is to be removed complete with the tie-rod end, continue as described in Section 34, paragraphs 3 and 4.
4 If the tie-rod is to be removed independently of the tie-rod end, loosen the tie-rod clamp bolt, which secures the tie-rod to the threaded adjuster pin on the tie-rod end.
5 Prise the locking plate from the tie-rod end-to-steering gear bolts, then unscrew and

33.4 Using a balljoint separator tool to disconnect the tie-rod end-to-suspension strut balljoint

remove the bolts, and recover the washers and spacer plate.

6 If the tie-rod is being removed complete with the tie-rod end, the assembly can now be withdrawn from the vehicle.

7 If the tie-rod is to be removed independently of the tie-rod end, note the position of the tie-rod end on the adjuster pin. Do this either, by marking the pin with paint or tape, or by counting the number of threads exposed, then unscrew the tie-rod from the tie-rod end, and withdraw it from the vehicle.

Refitting

8 Refitting is a reversal of removal, remembering the following points.

9 The tie-rod-to-steering gear bolt locking plate must be renewed on refitting.

10 If the tie-rod is being refitted complete with the tie-rod end, reconnect the tie-rod end balljoint to the suspension strut, and tighten a new self-locking nut to the specified torque.

11 If the tie-rod is being refitted with the tie-rod end already in place on the vehicle, screw the tie-rod onto the adjuster pin to approximately the same position as noted during removal, and tighten the clamp bolt.

12 On completion, check the front wheel alignment, as described in Section 35, and adjust if necessary. No harm will result from driving the vehicle a short distance to have the alignment checked.

35 Wheel alignment and steering angles - general

1 Accurate front wheel alignment is essential for precise steering and handling, and for even tyre wear. Before carrying out any checking or adjusting operations, make sure that the tyres are correctly inflated. Also check that all steering and suspension joints and linkages are in sound condition, and that the wheels are not buckled or distorted, particularly around the rims. It will also be necessary to have the vehicle positioned on flat, level ground, with enough space to push the car backwards and forwards through about half its length.

2 Front wheel alignment consists of four factors (see illustration):

Camber is the angle at which the roadwheels are set from the vertical, when viewed from the front or rear of the vehicle. Positive camber is the angle (in degrees) that the wheels are tilted outwards at the top from the vertical.

Castor is the angle between the steering axis and a vertical line when viewed from each side of the vehicle. Positive castor is indicated when the steering axis is inclined towards the rear of the vehicle at its upper end.

Steering axis inclination is the angle, when viewed from the front or rear of the vehicle, between the vertical and an imaginary line drawn between the upper and lower front suspension strut mountings.

Toe setting is the amount by which the distance between the front inside edges of the roadwheels differs from that between the rear inside edges, when measured at hub height. If the distance between the front edges is less than at the rear, the wheels are said to 'toe-in'. If it is greater than at the rear, the wheels are said to 'toe-out'.

3 Camber, castor and steering axis inclination are set during manufacture, and are not adjustable. Unless the vehicle has suffered accident damage, or there is gross wear in the suspension mountings or joints, it can be assumed that these settings are correct. If for any reason it is believed that they are not correct, the task of checking them should be left to a Vauxhall dealer, who will have the necessary special equipment needed to measure the small angles involved.

4 It is, however, within the scope of the home mechanic to check and adjust the front wheel toe setting. To do this, a tracking gauge must first be obtained. Two types of gauge are available, and can be obtained from motor accessory shops. The first type measures the distance between the front and rear inside edges of the roadwheels, as previously described, with the vehicle stationary. The second type, known as a 'scuff plate', measures the actual position of the contact surface of the tyre, in relation to the road surface, with the vehicle in motion. This is achieved by pushing or driving the front tyre over a plate, which then moves slightly according to the scuff of the tyre, and shows this movement on a scale. Both types have their advantages and disadvantages, but either can give satisfactory results if used correctly and carefully. Alternatively, a tracking gauge can be fabricated from a length of steel tubing, suitably cranked to clear the sump and clutch bellhousing, with a set screw and locknut at one end.

5 Many tyre specialists will also check toe settings free, or for a nominal charge.

6 Make sure that the steering is in the straight-ahead position when making measurements.

7 If adjustment is found to be necessary, clean the ends of the tie-rods in the area around the adjustment pin and clamp bolts.

8 Slacken the clamp bolts (one on each tie-rod balljoint, and one on each tie-rod), and

35.1 Wheel alignment and steering angles

turn the adjustment pin on each tie-rod by the same amount in the same direction. Only turn each pin by a quarter of a turn at a time before rechecking.

9 When adjustment is correct, tighten the clamp bolts to the specified torque. Check that the tie-rod lengths are equal to within 5.0 mm, and that the steering wheel spokes are in the correct straight-ahead position.

10

Notes

Chapter 11
Bodywork and fittings

Contents

Degrees of difficulty

| Easy, suitable for novice with little experience | | Fairly easy, suitable for beginner with some experience | | Fairly difficult, suitable for competent DIY mechanic | | Difficult, suitable for experienced DIY mechanic | | Very difficult, suitable for expert DIY or professional | |

Specifications

Torque wrench settings

	Nm	lbf ft
Front seat securing bolts	20	15
Seat belt mounting bolts	35	26
Seat belt height adjuster securing bolts	20	15
Tailgate hinge-to-body bolts	20	15

1 Bodywork information - general

The bodyshell and floorpan are manufactured from pressed-steel, and together make up the vehicle's structure, without the need for a separate chassis. The Astra is available in 4-door Saloon, 3- and 5-door Hatchback, 5-door Estate and 2-door Van body styles.

Various areas of the structure are strengthened to provide for suspension, steering and engine mounting points, and load distribution. One notable feature of all Astra models is the use of tubular reinforcing bars in the doors, to provide the occupants with additional protection if there is a side impact.

Extensive corrosion protection is applied to all new vehicles. Various anti-corrosion preparations are used, including galvanising, zinc phosphatisation, and PVC underseal. Protective wax is injected into the box sections and other hollow cavities.

Extensive use is made of plastic for peripheral components, such as the radiator grille, bumpers and wheel trims, and for much of the interior trim.

Interior fittings are to a high standard on all models, and a wide range of optional equipment is available throughout the range.

2 Maintenance of bodywork and underframe - general

Cleaning the vehicle's exterior

The general condition of a vehicle's bodywork is the one thing that significantly affects its value. Maintenance is easy but needs to be regular. Neglect, particularly after minor damage, can lead quickly to further deterioration and costly repair bills. It is important also to keep watch on those parts of the vehicle not immediately visible, for instance the underbody, inside all the wheel arches and the lower part of the engine compartment.

The basic maintenance routine for the bodywork is washing preferably with a lot of water, from a hose. This will remove all the loose solids that may have stuck to the vehicle. It is important to flush these off in such a way as to prevent grit from scratching the finish. The wheel arches and underbody need washing in the same way to remove any accumulated mud, which will retain moisture and tend to encourage rust, particularly in Winter, when it is essential that any salt (from that put down on the roads) is washed off. Paradoxically enough, the best time to clean the underbody and wheel arches is in wet weather, when the mud is thoroughly wet and soft. In very wet weather, the underbody is usually cleaned automatically of large accumulations; this is therefore a good time for inspection.

If the vehicle is very dirty, especially underneath or in the engine compartment, it is tempting to use one of the pressure-washers or steam-cleaners available on garage forecourts, while these are quick and effective, especially for the removal of the accumulation of oily grime which sometimes is allowed to become thick in certain areas, their usage does have some disadvantages. If caked-on dirt is simply blasted off the paintwork, its finish soon becomes scratched and dull, and the pressure can allow water to penetrate door and window seals and the lock mechanisms; if the full force of such a jet is directed at the vehicle's underbody, the wax-based protective coating can easily be damaged, and water (with whatever cleaning solvent is used) could be forced into crevices or components that it would not normally reach. Similarly, if such equipment is used to clean the engine compartment, water can be forced into the components of the fuel and electrical systems, and the protective coating can be removed that is applied to many small components during manufacture; this may therefore actually promote corrosion (especially inside electrical connectors) and initiate engine problems or other electrical faults. Also, if the jet is pointed directly at any of the oil seals, water can be forced past the seal lips and into the engine or transmission. Great care is required, therefore, if such equipment is used and, in general, regular cleaning by such methods should be avoided.

A much better solution in the long term is just to flush away as much loose dirt as possible using a hose alone, even if this leaves the engine compartment looking 'dirty'. If an oil leak has developed, or if any other accumulation of oil or grease is to be removed, there are one or two excellent grease solvents available that can be brush-applied. The dirt can then be simply hosed off. Take care to replace the wax-based protective coat, if this was affected by the solvent.

Normal washing of the vehicle's bodywork is best carried out using cold or warm water, with a proprietary vehicle shampoo, tar spots can be removed by using white spirit, followed by soapy water to remove all traces of spirit. Try to keep water out of the bonnet air inlets, and check afterwards that the heater air inlet box drain tube is clear, so that any water has drained out of the box.

After washing the paintwork, wipe off with a chamois leather to give an unspotted clear finish. A coat of clear protective wax polish will give added protection against chemical pollutants in the air. If the paintwork sheen has dulled or oxidised, use a cleaner/polisher combination to restore the brilliance of the shine. This requires a little effort, but such dulling is usually caused because regular washing has been neglected. Care needs to be taken with metallic paintwork, as special non-abrasive cleaner/polisher is required to avoid damage to the finish.

Any polished metals should be treated in the same way as paintwork.

Windscreens and windows can be kept clear of the smeary film that often appears with proprietary glass cleaner. Never use any form of wax or other body or chromium polish on glass.

Exterior paintwork and body panels check

Once the vehicle has been washed, and all tar spots and other surface blemishes have been cleaned off, check carefully all paintwork, looking closely for chips or scratches; check with particular care vulnerable areas such as the front (bonnet and spoiler) and around the wheel arches. Any damage to the paintwork must be rectified as soon as possible, to comply with the terms of the manufacturer's cosmetic and anti-corrosion warranties; check with a Vauxhall dealer for details.

If a chip or (light) scratch is found that is recent and still free from rust, it can be touched-up using the appropriate touch-up pencil; these can be obtained from Vauxhall dealers. Any more serious damage, or rusted stone chips, can be repaired as described in Section 4, but if damage or corrosion is so severe that a panel must be renewed, seek professional advice as soon as possible.

Always check that the door and ventilator opening drain holes and pipes are completely clear, so that water can drain out.

Underbody sealer check

The wax-based underbody protective coating should be inspected annually, preferably just before Winter. Wash the underbody down as thoroughly but gently as possible (see the above concerning steam cleaners, etc.) and any damage to the coating repaired. If any of the body panels are disturbed for repair or renewed, do not forget to replace the coating and to inject wax into door panels, sills, box sections, etc., to maintain the level of protection provided by the vehicle manufacturer.

3 Maintenance of upholstery and carpets - general

Mats and carpets should be brushed or vacuum-cleaned regularly, to keep them free of grit. If they are badly stained, remove them from the vehicle for scrubbing or sponging, and make quite sure they are dry before refitting. Seats and interior trim panels can be kept clean by wiping with a damp cloth. If they do become stained (which can be more apparent on light-coloured upholstery), use a little liquid detergent and a soft nail brush to scour the grime out of the grain of the material. Do not forget to keep the headlining clean in the same way as the upholstery. When using liquid cleaners inside the vehicle, do not over-wet the surfaces being cleaned. Excessive damp could get into the seams and padded interior, causing stains, offensive odours or even rot. If the inside of the vehicle gets wet accidentally, it is worthwhile taking some trouble to dry it out properly, particularly where carpets are involved. *Do not leave oil or electric heaters inside the vehicle for this purpose.*

4   Minor body damage repair - general

Repairs of minor scratches in bodywork

If the scratch is very superficial, and does not penetrate to the metal of the bodywork, repair is very simple. Lightly rub the area of the scratch with a paintwork renovator, or a very fine cutting paste, to remove loose paint from the scratch, and to clear the surrounding bodywork of wax polish. Rinse the area with clean water.

Apply touch-up paint to the scratch using a fine paint brush; continue to apply fine layers of paint until the surface of the paint in the scratch is level with the surrounding paintwork. Allow the new paint at least two weeks to harden, then blend it into the surrounding paintwork by rubbing the scratch area with a paintwork renovator or a very fine cutting paste. Finally, apply wax polish.

Where the scratch has penetrated right through to the metal of the bodywork, causing the metal to rust, a different repair technique is required. Remove any loose rust from the bottom of the scratch with a penknife, then apply rust-inhibiting paint to prevent the formation of rust in the future. Using a rubber or nylon applicator, fill the scratch with bodystopper paste. If required, this paste can be mixed with cellulose thinners to provide a very thin paste that is ideal for filling narrow scratches. Before the stopper-paste in the scratch hardens, wrap a piece of smooth cotton rag around the top of a finger. Dip the finger in cellulose thinners, and quickly sweep it across the surface of the stopper-paste in the scratch; this will ensure that the surface of the stopper-paste is slightly hollowed. The scratch can now be painted over as described earlier in this Section.

Repairs of dents in bodywork

When deep denting of the vehicle's bodywork has taken place, the first task is to pull the dent out, until the affected bodywork almost attains its original shape. There is little point in trying to restore the original shape completely, as the metal in the damaged area will have stretched on impact, and cannot be reshaped fully to its original contour. It is better

to bring the level of the dent up to a point that is about 3 mm below the level of the surrounding bodywork. In cases where the dent is very shallow anyway, it is not worth trying to pull it out at all. If the underside of the dent is accessible, it can be hammered out gently from behind, using a mallet with a wooden or plastic head. Whilst doing this, hold a block of wood firmly against the outside of the panel, to absorb the impact from the hammer blows and thus prevent a large area of the bodywork from being 'belled-out'.

Should the dent be in a section of the bodywork that has a double skin, or some other factor making it inaccessible from behind, a different technique is called for. Drill several small holes through the metal inside the area - particularly in the deeper section. Then screw long self-tapping screws into the holes, just sufficiently for them to gain a good purchase in the metal. Now the dent can be pulled out by pulling on the protruding heads of the screws with a pair of pliers.

The next stage of the repair is the removal of the paint from the damaged area, and from an inch or so of the surrounding 'sound' bodywork. This is accomplished most easily by using a wire brush or abrasive pad on a power drill, although it can be done just as effectively by hand, using sheets of abrasive paper. To complete the preparation for filling, score the surface of the bare metal with a screwdriver or the tang of a file, or alternatively, drill small holes in the affected area. This will provide a good 'key' for the filler paste.

To complete the repair, see the Section on filling and respraying.

Repairs of rust holes or gashes in bodywork

Remove all paint from the affected area, and from an inch or so of the surrounding 'sound' bodywork, using an abrasive pad or a wire brush on a power drill. If these are not available, a few sheets of abrasive paper will do the job most effectively. With the paint removed, you will be able to judge the severity of the corrosion, and therefore decide whether to renew the whole panel (if this is possible) or to repair the affected area. New body panels are not as expensive as most people think, and it is often quicker and more satisfactory to fit a new panel than to attempt to repair large areas of corrosion.

Remove all fittings from the affected area, except those which will act as a guide to the original shape of the damaged bodywork (e.g. headlight shells, etc.). Then, using tin snips or a hacksaw blade, remove all loose metal and any other metal badly affected by corrosion. Hammer the edges of the hole inwards, to create a slight depression for the filler paste.

Wire-brush the affected area to remove the powdery rust from the surface of the remaining metal. Paint the affected area with rust-inhibiting paint, if the back of the rusted area is accessible, treat this also.

Before filling can take place, it will be necessary to block the hole in some way. This can be achieved with aluminium or plastic mesh, or aluminium tape.

Aluminium or plastic mesh, or glass-fibre matting, is probably the best material to use for a large hole. Cut a piece to the approximate size and shape of the hole to be filled, then position it in the hole so that its edges are below the level of the surrounding bodywork. It can be retained in position by several blobs of filler paste around its periphery.

Aluminium tape should be used for small or very narrow holes. Pull a piece off the roll, trim it to the approximate size and shape required, then pull off the backing paper (if used) and stick the tape over the hole. It can be overlapped if the thickness of one piece is insufficient. Burnish down the edges of the tape with the handle of a screwdriver or similar, to ensure that the tape is securely attached to the metal underneath.

Bodywork repairs - filling and respraying

Before using this Section, see the Sections on dent, deep scratch, rust holes and gash repairs.

Many types of bodyfiller are available, but generally speaking, those proprietary kits that contain a tin of filler paste and a tube of resin hardener are best for this type of repair. A wide, flexible plastic or nylon applicator will be found invaluable for imparting a smooth and well-contoured finish to the surface of the filler.

Mix up a little filler on a clean piece of card or board - measure the hardener carefully (follow the maker's instructions on the pack), otherwise the filler will set too rapidly or too slowly. Using the applicator, apply the filler paste to the prepared area; draw the applicator across the surface of the filler to achieve the correct contour and to level the surface. When a contour that follows the original is achieved, stop working the paste. If you carry on too long, the paste will become sticky and begin to 'pick-up' on the applicator. Continue to add thin layers of filler paste at 20-minute intervals, until the level of the filler is just proud of the surrounding bodywork.

Once the filler has hardened, the excess can be removed using a metal plane or file. From then on, progressively-finer grades of abrasive paper should be used, starting with a 40-grade production paper, and finishing with a 400-grade wet-and-dry paper. Always wrap the abrasive paper around a flat rubber, cork, or wooden block - otherwise the surface of the filler will not be completely flat. During the smoothing of the filler surface, the wet-and-dry paper should be periodically rinsed in water. This will ensure that a very smooth finish is imparted to the filler at the final stage.

At this stage, the 'dent' should be surrounded by a ring of bare metal, which in

11

turn should be encircled by the finely 'feathered' edge of the good paintwork. Rinse the repair area with clean water, until all of the dust produced by the rubbing-down operation has gone.

Spray the whole area with a light coat of primer - this will show up any imperfections in the surface of the filler. Repair these imperfections with fresh filler paste or bodystopper, and again smooth the surface with abrasive paper. If bodystopper is used, it can be mixed with cellulose thinners, to form a thin paste that is ideal for filling small holes.

Repeat this spray-and-repair procedure until you are satisfied that the surface of the filler, and the feathered edge of the paintwork, are perfect. Clean the repair area with clean water, and allow to dry fully.

The repair area is now ready for final spraying. Paint spraying must be carried out in a warm, dry, windless and dust-free atmosphere. This condition can be created artificially if you have access to a large indoor working area, but if you are forced to work in the open, you will have to pick your day very carefully. If you are working indoors, dousing the floor in the work area with water will help to settle the dust that would otherwise be in the atmosphere. If the repair area is confined to one body panel, mask off the surrounding panels; this will help to minimise the effects of a slight mis-match in paint colours. Bodywork fittings (e.g. chrome strips, door handles, etc.), will also need to be masked off. Use genuine masking tape, and several thicknesses of newspaper, for the masking operations.

Before starting to spray, agitate the aerosol can thoroughly, then spray a test area (an old tin, or similar) until the technique is mastered. Cover the repair area with a thick coat of primer; the thickness should be built up using several thin layers of paint, rather than one thick one. Using 400-grade wet-and-dry paper, rub down the surface of the primer until it is smooth. While doing this, the work area should be thoroughly doused with water, and the wet-and-dry paper periodically rinsed in water. Allow to dry before spraying on more paint.

Spray on the top coat, again building up the thickness by using several thin layers of paint. Start spraying at one edge of the repair area, and then, using a side-to-side motion, work until the whole repair area and about 2 inches of the surrounding original paintwork is covered. Remove all masking material 10 to 15 minutes after spraying on the final coat of paint.

Allow the new paint at least two weeks to harden, then, using a paintwork renovator, or a very fine cutting paste, blend the edges of the paint into the existing paintwork. Finally, apply wax polish.

Plastic components

With the use of more and more plastic body components by the vehicle manufacturers (e.g. bumpers. spoilers, and in some cases major body panels), rectification of more serious damage to such items has become a matter of either entrusting repair work to a specialist in this field, or renewing complete components. Repair of such damage by the DIY owner is not feasible, owing to the cost of the equipment and materials required for effecting such repairs. The basic technique involves making a groove along the line of the crack in the plastic, using a rotary burr in a power drill. The damaged part is then welded back together, using a hot-air gun to heat up and fuse a plastic filler rod into the groove. Any excess plastic is then removed, and the area rubbed down to a smooth finish. It is important that a filler rod of the correct plastic is used, as body components can be made of a variety of different types (e.g. polycarbonate, ABS, polypropylene).

Damage of a less serious nature (abrasions, minor cracks, etc.), can be repaired by the DIY owner using a two-part epoxy filler repair material. Once mixed in equal proportions, this is used in similar fashion to the bodywork filler used on metal panels. The filler is usually cured in twenty to thirty minutes, ready for sanding and painting.

If the owner is renewing a complete component himself, or if he has repaired it with epoxy filler, he will be left with the problem of finding a paint for finishing which is compatible with the type of plastic used. At one time, the use of a universal paint was not possible, owing to the complex range of plastics encountered in body component applications. Standard paints, generally speaking, will not bond to plastic or rubber satisfactorily. However, it is now possible to obtain a plastic body parts finishing kit that consists of a pre-primer treatment, a primer and coloured top coat. Full instructions are normally supplied with a kit, but basically, the method of use is to first apply the pre-primer to the component concerned, and allow it to dry for up to 30 minutes. Then the primer is applied, and left to dry for about an hour before finally applying the special-coloured top coat. The result is a correctly coloured component, where the paint will flex with the plastic or rubber, a property that standard paint does not normally possess.

5 Major body damage repair - general

Where serious damage has occurred, or large areas need renewal due to neglect, it means that complete new panels will need welding-in; this is best left to professionals. If the damage is due to impact, it will also be necessary to check completely the alignment of the bodyshell; this can only be carried out accurately by a Vauxhall dealer using special jigs. If the body is left misaligned, it is primarily dangerous (as the car will not handle properly) and secondly, uneven stresses will be imposed on the steering, suspension and possibly transmission, causing abnormal wear or complete failure, particularly to items such as the tyres.

6 Front and rear bumpers - removal and refitting

Front bumper

Removal

1 The bumper is removed as a complete assembly with the front trim panel; on models with front foglights, disconnect the battery negative lead and disconnect the foglight wiring plugs.

2 For improved access, apply the handbrake, then jack up the front of the vehicle, and support securely on axle stands.

3 Remove the radiator grille, as described in Section 7.

4 Working under the wheel arches, remove the screws and/or clips, as applicable, securing the rear edges of the bumper to the wheel arch liners.

5 Unscrew the two screws securing each side of the bumper to the brackets on the body (see illustration).

6 Unscrew the two nuts (one at each side of the bumper) securing the bumper to the body front panel (see illustration). Recover the washers.

6.5 Front bumper side securing screws (arrowed)

6.6 Front bumper-to-body front panel securing nut

6.7 Removing a front bumper securing clip

6.12 Rear bumper securing screw and nut locations

6.14 Rear bumper-to-rear body panel securing nut - Hatchback model

7 Remove the four plastic clips securing the lower edge of the bumper to the lower body panel. To remove the clips, prise out the central pins, using a screwdriver if necessary, then pull the clips from the bumper **(see illustration)**.

8 Carefully withdraw the bumper from the vehicle.

Refitting

9 Refitting is a reversal of removal.

Rear bumper

Removal

10 The bumper is removed as a complete assembly with the rear trim panel.

11 On Saloon and Hatchback models,

remove the rear number plate light(s), as described in Chapter 12.

12 Working under the wheel arches, unscrew the two screws securing each side of the bumper to the brackets on the body **(see illustration)**.

13 Where applicable, remove the rear luggage compartment trim panel for access to the bumper-to-rear body panel nuts. On Estate and Van models, note that it will be necessary to lift the spare wheel cover for access to one of the bumper securing nuts.

14 Unscrew the two bumper-to-rear body panel nuts (one at each side of the bumper), **(see illustration)**. Recover the washers.

15 Carefully withdraw the bumper from the vehicle.

Refitting

16 Refitting is a reversal of removal.

---

7 Radiator grille - removal and refitting

Removal

1 Open the bonnet.

2 Carefully lever the top of the grille forwards to release the upper securing clips **(see illustration)**.

3 Using a screwdriver, carefully release the clips from each end of the grille, below the headlights **(see illustration)**.

4 Slide the grille towards the right-hand side of the vehicle, to release the lower securing clips, then lift the grille from the vehicle **(see illustration)**.

5 Where applicable, disconnect the fluid hoses from the headlight washer nozzles, which are integral with the grille panel.

6 Carefully manipulate the grille from the front panel, and withdraw it from the vehicle.

Refitting

7 Refitting is a reversal of removal, ensuring that all the clips are positively engaged.

---

8 Windscreen cowl panel - removal and refitting

Removal

1 Open the bonnet.

2 Remove the windscreen wiper arms, as described in Chapter 12.

3 Unscrew the two large nuts from the windscreen wiper arm spindles.

4 Prise the two screw covers from the cowl panel, and remove the securing screws **(see illustration)**.

5 Note how the cowl panel engages with the weatherstrip at the base of the windscreen. Then carefully release the ends of the cowl panel from the scuttle (the ends of the panel

7.2 Releasing a radiator grille upper securing clip

7.4 Radiator grille lower securing clip released from body front panel

8.4 Removing a windscreen cowl panel securing screw nut from the wiper arm spindle. Cowl panel securing screw arrowed

7.3 Radiator grille end securing clip released from below headlight

11

8.5 Removing the windscreen cowl panel

are secured with Velcro strips), and withdraw the panel from the vehicle **(see illustration)**.

Refitting

6 Refitting is a reversal of removal, remembering the following points.

7 Ensure that the panel is correctly engaged with the weatherstrip.

8 Make sure that the ends of the panel are securely held by the Velcro strips.

9 Refit the windscreen wiper arms as described in Chapter 12.

9 Bonnet - removal and refitting

Removal

1 Open the bonnet and support it in the fully open position.

2 Disconnect the windscreen washer fluid hose from the connector in the bonnet. It is advisable to tie a length of string to the connector, to prevent it from slipping into an inaccessible position in the bonnet.

3 If the original bonnet is to be refitted, mark the position of the hinges on the bonnet, to alignment on refitting.

4 Carefully pull back the insulation blocks from the bonnet hinges.

5 With the help of an assistant, support the weight of the bonnet, then unscrew the securing bolts from the hinges, and lift the bonnet from the vehicle. If the bonnet is to be refitted, rest it carefully on rags or cardboard, to avoid damaging the paint.

Refitting

6 Refitting is a reversal of removal, remembering the following points.

7 If a new bonnet is to be fitted, transfer all the serviceable fixings (rubber buffers, lock strikers, etc.) to it.

8 Where applicable, align the hinges with the previously made marks on the bonnet.

9 If the lock striker has been disturbed, adjust it to the dimension shown in Section 11, then tighten the locknut.

10 If necessary, adjust the hinge bolts and the front rubber buffers until a good fit is obtained with the bonnet shut.

10.6 Bonnet hinge-to-body fixing components

1	Bolt	4	Body bracket
2	Spring washer	5	Washer
3	Hinge	6	Nut

10 Bonnet hinge - removal and refitting

Note: *To secure the hinge on refitting, a new bolt and washer assembly will be required.*

Removal

1 Remove the bonnet, as described in Section 9.

2 Remove the windscreen cowl panel, as described in Section 8.

3 The bonnet hinges are riveted to the body panels, and to remove a hinge, it will be necessary to drill or grind off the rivet head.

4 With the rivet head removed, tap the rivet from the hinge assembly, and withdraw the hinge.

Refitting

5 When refitting the hinge, a bolt and washer assembly must be used to replace the rivet used originally.

6 Secure the hinge using the bolt and washer assembly (available from a Vauxhall dealer), ensuring that the components are located as shown **(see illustration)**.

7 Refit the windscreen cowl panel, referring to Section 8.

8 Refit the bonnet as described in Section 9.

11 Bonnet lock components - removal and refitting

Bonnet lock hook

Removal

1 The bonnet lock hook is riveted to the bonnet, and removal involves drilling out the rivet.

Refitting

2 Refitting is a reversal of removal, using a new rivet.

11.4 Bonnet lock striker adjustment

1	Striker	4	Locknut
2	Washer		X = 40 to 45 mm
3	Coil spring		

Lock striker

Removal

3 To remove the lock striker from the bonnet, loosen the locknut, then unscrew the striker, and recover the washer and spring.

Refitting

4 Refitting is a reversal of removal, but adjust the striker dimension as shown **(see illustration)**, before tightening the locknut.

Locking spring

Removal

5 Disconnect the end of the bonnet release cable from the spring, then unhook the end of the spring from the slot in the front body panel, taking care not to damage the paint.

Refitting

6 Refitting is a reversal of removal.

12 Bonnet release cable - removal and refitting

Removal

1 Open the bonnet, and support it in the fully open position.

2 Unscrew the release cable clip from the front body panel.

3 Disconnect the end of the release cable from the locking spring under the front body panel.

4 Disconnect the release cable from the release lever in the driver's footwell. If necessary, remove the release lever from its retainer for access to the cable end.

5 Pull the cable assembly through the grommet in the engine compartment bulkhead and into the engine compartment.

6 Note the routing of the cable, then release the cable from any remaining clips and cable-ties, and withdraw it from the engine compartment.

13.2 Front door wiring connector

13.3 Front door check-link roll-pin (1) and hinge pin (2)

14.2a Releasing a front door interior handle retaining clip

Refitting

7 Refitting is a reversal of removal, but ensure that the cable is correctly routed, and on completion, check the release mechanism for satisfactory operation.

13 Doors - removal, refitting and adjustment

Front door

Removal

1 To remove a door, open it fully and support it under its lower edge on blocks or axle stands covered with pads of rag.
2 Disconnect the wiring connector from the front edge of the door. To release the connector, twist the locking collar, then pull the connector from the socket in the door (see illustration).
3 Using a punch, drive the large roll-pin from the door check arm pivot (see illustration).
4 Where applicable, remove the plastic covers from the hinge pins, then drive out the pins using a punch. Have an assistant support the door as the pins are driven out, then withdraw the door from the vehicle.

Refitting

5 Refitting is a reversal of removal, using a new check-link roll-pin.

Adjustment

6 The door hinges are welded onto the door frame and the body pillar, so that there is no provision for adjustment or alignment.
7 If the door can be moved up and down on its hinges due to wear in the hinge pins or their holes, it may be possible to drill out the holes and fit slightly oversize pins. Consult a Vauxhall dealer for further advice.
8 Door closure may be adjusted by altering the position of the lock striker on the body pillar, using an Allen key or a hexagon bit.

Rear door

Removal

9 On models with central locking, Remove the door inner trim panel, as described in Section 51, and disconnect the wiring

connector inside the door. Note the routing of the wiring, and the location of the wiring connector, then carefully feed the wiring through the grommet in the front edge of the door.
10 Proceed as described in paragraphs 3 and 4.

Refitting

11 Refitting is a reversal of removal, using a new check-link roll-pin.
12 Where applicable, ensure that the wiring and the connector are routed and located as noted during removal.
13 Door handle and lock components removal and refitting

14 Door interior handle - removal and refitting

Removal

1 Remove the door inner trim panel, as described in Section 51.
2 Using a screwdriver, carefully release the retaining clips and pull the handle assembly from the door, then unhook the operating rod, and withdraw the assembly (see illustrations).

Refitting

3 Refitting is a reversal of removal, but check the mechanism for satisfactory operation before refitting the door inner trim panel, then refit the trim panel referring to Section 51.

15.2 Front door exterior handle securing nuts (1) and central locking microswitch (2)

14.2b Front door interior handle - retaining clips (arrowed)

15 Door exterior handles - removal and refitting

Front door handles

Removal

1 Remove the door inner trim panel, and peel back the plastic insulating sheet for access to the handle, as described in Section 51.
2 Unscrew the two nuts securing the exterior handle to the door (see illustration).
3 Where applicable, unclip the central locking microswitch from the rear edge of the exterior handle assembly.
4 Release the two lower retaining clips, then manipulate the outer plastic section of the exterior handle assembly through the outside of the door, and disconnect the operating rod (see illustration).

15.4 Withdrawing the outer section of a front door exterior handle

11

5 Withdraw the inner section of the exterior handle assembly from the inside of the door, and disconnect the lock cylinder operating rod.

Refitting

6 Refitting is a reversal of removal, but check the operation of the mechanism before refitting the door inner trim panel, and refit the trim panel referring to Section 51.

Rear door handles (Saloon and Hatchback models)

Removal

7 Remove the door inner trim panel, and peel back the plastic insulating sheet for access to the handle, as described in Section 51.
8 Pull the weatherstrips from the inside and outside lower edges of the window aperture.
9 Unscrew the upper window rear guide rail securing bolt, which is accessible at the rear edge of the window aperture.
10 Unscrew the lower window rear guide rail securing bolt (Torx type), which is accessible through the inner door skin, then withdraw the guide rail from the door. Where applicable, the weatherstrip can be left attached to the guide rail, in which case, position the guide rail to one side out of the way, taking care not to damage the vehicle paintwork.
11 Unscrew the two nuts securing the exterior handle to the door.
12 Release the two lower retaining clips, then manipulate the exterior handle assembly through the outside of the door, and disconnect the operating rods.

Refitting

13 Refitting is a reversal of removal, but check the operation of the mechanism before refitting the door inner trim panel, and refit the trim panel referring to Section 51.

Rear door handle (Estate models)

Removal

14 Remove the door inner trim panel, and peel back the plastic insulating sheet for access to the handle, as described in Section 51.
15 Unscrew the two nuts securing the exterior handle to the door.

16 Release the two lower retaining clips, then manipulate the exterior handle assembly through the outside of the door, and disconnect the operating rods.

Refitting

17 Refitting is a reversal of removal, but check the operation of the mechanism before refitting the door inner trim panel, and refit the trim panel referring to Section 51.

16 Door locks - removal and refitting

Front

Removal

1 Remove the door inner trim panel, and peel back the plastic insulating sheet from the rear edge of the door, as described in Section 51.
2 Unscrew the window rear guide rail securing bolt from the rear edge of the door, then manipulate the guide rail out through the lower aperture in the door.
3 Where applicable, reach in through the door aperture and unclip the plastic cover from the lock.
4 Working through the apertures in the door, disconnect the three operating rods from the lock assembly.
5 On models with central locking, disconnect the battery negative lead (if not already done), then reach in through the door aperture, and disconnect the wiring plug from the central locking motor **(see illustration)**.
6 Unscrew the three Torx screws securing the lock assembly to the rear edge of the door, then manipulate the lock assembly (complete with the lock button operating rod, and the central locking motor, where applicable) around the window regulator mechanism, and out through the lower door aperture **(see illustrations)**.

Refitting

7 Refitting is a reversal of removal, but check the operation of the door lock, handle and window regulator mechanisms before refitting the door trim panel, and refit the trim panel

referring to Section 51. If the lock operation is not satisfactory, note that the exterior handle operating rod can be adjusted by turning the knurled plastic adjuster wheel at the end of the rod.

Rear door (Saloon and Hatchback models)

Removal

8 Fully lower the window, then remove the door inner trim panel and the plastic insulating sheet, as described in Section 51.
9 Pull the weatherstrips from the inside and outside lower edges of the window aperture.
10 Unscrew the upper window rear guide rail securing bolt, which is accessible at the rear edge of the window aperture.
11 Unscrew the lower window rear guide rail securing bolt (Torx type), which is accessible through the inner door skin, then withdraw the guide rail from the door. Where applicable, the weatherstrip can be left attached to the guide rail, in which case, position the guide rail to one side out of the way, taking care not to damage the vehicle paintwork.
12 Where applicable, reach in through the door aperture, and unclip the plastic cover from the lock.
13 Working through the apertures in the door, disconnect the operating rods from the lock assembly.
14 On models with central locking, disconnect the battery negative lead (if not already done), and disconnect the wiring plug from the central locking motor.
15 Unscrew the three Torx screws securing the lock assembly to the rear edge of the door. Then manipulate the lock assembly (complete with the lock button operating rod, and the central locking motor, where applicable) around the window regulator mechanism, and out through the lower door aperture.

Refitting

16 Refitting is a reversal of removal, but check the operation of the door lock, handle and window regulator mechanisms before refitting the door trim panel, and refit the trim panel referring to Section 51. If the lock operation is not satisfactory, note that the

16.5 Disconnecting the central locking motor wiring plug from a front door lock

16.6a Unscrewing a front door lock securing screw

16.6b Withdrawing a front door lock assembly through the lower door aperture

17.2 Front door lock cylinder securing circlip (arrowed)

19.2a Removing the weatherstrip from the inside of the front door window aperture

19.2b Removing the weatherstrip from the outside of the front door window aperture (door mirror removed)

exterior handle operating rod can be adjusted by turning the knurled plastic adjuster wheel at the end of the rod.

Rear door (Estate models)

Removal

17 Fully lower the window, then remove the door inner trim panel and the plastic insulating sheet, as described in Section 51.
18 Working at the top of the window aperture, remove the two upper rear window rear guide rail securing screws.
19 Working at the bottom of the window aperture, remove the lower rear window guide securing screw, then remove the rear window guide securing bolt and nut, and withdraw the window guide upwards through the window aperture.
20 Proceed as described in paragraphs 12 to 15 inclusive.

Refitting

21 Refitting is a reversal of removal, but check the operation of the door lock, handle and window regulator mechanisms before refitting the door trim panel, and refit the trim panel referring to Section 51. If the lock operation is not satisfactory, note that the exterior handle operating rod can be adjusted by turning the knurled plastic adjuster wheel at the end of the rod.

17 Front door lock cylinder - removal and refitting

Removal

1 Remove the door exterior handle, as described in Section 15.
2 Insert the key into the lock, then extract the circlip from the end of the lock cylinder **(see illustration)**.
3 Withdraw the lock cylinder using the key, and recover the lever assembly.

Refitting

4 Refitting is a reversal of removal, but check the operation of the door lock, handle and window regulator mechanism before refitting

the door trim panel, and refit the trim panel referring to Section 51.

18 Lock striker - removal and refitting

Removal

1 The lock striker is screwed into the door pillar on the body.
2 Before removing the striker, mark its position, so that it can be refitted in exactly the same position.
3 To remove the striker, simply unscrew the securing screw using an Allen key or hexagon bit.

Refitting

4 Refitting is a reversal of removal, but if necessary, adjust the position of the striker to achieve satisfactory closing of the door.

19 Door window glass - removal and refitting

Front

Removal

1 Remove the door inner trim panel and the plastic insulating sheet, as described in Section 51.

19.3b . . . and withdrawing the rear guide rail

2 Pull the weatherstrips from the inside and outside lower edges of the window aperture. Note that on certain models, it may be necessary to remove the door mirror (see Section 29) to enable removal of the outside weatherstrip **(see illustrations)**.
3 Unscrew the window rear guide rail securing bolt from the rear edge of the door, then manipulate the guide rail out through the lower aperture in the door **(see illustrations)**.
4 Where applicable, reconnect the battery negative lead and the electric window switch wiring, and lower the window until the metal guide channel at the bottom edge of the window glass is accessible through the door aperture.
5 Prise the plastic end stop from the window glass guide channel **(see illustration)**.

19.3a Unscrewing the window rear guide rail securing bolt from the front door . . .

19.5 Prising the end stop from the front door window glass guide channel

11

19.6a Unscrewing a front door window lower guide rail securing bolt . . .

19.6b . . . and withdrawing the lower guide rail

19.7 Withdrawing the front door window glass

6 Unscrew the two securing bolts, and remove the window lower guide rail from the door (see illustrations).

7 Manipulate the window regulator mechanism as necessary, and tilt the window glass forwards until it can be withdrawn from outside the door through the window aperture (see illustration).

Refitting

8 Refitting is a reversal of removal, but adjust the angle of the lower guide rail by means of the two securing screws until smooth operation of the window is achieved, and refit the door inner trim panel referring to Section 51.

Rear (Saloon and Hatchback models)

Removal

9 Fully lower the window, then remove the door inner trim panel and the plastic insulating sheet, as described in Section 51.

10 Pull the weatherstrips from the inside and outside lower edges of the window aperture.

11 Unscrew the upper window rear guide rail securing bolt, which is accessible at the rear edge of the window aperture.

12 Unscrew the lower window rear guide rail securing bolt (Torx type), which is accessible through the inner door skin, then withdraw the guide rail from the door (see illustration). Where applicable, the weatherstrip can be left attached to the guide rail, in which case, position the guide rail to one side out of the

way, taking care not to damage the vehicle paintwork.

13 Manipulate the window regulator mechanism as necessary, and tilt the window glass forwards until it can be withdrawn from outside the door through the window aperture.

Refitting

14 Refitting is a reversal of removal, but refit the door inner trim panel referring to Section 51.

Rear sliding glass (Estate models)

Removal

15 Remove the rear glass, as described in paragraphs 9 and 10.

16 Remove the window regulator mechanism, as described in Section 20.

17 Working at the top of the window aperture, remove the two upper rear window rear guide rail securing screws.

18 Working at the bottom of the window aperture, remove the lower rear window guide securing screw, then remove the rear window guide securing bolt and nut, and withdraw the window guide upwards through the window aperture (see illustration).

19 Withdraw the window glass upwards through the window aperture.

Refitting

20 Refitting is a reversal of removal, but refit the window regulator mechanism as

described in Section 20, and refit the door inner trim panel referring to Section 51.

Rear window fixed glass (Estate models)

Removal

21 Remove the sliding glass, as described in paragraphs 15 to 19.

22 Pull the fixed glass forwards from its surround, and withdraw it from the door.

Refitting

23 Refitting is a reversal of removal.

20 Window regulator - removal and refitting

Front door

Removal

1 Lower the window approximately halfway, then remove the door inner trim panel and the plastic insulating sheet, as described in Section 51.

2 Support the window in the half-open position by placing a wooden prop under it, ensuring that the prop is clear of the regulator mechanism.

3 Drill out the four rivets securing the regulator mechanism to the door, using an 8.5 mm diameter drill (see illustration). Take care not to damage the door panel.

4 Prise the plastic end stop from the window glass guide channel.

19.12 Upper (1) and lower (2) rear door window rear guide rail securing bolts - Hatchback model

19.18 Rear door rear window guide fixings - Estate models

1 Regulator securing rivets 3 Nut and bolt
2 Screws

20.3 Drilling out a front door window regulator securing rivet

20.5 Front door window regulator securing rivets (1), and window lower guide rail securing bolts (2)

20.6 Disconnecting a front door electric window motor wiring plug

20.7 Withdrawing a front door window regulator assembly

5 Unscrew the two securing bolts, and remove the window lower guide rail from the door **(see illustration).**

6 On models with electric windows, disconnect the battery negative lead (if not already done), then disconnect the wiring plug from the window motor **(see illustration).**

7 Carefully manipulate the window regulator assembly out through the aperture in the door **(see illustration).**

Refitting

8 Refitting is a reversal of removal, remembering the following points.

9 Ensure that the regulator arms are correctly positioned in the guide rails before securing the regulator assembly to the door.

10 Secure the regulator assembly to the door, using new rivets **(see illustration).**

11 Adjust the angle of the lower guide rail by means of the two securing screws, until smooth operation of the window is achieved.

12 Refit the door inner trim panel referring to Section 51.

Rear door

Removal

13 Proceed as described in paragraphs 1 to 3 inclusive, and paragraphs 6 and 7, noting that the assembly is secured by five rivets (two upper and three lower rivets), **(see illustrations).**

Refitting

14 Refitting is a reversal of removal, remembering the following points.

15 Ensure that the regulator arm is correctly positioned in the guide rail before securing the regulator assembly to the door.

16 Secure the regulator assembly to the door using new rivets.

17 Check the regulator mechanism for satisfactory operation before refitting the door trim panel, then refit the panel referring to Section 51.

21 Boot lid (Saloon models) - removal and refitting

Removal

1 Open the boot lid fully.

2 On models with central locking, disconnect the battery negative lead, then disconnect the wiring from the lock motor. If the original boot lid is to be refitted, first tie a length of string to the end of the wiring. Feed the wiring through the boot lid, then untie the string, leaving it in position in the boot lid to assist refitting.

3 Mark the position of the hinges on the boot lid.

4 With the help of an assistant, support the weight of the boot lid, then unscrew the securing bolts from the hinges **(see illustration),** and lift the boot lid from the vehicle.

20.10 Fit new rivets to secure the front door window regulator assembly

Refitting

5 If a new boot lid is to be fitted, transfer all the serviceable fittings (rubber buffers, lock mechanism, etc.) to it.

6 Refitting is a reversal of removal, remembering the following points.

7 Align the hinges with the previously made marks on the boot lid.

8 Where applicable, draw the central locking motor wiring through the boot lid, using the string.

9 If necessary, adjust the hinge bolts and the rubber buffers until a good fit is obtained with the boot lid shut.

10 If necessary, adjust the position of the lock striker on the body, to achieve satisfactory lock operation.

20.13a Rear door window regulator assembly upper . . .

20.13b . . . and lower securing rivets (arrowed)

21.4 Boot lid hinge securing bolts (1) and central locking motor wiring (2) - Saloon model

11

22 Boot lid hinge -
removal and refitting

Removal

1 Remove the boot lid, as described in Section 21.
2 Remove the rear quarter trim panel, as described in Section 51.
3 Note the position of the hinge counterbalance spring in the bracket on the body, so that it can be refitted in its original position, then unhook the spring from the body **(see illustration)**. Use a lever to release the spring if necessary.
4 Unscrew the securing bolt **(see illustration)**, and remove the hinge from the body.

Refitting

5 Refitting is a reversal of removal, remembering the following points.
6 Ensure that the counterbalance spring is positioned as noted before removal.
7 Refit the boot lid as described previously in this Section 21.

23 Boot lid components -
removal and refitting

Handle
Removal

1 Open the boot lid, then remove the four securing screws, and withdraw the lock cylinder assembly cover panel.
2 Unscrew the two securing nuts, then withdraw the handle from outside the boot lid. Note that the securing nuts also secure the lock cylinder assembly to the boot lid.

Refitting

3 Refitting is a reversal of removal.

Lock
Removal

4 Proceed as described in paragraph 1.

22.3 Boot lid hinge spring (1) - note position of spring in bracket (2) - Saloon model

5 Unscrew the two securing bolts, and withdraw the lock from the boot lid **(see illustration)**.

Refitting

6 Refitting is a reversal of removal, but if necessary, adjust the position of the lock striker on the body, to achieve satisfactory lock operation.

Lock cylinder
Removal

7 Open the boot lid fully.
8 Remove the four securing screws, and withdraw the lock cylinder assembly cover panel.
9 Unscrew the two securing nuts **(see illustration)**, and withdraw the lock cylinder assembly, unhooking the lock operating rod(s) as the assembly is withdrawn. Note that the securing nuts also secure the boot lid handle.
10 No spare parts are available for the lock cylinder assembly, and if faulty, the complete assembly must be renewed.

Refitting

11 Refitting is a reversal of removal.

Lock striker
Removal

12 The lock striker is screwed into the lower body panel.
13 Remove the securing screws, then unclip the rear boot trim panel to expose the lock striker securing bolt **(see illustration)**.

22.4 Boot lid hinge-to-body securing bolt (arrowed) - Saloon model

14 Before removing the striker, mark its position, so that it can be refitted in exactly the same position.
15 To remove the striker, simply unscrew the securing screw.

Refitting

16 Refitting is a reversal of removal, but if necessary, adjust the position of the striker to achieve satisfactory closing of the boot lid.

24 Tailgate -
removal and refitting

Removal

1 Open the tailgate fully.
2 Disconnect the battery negative lead.
3 Remove the securing screws, and withdraw the tailgate rear trim panels.
4 Disconnect all the relevant wiring now exposed, and disconnect the washer fluid hose from the washer nozzle.
5 If the original tailgate is to be refitted, tie string to the ends of all the relevant wires, and if necessary the washer fluid hose, then feed the wiring and the hose through the top of the tailgate. Untie the string, leaving it in position in the tailgate to assist refitting.
6 Have an assistant support the weight of the tailgate, then disconnect the tailgate support struts from their mounting balljoints.

23.5 Boot lid lock - Saloon model

23.9 Lock cylinder securing nut (arrowed) - Saloon model

23.13 Boot lid lock striker securing bolt

24.7 Tailgate hinge pin securing clip (arrowed) - Hatchback model

26.2 Prising out a tailgate support strut balljoint clip - Hatchback model

26.14 Disconnecting a tailgate lock operating rod - Hatchback model

7 Prise the securing clips from the ends of the tailgate hinge pins **(see illustration)**.
8 With the tailgate adequately supported, tap the hinge pins from the hinges, using a punch, and carefully lift the tailgate from the vehicle.

Refitting

9 If a new tailgate is to be fitted, transfer all serviceable components (rubber buffers, lock mechanism, etc.) to it.
10 Refitting is a reversal of removal, remembering the following points.
11 If the original tailgate is being refitted, draw the wiring and washer fluid hose (where applicable) through the tailgate, using the string.
12 If necessary, adjust the rubber buffers to obtain a good fit when the tailgate is shut.
13 If necessary, adjust the position of the lock striker on the body, to achieve satisfactory lock operation.

25 Tailgate hinge - removal and refitting

Removal

1 Remove the tailgate as described previously in this Section 24.
2 Prise off the rear roof trim panel, taking care not to break the securing clips (see Section 48), and lower the rear headlining slightly for access to the tailgate hinge securing screws.

26.15 Removing the tailgate lock - Hatchback model

3 Mark the hinge position on the body.
4 Unscrew the securing screws, and withdraw the hinge.

Refitting

5 Refitting is a reversal of removal, remembering the following points.
6 Align the hinges with the previously made marks on the body.
7 Refit the tailgate as described previously in this Section 24.

26 Tailgate components - removal and refitting

Support strut

Removal

1 Open the tailgate fully, and have an assistant support it.
2 Release the strut from its mounting balljoints by prising the spring clips a little way out **(see illustration)**, and pulling the strut off the balljoints.

Refitting

3 Refitting is a reversal of removal.

Handle (Hatchback models)

Removal

4 Open the tailgate, then remove the securing screws and withdraw the tailgate rear trim panel.

26.18 Disconnecting an operating rod from the lock cylinder assembly - Hatchback model

5 Working through the aperture in the tailgate, unscrew the two securing nuts, then withdraw the handle from outside the tailgate. Note that the securing nuts also secure the lock cylinder assembly.

Refitting

6 Refitting is a reversal of removal.

Handle (Estate and Van models)

Removal

7 Proceed as described in paragraph 1.
8 Remove the tailgate lock cylinder assembly, as described later in this Section.
9 Remove the tailgate wiper motor, as described in Chapter 12.
10 Remove the rear number plate lights, as described in Chapter 12.
11 Working through the apertures in the tailgate, unscrew the four securing nuts, and withdraw the handle from outside the tailgate.

Refitting

12 Refitting is a reversal of removal, but refit the tailgate wiper motor as described in Chapter 12.

Lock (Estate and Van models)

Removal

13 Proceed as described in paragraph 1.
14 Working through the aperture in the tailgate, disconnect the operating rod(s) from the lock **(see illustration)**.
15 Unscrew the securing screws (three on Hatchback models, four on Estate models), and withdraw the lock **(see illustration)**.

Refitting

16 Refitting is a reversal of removal, but if necessary, adjust the position of the lock striker on the body, to achieve satisfactory lock operation.

Lock cylinder (Estate and Van models)

Removal

17 Remove the securing screws, and withdraw the tailgate rear trim panel.
18 Disconnect the operating rod(s) from the lock cylinder assembly **(see illustration)**.

11

26.19 Lock cylinder assembly securing nuts (arrowed) - Hatchback model

26.25 Tailgate lock striker - Hatchback model

27.5a Pull the securing clips from the studs in the footwell . . .

19 Unscrew the two securing nuts **(see illustration)**, and withdraw the lock cylinder assembly. Note that on Hatchback models, the securing nuts also secure the tailgate handle.

20 No spare parts are available for the lock cylinder assembly, and if faulty, the complete assembly must be renewed.

Refitting

21 Refitting is a reversal of removal.

Lock striker (Estate and Van models)

Removal

22 The lock striker is screwed into the lower body panel.

23 Where applicable, extract the securing screws, and remove the luggage compartment rear trim panel for access to the lock striker securing bolts.

24 Before removing the striker, mark its position, so that it can be refitted in exactly the same position.

25 To remove the striker, simply unscrew the securing screws **(see illustration)**.

Refitting

26 Refitting is a reversal of removal, but if necessary, adjust the position of the striker to achieve satisfactory closing of the tailgate.

27.5b . . . and pull the carpet back to expose the central locking electronic control unit (arrowed)

27 Central locking components - removal and refitting

Electronic control unit

Removal

1 The control unit is located behind the right-hand footwell side/sill trim panel.

2 Disconnect the battery negative lead.

3 Remove the footwell side/sill trim panel, as described in Section 51.

4 Where applicable, unscrew the two securing nuts, and pull the wiring plug bracket from the footwell.

5 Pull the two securing clips from the studs in the footwell, and pull the carpet back from the studs to expose the control unit **(see illustrations)**.

6 Unscrew the two securing screws, and lift the unit from its location in the footwell, then disconnect the wiring plug and withdraw the unit.

Refitting

7 Refitting is a reversal of removal.

Microswitches

Removal

8 The microswitches are mounted inside the front doors, at the rear of the exterior handle assemblies.

9 Remove the door inner trim panel, and peel back the plastic insulating sheet sufficiently to

27.10 Central locking operating microswitch (arrowed)

gain access to the exterior handle, as described in Section 51.

10 Unclip the microswitch from the rear edge of the exterior handle assembly, disconnect the switch wiring connector from the door wiring harness, then withdraw the switch **(see illustration)**.

Refitting

11 Refitting is a reversal of removal, but refit the door inner trim panel as described in Section 51.

Door motor

Removal

12 Remove the door lock, as described in Section 16.

13 Disconnect the lock operating rod from the motor.

14 Remove the two securing screws, and withdraw the motor from the lock assembly **(see illustration)**.

Refitting

15 Refitting is a reversal of removal.

Boot lid or tailgate motor

Removal

16 Disconnect the battery negative lead.

17 Open the boot or tailgate, as applicable.

18 Remove the securing screws, and withdraw the lock cylinder assembly cover (Saloon models), or the tailgate rear trim panel (Hatchback and Estate models).

27.14 Central locking motor securing screws (arrowed)

27.19 Disconnecting the wiring plug from the boot lid lock operating motor - Saloon model

27.20a Boot lid lock operating motor - Saloon model

27.20b Removing a tailgate lock operating motor - Hatchback model

19 Disconnect the wiring plug from the motor (see illustration).
20 Unscrew the two securing screws, and withdraw the motor from the boot lid or tailgate, as applicable, unhooking the lock operating rod as the motor is withdrawn (see illustrations).

Refitting

21 Refitting is a reversal of removal.

Fuel filler flap motor (Saloon and Estate models)

Removal

22 Disconnect the battery negative lead.
23 Release the right-hand luggage compartment side trim panel from the body, referring to Section 51.
24 Disconnect the motor wiring plug.
25 Remove the two securing screws, then carefully manipulate the motor from its location, disengaging the operating rod as the unit is withdrawn (see illustration).

Refitting

26 Refitting is a reversal of removal.

Fuel filler flap motor (Hatchback models)

Removal

27 Disconnect the battery negative lead.
28 Remove the luggage compartment right-

hand side trim panel, referring to Section 51.
29 Remove the right-hand rear light cluster, as described in Chapter 12.
30 Pull back the carpet from the wheel arch to expose the two lock motor bracket securing screws (see illustration).
31 Remove the securing screws, then carefully manipulate the motor and bracket assembly from its location, disengaging the operating rod as the unit is withdrawn. Manipulate the unit out through the rear light cluster aperture, and disconnect the wiring plug (see illustration).
32 The motor can be separated from the bracket by removing the securing screws.

Refitting

33 Refitting is a reversal of removal.

28 Electric window components - removal and refitting

Switches

Removal

1 The switches are located in the driver's and passenger's doors.
2 Remove the door inner trim panel, as described in Section 51.

27.25 Fuel filler flap operating motor securing screws (arrowed) - Saloon model

3 With the wiring connector disconnected, carefully prise the switch assembly from the trim panel (see illustration).

Refitting

4 Refitting is a reversal of removal, but refit the door inner trim panel as described in Section 51.

Window motors

Removal

5 Remove the door window regulator, as described in Section 20.
6 To remove the motor assembly from the

27.30 Pulling back the carpet to expose the fuel filler flap lock operating motor bracket securing screws - Hatchback model

27.31 Fuel filler flap operating motor viewed through rear light cluster aperture

28.3 Removing the electric window operating switch from the driver's door

11

28.6 Electric window operating motor securing screws (arrowed)

29.3 Door mirror trim panel freed from front edge of door - electric mirror

29.4 Unscrewing a door mirror securing screw - electric mirror

regulator, unscrew the three securing screws **(see illustration)**.

7 No spare parts are available for the motor assembly, and if faulty, the complete unit must be renewed.

Refitting

8 Refitting is a reversal of removal, but refit the regulator as described in Section 20.

29 Door mirror - removal and refitting

Removal

1 On models with electric mirrors, disconnect the battery negative lead.

2 Where applicable, on models with manually adjustable mirrors, pull off the adjuster lever.

3 Prise the mirror trim panel from the inside front edge of the door, and disconnect the wiring from the loudspeaker mounted in the trim panel **(see illustration)**.

4 Extract the three now-exposed securing screws, and withdraw the mirror assembly from the door. On models with electric mirrors, disconnect the wiring plug **(see illustration)**.

Refitting

5 Refitting is a reversal of removal, but ensure that the rubber weatherstrip is correctly located on the mirror housing.

30 Door mirror glass - removal and refitting

Removal

1 The mirror glass can be removed for renewal without removing the mirror. On models with electric mirrors, disconnect the battery negative lead before proceeding.

2 Carefully prise the glass from its balljoints using a screwdriver, and where applicable, disconnect the heater wires from the glass. Take care, as the glass is easily broken if forced **(see illustration)**.

Refitting

3 To refit, simply push the glass onto the balljoints (ensuring that the heater wires are connected, where applicable).

31 Electric mirror components - removal and refitting

Switch

Removal

1 The switch can be prised from the door inner trim panel, after removing the door inner trim panel (as described in Section 51) and disconnecting the wiring plug **(see illustration)**.

Refitting

2 After refitting the switch, refit the door inner trim panel as described in Section 51.

Motor

Removal

3 Remove the mirror glass, as described previously in this Section.

4 Extract the three motor securing screws, disconnect the wiring plug, then withdraw the motor.

Refitting

5 Refitting is a reversal of removal, but ensure that the wiring is routed behind the motor, to avoid interfering with the adjustment mechanism.

32 Interior mirror - removal and refitting

Removal

1 The mirror can be removed from its mounting plate on the windscreen, after unscrewing the mounting screw using a 2 mm Allen key.

2 The mounting plate is fixed to the windscreen using a special adhesive, and should not be disturbed unless necessary. Note that there is a risk of cracking the windscreen glass if an attempt is made to remove a securely bonded mounting plate.

Refitting

3 If necessary, the special adhesive required to fix the mounting plate to the windscreen can be obtained from a Vauxhall dealer.

33 Windscreen and rear window glass - general

Except for the rear quarter windows, all fixed glass is bonded in position, using a special adhesive.

Special tools, adhesives and expertise are required for successful removal and refitting of glass fixed by this method. Such work must therefore be entrusted to a Vauxhall dealer, a windscreen specialist, or other competent professional.

30.2 Prising the mirror glass from an electric mirror - heater wires arrowed

31.1 Removing the electric mirror operating switch from the door inner trim panel

34.2 Rear quarter window securing nuts (arrowed)

35.2a Extract the four securing screws . . .

35.2b . . . and withdraw the sunroof guide rail plastic surround

34 Rear quarter windows - removal and refitting

Note: *The manufacturers recommend the use of new plastic nuts to secure the glass on refitting.*

Removal

1 Remove the rear quarter trim panel, as described in Section 51.

2 Have an assistant support the quarter window from outside the vehicle, then unscrew the plastic securing nuts **(see illustration)**, and the bolts, and push the window from the body.

Refitting

3 Refitting is a reversal of removal, but ensure that the seal on the rear of the glass is seated correctly against the body as the window is fitted, and use new plastic nuts to secure the glass.

35 Sunroof glass panel - removal and refitting

Note: *The sunroof is a complex piece of equipment, consisting of a large number of components. It is strongly recommended that the sunroof mechanism is not disturbed unless necessary. If the sunroof mechanism is*

faulty, or requires overhaul, consult a Vauxhall dealer for advice.

Removal

1 Push the sunshade fully rearwards, and open the glass panel halfway.

2 Extract the four securing screws from the front edge of the guide rail plastic surround, and withdraw the surround down through the sunroof aperture **(see illustrations)**.

3 Move the glass panel forwards, and open it to its tilt position.

4 Prise the plastic trim strips from the guide rails, to expose the glass panel securing screws **(see illustration)**.

5 Extract the three securing screws from each guide rail **(see illustration)** and where applicable, recover the lockwashers.

6 Carefully lift the glass panel from the roof aperture, taking care not to damage the vehicle paintwork.

Refitting

7 Refitting is a reversal of removal, remembering the following points.

8 Before refitting the glass panel, measure the distance between the mounting flanges. Bend the flanges if necessary to achieve the required dimension **(see illustration)**.

35.4 Prising a plastic trim strip from the guide rail

9 Where applicable, ensure that the glass panel securing screw lockwashers engage with the locating pins on the guide rails.

10 Before fully tightening the glass panel securing screws, close the panel, and adjust its position to give the dimensions shown **(see illustration)**.

11 If a new glass panel has been fitted, peel off the protective foil on completion of adjustment.

36 Sunroof components - removal and refitting

Gutter

Removal

1 Remove the glass panel, as described in Section 35.

2 Extract the two securing screws, then lift the gutter from the roof aperture.

35.5 Loosening a glass panel securing screw

35.8 Sunroof glass panel mounting flange dimension

1 Mounting flange   A - A Cross-section
2 Nut   cutting point
3 Protective foil   Dimensions in mm

35.10 Sunroof glass panel fitting position

11

36.7 Sunshade spring clip locations (arrowed)

Refitting

3 Refit the gutter to the roof aperture at an angle, pushing it up to the stop on both sides until the retaining lugs engage with the gutter guides.
4 Refit and tighten the securing screws.
5 Refit and adjust the glass panel, as described in Section 35.

Sunshade

Removal

6 Remove the glass panel and the gutter, as described in Section 35.
7 Carefully prise the four sunshade spring clips out of the roof guides (using a plastic or wooden implement to avoid damage), then withdraw the sunshade from the guides **(see illustration)**.

Refitting

8 Refitting is a reversal of removal, but ensure that the spring clips engage correctly with the roof guides.

Crank drive

Removal

9 Prise out the trim, and unscrew the crank handle securing screw. Prise the crank from the drive spindle.
10 Disconnect the battery negative lead, then prise the courtesy light from the roof trim panel, and disconnect the wiring.
11 Remove the two trim panel securing screws, and withdraw the trim panel from the roof.

38.3 Engine undershield securing screw (arrowed)

12 Extract the two securing screws, and remove the crank drive assembly.

Refitting

13 Refitting is a reversal of removal, remembering the following points.
14 Before finally tightening the crank handle, the crank drive must be adjusted as follows.
15 Temporarily refit the crank handle, and position it so that it faces forwards, then depress the locking button.
16 Remove the crank handle and turn the crank drive pinion anti-clockwise by hand as far as the stop.
17 Refit the crank handle so that it faces directly forwards, then tighten the securing screw and refit the trim.

37 Wheel arch liners - general

The plastic wheel arch liners are secured by a combination of self-tapping screws and plastic nuts and clips. Removal and refitting is self-evident, remembering the following points.

Some of the securing clips may be held in place using a central pin, which must be tapped out to release the clip.

The clips are easily broken during removal, and it is advisable to obtain a few spare clips for possible use when refitting.

Certain models may have additional underbody shields and splashguards fitted, which may be attached to the wheel arch liners.

38 Engine undershield (if fitted) - removal and refitting

Removal

1 Apply the handbrake, then jack up the front of the vehicle, and support securely on axle stands.
2 Extract the two securing screws, and remove the oil filter access panel.
3 Working around the edges of the undershield, remove the self-tapping screws that secure the shield to the underbody, noting that some of the screws may also secure the wheel arch liners **(see illustration)**.
4 With the help of an assistant, pull the shield from the vehicle, and place it to one side to avoid damage.

Refitting

5 Refitting is a reversal of removal.

39 Fuel filler flap - removal and refitting

Removal

1 Open the flap for access to the two securing screws.
2 Remove the securing screws and withdraw the flap.

Refitting

3 Refitting is a reversal of removal.

40 Rear spoilers - removal and refitting

Boot lid (Saloon models)

Removal

1 Open the boot lid, then remove the securing screws, and withdraw the lock assembly cover panel.
2 Unscrew the three bolts and eight nuts securing the spoiler to the boot lid.
3 On certain models, the spoiler may be retained with adhesive tape, in which case great care mast be taken to avoid damage to the paintwork as the spoiler is removed. One solution is to heat the tape using a hot air gun or a hairdryer, until the heat softens the adhesive sufficiently to enable the spoiler to be easily removed. Take care that the heat does not damage the surrounding paintwork.
4 Withdraw the spoiler from the boot lid.

Refitting

5 Where applicable, clean off all traces of adhesive using white spirit, then wash the area with warm soapy water to remove all traces of spirit. If adhesive tape is used to secure the spoiler, ensure that the relevant surfaces are completely clean, and free from dirt and grease.
6 If adhesive tape is used to refit the spoiler, follow the instructions supplied for refitting (consult a Vauxhall dealer if necessary). It may be necessary to use a heat source, as during removal, to soften the adhesive before the tape is applied.
7 Refit the spoiler, ensuring that it is correctly aligned before pressing firmly into position, and tighten the securing nuts and bolts.
8 Refit the lock assembly cover panel on completion.

Tailgate spoiler (all except C 20 XE models)

Removal

9 Working outside the tailgate, remove the two spoiler securing screws.

10 Open the tailgate, and unscrew the two remaining screws from the corners of the tailgate **(see illustration)**.
11 Refer to paragraph 3.
12 Withdraw the spoiler.
13 The washer nozzle can be prised from the spoiler mounting bracket once the spoiler has been withdrawn.
14 The spoiler mounting bracket can be removed from the tailgate after unscrewing the securing nuts and screws.

Refitting

15 Where applicable, refit the spoiler mounting bracket and the washer nozzle, using a reversal of the removal procedure.
16 Refer to paragraphs 5 and 6.
17 Refit the spoiler, ensuring that it is correctly aligned before pressing firmly into position, and tighten the securing bolts.

Tailgate spoiler (C 20 XE models)

Removal

18 Open the tailgate, then remove the securing screws, and withdraw the tailgate upper inner trim panel.
19 Working inside the tailgate, and at the outer lower edge of the spoiler, remove the six bolts and four nuts securing the spoiler to the tailgate **(see illustration)**.
20 Proceed as described in paragraphs 11 to 14 inclusive.

Refitting

21 Proceed as described in paragraphs 15 to 17 inclusive.

41 Exterior body components - removal and refitting

Side strips

Removal

1 Apply masking tape along the edge of the strip to be removed, as an aid to correct alignment on refitting.
2 Using a hot air gun or a hairdryer, heat the trim strip until the heat softens the adhesive sufficiently to enable the trim strip to be easily removed. Take care that the heat does not damage the surrounding paintwork.

Refitting

3 Clean off all traces of adhesive using white spirit, then wash the area with warm soapy water to remove all traces of spirit. Ensure that the surface to which the new strip is to be fitted is completely clean, and free from dirt and grease.
4 Use the heat gun or hairdryer to heat the new trim strip to approximately 80°C, then peel off the protective foil, and press the trim strip firmly into position, using the masking

40.10 Tailgate spoiler securing screws (1) - all except C 20 XE models

tape as a guide. Remove the masking tape when the strip is secured.

Badges

Removal

5 The various badges are secured with adhesives. To remove them, either soften the adhesive using a hot air gun or hairdryer (taking care to avoid damage to the paintwork), or separate the badge from the body by 'sawing' through the adhesive using a length of nylon cord.

Refitting

6 Clean off all traces of adhesive using white spirit, then wash the area with warm soapy water to remove all traces of spirit. Ensure that the surface to which the new badge is to be fastened is completely clean, and free from grease and dirt.
7 Use the hot air gun to soften the adhesive on the new badge, then press it firmly into position.

42 Side skirts and additional spoilers - general

On certain models, body kits may be fitted, comprising side skirts and an additional tailgate spoiler.

43.1 Removing the securing screw from the outer seat rail trim

40.19 Tailgate spoiler fixings (arrowed) - C 20 XE models

These components are secured by a combination of screws, adhesive and rivets. Although the basic principles described in this Section for other similar components apply, it is advisable to entrust removal and refitting to a Vauxhall dealer or a bodywork specialist. Great care is required to avoid damage to the surrounding paintwork and the components themselves.

43 Front seats - removal and refitting

Warning: The seat belt tensioners fitted to the front seat assemblies may cause injury if triggered inadvertently. Before carrying out any work on the front seats, the safety fork must be inserted into the seat belt tensioner cylinder, to prevent the possibility of the tensioner being triggered (see paragraphs 3 and 4 below). Seats should always be transported and installed with the safety fork in place. If a seat is to be disposed of, the tensioner must be triggered before the seat is removed from the vehicle, by inserting the safety fork, and striking the tensioner tube sharply with a hammer. If the tensioner has been triggered due to a sudden impact or accident, the unit must be renewed, as it cannot be reset. Due to safety consider-ations, tensioner renewal should be entrusted to a Vauxhall dealer.

Note: *The manufacturers recommend the use of new bolts when refitting the seats.*

Removal

1 Remove the single securing screw from the front edge of the outer seat rail trim **(see illustration)**, then withdraw the trim.
2 Release the securing clips, and unclip the trim from the rear edge of the inner seat rail **(see illustration)**.

11

43.2 Releasing the clips from the inner seat rail trim piece

3 Locate the plastic safety fork for the seat belt tensioner, which is usually taped to the outside of the tensioner cylinder **(see illustration)**.
4 Insert the safety fork into the slot provided in the tensioner cylinder, ensuring that the fork engages securely.
5 Remove the four bolts that secure the seat rails to the floor, then withdraw the seat, complete with rails **(see illustrations)**. Recover the washers and plates.
6 Withdraw the seat, complete with the rails, from the vehicle.
7 The seat can be separated from the rails for attention to the adjustment mechanism.

Refitting

8 Refitting is a reversal of removal, remembering the following points.

43.5b Rear outer seat rail securing bolt - note washer and plate

43.9 Tightening sequence for front seat bolts

43.3 Inserting the safety fork into its slot in the seat belt tensioner cylinder

9 Use new seat securing bolts, and tighten them in the sequence shown **(see illustration)**.
10 Before refitting the trim panels to the seat rails, remove the safety fork from the seat belt tensioner cylinder, and tape it to the outside of the cylinder.

44 Rear seats - removal and refitting

Cushion

Removal

1 With the seats in their raised position, where applicable, unclip the trim panel from the front of the hinge **(see illustration)**.

43.5c Rear inner seat rail securing bolt

44.1 Removing the trim panel from a rear seat cushion hinge - note securing clip (arrowed)

43.5a Front outer seat rail securing bolt (1) - note seat belt tensioner safety fork (2) engaged in slot

2 Prise the securing clips from the ends of the hinge pins **(see illustration)**, then withdraw the pins from the hinges.
3 With the hinge pins removed, the seat cushion can be withdrawn from the vehicle.

Refitting

4 Refitting is a reversal of removal.

Back

Removal

5 Fold down the seat back.
6 Carefully release the securing clips, using a forked tool or a screwdriver, and pull back the trim covering the hinges on the seat back.
7 Unscrew the two bolts at each side, securing the seat back to the hinges, then withdraw the seat back from the vehicle.

Refitting

8 Refitting is a reversal of removal.

45 Front seat belt tensioner system - general

1 All models are fitted with a front seat belt tensioner system, which is designed to instantaneously take up any slack in the seat belt in the case of a sudden frontal impact, therefore reducing the possibility of injury to the front seat occupants. Each front seat is fitted with

44.2 Rear seat cushion hinge pin securing clip (arrowed)

45.1 Front seat belt tensioner system

1 Spring   2 Cable   3 Fulcrum

its own system, the components of which are mounted in the seat frame **(see illustration)**.

2 The seat belt tensioner is triggered by a frontal impact causing a deceleration of six times the force of gravity or greater. Lesser impacts, including impacts from behind, will not trigger the system.

3 When the system is triggered, a pre-tensioned spring draws back the seat belt through a cable attached to a fulcrum, which acts on the seat belt stalk mounted on the seat frame. The cable and fulcrum can move by up to 80.0 mm, which therefore reduces the slack in the seat belt around the shoulders and waist of the occupant by a similar amount.

4 There is a risk of injury if the system is triggered inadvertently when working on the vehicle, and it is therefore strongly recommended that any work involving the seat belt tensioner system is entrusted to a Vauxhall dealer. Refer to the warning given at the beginning of Section 43 before contemplating any work on the front seats.

46 Seat belts - removal and refitting

Front belt (except 3-door Hatchback)

Removal

1 Remove the B-pillar lower trim panel, as described in Section 51.

2 Prise off the trim, and unbolt the seat belt upper mounting from the B-pillar. Recover the spacer.

3 Unbolt the lower seat belt mounting from the body, and recover the spacer and washers, noting their locations.

46.4 B-pillar lower trim panel removed to expose inertia reel unit and seat belt lower mounting securing bolts (arrowed)

4 Unscrew the securing bolt **(see illustration)**, withdraw the inertia reel unit from the B-pillar, then withdraw the seat belt assembly from the vehicle.

Refitting

5 Refitting is a reversal of removal, but make sure that the belt is fitted untwisted, and ensure that the washers and spacers on the upper and lower mountings are fitted as noted before removal. Tighten all fixings to the specified torque.

Front belt (3-door Hatchback models)

Removal

6 Prise off the trim, and unbolt the seat belt upper mounting from the B-pillar. Recover the spacer.

7 Remove the rear side trim panel, as described in Section 51.

8 Unscrew the securing bolt, withdraw the inertia reel unit from the B-pillar, then withdraw the seat belt assembly from the vehicle.

Refitting

9 Refitting is a reversal of removal, but tighten all fixings to the specified torque.

Rear belts

Removal

10 Fold the rear seat cushion forwards for access to the seat belt lower mountings.

46.18a Rear seat belt inertia reel securing bolt (arrowed) - 5-door Hatchback model

46.13 Prising the trim from a rear seat belt upper mounting

11 Prise up the carpet to expose the seat belt lower mounting bolt(s), then unscrew the relevant bolt(s) from the floor. Note the location of any spacers and washers on the mounting bolt(s).

12 If removing one of the side inertia reel seat belts, continue as follows.

13 Prise off the trim, and unbolt the seat belt upper mounting from the body pillar **(see illustration)**. Recover the spacer.

14 On Saloon and 5-door Hatchback models, remove the rear quarter trim panel, as described in Section 51.

15 On 3-door Hatchback models, remove the rear parcel shelf support panel, as described in Section 51.

16 On Estate and Van models, remove the luggage compartment side trim panel, referring to Section 51.

17 On Saloon models, remove the luggage compartment side trim panel, referring to Section 51.

18 Unscrew the inertia reel unit securing bolt - accessible from the luggage compartment on Saloon models **(see illustrations)** - remove the inertia reel unit from the body, then withdraw the seat belt assembly from the vehicle.

Refitting

19 Refitting is a reversal of removal, but make sure that the belt is fitted untwisted, and ensure that the washers and spacers on the upper (where applicable) and lower mountings

46.18b Rear seat belt inertia reel securing bolt (arrowed) - Saloon model

11

46.19 Fitting a rear seat belt upper mounting spacer and washer

47.4 Rear seat belt height adjuster assembly

48.4 Using a forked tool to remove a trim panel securing clip

are fitted as noted before removal **(see illustration)**. Tighten all fixings to the specified torque.

47 Seat belt height adjusters - removal and refitting

Front

Removal

1 Remove the B-pillar upper trim panel, as described in Section 51.

2 Remove the two Torx type securing bolts, and withdraw the height adjuster assembly from the B-pillar.

Refitting

3 Refitting is a reversal of removal, but ensure that the height adjuster is fitted the correct way up. The top of the adjuster is marked with two arrows, which should point towards the vehicle roof.

Rear

General

4 The procedure is as described for the front seat belt height adjuster, but for access to the height adjuster, remove the rear quarter trim panel (see Section 51) instead of the B-pillar trim panel **(see illustration)**.

48 Interior trim panels - general

1 The interior trim panels are all secured using either screws or various types of plastic fasteners.

2 To remove a panel, study it carefully, noting how it is secured. Often, other panels or ancillary components must be removed before a particular panel can be withdrawn, such as seat belt mountings, grab handles, etc.

3 Once any such components have been removed, check that there are no other panels overlapping the one to be removed; usually there is a sequence that has to be followed,

which will become obvious on close inspection.

4 Remove all obvious fasteners, such as screws, many of which may have plastic covers fitted. If the panel cannot be freed, it is probably secured by hidden clips or fasteners on the rear of the panel. Such fasteners are usually situated around the edge of the panel, and can be prised up to release them. Note that plastic clips can break quite easily so it is advisable to have a few replacement clips of the correct type available for refitting. Generally, the best way of releasing such clips is to use a forked tool **(see illustration)**. If this is not available, an old, broad-bladed screwdriver with the edges rounded-off and wrapped in insulating tape will serve as a good substitute.

5 The following Section and the accompanying illustrations and photographs describe removal and refitting of all the major trim panels. Note that the type and number of fasteners used often varies during the production run of a particular model, and differences may be noted to the procedures provided for certain vehicles.

6 When removing a panel, **never** use excessive force, or the panel may be damaged. Always check carefully that all fasteners have been removed or released before attempting to withdraw a panel.

7 Refitting is the reverse of the removal procedure; secure the fasteners by pressing them firmly into place, and ensure that all disturbed components are correctly secured to prevent rattles. If adhesives were found at any point during removal, use white spirit to remove all traces of old adhesive, then wash off all traces of spirit using soapy water. Use a trim adhesive (a Vauxhall dealer should be able to recommend a proprietary product) on reassembly.

49 Carpets - general

The passenger compartment floor carpet is divided into two pieces, front and rear, and each section is secured by plastic clips.

Carpet removal and refitting is reasonably

straightforward, but very time-consuming because many of the adjoining trim panels must be removed first, as must components such as the seats and their mountings, the centre console, etc.

50 Headlining - general

The headling is clipped to the roof, and can be withdrawn only once all fittings such as the grab handles, sunvisors, sunroof trim (where applicable), door pillar trim panels, rear quarter trim panels, weatherstrips, etc., have been removed or prised clear.

Note that headlining removal requires considerable skill and patience if it is to be carried out without damage, and is therefore best entrusted to an expert.

51 Inner trim panels - removal and refitting

Front door

Removal

1 Disconnect the battery negative lead.

2 Prise the trim plate from the door lock button in the top rear edge of the door, then pull the lock button from the operating rod **(see illustrations)**.

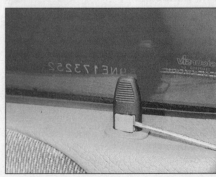

51.2a Prise the trim plate from the door lock button . . .

51.2b . . . and pull the lock button from the operating rod

51.5 Unscrewing the front door inner trim panel upper securing screw

51.6a Removing a front door inner trim panel lower securing screw

3 On models with manually operated windows, release the securing clip, and remove the window regulator handle. To release the securing clip, insert a length of wire with a hooked end between the handle and the trim bezel on the door trim panel, and manipulate it to free the securing clip from the handle. Take care not to damage the door trim panel. Recover the trim bezel.

4 Where applicable (manually adjustable mirrors), pull off the door mirror adjuster lever, then prise the door mirror trim panel from the door, and disconnect the wiring from the loudspeaker mounted in the trim panel.

5 Prise the door mirror switch (driver's door), electric window switch (passenger door), or the blanking plate, as applicable, from the door handle surround to expose the upper door trim panel securing screw. Remove the screw (see illustration).

6 Remove the five remaining trim panel securing screws, which are located along the bottom edge of the door (three screws), and around the bottom edge of the armrest (two screws), (see illustrations).

7 The plastic clips securing the trim panel to the door must now be released. This can be done using a screwdriver, but it is preferable to use a forked tool, to minimise the possibility of damage to the trim panel and the clips. The clips are located around the outer edge of the trim panel.

8 Once the clips have been released, pull the trim panel away from the door.

9 When working on models with electric door mirrors and/or electric windows, it will be necessary to disconnect the wiring plugs as the trim panel is withdrawn. Note the position of the wiring connector(s) in the bracket(s) on the door (see illustrations).

10 Withdraw the trim panel from the door.

11 The plastic insulating sheet can be peeled from the door (see illustration). Peel the sheet back slowly to prevent damage to the sealant, and take care not to damage the sheet.

Refitting

12 Refitting is a reversal of removal, remembering the following points.

13 If the plastic insulating sheet has been removed from the door, make sure that it is refitted intact, and securely fixed to the door.

51.6b Removing a front door inner trim panel securing screw from armrest/handgrip

If the sheet was removed carefully, there should be no need to use new sealant when refitting the sheet. If the sheet is damaged or detached, rainwater may leak into the vehicle or damage the door trim.

14 Where applicable, ensure that the wiring connector(s) is/are positioned correctly in the bracket(s) on the door before refitting the trim panel.

15 Ensure that all the trim panel securing clips engage as the panel is refitted, and if any of the clips were broken during removal, renew them on refitting.

Rear door

Removal

16 Proceed as described in paragraphs 2 and 3 (see illustration).

51.9a Front door inner trim panel removed to expose wiring connectors

51.9b Electric door mirror wiring connector locates under foam padding

51.11 Peeling the plastic insulating sheet from the door

51.16 Removing the rear window regulator handle - securing clip arrowed

11

51.17 Removing the plastic surround from the rear door interior handle

51.18 Removing the trim panel from the edge of the rear door window aperture

51.19 Removing a rear door inner trim panel securing screw

17 Prise the plastic surround from the door interior handle **(see illustration)**.
18 Prise the trim panel from the lower rear edge of the window aperture **(see illustration)**.
19 Remove the four trim panel securing screws. Two are located at the bottom edge of the door, and two are located under the armrest **(see illustration)**.
20 Proceed as described in paragraphs 7 and 8.
21 Withdraw the trim panel from the door.

Refitting

22 Proceed as described in paragraphs 12 to 15 inclusive.

Front footwell side/sill trim panel

Removal

23 Working along the sill, prise down the three cover panels, and remove the three securing screws **(see illustration)**.
24 Working at the upper front edge of the panel, prise out the cover and extract the remaining securing screw, then withdraw the panel **(see illustrations)**.

Refitting

25 Refitting is a reversal of removal.

Rear sill trim panel (except 3-door Hatchback)

Removal

26 Fold the rear seat cushion forwards.
27 Working along the sill, prise down the two cover panels and remove the two securing screws, then withdraw the panel.

Refitting

28 Refitting is a reversal of removal.

Rear sill trim panel (3-door Hatchback models)

Removal

29 Prise down the covers, and remove the two rear securing screws from the front footwell side/sill trim panel.
30 Prise down the cover, and unscrew the bolt securing the seat belt lower mounting rail to the sill. Recover the spacer plate **(see illustration)**.
31 Pull the rear of the seat belt mounting rail from the hole in the sill trim panel and slip the lower end of the seat belt webbing from the rail **(see illustration)**.
32 Fold the rear seat cushion forwards.
33 Prise out the covers, and extract the two trim panel securing screws then carefully withdraw the panel, sliding the front edge of

51.23 Unscrewing a front footwell side/sill trim panel securing screw

51.24a Removing the cover from the front footwell side/sill trim panel securing screw

51.24b Removing a front footwell side/sill trim panel (front seat removed)

51.30 Removing the seat belt mounting rail securing bolt and spacer plate - 3-door Hatchback model

51.31 Removing the seat belt mounting rail - 3-door Hatchback model

51.33a Remove the rear sill trim panel rear...

51.33b ... and front securing screws ...

51.33c ... and withdraw the panel - 3-door Hatchback model

the panel from under the front footwell side/sill trim panel **(see illustrations)**.

Refitting

34 Refitting is a reversal of removal, tightening the seat belt mounting rail bolt to the specified torque.

A-pillar trim panel

Removal

35 Prise out the cover, and remove the securing screw from the top of the trim panel.
36 Carefully prise the panel from the pillar to release the two securing clips **(see illustration)**.

Refitting

37 Refitting is a reversal of removal.

B-pillar lower trim panel (except 3-door Hatchback)

Removal

38 Prise down the cover, and remove the front securing screw from the rear sill trim panel.
39 Open the front and rear doors, and prise the weatherstrips from the edges of the B-pillar.
40 Carefully prise the panel from the pillar, recovering the securing clips, where applicable.

Refitting

41 Refitting is a reversal of removal.

B-pillar upper trim panel (except 3-door Hatchback)

Removal

42 Remove the B-pillar lower trim panel, as described previously in this Section.
43 Prise off the trim, and unbolt the seat belt upper mounting from the B-pillar. Recover the spacer.
44 Prise out the covers, and remove the two securing screws from the upper trim panel (one at the top and one at the bottom) **(see illustration)**.
45 Carefully prise the panel from the pillar.

Refitting

46 Refitting is a reversal of removal, tightening the seat belt mounting to the specified torque.

B-pillar upper trim panel (3-door Hatchback models)

Removal

47 Remove the rear side trim panel, as described later in this Section.
48 Prise off the trim, and unbolt the seat belt

upper mounting from the B-pillar. Recover the spacer.
49 Extract the two securing screws, and remove the grab handle from the top of the B-pillar upper trim panel.
50 Extract the securing screw, and remove the coat hook from the B-pillar **(see illustration)**.
51 Prise out the cover, and remove the lower securing screw from the trim panel.
52 Carefully prise the panel from the body, releasing the clip from the rear end of the panel as it is withdrawn.

Refitting

53 Refitting is a reversal of removal, tightening the seat belt mounting to the specified torque.

Rear side trim panel (3-door Hatchback models)

Removal

54 Remove the rear sill trim panel, as described previously in this Section.
55 Open the door, and carefully pull the weatherstrip from the front of the rear trim panel.

51.36 A-pillar trim panel fixings

1 Screw and cover   2 Clips

51.44 B-pillar upper trim panel fixings - all models except 3-door Hatchback

1 Rear sill panel securing screw
2 Seat belt upper mounting bolt
3 Weather seals
4 Trim panel securing screws

51.50 B-pillar upper trim panel fixings - 3-door Hatchback models

1 Seat belt upper mounting bolt
2 Coat hook
3 Grab handle
4 Trim panel securing screws
5 Trim panel securing clip

11

51.56 Unscrewing a rear side trim panel securing screw - 3-door Hatchback model

51.57 Rear side trim panel removed to expose securing clips (arrowed - viewed through rear window) - 3-door Hatchback model

51.69 Rear quarter trim panel securing screw locations (arrowed) - Saloon model

56 Prise out the cover, and remove the securing screw from the rear of the side trim panel **(see illustration)**.

57 Carefully pull the panel from the body to release the securing clips **(see illustration)**.

Refitting

58 Refitting is a reversal of removal.

Rear parcel shelf support panel (3-door Hatchback models)

Removal

59 Open the tailgate, then remove the parcel shelf, and fold the rear seat back forwards.

51.70 Rear quarter trim panel removed to show two of the securing clips (arrowed) - Saloon model

51.74 Rear quarter (C-pillar) trim panel fixings - 3-door Hatchback models

1 *Seat belt upper mounting*
2 *Trim panel securing screws and covers*

60 Working in the luggage compartment, disconnect the wiring from the loudspeaker.
61 Working inside the rear of the vehicle, where applicable prise out the cover, and remove the trim panel securing screw.
62 Working in the luggage compartment, remove the five remaining panel securing screws.
63 Carefully pull the panel from the body, releasing the retaining clip at the front of the panel as it is pulled free.
64 Pass the seat belt webbing and the wiring through the holes in the panel, and withdraw the panel from the vehicle.

Refitting

65 Refitting is a reversal of removal.

Rear quarter trim panel (Saloon models)

Removal

66 Fold the rear seat back forwards.
67 Prise off the trim, and unbolt the seat belt upper mounting from the C-pillar. Recover the spacer.
68 Open the rear door, and carefully prise the weatherstrip from the front edge of the trim panel.
69 Where applicable, prise out the covers, and remove the three trim panel securing screws (two upper screws, and one lower screw), **(see illustration)**.

51.81 Rear quarter trim panel securing screws (arrowed) - 5-door Hatchback model

70 Carefully pull the panel from the body to release the securing clips, passing the seat belt webbing through the slot in the panel as it is withdrawn **(see illustration)**.

Refitting

71 Refitting is a reversal of removal, tightening the seat belt mounting to the specified torque.

Rear quarter (C-pillar) trim panel (3-door Hatchback models)

Removal

72 Prise off the trim, and unbolt the seat belt upper mounting from the C-pillar. Recover the spacer.
73 Open the tailgate, and carefully prise the weatherstrip from the rear edge of the trim panel.
74 Prise out the covers, remove the three securing screws, then withdraw the panel **(see illustration)**.

Refitting

75 Refitting is a reversal of removal, tightening the seat belt mounting to the specified torque.

Rear quarter trim panel (5-door Hatchback models)

Removal

76 Remove the rear parcel shelf, and fold the rear seat back forwards.
77 Prise off the trim, and unbolt the seat belt upper mounting from the C-pillar. Recover the spacer.
78 Open the rear door and the tailgate, and carefully prise the weatherstrips from the edges of the trim panel.
79 Working in the luggage compartment, disconnect the wiring from the loudspeaker.
80 Working inside the rear of the vehicle, where applicable prise out the covers, and remove the four trim panel securing screws.
81 Working in the luggage compartment, remove the five remaining panel securing screws **(see illustration)**.

82 Carefully pull the panel from the body, releasing the retaining clip at the front of the panel as it is pulled free **(see illustration)**.
83 Pass the seat belt webbing and the wiring through the holes in the panel, and withdraw the panel from the vehicle.

Refitting

84 Refitting is a reversal of removal, tightening the seat belt mounting to the specified torque.

Rear quarter trim panel (Estate models)

Removal

85 Fold the rear seat back forwards.
86 Prise off the trim, and unbolt the seat belt upper mounting from the C-pillar. Recover the spacer.
87 Open the rear door and the tailgate, and carefully prise the weatherstrips from the edges of the trim panel.
88 Where applicable, remove the luggage retaining net and the luggage compartment cover.
89 Prise off the covers, and remove the three trim panel securing screws.
90 Carefully pull the panel from the body to release the securing clips, and withdraw the panel from the vehicle **(see illustration)**.

Refitting

91 Refitting is reversal of removal, tightening the seat belt mounting to the specified torque.

51.82 Removing the rear quarter trim panel - 5-door Hatchback model

quarter trim panel, as described in Section 51 **(see illustration)**.
3 Various fittings, such as the luggage compartment light, and the first aid kit retaining strap bolt, may have to be removed before certain panels can be freed.

53 Centre console - removal and refitting

Removal

1 Disconnect the battery negative lead.
2 Carefully prise the rear ashtray from the centre console.
3 Similarly, remove the central storage tray from the centre console **(see illustration)**. Note that on models fitted with heated front seats and/or electronic traction control, it will be necessary to disconnect the battery negative lead and then disconnect the wiring from the relevant switches located in the storage tray, before the tray can be removed.
4 Release the handbrake lever gaiter from the centre console, and on manual gearbox models, release the gear lever gaiter from the centre console.
5 On models with automatic transmission, release the transmission selector cover from

51.90 Rear quarter trim panel fixings - Estate models

1 Securing screws and covers
2 Clips

52.2 Removing the luggage compartment side trim panel - 5-door Hatchback model

the centre console (the cover is secured by clips at either side). Pull the illumination light bulbholder from the selector cover, and disconnect the transmission 'Winter' mode switch wiring connector.
6 Remove the two securing screws from the rear ashtray housing **(see illustration)**.
7 Remove the two securing screws from the central storage tray housing **(see illustration)**.
8 Remove the two screws from the front of the centre console assembly one screw on

52 Luggage compartment, tailgate and boot lid trim panels - general

1 The luggage compartment trim panels on all models are secured by a combination of plastic clips and/or screws. Removal and refitting of the panels is self-explanatory, remembering the points made in Section 48, and the following additional points.
2 To remove the luggage compartment side trim panel on Hatchback and Estate models, it will first be necessary to remove the rear

53.3 Removing the central storage tray from the centre console

53.6 Rear ashtray removed to expose rear centre console securing screws

53.7 Central storage tray removed to expose centre console securing screws (arrowed)

11

53.8 Centre console front securing screw

54.7 Releasing the centre facia ventilation vent flap actuating rod

54.8 Unscrewing a facia centre panel lower securing screw

54.9a Pull off the heater switch knobs . . .

54.9b . . . and extract the facia centre panel securing screws

54.11 Unscrewing a facia centre panel upper securing screw

54.12 Multi-function display removed to expose facia centre panel securing screws (arrowed)

54.13 Removing the facia centre panel securing clip

each side **(see illustration)**. Then slide the assembly rearwards, and pull the cigarette lighter plug and the illumination bulb from the rear of the assembly.

9 Withdraw the assembly, manipulating the gear lever gaiter/selector lever and cover (as applicable) through the aperture in the centre console, and sliding the handbrake lever gaiter from the assembly as it is withdrawn.

Refitting

10 Refitting is a reversal of removal.

54 Facia centre panel assembly - removal and refitting

Note: When removing facia panels, note the locations of the securing screws, as several different types of screw are used.

Removal

1 Disconnect the battery negative lead.
2 Remove the steering column shrouds and the instrument panel surround, as described in Section 55.
3 Remove the lighting control stalk (right-hand-drive models), or the wash/wipe control stalk (left-hand-drive models), as applicable, as described in Chapter 12.
4 Remove the hazard warning light switch, as described in Chapter 12.
5 Remove the radio/cassette player, and the

multi-function display, as described in Chapter 12.
6 Remove the centre facia ventilation nozzles, as described in Chapter 3.
7 Working through the centre facia ventilation nozzle apertures, carefully release the securing clip, using a screwdriver or a similar tool, and disconnect the vent flap actuating rod **(see illustration)**.
8 Remove the two lower facia panel securing screws, visible at the bottom of the panel **(see illustration)**.
9 Carefully pull off the heater air distribution and temperature control switch knobs, to expose two of the facia panel securing screws, then extract the screws **(see illustrations)**.
10 Turn the heater blower switch knob to position '3', then insert a small screwdriver or a rod through the hole in the bottom of the switch knob to depress the knob retaining clip. Pull the knob from the switch.
11 Remove the two upper facia panel securing screws, accessible through the centre facia ventilation nozzle apertures **(see illustration)**.
12 Remove the two centre facia panel securing screws, accessible through the multi-function display aperture **(see illustration)**.
13 Carefully pull out the facia panel securing clip, accessible from behind the right-hand side (right-hand-drive models), or the left-hand side (left-hand-drive models) of the panel, as applicable **(see illustration)**.

54.14a Facia centre panel securing screws (arrowed)

54.14b Withdrawing the facia centre panel assembly

54.14c Disconnecting the radio/cassette unit wiring plug . . .

14 The facia centre panel assembly can now be carefully withdrawn from the facia. As the assembly is withdrawn, disconnect the radio aerial lead, the radio/cassette unit wiring plug, and the hazard warning light switch wiring plug from the rear of the assembly **(see illustrations)**.

Refitting

15 Refitting is a reversal of removal, remembering the following points.
16 Make sure that all electrical plugs are securely reconnected to the rear of the assembly, and as the assembly is refitted, feed the multi-function display wiring through the multi-function display aperture, to aid subsequent reconnection.
17 Ensure that the centre vent flap actuating

rod is securely reconnected, before refitting the ventilation nozzles.

55 Steering column shrouds - removal and refitting

Removal

1 Disconnect the battery negative lead.
2 Turn the steering wheel to expose the two front steering column shroud securing screw covers.
3 Prise out the covers, then remove the securing screws **(see illustrations)**.
4 Working under the lower steering column shroud, remove the three lower securing

screws, noting their locations, as the screws are of different lengths **(see illustration)**.
5 Pull the rubber grommet from the ignition switch.
6 Unclip the lower shroud from the upper shroud (two clips at the back, and one each side), and withdraw the lower shroud **(see illustration)**.
7 Unhook the stalk switch gaiters from the upper shroud, and withdraw the upper shroud **(see illustration)**.

Refitting

8 Refitting is a reversal of removal, but ensure that the stalk switch gaiters and ignition switch grommet are correctly located, and make sure that the lower shroud securing screws are refitted to their original locations.

54.14d . . . and the hazard warning light switch wiring plug from the rear of the facia centre panel assembly

55.3a Prise out the covers . . .

55.3b . . . to expose the front steering column shroud securing screws

55.4 Unscrewing a steering column shroud lower securing screw

55.6 Withdrawing the lower steering column shroud

55.7 Withdrawing the upper steering column shroud

11

56.2a Unscrewing an instrument panel surround lower securing screw

56.2b Withdrawing the instrument panel surround

57.4 Withdrawing the glovebox assembly

56 Instrument panel surround - removal and refitting

Removal

1 Remove the steering column shrouds, as described earlier in this Section 55.
2 Where applicable, prise out the screw covers, then remove the four (two upper and two lower) securing screws, and withdraw the instrument panel surround (see illustrations).

Refitting

3 Refitting is a reversal of removal.

57 Glovebox - removal and refitting

Note: *If an airbag is fitted, read the warning in Chapter 12, before starting work.*

Removal

1 With the glovebox lid closed, unscrew the two lower securing screws, which are accessible below the glovebox.
2 Open the glovebox lid, and prise the glovebox light from its location in the side of the glovebox. Disconnect the wiring, and remove the light assembly.
3 Unscrew the two upper securing screws, which are now accessible at the top of the glovebox.
4 Withdraw the glovebox from the facia, feeding the light through the aperture in the side of the glovebox as it is withdrawn (see illustration).

Refitting

5 Refitting is a reversal of removal.

58 Glovebox lock cylinder - removal and refitting

Removal

1 Squeeze the two securing lugs together, and remove the cover from the glovebox catch.
2 Insert the key into the lock cylinder, then turn the key and cylinder to the locked

position, and pull the lock cylinder from its housing using the key.

Refitting

3 Refitting is a reversal of removal.

59 Footwell lower trim panels - removal and refitting

Removal

1 The footwell lower trim panels are attached to the bottom of the facia by plastic securing clips.
2 To remove a panel, release the clips by turning them with a screwdriver, then withdraw the panel from underneath the facia.

Refitting

3 Refitting is a reversal of removal.

60 Facia assembly - removal and refitting

Removal

1 Disconnect the battery negative lead.
2 Remove the centre console, as described in Section 53.
3 Remove the facia centre panel assembly, the steering column shrouds, the footwell lower trim panels, the glovebox, and the instrument panel surround, as described in earlier Sections.
4 Remove the heater/ventilation control unit, and the driver's side ventilation nozzle housing, as described in Chapter 3.
5 Remove the steering wheel, as described in Chapter 10.

6 Remove the steering column stalk switches, the instrument panel, and the fusebox, as described in Chapter 12.
7 Open the front doors, then prise out the covers, and unscrew the two securing screws from each side of the facia.
8 Working under the centre of the facia, unscrew the two lower facia securing screws from the mounting bracket (see illustration).
9 Remove the windscreen wiper motor and linkage, as described in Chapter 12.
10 Unscrew the three facia panel securing bolts from the engine compartment bulkhead (see illustration).
11 With the aid of an assistant, withdraw the facia assembly into the interior of the vehicle, and carefully disconnect all wiring and hoses from the rear of the facia.
12 Check that all relevant wiring and hoses have been disconnected, then manipulate the facia out through one of the front door apertures.

Refitting

13 Refitting is a reversal of removal, remembering the following points.
14 Make sure that all relevant wiring and hoses are securely reconnected, and routed so that they are not under strain.
15 Refit the windscreen wiper motor and linkage as described in Chapter 12.
16 Refit the instrument panel as described in Chapter 12.
17 Refit the steering wheel as described in Chapter 10.
18 Refit the heater/ventilation control unit, and the driver's side ventilation nozzle housing, as described in Chapter 3.
19 Refit the facia centre panel assembly, as described in Section 54.

60.8 Facia internal fixing screws (arrowed)

60.10 Facia panel bulkhead fixing bolts (arrowed)

Chapter 12
Body electrical systems

Contents

Degrees of difficulty

Easy, suitable for novice with little experience	**Fairly easy,** suitable for beginner with some experience	**Fairly difficult,** suitable for competent DIY mechanic	**Difficult,** suitable for experienced DIY mechanic	**Very difficult,** suitable for expert DIY or professional 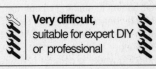

12

Specifications

System type	12-volt, negative earth

Fuses - fusebox with 30 fuse locations

Fuse No	Rating (amps)	Circuit(s) protected
1	20	Central door locking
2	20	Fuel pump
3	30	Horn, windscreen and tailgate wash/wipe systems
4	10	Left-hand headlight dipped beam, left-hand headlight aim adjustment motor, bulb failure sensor
5	10	Right-hand headlight dipped beam, right-hand headlight aim adjustment motor, bulb failure sensor
6	10	Automatic transmission ECU, anti-lock braking system ECU
7	10	Warning lights, 'headlights on' warning buzzer, electric mirrors, glovebox light, radio/cassette player, facia switch illumination bulbs, heated rear window
8	20	Tow bar coupling
9		Unused
10		Unused
11		Unused
12	10	Left-hand headlight main beam
13	10	Right-hand headlight main beam, headlight main beam warning light
14	15	TC control unit
15	30	Electric window motors
16		Unused
17	20	Front foglights
18	10	Left-hand sidelight, left-hand tail light, bulb failure sensor
19	10	Right-hand sidelight, right-hand tail light, number plate light(s), bulb failure sensor, facia switch illumination bulbs, centre console switch illumination bulbs, radio/cassette player, headlight washer pump, 'headlights on' warning buzzer
20	20	Central door locking, carburettor automatic choke, automatic transmission switch, reversing lights, cigarette lighter, seat heating
21		Unused
22	10	Anti-theft alarm horn
23		Unused
24	20	Electric aerial, direction indicators, radio/cassette player, interior lights
25	10	Automatic transmission ECU
26		Unused
27	10	Daytime running lights (Norway and Sweden only)
28	15	Brake lamps, ABS/TC/AT control units, hazard warning switch
29	10	Rear foglamps and switch
30	20	Heated rear window

Fuses - fusebox with 28 fuse locations

All fuse ratings and circuits protected as for fusebox with 30 fuse locations, except for the following.

Fuse No	Rating (amps)	Circuit(s) protected
9	15	Electronic traction control ECU
10	30	Electric window motors
11	10	Rear foglights
14	30	Heater blower motor
15	30	Cooling fan
16	30	Heated rear window
22		Unused
23	30	Headlight washer system

Torque wrench settings

	Nm	lbf ft
Airbag unit to steering wheel	10	7
Airbag control unit	10	7
Brackets, passenger airbag	22	16
Passenger airbag to bracket	8	6
Steering wheel to column	25	18

1 Electrical fault-finding information - general

Note: *Refer to the precautions given in 'Safety first!' and in Chapter 5, before starting work. The following tests relate to testing of the main electrical circuits, and should not be used to test delicate electronic circuits (such as engine management systems, anti-lock braking systems, etc.), particularly where an electronic control module is used. Refer to Chapter 4B, for precautions to be observed when working on models fitted with electronic control units.*

General

1 A typical electrical circuit consists of an electrical component, any switches, relays, motors, fuses, fusible links or circuit breakers related to that component, and the wiring and connectors that link the component to both the battery and the chassis. To help to pinpoint a problem in an electrical circuit, wiring diagrams are included at the end of this manual.

2 Before attempting to diagnose an electrical fault, first study the appropriate wiring diagram to obtain a complete understanding of the components included in the particular circuit concerned. The possible sources of a fault can be narrowed down by noting if other components related to the circuit are operating properly. If several components or circuits fail at one time, the problem is likely to be related to a shared fuse or earth connection.

3 Electrical problems usually stem from simple causes, such as loose or corroded connections, a faulty earth connection, a blown fuse, a melted fusible link, or a faulty relay (refer to Section 4 for details of testing relays). Visually inspect the condition of all fuses, wires and connections in a problem circuit before testing the components. Use the wiring diagrams to determine which terminal connections will need to be checked, to pinpoint the trouble-spot.

4 The basic tools required for electrical fault-finding include a circuit tester or voltmeter (a 12-volt bulb with a set of test leads can also be used for certain tests); a self-powered test light (sometimes known as a continuity tester); an ohmmeter (to measure resistance); a battery and set of test leads; and a jumper wire, preferably with a circuit breaker or fuse incorporated, which can be used to bypass suspect wires or electrical components. Before attempting to locate a problem with test instruments, use the wiring diagram to determine where to make the connections.

5 To find the source of an intermittent wiring fault (usually due to a poor or dirty connection, or damaged wiring insulation), a 'wiggle' test can be performed on the wiring. This involves wiggling the wiring by hand to see if the fault occurs as the wiring is moved. It should be possible to narrow down the source of the fault to a particular section of wiring. This method of testing can be used in conjunction with any of the tests described in the following sub-Sections.

6 Apart from problems due to poor connections, two basic types of fault can occur in an electrical circuit - open-circuit, or short-circuit.

7 Open-circuit faults are caused by a break somewhere in the circuit, which prevents current from flowing. An open-circuit fault will prevent a component from working, but will not cause the relevant circuit fuse to blow.

8 Short-circuit faults are caused by a 'short' somewhere in the circuit, which allows the current flowing in the circuit to 'escape' along an alternative route, usually to earth. Short-circuit faults are normally caused by a breakdown in wiring insulation, which allows a feed wire to touch either another wire, or an earthed component such as the bodyshell. A short-circuit fault will normally cause the relevant circuit fuse to blow.

Finding an open-circuit

9 To check for an open-circuit, connect one lead of a circuit tester or voltmeter to either the negative battery terminal or a known good earth.

10 Connect the other lead to a connector in the circuit being tested, preferably nearest to the battery or fuse.

11 Switch on the circuit, remembering that some circuits are live only when the ignition switch is moved to a particular position.

12 If voltage is present (indicated either by the tester bulb lighting or a voltmeter reading, as applicable), this means that the section of the circuit between the relevant connector and the battery is problem-free.

13 Continue to check the remainder of the circuit in the same fashion.

14 When a point is reached at which no voltage is present, the problem must lie between that point and the previous test point with voltage. Most problems can be traced to a broken, corroded or loose connection.

Finding a short-circuit

15 To check for a short-circuit, first disconnect the load (s), from the circuit (loads are the components that draw current from a circuit, such as bulbs, motors, heating elements, etc.).

16 Remove the relevant fuse from the circuit, and connect a circuit tester or voltmeter to the fuse connections.

17 Switch on the circuit, remembering that some circuits are live only when the ignition switch is moved to a particular position.

18 If voltage is present (indicated either by the tester bulb lighting or a voltmeter reading, as applicable), this means that there is a short-circuit.

19 If no voltage is present, but the fuse still blows with the load(s) connected, this indicates an internal fault in the load(s).

Finding an earth fault

20 The battery negative terminal is connected to 'earth' - the metal of the engine/transmission and the car body - and most systems are wired so that they only receive a positive feed, the current returning through the metal of the car body. This means that the component mounting and the body form part of that circuit. Loose or corroded mountings can therefore cause a range of electrical faults, ranging from total failure of a circuit, to a puzzling partial fault. In particular, lights may shine dimly (especially when another circuit sharing the same earth point is in operation), motors (e.g. wiper motors or the radiator cooling fan motor) may run slowly, and the operation of one circuit may have an apparently unrelated effect on another. Note that on many vehicles, earth straps are used between certain components, such as the engine/transmission and the body, usually where there is no metal-to-metal contact between components due to flexible rubber mountings, etc.

21 To check whether a component is properly earthed, disconnect the battery, and connect one lead of an ohmmeter to a known good earth point. Connect the other lead to the wire or earth connection being tested. The resistance reading should be zero; if not, check the connection as follows.

22 If an earth connection is thought to be faulty, dismantle the connection, and clean back to bare metal both the bodyshell and the wire terminal or the component earth connection mating surface. Be careful to remove all traces of dirt and corrosion, then use a knife to trim away any paint, so that a clean metal-to-metal joint is made. On reassembly, tighten the joint fasteners securely; if a wire terminal is being refitted, use serrated washers between the terminal and the bodyshell, to ensure a clean and secure connection. When the connection is re-made, prevent the onset of corrosion in the future by applying a coat of petroleum jelly or silicone-based grease. Alternatively, (at regular intervals) spray on a proprietary ignition sealer or a water-dispersant lubricant.

2 Fusebox - removal and refitting

Removal

1 Disconnect the battery negative lead.

2 Pull off the fusebox cover.

3 Unscrew the two securing screws **(see illustration)**, then release the assembly from

2.3 Fusebox cover removed to expose securing screws (arrowed)

the retaining brackets, and lower the assembly sufficiently to enable the wiring plugs to be disconnected.

4 Disconnect the wiring plugs, carefully noting their locations if there is likely to be any confusion on refitting, then withdraw the assembly from the facia.

Refitting

5 Refitting is a reversal of removal.

3 Fuses - testing, removal and refitting

Testing

1 Fuses are designed to break a circuit when a predetermined current is reached, to protect components that may be damaged by excessive current flow. Any excessive current flow will be due to a fault in the circuit - usually a short-circuit (see Section 1).

2 The main fuses are located in the fusebox, at the lower driver's side: of the facia, under a removable cover.

3 On certain models, additional fuses are located in a secondary fusebox mounted on the engine compartment bulkhead **(see illustration)**.

4 The circuits protected by the various fuses are marked on the inside of the panel cover.

5 A blown fuse can be recognised from its melted or broken wiring.

Removal

6 To remove a fuse, first ensure that the relevant circuit is switched off.

7 Pull off the fusebox cover, and pull the relevant fuse from its location in the fusebox.

Refitting

8 Before renewing a blown fuse, try to trace and rectify the cause, and always use a fuse of the correct rating. Fuses rarely blow without good reason - do not renew the same fuse more than once without finding the source of the problem. If the same fuse is blowing regularly, it could be that the associated wiring is getting too hot, with attendant fire risks (see *"Safety first!"*). Never substitute a fuse of a higher rating, or make temporary repairs using wire or metal foil, as more serious damage or even fire could result.

9 Note that the fuses are colour-coded as follows. Refer to the Specifications for details of the fuse ratings and the circuits protected.

Red	10A
Blue	15A
Yellow	20A
Green	30A

3.3 Removing the cover from the secondary fusebox on the engine compartment bulkhead - C 20 XE model

4 Relays - general

General

1 A relay is an electrically operated switch, which is used for the following reasons.

a) *A relay can switch a heavy current remotely from the circuit in which the current is flowing, therefore allowing the use of lighter gauge wiring and switch contacts.*

A Left-hand sill panel
  1 Traction control ECU
B Fusebox - front view
  1 Door mirror heater relay
  2 Direction indicator relay
  3 Tailgate wash/wipe relay
  4 Front foglight relay
  5 Rear foglight relay
  6 Windscreen wash/wipe relay
  7 Heated rear window relay
  8 Warning buzzer
  9 Diagnostic plug
C Fusebox - rear view
  1 Cooling fan fuse
  2 Starter motor relay
  3 Heater blower motor fuse
D Fusebox - rear view
  1 Starter motor relay
  2 Anti-theft alarm fuse
F Right-hand footwell
  1 Central door locking ECU
  2 Anti-theft alarm ECU
G Right-hand footwell
  1 Engine management ECU
  2 Fuel pump relay
I Steering column bracket
  1 Driving light relay (Sweden and Norway only)

H. 26715

4.2a Schematic vie w of fuse and relay locations

A **Left-hand rear wing**
   1 *Electric aerial relay*
B **Engine compartment**
   bulkhead
   1 *Hea dlight wash*
      system fuse
   2 *Headlight wash*
      system relay
   3 *Horn relay*
   4 *Horn fuse*
C **Engine compartment**
   1 *Anti-lock braking*
      system ECU

4.2b Schematic view of fuse and relay locations

4.2c Relays located above fuses in fusebox

b) *A relay can receive more than one control input, unlike a mechanical switch.*
c) *A relay can have a 'timer' function e.g., intermittent wiper relay.*

2 The main relays are located in the fusebox, above the fuses **(see illustrations)**. Additional relays are located in various positions, as shown in the accompanying illustrations.

3 If a circuit controlled by a relay develops a fault, and the relay is suspect, operate the circuit. If the relay is functioning, it should be possible to hear the relay click as it is energised. If this is the case, the fault lies with the components or wiring in the system. If the relay is not being energised, then either the relay is not receiving a main supply or switching voltage, or the relay itself is faulty. (Do not overlook the relay socket terminals when tracing faults.) Testing is by the substitution of a known good unit, but be careful; while some relays are identical in appearance and in operation, others look similar, but perform different functions.

5 Ignition switch - removal and refitting

Removal

1 Disconnect the battery negative lead.
2 Remove the steering column shrouds, as described in Chapter 11.
3 The ignition switch is secured to the steering lock housing by two grub screws.
4 Disconnect the wiring, and remove the screws to extract the switch **(see illustrations)**. It is recommended that the switch and the lock cylinder are not both removed at the same time, or their mutual alignment will be lost.

Refitting

5 Refitting is a reversal of removal.

6 Steering column stalk switches - removal and refitting

Removal

1 Disconnect the battery negative lead.
2 Remove the steering column shrouds, as described in Chapter 11.
3 Depress the retaining clips, and release the relevant switch from the steering column **(see illustration)**.
4 Disconnect the wiring plug(s) and withdraw the switch **(see illustration)**.

Refitting

5 Refitting is a reversal of removal.

5.4a Ignition switch grub screw location (arrowed)

5.4b Disconnecting the wiring plug from the ignition switch

6.3 Withdrawing a stalk switch from the steering column

6.4 Disconnecting a stalk switch wiring plug

12

7.2 Releasing the lighting switch knob retaining clip

7.3 Removing the lighting switch

7 Lighting switch - removal and refitting

Removal

1 Disconnect the battery negative lead.
2 Insert a small screwdriver or rod through the hole in the bottom of the switch knob to depress the knob retaining clip **(see illustration)**. Pull the knob from the switch.
3 Press the two now-exposed switch securing clips towards the switch spindle **(see illustration)**, then pull the switch from the facia and disconnect the wiring plug.
4 Note that the switch assembly cannot be dismantled, and if any part of the switch is faulty, the complete assembly must be renewed.

Refitting

5 Refitting is a reversal of removal.

8 Facia push-button switches - removal and refitting

Removal

1 Disconnect the battery negative lead.
2 Using a screwdriver, carefully prise the switch from the facia, taking care not to

damage the facia trim, and where applicable disconnect the wiring plug **(see illustrations)**.

Refitting

3 Refitting is a reversal of removal.

9 Hazard warning flasher switch - removal and refitting

Removal

1 Disconnect the battery negative lead.
2 Move the switch to the 'on' position.
3 Using a screwdriver, carefully prise off the switch button to expose the switch.
4 Again using a screwdriver, carefully prise the switch from its housing.

Refitting

5 Refitting is a reversal of removal.

10 Horn switch - general

1 Carefully prise the centre pad from the steering wheel, and disconnect the wire.
2 The horn switch contact assembly can be removed from the centre of the steering wheel, after removing the steering wheel as described in Chapter 10.

11 Brake light switch - removal and refitting

Removal

1 Disconnect the battery negative lead.
2 Working in the driver's footwell, release the securing clips, and remove the lower trim panel.
3 The switch is mounted in a bracket next to the steering column, at the top of the brake pedal.
4 Disconnect the wiring plug from the switch.
5 Twist the switch anti-clockwise, and withdraw it from the bracket **(see illustration)**.

Refitting

6 Refitting is a reversal of removal, but note that the brake lights should come on when the brake pedal is pressed down by about 15.0 to 20.0 mm. The switch can only be adjusted by carefully bending the mounting bracket, but this is not recommended.

12 Courtesy light switches - removal and refitting

Removal

1 The courtesy light switches are located in the door pillars, at the front of the doors.
2 Disconnect the battery negative lead.
3 Open the relevant door.
4 Remove the securing screw, then pull the switch from the door pillar, and disconnect the wiring. If there is a danger of the wiring falling back inside the door pillar, tie a piece of string to it.

Refitting

5 Refitting is a reversal of removal.

8.2a Carefully prise the switch free . . .

8.2b . . . and withdraw it from the facia

11.5 Brake light switch location (arrowed) - twist switch anti-clockwise to remove

13.1a Removing the luggage compartment light switch securing screw - Hatchback model

13.1b Luggage compartment light switch location - Saloon model

15.2 Disconnecting the wiring plug from a headlight bulb

13 Luggage compartment light switch - general

1 The switch is located at the bottom of the tailgate on Hatchback, Estate and Van models, and at the front left-hand corner of the luggage compartment on Saloon models **(see illustrations)**.
2 Removal and refitting is as described previously in Section 12, for the courtesy light switches.

14 Glovebox light switch - general

1 The switch is integral with the light assembly, and is operated by the left-hand glovebox hinge.
2 Removal and refitting of the assembly is described in Section 15.

15 Bulbs (exterior lights) - general and renewal

General

1 Whenever a bulb is renewed, note the following points.

a) *Disconnect the battery negative lead before starting work.*
b) *Remember that if the light has recently been in use, the bulb may be extremely hot.*
c) *Always check the bulb contacts and/or holder (as applicable). Ensure that there is clean metal-to-metal contact between the bulb contacts and the contacts in the holder, and/or the holder and the wiring plug. Clean off any corrosion or dirt before fitting a new bulb.*
d) *Always ensure that the new bulb is of the correct rating, and that it is completely clean before fitting; this applies particularly to headlight bulbs.*

Renewal

Headlight

Note: *It may be necessary to remove the air filter assembly, to replace the drivers side headlight bulb (refer to Chapter 4A) .*
2 Working in the engine compartment, pull the wiring plug from the rear of the headlight bulb **(see illustration)**.
3 Pull the rubber cover from the rear of the headlight.
4 Release the bulb retaining spring clip, then grasp the bulb by its contacts and carefully withdraw it from the headlight unit **(see illustration)**.
5 When handling the new bulb, use a tissue or clean cloth to avoid touching the glass with

the fingers; moisture and grease from the skin can cause blackening and rapid failure of this type of bulb. If the glass is accidentally touched, wipe it clean using methylated spirit.
6 Refitting is a reversal of removal, but make sure that the locating lugs on the bulb engage with the cut-outs in the headlight reflector, and ensure that the rubber cover is securely located over the rear of the headlight unit.

Front sidelight

7 Working in the engine compartment, locate the sidelight bulbholder, which is positioned in the lower rear of the headlight unit, on the side nearest the radiator grille.
8 Push the bulbholder into the headlight unit, and twist it anti-clockwise to remove it **(see illustration)**.
9 The bulb is a push-fit in the holder.
10 Refitting is a reversal of removal.

Front direction indicator light

11 Working in the engine compartment, loosen, but do not remove the screw securing the top of the direction indicator unit to the headlight **(see illustration)**.
12 Withdraw the direction indicator unit forwards from the front wing, taking care not to strain the wiring **(see illustration)**.
13 Push the bulbholder into the light unit, and twist it anti-clockwise to remove it.
14 The bulb is a bayonet fit in the bulbholder.
15 Refitting is a reversal of removal.

15.4 Removing a headlight bulb

15.8 Removing a sidelight bulbholder

15.11 Loosening a front direction indicator unit securing screw

12

15.12 Front direction indicator unit withdrawn, exposing securing screw (arrowed)

15.16 Removing the front direction indicator side repeater light lens

15.20 Removing the rear cover from a front foglight

Front direction indicator side repeater light

16 Twist the light lens anti-clockwise, and pull it from the light **(see illustration)**.
17 The bulb is a push-fit in the light.
18 Refitting is a reversal of removal, but ensure that the rubber sealing ring is correctly seated between the lens and the body panel.

Front foglight

19 To improve access, apply the handbrake, then jack up the front of the vehicle, and support securely on axle stands.
20 Remove the plastic cover from the rear of the light unit by twisting it anti-clockwise, and pulling it free **(see illustration)**.

21 Release the retaining clip, then withdraw the bulb and disconnect the wiring.
22 Refitting is a reversal of removal.

Rear light cluster

23 Working in the luggage compartment, unclip the cover from the rear of the light unit.
24 On Saloon and Hatchback models, release the securing lug, and on Estate and Van models, squeeze the two securing clips towards the centre of the bulbholder, then withdraw the bulbholder from the light unit, taking care not to strain the wiring **(see illustrations)**.
25 The bulbs are a bayonet fit in the bulbholder **(see illustration)**. Note that the

brake/tail light bulb has offset bayonet pins, so that it can only be fitted in one position; ensure that the correct type of replacement is obtained.
26 Refitting is a reversal of removal.

Rear number plate light - Saloon and Hatchback models (except C 20 XE models)

27 Using a thin-bladed screwdriver, carefully prise the light surround from the bumper **(see illustration)**.
28 Pull the light assembly from the bumper, taking care not to strain the wiring.
29 Unclip the cover from the light unit, to expose the bulb **(see illustration)**.
30 The bulb is a bayonet fit in the light unit.
31 Refitting is a reversal of removal.

Rear number plate light - Saloon and hatchback models (C 20 XE models)

32 Proceed as described in paragraph 27.
33 Remove the bulb by carefully prising it from its location with a screwdriver.
34 Refitting is a reversal of removal.

Rear number plate light - Estate and Van models

35 Remove the two screws securing the relevant light to the tailgate handle assembly, and lower the light from the tailgate.
36 Carefully prise the bulb from the light.
37 Refitting is a reversal of removal.

15.24a Rear light bulbholder securing lug (arrowed) - Hatchback model

15.24b Removing a rear light bulbholder - Saloon model

15.25 Removing a rear light bulb - Hatchback model

15.27 Prising the rear number plate light surround from the bumper - Hatchback model

15.29 Removing the cover from the rear number plate light unit

16.2a Withdrawing the front courtesy light to expose the bulb

16.2b Prising a rear reading light from its location

16.3 Unclipping the shield from a rear reading light bulb

16 Bulbs (interior lights) - general and renewal

General

1 Refer to Section 15, paragraph 1.

Renewal

Courtesy lights and rear reading lights

2 Using a thin-bladed screwdriver, carefully prise the light from its location (see illustrations).
3 Where applicable, unclip the shield from the bulb, then remove the bulb by carefully prising it from the contacts in the light unit (see illustration).
4 Refitting is a reversal of removal.

Glovebox light

5 Proceed as described previously in this Section for the courtesy light (see illustration).

Luggage compartment light

6 Proceed as described previously in this Section for the courtesy light (see illustration).

Instrument illumination and warning light bulbs

7 The procedure is described in Section 21.

Heater/ventilation control illumination light bulb

8 The procedure is described as part of the heater/ventilation control unit removal and refitting procedure in Chapter 3.

Cigarette lighter illumination light bulb

9 The procedure is described as part of the cigarette lighter removal and refitting procedure in Section 26.

Facia panel/centre console switch illumination bulbs

10 If a bulb fails in one of these switches, the complete switch assembly must be renewed as described in Section 8, as no individual spare parts are available.

17 Exterior light units - removal and refitting

Headlight unit

Removal

1 Disconnect the battery negative lead.
2 Remove the radiator grille panel, as described in Chapter 11.
3 Working in the engine compartment, loosen, but do not remove the screw securing the top of the direction indicator unit to the headlight.
4 Withdraw the direction indicator unit forwards from the front wing, and disconnect the wiring plug.
5 Disconnect the wiring plugs from the headlight bulb, sidelight bulb, and headlight aim adjustment motor.

16.5 Glovebox light assembly withdrawn from its location

6 Remove the three securing screws (two upper screws, and a single lower screw), and withdraw the headlight unit (see illustrations).
7 Except for bulbs and the aim adjustment motor, no headlight components are available separately, and if faulty or damaged, the complete unit must be renewed.

Refitting

8 Refitting is a reversal of removal, but on completion have the headlight beam alignment checked, referring to Section 18.

Front direction indicator unit

Removal

9 Disconnect the battery negative lead.
10 Proceed as described in paragraphs 3 and 4.

16.6 Withdrawing a luggage compartment light bulb

17.6a Headlight securing screws (arrowed)

17.6b Withdrawing a headlight

12

17.15 Removing a front direction indicator side repeater light

Refitting

11 Refitting is a reversal of removal.

Front direction indicator side repeater light

Removal

12 Disconnect the battery negative lead.
13 Remove the wheel arch liner, as described in Chapter 11.
14 Working in the engine compartment, locate the repeater light wiring connector, and separate the two halves of the connector.
15 Working under the wheel arch, depress the retaining tabs and manipulate the light unit through the outside of the wing, pulling the wiring and the grommet from the inner wing panel **(see illustration)**.
16 The lens can be removed from the light by twisting it to release the retaining clips.
17 Check the condition of the rubber sealing ring, and renew if necessary.

Refitting

18 Refitting is a reversal of removal.

Front foglight

Removal

19 Disconnect the battery negative lead.
20 For improved access, apply the handbrake, then jack up the front of the vehicle, and support securely on axle stands.

17.22 Front foglight lower securing screws (1) and wiring plug (2)

21 Working behind the front spoiler, disconnect the foglight wiring plug.
22 Unscrew the three securing screws (two at the bottom of the light, and one well hidden above the light), and withdraw the light from the front bumper/spoiler assembly **(see illustration)**.

Refitting

23 Refitting is a reversal of removal.

Rear light cluster

Removal

24 Disconnect the battery negative lead.
25 Working in the luggage compartment, unclip the cover from the rear of the light unit.
26 On Saloon and Hatchback models, release the securing lug, and on Estate and Van models, squeeze the two securing clips towards the centre of the bulbholder. Then withdraw the bulbholder from the light unit, taking care not to strain the wiring.
27 On Saloon and Hatchback models, remove the four light cluster securing screws, and on Estate and Van models, remove the three securing screws (one upper screw, and two lower screws). Then withdraw the light cluster from outside the rear wing panel **(see illustrations)**.
28 Note that the lens cannot be renewed separately, and if damaged, the complete light cluster must be renewed.

Refitting

29 Refitting is a reversal of removal.

Rear number plate light - Saloon and Hatchback models

Removal

30 Using a thin-bladed screwdriver, carefully prise the light surround from the bumper.
31 Pull the light assembly from the bumper, and disconnect the wiring.

Refitting

32 Refitting is a reversal of removal.

Rear number plate light - Estate and Van models

Removal

33 Remove the two screws securing the relevant light assembly to the tailgate handle.
34 Pull the light assembly from the handle, and disconnect the wiring.

Refitting

35 Refitting is a reversal of removal.

18 Headlight beam alignment - general

1 It is advisable to have the headlight beam alignment checked and if necessary adjusted by a Vauxhall dealer using optical beam-setting equipment. Correct alignment of the headlight beams is most important, not only to ensure good vision for the driver, but also to protect other drivers from being dazzled.
2 The headlight beam height may be adjusted to compensate for the load being carried by using the headlight aim adjustment control on the facia. The settings provided by this control are as follows:

0   Driver's seat occupied.
1   All seats occupied.
2   All seats occupied and load in luggage compartment
3   Driver's seat occupied and load in luggage compartment.

3 In an emergency, adjustment of the headlights may be made by turning the adjuster screws on the top and rear of each headlight unit. The top screw controls horizontal adjustment, and the rear screw controls vertical adjustment **(see illustration)**.

18.3 Headlight beam adjustment screws

A   Vertical adjustment
B   Horizontal adjustment

17.27a Rear light cluster securing screws (arrowed) - Saloon model

17.27b Removing a rear light cluster - Hatchback model

19.3 Remove the sidelight bulbholder, turn the headlight aim adjustment motor, and push the reflector assembly to one side

19.4 Pull the headlight aim adjustment motor from the headlight - 'Carello' type headlight

19.5 Release the headlight aim adjustment motor balljoint using a screwdriver - 'Bosch' type headlight

4 If an adjustment is made, the alignment should be checked using beam-setting equipment at the earliest opportunity. Note that when using beam-setting equipment, the headlight aim adjustment control should be set to position '0'.

19 Headlight aim adjustment motor - removal and refitting

Removal

1 Remove the headlight unit, as described in Section 17.
2 Remove the sidelight bulbholder assembly, referring to Section 15 if necessary.
3 Turn the motor through approximately 60° towards the top of the headlight. Then carefully push the headlight reflector assembly away from the motor, and hold it in position, so that the motor and the balljoint are pushed partially out of the headlight assembly **(see illustration)**.
4 On models with 'Carello' type headlights, carefully pull the motor and balljoint assembly from the headlight **(see illustration)**.
5 On models with 'Bosch' type headlights, release the balljoint using a small screwdriver, then carefully pull the motor and balljoint assembly from the headlight **(see illustration)**.

Refitting

6 Carefully push the headlight reflector assembly away from the motor location, ensuring that on models with 'Carello' type headlights, the ball socket is open, as shown **(see illustration)**, (otherwise irreparable damage could be caused to the headlight). Also hold the reflector in position while pushing the motor balljoint into place.
7 With the balljoint reconnected, lock the motor in position by twisting it towards the bottom of the headlight.
8 Refit the sidelight bulbholder, then refit the headlight as described in Section 17.

20 Instrument panel - removal and refitting

Removal

1 Disconnect the battery negative lead.
2 Working in the engine compartment, unscrew the securing sleeve, and disconnect the speedometer cable from the gearbox/transmission.
3 Remove the steering column shrouds, as described in Chapter 11.
4 Where applicable, prise out the screw covers, then remove the four (two upper and

19.6 The ball socket (1) must be open before pushing the headlight aim adjustment motor balljoint into place - 'Carello' type headlight

two lower) securing screws, and withdraw the instrument panel surround.
5 Remove the three (one upper and two lower) instrument panel securing screws **(see illustration)**, and carefully pull the instrument panel forwards from the facia.
6 Push down (towards the back of the speedometer) on the catch securing the speedometer cable to the rear of the speedometer, and release the speedometer cable **(see illustration)**.
7 Release the retaining clips, and disconnect the wiring plugs from the rear of the instrument panel **(see illustration)**.
8 Withdraw the instrument panel.

20.5 Unscrewing a lower instrument panel securing screw

20.6 Speedometer cable disconnected from speedometer

20.7 Disconnecting a wiring plug from the rear of the instrument panel

12

21.2 Warning light bulb withdrawn from its location in the instrument panel

21.5 Pulling the instrument panel voltage stabiliser from the printed circuit board

21.8 Releasing an instrument panel shroud retaining clip

Refitting

9 Refitting is a reversal of removal, but ensure that the speedometer cable is not twisted or kinked between the instrument panel and the bulkhead as the panel is refitted.

21 Instrument panel components - general, removal and refitting

General

1 With the instrument panel removed as described in Section 20, continue as follows.

Panel illumination and warning light bulbs

Removal

2 Twist the relevant bulbholder anti-clockwise, and withdraw it from the printed circuit board on the rear of the instrument panel (see illustration).

3 The bulbs are integral with the bulbholders, and must be renewed as a unit.

Refitting

4 Refitting is a reversal of removal.

Voltage stabiliser

Removal

5 Remove the single securing screw from the rear of the instrument panel, then pull the voltage stabiliser from the contacts on the printed circuit board (see illustration).

21.11 Rear view of instrument panel - model with tachometer

1 Fuel and temperature gauge securing nuts
2 Tachometer securing nuts
3 Speedometer securing screws
4 Voltage stabiliser securing screw

Refitting

6 Refitting is a reversal of removal, but take care not to damage the contacts on the voltage stabiliser and printed circuit board.

Fuel and temperature gauges - models without tachometer

Removal

7 Pull the tripmeter reset pin from the front of the panel.

8 Release the two retaining clips at the top of the panel, and remove the panel shroud (see illustration).

9 Unscrew the two securing nuts, and withdraw the relevant gauge through the front of the instrument panel.

Refitting

10 Refitting is a reversal of removal.

Fuel and temperature gauge assembly - models with tachometer

11 The procedure is as described in paragraphs 7 to 10 inclusive, except that the gauge assembly is secured by four nuts (see illustration).

Tachometer

12 The procedure is as described in paragraphs 7 to 10 inclusive, except that the tachometer is secured by three nuts.

Speedometer

Removal

13 Proceed as described in paragraphs 7 and 8.

22.3 Removing the rubber mat from the tray in front of the clock/multi-function display

14 Extract the four securing screws from the rear of the panel, and withdraw the speedometer from the front of the panel.

Refitting

15 Refitting is a reversal of removal.

Printed circuit board

Removal

16 Remove all bulbs and instruments, and the voltage stabiliser, as described previously in this Section.

17 Carefully peel the printed circuit board from the instrument panel.

Refitting

18 Refitting is a reversal of removal, but ensure that the printed circuit board is seated correctly on the rear of the instrument panel.

22 Clock/multi-function display - removal and refitting

Removal

1 Disconnect the battery negative lead.

2 Remove the radio/cassette player, as described in Section 34.

3 Remove the rubber mat from the tray in front of the clock/multifunction display (see illustration).

4 Remove the two central now-exposed screws (see illustration).

22.4 Unscrewing a clock/multifunction display securing screw

22.5 Pushing the clock/multifunction display from the facia

5 Reach up through the radio/cassette player aperture, and push the clock/multi-function display from the facia **(see illustration)**.
6 Disconnect the wiring plug, and withdraw the unit.

Refitting

7 Refitting is a reversal of removal, but refit the radio/cassette player as described in Section 34.

23 Auxiliary warning system - general

The auxiliary warning system displays information on the multifunction display, to warn the driver of low engine oil level, low engine coolant level, low washer fluid level, brake pad wear, brake light bulb failure, and dipped headlight beam/tail light bulb failure.
Warnings are displayed automatically on the multi-function display, and the warnings will override any other information displayed.
Removal and refitting procedures for the auxiliary warning system components are given in Section 24.

24 Auxiliary warning system components - removal and refitting

Control module

1 The control module is integral with the multi-function display. Refer to Section 22 for details of removal and refitting.

Multi-function display

2 Refer to Section 22.

Coolant level sensor

Note: *Refer to the precautions in Chapter 3, before removing the sensor.*

Removal

3 The coolant level sensor is integral with the expansion tank filler cap.
4 Before removing the filler cap/coolant level sensor assembly, disconnect the battery negative lead, and disconnect the wiring plug from the top of the sensor.

Refitting

5 Refitting is a reversal of removal.

Washer fluid level sensor

Removal

6 If possible, drain the fluid reservoir by operating the washers, to minimise fluid loss when the level sensor is removed.
7 Disconnect the battery negative lead.
8 Disconnect the wiring plug from the sensor, which is mounted in the side of the washer fluid reservoir.
9 Unscrew the sensor from the reservoir.

Refitting

10 Refitting is a reversal of removal.

Brake fluid level sensor

Note: *Refer to the Precautions in Chapter 9, before removing the sensor.*

Removal

11 The brake fluid level warning sensor is integral with the brake hydraulic fluid reservoir filler cap.
12 Before removing the filler cap/level sensor assembly, disconnect the battery negative lead, and disconnect the wiring plug from the top of the sensor.

Refitting

13 Refitting is a reversal of removal.

Brake pad wear sensors

14 The sensors take the form of wires located in the front brake pads.
15 Removal and refitting are described in Chapter 9 as part of the front brake pad renewal procedure.

Outside air temperature sensor

Removal

16 The sensor is clipped into the lower edge of the front spoiler.
17 Disconnect the battery negative lead.
18 For improved access, apply the handbrake, then jack up the front of the vehicle, and support securely on axle stands.
19 Unclip the sensor from the spoiler, then disconnect the wiring connector, noting its location **(see illustration)**.

Refitting

20 Refitting is a reversal of removal, ensuring that the wiring connector is located as noted before removal.

24.19 Unclipping the outside air temperature sensor from the spoiler

25 Trip computer - general

The trip computer displays information on the multi-function display, to indicate fuel consumption, average speed, range, outside air temperature, and elapsed time (stopwatch). The information to be displayed is selected using two push-buttons on the end of the right-hand steering column stalk switch.
The trip computer operates in conjunction with the auxiliary warning system, and any warning display will take priority over the trip computer display.
Details for removal and refitting of the auxiliary warning system components are given in Section 24.

26 Cigarette lighter - removal and refitting

Removal

1 Disconnect the battery negative lead.
2 Remove the centre console, as described in Chapter 11.
3 To remove the cigarette lighter assembly, simply pull it from the illumination ring assembly. The illumination ring assembly can be removed, by pulling it from the housing after depressing the retaining clips.

Refitting

4 Refitting is a reversal of removal.

27 Horn - removal and refitting

Models with single-tone horn

Removal

1 Disconnect the battery negative lead.
2 Remove the radiator grille, as described in Chapter 11.
3 Disconnect the wiring from the rear of the horn.
4 Unscrew the securing nut, and withdraw the horn from its bracket **(see illustration)**.

27.4 Horn location viewed with radiator grille panel removed (securing nut arrowed) - model with single-tone horn

12

27.9 Horn location (arrowed) - model with multi-tone horns

29.2a Unscrewing a windscreen wiper arm securing nut

29.2b Removing the tailgate wiper arm securing nut and washer - Hatchback model

Refitting

5 Refitting is a reversal of removal.

Models with multi-tone horns

Removal

6 Disconnect the battery negative lead.

7 Apply the handbrake, then jack up the front of the vehicle, and support securely on axle stands.

8 Working at the front of the left-hand wheel arch, disconnect the wiring from the relevant horn.

9 Unscrew the relevant securing nut, and withdraw the horn from its bracket **(see illustration)**.

10 On certain models, access to the horn mounting nuts may be easier if the complete horn assembly is first removed by unscrewing the bracket securing nut.

Refitting

11 Refitting is a reversal of removal.

28 Speedometer drive cable - removal and refitting

Removal

1 Remove the instrument panel, as described in Section 20.

2 Carefully pull the speedometer cable through the bulkhead into the engine compartment, noting its routing. It will probably be necessary to prise the cable grommet from the bulkhead.

3 The cable can now be withdrawn from the vehicle, noting its routing so that it can be refitted in the same position.

Refitting

4 Refitting is a reversal of removal, ensuring that the cable is correctly routed. Make sure that the cable is not kinked or twisted between the instrument panel and the bulkhead as the instrument panel is refitted, and ensure that the cable grommet is securely located in the bulkhead.

29 Wiper arms - removal and refitting

Removal

1 The wiper motor should be in the parked position before removing the wiper arm.

> **HAYNES HiNT**
> *Mark the position of the blade on the glass with adhesive tape, as a guide to refitting.*

2 Lift the hinged cover, and remove the nut and washer securing the arm to the spindle **(see illustrations)**.

3 Prise the arm from the spindle, using a screwdriver if necessary - take care not to damage the trim or paintwork.

Refitting

4 Refitting is a reversal of removal, positioning the arms so that the blades align with the tape applied to the glass before removal. Note that the driver's side windscreen wiper blade is fitted with a wind deflector.

30 Windscreen wiper motor and linkage - removal and refitting

Removal

1 Disconnect the battery negative lead.

2 Remove the windscreen wiper arms referring to Section 29.

3 Remove the scuttle water deflector panels, noting how they are located over the flanges on the scuttle **(see illustrations)**.

4 Remove the windscreen cowl panel, as described in Chapter 11.

5 Disconnect the wiring plug from the motor **(see illustration)**.

6 Unscrew the three securing bolts, and withdraw the complete motor and linkage assembly from the scuttle **(see illustration)**.

30.3a Removing the front . . .

30.3b . . . and rear water deflector panels from the scuttle

30.5 Disconnecting the wiring plug from the windscreen wiper motor

30.6 Withdrawing the windscreen wiper motor and linkage assembly

Refitting

7 Refitting is a reversal of removal, remembering the following points.
8 Refit the windscreen cowl panel, as described in Chapter 11.
9 Refit the windscreen wiper arms referring to Section 29.

---

31 Tailgate wiper motor and linkage - removal and refitting

Removal

1 Disconnect the battery negative lead.
2 Remove the tailgate wiper arm, as described in Section 29.
3 Remove the plastic cover from the end of the wiper spindle, then unscrew the spindle nut and recover the washer **(see illustration)**.
4 Remove the tailgate trim panel, as described in Chapter 11.
5 Locate the motor wiring connector, and separate the two halves of the connector **(see illustration)**.
6 Unscrew the two securing bolts, noting the locations of any earth wires secured by the bolts **(see illustration)**, and withdraw the motor assembly from the tailgate. Note that the spindle mounting rubbers may be released from the tailgate as the assembly is withdrawn.

Refitting

7 Refitting is a reversal of removal, ensuring that the spindle mounting rubbers are correctly located in the tailgate aperture, and that any earth wires are located as noted before removal.

---

32 Windscreen/tailgate washer system components - removal and refitting

Fluid reservoir

Removal

1 Disconnect the battery negative lead.
2 Working in the engine compartment, disconnect the wiring plug(s) from the fluid pump(s) in the reservoir.
3 Disconnect the fluid hose(s) from the pump(s). Be prepared for fluid spillage.
4 Remove the securing screw from the front right-hand edge of the reservoir, and withdraw the reservoir from the engine compartment.

Refitting

5 Refitting is a reversal of removal.

Fluid pump

Removal

6 Disconnect the battery negative lead.
7 Working in the engine compartment, disconnect the wiring plug from the pump.
8 Disconnect the fluid hose(s) from the pump. Be prepared for fluid spillage.
9 Pull the pump from the reservoir, being prepared for fluid spillage if the reservoir still contains fluid.

Refitting

10 Examine the condition of gauze filter at the end of the pump pick-up tube, and clean or renew if necessary.
11 Refitting is a reversal of removal, ensuring that the pump is securely seated in the reservoir.

Windscreen washer nozzle

Removal

12 Carefully prise the nozzle from the bonnet, taking care not to damage the paintwork.

---

13 Disconnect the fluid hose, and withdraw the nozzle.

Refitting

14 To refit, reconnect the washer hose to the nozzle, and push the nozzle into its locating hole.
15 The nozzle can be adjusted by inserting a pin into the jet, and swivelling it to the required position.

Tailgate washer nozzle - Hatchback models

Removal

16 The washer nozzle can be removed after removing the tailgate spoiler as described in Chapter 11. Take care to prevent the end of the fluid hose from dropping into the tailgate.

Refitting

17 Refitting is a reversal of removal, but refit the spoiler as described in Chapter 11, and note that the nozzle can be adjusted by inserting a pin into the jet and swivelling it to the desired position.

Tailgate washer nozzle - Estate models

Removal

18 Open the tailgate, and remove the upper tailgate interior trim panel, referring to Chapter 11.
19 Disconnect the fluid hose from the rear of the nozzle, then push the nozzle out through the tailgate.

Refitting

20 Refitting is a reversal of removal.

---

33 Headlight washer system components - removal and refitting

Washer nozzles

Removal

1 Remove the radiator grille, as described in Chapter 11.
2 Remove the two securing screws, and withdraw the nozzles from the radiator grille.

31.3 Removing the plastic cover from the tailgate wiper spindle - Hatchback model

31.5 Tailgate wiper motor wiring connector - Hatchback model

31.6 Tailgate wiper motor securing bolts (arrowed)

34.3 Unscrewing a grub screw from the radio/cassette player

34.5 Withdrawing the radio/cassette player from the facia

35.4 Removing a front treble loudspeaker from the mirror trim panel

Refitting

3 Refitting is a reversal of removal.
4 The nozzles can be adjusted by inserting a pin into the jet, and swivelling it to the desired position.

Reservoir

Removal

5 The headlight washer fluid reservoir is located at the rear left-hand corner of the engine compartment.
6 Disconnect the battery negative lead.
7 Working in the engine compartment, unscrew the filler neck from the top of the reservoir.
8 Remove the wheel arch liner, as described in Chapter 11.
9 Remove the three reservoir securing screws, and manipulate the reservoir as necessary to disconnect the pump wiring plug and the fluid hose. Be prepared for fluid spillage as the hose is disconnected.
10 Withdraw the reservoir from under the wheel arch.

Refitting

11 Refitting is a reversal of removal.

Washer pump

Removal

12 Remove the fluid reservoir, as described previously in this Section.
13 Pull the pump from the reservoir, being prepared for fluid spillage if the reservoir still contains fluid.

Refitting

14 Examine the condition of the pump-to-reservoir sealing grommet, and renew if necessary.
15 Refitting is a reversal of removal.

---

34 Radio/cassette player - removal and refitting

Removal

1 All the radio/cassette players have DIN standard fixings. Two special tools, obtainable from in-car entertainment specialists, are required for removal.
2 Disconnect the battery negative lead.
3 Unscrew the four grub screws from the corners of the radio/cassette player, using an Allen key or hexagon bit **(see illustration)**.
4 Insert the tools into the holes exposed by removal of the grub screws, and push them until they snap into place. Pull the tools rearwards (away from the facia) to release the unit.
5 Pull the unit forwards, and withdraw it from the facia **(see illustration)**.

Refitting

6 To refit the radio/cassette player, simply push the unit into the facia until the retaining lugs snap into place, then refit the grub screws.

---

35 Speakers - removal and refitting

Front treble speaker ('tweeter')

Removal

1 Disconnect the battery negative lead.
2 Carefully prise the door mirror trim panel from the door.
3 Disconnect the wiring plug from the speaker.
4 Carefully push the speaker from its location in the trim panel **(see illustration)**.

Refitting

5 Refitting is a reversal of removal.

Front bass speaker ('woofer')

Removal

6 Disconnect the battery negative lead.
7 Carefully unclip the speaker trim panel from the door to expose the speaker **(see illustration)**.
8 Remove the three securing screws, then withdraw the speaker from the door and disconnect the wiring.

Refitting

9 Refitting is a reversal of removal.

Rear speaker - Saloon models

Removal

10 Disconnect the battery negative lead.
11 Working in the luggage compartment, disconnect the wiring plug from the speaker.
12 Working inside the vehicle, carefully prise the speaker cover from the rear parcel shelf (slide the cover towards the centre of the vehicle to remove it), **(see illustration)**.
13 Unscrew the four now-exposed speaker securing screws, and carefully withdraw the speaker into the luggage compartment **(see illustration)**.

Refitting

14 Refitting is a reversal of removal.

35.7 Removing the front bass loudspeaker trim panel from the door

35.12 Removing the rear loudspeaker cover from the parcel shelf (viewed through rear window) - Saloon model

Rear speaker - Hatchback models

Removal

15 Disconnect the battery negative lead.
16 Working in the luggage compartment, disconnect the wiring plug from the speaker.
17 Remove the four securing screws, and withdraw the speaker from under the rear parcel shelf (see illustration).

Refitting

18 Refitting is a reversal of removal.

Rear speaker - Estate and Van models

Removal

19 Disconnect the battery negative lead.
20 Remove the tailgate lower trim panel, as described in Chapter 11.
21 Remove the three securing screws, then withdraw the speaker from the tailgate, and disconnect the wiring.

Refitting

22 Refitting is a reversal of removal.

36 Radio aerial - removal and refitting

Saloon models

Removal

1 On models fitted with an electrically operated aerial, make sure that the aerial is fully retracted, then disconnect the battery negative lead.
2 Remove the luggage compartment rear trim panel, and the left-hand side trim panel, as described in Chapter 11.
3 Where applicable, remove the screw securing the aerial earth lead to the body panel.
4 Remove the screw securing the lower end of the aerial to the body panel. Then pull the aerial through the grommet in the rear wing panel, and lower it sufficiently to disconnect the aerial lead and, where applicable, the motor wiring plug.
5 Withdraw the aerial into the luggage compartment.

Refitting

6 Refitting is a reversal of removal, but ensure that the aerial grommet is correctly seated in the rear wing panel.

Hatchback models

Removal

7 Proceed as described in paragraphs 1 and 2.
8 Remove the left-hand rear light cluster, as described in Section 17.
9 Proceed as described in paragraphs 3 and 4 (see illustrations).

35.13 Removing a rear loudspeaker securing screw (viewed through rear window) - Saloon model

10 Carefully manipulate the aerial assembly to enable it to be withdrawn from the vehicle through the rear light cluster aperture (see illustration).

Electric aerial mast

Removal

11 The mast on 'factory fitted', fully automatic electric aerials, can be replaced separately.
12 Extend the aerial as far as possible, by switching on the radio.
13 Unscrew the mounting nut.
14 Pull the sprung sleeve upwards and clear of its base.
15 The assembly can now be removed from

35.17 Removing a rear loudspeaker - Hatchback model

the clutch mechanism, by pulling the assembly upwards.

Refitting

16 Insert the ball end of the mast assembly into the base.
17 Carefully push the mast assembly down as far as possible, until it engages into the clutch mechanism.
18 Switch the radio off to retract the aerial.
19 If the aerial does not fully retract into its base, guide the remaining mast into the base by hand.
20 Insert the sprung sleeve into the base and tighten the mounting nut.
21 Check the aerial works properly by turning the radio on and off a few times.
22 Refer to paragraph 6.

36.9a Electric aerial earth lead (arrowed) - Hatchback model

36.9b Lower the aerial to disconnect the aerial lead (arrowed) . . .

36.9c . . . and the motor wiring plug - Hatchback model

36.10 Withdrawing the aerial assembly through the rear light cluster aperture - Hatchback model

12

37.2 Anti-theft alarm system components

1 *Electronic control unit*
2 *Radio/cassette sensor*
3 *Bonnet switch*
4 *Ignition switch*
5 *LED integral with courtesy light*
6 *Tailgate/boot lid switch*
7 *Door lock switch*
8 *Relay (isolates starter motor)*
9 *Courtesy light switch*
10 *Horn*

38.1 Anti-theft alarm electronic control unit location (arrowed) in right-hand footwell

Estate and C 20 XE models

Removal

23 Remove the headlining, referring to Chapter 11.
24 Working through the access hole in the roof, disconnect the aerial lead from the base of the aerial.
25 Unscrew the aerial securing nut, and withdraw the aerial from the roof.

Refitting

26 Refitting is a reversal of removal.

37 Anti-theft alarm system - general

1 Certain models are fitted with an anti-theft alarm system as standard equipment.
2 The alarm system operates in conjunction with the central locking system switches, and is triggered by opening of the doors, bonnet, and boot lid/tailgate, or by interference with the radio/cassette player **(see illustration)**.
3 The alarm features a self-diagnostic function, and any faults should be referred to a Vauxhall dealer, who will have access to the necessary specialist diagnostic equipment.

38 Anti-theft alarm system components - removal and refitting

Electronic control unit

Removal

1 The control unit is located behind the right-hand footwell side/sill trim panel **(see illustration)**.
2 Disconnect the battery negative lead.
3 Remove the footwell side/sill trim panel, as described in Chapter 11.

4 Unscrew the two plastic securing nuts, then lift the control unit from the footwell, disconnect the wiring plug, and withdraw the unit.

Refitting

5 Refitting is a reversal of removal.

Bonnet switch

Removal

6 Disconnect the battery negative lead.
7 Using a screwdriver, carefully release the securing clip, and withdraw the switch from its bracket on the suspension turret **(see illustration)**.
8 Disconnect the wiring plug, and withdraw the switch.

Refitting

9 Refitting is a reversal of removal.

Horn

Removal

10 The horn is located on the left-hand inner front wing panel, next to the battery **(see illustration)**.
11 Disconnect the battery negative lead, then disconnect the wiring from the horn.
12 Unscrew the securing nut, and withdraw the horn from its mounting bracket. Alternatively, unscrew the securing bolt, and withdraw the mounting bracket complete with the horn.

Refitting

13 Refitting is a reversal of removal.

38.7 Anti-theft alarm bonnet switch (arrowed)

38.10 Anti-theft alarm horn (arrowed)

39 Airbag - general

Warning: Before starting any work on airbag or related components, disconnect the battery. Cover the battery's terminals and wait a minimum of 1 minutes as a precaution against accidental firing of the airbag unit. This period ensures that any stored energy in the back-up capacitor is dissipated. Handle the airbag unit with extreme care as a precaution against personal injury, and always hold it with the cover facing away from the body. If in doubt concerning any proposed work involving the airbag unit or its control circuitry, consult a Vauxhall dealer or other qualified specialist.

1 During 1993 models were available with an airbag that is designed to prevent serious chest and head injuries to the driver during an accident. A similar bag for the front seat passenger was also available on certain models. Sensors in the centre of the car measure the vehicle deceleration rate and pass these signals to a microprocessor. This unit analyses the sensor data and compares the information with pre-programmed values stored in its memory, triggering the airbag if the deceleration is severe. The airbag is inflated in 50 milliseconds by a gas generator that forces the bag out of the module cover in the centre of the steering wheel.

2 No repairs are possible on the airbag unit or its associated parts. The contents of the following Sections are confined to removal and refitting of the airbag, purely for access to other non-related components.

3 Should a fault be suspected on the airbag unit, indicated by the warning light on the instrument panel, or if the car has been involved in an accident, however minor, consult a Vauxhall dealer immediately. Do not attempt to dismantle any of the airbag components or carry out any work whatsoever, other than the procedures described in the following Sections.

4 On vehicles fitted with a passenger side airbag, **do not** fit accessories in the airbag zone. Items like telephones, cassette storage boxes, additional mirrors, etc., can be ripped off and cause serious injury, if the airbag inflates.

40 Airbag unit, driver's side - removal and refitting

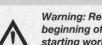

Warning: Read warning at the beginning of Section 39, before starting work. Stand the unit with the cover uppermost and do not expose it to heat sources more than 100°C. Do not attempt to open or repair the airbag unit, or apply any voltage to it. Do not use any airbag unit that is visibly damaged or has been tampered with.

Note: *On power steering models in particular, it will be advantageous to jack up the front of the car and support it on axle stands placed under the body side members, so that the steering wheel can be turned more easily.*

Removal

1 Disconnect the battery negative lead and cover the battery terminal. Wait a minimum of 1 minute.
2 With the steering wheel positioned in the straight-ahead position, turn it 90° clockwise so that the left-hand spoke is accessible from the rear.
3 Using a Torx type socket, undo the first airbag retaining bolt from the underside of the steering wheel.
4 Turn the steering wheel 180° anti-clockwise so that the right-hand spoke is accessible from the rear.
5 Undo the second retaining bolt from the rear of the steering wheel.
6 Return the steering wheel to the straight-ahead position then carefully lift up the airbag unit.
7 Disconnect the wiring plug and remove the airbag from the car.

Refitting

8 Refitting is a reversal of removal.

41 Steering wheel (with airbag) - removal and refitting

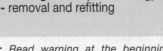

Note: *Read warning at the beginning of Section 39, before starting work. A two-legged puller will be required for this operation. Note also that the steering wheel is a very tight fit on the shaft.*

Removal

1 Remove the airbag unit as described previously.
2 Remove the steering column shrouds, as described in Chapter 11.
3 Remove the cable-tie and disconnect the plug connection for the contact unit and horn.
4 Ensure that the steering wheel is in the straight ahead position.
5 Using a screwdriver, prise back the tabs on the lockwasher securing the steering wheel retaining nut.
6 Unscrew and remove the steering wheel retaining nut and the lockwasher.
7 Make alignment marks between the steering wheel and the end of the column shaft.
8 A suitably small two-legged puller must now be fitted to the steering wheel to pull it from the column shaft.

Refitting

9 Begin refitting by positioning the steering wheel on the column shaft, ensuring that the marks made on removal are aligned, and that the wheel correctly engages with the airbag contact unit. It may be necessary to tap the steering wheel fully home on the column shaft using a metal tube and socket.
10 Reconnect the horn wiring.
11 Refit the lockwasher and the steering wheel retaining nut, and tighten the nut to the specified torque. Bend up the lockwasher to secure.
12 Refit the two screws securing the airbag contact unit.
13 Refit the airbag as described previously.

42 Airbag contact unit - removal and refitting

Note: *Read warning at the beginning of Section 39, before starting work.*

Removal

1 Remove the airbag and the steering wheel as described previously.
2 Remove the steering column upper and lower shrouds, referring to Chapter 10, if necessary.
3 Disconnect the contact unit wiring plug below the steering column and withdraw the contact unit from the column, noting its fitted position as a guide to reassembly **(see illustration)**.

Refitting

4 Before refitting the contact unit, ensure that the front wheels are in the straight-ahead position.
5 Place the contact unit on the column in the correct position as noted during removal.
6 Route the wiring harness under the steering column lock/ignition switch and connect the wiring plug.
7 Refit the steering column shrouds.
8 Refit the steering wheel and airbag as described previously.

42.3 Removing the steering wheel airbag contact unit

43.7 Removing the passenger airbag unit

45.3 Location of the airbag control unit

45 Airbag control unit - removal and refitting

Note: *Read warning at the beginning of Section 39, before starting work.*

Removal

1 Disconnect the battery negative lead and cover the battery terminal to prevent accidental reconnection.
2 Remove the centre console rear section as described in Chapter 11.
3 Disconnect the control unit wiring plug, then undo the three nuts and remove the unit from the car **(see illustration)**.

Refitting

4 Refitting is a reversal of removal.

43 Airbag unit, passenger's side - removal and refitting

Note: *Read the warning at the beginning of Section 39, before starting work. If the airbag has been deployed, the units brackets must be replaced. The securing nuts must be replaced when refitting.*

Removal

1 Disconnect the battery, cover the terminals and wait at least 1 minute.
2 Remove the scuttle panel and glovebox assembly. Refer to Chapter 11, for further details.
3 Remove the right hand and mixed ventilation air duct.
4 Remove the passenger side storage tray and footwell panelling.
5 Disconnect the plug connections.
6 Unbolt the six nuts from the two side brackets.
7 Remove the airbag unit **(see illustration)**.

Refitting

8 Refitting is a reversal of removal. Use new

nuts and tighten them to the specific torque. See Specifications.

44 Bracket, passenger airbag unit - removal and refitting

Note: *Read the warning at the beginning of Section 39, before starting work. New airbag to brackets nuts will be required.*

Removal

1 Remove the passenger side airbag unit as described in Section 43.
2 Remove the pollen filter and disconnect the fan motor wiring plug.
3 Drain cooling system (referring to Chapter 3) and disconnect the heater hoses from the heater radiator.
4 Disconnect the vacuum hose, remove the pollen filter and air distribution housing assemblies.
5 Detach the instrument panel padding and pull it forwards approximately 4 ins (10 cm).
6 The brackets can now be unbolted.

Refitting

7 Refitting is a reversal of removal. Use new nuts to secure the airbag unit to the brackets.

46 Wiring diagrams - explanatory notes

1 Two wiring diagrams are provided, one diagram for early models with 30 fuses in the fusebox, and one for later models with 28 fuses in the fusebox **(see illustration)**.
2 The wiring diagrams are of the current flow type, each circuit being shown in the simplest possible form. Note that since the diagrams were originally produced in Germany (to the DIN standard), all wire colours and abbreviations used on the diagrams are in German; refer to the information given above the diagram key for clarification.
3 The bottom line of the diagram represents the earth (or negative) connection; the numbers below this line are track numbers, enabling circuits and components to be located using the key.
4 The lines at the top of the diagram represent live feed (or positive) connection points. The line marked '30' is live at all times, that marked '15' is live only when the ignition is switched on.
5 Numbers on the diagram that are framed in square boxes at the end of a wire indicate the track reference number at which that particular wire is continued. At the point indicated, another framed number will appear, referring back to the previous circuit.

46.1 Early and later type fuseboxes

A Early models with 30 fuses   B Later models with 28 fuses

Explanation of abbreviations used

Note: *The following list is included for guidance only - a comprehensive list was not available at time of writing.*

ABS	Anti-lock braking system	HW	Rear screen wiper	PBSL	Parking/brake lockout
AC	Air conditioning	HZG	Heating	P/N	Park/Neutral (starter inhibitor -
AT	Automatic transmission	INS	Instrument		automatic transmission)
ATC	Automatic temperature control	IRL	Interior light	POT	Potentiometer
AZV	Trailer hitch	KAT	Catalytic converter	RC	Ride control
BR	On-board computer	KBS	Wiring harness	RFS	Reversing lights
CC	Check control	KV	Contact, distributor	RHD	Right-hand drive
CRC	Cruise control	L3.1	Fuel injection (Bosch L3.1-Jetronic)	S	Sweden
D	Diesel	LCD	LCD instrument	SD	Sliding sunroof
DID	Dual information display	LHD	Left-hand drive	SH	Seat heating
DIS	Direct ignition system	LWR	Headlamp range control	SRA	Headlight washer
DS	Theft protection	M1.5	Fuel injection (Bosch Motronic	TANK	Fuel gauge
DWA	Anti-theft warning system		M1.5)	TD	Turbodiesel
DZM	Tachometer	M2.5	Fuel injection (Bosch Motronic	TEMP	Temperature gauge
EFC	Electric folding roof (Convertible)		M2.5)	TFL	Day running lights
EKS	Pinch guard (electric windows)	MID	Multi-information display	TKS	Door courtesy light switch
EMP	Radio/cassette	MOT	Motronic system (general)	TSZI	High-energy ignition (HEI)
ETC	Electronic traction control	MT	Manual transmission	VGS	Carburettor
EUR	Euronorm engine	MUL	Fuel injection (Multec)	WEG	Mileometer frequency sensor
EZ +	El Plus with self-diagnosis	N	Norway	WHR	Vehicle level control
EZV	Ecotronic	NSL	Rear foglight	WS	Warning buzzer
FH	Electric windows	NSW	Foglight	ZV	Central locking
GB	Great Britain	OEL	Oil level check (oil pressure)	ZYL	Cylinder
HRL	Luggage compartment lamp	OPT	Optional equipment	4WD	Four-wheel-drive
HS	Heated rear window				

Wiring identification

Example: GE WS 1.5
GE - Basic colour
WS - Identification colour
1.5 - Wirecross-section (mm²)

Colour code

BL	Blue	GN	Green	HBL	Light blue	RT	Red	VI	Violet
BR	Brown	GR	Grey	LI	Lilac	SW	Black	WS	White
GE	Yellow						

Circuit interconnections

A framed number - eg 180 - refers to a grid reference (track) at which the circuit is continued

12

Key to wiring diagrams

Not all items fitted to all models *Models with earlier 30-fuse type fusebox* **Models with later 28-fuse type fusebox*

No	Description	Track
E01	Sidelight, left	604
E02	Tail light, left	501, 602
E03	Number plate light	613 to 616
E04	Sidelight, right	609
E05	Tail light, right	503, 611
E07	Headlight main beam, left	629
E08	Headlight main beam, right	631
E09	Headlight dipped beam, left	505, 630
E10	Headlight dipped beam, right	507, 632
E11	Instrument lighting	546
E12	Automatic transmission selector illumination	296, 297
E13	Luggage compartment light	687
E14	Interior light	689, 750, 752
E15	Glovebox light	857
E16	Cigarette lighter illumination	855
E17	Reversing light, left	698
E18	Reversing light, right	699
E19	Heated rear window	756
E20	Foglight, front left	650
E21	Foglight, front right	651
E24	Foglight, rear left	645
E25	Seat heating, left	860
E27	Rear reading light, left	692
E28	Rear reading light, right	694
E30	Seat heating, right	864
E34	Heater control illumination	756
E39	Foglight, rear right	646
F01 to F30	Fuses in fusebox	Various
F14**	Heater blower fuse ('maxi' type)	762
F35	Voltage stabiliser	548
F36	Fuel filter heating fuse (diesel, engine compartment)	450, 495
F38**	Anti-theft alarm horn fuse	743
F41	Glow plug fuse ('maxi' type, engine compartment)	440, 487
F42	Fuse, radiator cooling fan	120
F45	Horn fuse	830
F46*	Heater blower fuse ('maxi' type)	762
F48*	Anti-theft alarm horn fuse	743
G01	Battery	100
G02	Alternator	115
G06	Alternator (diesel)	469 to 472
H01	Radio/cassette	571 to 587
H02	Horn (single-tone)	826
H03	Direction indicator warning light	554
H04	Oil pressure warning light	561
H05	Brake fluid warning light	563
H06	Hazard flashers warning light	674
H07	Alternator/no-charge warning light	565
H08	Headlight main beam warning light	558
H09	Stop-light, left	509, 659
H10	Stop-light, right	511, 660
H11	Direction indicator light, front left	675
H12	Direction indicator light, rear left	676
H13	Direction indicator light, front right	683
H14	Direction indicator light, rear right	684
H15	Low fuel/fuel reserve warning light	551
H16	Glow plug warning light	539
H17	Trailer direction indicator warning light	542
H18	Horn (twin-tone)	830
H19	Headlights 'on' warning buzzer	695, 696
H21	Handbrake 'on' warning light	566
H25	Heated mirror warning light	842
H26	ABS warning light	537
H30	Engine warning light	559

No	Description	Track
H33	Direction indicator side repeater light left	679
H34	Direction indicator side repeater light right	681
H37	Loudspeaker, front left	576, 577
H38	Loudspeaker, front right	581 582
H39	Loudspeaker, rear left	576 577
H40	Loudspeaker, rear right	581, 582
H42	Automatic transmission warning light	540
H47	Anti-theft alarm horn	743
H48	Horn (twin-tone)	832
H51	Electronic traction control (ETC) warning light	538
H52	Tweeter, front left	576
H53	Tweeter, front right	581
K01	Heated rear window relay	756, 757
K03	Relay, starter (anti-theft warning unit, 70A)	111, 112
K05	Front foglight relay	651, 652
K08	Intermittent wiper relay (windscreen)	803 to 806
K10	Direction indicator flasher unit	670 to 672
K20	Ignition module/ignition coil	137 to 141, 170 to 172, 239, 240, 302, 303, 362 to 365
K25	Glow time relay (70A)	437 to 440
K30	Intermittent wiper relay (tailgate)	813 to 815
K35	Heated mirror relay	847 to 849
K37	Central door locking control unit	705 to 711
K57	Multec single-point control unit	175 to 194, 211 to 230, 242 to 261
K58	Fuel pump relay (Multec single-point)	196, 197, 231, 232, 261, 262, 332, 333
K59	Day running light relay	619 to 625
K61	Motronic control unit	367 to 397, 402 to 426
K63	Twin-tone horn relay	829, 830
K68	Fuel injection unit relay	395 to 399, 428 to 432
K76	Glow time control unit	479 to 484
K77	Glow plug relay	486, 487
K78	Pre-resistor relay	489, 490
K79	Charging indicator relay	472 to 474
K80	Fuel filter heating relay (diesel)	449, 450, 494, 495
K82	Engine speed relay	444, 445
K85	Automatic transmission control unit	271 to 294
K89	Rear foglight relay	639 to 641
K91	Multec multi-point control unit	305 to 332, 345
K94	Anti-theft alarm control unit	737 to 750
K95	ETC system control unit	926 to 941
K97	Headlight washer delay relay	820 to 822
L01	Ignition coil	138, 172, 205, 239, 303, 362, 406
L02	Ignition coil (DIS)	338 to 343
M01	Starter motor	105, 106
M02	Windscreen wiper motor	801 to 804
M03	Heater blower motor	761 to 763
M04*	Radiator cooling fan motor	120, 123
M04**	Radiator cooling fan motor	120, 123, 127
M08	Tailgate wiper motor	811 to 813
M15	Electric window motor, front passenger door	783, 785
M18	Central locking motor, driver's door	706 to 709
M19	Central locking motor, left rear door	717 to 719
M20	Central locking motor, right rear door	721 to 723
M21	Fuel pump	197, 232, 262, 333, 399, 429
M24	Headlight washer pump	822
M26	Electric aerial motor	587, 588
M26.1	Electric aerial motor relay	590
M30	Electric mirror (driver's side)	838 to 841
M31	Electric mirror (passenger side)	844 to 847
M32	Central locking motor, front passenger door	717 to 720
M33	Idle speed actuator/power unit	377, 378, 414, 415
M39	Headlight levelling motor, left	592 to 594
M40	Headlight levelling motor, right	596 to 598
M41	Central locking motor, fuel filler flap	725, 726

Key to wiring diagrams (continued)

Not all items fitted to all models   *Models with earlier 30-fuse type fusebox*   **Models with later 28-fuse type fusebox**

No	Description	Track
M47	Electric window motor, driver's door	773 to 776
M55	Windscreen/tailgate washer pump	817
M60	Central locking motor, boot lid/tailgate	726, 728
M65	Throttle valve actuator (ETC system)	930 to 934
M66	Idle air stepper motor	178 to 181, 215 to 218, 249 to 252, 314 to 317
P01	Fuel gauge	550
P02	Coolant temperature gauge	553
P04	Fuel level sensor	550
P05	Coolant temperature sensor	553
P07	Tachometer	543
P12	Coolant temperature sensor	371 to 373, 413
P13	Ambient air temperature sensor	524
P14	Distance sensor	478, 479
P17	Wheel sensor, front left	910, 953
P18	Wheel sensor, front right	913, 956
P19	Wheel sensor, rear left	916, 959
P20	Wheel sensor, rear right	919, 962
P21	Distance sensor	556
P23	MAP sensor	188 to 190, 217 to 219, 249 to 251, 319 to 321
P25	Bulb test sensor	500 to 513
P27	Brake pad wear sensor, front left	516
P28	Brake pad wear sensor, front right	516
P29	Inlet manifold temperature sensor	315, 410
P30	Coolant temperature sensor	186, 215, 247, 317
P32	Exhaust gas oxygen sensor (heated)	392, 393, 426, 427
P33	Exhaust gas oxygen sensor	190, 229, 256, 330
P34	Throttle valve potentiometer	191 to 193, 221 to 223, 252 to 254, 323 to 325, 411, 412
P35	Crankshaft impulse sensor	244 to 246, 311 to 313, 381, 383, 421 to 423
P38	Automatic transmission fluid temperature sensor	290
P44	Air mass meter	394 to 398, 417 to 419
P45	Automatic transmission engine speed sensor	287, 288
P46	Knock sensor	385, 386
P47	Hall sensor (cylinder identification)	388, 389
P48	Automatic transmission distance sensor	285, 286
P55	Coolant temperature sensor	482
P57	Aerial	587
P58	Anti-theft alarm glass breakage sensor, rear left	754
P59	Anti-theft alarm glass breakage sensor, rear right	754
R02	Carburettor pre-heating	135
R03	Cigarette lighter	854
R05	Glow plugs	438 to 440, 485 to 487
R19*	Pre-resistor, radiator cooling fan motor	123
R19**	Pre-resistor, radiator cooling fan motor	123, 127
R22	Glow plug pre-resistor	490
S01	Ignition/starter switch	105, 106
S02	Light switch assembly	
S02.1	Light switch	604 to 607
S02.2	Interior light switch	689
S02.3	Instrument lighting dimmer	533
S03	Heater blower/heated rear window switch	760 to 764
S05	Direction indicator switch assembly	
S05.2	Headlight dipped beam switch	630 to 631
S05.3	Direction indicator switch	682 to 684
S07	Reversing light switch	698
S08	Stop-light switch	660
S09	Wiper switch assembly	
S09.2	Intermittent wiper switch (windscreen)	801 to 804
S09.5	Tailgate wash/wipe switch	814 to 816
S010	Automatic transmission selector switch	271 to 277
S011	Brake fluid level switch	563
S013	Handbrake 'on' switch	566
S014	Oil pressure sender/switch	561

No	Description	Track
S015	Luggage compartment light switch	687
S017	Courtesy light switch, front passenger door	694
S021	Front foglight switch	652 to 654
S022	Rear foglight switch	645 to 647
S029**	Coolant temperature switch	120
S030	Seat heating switch, front left	860 to 862
S031	Courtesy light switch, left rear door	691
S032	Courtesy light switch, right rear door	692
S033	ETC system switch	929, 930
S034	Multi-information display switch	526, 527
S037	Electric window switch assembly (in driver's door)	
S037.1	Electric window switch, driver's window	774, 775
S037.2	Electric window switch, passenger window	772 to 777
S041	Anti-theft locking switch, driver's door	702 to 704
S042	Front passenger door locking switch	714
S047	Courtesy light switch, driver's door	695, 696
S052	Hazard warning light (hazard flashers) switch	672 to 676
S055	Seat heating switch, front right	864 to 866
S064	Horn switch	826
S068	Electric mirror switch assembly	
S068.1	Electric mirror adjustment switch	836 to 840
S068.2	Electric mirror heating switch	842
S068.3	Electric mirror left/right selector switch	836 to 841
S078	Electric window switch assembly (in passenger door)	782 to 785
S082	Washer fluid level switch	518
S088*	Coolant temperature switch	119 to 124
S088**	Coolant temperature switch	123 to 128
S093	Coolant level switch	520
S095	Engine oil level switch	522
S098	Headlight levelling switch	591 to 593
S104	Automatic transmission kickdown switch	289
S105	Automatic transmission 'Winter' switch	293 to 295
S106	Automatic transmission 'Economy'/'Sport' switch	288
S107	Throttle valve switch	374 to 379
S120	Anti-theft alarm bonnet switch	739
S127	Boot lid/tailgate central locking switch	735
U04	ABS hydraulic unit	
U04.1	Pump motor relay	902, 903, 945, 946
U04.2	Solenoid valve relay	904, 905, 947, 948
U04.3	Pump motor	902, 945
U04.4	Diode	905, 948
U04.5	Solenoid valve, front left	909, 952
U04.6	Solenoid valve, front right	911, 954
U04.7	Solenoid valve, rear axle	913, 956
U04.8	ABS control unit	906 to 912, 949 to 963
U12	Heated fuel filter assembly	449, 450, 494, 495
U13	Automatic transmission solenoid valve block	280 to 283
U14	Clock display unit	515 to 533
U15	Clock/radio display unit	515 to 533
U16	Clock/radio/computer display unit	515 to 533
U17	Aerial amplifier	584, 585
V01	Brake fluid level test bulb diode	564
V03	Anti-theft alarm light/diode	749
X01	Trailer socket	606, 607, 657, 658
X02 to X90	Wiring connectors	Various
Y05	Fuel solenoid valve	442, 476
Y07	Fuel injectors	323 to 330, 380 to 387, 416 to 423
Y10	Distributor (HEI system)	174 to 179
Y23	Distributor (HEI system)	140 to 144, 201 to 208
Y30	Cold start acceleration valve	445
Y32	Single-point fuel injector	181, 212, 244
Y33	Distributor (MHDI system)	237, 303 to 305, 361 to 363, 401
Y34	Fuel tank ventilation valve	391, 422

12

Wiring diagram for models with 30 fuses in fusebox (up to approximately February 1992)

Wiring diagram for models with 30 fuses in fusebox (up to approximately February 1992) – continued

12

Wiring diagram for models with 30 fuses in fusebox (up to approximately February 1992) – continued

Wiring diagram for models with 30 fuses in fusebox (up to approximately February 1992) – continued

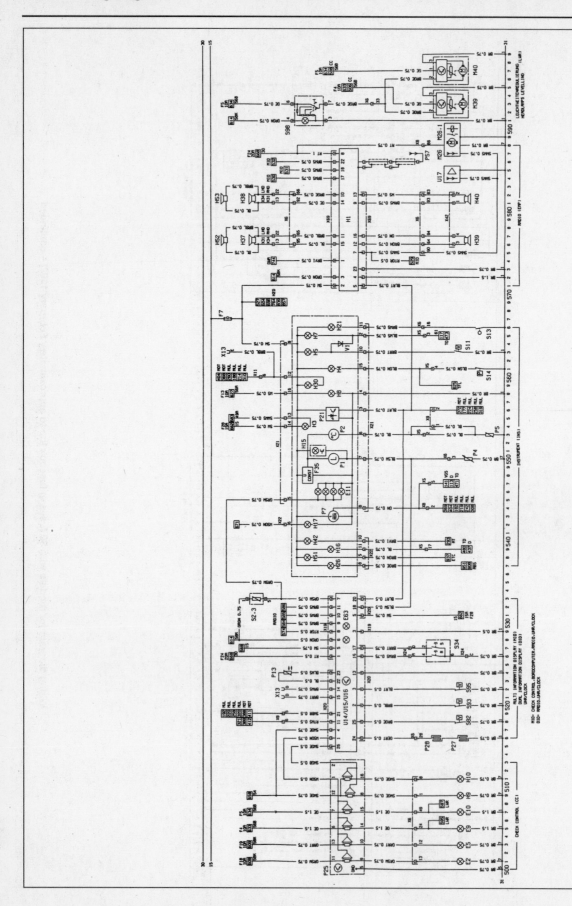

Wiring diagram for models with 30 fuses in fusebox (up to approximately February 1992) – continued

Wiring diagram for models with 30 fuses in fusebox (up to approximately February 1992) – continued

Wiring diagram for models with 30 fuses in fusebox (up to approximately February 1992) – continued

Wiring diagram for models with 30 fuses in fusebox (up to approximately February 1992) – continued

12

Wiring diagram for models with 30 fuses in fusebox (up to approximately February 1992) – continued

Wiring diagram for models with 28 fuses in fusebox (from approximately March 1992)

Wiring diagram for models with 28 fuses in fusebox (from approximately March 1992) – continued

Wiring diagram for models with 28 fuses in fusebox (from approximately March 1992) – continued

Wiring diagram for models with 28 fuses in fusebox (from approximately March 1992) – continued

Wiring diagram for models with 28 fuses in fusebox (from approximately March 1992) – continued

12

Wiring diagram for models with 28 fuses in fusebox (from approximately March 1992) – continued

Wiring diagram for models with 28 fuses in fusebox (from approximately March 1992) – continued

Wiring diagram for models with 28 fuses in fusebox (from approximately March 1992) – continued

Wiring diagram for models with 28 fuses in fusebox (from approximately March 1992) – continued

12

Notes

Dimensions and Weights

Note: *All figures and dimensions are approximate and may vary according to model. Refer to manufacturer's data for exact figures.*

Overall length *
Saloon models . . . . 4239 mm
Hatchback models (except DOHC models) . . . . 4051 mm
DOHC models . . . . 4086 mm
Estate and Van models . . . . 4278 mm

Overall width *
All models . . . . 1688 mm
All models (including door mirrors) . . . . 1795 mm

Overall height (unladen) *
Saloon and Hatchback models . . . . 1410 mm
Estate models (without roof rails) . . . . 1475 mm
Estate models (with roof rails) . . . . 1525 mm
Van models (without roof rails) . . . . 1490 mm
Van models (with roof rails) . . . . 1540 mm

Wheelbase *
All models . . . . 2517 mm

Turning circle
All models . . . . 9.8 metres

Ground clearance (minimum) *
All models . . . . 130 mm

Weights

Kerb weight *
Saloon models . . . . 960 to 1090 kg
Hatchback models . . . . 930 to 1125 kg
Estate models . . . . 995 to 1127 kg
Van models . . . . 1030 to 1050 kg
* *Exact kerb weights depend upon model and specification.*

Maximum gross vehicle weight
All models . . . . Refer to VIN plate

Maximum roof rack load
All models . . . . 100 kg

Maximum towing hitch downward load (noseweight)
All models . . . . 75 kg

Maximum towing weights
All models . . . . Refer to dealer for latest recommendations

Conversion Factors

Length (distance)

Inches (in)	x 25.4	= Millimetres (mm)	x 0.0394	=	Inches (in)
Feet (ft)	x 0.305	= Metres (m)	x 3.281	=	Feet (ft)
Miles	x 1.609	= Kilometres (km)	x 0.621	=	Miles

Volume (capacity)

Cubic inches (cu in; in^3)	x 16.387	= Cubic centimetres (cc; cm^3)	x 0.061	=	Cubic inches (cu in; in^3)
Imperial pints (Imp pt)	x 0.568	= Litres (l)	x 1.76	=	Imperial pints (Imp pt)
Imperial quarts (Imp qt)	x 1.137	= Litres (l)	x 0.88	=	Imperial quarts (Imp qt)
Imperial quarts (Imp qt)	x 1.201	= US quarts (US qt)	x 0.833	=	Imperial quarts (Imp qt)
US quarts (US qt)	x 0.946	= Litres (l)	x 1.057	=	US quarts (US qt)
Imperial gallons (Imp gal)	x 4.546	= Litres (l)	x 0.22	=	Imperial gallons (Imp gal)
Imperial gallons (Imp gal)	x 1.201	= US gallons (US gal)	x 0.833	=	Imperial gallons (Imp gal)
US gallons (US gal)	x 3.785	= Litres (l)	x 0.264	=	US gallons (US gal)

Mass (weight)

Ounces (oz)	x 28.35	= Grams (g)	x 0.035	=	Ounces (oz)
Pounds (lb)	x 0.454	= Kilograms (kg)	x 2.205	=	Pounds (lb)

Force

Ounces-force (ozf; oz)	x 0.278	= Newtons (N)	x 3.6	=	Ounces-force (ozf; oz)
Pounds-force (lbf; lb)	x 4.448	= Newtons (N)	x 0.225	=	Pounds-force (lbf; lb)
Newtons (N)	x 0.1	= Kilograms-force (kgf; kg)	x 9.81	=	Newtons (N)

Pressure

Pounds-force per square inch (psi; lbf/in^2; lb/in^2)	x 0.070	= Kilograms-force per square centimetre (kgf/cm^2; kg/cm^2)	x 14.223	=	Pounds-force per square inch (psi; lbf/in^2; lb/in^2)
Pounds-force per square inch (psi; lbf/in^2; lb/in^2)	x 0.068	= Atmospheres (atm)	x 14.696	=	Pounds-force per square inch (psi; lbf/in^2; lb/in^2)
Pounds-force per square inch (psi; lbf/in^2; lb/in^2)	x 0.069	= Bars	x 14.5	=	Pounds-force per square inch (psi; lbf/in^2; lb/in^2)
Pounds-force per square inch (psi; lbf/in^2; lb/in^2)	x 6.895	= Kilopascals (kPa)	x 0.145	=	Pounds-force per square inch (psi; lbf/in^2; lb/in^2)
Kilopascals (kPa)	x 0.01	= Kilograms-force per square centimetre (kgf/cm^2; kg/cm^2)	x 98.1	=	Kilopascals (kPa)
Millibar (mbar)	x 100	= Pascals (Pa)	x 0.01	=	Millibar (mbar)
Millibar (mbar)	x 0.0145	= Pounds-force per square inch (psi; lbf/in^2; lb/in^2)	x 68.947	=	Millibar (mbar)
Millibar (mbar)	x 0.75	= Millimetres of mercury (mmHg)	x 1.333	=	Millibar (mbar)
Millibar (mbar)	x 0.401	= Inches of water (inH$_2$O)	x 2.491	=	Millibar (mbar)
Millimetres of mercury (mmHg)	x 0.535	= Inches of water (inH$_2$O)	x 1.868	=	Millimetres of mercury (mmHg)
Inches of water (inH$_2$O)	x 0.036	= Pounds-force per square inch (psi; lbf/in^2; lb/in^2)	x 27.68	=	Inches of water (inH$_2$O)

Torque (moment of force)

Pounds-force inches (lbf in; lb in)	x 1.152	= Kilograms-force centimetre (kgf cm; kg cm)	x 0.868	=	Pounds-force inches (lbf in; lb in)
Pounds-force inches (lbf in; lb in)	x 0.113	= Newton metres (Nm)	x 8.85	=	Pounds-force inches (lbf in; lb in)
Pounds-force inches (lbf in; lb in)	x 0.083	= Pounds-force feet (lbf ft; lb ft)	x 12	=	Pounds-force inches (lbf in; lb in)
Pounds-force feet (lbf ft; lb ft)	x 0.138	= Kilograms-force metres (kgf m; kg m)	x 7.233	=	Pounds-force feet (lbf ft; lb ft)
Pounds-force feet (lbf ft; lb ft)	x 1.356	= Newton metres (Nm)	x 0.738	=	Pounds-force feet (lbf ft; lb ft)
Newton metres (Nm)	x 0.102	= Kilograms-force metres (kgf m; kg m)	x 9.804	=	Newton metres (Nm)

Power

Horsepower (hp)	x 745.7	= Watts (W)	x 0.0013	=	Horsepower (hp)

Velocity (speed)

Miles per hour (miles/hr; mph)	x 1.609	= Kilometres per hour (km/hr; kph)	x 0.621	=	Miles per hour (miles/hr; mph)

Fuel consumption*

Miles per gallon (mpg)	x 0.354	= Kilometres per litre (km/l)	x 2.825	=	Miles per gallon (mpg)

Temperature

Degrees Fahrenheit = (°C x 1.8) + 32   Degrees Celsius (Degrees Centigrade; °C) = (°F - 32) x 0.56

It is common practice to convert from miles per gallon (mpg) to litres/100 kilometres (l/100km), where mpg x l/100 km = 282

Spare parts are available from many sources, for example: Vauxhall dealers, other garages and accessory shops, and motor factors. Our advice regarding spare part sources is as follows.

Officially appointed Vauxhall dealers

This is the best source of parts that are peculiar to your car and are otherwise not generally available (e.g. complete cylinder heads, transmission components, badges, interior trim, etc.). It is also the only place at which you should buy parts if your vehicle is still under warranty - use of non-Vauxhall components may invalidate the warranty. To be sure of obtaining the correct parts it will always be necessary to give the storeman your car's vehicle identification number, and if possible, to take the "old" parts along for positive identification. Remember that many parts are available on a factory exchange scheme - any parts returned should always be clean! It obviously makes good sense to go straight to the specialists on your car for this type of part for they are best equipped to supply you.

Other garages and accessory shops

These are often very good places to buy materials and components needed for the maintenance of your car (e.g. oil filters, spark plugs, bulbs, drivebelts, oils and greases, touch-up paint, filler paste, etc.). They also sell general accessories, usually have convenient opening hours, charge lower prices and can often be found not far from home.

Motor factors

Good factors will stock all the more important components that wear out relatively quickly (e.g. clutch components, pistons, valves, exhaust systems, brake cylinders/pipes/hoses/seals/shoes and pads, etc.). Motor factors will often provide new or reconditioned components on a part exchange basis - this can save considerable amount of money.

Vehicle Identification

Modifications are a continuing and unpublished process in vehicle manufacture, quite apart from major model changes. Spare parts manuals and lists are compiled upon a numerical basis, the individual vehicle numbers being essential to correct identification of the component required.

When ordering spare parts, always give as much information as possible. Quote the car model, year of manufacture and vehicle identification and/or engine numbers as appropriate.

The *vehicle identification plate* is riveted on top of the front body panel and includes the Vehicle Identification Number (VIN), vehicle weight information and paint and trim colour codes.

The *Vehicle Identification Number (VIN)* is given on the vehicle identification plate and is also stamped into the body floor panel between the driver's seat and the door sill panel; lift the flap in the carpet to see it.

The engine number is stamped on a horizontal flat located on the exhaust manifold side of the cylinder block, at the distributor end.

During 1995, Vauxhall introduced 'Car pass'. This is a card, which is issued to the customer when the car is first bought. It contains important information, e.g. VIN number, key number and radio code. It also includes a special code for diagnostic equipment, therefore it must be kept in a secure place and not in the vehicle.

The Vehicle Identification Number (VIN) plate (1) and engine number (2) locations

The VIN is stamped on the floor next to the driver's seat

Whenever servicing, repair or overhaul work is carried out on the car or its components, observe the following procedures and instructions. This will assist in carrying out the operation efficiently and to a professional standard of workmanship.

Joint mating faces and gaskets

When separating components at their mating faces, never insert screwdrivers or similar implements into the joint between the faces in order to prise them apart. This can cause severe damage which results in oil leaks, coolant leaks, etc upon reassembly. Separation is usually achieved by tapping along the joint with a soft-faced hammer in order to break the seal. However, note that this method may not be suitable where dowels are used for component location.

Where a gasket is used between the mating faces of two components, a new one must be fitted on reassembly; fit it dry unless otherwise stated in the repair procedure. Make sure that the mating faces are clean and dry, with all traces of old gasket removed. When cleaning a joint face, use a tool which is unlikely to score or damage the face, and remove any burrs or nicks with an oilstone or fine file.

Make sure that tapped holes are cleaned with a pipe cleaner, and keep them free of jointing compound, if this is being used, unless specifically instructed otherwise.

Ensure that all orifices, channels or pipes are clear, and blow through them, preferably using compressed air.

Oil seals

Oil seals can be removed by levering them out with a wide flat-bladed screwdriver or similar implement. Alternatively, a number of self-tapping screws may be screwed into the seal, and these used as a purchase for pliers or some similar device in order to pull the seal free.

Whenever an oil seal is removed from its working location, either individually or as part of an assembly, it should be renewed.

The very fine sealing lip of the seal is easily damaged, and will not seal if the surface it contacts is not completely clean and free from scratches, nicks or grooves. If the original sealing surface of the component cannot be restored, and the manufacturer has not made provision for slight relocation of the seal relative to the sealing surface, the component should be renewed.

Protect the lips of the seal from any surface which may damage them in the course of fitting. Use tape or a conical sleeve where possible. Lubricate the seal lips with oil before fitting and, on dual-lipped seals, fill the space between the lips with grease.

Unless otherwise stated, oil seals must be fitted with their sealing lips toward the lubricant to be sealed.

Use a tubular drift or block of wood of the appropriate size to install the seal and, if the seal housing is shouldered, drive the seal down to the shoulder. If the seal housing is unshouldered, the seal should be fitted with its face flush with the housing top face (unless otherwise instructed).

Screw threads and fastenings

Seized nuts, bolts and screws are quite a common occurrence where corrosion has set in, and the use of penetrating oil or releasing fluid will often overcome this problem if the offending item is soaked for a while before attempting to release it. The use of an impact driver may also provide a means of releasing such stubborn fastening devices, when used in conjunction with the appropriate screwdriver bit or socket. If none of these methods works, it may be necessary to resort to the careful application of heat, or the use of a hacksaw or nut splitter device.

Studs are usually removed by locking two nuts together on the threaded part, and then using a spanner on the lower nut to unscrew the stud. Studs or bolts which have broken off below the surface of the component in which they are mounted can sometimes be removed using a stud extractor. Always ensure that a blind tapped hole is completely free from oil, grease, water or other fluid before installing the bolt or stud. Failure to do this could cause the housing to crack due to the hydraulic action of the bolt or stud as it is screwed in.

When tightening a castellated nut to accept a split pin, tighten the nut to the specified torque, where applicable, and then tighten further to the next split pin hole. Never slacken the nut to align the split pin hole, unless stated in the repair procedure.

When checking or retightening a nut or bolt to a specified torque setting, slacken the nut or bolt by a quarter of a turn, and then retighten to the specified setting. However, this should not be attempted where angular tightening has been used.

For some screw fastenings, notably cylinder head bolts or nuts, torque wrench settings are no longer specified for the latter stages of tightening, "angle-tightening" being called up instead. Typically, a fairly low torque wrench setting will be applied to the bolts/nuts in the correct sequence, followed by one or more stages of tightening through specified angles.

Locknuts, locktabs and washers

Any fastening which will rotate against a component or housing during tightening should always have a washer between it and the relevant component or housing.

Spring or split washers should always be renewed when they are used to lock a critical component such as a big-end bearing retaining bolt or nut. Locktabs which are folded over to retain a nut or bolt should always be renewed.

Self-locking nuts can be re-used in non-critical areas, providing resistance can be felt when the locking portion passes over the bolt or stud thread. However, it should be noted that self-locking stiffnuts tend to lose their effectiveness after long periods of use, and should then be renewed as a matter of course.

Split pins must always be replaced with new ones of the correct size for the hole.

When thread-locking compound is found on the threads of a fastener which is to be re-used, it should be cleaned off with a wire brush and solvent, and fresh compound applied on reassembly.

Special tools

Some repair procedures in this manual entail the use of special tools such as a press, two or three-legged pullers, spring compressors, etc. Wherever possible, suitable readily-available alternatives to the manufacturer's special tools are described, and are shown in use. In some instances, where no alternative is possible, it has been necessary to resort to the use of a manufacturer's tool, and this has been done for reasons of safety as well as the efficient completion of the repair operation. Unless you are highly-skilled and have a thorough understanding of the procedures described, never attempt to bypass the use of any special tool when the procedure described specifies its use. Not only is there a very great risk of personal injury, but expensive damage could be caused to the components involved.

Environmental considerations

When disposing of used engine oil, brake fluid, antifreeze, etc, give due consideration to any detrimental environmental effects. Do not, for instance, pour any of the above liquids down drains into the general sewage system, or onto the ground to soak away. Many local council refuse tips provide a facility for waste oil disposal, as do some garages. If none of these facilities are available, consult your local Environmental Health Department, or the National Rivers Authority, for further advice.

With the universal tightening-up of legislation regarding the emission of environmentally-harmful substances from motor vehicles, most vehicles have tamperproof devices fitted to the main adjustment points of the fuel system. These devices are primarily designed to prevent unqualified persons from adjusting the fuel/air mixture, with the chance of a consequent increase in toxic emissions. If such devices are found during servicing or overhaul, they should, wherever possible, be renewed or refitted in accordance with the manufacturer's requirements or current legislation.

OIL CARE

FOLLOW THE CODE

OIL BANK LINE
0800 66 33 66

Note: It is antisocial and illegal to dump oil down the drain. To find the location of your local oil recycling bank, call this number free.

The jack supplied with the vehicle tool kit should only be used for changing roadwheels. When carrying out any other kind of work, raise the vehicle using a hydraulic jack, and always supplement the jack with axle stands positioned under the vehicle jacking points.

When jacking up the vehicle with a trolley jack, position the jack head under one of the relevant jacking points (note that the jacking points for use with a hydraulic jack are different to those for use with the vehicle jack). **Do not** jack the vehicle under the sump or any of the steering or suspension components. Supplement the jack using axle stands. The jacking points and axle stand positions are shown in the accompanying illustrations. **Never** *work under, around, or near a raised vehicle, unless it is adequately supported in at least two places.*

Front jacking point for hydraulic jack or axle stands

Rear jacking point for hydraulic jack or axle stands

Axle stands should be placed under, or adjacent to the jacking point (arrowed)

Using a trolley jack and block of wood under the centre of the front subframe

Radio/cassette Anti-theft System - Precaution

The radio/cassette unit fitted as standard equipment by Vauxhall is equipped with a built-in security code, to deter thieves. If the power source to the unit is cut, the anti-theft system will activate. Even if the power source is immediately reconnected, the radio/cassette unit will not function until the correct security code has been entered. Therefore, if you do not know the correct security code for the radio/cassette unit, **do not** disconnect the battery negative terminal of the battery, or remove the radio/cassette unit from the vehicle.

Refer to the Audio handbook supplied in the owners handbook pack, for further details of how to use the code.

If you should loose or forget the code, seek the advice of your Vauxhall dealer. On presentation of proof of ownership, a Vauxhall dealer will be able to unlock the unit and provide you with a new security code.

Introduction

A selection of good tools is a fundamental requirement for anyone contemplating the maintenance and repair of a motor vehicle. For the owner who does not possess any, their purchase will prove a considerable expense, offsetting some of the savings made by doing-it-yourself. However, provided that the tools purchased meet the relevant national safety standards and are of good quality, they will last for many years and prove an extremely worthwhile investment.

To help the average owner to decide which tools are needed to carry out the various tasks detailed in this manual, we have compiled three lists of tools under the following headings: *Maintenance and minor repair, Repair and overhaul*, and *Special*. Newcomers to practical mechanics should start off with the *Maintenance and minor repair* tool kit, and confine themselves to the simpler jobs around the vehicle. Then, as confidence and experience grow, more difficult tasks can be undertaken, with extra tools being purchased as, and when, they are needed. In this way, a *Maintenance and minor repair* tool kit can be built up into a *Repair and overhaul* tool kit over a considerable period of time, without any major cash outlays. The experienced do-it-yourselfer will have a tool kit good enough for most repair and overhaul procedures, and will add tools from the *Special* category when it is felt that the expense is justified by the amount of use to which these tools will be put.

Maintenance and minor repair tool kit

The tools given in this list should be considered as a minimum requirement if routine maintenance, servicing and minor repair operations are to be undertaken. We recommend the purchase of combination spanners (ring one end, open-ended the other); although more expensive than open-ended ones, they do give the advantages of both types of spanner.

☐ *Combination spanners:*
  Metric - 8 to 19 mm inclusive
☐ *Adjustable spanner - 35 mm jaw (approx.)*
☐ *Spark plug spanner (with rubber insert) - petrol models*
☐ *Spark plug gap adjustment tool - petrol models*
☐ *Set of feeler gauges*
☐ *Brake bleed nipple spanner*
☐ *Screwdrivers:*
  Flat blade - 100 mm long x 6 mm dia
  Cross blade - 100 mm long x 6 mm dia
☐ *Combination pliers*
☐ *Hacksaw (junior)*
☐ *Tyre pump*
☐ *Tyre pressure gauge*
☐ *Oil can*
☐ *Oil filter removal tool*
☐ *Fine emery cloth*
☐ *Wire brush (small)*
☐ *Funnel (medium size)*

Repair and overhaul tool kit

These tools are virtually essential for anyone undertaking any major repairs to a motor vehicle, and are additional to those given in the *Maintenance and minor repair* list. Included in this list is a comprehensive set of sockets. Although these are expensive, they will be found invaluable as they are so versatile - particularly if various drives are included in the set. We recommend the half-inch square-drive type, as this can be used with most proprietary torque wrenches.

The tools in this list will sometimes need to be supplemented by tools from the *Special* list:

☐ *Sockets (or box spanners) to cover range in previous list (including Torx sockets)*
☐ *Reversible ratchet drive (for use with sockets)*
☐ *Extension piece, 250 mm (for use with sockets)*
☐ *Universal joint (for use with sockets)*
☐ *Torque wrench (for use with sockets)*
☐ *Self-locking grips*
☐ *Ball pein hammer*
☐ *Soft-faced mallet (plastic/aluminium or rubber)*
☐ *Screwdrivers:*
  Flat blade - long & sturdy, short (chubby), and narrow (electrician's) types
  Cross blade – Long & sturdy, and short (chubby) types
☐ *Pliers:*
  Long-nosed
  Side cutters (electrician's)
  Circlip (internal and external)
☐ *Cold chisel - 25 mm*
☐ *Scriber*
☐ *Scraper*
☐ *Centre-punch*
☐ *Pin punch*
☐ *Hacksaw*
☐ *Brake hose clamp*
☐ *Brake/clutch bleeding kit*
☐ *Selection of twist drills*
☐ *Steel rule/straight-edge*
☐ *Allen keys (inc. splined/Torx type)*
☐ *Selection of files*
☐ *Wire brush*
☐ *Axle stands*
☐ *Jack (strong trolley or hydraulic type)*
☐ *Light with extension lead*

Sockets and reversible ratchet drive

Valve spring compressor

Spline bit set

Piston ring compressor

Clutch plate alignment set

Special tools

The tools in this list are those which are not used regularly, are expensive to buy, or which need to be used in accordance with their manufacturers' instructions. Unless relatively difficult mechanical jobs are undertaken frequently, it will not be economic to buy many of these tools. Where this is the case, you could consider clubbing together with friends (or joining a motorists' club) to make a joint purchase, or borrowing the tools against a deposit from a local garage or tool hire specialist. It is worth noting that many of the larger DIY superstores now carry a large range of special tools for hire at modest rates.

The following list contains only those tools and instruments freely available to the public, and not those special tools produced by the vehicle manufacturer specifically for its dealer network. You will find occasional references to these manufacturers' special tools in the text of this manual. Generally, an alternative method of doing the job without the vehicle manufacturers' special tool is given. However, sometimes there is no alternative to using them. Where this is the case and the relevant tool cannot be bought or borrowed, you will have to entrust the work to a dealer.

☐ Valve spring compressor
☐ Valve grinding tool
☐ Piston ring compressor
☐ Piston ring removal/installation tool
☐ Cylinder bore hone
☐ Balljoint separator
☐ Coil spring compressors (where applicable)
☐ Two/three-legged hub and bearing puller
☐ Impact screwdriver
☐ Micrometer and/or vernier calipers
☐ Dial gauge
☐ Stroboscopic timing light
☐ Dwell angle meter/tachometer
☐ Universal electrical multi-meter
☐ Cylinder compression gauge
☐ Hand-operated vacuum pump and gauge
☐ Clutch plate alignment set
☐ Brake shoe steady spring cup removal tool
☐ Bush and bearing removal/installation set
☐ Stud extractors
☐ Tap and die set
☐ Lifting tackle
☐ Trolley jack

Buying tools

Reputable motor accessory shops and superstores often offer excellent quality tools at discount prices, so it pays to shop around.

Remember, you don't have to buy the most expensive items on the shelf, but it is always advisable to steer clear of the very cheap tools. Beware of 'bargains' offered on market stalls or at car boot sales. There are plenty of good tools around at reasonable prices, but always aim to purchase items which meet the relevant national safety standards. If in doubt, ask the proprietor or manager of the shop for advice before making a purchase.

Care and maintenance of tools

Having purchased a reasonable tool kit, it is necessary to keep the tools in a clean and serviceable condition. After use, always wipe off any dirt, grease and metal particles using a clean, dry cloth, before putting the tools away. Never leave them lying around after they have been used. A simple tool rack on the garage or workshop wall for items such as screwdrivers and pliers is a good idea. Store all normal spanners and sockets in a metal box. Any measuring instruments, gauges, meters, etc, must be carefully stored where they cannot be damaged or become rusty.

Take a little care when tools are used. Hammer heads inevitably become marked, and screwdrivers lose the keen edge on their blades from time to time. A little timely attention with emery cloth or a file will soon restore items like this to a good finish.

Working facilities

Not to be forgotten when discussing tools is the workshop itself. If anything more than routine maintenance is to be carried out, a suitable working area becomes essential.

It is appreciated that many an owner-mechanic is forced by circumstances to remove an engine or similar item without the benefit of a garage or workshop. Having done this, any repairs should always be done under the cover of a roof.

Wherever possible, any dismantling should be done on a clean, flat workbench or table at a suitable working height.

Any workbench needs a vice; one with a jaw opening of 100 mm is suitable for most jobs. As mentioned previously, some clean dry storage space is also required for tools, as well as for any lubricants, cleaning fluids, touch-up paints etc, which become necessary.

Another item which may be required, and which has a much more general usage, is an electric drill with a chuck capacity of at least 8 mm. This, together with a good range of twist drills, is virtually essential for fitting accessories.

Last, but not least, always keep a supply of old newspapers and clean, lint-free rags available, and try to keep any working area as clean as possible.

Micrometer set

Dial test indicator ("dial gauge")

Stroboscopic timing light

Compression tester

Stud extractor set

This is a guide to getting your vehicle through the MOT test. Obviously it will not be possible to examine the vehicle to the same standard as the professional MOT tester. However, working through the following checks will enable you to identify any problem areas before submitting the vehicle for the test.

Where a testable component is in borderline condition, the tester has discretion in deciding whether to pass or fail it. The basis of such discretion is whether the tester would be happy for a close relative or friend to use the vehicle with the component in that condition. If the vehicle presented is clean and evidently well cared for, the tester may be more inclined to pass a borderline component than if the vehicle is scruffy and apparently neglected.

It has only been possible to summarise the test requirements here, based on the regulations in force at the time of printing. Test standards are becoming increasingly stringent, although there are some exemptions for older vehicles. For full details obtain a copy of the Haynes publication Pass the MOT! (available from stockists of Haynes manuals).

An assistant will be needed to help carry out some of these checks.

The checks have been sub-divided into four categories, as follows:

1 Checks carried out **FROM THE DRIVER'S SEAT**

2 Checks carried out **WITH THE VEHICLE ON THE GROUND**

3 Checks carried out **WITH THE VEHICLE RAISED AND THE WHEELS FREE TO TURN**

4 Checks carried out on **YOUR VEHICLE'S EXHAUST EMISSION SYSTEM**

---

1 Checks carried out **FROM THE DRIVER'S SEAT**

Handbrake

☐ Test the operation of the handbrake. Excessive travel (too many clicks) indicates incorrect brake or cable adjustment.

☐ Check that the handbrake cannot be released by tapping the lever sideways. Check the security of the lever mountings.

Footbrake

☐ Depress the brake pedal and check that it does not creep down to the floor, indicating a master cylinder fault. Release the pedal, wait a few seconds, then depress it again. If the pedal travels nearly to the floor before firm resistance is felt, brake adjustment or repair is necessary. If the pedal feels spongy, there is air in the hydraulic system which must be removed by bleeding.

☐ Check that the brake pedal is secure and in good condition. Check also for signs of fluid leaks on the pedal, floor or carpets, which would indicate failed seals in the brake master cylinder.

☐ Check the servo unit (when applicable) by operating the brake pedal several times, then keeping the pedal depressed and starting the engine. As the engine starts, the pedal will move down slightly. If not, the vacuum hose or the servo itself may be faulty.

Steering wheel and column

☐ Examine the steering wheel for fractures or looseness of the hub, spokes or rim.

☐ Move the steering wheel from side to side and then up and down. Check that the steering wheel is not loose on the column, indicating wear or a loose retaining nut. Continue moving the steering wheel as before, but also turn it slightly from left to right.

☐ Check that the steering wheel is not loose on the column, and that there is no abnormal

movement of the steering wheel, indicating wear in the column support bearings or couplings.

Windscreen and mirrors

☐ The windscreen must be free of cracks or other significant damage within the driver's field of view. (Small stone chips are acceptable.) Rear view mirrors must be secure, intact, and capable of being adjusted.

290mm

Seat belts and seats

Note: *The following checks are applicable to all seat belts, front and rear.*

☐ Examine the webbing of all the belts (including rear belts if fitted) for cuts, serious fraying or deterioration. Fasten and unfasten each belt to check the buckles. If applicable, check the retracting mechanism. Check the security of all seat belt mountings accessible from inside the vehicle.

☐ The front seats themselves must be securely attached and the backrests must lock in the upright position.

Doors

☐ Both front doors must be able to be opened and closed from outside and inside, and must latch securely when closed.

2 Checks carried out WITH THE VEHICLE ON THE GROUND

Vehicle identification

☐ Number plates must be in good condition, secure and legible, with letters and numbers correctly spaced – spacing at (A) should be twice that at (B).

☐ The VIN plate and/or homologation plate must be legible.

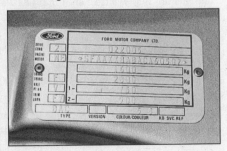

Electrical equipment

☐ Switch on the ignition and check the operation of the horn.

☐ Check the windscreen washers and wipers, examining the wiper blades; renew damaged or perished blades. Also check the operation of the stop-lights.

☐ Check the operation of the sidelights and number plate lights. The lenses and reflectors must be secure, clean and undamaged.

☐ Check the operation and alignment of the headlights. The headlight reflectors must not be tarnished and the lenses must be undamaged.

☐ Switch on the ignition and check the operation of the direction indicators (including the instrument panel tell-tale) and the hazard warning lights. Operation of the sidelights and stop-lights must not affect the indicators - if it does, the cause is usually a bad earth at the rear light cluster.

☐ Check the operation of the rear foglight(s), including the warning light on the instrument panel or in the switch.

Footbrake

☐ Examine the master cylinder, brake pipes and servo unit for leaks, loose mountings, corrosion or other damage.

☐ The fluid reservoir must be secure and the fluid level must be between the upper (**A**) and lower (**B**) markings.

☐ Inspect both front brake flexible hoses for cracks or deterioration of the rubber. Turn the steering from lock to lock, and ensure that the hoses do not contact the wheel, tyre, or any part of the steering or suspension mechanism. With the brake pedal firmly depressed, check the hoses for bulges or leaks under pressure.

Steering and suspension

☐ Have your assistant turn the steering wheel from side to side slightly, up to the point where the steering gear just begins to transmit this movement to the roadwheels. Check for excessive free play between the steering wheel and the steering gear, indicating wear or insecurity of the steering column joints, the column-to-steering gear coupling, or the steering gear itself.

☐ Have your assistant turn the steering wheel more vigorously in each direction, so that the roadwheels just begin to turn. As this is done, examine all the steering joints, linkages, fittings and attachments. Renew any component that shows signs of wear or damage. On vehicles with power steering, check the security and condition of the steering pump, drivebelt and hoses.

☐ Check that the vehicle is standing level, and at approximately the correct ride height.

Shock absorbers

☐ Depress each corner of the vehicle in turn, then release it. The vehicle should rise and then settle in its normal position. If the vehicle continues to rise and fall, the shock absorber is defective. A shock absorber which has seized will also cause the vehicle to fail.

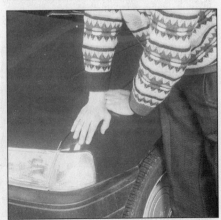

Exhaust system

☐ Start the engine. With your assistant holding a rag over the tailpipe, check the entire system for leaks. Repair or renew leaking sections.

3 Checks carried out
WITH THE VEHICLE RAISED AND THE WHEELS FREE TO TURN

Jack up the front and rear of the vehicle, and securely support it on axle stands. Position the stands clear of the suspension assemblies. Ensure that the wheels are clear of the ground and that the steering can be turned from lock to lock.

Steering mechanism

☐ Have your assistant turn the steering from lock to lock. Check that the steering turns smoothly, and that no part of the steering mechanism, including a wheel or tyre, fouls any brake hose or pipe or any part of the body structure.
☐ Examine the steering rack rubber gaiters for damage or insecurity of the retaining clips. If power steering is fitted, check for signs of damage or leakage of the fluid hoses, pipes or connections. Also check for excessive stiffness or binding of the steering, a missing split pin or locking device, or severe corrosion of the body structure within 30 cm of any steering component attachment point.

Front and rear suspension and wheel bearings

☐ Starting at the front right-hand side, grasp the roadwheel at the 3 o'clock and 9 o'clock positions and shake it vigorously. Check for free play or insecurity at the wheel bearings, suspension balljoints, or suspension mountings, pivots and attachments.
☐ Now grasp the wheel at the 12 o'clock and 6 o'clock positions and repeat the previous inspection. Spin the wheel, and check for roughness or tightness of the front wheel bearing.

☐ If excess free play is suspected at a component pivot point, this can be confirmed by using a large screwdriver or similar tool and levering between the mounting and the component attachment. This will confirm whether the wear is in the pivot bush, its retaining bolt, or in the mounting itself (the bolt holes can often become elongated).

☐ Carry out all the above checks at the other front wheel, and then at both rear wheels.

Springs and shock absorbers

☐ Examine the suspension struts (when applicable) for serious fluid leakage, corrosion, or damage to the casing. Also check the security of the mounting points.
☐ If coil springs are fitted, check that the spring ends locate in their seats, and that the spring is not corroded, cracked or broken.
☐ If leaf springs are fitted, check that all leaves are intact, that the axle is securely attached to each spring, and that there is no deterioration of the spring eye mountings, bushes, and shackles.

☐ The same general checks apply to vehicles fitted with other suspension types, such as torsion bars, hydraulic displacer units, etc. Ensure that all mountings and attachments are secure, that there are no signs of excessive wear, corrosion or damage, and (on hydraulic types) that there are no fluid leaks or damaged pipes.
☐ Inspect the shock absorbers for signs of serious fluid leakage. Check for wear of the mounting bushes or attachments, or damage to the body of the unit.

Driveshafts (fwd vehicles only)

☐ Rotate each front wheel in turn and inspect the constant velocity joint gaiters for splits or damage. Also check that each driveshaft is straight and undamaged.

Braking system

☐ If possible without dismantling, check brake pad wear and disc condition. Ensure that the friction lining material has not worn excessively, (A) and that the discs are not fractured, pitted, scored or badly worn (B).

☐ Examine all the rigid brake pipes underneath the vehicle, and the flexible hose(s) at the rear. Look for corrosion, chafing or insecurity of the pipes, and for signs of bulging under pressure, chafing, splits or deterioration of the flexible hoses.
☐ Look for signs of fluid leaks at the brake calipers or on the brake backplates. Repair or renew leaking components.
☐ Slowly spin each wheel, while your assistant depresses and releases the footbrake. Ensure that each brake is operating and does not bind when the pedal is released.

□ Examine the handbrake mechanism, checking for frayed or broken cables, excessive corrosion, or wear or insecurity of the linkage. Check that the mechanism works on each relevant wheel, and releases fully, without binding.

□ It is not possible to test brake efficiency without special equipment, but a road test can be carried out later to check that the vehicle pulls up in a straight line.

Fuel and exhaust systems

□ Inspect the fuel tank (including the filler cap), fuel pipes, hoses and unions. All components must be secure and free from leaks.

□ Examine the exhaust system over its entire length, checking for any damaged, broken or missing mountings, security of the retaining clamps and rust or corrosion.

Wheels and tyres

□ Examine the sidewalls and tread area of each tyre in turn. Check for cuts, tears, lumps, bulges, separation of the tread, and exposure of the ply or cord due to wear or damage. Check that the tyre bead is correctly seated on the wheel rim, that the valve is sound and

properly seated, and that the wheel is not distorted or damaged.

□ Check that the tyres are of the correct size for the vehicle, that they are of the same size and type on each axle, and that the pressures are correct.

□ Check the tyre tread depth. The legal minimum at the time of writing is 1.6 mm over at least three-quarters of the tread width. Abnormal tread wear may indicate incorrect front wheel alignment.

Body corrosion

□ Check the condition of the entire vehicle structure for signs of corrosion in load-bearing areas. (These include chassis box sections, side sills, cross-members, pillars, and all suspension, steering, braking system and seat belt mountings and anchorages.) Any corrosion which has seriously reduced the thickness of a load-bearing area is likely to cause the vehicle to fail. In this case professional repairs are likely to be needed.

□ Damage or corrosion which causes sharp or otherwise dangerous edges to be exposed will also cause the vehicle to fail.

4 Checks carried out on YOUR VEHICLE'S EXHAUST EMISSION SYSTEM

Petrol models

□ Have the engine at normal operating temperature, and make sure that it is in good tune (ignition system in good order, air filter element clean, etc).

□ Before any measurements are carried out, raise the engine speed to around 2500 rpm, and hold it at this speed for 20 seconds. Allow

the engine speed to return to idle, and watch for smoke emissions from the exhaust tailpipe. If the idle speed is obviously much too high, or if dense blue or clearly-visible black smoke comes from the tailpipe for more than 5 seconds, the vehicle will fail. As a rule of thumb, blue smoke signifies oil being burnt (engine wear) while black smoke signifies unburnt fuel (dirty air cleaner element, or other carburettor or fuel system fault).

□ An exhaust gas analyser capable of measuring carbon monoxide (CO) and hydrocarbons (HC) is now needed. If such an instrument cannot be hired or borrowed, a local garage may agree to perform the check for a small fee.

CO emissions (mixture)

□ At the time of writing, the maximum CO level at idle is 3.5% for vehicles first used after August 1986 and 4.5% for older vehicles. From January 1996 a much tighter limit (around 0.5%) applies to catalyst-equipped vehicles first used from August 1992. If the CO level cannot be reduced far enough to pass the test (and the fuel and ignition systems are otherwise in good condition) then the carburettor is badly worn, or there is some problem in the fuel injection system or catalytic converter (as applicable).

HC emissions

□ With the CO emissions within limits, HC emissions must be no more than 1200 ppm (parts per million). If the vehicle fails this test at idle, it can be re-tested at around 2000 rpm; if the HC level is then 1200 ppm or less, this counts as a pass.

□ Excessive HC emissions can be caused by oil being burnt, but they are more likely to be due to unburnt fuel.

Diesel models

□ The only emission test applicable to Diesel engines is the measuring of exhaust smoke density. The test involves accelerating the engine several times to its maximum unloaded speed.

Note: *It is of the utmost importance that the engine timing belt is in good condition before the test is carried out.*

□ Excessive smoke can be caused by a dirty air cleaner element. Otherwise, professional advice may be needed to find the cause.

Engine

- ☐ Engine fails to rotate when attempting to start
- ☐ Engine rotates, but will not start
- ☐ Engine difficult to start when cold
- ☐ Engine difficult to start when hot
- ☐ Starter motor noisy or excessively rough in engagement
- ☐ Engine starts, but stops immediately
- ☐ Engine idles erratically
- ☐ Engine misfires at idle speed
- ☐ Engine misfires throughout the driving speed range
- ☐ Engine hesitates on acceleration
- ☐ Engine stalls
- ☐ Engine lacks power
- ☐ Engine backfires
- ☐ Oil pressure warning light illuminated with engine running
- ☐ Engine runs-on after switching off
- ☐ Engine noises

Cooling system

- ☐ Overheating
- ☐ Overcooling
- ☐ External coolant leakage
- ☐ Internal coolant leakage
- ☐ Corrosion

Fuel and exhaust systems

- ☐ Excessive fuel consumption
- ☐ Fuel leakage and/or fuel odour
- ☐ Excessive noise or fumes from exhaust system

Clutch

- ☐ Pedal travels to floor - no pressure or very little resistance
- ☐ Clutch fails to disengage (unable to select gears)
- ☐ Clutch slips (engine speed increases, with no increase in vehicle speed)
- ☐ Judder as clutch is engaged
- ☐ Noise when depressing or releasing clutch pedal

Manual transmission

- ☐ Noisy in neutral with engine running
- ☐ Noisy in one particular gear
- ☐ Difficulty engaging gears
- ☐ Jumps out of gear
- ☐ Vibration
- ☐ Lubricant leaks

Automatic transmission

- ☐ Fluid leakage
- ☐ Transmission fluid brown, or has burned smell
- ☐ General gear selection problems
- ☐ Transmission will not downshift (kickdown) with accelerator pedal fully depressed
- ☐ Engine will not start in any gear, or starts in gears other than Park or Neutral
- ☐ Transmission slips, shifts roughly, is noisy, or has no drive in forward or reverse gears

Driveshafts

- ☐ Clicking or knocking noise on turns (at slow speed on full-lock)
- ☐ Vibration when accelerating or decelerating

Braking system

- ☐ Vehicle pulls to one side under braking
- ☐ Noise (grinding or high-pitched squeal) when brakes applied
- ☐ Excessive brake pedal travel
- ☐ Brake pedal feels spongy when depressed
- ☐ Excessive brake pedal effort required to stop vehicle
- ☐ Judder felt through brake pedal or steering wheel when braking
- ☐ Brakes binding
- ☐ Rear wheels locking under normal braking

Suspension and steering

- ☐ Vehicle pulls to one side
- ☐ Wheel wobble and vibration
- ☐ Excessive pitching and/or rolling around corners, or during braking
- ☐ Wandering or general instability
- ☐ Excessively stiff steering
- ☐ Excessive play in steering
- ☐ Lack of power assistance
- ☐ Tyre wear excessive

Electrical system

- ☐ Battery will not hold a charge for more than a few days
- ☐ Ignition/no-charge warning light remains illuminated with engine running
- ☐ Ignition/no-charge warning light fails to come on
- ☐ Lights inoperative
- ☐ Instrument readings inaccurate or erratic
- ☐ Horn inoperative, or unsatisfactory in operation
- ☐ Windscreen/tailgate wipers inoperative, or unsatisfactory in operation
- ☐ Windscreen/tailgate washers inoperative, or unsatisfactory in operation
- ☐ Electric windows inoperative, or unsatisfactory in operation
- ☐ Central locking system inoperative, or unsatisfactory in operation

Introduction

The vehicle owner who does his or her own maintenance according to the recommended service schedules should not have to use this section of the manual very often. Modern component reliability is such that, provided those items subject to wear or deterioration are inspected or renewed at the specified intervals, sudden failure is comparatively rare. Faults do not usually just happen as a result of sudden failure, but develop over a period of time. Major mechanical failures in particular are usually preceded by characteristic symptoms over hundreds or even thousands of miles. Those components that do occasionally fail without warning are often small and easily carried in the vehicle.

With any fault-finding, the first step is to decide where to begin investigations. Sometimes this is obvious, but on other occasions, a little detective work will be necessary. The owner who makes half a dozen haphazard adjustments or replacements may be successful in curing a fault (or its symptoms). However, will be none the wiser if the fault recurs, and ultimately may have spent more time and money than was necessary. A calm and logical approach will be found to be more satisfactory in the long run. Always take into account any warning signs or abnormalities that may have been noticed in the period preceding the fault - power loss, high or low gauge readings, unusual smells, etc. - and remember that failure of components such as fuses or spark plugs may only be pointers to some underlying fault.

The pages that follow provide an easy-reference guide to the more common problems that may occur during the operation of the vehicle. These problems and their possible causes are grouped under headings denoting various components or systems, such as Engine, Cooling system, etc. The Chapter and/or Section that deals with the problem is also shown in brackets. Whatever the fault, certain basic principles apply. These are as follows:

Verify the fault. This is simply a matter of being sure that you know what the symptoms are before starting work. This is particularly important if you are investigating a fault for someone else, who may not have described it very accurately.

Do not overlook the obvious. For example, if the vehicle will not start, is there petrol in the tank? (Do not take anyone else's word on this particular point, and do not trust the fuel gauge either!) If an electrical fault is indicated, look for loose or broken wires before digging out the test gear.

Cure the disease, not the symptom. Substituting a flat battery with a fully charged one will get you off the hard shoulder, but if the underlying cause is not attended to, the new battery will go the same way. Similarly, changing oil-fouled spark plugs for a new set will get you moving again, but remember that the reason for the fouling (if it was not simply an incorrect grade of plug) will have to be established and corrected.

Do not take anything for granted. Particularly, do not forget that a "new" component may itself be defective (especially if it's been rattling around in the boot for months). Also do not leave components out of a fault diagnosis sequence just because they are new or recently fitted. When you do finally diagnose a difficult fault, you will probably realise that all the evidence was there from the start.

Engine

Engine fails to rotate when attempting to start

- [ ] Battery terminal connections loose or corroded (*"Weekly checks"*).
- [ ] Battery discharged or faulty (Chapter 5).
- [ ] Broken, loose or disconnected wiring in the starting circuit (Chapter 5).
- [ ] Defective starter solenoid or switch (Chapter 5).
- [ ] Defective starter motor (Chapter 5).
- [ ] Starter pinion or flywheel ring gear teeth loose or broken (Chapters 2A and 5).
- [ ] Engine earth strap broken or disconnected (Chapter 5).

Engine rotates, but will not start

- [ ] Fuel tank empty.
- [ ] Battery discharged (engine rotates slowly), (Chapter 5).
- [ ] Battery terminal connections loose or corroded (*"Weekly checks"*).
- [ ] Ignition components damp or damaged (Chapters 1 and 5).
- [ ] Broken, loose or disconnected wiring in the ignition circuit (Chapters 1 and 5).
- [ ] Worn, faulty or incorrectly gapped spark plugs (Chapter 1).
- [ ] Choke mechanism incorrectly adjusted, worn or sticking - carburettor models (Chapter 4A).
- [ ] Faulty fuel cut-off solenoid - carburettor models (Chapter 4A).
- [ ] Fuel injection system fault - fuel-injected models (Chapter 4B).
- [ ] Major mechanical failure (e.g. camshaft drive), (Chapter 2A or 2B).

Engine difficult to start when cold

- [ ] Battery discharged (Chapter 5).
- [ ] Battery terminal connections loose or corroded (*"Weekly checks"*).
- [ ] Worn, faulty or incorrectly gapped spark plugs (Chapter 1).
- [ ] Choke mechanism incorrectly adjusted, worn or sticking - carburettor models (Chapter 4A).
- [ ] Fuel injection system fault - fuel-injected models (Chapter 4B).
- [ ] Other ignition system fault (Chapters 1 and 5).
- [ ] Low cylinder compressions (Chapter 2A).

Engine difficult to start when hot

- [ ] Air filter element dirty or clogged (Chapter 1).
- [ ] Choke mechanism incorrectly adjusted, worn or sticking - carburettor models (Chapter 4A).
- [ ] Fuel injection system fault - fuel-injected models (Chapter 4B).
- [ ] Low cylinder compressions (Chapter 2A).

Starter motor noisy or excessively rough in engagement

- [ ] Starter pinion or flywheel ring gear teeth loose or broken (Chapters 2A and 5).
- [ ] Starter motor mounting bolts loose or missing (Chapter 5).
- [ ] Starter motor internal components worn or damaged (Chapter 5).

Engine starts, but stops immediately

- [ ] Loose or faulty electrical connections in the ignition circuit (Chapters 1 and 5).
- [ ] Vacuum leak at the carburettor/throttle body or inlet manifold (Chapter 4A or 4B).
- [ ] Blocked carburettor jet(s) or internal passages - carburettor models (Chapter 4A).
- [ ] Blocked injector/fuel injection system fault - fuel-injected models (Chapter 4B).

Engine idles erratically

- [ ] Air filter element clogged (Chapter 1).
- [ ] Vacuum leak at the carburettor/throttle body, inlet manifold or associated hoses (Chapter 4A or 4B).
- [ ] Worn, faulty or incorrectly gapped spark plugs (Chapter 1).
- [ ] Uneven or low cylinder compressions (Chapter 2A).
- [ ] Camshaft lobes worn (Chapter 2A or 2B).
- [ ] Timing belt incorrectly tensioned (Chapter 2A or 2B).
- [ ] Blocked carburettor jet(s) or internal passages - carburettor models (Chapter 4A).
- [ ] Blocked injector/fuel injection system fault - fuel-injected models (Chapter 4B).

Engine misfires at idle speed

- [ ] Worn, faulty or incorrectly gapped spark plugs (Chapter 1).
- [ ] Faulty spark plug HT leads (Chapter 1).
- [ ] Vacuum leak at the carburettor/throttle body, inlet manifold or associated hoses (Chapter 4A or 4B).
- [ ] Blocked carburettor jet(s) or internal passages - carburettor models (Chapter 4A).
- [ ] Blocked injector/fuel injection system fault - fuel-injected models (Chapter 4B).
- [ ] Distributor cap cracked or tracking internally (where applicable), (Chapter 1).
- [ ] Uneven or low cylinder compressions (Chapter 2A).
- [ ] Disconnected, leaking, or perished crankcase ventilation hoses (Chapter 4C).

Engine misfires throughout the driving speed range

- [ ] Fuel filter choked (Chapter 1).
- [ ] Fuel pump faulty, or delivery pressure low (Chapter 4A or 4B).
- [ ] Fuel tank vent blocked, or fuel pipes restricted (Chapter 4A or 4B).
- [ ] Vacuum leak at the carburettor/throttle body, inlet manifold or associated hoses (Chapter 4A or 4B).
- [ ] Worn, faulty or incorrectly gapped spark plugs (Chapter 1).
- [ ] Faulty spark plug HT leads (Chapter 1).
- [ ] Distributor cap cracked or tracking internally (where applicable), (Chapter 1).
- [ ] Faulty ignition coil (Chapter 5).
- [ ] Uneven or low cylinder compressions (Chapter 2A).
- [ ] Blocked carburettor jet(s) or internal passages - carburettor models (Chapter 4A).
- [ ] Blocked injector/fuel injection system fault - fuel-injected models (Chapter 4B).

Engine hesitates on acceleration

- [ ] Worn, faulty or incorrectly gapped spark plugs (Chapter 1).
- [ ] Vacuum leak at the carburettor/throttle body, inlet manifold or associated hoses (Chapter 4A or 4B).
- [ ] Blocked carburettor jet(s) or internal passages - carburettor models (Chapter 4A).
- [ ] Blocked injector/fuel injection system fault - fuel-injected models (Chapter 4B).

Engine stalls

- [ ] Vacuum leak at the carburettor/throttle body, inlet manifold or associated hoses (Chapter 4A or 4B).
- [ ] Fuel filter choked (Chapter 1).
- [ ] Fuel pump faulty, or delivery pressure low (Chapter 4A or 4B).
- [ ] Fuel tank vent blocked, or fuel pipes restricted (Chapter 4A or 4B).
- [ ] Blocked carburettor jet(s) or internal passages - carburettor models (Chapter 4A).
- [ ] Blocked injector/fuel injection system fault - fuel-injected models (Chapter 4B).

Engine lacks power

- [ ] Timing belt incorrectly fitted or tensioned (Chapter 2A or 2B).
- [ ] Fuel filter choked (Chapter 1).
- [ ] Fuel pump faulty, or delivery pressure low (Chapter 4A or 4B).
- [ ] Uneven or low cylinder compressions (Chapter 2A).
- [ ] Worn, faulty or incorrectly gapped spark plugs (Chapter 1).
- [ ] Vacuum leak at the carburettor/throttle body, inlet manifold or associated hoses (Chapter 4A or 4B).
- [ ] Blocked carburettor jet(s) or internal passages - carburettor models (Chapter 4A).
- [ ] Blocked injector/fuel injection system fault - fuel-injected models (Chapter 4B).
- [ ] Brakes binding (Chapters 1 and 9).
- [ ] Clutch slipping (Chapter 6).

Engine backfires

- [ ] Timing belt incorrectly fitted or tensioned (Chapter 2A or 2B).
- [ ] Vacuum leak at the carburettor/throttle body, inlet manifold or associated hoses (Chapter 4A or 4B).
- [ ] Blocked carburettor jet(s) or internal passages - carburettor models (Chapter 4A).
- [ ] Blocked injector/fuel injection system fault - fuel-injected models (Chapter 4B).

Oil pressure warning light illuminated with engine running

- [ ] Low oil level, or incorrect oil grade (*"Weekly checks"*).
- [ ] Faulty oil pressure warning light switch (Chapter 5).
- [ ] Worn engine bearings and/or oil pump (Chapter 2A).
- [ ] High engine operating temperature (Chapter 3).
- [ ] Oil pressure relief valve defective (Chapter 2A).
- [ ] Oil pick-up strainer clogged (Chapter 2A).

Engine runs-on after switching off

- [ ] Excessive carbon build-up in engine (Chapter 2A).
- [ ] High engine operating temperature (Chapter 3).
- [ ] Faulty fuel cut-off solenoid - carburettor models (Chapter 4A).
- [ ] Fuel injection system fault - fuel-injected models (Chapter 4B).

Engine noises

Pre-ignition (pinking) or knocking during acceleration or under load

- [ ] Ignition timing incorrect/ignition system fault (Chapters 1 and 5).
- [ ] Incorrect grade of spark plug (Chapter 1).
- [ ] Incorrect grade of fuel (Chapter 1).
- [ ] Vacuum leak at the carburettor/throttle body, inlet manifold or associated hoses (Chapter 4A or 4B).
- [ ] Excessive carbon build-up in engine (Chapter 2A).
- [ ] Blocked carburettor jet(s) or internal passages - carburettor models (Chapter 4A).
- [ ] Blocked injector/fuel injection system fault - fuel-injected models (Chapter 4B).

Whistling or wheezing noises

- [ ] Leaking inlet manifold or carburettor/throttle body gasket (Chapter 4A or 4B).
- [ ] Leaking exhaust manifold gasket or pipe-to-manifold joint (Chapter 4C).
- [ ] Leaking vacuum hose (Chapters 4A, 4B, 4C, 5, 9 and 12).
- [ ] Blowing cylinder head gasket (Chapter 2A or 2B).

Tapping or rattling noises

- [ ] Worn valve gear or camshaft (Chapter 2A or 2B).
- [ ] Ancillary component fault (coolant pump, alternator, etc.) (Chapters 3, 5, etc.).

Knocking or thumping noises

- [ ] Worn big-end bearings (regular heavy knocking, perhaps less under load), (Chapter 2A or 2B).
- [ ] Worn main bearings (rumbling and knocking, perhaps worsening under load), (Chapter 2A or 2B).
- [ ] Piston slap (most noticeable when cold), (Chapter 2A).
- [ ] Ancillary component fault (coolant pump, alternator, etc.) (Chapters 3, 5, etc.).

Cooling system

Overheating

☐ Insufficient coolant in system (*"Weekly checks"*).
☐ Thermostat faulty (Chapter 3).
☐ Radiator core blocked, or grille restricted (Chapter 3).
☐ Electric cooling fan or thermoswitch faulty (Chapter 3).
☐ Pressure cap faulty (Chapter 3).
☐ Ignition timing incorrect/ignition system fault (Chapters 1 and 5).
☐ Inaccurate temperature gauge sender unit (Chapter 3).
☐ Airlock in cooling system (Chapter 1).

Overcooling

☐ Thermostat faulty (Chapter 3).
☐ Inaccurate temperature gauge sender unit (Chapter 3).

Internal coolant leakage

☐ Leaking cylinder head gasket (Chapter 2A or 2B).
☐ Cracked cylinder head or cylinder bore (Chapter 2A or 2B).

External coolant leakage

☐ Deteriorated or damaged hoses or hose clips (Chapter 1).
☐ Radiator core or heater matrix leaking (Chapter 3).
☐ Pressure cap faulty (Chapter 3).
☐ Water pump seal leaking (Chapter 3).
☐ Boiling due to overheating (Chapter 3).
☐ Core plug leaking (Chapter 2A).

Corrosion

☐ Infrequent draining and flushing (Chapter 1).
☐ Incorrect coolant mixture or inappropriate coolant type (Chapter 1).

Fuel and exhaust systems

Excessive fuel consumption

☐ Air filter element dirty or clogged (Chapter 1).
☐ Choke cable incorrectly adjusted, or choke sticking - carburettor models (Chapter 4A).
☐ Fuel injection system fault - fuel injected models (Chapter 4B).
☐ Ignition timing incorrect/ignition system fault (Chapters 1 and 5).
☐ Tyres under-inflated (*"Weekly checks"*).

Fuel leakage and/or fuel odour

☐ Damaged or corroded fuel tank, pipes or connections (Chapter 4A or 4B).
☐ Carburettor float chamber flooding (float height incorrect) - carburettor models (Chapter 4A).

Excessive noise or fumes from exhaust system

☐ Leaking exhaust system or manifold joints (Chapters 1 and 4C).
☐ Leaking, corroded or damaged silencers or pipe (Chapters 1 and 4C).
☐ Broken mountings causing body or suspension contact (Chapter 1).

Clutch

Pedal travels to floor - no pressure or very little resistance

☐ Broken clutch cable (Chapter 6).
☐ Incorrect clutch cable adjustment (Chapter 6).
☐ Broken clutch release bearing or fork (Chapter 6).
☐ Broken diaphragm spring in clutch pressure plate (Chapter 6).

Noise when depressing or releasing clutch pedal

☐ Worn clutch release bearing (Chapter 6).
☐ Worn or dry clutch pedal bushes (Chapter 6).
☐ Faulty pressure plate assembly (Chapter 6).
☐ Pressure plate diaphragm spring broken (Chapter 6).
☐ Broken clutch disc cushioning springs (Chapter 6).

Clutch slips (engine speed increases, with no increase in vehicle speed).

☐ Incorrect clutch cable adjustment (Chapter 6).
☐ Clutch disc linings excessively worn (Chapter 6).
☐ Clutch disc linings contaminated with oil or grease (Chapter 6).
☐ Faulty pressure plate or weak diaphragm spring (Chapter 6).

Clutch fails to disengage (unable to select gears).

☐ Incorrect clutch cable adjustment (Chapter 6).
☐ Clutch disc sticking on transmission input shaft splines (Chapter 6).
☐ Clutch disc sticking to flywheel or pressure plate (Chapter 6).
☐ Faulty pressure plate assembly (Chapter 6).
☐ Clutch release mechanism worn or incorrectly assembled (Chapter 6).

Judder as clutch is engaged

☐ Clutch disc linings contaminated with oil or grease (Chapter 6).
☐ Clutch disc linings excessively worn (Chapter 6).
☐ Clutch cable sticking or frayed (Chapter 6).
☐ Faulty or distorted pressure plate or diaphragm spring (Chapter 6).
☐ Worn or loose engine or transmission mountings (Chapter 2A or 2B).
☐ Clutch disc hub or transmission input shaft splines worn (Chapter 6).

Manual transmission

Noisy in neutral with engine running
☐ Input shaft bearings worn (noise apparent with clutch pedal released, but not when depressed), (Chapter 7A).*
☐ Clutch release bearing worn (noise apparent with clutch pedal depressed, possibly less when released), (Chapter 6).

Noisy in one particular gear
☐ Worn, damaged or chipped gear teeth (Chapter 7A).*

Difficulty engaging gears
☐ Clutch fault (Chapter 6).
☐ Worn or damaged gear linkage (Chapter 7A).
☐ Incorrectly adjusted gear linkage (Chapter 7A).
☐ Worn synchroniser units (Chapter 7A).*

Vibration
☐ Lack of oil (Chapter 1).
☐ Worn bearings (Chapter 7A).*

Jumps out of gear
☐ Worn or damaged gear linkage (Chapter 7A).
☐ Incorrectly adjusted gear linkage (Chapter 7A).
☐ Worn synchroniser units (Chapter 7A).*
☐ Worn selector forks (Chapter 7A).*

Lubricant leaks
☐ Leaking differential output oil seal (Chapter 7A).
☐ Leaking housing joint (Chapter 7A).*
☐ Leaking input shaft oil seal (Chapter 7A).*

* Although the corrective action necessary to remedy the symptoms described is beyond the scope of the home mechanic, the above information should be helpful in isolating the cause of the condition. This should enable the owner can communicate clearly with a professional mechanic.

Automatic transmission

Note: Due to the complexity of the automatic transmission, it is difficult for the home mechanic to properly diagnose and service this unit. For problems other than the following, the vehicle should be taken to a dealer service department or automatic transmission specialist. Do not be too hasty in removing the transmission if a fault is suspected, as most of the testing is carried out with the unit still fitted.

Fluid leakage
☐ Automatic transmission fluid is usually dark in colour. Fluid leaks should not be confused with engine oil, which can easily be blown onto the transmission by airflow.
☐ To determine the source of a leak, first remove all built-up dirt and grime from the transmission housing and surrounding areas using a degreasing agent, or by steam-cleaning. Drive the vehicle at low speed, so airflow will not blow the leak far from its source. Raise and support the vehicle, and determine where the leak is coming from. The following are common areas of leakage:
a) Fluid pan or "sump" (Chapter 1 and 7B).
b) Dipstick tube (Chapter 1 and 7B).
c) Transmission-to-fluid cooler pipes/unions (Chapter 7B).

Transmission fluid brown, or has burned smell
☐ Transmission fluid level low, or fluid in need of renewal (Chapter 1).

Transmission will not downshift (kickdown) with accelerator pedal fully depressed
☐ Low transmission fluid level (Chapter 1).
☐ Incorrect selector cable adjustment (Chapter 7B).

Engine will not start in any gear, or starts in gears other than Park or Neutral
☐ Incorrect starter/inhibitor switch adjustment (Chapter 7B).
☐ Incorrect selector cable adjustment (Chapter 7B).

General gear selection problems
☐ Chapter 7B deals with checking and adjusting the selector cable on automatic transmissions. The following are common problems that may be caused by a poorly adjusted cable:
a) Engine starting in gears other than Park or Neutral.
b) Indicator panel indicating a gear other than the one actually being used.
c) Vehicle moves when in Park or Neutral.
d) Poor gear shift quality or erratic gear changes.

☐ Refer to Chapter 7B for the selector cable adjustment procedure.

Transmission slips, shifts roughly, is noisy, or has no drive in forward or reverse gears
☐ There are many probable causes for the above problems, but the home mechanic should be concerned with only one possibility - fluid level. Before taking the vehicle to a dealer or transmission specialist, check the fluid level and condition of the fluid as described in Chapter 1. Correct the fluid level as necessary, or change the fluid and filter if needed. If the problem persists, professional help will be necessary.

Driveshafts

Clicking or knocking noise on turns (at slow speed on full-lock)
☐ Lack of constant velocity joint lubricant, possibly due to damaged gaiter (Chapter 8).
☐ Worn outer constant velocity joint (Chapter 8).

Vibration when accelerating or decelerating
☐ Worn inner constant velocity joint (Chapter 8).
☐ Bent or distorted driveshaft (Chapter 8).

Braking system

Note: *Before assuming that a brake problem exists, make sure that the tyres are in good condition and correctly inflated, that the front wheel alignment is correct, and that the vehicle is not loaded with weight in an unequal manner. Apart from checking the condition of all pipe and hose connections, any faults occurring on the anti-lock braking system should be referred to a Peugeot dealer for diagnosis.*

Vehicle pulls to one side under braking

- [ ] Worn, defective, damaged or contaminated brake pads/shoes on one side (Chapters 1 and 9).
- [ ] Seized or partially seized front brake caliper/wheel cylinder piston (Chapters 1 and 9).
- [ ] A mixture of brake pad/shoe lining materials fitted between sides (Chapters 1 and 9).
- [ ] Brake caliper or backplate mounting bolts loose (Chapter 9).
- [ ] Worn or damaged steering or suspension components (Chapters 1 and 10).

Noise (grinding or high-pitched squeal) when brakes applied

- [ ] Brake pad or shoe friction lining material worn down to metal backing (Chapters 1 and 9).
- [ ] Excessive corrosion of brake disc or drum. This may be apparent after the vehicle has been standing for some time (Chapters 1 and 9).
- [ ] Foreign object (stone chipping, etc.) trapped between brake disc and shield (Chapters 1 and 9).

Excessive brake pedal travel

- [ ] Inoperative rear brake self-adjust mechanism - drum brakes (Chapters 1 and 9).
- [ ] Faulty master cylinder (Chapter 9).
- [ ] Air in hydraulic system (Chapters 1 and 9).
- [ ] Faulty vacuum servo unit (Chapter 9).

Brake pedal feels spongy when depressed

- [ ] Air in hydraulic system (Chapters 1 and 9).
- [ ] Deteriorated flexible rubber brake hoses (Chapters 1 and 9).
- [ ] Master cylinder mounting nuts loose (Chapter 9).
- [ ] Faulty master cylinder (Chapter 9).

Excessive brake pedal effort required to stop vehicle

- [ ] Faulty vacuum servo unit (Chapter 9).
- [ ] Disconnected, damaged or insecure brake servo vacuum hose (Chapter 9).
- [ ] Primary or secondary hydraulic circuit failure (Chapter 9).
- [ ] Seized brake caliper or wheel cylinder piston(s) (Chapter 9).
- [ ] Brake pads or brake shoes incorrectly fitted (Chapters 1 and 9).
- [ ] Incorrect grade of brake pads or brake shoes fitted (Chapters 1 and 9).
- [ ] Brake pads or brake shoe linings contaminated (Chapters 1 and 9).

Judder felt through brake pedal or steering wheel when braking

- [ ] Excessive run-out or distortion of discs/drums (Chapters 1 and 9).
- [ ] Brake pad or brake shoe linings worn (Chapters 1 and 9).
- [ ] Brake caliper or brake backplate mounting bolts loose (Chapter 9).
- [ ] Wear in suspension or steering components or mountings (Chapters 1 and 10).

Brakes binding

- [ ] Seized brake caliper or wheel cylinder piston(s) (Chapter 9).
- [ ] Incorrectly adjusted handbrake mechanism (Chapter 9).
- [ ] Faulty master cylinder (Chapter 9).

Rear wheels locking under normal braking

- [ ] Rear brake shoe linings contaminated (Chapters 1 and 9).
- [ ] Faulty brake pressure regulator (Chapter 9).

Suspension and steering

Note: *Before diagnosing suspension or steering faults, be sure that the trouble is not due to incorrect tyre pressures, mixtures of tyre types, or binding brakes.*

Vehicle pulls to one side

- [ ] Defective tyre (*"Weekly checks"*).
- [ ] Excessive wear in suspension or steering components (Chapters 1 and 10).
- [ ] Incorrect front wheel alignment (Chapter 10).
- [ ] Accident damage to steering or suspension components (Chapter 1).

Excessive pitching and/or rolling around corners, or during braking

- [ ] Defective shock absorbers (Chapters 1 and 10).
- [ ] Broken or weak spring and/or suspension component (Chapters 1 and 10).
- [ ] Worn or damaged anti-roll bar or mountings (Chapter 10).

Wandering or general instability

- [ ] Incorrect front wheel alignment (Chapter 10).
- [ ] Worn steering or suspension joints, bushes or components (Chapters 1 and 10).
- [ ] Roadwheels out of balance (Chapters 1 and 10).
- [ ] Faulty or damaged tyre (*"Weekly checks"*).
- [ ] Wheel bolts loose (Chapters 1 and 10).
- [ ] Defective shock absorbers (Chapters 1 and 10).

Excessively stiff steering

- [ ] Lack of steering gear lubricant (Chapter 10).
- [ ] Seized track rod end balljoint or suspension balljoint (Chapters 1 and 10).
- [ ] Broken or incorrectly adjusted auxiliary drivebelt - power steering (Chapter 1).
- [ ] Incorrect front wheel alignment (Chapter 10).
- [ ] Steering rack or column bent or damaged (Chapter 10).

Suspension and steering (continued)

Wheel wobble and vibration

- ☐ Front roadwheels out of balance (vibration felt mainly through the steering wheel), (Chapters 1 and 10).
- ☐ Rear roadwheels out of balance (vibration felt throughout the vehicle), (Chapters 1 and 10).
- ☐ Roadwheels damaged or distorted (Chapters 1 and 10).
- ☐ Faulty or damaged tyre (*"Weekly checks"*).
- ☐ Worn steering or suspension joints, bushes or components (Chapters 1 and 10).
- ☐ Wheel bolts loose (Chapters 1 and 10).

Excessive play in steering

- ☐ Worn steering column intermediate shaft universal joint (Chapter 10).
- ☐ Worn steering track rod end balljoints (Chapters 1 and 10).
- ☐ Worn rack-and-pinion steering gear (Chapter 10).
- ☐ Worn steering or suspension joints, bushes or components (Chapters 1 and 10).

Lack of power assistance

- ☐ Broken or incorrectly adjusted auxiliary drivebelt (Chapter 1).
- ☐ Incorrect power steering fluid level (*"Weekly checks"*).
- ☐ Restriction in power steering fluid hoses (Chapter 1).
- ☐ Faulty power steering pump (Chapter 10).
- ☐ Faulty rack-and-pinion steering gear (Chapter 10).

Tyre wear excessive

Tyres worn on inside or outside edges

- ☐ Tyres under-inflated (wear on both edges), (*"Weekly checks"*).
- ☐ Incorrect camber or castor angles (wear on one edge only), (Chapter 10).
- ☐ Worn steering or suspension joints, bushes or components (Chapters 1 and 10).
- ☐ Excessively hard cornering.
- ☐ Accident damage.

Tyre treads exhibit feathered edges

- ☐ Incorrect toe setting (Chapter 10).

Tyres worn in centre of tread

- ☐ Tyres over-inflated (*"Weekly checks"*).

Tyres worn on inside and outside edges

- ☐ Tyres under-inflated (*"Weekly checks"*).

Tyres worn unevenly

- ☐ Tyres/wheels out of balance (Chapter 1).
- ☐ Excessive wheel or tyre run-out (Chapter 1).
- ☐ Worn shock absorbers (Chapters 1 and 10).
- ☐ Faulty tyre (*"Weekly checks"*).

Electrical system

Note: *For problems associated with the starting system, refer to the faults listed under "Engine" earlier in this Section.*

Battery will not hold a charge for more than a few days

- ☐ Battery defective internally (Chapter 5).
- ☐ Battery terminal connections loose or corroded (*"Weekly checks"*).
- ☐ Auxiliary drivebelt worn or incorrectly adjusted (Chapter 1).
- ☐ Alternator not charging at correct output (Chapter 5).
- ☐ Alternator or voltage regulator faulty (Chapter 5).
- ☐ Short-circuit causing continual battery drain (Chapters 5 and 12).

Ignition/no-charge warning light remains illuminated with engine running

- ☐ Auxiliary drivebelt broken, worn, or incorrectly adjusted (Chapter 1).
- ☐ Alternator brushes worn, sticking, or dirty (Chapter 5).
- ☐ Alternator brush springs weak or broken (Chapter 5).
- ☐ Internal fault in alternator or voltage regulator (Chapter 5).
- ☐ Broken, disconnected, or loose wiring in charging circuit (Chapter 5).

Ignition/no-charge warning light fails to come on

- ☐ Warning light bulb blown (Chapter 12).
- ☐ Broken, disconnected, or loose wiring in warning light circuit (Chapter 12).
- ☐ Alternator faulty (Chapter 5).

Lights inoperative

- ☐ Bulb blown (Chapter 12).
- ☐ Corrosion of bulb or bulbholder contacts (Chapter 12).
- ☐ Blown fuse (Chapter 12).
- ☐ Faulty relay (Chapter 12).
- ☐ Broken, loose, or disconnected wiring (Chapter 12).
- ☐ Faulty switch (Chapter 12).

Instrument readings inaccurate or erratic

Instrument readings increase with engine speed

- ☐ Faulty voltage regulator (Chapter 12).

Fuel or temperature gauges give no reading

- ☐ Faulty gauge sender unit (Chapters 3, 4A and 4B).
- ☐ Wiring open-circuit (Chapter 12).
- ☐ Faulty gauge (Chapter 12).

Fuel or temperature gauges give continuous maximum reading

- ☐ Faulty gauge sender unit (Chapters 3, 4A and 4B).
- ☐ Wiring short-circuit (Chapter 12).
- ☐ Faulty gauge (Chapter 12).

Horn inoperative, or unsatisfactory in operation

Horn operates all the time

- ☐ Horn push either earthed or stuck down (Chapter 12).
- ☐ Horn cable-to-horn push earthed (Chapter 12).

Horn fails to operate

- ☐ Blown fuse (Chapter 12).
- ☐ Cable or cable connections loose, broken or disconnected (Chapter 12).
- ☐ Faulty horn (Chapter 12).

Horn emits intermittent or unsatisfactory sound

- ☐ Cable connections loose (Chapter 12).
- ☐ Horn mountings loose (Chapter 12).
- ☐ Faulty horn (Chapter 12).

Electrical system (continued)

Windscreen/tailgate wipers inoperative, or unsatisfactory in operation

Wipers fail to operate, or operate very slowly

☐ Wiper blades stuck to screen, or linkage seized or binding (Chapters 1 and 12).
☐ Blown fuse (Chapter 12).
☐ Cable or cable connections loose, broken or disconnected (Chapter 12).
☐ Faulty relay (Chapter 12).
☐ Faulty wiper motor (Chapter 12).

Wiper blades sweep over too large or too small an area of the glass

☐ Wiper arms incorrectly positioned on spindles (Chapter 1).
☐ Excessive wear of wiper linkage (Chapter 12).
☐ Wiper motor or linkage mountings loose or insecure (Chapter 12).

Wiper blades fail to clean the glass effectively

☐ Wiper blade rubbers worn or perished (Chapter 1).
☐ Wiper arm tension springs broken, or arm pivots seized (Chapter 12).
☐ Insufficient windscreen washer additive to adequately remove road film (Chapter 1).

Windscreen/tailgate washers inoperative, or unsatisfactory in operation

One or more washer jets inoperative

☐ Blocked washer jet (Chapter 1).
☐ Disconnected, kinked or restricted fluid hose (Chapter 12).
☐ Insufficient fluid in washer reservoir (Chapter 1).

Washer pump fails to operate

☐ Broken or disconnected wiring or connections (Chapter 12).
☐ Blown fuse (Chapter 12).
☐ Faulty washer switch (Chapter 12).
☐ Faulty washer pump (Chapter 12).

Washer pump runs for some time before fluid is emitted from jets

☐ Faulty one-way valve in fluid supply hose (Chapter 12).

Electric windows inoperative, or unsatisfactory in operation

Window glass will only move in one direction

☐ Faulty switch (Chapter 12).

Window glass slow to move

☐ Regulator seized or damaged, or in need of lubrication (Chapter 11).
☐ Door internal components or trim fouling regulator (Chapter 11).
☐ Faulty motor (Chapter 12).

Window glass fails to move

☐ Blown fuse (Chapter 12).
☐ Faulty relay (Chapter 12).
☐ Broken or disconnected wiring or connections (Chapter 12).
☐ Faulty motor (Chapter 12).

Central locking system inoperative, or unsatisfactory in operation

Complete system failure

☐ Blown fuse (Chapter 12).
☐ Faulty relay (Chapter 12).
☐ Broken or disconnected wiring or connections (Chapter 12).
☐ Faulty control module (Chapter 12).

Latch locks but will not unlock, or unlocks but will not lock

☐ Faulty master switch (Chapter 12).
☐ Broken or disconnected latch operating rods or levers (Chapter 11).
☐ Faulty relay (Chapter 12).
☐ Faulty control module (Chapter 12).

One solenoid/motor fails to operate

☐ Broken or disconnected wiring or connections (Chapter 12).
☐ Faulty solenoid/motor (Chapter 12).
☐ Broken, binding or disconnected latch operating rods or levers (Chapter 11).
☐ Fault in door latch (Chapter 11).

A

ABS (Anti-lock brake system) A system, usually electronically controlled, that senses incipient wheel lockup during braking and relieves hydraulic pressure at wheels that are about to skid.

Air bag An inflatable bag hidden in the steering wheel (driver's side) or the dash or glovebox (passenger side). In a head-on collision, the bags inflate, preventing the driver and front passenger from being thrown forward into the steering wheel or windscreen.

Air cleaner A metal or plastic housing, containing a filter element, which removes dust and dirt from the air being drawn into the engine.

Air filter element The actual filter in an air cleaner system, usually manufactured from pleated paper and requiring renewal at regular intervals.

Air filter

Allen key A hexagonal wrench which fits into a recessed hexagonal hole.

Alligator clip A long-nosed spring-loaded metal clip with meshing teeth. Used to make temporary electrical connections.

Alternator A component in the electrical system which converts mechanical energy from a drivebelt into electrical energy to charge the battery and to operate the starting system, ignition system and electrical accessories.

Alternator (exploded view)

Ampere (amp) A unit of measurement for the flow of electric current. One amp is the amount of current produced by one volt acting through a resistance of one ohm.

Anaerobic sealer A substance used to prevent bolts and screws from loosening. Anaerobic means that it does not require oxygen for activation. The Loctite brand is widely used.

Antifreeze A substance (usually ethylene glycol) mixed with water, and added to a vehicle's cooling system, to prevent freezing of the coolant in winter. Antifreeze also contains chemicals to inhibit corrosion and the formation of rust and other deposits that

would tend to clog the radiator and coolant passages and reduce cooling efficiency.

Anti-seize compound A coating that reduces the risk of seizing on fasteners that are subjected to high temperatures, such as exhaust manifold bolts and nuts.

Anti-seize compound

Asbestos A natural fibrous mineral with great heat resistance, commonly used in the composition of brake friction materials. Asbestos is a health hazard and the dust created by brake systems should never be inhaled or ingested.

Axle A shaft on which a wheel revolves, or which revolves with a wheel. Also, a solid beam that connects the two wheels at one end of the vehicle. An axle which also transmits power to the wheels is known as a live axle.

Axle assembly

Axleshaft A single rotating shaft, on either side of the differential, which delivers power from the final drive assembly to the drive wheels. Also called a driveshaft or a halfshaft.

B

Ball bearing An anti-friction bearing consisting of a hardened inner and outer race with hardened steel balls between two races.

Bearing

Bearing The curved surface on a shaft or in a bore, or the part assembled into either, that permits relative motion between them with minimum wear and friction.

Big-end bearing The bearing in the end of the connecting rod that's attached to the crankshaft.

Bleed nipple A valve on a brake wheel cylinder, caliper or other hydraulic component that is opened to purge the hydraulic system of air. Also called a bleed screw.

Brake bleeding

Brake bleeding Procedure for removing air from lines of a hydraulic brake system.

Brake disc The component of a disc brake that rotates with the wheels.

Brake drum The component of a drum brake that rotates with the wheels.

Brake linings The friction material which contacts the brake disc or drum to retard the vehicle's speed. The linings are bonded or riveted to the brake pads or shoes.

Brake pads The replaceable friction pads that pinch the brake disc when the brakes are applied. Brake pads consist of a friction material bonded or riveted to a rigid backing plate.

Brake shoe The crescent-shaped carrier to which the brake linings are mounted and which forces the lining against the rotating drum during braking.

Braking systems For more information on braking systems, consult the *Haynes Automotive Brake Manual*.

Breaker bar A long socket wrench handle providing greater leverage.

Bulkhead The insulated partition between the engine and the passenger compartment.

C

Caliper The non-rotating part of a disc-brake assembly that straddles the disc and carries the brake pads. The caliper also contains the hydraulic components that cause the pads to pinch the disc when the brakes are applied. A caliper is also a measuring tool that can be set to measure inside or outside dimensions of an object.

Camshaft A rotating shaft on which a series of cam lobes operate the valve mechanisms. The camshaft may be driven by gears, by sprockets and chain or by sprockets and a belt.

Canister A container in an evaporative emission control system; contains activated charcoal granules to trap vapours from the fuel system.

Canister

Carburettor A device which mixes fuel with air in the proper proportions to provide a desired power output from a spark ignition internal combustion engine.

Carburettor

Castellated Resembling the parapets along the top of a castle wall. For example, a castellated balljoint stud nut.

Castellated nut

Castor In wheel alignment, the backward or forward tilt of the steering axis. Castor is positive when the steering axis is inclined rearward at the top.

Catalytic converter A silencer-like device in the exhaust system which converts certain pollutants in the exhaust gases into less harmful substances.

Catalytic converter

Circlip A ring-shaped clip used to prevent endwise movement of cylindrical parts and shafts. An internal circlip is installed in a groove in a housing; an external circlip fits into a groove on the outside of a cylindrical piece such as a shaft.

Clearance The amount of space between two parts. For example, between a piston and a cylinder, between a bearing and a journal, etc.

Coil spring A spiral of elastic steel found in various sizes throughout a vehicle, for example as a springing medium in the suspension and in the valve train.

Compression Reduction in volume, and increase in pressure and temperature, of a gas, caused by squeezing it into a smaller space.

Compression ratio The relationship between cylinder volume when the piston is at top dead centre and cylinder volume when the piston is at bottom dead centre.

Constant velocity (CV) joint A type of universal joint that cancels out vibrations caused by driving power being transmitted through an angle.

Core plug A disc or cup-shaped metal device inserted in a hole in a casting through which core was removed when the casting was formed. Also known as a freeze plug or expansion plug.

Crankcase The lower part of the engine block in which the crankshaft rotates.

Crankshaft The main rotating member, or shaft, running the length of the crankcase, with offset "throws" to which the connecting rods are attached.

Crankshaft assembly

Crocodile clip See Alligator clip

D

Diagnostic code Code numbers obtained by accessing the diagnostic mode of an engine management computer. This code can be used to determine the area in the system where a malfunction may be located.

Disc brake A brake design incorporating a rotating disc onto which brake pads are squeezed. The resulting friction converts the energy of a moving vehicle into heat.

Double-overhead cam (DOHC) An engine that uses two overhead camshafts, usually one for the intake valves and one for the exhaust valves.

Drivebelt(s) The belt(s) used to drive accessories such as the alternator, water pump, power steering pump, air conditioning compressor, etc. off the crankshaft pulley.

Accessory drivebelts

Driveshaft Any shaft used to transmit motion. Commonly used when referring to the axleshafts on a front wheel drive vehicle.

Driveshaft

Drum brake A type of brake using a drum-shaped metal cylinder attached to the inner surface of the wheel. When the brake pedal is pressed, curved brake shoes with friction linings press against the inside of the drum to slow or stop the vehicle.

Drum brake assembly

E

EGR valve A valve used to introduce exhaust gases into the intake air stream.

EGR valve

Electronic control unit (ECU) A computer which controls (for instance) ignition and fuel injection systems, or an anti-lock braking system. For more information refer to the *Haynes Automotive Electrical and Electronic Systems Manual*.

Electronic Fuel Injection (EFI) A computer controlled fuel system that distributes fuel through an injector located in each intake port of the engine.

Emergency brake A braking system, independent of the main hydraulic system, that can be used to slow or stop the vehicle if the primary brakes fail, or to hold the vehicle stationary even though the brake pedal isn't depressed. It usually consists of a hand lever that actuates either front or rear brakes mechanically through a series of cables and linkages. Also known as a handbrake or parking brake.

Endfloat The amount of lengthwise movement between two parts. As applied to a crankshaft, the distance that the crankshaft can move forward and back in the cylinder block.

Engine management system (EMS) A computer controlled system which manages the fuel injection and the ignition systems in an integrated fashion.

Exhaust manifold A part with several passages through which exhaust gases leave the engine combustion chambers and enter the exhaust pipe.

Exhaust manifold

F

Fan clutch A viscous (fluid) drive coupling device which permits variable engine fan speeds in relation to engine speeds.

Feeler blade A thin strip or blade of hardened steel, ground to an exact thickness, used to check or measure clearances between parts.

Feeler blade

Firing order The order in which the engine cylinders fire, or deliver their power strokes, beginning with the number one cylinder.

Flywheel A heavy spinning wheel in which energy is absorbed and stored by means of momentum. On cars, the flywheel is attached to the crankshaft to smooth out firing impulses.

Free play The amount of travel before any action takes place. The "looseness" in a linkage, or an assembly of parts, between the initial application of force and actual movement. For example, the distance the brake pedal moves before the pistons in the master cylinder are actuated.

Fuse An electrical device which protects a circuit against accidental overload. The typical fuse contains a soft piece of metal which is calibrated to melt at a predetermined current flow (expressed as amps) and break the circuit.

Fusible link A circuit protection device consisting of a conductor surrounded by heat-resistant insulation. The conductor is smaller than the wire it protects, so it acts as the weakest link in the circuit. Unlike a blown fuse, a failed fusible link must frequently be cut from the wire for replacement.

G

Gap The distance the spark must travel in jumping from the centre electrode to the side

Adjusting spark plug gap

electrode in a spark plug. Also refers to the spacing between the points in a contact breaker assembly in a conventional points-type ignition, or to the distance between the reluctor or rotor and the pickup coil in an electronic ignition.

Gasket Any thin, soft material - usually cork, cardboard, asbestos or soft metal - installed between two metal surfaces to ensure a good seal. For instance, the cylinder head gasket seals the joint between the block and the cylinder head.

Gasket

Gauge An instrument panel display used to monitor engine conditions. A gauge with a movable pointer on a dial or a fixed scale is an analogue gauge. A gauge with a numerical readout is called a digital gauge.

H

Halfshaft A rotating shaft that transmits power from the final drive unit to a drive wheel, usually when referring to a live rear axle.

Harmonic balancer A device designed to reduce torsion or twisting vibration in the crankshaft. May be incorporated in the crankshaft pulley. Also known as a vibration damper.

Hone An abrasive tool for correcting small irregularities or differences in diameter in an engine cylinder, brake cylinder, etc.

Hydraulic tappet A tappet that utilises hydraulic pressure from the engine's lubrication system to maintain zero clearance (constant contact with both camshaft and valve stem). Automatically adjusts to variation in valve stem length. Hydraulic tappets also reduce valve noise.

I

Ignition timing The moment at which the spark plug fires, usually expressed in the number of crankshaft degrees before the piston reaches the top of its stroke.

Inlet manifold A tube or housing with passages through which flows the air-fuel mixture (carburettor vehicles and vehicles with throttle body injection) or air only (port fuel-injected vehicles) to the port openings in the cylinder head.

J

Jump start Starting the engine of a vehicle with a discharged or weak battery by attaching jump leads from the weak battery to a charged or helper battery.

L

Load Sensing Proportioning Valve (LSPV) A brake hydraulic system control valve that works like a proportioning valve, but also takes into consideration the amount of weight carried by the rear axle.

Locknut A nut used to lock an adjustment nut, or other threaded component, in place. For example, a locknut is employed to keep the adjusting nut on the rocker arm in position.

Lockwasher A form of washer designed to prevent an attaching nut from working loose.

M

MacPherson strut A type of front suspension system devised by Earle MacPherson at Ford of England. In its original form, a simple lateral link with the anti-roll bar creates the lower control arm. A long strut - an integral coil spring and shock absorber - is mounted between the body and the steering knuckle. Many modern so-called MacPherson strut systems use a conventional lower A-arm and don't rely on the anti-roll bar for location.

Multimeter An electrical test instrument with the capability to measure voltage, current and resistance.

N

NOx Oxides of Nitrogen. A common toxic pollutant emitted by petrol and diesel engines at higher temperatures.

O

Ohm The unit of electrical resistance. One volt applied to a resistance of one ohm will produce a current of one amp.

Ohmmeter An instrument for measuring electrical resistance.

O-ring A type of sealing ring made of a special rubber-like material; in use, the O-ring is compressed into a groove to provide the sealing action.

O-ring

Overhead cam (ohc) engine An engine with the camshaft(s) located on top of the cylinder head(s).

Overhead valve (ohv) engine An engine with the valves located in the cylinder head, but with the camshaft located in the engine block.

Oxygen sensor A device installed in the engine exhaust manifold, which senses the oxygen content in the exhaust and converts this information into an electric current. Also called a Lambda sensor.

P

Phillips screw A type of screw head having a cross instead of a slot for a corresponding type of screwdriver.

Plastigage A thin strip of plastic thread, available in different sizes, used for measuring clearances. For example, a strip of Plastigage is laid across a bearing journal. The parts are assembled and dismantled; the width of the crushed strip indicates the clearance between journal and bearing.

Plastigage

Propeller shaft The long hollow tube with universal joints at both ends that carries power from the transmission to the differential on front-engined rear wheel drive vehicles.

Proportioning valve A hydraulic control valve which limits the amount of pressure to the rear brakes during panic stops to prevent wheel lock-up.

R

Rack-and-pinion steering A steering system with a pinion gear on the end of the steering shaft that mates with a rack (think of a geared wheel opened up and laid flat). When the steering wheel is turned, the pinion turns, moving the rack to the left or right. This movement is transmitted through the track rods to the steering arms at the wheels.

Radiator A liquid-to-air heat transfer device designed to reduce the temperature of the coolant in an internal combustion engine cooling system.

Refrigerant Any substance used as a heat transfer agent in an air-conditioning system. R-12 has been the principle refrigerant for many years; recently, however, manufacturers have begun using R-134a, a non-CFC substance that is considered less harmful to

the ozone in the upper atmosphere.

Rocker arm A lever arm that rocks on a shaft or pivots on a stud. In an overhead valve engine, the rocker arm converts the upward movement of the pushrod into a downward movement to open a valve.

Rotor In a distributor, the rotating device inside the cap that connects the centre electrode and the outer terminals as it turns, distributing the high voltage from the coil secondary winding to the proper spark plug. Also, that part of an alternator which rotates inside the stator. Also, the rotating assembly of a turbocharger, including the compressor wheel, shaft and turbine wheel.

Runout The amount of wobble (in-and-out movement) of a gear or wheel as it's rotated. The amount a shaft rotates "out-of-true." The out-of-round condition of a rotating part.

S

Sealant A liquid or paste used to prevent leakage at a joint. Sometimes used in conjunction with a gasket.

Sealed beam lamp An older headlight design which integrates the reflector, lens and filaments into a hermetically-sealed one-piece unit. When a filament burns out or the lens cracks, the entire unit is simply replaced.

Serpentine drivebelt A single, long, wide accessory drivebelt that's used on some newer vehicles to drive all the accessories, instead of a series of smaller, shorter belts. Serpentine drivebelts are usually tensioned by an automatic tensioner.

Serpentine drivebelt

Shim Thin spacer, commonly used to adjust the clearance or relative positions between two parts. For example, shims inserted into or under bucket tappets control valve clearances. Clearance is adjusted by changing the thickness of the shim.

Slide hammer A special puller that screws into or hooks onto a component such as a shaft or bearing; a heavy sliding handle on the shaft bottoms against the end of the shaft to knock the component free.

Sprocket A tooth or projection on the periphery of a wheel, shaped to engage with a chain or drivebelt. Commonly used to refer to the sprocket wheel itself.

Starter inhibitor switch On vehicles with an

automatic transmission, a switch that prevents starting if the vehicle is not in Neutral or Park.

Strut See MacPherson strut.

T

Tappet A cylindrical component which transmits motion from the cam to the valve stem, either directly or via a pushrod and rocker arm. Also called a cam follower.

Thermostat A heat-controlled valve that regulates the flow of coolant between the cylinder block and the radiator, so maintaining optimum engine operating temperature. A thermostat is also used in some air cleaners in which the temperature is regulated.

Thrust bearing The bearing in the clutch assembly that is moved in to the release levers by clutch pedal action to disengage the clutch. Also referred to as a release bearing.

Timing belt A toothed belt which drives the camshaft. Serious engine damage may result if it breaks in service.

Timing chain A chain which drives the camshaft.

Toe-in The amount the front wheels are closer together at the front than at the rear. On rear wheel drive vehicles, a slight amount of toe-in is usually specified to keep the front wheels running parallel on the road by offsetting other forces that tend to spread the wheels apart.

Toe-out The amount the front wheels are closer together at the rear than at the front. On front wheel drive vehicles, a slight amount of toe-out is usually specified.

Tools For full information on choosing and using tools, refer to the *Haynes Automotive Tools Manual*.

Tracer A stripe of a second colour applied to a wire insulator to distinguish that wire from another one with the same colour insulator.

Tune-up A process of accurate and careful adjustments and parts replacement to obtain the best possible engine performance.

Turbocharger A centrifugal device, driven by exhaust gases, that pressurises the intake air. Normally used to increase the power output from a given engine displacement, but can also be used primarily to reduce exhaust emissions (as on VW's "Umwelt" Diesel engine).

U

Universal joint or U-joint A double-pivoted connection for transmitting power from a driving to a driven shaft through an angle. A U-joint consists of two Y-shaped yokes and a cross-shaped member called the spider.

V

Valve A device through which the flow of liquid, gas, vacuum, or loose material in bulk may be started, stopped, or regulated by a movable part that opens, shuts, or partially obstructs one or more ports or passageways. A valve is also the movable part of such a device.

Valve clearance The clearance between the valve tip (the end of the valve stem) and the rocker arm or tappet. The valve clearance is measured when the valve is closed.

Vernier caliper A precision measuring instrument that measures inside and outside dimensions. Not quite as accurate as a micrometer, but more convenient.

Viscosity The thickness of a liquid or its resistance to flow.

Volt A unit for expressing electrical "pressure" in a circuit. One volt that will produce a current of one ampere through a resistance of one ohm.

W

Welding Various processes used to join metal items by heating the areas to be joined to a molten state and fusing them together. For more information refer to the *Haynes Automotive Welding Manual*.

Wiring diagram A drawing portraying the components and wires in a vehicle's electrical system, using standardised symbols. For more information refer to the *Haynes Automotive Electrical and Electronic Systems Manual*.

Haynes Manuals – The Complete List

Title	Book No.
ALFA ROMEO	
Alfa Romeo Alfasud/Sprint (74 - 88)	0292
Alfa Romeo Alfetta (73 - 87)	0531
AUDI	
Audi 80 (72 - Feb 79)	0207
Audi 80, 90 (79 - Oct 86) & Coupe (81 - Nov 88)	0605
Audi 80, 90 (Oct 86 - 90) & Coupe (Nov 88 - 90)	1491
Audi 100 (69 - Sept 76)	0162
Audi 100 (Oct 76 - Oct 82)	0428
Audi 100 (Oct 82 - 90) & 200 (Feb 84 - Oct 89)	0907
AUSTIN	
Austin Allegro 1100, 1300, 1.0, 1.1 & 1.3 (73 - 82)	0164
Austin Ambassador (82 - 84)	0871
Austin/MG Maestro 1.3 & 1.6 (petrol)(83 - 95)	0922
Austin Maxi (69 - 81)	0052
Austin/MG Metro (80 - May 90)	0718
Austin Montego 1.3 & 1.6 (84 - 94)	1066
Austin/MG Montego 2.0 (petrol)(84 - 95)	1067
Mini (59 - 69)	0527
Mini (69 - 95)	0646
Austin/Rover Diesel Engine 2.0 litre (86 - 93)	1857
BEDFORD	
Bedford CF (petrol)(69 - 87)	0163
Bedford HA Van (64 - 83)	0607
Bedford Rascal (86 - Oct 94)	3015
BL	
BL Princess & BLMC 18-22 (75 - 82)	0286
BMW	
BMW 316, 320 & 320i (4-cyl)(75 - Feb 83)	0276
BMW 320, 320i, 323i & 325i (6-cyl) (Oct 77 - Sept 87)	0815
BMW 520i & 525e (Oct 81 - June 88)	1560
BMW 525, 528 & 528i (73 - Sept 81)	0632
BMW 3 Series (sohc, petrol)(81 - 93)	1948
BMW 5 Series (sohc, petrol)(81 - 93)	1948
BMW 1500, 1502, 1600, 1602 & 2000 (59 - 77)	0240
CITROEN	
Citroën 2CV, Ami & Dyane (67 - 90)	0196
Citroën AX (petrol & diesel)(87 - 94)	3014
Citroën BX (83 - 94)	0908
Citroën CX (75 - 88)	0528
Citroën GS & GSA (71 - 85)	0290
Citroën Visa (79 - 88)	0620
Citroën Xantia (petrol & diesel)(93 - Oct 95)	3082
Citroën ZX (diesel)(91 - 93)	1922
Citroën ZX (petrol)(91 - 94)	1881
Citroën Diesel Engines 1.7 & 1.9 litres (84 - 94)	1379
COLT	
Colt 1200, 1250 & 1400 (79 - May 84)	0600
Colt Galant (74 - 78) & Celeste (76 - 81)	0236
Colt Lancer (74 - 77)	0419
DAIMLER	
Daimler Sovereign (68 - Oct 86)	0242
Daimler Double Six (72 - 88)	0478

Title	Book No.
DATSUN (see also **Nissan**)	
Datsun 120Y (73 - Aug 78)	0228
Datsun 1300, 1400 & 1600 (69 - Aug 72)	0123
Datsun Cherry (71 - 76)	0195
Datsun Cherry (79 - Sept 82)	0679
Datsun Pick-up (75 - 78)	0277
Datsun Sunny (Aug 78 - May 82)	0525
Datsun Violet (78 - 82)	0430
FIAT	
Fiat 124 (66 - 75)	0080
Fiat 126 (73 - 87)	0305
Fiat 127 (71 - 83)	0193
Fiat 500 (57 - 73)	0090
Fiat 850 (64 - 81)	0038
Fiat Panda (81 - 95)	0793
Fiat Regata (84 - 88)	1167
Fiat Strada (79 - 88)	0479
Fiat Tipo (88 - 91)	1625
Fiat Uno (82 - 93)	0923
Fiat X1/9 (74 - 89)	0273
FORD	
Ford Capri II & III 1.6 & 2.0 (74 - 87)	0283
Ford Capri II & III 2.8 & 3.0 (74 - 87)	1309
Ford Cortina Mk III 1300 & 1600 (70 - 76)	0070
Ford Cortina Mk III 1600 & 2000 (70 - 76)	0295
Ford Cortina Mk IV & V 1.6 & 2.0 (76 - 83)	0343
Ford Cortina Mk IV & V 2.3 V6 (77 - 83)	0426
Ford Escort (75 - Aug 80)	0280
Ford Escort Mk II Mexico, RS 1600 & RS 2000 (75 - 80)	0735
Ford Escort fwd (Sept 80 - Sept 90)	0686
Ford Escort (Sept 90 - Feb 95)	1737
Ford Fiesta (inc. XR2)(76 - Aug 83)	0334
Ford Fiesta (inc. XR2)(Aug 83 - Feb 89)	1030
Ford Fiesta (Feb 89 - 93)	1595
Ford Granada (Sept 77 - Feb 85)	0481
Ford Granada (Mar 85 - 94)	1245
Ford Mondeo (93 - 95)	1923
Ford Orion (83 - Sept 90)	1009
Ford Orion (Sept 90 - Feb 95)	1737
Ford Sierra 1.3, 1.6, 1.8 & 2.0 (82 - 93)	0903
Ford Sierra 2.3, 2.8 & 2.9 (82 - 91)	0904
Ford Scorpio (Mar 85 - 94)	1245
Ford Transit Mk 1 (diesel)(65 - Feb 78)	0418
Ford Transit Mk 1 (petrol)(65 - Feb 78)	0377
Ford Transit Mk 2 (petrol)(78 - Jan 86)	0719
Ford Transit Mk 3 (petrol)(Feb 86 - 89)	1468
Ford Transit (diesel)(Feb 86 - 95)	3019
Ford Diesel Engines 1.6 & 1.8 litre (fwd)(84 - 95)	1172
Ford Diesel Engines 2.1, 2.3 & 2.5 litres (77 - 90)	1606
Ford Vehicle Carburettors	1783
FREIGHT ROVER	
Sherpa (74 - 87)	0463
HILLMAN	
Hillman Avenger (70 - 82)	0037
Hillman Minx & Husky (56 - 75)	0009
HONDA	
Honda Accord (76 - Feb 84)	0351
Honda Accord (Feb 84 - Oct 85)	1177

Title	Book No.
Honda Civic 1200 (73 - 79)	0160
Honda Civic (Feb 84 - Oct 87)	1226
JAGUAR	
Jaguar E Type (61 - 72)	0140
Jaguar MkI & II, 240 & 340 (55 - 69)	0098
Jaguar XJ6, XJ & Sovereign (68 - Oct 86)	0242
Jaguar XJ12, XJS & Sovereign (72 - 88)	0478
LADA	
Lada 1200, 1300, 1500 & 1600 (74 - 91)	0413
Lada Samara (87 - 91)	1610
LANCIA	
Lancia Beta (73 - 80)	0533
LAND ROVER	
Land Rover Series II, IIA & III (petrol)(58 - 85)	0314
Land Rover Series IIA & III (diesel)(58 - 85)	0529
Land Rover 90, 110 & Defender (diesel)(83 - 95)	3017
Land Rover Discovery (diesel)(89 - 95)	3016
MAZDA	
Mazda 323 rwd (77 - Apr 86)	0370
Mazda 323 fwd (Mar 81 - Oct 89)	1608
Mazda 626 fwd (May 83 - Sept 87)	0929
Mazda B-1600, B-1800 & B-2000 Pick-up (72 - 88)	0267
Mazda RX-7 (79 - 85)	0460
MERCEDES-BENZ	
Mercedes-Benz 190 & 190E (83 - 87)	0928
Mercedes-Benz 200, 240, 300 (diesel) (Oct 76 - 85)	1114
Mercedes-Benz 250 & 280 (68 - 72)	0346
Mercedes-Benz 250 & 280 (123 Series) (Oct 76 - 84)	0677
MG	
MG Maestro 1.3 & 1.6 (83 - 95)	0922
MG Metro (80 - May 90)	0718
MG Montego 2.0 (84 - 95)	1067
MG Midget & AH Sprite (58 - 80)	0265
MGB (62 - 80)	0111
MITSUBISHI	
Mitsubishi Shogun & L200 Pick-Ups (83 - 94)	1944
Mitsubishi 1200, 1250 & 1400 (79 - May 84)	0600
MORRIS	
Morris Ital 1.3 (80 - 84)	0705
Morris Marina 1700 (78 - 80)	0526
Morris Marina 1.8 (71 - 78)	0074
Morris Minor 1000 (56 - 71)	0024
NISSAN (See also Datsun)	
Nissan Bluebird 160B & 180B (rwd) (May 80 - May 84)	0957
Nissan Bluebird fwd (May 84 - Mar 86)	1223
Nissan Bluebird T12 & T72 (Mar 86 - 90)	1473
Nissan Cherry N12 (Sept 82 - 86)	1031
Nissan Micra K10 (83 - Jan 93)	0931
Nissan Primera (90 - 95)	1851
Nissan Stanza (82 - 86)	0824
Nissan Sunny B11 (May 82 - Oct 86)	0895
Nissan Sunny (Oct 86 - Mar 91)	1378
OPEL	
Opel Ascona & Manta B Series (Sept 75 - 88)	0316

Title	Book No.
Opel Kadett C Series (Nov 73 - Nov 79)	0395
Opel Kadett D Series (fwd)(Nov 79 - Oct 84)	0634
PEUGEOT	
Peugeot 106 (petrol & diesel)(91 - 94)	1882
Peugeot 205 (83 - 95)	0932
Peugeot 305 (78 - 89)	0538
Peugeot 306 (petrol & diesel)(93 - 95)	3073
Peugeot 309 (86 - 93)	1266
Peugeot 405 (88 - 95)	1559
Peugeot 405 (diesel)(88 - 96)	3198
Peugeot 504 (68 - 82)	0161
Peugeot 504 (diesel)(74 - 82)	0663
Peugeot 505 (79 - 89)	0762
Peugeot Diesel Engines 1.7 & 1.9 litres (82 - 94)	0950
Peugeot Diesel Engines 2.0, 2.1, 2.3 & 2.5 litres (74 - 90)	1607
PORSCHE	
Porsche 911 (65 - 85)	0264
Porsche 924 & 924 Turbo (76 - 85)	0397
RANGE ROVER	
Range Rover V8 (70 - Oct 92)	0606
RELIANT	
Reliant Robin & Kitten (73 - 83)	0436
RENAULT	
Renault 4 (61 - 86)	0072
Renault 5 (72 - Feb 85)	0141
Renault 5 (Feb 85 - 95)	1219
Renault 6 (68 - 79)	0092
Renault 9 & 11 (82 - 89)	0822
Renault 12 (70 - 80)	0097
Renault 14 (77 - 83)	0362
Renault 15 & 17 (72 - 79)	0763
Renault 16 (65 - 79)	0081
Renault 18 (79 - 86)	0598
Renault 19 (petrol)(89 - 94)	1646
Renault 19 (diesel)(89 - 95)	1946
Renault 21 (86 - 94)	1397
Renault 25 (84 - 86)	1228
Renault Clio (petrol)(91 - 93)	1853
Renault Clio (diesel)(91 - 95)	3031
Renault Fuego (80 - 86)	0764
ROVER	
Rover 213 & 216 (84 - 89)	1116
Rover 214 & 414 (Oct 89 - 92)	1689
Rover 216 & 416 (Oct 89 - 92)	1830
Rover 820, 825 & 827 (petrol)(86 - 95)	1380
Rover 2000, 2300 & 2600 (77 - 87)	0468
Rover 3500 (76 - 87)	0365
Rover Metro (May 90 - 91)	1711
Rover Diesel Engine 2.0 litre (86 - 93)	1857
SAAB	
Saab 95 & 96 (66 - 76)	0198
Saab 99 (69 - 79)	0247
Saab 90, 99 & 900 (79 - Sept 93)	0765
Saab 9000 (4-cyl)(85 - 95)	1686
SEAT	
Seat Ibiza & Malaga (85 - 92)	1609
SIMCA	
Simca 1100 & 1204 (67 - 79)	0088
Simca 1301 & 1501 (63 - 76)	0199
SKODA	
Skoda 1000 & 1100 (64 - 78)	0303

Title	Book No.
Skoda Estelle 105, 120, 130 & 136 (77 - 89)	0604
Skoda Favorit (89 - 92)	1801
SUBARU	
Subaru 1600 (77 - Oct 79)	0237
Subaru 1600 & 1800 (Nov 79 - 90)	0995
SUZUKI	
Suzuki SJ Series, Samurai & Vitara (82 - 94)	1942
Suzuki Supercarry (86 - Oct 94)	3015
TALBOT	
Talbot Alpine, Solara, Minx & Rapier (75 - 86)	0337
Talbot Horizon (78 - 86)	0473
Talbot Samba (82 - 86)	0823
Talbot Sunbeam (77 - 82)	0435
TOYOTA	
Toyota 2000 (75 - 77)	0360
Toyota Celica (78 - Jan 82)	0437
Toyota Celica (Feb 82 - Sept 85)	1135
Toyota Corolla (rwd)(80 - 85)	0683
Toyota Corolla (fwd)(Sept 83 - Sept 87)	1024
Toyota Corolla (Sept 87 - 92)	1683
Toyota Hi-Ace & Hi-Lux (69 - Oct 83)	0304
Toyota Starlet (78 - Jan 85)	0462
TRIUMPH	
Triumph Acclaim (81 - 84)	0792
Triumph GT6 (62 - 74)	0112
Triumph Herald (59 - 71)	0010
Triumph Spitfire (62 - 81)	0113
Triumph Stag (70 - 78)	0441
Triumph TR2, 3, 3A, 4 & 4A (52 - 67)	0028
Triumph TR7 (75 - 82)	0322
Triumph Vitesse (62 - 74)	0112
VAUXHALL	
Vauxhall Astra (80 - Oct 84)	0635
Vauxhall Astra & Belmont (Oct 84 - Oct 91)	1136
Vauxhall Astra (Oct 91 - Oct 92)	1832
Vauxhall Carlton (Oct 78 - Oct 86)	0480
Vauxhall Carlton (Nov 86 - 93).	1469
Vauxhall Cavalier 1300 (77 - July 81)	0461
Vauxhall Cavalier 1600, 1900 & 2000 (75 - July 81)	0315
Vauxhall Cavalier (fwd)(81 - Oct 88)	0812
Vauxhall Cavalier (Oct 88 - 94)	1570
Vauxhall Chevette (75 - 84)	0285
Vauxhall Corsa (Mar 93 - 94)	1985
Vauxhall Magnum (73 - 77)	0294
Vauxhall Nova (83 - 93)	0909
Vauxhall Rascal (86 - Oct 94)	3015
Vauxhall Victor & VX4/90 FD Series (67 - 72)	0053
Vauxhall Viva HC (70 - 79)	0047
Vauxhall Diesel Engines 1.6 & 1.7 litres (82 - 94)	1222
VOLKSWAGEN	
VW Beetle 1200 (54 - 77)	0036
VW Beetle 1300 & 1500 (65 - 75)	0039
VW Beetle 1302 & 1302S (70 - 72)	0110
VW Beetle 1303, 1303S & GT (72 - 75)	0159
VW Golf 'Mk 1' 1.1 & 1.3 (74 - June 84)	0716
VW Golf 'Mk 1' 1.5, 1.6 & 1.8 (74 - 85)	0726
VW Golf 'Mk 1' (diesel)(78 - June 84)	0451
VW Golf 'Mk 2' (Mar 84 - 92)	1081
VW Golf 'Mk 3' (petrol & diesel)(Feb 92 - 95)	3097

Title	Book No.
VW Jetta 'Mk 1' 1.1 & 1.3 (74 - June 84)	0716
VW Jetta 'Mk 1' 1.5, 1.6 & 1.8 (74 - 85)	0726
VW Jetta 'Mk 1' (diesel)(78 - June 84)	0451
VW Jetta 'Mk 2' (Mar 84 - 92)	1081
VW LT vans & light trucks (76 - 87)	0637
VW Passat (73 - Sept 81)	0238
VW Passat (Sept 81 - May 88)	0814
VW Passat (May 88 - 91)	1647
VW Polo & Derby (76 - Jan 82)	0335
VW Polo (82 - Oct 90)	0813
VW Santana (Sept 81 - May 88)	0814
VW Scirocco 'Mk 1' 1.5, 1.6 & 1.8 (74 - 85)	0726
VW Scirocco (82 - 90)	1224
VW Transporter 1600 (68 - 79)	0082
VW Transporter 1700, 1800 & 2000 (72 - 79)	0226
VW Transporter with air-cooled engine (79 - 82)	0638
VW Type 3 (63 - 73)	0084
VW Vento (petrol & diesel)(Feb 92 - 95)	3097
VOLVO	
Volvo 66 & 343, Daf 55 & 66 (68 - 79)	0293
Volvo 142, 144 & 145 (66 - 74)	0129
Volvo 240 Series (74 - 93)(2nd Edition)	0270
Volvo 262, 264 & 260/265 (75 - 85)	0400
Volvo 340, 343, 345 & 360 (76 - 91)	0715
Volvo 440, 460 & 480 (87 - 92)	1691
Volvo 740 & 760 (petrol)(82 - 91)	1258
YUGO/ZASTAVA	
Yugo/Zastava (81 - 90)	1453

NEW TECH BOOKS	
Automotive Brake Manual	3050
Automotive Electrical & Electronic Systems	3049
Automotive Tools Manual	3052
Automotive Welding Manual	3053

SPECIAL INTEREST AUTOMOTIVE BOOKS	
Automotive Fuel Injection Systems	9755
Car Bodywork Repair Manual	9864
Caravan Manual	9894
Dishwasher Manual (New Edition)	9866
Ford Vehicle Carburettors	1783
Haynes Technical Data Book ('87 to '96)	1996
How To Keep Your Car Alive	9868
In-Car Entertainment Manual (2nd Edition)	9862
Japanese Vehicle Carburettors	1786
Kitcar Builder's Manual (2nd Edition)	H898
Pass the MOT!	9861
Small Engine Repair Manual	1755
Solex & Pierburg Carburettors	1785
SU Carburettors	0299
Weber Carburettors (to '79)	0393
Weber Carburettors ('79 to '91)	1784

All the manuals featured on these pages are available through good motor accessory shops and book stores. In case of difficulty, contact **Haynes Publishing** on 01963 440635

001/11/95

Preserving Our Motoring Heritage

<
The Model J Duesenberg Derham Tourster. Only eight of these magnificent cars were ever built – this is the only example to be found outside the United States of America

Almost every car you've ever loved, loathed or desired is gathered under one roof at the Haynes Motor Museum. Over 300 immaculately presented cars and motorbikes represent every aspect of our motoring heritage, from elegant reminders of bygone days, such as the superb Model J Duesenberg to curiosities like the bug-eyed BMW Isetta. There are also many old friends and flames. Perhaps you remember the 1959 Ford Popular that you did your courting in? The magnificent 'Red Collection' is a spectacle of classic sports cars including AC, Alfa Romeo, Austin Healey, Ferrari, Lamborghini, Maserati, MG, Riley, Porsche and Triumph.

A Perfect Day Out

Each and every vehicle at the Haynes Motor Museum has played its part in the history and culture of Motoring. Today, they make a wonderful spectacle and a great day out for all the family. Bring the kids, bring Mum and Dad, but above all bring your camera to capture those golden memories for ever. You will also find an impressive array of motoring memorabilia, a comfortable 70 seat video cinema and one of the most extensive transport book shops in Britain. The Pit Stop Cafe serves everything from a cup of tea to wholesome, home-made meals or, if you prefer, you can enjoy the large picnic area nestled in the beautiful rural surroundings of Somerset.

>
John Haynes O.B.E., Founder and Chairman of the museum at the wheel of a Haynes Light 12.

<
Graham Hill's Lola Cosworth Formula 1 car next to a 1934 Riley Sports.

The Museum is situated on the A359 Yeovil to Frome road at Sparkford, just off the A303 in Somerset. It is about 40 miles south of Bristol, and 25 minutes drive from the M5 intersection at Taunton.

Open 9.30am - 5.30pm (10.00am - 4.00pm Winter) 7 days a week, *except Christmas Day, Boxing Day and New Years Day*
Special rates available for schools, coach parties and outings Charitable Trust No. 292048